As Time Goes By

Also by Laurence Leamer:

The Paper Revolutionaries
Playing for Keeps in Washington
Assignment
Ascent: The Spiritual and Physical Quest of Willi Unsoeld
Make-Believe: The Story of Nancy and Ronald Reagan

AS TIME GOES BY

The Life of Ingrid Bergman

LAURENCE LEAMER

1817

HARPER & ROW, PUBLISHERS, New York

Cambridge, Philadelphia, San Francisco, London
Mexico City, São Paulo, Singapore, Sydney

Jo Vesna

Portions of this book have been published, in slightly different form, in *People* and *The National Enquirer*.

Grateful acknowledgment is made for permission to reprint excerpts from *Ingrid Bergman: My Story,* by Ingrid Bergman and Alan Burgess. Copyright © 1980 by Ingrid Bergman and Alan Burgess. Reprinted by permission of Delacorte Press.

Photo credits appear on page 424.

FIRST EDITION

Designer: Charlotte Staub

Library of Congress Cataloging-in-Publication Data

Leamer, Laurence.
  As time goes by.

  Bibliography: p.
  Includes index.
  1. Bergman, Ingrid, date.   2. Actors—
Sweden—Biography. I.Title.
PN2778.B43L43   1986   791.43'028'0924   [B] 85-45207
ISBN 0-06-015485-3

86 87 88 89 90 MPC 10 9 8 7 6 5 4 3 2 1

Contents

Illustrations follow pages 184 and 248

The Star Who Had Everything

The plane soared high over the Atlantic Ocean, carrying Ingrid Bergman toward Rome.

Ingrid enjoyed few things as much as traveling, encapsulated in the moment, with neither past nor future. Ten years before, she had sailed westward on the *Queen Mary* to begin her film life in America. Many times she had ridden the *20th Century Limited* and the *Super Chief* across America. She had flown between New York and Hollywood too, once in Howard Hughes's private plane. She had journeyed to the lodge at Sun Valley with Dr. Petter Lindstrom, her husband, and Clark Gable, Gary Cooper, and Ernest Hemingway. She had sat in the front seat of a Mercedes, speeding across war-ravaged Germany. Now she was traveling once again, on a twenty-hour flight in the spring of 1949 to make a movie with Roberto Rossellini, the master of the new Italian cinema.

In recent years, Ingrid had become the most popular movie star in America and perhaps the world. Three months earlier, a seventy-five-foot-tall image of Ingrid in white plastic armor as Joan of Arc had risen above Times Square. Ingrid stood equally far above the scandals and gossipmongering of Hollywood. The Swedish-born actress had become a symbol of goodness, a vulnerable woman yet one full of moral strength.

When Ingrid played women of questionable virtue, such as Clio Dulaine in *Saratoga Trunk* or Alicia Huberman in *Notorious*, her innate goodness seemed to show through, a beacon of pure, transcendent light. And when she played women of high virtue, Maria in *For Whom the Bell Tolls* or Sister Benedict in *The Bells of St. Mary's*, she appeared to be displaying aspects of herself.

At a time when the moral standards of Main Street America were being challenged at every turn, here at least was one star with whom decent, moral people could identify. Unlike so many of her colleagues, Ingrid was never the subject of scandal, of sordid gossip beyond the pale of Hollywood. Everyone who read the movie magazines or the columnists knew that Ingrid lived happily in Hollywood with Petter and their daughter, Pia.

Now, however, as TWA flight 916 droned through the night, Ingrid was taking an enormous chance. She talked amiably to Ellen Neuwald, her secretary, never letting on that she was going to Italy not only to make a film but to meet her lover.

A month before, Rossellini had visited Hollywood to arrange for the film that he and Ingrid would make now on the island of Stromboli, off the coast of Italy. Roberto had stayed with Ingrid and Petter in their house in Beverly Hills. Ingrid was mesmerized by the Italian director. She had been planning to have a new baby with Petter, a boy that she had already named Pelle, but she couldn't stand the thought any longer.

Always before, Ingrid had been able to control her affairs, ending them when she wanted to end them, often using her lovers to help perfect her roles and her films, always, in the end, returning to her husband and daughter. This time, too, she wanted to use Roberto to make a fine film on Stromboli. But she wasn't thinking any longer. Without a word to Petter, she had cleared out many of her clothes and furs, jewelry and clippings books. When she left, she hadn't let on to Pia that it might be months before she returned. She couldn't stand unpleasantness. She wanted to be in Rome, in Roberto's arms, and to make a memorable film.

She had no idea that she was about to become the center of the greatest celebrity scandal of the postwar period. More than that, Ingrid would become part of contemporary social history, helping to define an era both in the United States and in Europe.

Here was a woman who had everything that the most powerful country in the world could give. Fame. Fortune. Adulation. Home. Family. Here was a star whose adopted country had made her the symbol of all womanhood, the ideal of female virtue and beauty. And she was about to abandon America, to abandon herself. She was going to leave her husband and daughter and run off with a married Italian director.

If Ingrid Bergman would leave all that, then what was happening in the United States? She had betrayed America, and to many Americans she would become a moral bellwether of the McCarthy period. She would be viewed as a symbol of Hollywood's social and moral betrayal, part of a third column undermining America's traditional values.

In Italy, Ingrid would become an even more complicated symbol. A huge crowd was already gathering at Ciampino airport, outside Rome. To the Italians there was no Hollywood star like Ingrid Bergman. She was Sister Benedict. She was Joan of Arc. She was the biggest star of them all. She was flying into Rome to make not a Hollywood film but an Italian film. And she was making not a big film at Cinecittà, the new "Hollywood on the Tiber," but a modern neorealistic Italian film on location on one of the most remote islands in Italy. Further, she was making the film not with just any successful

2

director but with Roberto Rossellini, a man whose love affairs were discussed almost as avidly as his films. It was a moment to be anticipated and savored.

"Italy had just come out of the war," says Federico Fellini, the great Italian director, who was working then with Rossellini. "The people were starved. There were disasters. The figure of Ingrid was like an ambassadress of well-being. She was very familiar, like all the myths of Hollywood, like Clark Gable, like Gary Cooper, like Mickey Mouse.

"You could expect anything from her. She gave this feeling of being a fairy queen who could make little miracles. She was more like a Walt Disney character. This was the fascination. For Italians, who are so deeply touched by the Catholic Church and the figure of the Virgin Mary, she was someone who reminded you of an American saint."

The TWA clipper approached the airport, searchlights playing across the silver hull. The plane glided down, and as it taxied on the tarmac, the crowd pushed forward. All the other passengers filed out. Then Roberto marched up the portable stairs and greeted Ingrid with a kiss and a bouquet of roses that would have engulfed a smaller woman. Ingrid stepped out of the plane and smiled, and it was as if she were a searchlight, illuminating the night. She looked at the great crowd that stared upward, cheering and yelling. Then Ingrid descended, and within a few weeks nothing was the same.

CHAPTER ONE

"Papa, Papa, That's What I'm Going to Do"

On Saturday afternoons much of Stockholm paraded along Strandvägen, the most elegant of the capital's avenues. Young children hopped across the cobblestone quays. Old men ambled along who had been young in the 1880s, when the avenue was still a rude seafront and the shouts and curses of the boatmen were sharp and the odors of herring and coal dust strong. There were proud Swedish burghers who had made fortunes in herring, coal, lumber, and steel, and lived in the great new apartment houses along Strandvägen. Well-known actors and actresses from the Royal Dramatic Theater, whose sumptuous new performance hall stood at the head of the avenue, strutted past, enjoying the spectacle of themselves. Lovers strolled toward the Gröna Lund amusement park, across the bridge in Djurgården. Couples looked at the goods in shopwindows.

Strollers who glanced into the window of the photography shop at No. 3 Strandvägen saw a display that contrasted with the resolutely impersonal tone of the street: a silver baby shoe, and a picture of a mother and her small daughter. The robust, full-bodied young matron had broad eyebrows over small, quizzical eyes, and a mouth that seemed to be smiling at a secret joke. As for the angelic little girl, she had her mother's eyebrows, and a face that peered out on the world with serenity.

It was a scene of such domestic bliss and warmth that a passerby might be forgiven a moment of envy. But the silver shoe and the photo constituted a kind of shrine, a memorial to a family scene that had lasted not much longer than the clicking of a camera. For the mother now was dead.

Ingrid Bergman was only three years old when her thirty-four-year-old mother, Friedel Adler Bergman, died of a liver ailment. Ingrid had no real memories of her—only photographs, grainy film footage, a portrait, love letters, and the anecdotes of others. She could understand, though, why her German-born mother would have fallen so much in love with her father, Justus Samuel Bergman.

Justus Bergman was the eleventh of thirteen children; his father was a schoolteacher and an organist in Slätthög. *Berg* means "rock" in Swedish, and the Bergmans were for the most part practical, responsible people. Ingrid's father was an exception, a bohemian with the sensuous eyes of the boulevardier and the métier of an artist. Friedel Adler had been vacationing in Sweden a few summers after the turn of the century when she had come upon Justus painting in the woods outside Stockholm. Friedel was born in Lütjenburg, near the Baltic Sea, not far from Sweden; her father was a wheelwright, and she was the second of three daughters. Friedel was a pretty, maternal-looking woman, as resolutely practical and earthbound as her husband-to-be was impractical and whimsical. In the most out-of-character act of her short life, she fell in love with Justus.

Friedel was not only lovely but, as a foreigner, doubly unusual. In those years Sweden was a country that, as a 1914 government publication expressed it, rejoiced in "a rare degree of ethnographical homogeneity." Among the five and a half million Swedes there were only forty thousand residents from other nations.

Back in Hamburg, where she now lived, Friedel's family issued threefold objections. In the first place, Justus was not German but a mere Swede. He was Friedel's senior by thirteen years, and in all those years he had achieved no position or wealth.

But love is love, and Justus gave Friedel an engagement ring. In order to fool her family she wore the ring around her neck during the day and on her finger only in the privacy of her room at night. When the Adlers discovered the ruse, they exacted their harsh price: the couple could marry only when Justus had achieved a position of responsibility and substance worthy of an Adler. And thus Justus opened his photographic store at No. 3 Strandvägen, where he worked for seven years before he was deemed worthy to marry Friedel.

Ingrid believed that if her father had developed his artistic abilities, he might have become a painter of great stature. Her belief testified more to a daughter's loyalty than to artistic judgment. Justus was perhaps fortunate to be able to dream what he might have been, while prospering in a business that allowed his artistic bent a certain freedom. Some of his paintings remain; that he gave many of them away was possibly not as much a measure of generosity as absence of patrons.

Whatever his merits as a painter, Justus was a man of charm and aestheticism. Despite his lack of business acumen, his shop prospered. He took pictures, developed film, sold cameras and frames. He even had a device by which a customer could snap his own passport photograph. Justus was eventually successful enough to hire two full-time employees, and he played the grand *patron*, visiting the store when he saw fit.

The Bergmans lived in a large apartment on the sixth and top floor above the store. No. 3 Strandvägen is not quite as grand a structure as No. 21, modeled after a palace in Zaragoza, but nonetheless is an imposing structure, with small balconies facing the water, a smooth plaster front, and a tarred roof bordered by copper trim and great turrets. It is the sort of building along Strandvägen that Justus's bohemian colleagues derided as hopelessly bourgeois.

Like all the apartments in the building, the Bergmans' home was large and comfortable. There were half a dozen large rooms, an atelier for Justus's painting, and a small kitchen, space enough for a family far larger than the three Bergmans. Friedel had, in fact, been pregnant two times before the birth of Ingrid. One child had died at birth, the second after a week of life.

Ingrid was a gift, and from her birth, on August 29, 1915, her parents adored her. She was named after the two-year-old Swedish princess. On her first birthday, Justus took his family to a park to film them. Little Ingrid in a white dress kissed her kneeling mother. Then her father walked down the path, debonair in a three-piece suit, hat, and cane. He knelt down too, and she kissed him, her face hidden behind the brim of his hat. For her second birthday, Justus made another film. Ingrid stood in a white dress. She placed her arms around her kneeling mother's neck, touching the hem of her long, full skirt. Her mother kissed her. Ingrid shook her hand and curtsied, and then curtsied again, as if she had learned a new trick.

The next time Justus took home movies, three-year-old Ingrid wore a dark coat and carried white flowers. And as her father filmed her, she placed the flowers on her mother's grave.

Justus might have reverted to a more unconventional life-style. But a good Swedish daughter had to be brought up with all the strictures of the bourgeois life. And thus Ingrid's forty-nine-year-old Aunt Ellen descended on No. 3 Strandvägen. Ellen was the only one of Justus's twelve siblings not to marry. She had turned to God and to a life of service to her brothers and sisters. Ellen had a heart condition and rarely left the apartment. The aunt was a stern spinster indeed, a Lutheran who could smell the taint of sin in the most innocent of passions, and see the fires of hell nipping at the feet of the godless. "That's the devil sitting on your back," she would tell her niece.

One afternoon, a number of years after Friedel's death, the mother of one of Ingrid's school playmates telephoned to invite her daughter's friend to play.

"Is Mrs. Bergman there?" she asked.

"She's gone to God," Aunt Ellen answered, as if the sod were still fresh on her grave.

In the summers Justus left his daughter in Hamburg with her grandparents and aunts. To the Adlers, godliness was next to cleanliness, and they lectured and prodded their grandchild like Prussian drill sergeants. When her father returned from his summer wanderings, she fled into his arms as if only there she could find respite from imposed order and routine.

Her father was not the patriarch of their tiny family. He was her mentor and friend and companion. He spoiled her, doled out affection and treats in grand dollops. She was one of Justus's favorite photographic subjects. When she could not have been more than six or seven, she dressed up in her father's coat, hat, and glasses, and was photographed reading the daily paper, a slight smirk on her face.

Justus was a man of many interests. He was in a choir that made two trips to America. He loved music so much that he dreamed his daughter might become an opera singer. In Sweden as elsewhere, there is a whole industry based on parents' artistic aspirations for their children, one that gives far more pleasure to parents than it does to children. But Ingrid enjoyed taking piano lessons and singing for her father, as he sat puffed up with pride.

Better yet, Ingrid loved to act in front of Justus, to light up his face with her words and gestures. To Ingrid, acting meant joy and pleasure for herself and for those around her, a journey out of the mundane rites of daily existence. When she was alone she acted too, creating a world of wondrous characters and stories.

Alas, Ingrid could not always act and in acting forget that she was a shy, motherless child. And her days were full of an immense sense of aloneness.

Ensamhet, loneliness, is a great theme of Swedish culture. In the twentieth century, when people complained of isolation and alienation as they would of toothache, the greatest Swedish playwrights and filmmakers seemed to be speaking a peculiarly modern idiom. But in Sweden that *ensamhet* has roots not only in the psyche but in the land, not only in Freudian psychology but in the past.

Sweden is a small country with a small population. Yet it is a land of vast empty spaces, of stark panoramas, of foreboding that might have made another people huddle together. For the most part, though, Swedes have lived as apart from one another as possible. In the villages and countryside where most of them dwelt, the houses were usually set apart. In the growing towns and cities of Ingrid's early years, the Swedes brought their loneliness with them.

Justus sent his daughter to the Palmgrenska Samskolan, the most prestigious girls' school in Stockholm. The five-story yellow-brick structure was a solid, stolid building for a solid, stolid education. Ingrid was not a good student or a particularly popular one.

"She was a sad child and so shy," remembers Disa Lauhren, one of her classmates. "But when she played she always played like a star. We had a little playhouse at my house. We made a fire in the stove and we played with the food and made little pancakes. But all the time Ingrid was outside by herself, acting."

Preferable by far to play a princess, a policeman, a dog, a bird—anything but a motherless little girl. Then when Ingrid was nine Greta Danielsson arrived in the apartment on Strandvägen to be Ingrid's governess. As a tonic for his daughter, Justus had wanted a happy person, and in eighteen-year-old

Greta he had found that and more. "I think her father wanted someone to be an older sister to her," Greta says. "And I think we were sisters. She was very happy."

Greta came from Norrtäije, a little town outside Stockholm. She had dreams of being an opera singer. She helped Ingrid not only with schoolwork but with her piano lessons. In the evenings, Greta, Ingrid, and her father sat around the piano, playing and singing.

"He had a beautiful voice," Greta remembers. "I accompanied him. And we would go for promenades, the three of us."

Greta had a fresh beauty and was full of gentle goodness. She was the youth and laughter that the house so lacked. Greta was always there waiting when Ingrid walked home from school.

"Where have you been?" asked Greta one day when Ingrid arrived very late.

"There was a little bird that died, and we had to bury it in the park. And we had to sing."

"What did you sing?" Greta asked.

"The only song I knew was 'Glad as a Bird in the Morning.'"

Justus was fifty-three years old when the teenage governess entered the house in 1924. Almost three times Greta's age, he at first cared for her with paternal affection. But as the months went by he loved her less and less as a daughter. A typical Strandvägen gentleman would have flirted harmlessly with his child's governess before tucking the whole matter tightly back into his psyche. After all, it was simply not done to have an affair with a teenage governess. Or if it was done, it was done with the saving grace of hypocrisy, quietly, a little passion fitfully enjoyed. But Justus was a lonely romantic with a bohemian soul. Under the nose of Aunt Ellen, who could sniff even a hint of impropriety, a romance began.

In the summer, Justus, Greta, and Ingrid went to Aunt Ellen's tiny summer house outside Stockholm and swam in the lake. They were a happy frolicking threesome—her father, who was not a strong, disciplining parental figure but, as she said later, "like a big brother"; and Greta; not a figure of authority either, but, as she saw it, "an older sister"; and Ingrid, who accepted this ménage as natural and good.

As soon as Aunt Ellen and the other relatives learned about the affair, they were outraged. "Do you know where your father is?" they chided Ingrid, as she remembered years later. "He's not at home with you, is he?"

"No, he isn't, but it doesn't make any difference. I am very busy with my homework. I know he'll be along later."

"You *do* know where he is. He is with *her*."

"I don't mind! I am glad he is with Greta! I'm glad."

Justus's love cost Greta dearly.

"We fell in love and it was very difficult," Greta says. "He was so handsome. We had so much to speak about. I cared for him very much, but I was

8

much younger. He wanted to marry me. It was very difficult for me. If we had married, her aunt said that she would not stay. She wanted to stay with Ingrid. And I understood that. I said marriage is impossible. I began in a singing academy, but I continued to see Ingrid and her father very often."

In the name of propriety and morality, Aunt Ellen and the others drove Greta out of the house. And with it they drove out most of whatever lightness and gaiety there had been in Ingrid's home.

Soon afterward, when Ingrid was twelve years old, her father came to her holding an X-ray plate. "You see, this is a cancer growing here," he said gently. "And, darling, pretty soon I won't be able to get any food down into my stomach, so you see that's serious."

Justus heard of a doctor in Bavaria who had a miraculous new cure for cancer. He wanted to journey there. Even if his trip was futile, he would save Ingrid from observing the agony of his decline, while spending a few months freed from the constraints of his Strandvägen life. He asked Greta to put aside her singing career and go off with him.

"He was very, very sick," Greta recalls. "The doctor said he didn't have a long time to live. His sister cried. He said I must go. I was studying singing in school. I traveled to Germany with him, but there was nothing to do. He couldn't eat. He could only eat a little bouillon. We lived on a farm. But they had no chickens and I wanted to cook bouillon. I found chickens on another farm.

"Perhaps he thought that in Germany he could be better. But it was not only that. His brothers and sisters were all so sorry and cried so much. He thought I could give him a little life. He tried to be good and so did I. He was very, very ill."

When Justus and Greta returned, Ingrid's chubby, prosperous-looking father was replaced by a thin old man. The end was near, but Aunt Ellen and the other Swedish relatives would not have Greta hovering around. Not until Ingrid's aunt from Germany, Frau Elsa Adler, arrived for the death watch was Greta allowed to return. Frau Adler was a formidable woman, not used to being contradicted. Ingrid called her Aunt Mutti, German for "mother," and the woman was like a German mother to Ingrid.

In his last weeks Justus set his life in order. He had Greta and Aunt Mutti round up all his paintings so that he could give them away. He handed Greta the key to his atelier and asked her to destroy his papers. Greta burned the documents without reading a page of what she thought were personal journals.

Ingrid and Greta sat at his bedside. "I remember my Father turned his head to look at Greta, and then he turned his head to look at me, and I smiled at him," Ingrid said. "And that was the end."

For six months Ingrid lived with her fat, aging Aunt Ellen alone in the large apartment. Then one night Ingrid heard her aunt calling out in the dark: "I feel really ill." She asked Ingrid to telephone her brother. "Read the Bible to me. Read the Bible," she whispered. "I'm going to die. I'm going to die. Oh, why don't they come, why don't they come?"

Ingrid was supposed to throw the key out the window, but she had forgotten. And when her uncle finally burst into the room, Ingrid was holding Aunt Ellen in her arms. The old lady, gasping her last, was the black color of death.

Ingrid moved in with her Uncle Otto and Aunt Hulda and five cousins. The apartment was within walking distance of her home on Strandvägen, but it was a world apart. Her father had been an artist; to a loving daughter, the fact that he rarely sold a painting didn't matter. Theirs had been an artistic home, with the smell of oil paint drifting out of the atelier, and singing frequently sounding from the living room. The only singing at her aunt and uncle's was of Lutheran church hymns. There was no painting either, and when Ingrid dreamed of her father and her old life, she dreamed of an artistic life as well.

Uncle Otto had a frameshop and fancied himself an inventor, but his most persistent inventions were his reasons for never making a decent living. Aunt Hulda was the backbone of the family, a genius at making the soup go further, and patching a winter coat. She slept on a tiny portable bed in a windowless corridor, while her two girls shared one bedroom, and her three boys slept in others. Ingrid had the largest bedroom to herself, furnished with pieces from the old home, including the piano.

The whole family depended upon Ingrid's father's business and thus Ingrid merited the biggest room. Even the family's summer vacations were spent at the small house on Lake Mälaren that Ingrid had inherited from her Aunt Ellen. All these were subtleties on which Ingrid hardly ever reflected.

Ingrid's closest friend in the home was her cousin Britt, two years her junior, who would remain a friend all her life. "In our house she was just a sister," Britt reflects. "We took it for granted. We were fine together. She was very sensitive as a girl, and I had a feeling that she felt very much. She had her fantasy. She lived in another world."

When she was about eleven, her father had taken Ingrid to the theater. At the first intermission, she had announced, "Papa, Papa, that's what I'm going to do." Her home on Strandvägen had been no more than a hundred yards from the greatest Swedish theater, the Royal Dramatic. The magical theatrical world began not in the theater but out where Ingrid could see it, on the marble steps of the gracious building, where there arrived each evening gentlemen in evening dress, and ladies in long gowns.

Ingrid's new home was not far from Stockholm's film palace, the Röda Kvarn (Red Mill). Built in 1915, the year of Ingrid's birth, the great movie theater was as elegant as an opera house; music for the silent films was provided by one of the best orchestras in Stockholm. The well-dressed audience sat watching not only Charlie Chaplin, Mary Pickford, and other foreign performers, but films by the two Swedish masters Victor Sjöström and Mauritz Stiller.

At school Ingrid was not only shy, tall, and gawky but a poor student who had a hard time mastering the multiplication tables. While the other girls might dream of boys, Ingrid dreamed of stages and theaters. Increasingly, Ingrid retreated into her fantasy world, more real to her than quotidian existence. She went to her room, shut the door, and played different roles, as if she were trying on costumes—the golden brocade of a princess, a beggar's gray rags, a nurse's crisp outfit. She dreamed, as she wrote in her diary, that "one day I would stand at the Oscar Theater and the public would sit there and see this new Sarah Bernhardt." She dreamed that she might "play against Gösta Ekman [a famous actor], who was my ideal." She dreamed of standing in front of an audience, mesmerizing them with poems and drama, creating characters and voices.

Often on Sundays, Ingrid went to supper at the home of her father's old friend the florist Gunnar Spångberg. After dinner Spångberg would ask Ingrid to perform for his friends. Ingrid enjoyed the attention and the applause, and looked forward to the soirees and her chance to please and amuse a roomful of adults.

At school one Christmas, the students in her class could not do their exercises because the gymnasium had been turned into a stage for the senior play. As they sat waiting out the hour, Ingrid leaped to the stage and offered to put on a play for her peers. With six of her classmates drafted into subsidiary roles, Ingrid performed *The Green Elevator*, a play about a love triangle. Partway through the drama, the teacher returned and ordered the students outside. Ingrid finished her performance in the park, standing on a bench.

"If you remember Ingrid as a child, you remember her as an actress," says Disa Lauhren, her classmate. "When it was raining outside, one girl played the piano and Ingrid read poems. She was very quiet, but when she did it, that was the real Ingrid."

Uncle Otto tried to dissuade Ingrid from trying to become an actress. "My father was a very religious man," Britt says. "He thought they met bad people in the theater. He tried to get her interested in other things." Uncle Otto had lived a life mired in disappointment. He might well have thought that Ingrid's prospects as an actress were woeful, and wanted to shelter her. After all, she was too unassuming, too timid, ever to grace a stage. She had even developed a nervous condition. Sometimes her lips, eyelids, and fingers became so terribly swollen that she was almost grotesque.

When Ingrid talked of acting she was full of a breathless incredulity and innocence. She was, nonetheless, a mountain of ambition, the size of which was hidden, perhaps even from Ingrid herself. It was as if she had set out to climb a modest, gentle knoll, and saw rising above her another and then another climb, steeper, more challenging, rising to a sheer summit.

In later years Ingrid insisted that she had begun her journey upward from a pit of loneliness and unhappiness. Although her Uncle Otto and Aunt Hulda could not provide an idyllic family life for their orphaned niece, her memories of unhappiness were partially an actress's gift for self-dramatization. Those who knew her most intimately during those years do not remember such desperate unhappiness. "I never had the feeling she was unhappy," recalls Britt. "I think that Ingrid exaggerated the feeling of unhappiness." Greta Danielsson, a more dispassionate observer, makes the same observation: "I think she was happy as a child. But she was at a difficult age when she came to her uncle's. There were so many children, and before she had been the only one."

Greta was the only person Ingrid knew who had made even a modest start in her chosen métier. Greta had gone back to studying music, hoping for a career in opera. She was a lovely young woman, and someone at a film studio had offered her work. She worked as an extra and even had a few small roles. Although she had the prospect of a larger career in films, she wasn't interested. She simply wanted money to pursue her singing.

All Ingrid could talk about was theater and films, films and theater. One day Greta offered to take her out to the studio. She even arranged for fifteen-year-old Ingrid to work as an extra.

The Svensk Filmindustri (Swedish Film Industry) studios lay on the outskirts of Stockholm, on land that two decades before had been an ostrich farm. On that morning in late 1931 when Ingrid journeyed through the studio portals, the first golden age of Swedish film was as much a thing of the past as were ostrich feathers on ladies' hats. With the advent of sound there was a new market for provincial, Swedish-language films. Most of the better films were from America. It was what a French film historian of Swedish film calls an "age of lethargy." Even the two masters of early Swedish films had journeyed to Hollywood. Victor Sjöström had made the classic western *The Wind* before returning to Sweden. Mauritz Stiller had traveled westward too, taking his protégée Greta Garbo with him. He had been as much a failure as Garbo would prove a success, and had come back to Stockholm to die in 1928.

Svensk Filmindustri was the giant of the industry, with a captive market in its own chain of theaters. Every little town and village had its movie theater. For centuries the Swedes had been a poor farming people whose often austere, unyielding spirit matched the austere, unyielding land. But then there had been a great migration, not only to the cities but also to America. The first trickles of industrial wealth were reaching even the tiniest villages. Those in the rural reaches of the land sought entertainment and knowledge that the parish pastors could not provide. "The cinema was the church in the village," says Rune Waldekranz, the Swedish film historian.

If the cinema was the new church, it was primarily preaching comedy and tedious drama. For Ingrid's debut as an extra, she and a dozen other young women were doused in heavy yellow makeup. Wearing fur-trimmed wool coats, they were lined up along a brick wall, beside a sign saying "MODEHUSET ESTELLE" (Estelle Fashion House). The director turned to the young women, who were so pretty and well-fed that they might have been modeling winter coats. He told them they were playing desperate unemployed women applying for a job. They were to act appropriately hungry and fretful. Ingrid was in the second row. She was supposed to look forward. Instead, Ingrid turned slightly toward the camera. When the scene was shot, she was the only one of the thirteen extras whose full face appeared.

Ingrid was finished for the day, and it was only ten-thirty. She was not about to leave. She spent hours wandering the lot, visiting the various sets and films, still wearing her makeup. Late in the afternoon, when almost everyone else had left, a production assistant came upon Ingrid and gave her ten kronor for her work.

"She was so fascinated that she didn't want to leave," Greta says. "She was so happy. She said, 'I must be an actress.' "

If Ingrid was to become a great actress, there was only one place to begin: the school of the Royal Dramatic Theater. Founded by King Gustavus III in 1788, the Royal Dramatic is Sweden's national theater. The opulent four-tiered theater was often not a stage upon which one saw the world or saw into the world, but where one came to be seen and fitfully amused. Indeed, during the early 1930s the theater was playing primarily comedies and other light works. And yet Strindberg's *Master Olaf* had opened the new theater in 1908, and Eugene O'Neill's *Strange Interlude* had premiered there in 1928. These were plays full of truths so fierce and dark that one could imagine the elegant patrons plunging out into the winter winds almost with relief.

As an academy for actors, the Royal Dramatic School is almost unique in the western world. The school is so tiny, the competition so fierce, the training so rigorous, and the opportunities so great, that admission almost guarantees one a successful career in the theater.

In 1933 there were seventy-five would-be actors and actresses trying out for the eight places. Entrance depended not on references, school records, or past performances but on an audition before directors and others of the Royal Dramatic Theater. In later years Ingrid would suggest that she had been a helpless naïf who had made her way into the theater by luck and pluck. It was, however, almost as if Ingrid were two people. There was the timid, mousy child-woman who lived in the corners of life, in her room, in the back row at school. Her greatest gift was a quiet cunning, her greatest accomplishment the creation of the other, the public, Ingrid.

Ingrid was a young woman of substantial resources, and she prepared for the audition with great savvy and dedication. Ingrid had her own private drama teacher, Gabriel Alw, who prepared her for every aspect of her audition. She took private gymnastics lessons from Ruth Kylberg, who worked with the students at the Royal Dramatic School. She went to Ruth's apartment on Strandvägen and worked out in a room full of mirrors, bars, and paintings by her instructor's husband.

Ingrid's first audition was one of the great moments of her professional life, and in later years she loved talking about that day. When a great public performer makes an entrance, the audience *knows* that something has changed, that the play, the set, the auditorium, the stadium, is not the same. All that before a word is uttered. In her memory, her entrance onto the great stage became such a moment. In 1959 she told Joseph Steele, her biographer, that she had played the boy in Rostand's *L'Aiglon*. She was expecting applause from the twenty judges, but when she finished she was greeted only by silence. Two days afterward, Ingrid learned that she had been chosen. Only much later did she learn that the jury was so moved by her stunning performance that they had been unable to applaud. "They just sat there till the lights were turned on, and then the mood burst and they cheered," Ingrid recalled. "But I had already left the theater."

In her autobiography Ingrid had a different story to tell. She said that she had played a feisty, daring peasant girl in a play by a Hungarian playwright of such obscurity that she could remember neither the play nor the playwright. "A run and a leap into the air, and there I am in the middle of the stage with that big gay laugh that's supposed to stop them dead in their tracks," she remembered.

In her acting as well as in her personal life, Ingrid always seemed to be observing herself, reflecting upon her reflection. "I pause, and get out my first line," Ingrid recalled. "Then I take a quick glance down over the footlights at the jury. And I can't believe it! They are paying not the slightest attention to me. . . . I hear the voice of the chairman of the jury: 'Stop it, stop it. That's enough.' " According to Ingrid, years later one of the judges told her that she had been stopped because "the minute you leapt out of the wings and onto the stage, and stood there laughing at us, we turned round and said to each other, 'Well, we don't have to listen to her, she's in! Look at that security. Look at that stage presence.' "

Rarely, alas, is life so dramatic, are triumphs so pure, achievements so singular, as Ingrid would have it. Although there is no one left who re-members that August 1933 occasion, in 1946, when Ingrid was probably the most popular star in the world, an American reporter went to Stockholm to write about the Royal Dramatic School. He discovered that Ingrid had first performed a scene from *The Tower of the Conscience*, "with only minor slips." Like the other candidates, she went on to do two other pieces, choosing Rostand's *L'Aiglon* and Strindberg's *Dream Play*. One of the judges noted: "While she has too much the appearance of a country girl, she is very natural, and is the type that does not use make-up on her face or on her mind."

Ingrid had stood out well enough to be chosen one of the eight new students, but she had not stood out from her peers like a beacon in the night. Ingrid's greatest creation was herself, and on that stage that day she had made the first public performance of her Ingrid Bergman. The judge had noted her "country girl" appearance and her naturalness, but she was city born and city bred, with her own dramatics and gymnastics teachers. And she was now on her way to becoming a full-fledged actress.

CHAPTER TWO

"Oh, She Starts Well, Doesn't She?"

Two months after she entered the Royal Dramatic School, eighteen-year-old Ingrid sat with one of her cousins and two other friends at the Grand Hotel. As a little girl Ingrid could look out her window on Strandvägen and see the tall spire of the greatest hotel in all Sweden, a noble building that would not have been out of place along the Grand Canal in Venice. Here the world's artistic greats and Nobel Prize recipients stayed when they came to Stockholm. But Ingrid had never entered the lobby, much less sat in one of the Grand's fine restaurants.

Her cousin had arranged a date for Ingrid with a successful young dentist, Petter Aron Lindstrom,[*] called Aron since childhood. It was a measure of how much, and how positively, Ingrid's life was changing that she was having dinner at such a place, even if her blind date was a half hour late. Since she had entered the Royal Dramatic School, her face had stopped puffing up, and her hands no longer looked distended. She had only a couple of years before appeared a gawky adolescent, but now she was beautiful, glowing with youth and health. She was no dainty little thing, but a full-bodied robust young woman five feet nine inches tall, weighing around 130 pounds. In many respects she looked like a thousand other pretty Swedish girls, but there was an extraordinary quality to her appearance. Those who thought that beauty is only skin deep had only to look on Ingrid to feel that they were wrong. She seemed not only to look good but to be good, and to have a goodness that needed to be protected against the mean assaults of everyday life.

The revolving doors whirled once again, and through them walked a handsome six-foot-two-inch-tall young man who Ingrid knew immediately was her date. Petter Aron walked briskly toward them, his posture as straight as if he had a lamppost for a backbone.

Petter apologized for his tardiness, and was introduced to Ingrid.

"I like your hair," Petter said, as Ingrid remembered years later. "What a deep voice you have . . . what a beautiful voice."

---

[*] In the United States, Dr. Lindstrom's first name was often to be rendered as Peter.

Petter was a forceful young man with a confident, even cocky, air. He had light-brown hair and exuded a sense of cleanliness and order and good health. As Ingrid soon discovered, Petter was a wonderful dancer and he spun Ingrid across the floor with exuberant grace. If he had burdened Ingrid with all his accomplishments, he would have left her little room to talk. Petter had studied dentistry in Sweden and in Germany, and at the age of twenty-six had the only doctor of medical dentistry degree in all Sweden. He had spent a summer north of the Arctic Circle working in a tuberculosis sanatorium that provided dental treatment to Laplanders. He had published research papers, and was in private practice. He was also an associate professor at the Dental College of the Karolinska Institute in Stockholm. As if that wasn't enough, he was a medical student at the same institute where he was an instructor.

Petter was known as a stern, rigorous, and dedicated teacher; woe betide the hapless student who came to his class unprepared. Outside of his work he was a frolicking punster who turned the humor on himself as often as on others. He was an athlete, a champion boxer and skier, a man who enjoyed hiking with a knapsack full of rocks and challenging the unwary to arm-wrestling matches that he almost always won. It was not only sports that interested Petter; he also knew artists and writers, and found time to go to concerts and the theater.

Petter called Ingrid a few days later and they began dating. Their backgrounds were very different. Petter had grown up in Stöde, a large village of six hundred in north central Sweden. Most of the people in the village earned their living from farming or lumber, but Petter's father was the provincial landscape architect. The family house was a simple two-story structure, set off on several acres of land.

The Swedes are not a people who look kindly on pretense or ostentation, and the house was neither more nor less grand than the others in the village. The Swedish philosopher of egalitarianism is nature herself, who gives the land short, brilliant summers, time and light during most of Sweden's history to scurry and scamper to grow and harvest enough for the harsh, unyielding winter.

"When I was growing up there were many homeless, hungry people traveling through," Petter says. "My parents let them stay in the barn, sleeping in the hay, and gave them porridge to eat. It wasn't for religious reasons but because that was the family attitude. My mother did want me perhaps to grow up and become a priest because that was the most honored position in the town."

There is an old Swedish saying, "Neighbors are brothers," and though Petter did not become a priest, he was a man who was forever reaching out, helping people. It was almost a compulsion with him. Even when Ingrid first knew him there were many people whom he was helping with advice, money, treatment, or time.

Petter was a man of great pride, the pride that the Lutheran priests railed against in their Sunday sermons. But pride was the sinew of all Petter's virtues. He was proudly virtuous, proudly generous, proudly humane, proudly caring, and proudly loving. He was a good man and he knew it, and the proof of his goodness, and ample proof there was, was in his daily actions.

Petter was living in Stockholm, but he remained in many respects a man of Stöde. Life there had been tough, simple, and good: a sauna at the town steam bath on the weekends, nude bathing in the summer (the men and the women separated), sports year round. Despite his degrees and his ambition, Petter, too, sought a life that was tough, simple, and good.

Ingrid had already had one involvement, with an artist, and she was suddenly being courted by many young men. "She was absolutely natural in some things," Britt reminisces. "Many of the boys from the theater fell in love with her. They called and stood outside the window. But her career came first."

Petter was eight and a half years older than Ingrid, but in those days that was not a dramatic difference. Petter was one of the most eligible bachelors in Stockholm, and it was no wonder that Ingrid would be flattered by his attention. Moreover, if love begins sometimes with a wondrous dizzying leaving of the senses, it also often begins with calculations, as if one were weighing a pound of bacon.

Ingrid was not interested in mere boys. She had her career to think about. Petter was a listener. Love is in the details, and he sat there as she went on endlessly about the theater and the school. He was a man who liked to take care of things, and he freed Ingrid from worrying about many of the boring details of adult life. He thought about her, advised her. He was there waiting for her when she needed him. He had a substance and a background that were real and deep. He was funny and witty and caring. He was endlessly solicitous of Ingrid.

If Petter was not a womanizer, it was as much because of his sense of his own worth as of his personal morality. Petter understood Ingrid's value. She had a loveliness beyond loveliness. She was an adornment for any man—sweet, and innocent, and alone. He could do no better. If she did not seem especially smart to him, and didn't know even her multiplication tables, that didn't matter. If she wasn't as broadly interested in the world as he was, that didn't matter either. He was the man and he was concerned enough about the world for both of them.

Even before they professed their love, Ingrid had the first crisis of her professional life. A month or so after her meeting Petter, one of the judges at her audition, Alf Sjöberg, offered her a large role in the play he was directing. At the Royal Dramatic School, acting was a profession that required several years of apprenticeship. Any third-year student would have coveted such a role. It was almost unheard of to give a freshman any role, let alone a big one.

The young actors and actresses behaved as if they were a band of brothers and sisters of the arts, sharing equally of the bread of theater. Alas, there are good parts and bad parts and no parts at all. Ingrid's good fortune brought forth a plague of jealousy. "I was so hated, they actually attacked me physically," Ingrid said years later. "I was kicked, while one girl began hitting me over the head." Ingrid had a penchant for self-dramatization, and Petter has no memory of her ever talking of a physical attack. The slings and arrows of outrageous fortune may have been merely verbal, pricking her ego and not her skin. But in order to quell the uproar, the role was taken away from her.

The sting of unfairness had wakened her to the realities of a world where there are more prize seekers than prizes, where being best is sometimes not good enough. Ingrid fell back into the anonymity of the freshman class, but she believed that she was "still hated by the older girls."

If those around her radiated hate, at least that was a mark of their attention. Her classmates surely did not shower Ingrid with as much hatred as she imagined. Her peers were doubtless as involved with themselves and their careers as Ingrid. What impressed her fellow students was Ingrid's self-confidence and determination. One day when the students were discussing if they dared to go out to the film studio and try for a part, Ingrid reputedly piped up: "Ha! Try for a role! It's they who should come looking for us."

What is striking is how few memories her fellow students have of Ingrid. Signe Hasso, the Swedish actress, was one of those older girls who allegedly hated Ingrid. Yet Hasso states that she did not know her at all, a remarkable achievement in a school with less than thirty students. "I was so busy I never saw anyone," she says. Frank Sundstrom, the actor and director, was a schoolmate who was photographed with Ingrid in the class picture; he says that he never met her. Gunnar Björnstrand, the actor known best for his work with Ingmar Bergman, says that he has almost no memories of his classmate.

When the school year was over, many of her fellow students went on an inexpensive tour to study theater in Russia, but Ingrid stayed in Stockholm. "I really should have gone," she said later. "But I had fallen in love with Petter Lindstrom. I didn't want to stay away from him."

Ingrid had begun to use Petter as an excuse. She had other reasons not to go. She had few friends at the school; she surely could not relish spending twenty-four hours a day with young actresses who she felt hated her. She was growing bored and frustrated with mere classes. Probably most important, she had other ideas for her career, ideas that she dared not talk of too openly.

Women were not supposed to parade their ambition nakedly, boasting of their aspirations, proudly announcing their grand goals. Ingrid had to garb her intentions in more modest dress. She played the sweet ingenue, but she was full of fierce determination to succeed in her chosen métier.

Ingrid went to see Gunnar Spångberg, in whose house on Sunday evenings she had once so happily performed. Many actors and actresses bought flowers at Gunnar's shop near the Royal Dramatic Theater. Ingrid wanted Spångberg to ask one of these customers to help her get a small part at the film studio. Spångberg was delighted to help Ingrid, but he was a florist, after all, not part of the theatrical world. Ingrid, her innocence and naïveté still intact, knew the customer to ask: Karin Swanström, the artistic director of Svensk Filmindustri.

Wouldn't it be nice if Gunnar gave Miss Swanström a bunch of roses and then asked if young Ingrid might come out to the studio to seek advice? That was the neatest touch of all, to ask not for even an extra's role but only for advice. Gunnar told the artistic director that Ingrid was his little girl, the daughter of his best friend, and an orphan. It was a tale more poignant by far than half the melodramas being produced at the studio, and Miss Swanström agreed to see Ingrid the next day.

Ingrid knew how to make people want to help her, to make her success seem theirs as well. Miss Swanström fancied herself a *grande dame* and was not immune to the more subtle forms of flattery. The next morning she not only gave Ingrid "advice," but listened to her reciting poetry, and set up a screen test the following day.

Before arriving at the studio for the ten o'clock screen test, Ingrid got off the tram at the small cemetery where her parents were buried. Ingrid was not sure that she believed in God, but she did believe in her own ability as an actress. She sat and prayed not to God but to her father, and not for success either, but merely that she not be nervous.

When Ingrid arrived at the film studio, she was met by Gustav Molander, a leading director. Ingrid was flushed with excitement and anticipation. She had no lines to recite. She merely had to sit while the camera played over her, as she turned her head, smiled, or scowled.

A screen actor must concentrate absolutely and yet appear relaxed. Thus as Ingrid sat there, so sweetly, so obligingly, she was acting as much as if she had been standing reciting before a vast audience. She was exuding those inexplicable qualities that would make her a star: a femininity that was at once sensuous and innocent, a smile that was as warm as a winter's hearth, a fresh milky beauty that lay on her countenance like the morning's dew—a magical quality that enhanced the film with life, and seemed to enhance those who watched her.

The camera had the only eye that mattered. The film was the only judge and jury. Not until Molander saw the rushes the next day did he know for sure what a find this Ingrid Bergman was. As Ingrid sat watching herself, she was the professional critiquing her performance as if she were watching another person. "I didn't look very good, did I?" Ingrid said, confident enough to want not simply reassurance but the truth. "I think if I did some more I could be better later."

One of the films about to be shot that had a possible role for Ingrid was *The Count of the Monk's Bridge*, directed by Edvin Adolphson, who also played the lead. This was Adolphson's first chance to direct. He would have preferred a serious drama, and not a madcap comedy, a popular genre in Sweden during the 1930s. Adolphson assembled as fine a group of comedic talent as possible. The only remaining role was the ingenue. The first-time director was seeking a hard-nosed girl with character.

Ingrid was one possibility, but Adolphson had bittersweet memories of the studio's newest starlet. The previous year Adolphson had starred in a play in which Ingrid had been an extra. In his memoirs the director wrote that Ingrid and another student "had destroyed a scene for Inga Tidblad and me in Sheridan's play *The Rivals.* Inga and I had a big scene on a park sofa with people walking in the background. Just when the important dialogue was taking place, two elegant ladies with umbrellas and wide 18th century crinolines came and giggled in front of our sofa so that the public could see neither Inga nor me. . . . One was Ingrid Bergman."

In theater, an extra upstaging a lead character is the sin against the holy ghost. Ingrid was roundly reprimanded. But her behavior certainly displayed hard-nosed character. Adolphson gave her the part.

When Ingrid arrived for her first day's work, no one at the studio was as curious about her as Birgit Tengroth. Although she was Ingrid's age, Birgit was already a popular actress with half a decade of filmmaking behind her. In almost any other profession, Birgit would have viewed the future with confidence. But she was haunted by the specter of Ingrid Bergman and the dread thought that her own career might soon be over.

Two years before, Birgit's gymnastics teacher had told her about a high school student who looked like her and who would be trying out for the Royal Dramatic School. That had been enough to ruin Birgit's day. Then, recently, when she had demanded a higher salary for her current picture, she had been told that "there was a girl enough like me to be used to take my place." And now this Ingrid Bergman had a part that Birgit believed should have been hers.

Birgit felt worn out, old. She was no hapless paranoid, but a perfect product of her chosen profession. For five years she had been primped and pampered, made the center of the universe, as indispensable as the sun itself. Now, suddenly, "the new Birgit Tengroth" had arrived as if Birgit was only the caretaker of her own being.

No wonder, then, that as Birgit sat in her quarters, next to Ingrid's new dressing room, she felt only anguish and self-doubt. Even Ingrid's arrival that morning had been spectacular. No star or would-be star had ever wheeled into the studio on a bicycle, wearing sunglasses. It was as dramatic and unexpected an entrance as if Ingrid had arrived in a horse-drawn chariot.

Ingrid seemed to be totally devoid of the self-doubt that is endemic to film acting. "I was crushed, I sat in my dressing room with my troubles and a feeling of anguish," Birgit wrote later. "I heard her come up the stairs and into the dressing room corridor, and then she picked up the telephone, called up the restaurant and asked for two sandwiches, one with liver pate and one with veal, and then her strong laugh saying 'I love to eat and sleep.' "

Birgit might not have been so intimidated by Ingrid if she had reflected further on what she had just observed. A young woman who wolfs down sandwiches could be a compulsive eater. It might have occurred to Birgit, too, that the studio lay outside Stockholm. If Ingrid had bicycled all the way from her apartment, she had gotten up early indeed. Ingrid and Petter, in fact, later found it a wonderful joke: Ingrid would drive out near the studio, park the car, and then ride her bicycle the last few hundred yards, arriving with a wind-blown, miraculous freshness.

In *The Count of the Monk's Bridge*, Ingrid played a maid whose boyfriend and his disreputable friends lead the Stockholm police a merry chase through the capital's bohemian districts. The plot was a thin strand on which to drape one madcap scene after another. In one scene on the first day of shooting, Tollie Zellman, a leading comedienne, wrapped a fish for a customer while another customer, Ingrid, looked on. While the shot was being set up, Ingrid proceeded to show the talented and seasoned Miss Zellman how one properly wraps a fish.

Tollie looked first at the director and then at Ingrid, her measured glance more telling than any dialogue.

"And who's this?" the comedienne asked rhetorically, as Adolphson looked on, richly amused.

"Well, she's a young girl who's just started."

"Oh, she starts well, doesn't she?"

Part of the film was shot on the streets of Stockholm. "Adolphson was a dark sort of demoniac fellow," recalled Åke Dahlqvist, the cameraman. "On one occasion when we were working on the streets, he needed some faces in the shot. And he screamed, 'You bloody old hags, put your faces out of the windows.' And all these faces appeared."

In her first role Ingrid was merely another strand holding up the comic scenes, yet she made the most of it. "Edvin says very little except to tell me that I should go very far because of my impudence and audacity," she wrote in her diary.

Starting well was a matter of how Ingrid looked as well as how she acted. Dahlqvist, the cameraman on this and six of Ingrid's other Swedish films, was as responsible as anyone for creating what became the Bergman look. Dahlqvist had photographed the screen test that the decade before had led Greta Garbo to Hollywood. He had a tender, lyrical way of photographing women. "More as an experiment than anything else, at the studio they took special still pictures of Ingrid to show that her face was evenly balanced," Dahlqvist said. "They then took two right sides and two left sides, and the face looked the same. When they tried that with other actresses, they often got horrifying results.

"But in photographing her one side of her face was lit stronger than the other side. I did that. You had to be careful. I tried to avoid one profile. I thought that if I did an extreme profile it was too sharp."

22

As soon as Ingrid finished *The Count of the Monk's Bridge*, she was offered a studio contract. That would mean leaving drama school. In the 1920s Garbo had left the Royal Dramatic School early, but it was highly unusual. To make it an even more difficult decision, Ingrid had been hired at the film studio by Gustav Molander, whose brother, Olof, was the new head of the Royal Dramatic Theater and School. The fact that the Molanders were brothers was one of God's little jokes. Their competitiveness and jealousy bordered on hatred.

Olof was like an Old Testament patriarch who saw the true faith threatened by a false and glittery sect. He had begun to revitalize the Royal Dramatic Theater, bringing it into one of its most creative periods. The year before, he had staged O'Neill's *Mourning Becomes Electra*, and he was preparing a new, more realistic version of Strindberg's *Dream Play*. Olof Molander considered it unthinkable that a serious student of acting would give up *this* for his brother's fiefdom: mere money, celebrity, and the ersatz of the Swedish film industry.

If Ingrid had remained in school, she would have learned the discipline and techniques of the theater and might have become a great stage actress. At least that is what Olof Molander told her when she went in to tell him her decision not to return in September. He ranted at her, in turns threatening, flattering, and cajoling, finally simply forbidding her to leave the school.

Ingrid had made up her mind. "I don't see how you can forbid me," she remembered saying. "We have no contract between us. You accepted me. The lessons are free. I don't pay anything, and I don't get paid."

Ingrid left that day, with Olof's prophecies ringing in her ears like curses. Although Ingrid took drama lessons on her own, Olof Molander was in part correct. She never did receive the formal training or theatrical apprenticeship of so many of her contemporaries that makes the Swedish acting community such a brilliant repertory company. Ingrid was similar to so many young screen actors in America today. She had to rely on her instincts, on whatever technique she could pick up as she went along, and on her personality.

Ingrid had hardly finished *The Count of the Monk's Bridge* when she began her second film, *Ocean Breakers*, a melodramatic tale in which she played a fisherman's daughter, seduced and impregnated by a married minister. *Ocean Breakers* was considered one of the best Swedish films of the year, good enough to be sent as a Swedish entry to the Venice Film Festival in the summer of 1935.

"One did believe in her tenderness and faithfulness," said the critic for the *Stockholm Daily*. Around her image on the screen there was a penumbra of goodness and caring that stayed no matter whom she played.

In her third film, *The Family Swedenhielms*, Ingrid played alongside Gösta Ekman, one of the most distinguished names in Swedish cinema, and Ingrid's idol. For the first time Ingrid saw how the image and the reality could be totally at odds. Ekman appeared a good family man, but he was homosexual and a drug addict. "Ekman told Ingrid that it didn't matter what people say about you, but what matters is that they talk about you," Petter says. "She learned that from her idol, and she said it all the time."

In *The Family Swedenhielms* Ingrid was cast as the rich girlfriend of a brilliant scientist, played by Ekman. The scientist, falsely accused of forgery, turns down the Nobel Prize, but love and truth triumph, and Ingrid carries on, noble and selfless. She seemed to glow with character, as if her beauty grew out of intrinsic goodness. In *Walpurgis Night*, Ingrid's fourth film, her role had similarities to that in *Ocean Breakers*. Once again Ingrid found herself innocently involved in an illicit affair with her married boss. Her lover's wife becomes pregnant, gets an abortion, kills her blackmailer, and commits suicide. Loyal Ingrid is waiting when her lover returns from the Foreign Legion, where he has fled, and they marry and raise a family.

For her fifth film, a comedy called *On the Sunny Side*, Ingrid was cast as an orphan from a good family who marries a rich older gentleman and goes to live on his estate. Her husband, played by Lars Hanson, fears that his young bride may be bored by the tranquil country life. He invites her old flame, a bohemian writer played by Edvin Adolphson, to liven up Ingrid's days. The triangle creates enough friction to light a fire, but inevitably love and virtue triumph.

Day after day Ingrid journeyed out to the studios, playing one role after another. Fame was still a mystery that had not touched her. There is a curious time warp in a film career, and Ingrid had already completed three films when *The Count of the Monk's Bridge* premiered at Stockholm's Skandia Theater on January 21, 1935. Ingrid received respectable reviews, but none of her early films were sensational successes that in one fell swoop carried her to stardom. Yet she was becoming a figure of major importance at the studio, and a favorite among Stockholm moviegoers. Her name and face were familiar to audiences in the far villages of Sweden. Even Hollywood was taking its first small notice of Ingrid Bergman. *Variety*, the entertainment industry's premier trade journal, noted in its review of *On the Sunny Side* on September 16, 1936, that Eva Bergh, played by Ingrid, was "one of the better characterizations in the play . . . pretty and capable, rating a Hollywood berth."

By far the most important of Ingrid's early movies was *Intermezzo*, so much so that she considered it one of the three films on which her career was based (*Casablanca* and *Autumn Sonata* were the others). Not only was *Intermezzo* a great, much deserved success, but it indelibly defined Ingrid's film persona. Gösta Ekman played Holger Brandt, a world-famous violinist who falls in love with Anita Hoffman, a beautiful young pianist, played by Ingrid. Brandt leaves his family and runs off with Anita. The couple travel through Europe, where Anita serves as Brandt's accompanist. As much as she loves him, Anita realizes that their love cannot go on. So she steals away. Brandt returns to his eternally patient wife and family. His daughter is struck by a car when she runs across the street to meet her errant father, but she presumably recovers.

Gösta Ekman had by far the largest part in the film. *Intermezzo* should have been *his* film, his drama of moral redemption. But from the moment

Ingrid appears on the screen, looking as if she is made of warm milk and strawberries, *Intermezzo* is Ingrid's film. The haunting, poignant strains of the theme music become her theme, the music of her soul. She haunts the screen even when her scenes are finished. "It wasn't just a *pilsnerfilm* [beer movie]," Ingrid told a Swedish interviewer at the end of her career. "It was so well written that you felt pity for everybody."

The exquisite melancholy of *Intermezzo* is irresistible. When the film opened on November 16, 1936, at the Red Mill Theater, the Stockholm *Daily News* reported that at the end the audience sat silent, not wanting to break the spell with applause.

Ingrid had enraptured the audience in what was becoming an almost familiar role. In three of her first six films Ingrid played an innocent woman involved in an illicit affair. In the fourth she was the catalyst for what could have developed into an adulterous affair. In these films her innocence is based on a mixture of ignorance and the exoneration of pure emotion. For her audience she sanctified behavior that the moral dictates of her time considered slightly sordid or improper. It was a role she would play again and again.

At the end of *Intermezzo*, Ingrid is off somewhere, pursuing her career. This, too, became the ending in so many Ingrid Bergman films: Ingrid running off, getting on a plane, leaving a school, her daughter's home, a royal appointment, running off, running away, running on.

As Ingrid's career blossomed, she kept her personal and professional lives totally separate. Like most actors and actresses, Ingrid was always talking about her dear friends in the theatrical world, praising them extravagantly in public, gushing over them. But she had no real friends in film, no one she totally trusted, no gang of buddies that she met at the Opera café for ice cream and conversation. Her personal life meant one person: Petter Lindstrom. Ingrid was Petter's *fästmö*, a peculiarly Swedish word that means steady girlfriend but with at least some presumption of sexual intimacy.

There were those who felt that Petter was too prideful about Ingrid, too much the man of the world bestowing a precious heritage on a young woman. Ingrid did not take Petter out to the studio, or to her film openings. Petter was as busy as Ingrid and every bit as ambitious, studying medicine while continuing to teach and practice dentistry. In the evenings, when Ingrid was busy memorizing her lines for the next day's shooting, Petter was studying medical books. But on the weekends they often went off on long hikes.

Ingrid was only mildly interested in what went on outside the walls of the film studio. She constantly talked to Petter about films and the theater. She rarely read books, and she knew practically nothing about the darkening world of European politics, or of neighboring Europe, where Adolf Hitler had just become chancellor. She rarely cooked, and she threw up her arms at the idea of managing the house.

Petter took care of all the busy work of Ingrid's life. He left her free to do what she did best. She could be honest and open with him. And in his company she often became a radiant, childlike person.

On July 4, 1935, Ingrid and Petter left Stockholm on their first trip together, to drive to northern Norway. They bought a diary before their trip and intended to save it to read again in old age. In a pension they had dinner and rented two rooms with a door between them but used only the smaller bedroom.

Petter called Ingrid "Kat" (kitten), and a kitten she was. During the second night of the trip a black cat entered their bedroom. Ingrid felt like a true cat and she wondered whether the second cat meant good luck. "The cat was trying to replace the true cat," she wrote. "But I was sticking hard to Petter's stomach. Even in the morning the other cat was still lying there. We woke up partly from our sleep. Petter wanted to tell me that the other cat was still there. And kind as he usually is, he was trying to help both cats."

Northward they drove in the northern lights. With each day's journey the roads grew more empty, until they were practically alone. Petter took pictures of Ingrid sunning herself on the rocks. They pitched their tent one evening next to a rushing stream and did not crawl out until noon the next day. Ingrid waited as Petter went to help a couple with car trouble. As she sat waiting for Petter to return, Ingrid wrote: "He does that maybe to impress me, and that he's really doing to a high degree. I think he's so sweet, and I do love him so much."

Ingrid had no mother to pass judgment on Petter, no father to ask for his daughter's hand. Petter did not make a formal proposal; nor did he have to, for it seemed to both of them that their fates were as intertwined as two flowers that have grown together. Her mother's lucky number was seven. Ingrid wanted to become formally engaged the following year on the seventh day of the seventh month. She wanted to do it in Hamburg, her mother's birthplace. Petter adored Ingrid, and he would have traveled to Lhasa if that had been his fiancée's choice. And so early in July 1936 they drove to Hamburg.

Ingrid's worldly, sophisticated relatives, the Adlers, were doing well in the first years of the Thousand Year Reich. "They all were there and they raised their arms, saying 'Heil Hitler,' " remembers Petter. "So did Ingrid. I just said hello and I said to her, 'If you do that again I am returning to Sweden.' But she said, ' "Heil Hitler" is just a greeting.'

"The day after we arrived, the morning before we were to have an engagement party, Frau Adler took me aside and said, 'I have to explain why we have to change your name.' Then Frau Adler said, 'We can't have a Jewish name in our family.'

" 'Oh,' I said. What could I say?

" 'I don't ever want to hear you called Aron again,' Ingrid said.

"I went along because though I had been called Aron all my life, my first name was really Petter, on both my birth certificate and my passport."

On the seventh day of the seventh month, Ingrid and Petter stood in the same church where Ingrid's parents had been married. They exchanged platinum engagement rings that had two wavering lines engraved on them, growing apart but then always converging again.

Ingrid had been delighted to come to Hamburg almost every summer since she was a child. She especially admired and trusted her mother's older sister, Frau Elsa Adler. Unlike Ingrid's Swedish Uncle Otto and Aunt Hulda, her Aunt Mutti was a sophisticated woman. Petter felt differently. He loved Ingrid like a precious gift, but he was a man of stern moral fiber, and he was taken aback by his German relatives-to-be. Aunt Mutti was married to a wealthy French planter, who lived in Haiti. Ingrid's aunt hadn't liked the Caribbean island. She had returned to Germany, leaving her two sons with their father.

Like any good Swedish Lutheran, Petter believed that when you were married you were married. "Ingrid was brought up in an atmosphere where sex wasn't important, and not only in her immediate family," Petter reflected years later. "When I came to visit, Frau Adler hadn't seen her husband for ten years. She was living with a man. He took us to show his bedroom. There was a bedroom with the biggest bed I've ever seen, the bed shaped like an enormous heart."

What troubled Petter far more were the family's political attitudes. "The man Frau Adler was living with was a high Nazi who was selling uniforms to the SS. Ingrid was brought in with these people who heiled Hitler and in Hamburg she would heil Hitler herself. Frau Adler had left a mark on her. I wanted her to read a book about Nazism, but she wouldn't. She had no real interest in politics."

Ingrid would later write that she had refused to heil Hitler, and whether she did or not, she certainly was not a devotee of Nazism. She didn't care about politics, except as far as they might advance her career. In the mid 1930s, however, she did appear deaf to the sounds of the new Germany—the roll of drums, the clang of steel, and the cadences of marching feet. She was an actress, and she was fascinated by the pure theater of Nazi Germany.

But Ingrid gave little thought to Germany, and the newly engaged couple were soon back in Stockholm.

On August 29, for Ingrid's twenty-first birthday, Petter bought her a spectacular present: a silver fox coat. Alone in her apartment, Ingrid opened the gift. She was not an extravagant woman and she hadn't dared to think that Petter would give her such a gift. Rushing to the phone to thank her fiancé, she tripped and broke her ankle.

At the Serafimer Hospital, Ingrid had many guests, including the actress Birgit Tengroth. The year before, Birgit had been in the hospital for a mysterious, though temporary, condition. Her face had swollen, and she had rested in bed looking despondently at her distorted image in a hand mirror. That was punishment enough, but what had truly exasperated her was the arrival of

Ingrid in a yellow sweater as sunny as her mood. "How happy I am," Ingrid had said, hardly the desired greeting. "This is for you." She pushed a tin of cookies at Birgit.

War is war, and today Birgit brought Ingrid an enormous box of chocolates. "Thank you," Ingrid said. "I've already got lots of boxes." Just then Ingrid's lunch was brought in. She lustily inhaled the food odors. "How nice it smells," Ingrid said, never one to belittle the obvious. "And how dangerous it is with good food."

Ingrid proceeded to eat a full meal, before turning to her knitting. "How happy I am now, knitting a sweater for my cousin," Ingrid said, as if there was nothing in the world she would like better than to be sitting here in a hospital bed, her plastered leg up in the air.

"I was [jealous] but it was not just a case of simple 'jalousie de métier,' " Birgit wrote later. "I was envious of her coolness and freshness, envious that she was so bright and real, envious at her wonderful ability to meet problems with a ringing laugh. She said to me once, 'I will never survive a bad review.' But she never got a bad review. And she knew she wouldn't get one. How on earth did she do it? She had a secret knowledge about success of which every friend had to be envious."

As a prominent actress Ingrid had already far outdistanced her erstwhile rival. Both Ingrid and Birgit were part of a small company of leading actors and directors who formed a theatrical company to keep busy during the winter. Ingrid was busier than most of the other cast members. She was the only member of the group in an active production at the film studio. Yet not only did she take part in the first production, *Jean*, a political comedy by the Hungarian playwright Bus-Feketes, but she played the lead.

"All of us were directors for the only employed actor, Ingrid Bergman, who for the first time went on stage in a big part," Edvin Adolphson wrote in his memoirs. In this profession where jealousy perfumes the air like the scent of cedar in old Lebanon, Ingrid was able to make people want to help her, to lift her high above them. Birgit Tengroth watched this spectacle in awed befuddlement from an excellent seat. Dressed in a prim outfit and frilly mini-apron, and carrying a silver calling-card tray, Birgit played Ingrid's maid. "She [Ingrid] played a young girl of good family who falls in love with her man servant but has character enough to renounce her love," Birgit recalled. "The part was made for her. Ingrid was a child of the secure world. She didn't make any mistakes with servants. And she had nerves as strong as wires from the Royal telegraph."

Like almost everything else Ingrid touched, the play was a great success and ran well into the spring. By then Ingrid was busy at the studio with her new film, *Dollar*, a romantic comedy directed by Gustav Molander. Ingrid played a gorgeous actress married to a highly successful businessman.

Edvin Adolphson was one of her co-stars. The actor/director had become a problem for Ingrid, making passes with unrelenting persistence. One eve-ning the film company arranged a formal dinner after the play. Any young star would have known that attendance at such an occasion was mandatory; not Ingrid.

When Ingrid told Adolphson that she was not going, he became infur-iated. Ingrid wrote Petter that Adolphson had at times been acting crazy. He had been so looking forward to a great evening and was half sick with love. "He is telephoning and writing more and more, as soon as there is a pause," she wrote. "I almost took the life away from him tonight. Surely he never had experienced something like that in his love-seeking life."

Ingrid had something else on her mind: her wedding. She wanted it for the seventh of July, but as the film production lagged, the date had to be changed until the tenth.

She wrote Petter from the studio twelve days before the wedding, saying that she was "devilishly lonesome." "Little golden kitten of mine, my every-thing on this earth, my wonderful, great and only love . . . If I could only get a little kiss from you that I can suck on. Don't ever leave me. I shall never leave you. How crazy I am about you."

"How many hours do I have left as a miss?" Ingrid asked as she stood on the veranda of the Lindstroms' old house in Stöde.

"Three," Petter said. Ingrid and Petter had become engaged in Hamburg, but they would be married in Stöde, symbolizing even more strongly that Ingrid was entering into Petter's family. Petter was a small-town boy who had gone to the big city and triumphed a hundredfold, returning with his beautiful movie actress bride. It was a story that the townspeople might see at the movie theater.

Though Ingrid and Petter shared visions of a rich and blissful married life, they had grown up with profoundly different experiences of the way men and women live together. When he thought of what a marriage should be, Petter looked no further than his own family. His father was the man of the house, the patriarch. Petter had never seen his mother and father argue. He loved and admired his parents, and he wanted his own life to honor them.

Ingrid could not remember what it was to have a mother and father and a happy home life. She had seen how happy her father had been with Greta, but Greta was more an older sister than a mother figure. And that wasn't a marriage anyway. At Aunt Hulda's, Ingrid had been part of a real family, but she was treated as the rich relative and given a private room. In Germany, Ingrid had seen her beloved Aunt Mutti living in an adulterous relationship. Throughout her young life, Ingrid had been emotionally uprooted. From all that Ingrid had seen and felt, words like "fidelity," "loyalty," and "devotion" might not have quite the same meanings that they had to Petter.

In those years the villagers of Sweden were the most ceremonial of people, as if rituals well performed will placate the gods. They sent the dead on their way with stark formality. Their weddings were full of such grace and solemnity and high seriousness that the marriage the newlyweds were sanctifying had better be a perfect one, untainted by lust, jealousy, pride, or covetousness.

By the appointed hour of 4 P.M. on July 10, 1937, the church was full. This was one of the biggest events in Stöde's history. Villagers and dignitaries squeezed into the pews. A few younger people stood against the walls. Everyone was dressed in his or her best, the ladies in their fanciest hats and best cotton dresses, the men in suits pressed until the creases were razor sharp, the minister in a white cloak and dark vestments.

Most of the people in the church had known Petter for years, but in his elegant morning suit, fitting so perfectly on his slim frame, the long coat set off by a boutonniere, he looked a young prince.

As for Ingrid, she could have stepped off the screen, playing an ethereal bride of transcendent beauty. She wore a long white silk gown that fell to her white shoes. Her light-brown hair was crowned by a Juliet cap from which flowed a veil of silky white mesh. In her arm she carried a spray of orchids, lilies of the valley, and stephanotises. Although the wedding was supposed to be private, one young reporter, Barbro ("Bang") Alving, had shown up. Bang thought that the congregation "sometimes behaved as if it were in a theater," at this wedding in which "the most popular film star in Sweden was no longer Ingrid Bergman but Mrs. Ingrid Lindstrom."

The newlyweds sped southward on a honeymoon trip to Norway and then to England. In Stockholm they discovered their picture on the cover of the *Daily News*; they were shown leaving the church in Stöde. "MOST BEAUTIFUL AND PRIVATE BRIDE IN SWEDEN SHOWS A LACK OF PUBLIC PRESENCE" was the headline of Bang's long, loving article. If the camera was one friend that never betrayed Ingrid, publicity was the other. A star who had sought publicity for her wedding would never imagine that she would find the account on the front page of a leading newspaper. Ingrid was having it both ways, privacy and publicity.

"I think I should send this Bang a picture postcard," Petter remembers Ingrid saying on the honeymoon. "She may become important." For all Ingrid's unspoiled qualities, she had the attributes of a young politician, developing her own constituencies and clients. Mixed motives are usually the most durable, and Bang soon became a friend, and a writer of articles about Ingrid.

There was a seemingly guileless quality to the public Ingrid, and her new husband didn't know quite what to make of it. He knew the private Ingrid, who, as he remembered years later, was fiercely jealous of Birgit Tengroth and Signe Hasso and other actresses. It didn't matter that Ingrid had outdistanced them as a movie star; she still, as Petter saw it, felt threatened. Petter knew an Ingrid, too, who could say the strangest things.

According to Petter, one day when they had been married only a few weeks, Ingrid turned to him and said, "I'd like to make love with at least one man of each race."

Petter considered the remark a total non sequitur.

CHAPTER THREE

Destined for Hollywood

"*M*en make women helpless by deciding and telling them what to do," Ingrid reflected years later. "Men in my life taught me to be dependent, beginning with my father, and after that Uncle Otto, who didn't want me to become an actress, and then Petter, even before our engagement—not that it was Petter's fault. I was the one who asked him for advice and help in those early days."

Men had not taught Ingrid to be dependent as much as to create the illusion of dependency. Like many widowed or divorced fathers, Justus Bergman had lavished attention and affection on his only daughter. He had praised her artistic gifts, and sung her praises to friends and relatives. Ingrid had learned that the best way to get things from her father was to manipulate him, to make him think everything was his idea. As for Uncle Otto, here was a man full of high moral preaching and precepts who was a weak and ineffectual person, unable even to provide a decent living for his own family. Ingrid had listened politely to her uncle, and then done as she pleased.

Ingrid had learned to use people without appearing to use them, while maintaining her persona of naïveté and goodness. Much of this was done not consciously but with the intuitiveness of a brilliant politician. She grasped that people in the arts enjoyed having protégées, boasting that they had "made" a career. Ingrid had already had several mentors, among them Karin Swanström and Gustav Molander, mentors whom at an appropriate moment she was willing to discard.

Petter was her mentor as well. He was a strong, dominant man. He was also a slave to love, in sweet and gentle bondage. He had even given up his name Aron at Ingrid's demand. Ingrid had Petter help her to create *herself*, the person who became Ingrid Bergman. She had him chide her for overeating, slouching, and wrinkling her forehead. She even devised a signal so that Petter could alert her if she was talking too much at a party.

In those early years Petter was only doing what Ingrid asked him to do.

And with their success in evolving Ingrid's persona, they were creating an actress, a star far different from the woman he thought he had married.

Ingrid had large areas of her life about which she was absolutely incompetent and in which she had no intention of developing a competency. If Petter had not taken care of such matters, Ingrid would have found someone else to do so. Petter handled the household affairs, supervised the maid and the money, primarily because Ingrid had no interest in cooking and managing the house.

"I had the strong feeling that he admired her a great deal," says Elsa Holm, a close friend, whose husband, Cyril, was Ingrid's lawyer. "It was not my ideal of communication between man and wife. He admired her. And I wouldn't have liked my husband to be like that."

If it is possible to love a woman too much, then Petter loved Ingrid too much, or rather her glorious image, and he could no more communicate with that image than talk to an image on the screen.

Petter would do anything for his Ingrid, and she used him to handle many of the unpleasant, onerous duties and conflicts of her professional life. Ingrid had never lived in a house where family members faced up to their conflicts in discussion or debate or rowdy arguments. She couldn't stand unpleasantness, and again like a successful politician, Ingrid let others take the blame for her demands and mistakes. It was never Ingrid who wanted something changed; it was always Petter or someone else. And Petter was only too forceful in protecting his Ingrid.

Yet Petter did not go to the studios, the openings, the movie parties, largely because Ingrid had segregated her life. "Ingrid made nine pictures in Sweden," Petter says. "I never visited a set. I never met any of the actors and actresses. I never saw a contract. I never had anything to do with her films."

In fact, in Ingrid's next film, *A Woman's Face*, Petter gave a technical hand to his wife's career. Ingrid played a young woman whose face has been hideously burned in a fire. Petter built a brace for Ingrid to wear inside her mouth, which distorted her left cheek. "Gustav Molander, the director, wanted one side of the face normal, the other distorted," remembered Dahlqvist, the cameraman. "So the husband built this thing inside her mouth to twist her face. It punctured the inside of the mouth, so he had to change it." According to Petter, his invention was not the problem; it was that Ingrid insisted on wearing the device all the time.

A Woman's Face, later remade in Hollywood starring Joan Crawford, was a film that Ingrid very much wanted to make. As Anna Holm, Ingrid portrayed a woman scarred internally far more than externally. Anna is a mean-spirited, graceless, mistrustful leader of a gang of blackmailers. A prominent plastic surgeon whom she is attempting to blackmail offers to perform an operation to redo her scarred countenance.

Anna Holm was an extraordinary role and Ingrid gave a performance touched with brilliance. As the scarred and tortured Anna, Ingrid holds her hand up to her face, shielding her ugliness from the world. Her back is slightly hunched, her head tilted. She sneers at the world, her pain palpable. Even after the successful operation, Ingrid holds her gleaming countenance in check, psychic scars still visible, a gash deeper than the physical. And then as she slowly enters into life and love and human concerns, her beauty begins to light up her face. A year later, when *A Woman's Face* played in New York, the *World-Telegram* wrote that "Ingrid Bergman is another Garbo . . . as good as Garbo in her earliest efforts."

In order to do *A Woman's Face*, a role that went so much against her usual casting, Ingrid had to agree to make *Only One Night*, a film that she considered "junk," but one that was perfect typecasting. Ingrid had become known in Sweden as the *herrgårdsflicka*, the manor house girl, a phrase that may have been coined by Rune Waldekranz in a review. The manor house girl was an upper-class woman living on a country estate, beautiful but almost untouchable. *Only One Night* begins at a traveling circus where a handsome roustabout, played by Edvin Adolphson, leaves his mistress to claim his inheritance as the illegitimate son of an aging, wealthy aristocrat. On his father's estate, Adolphson falls in love with Ingrid, who rebukes his crude drunken attempt at seduction. Realizing that he would be happier in the circus, he leaves the estate to marry his old sweetheart.

Only One Night was largely turgid melodrama, but Ingrid's mere presence seemed enough to make a film memorable. Her beauty was now fully mature, a breathtaking, ethereal beauty that seemed to exist beyond time and space. It was a beauty that would have proved irresistible to most leading men, and Adolphson's seduction scenes may have existed not only on the screen. "Adolphson put his two arms around her to protect her," said another actor in the film, "but I knew his motives. I thought it was awful. He was well known as just taking the girls. He was big and strong and she fell for it. Ingrid always wanted someone strong."

"I remember when Petter and Ingrid were newly married and we went out to their flat," says Elsa Holm. "Ingrid was upset because Edvin Adolphson was trying to flirt with her. She told Petter that he should say that if they were going to continue with the film he should act properly. She was very upset. And she told Petter to take care of things. She didn't want to meet the problem herself. She pushed Petter to do it."

Ingrid was one of the most popular stars in Sweden, but her aspirations extended beyond Scandinavia. Hollywood was the greatest capital of cinema, but the new Germany was a major and growing power in filmmaking, seeking to supplant Hollywood in the world's imagination. Ingrid knew German. Indeed, she was half German. Early in 1938, despite what Petter calls his strong opposition, Ingrid signed a three-picture contract with UFA, the major German film company. Her first role was to be in a fluffy, rather mindless comedy, *The Four Companions*, but then she would star in a role she richly coveted: Charlotte Corday, the eighteenth-century Frenchwoman who assassinated Jean-Paul Marat, the revolutionary leader.

Ingrid was pregnant, and another woman might have taken time off. She saw no reason, however, why she couldn't have her career and her child. When Ingrid entered Berlin to begin filming, Hitler's troops had just marched into Austria. German planes were flying against Loyalist Spain. George Orwell wrote in that summer of 1938 that it was an age of "rubber truncheons and concentration camps." But Ingrid noted little—and understood even less—of what was going on around her. She was unaware that her presence gave credibility to the Nazi regime.

Ingrid was not the only Swedish actress to make films in Germany. Sarah Leander was a major UFA star. Kristina Söderbaum, who later made the notorious *Jew Süss*, had married a German director and was more German than Swedish. Signe Hasso made a film for the Germans as well.

In later years Ingrid would say she had been frightened by what she had seen in Berlin: "Karl Fröhlich took me to one of those great Nazi rallies in Berlin to impress me, I suppose. An enormous stadium, floodlights, band, steel-helmeted storm troopers . . . and there's Hitler beaming. Then the *Sieg Heil* with their arms stretched out in the Nazi salute. I just looked round in amazement. And Karl Fröhlich almost had a fit. He whispered in sheer terror, 'My God, you're not doing the Heil Hitler Salute!' and I retorted, 'Why should I? You're all doing it so well without me.' . . . I never did raise my arm in a Nazi salute, and later in the privacy of his office I protested, 'But I'm a Swedish actress only here for a few weeks.' "

Petter has a different recollection of his wife's attitude. "Ingrid knew that Goebbels was not only Minister of Information but the head of the studio. When Frau Adler took her to a Nazi meeting to hear Goebbels in Hamburg, she said it was a fantastic speech."

Ingrid wanted to get on with her work. It was not an unusual posture for an actress. Movie stars are damned if they take political stands, pilloried for abusing their fame. And they are damned if they remain silent, indifferent citizens selfishly hoarding their celebrity. However, Ingrid's persona of sheer goodness made audiences want to believe that she stood on the side of right and goodness regarding the great issues of her day. In Germany as in later years, she was supremely indifferent to the political world around her.

While Ingrid was in Berlin, Petter spent hours looking for a new house to rent for his family, often in the company of Cyril and Elsa Holm. "He was always looking for the best for Ingrid," Elsa says. "He wanted the most beautiful house."

Petter was devoted to his young bride. "I gave her more jewelry than I could afford," Petter recalls. One of his patients was a jeweler to the crown. In exchange for Petter's services, Mr. Carleman sold him several exquisite pieces at cost, including a diamond ring with small stones on either side, and a large aquamarine mounted on a platinum ring.

One day when Ingrid returned from the studio to the Adlon Hotel, she found Petter sitting in the lobby. He had come from Stockholm and taken up residence in a shabby hotel across the street from the luxurious Adlon. "I suddenly realized how lonely you'd be on your own," Ingrid remembered him saying. "And how nervous, because you don't know how to handle people. . . . But don't tell anybody I'm here, because I know these film people. They don't want husbands around."

Such an act, as generous as it was, might have seemed almost pathetic in a lesser man, a man without his own identity and profession. Despite all Petter's pride and ambition, he was willing to subjugate himself to Ingrid and her career. He wanted her to be so much, to become so much.

The Four Companions was by no means a piece of Nazi propaganda. The film chronicled the adventures of four young women in an advertising agency, and was thin gruel, indeed, for an actress with Ingrid's aspirations. For the shooting Ingrid's stomach was bound up like a maiden's foot in imperial China. On the weekend Petter and a clearly pregnant Ingrid walked the streets of the great city, Petter surreptitiously taking pictures of the Third Reich, posing Ingrid in front of Jewish-owned stores slashed with swastikas, and other evidence of the new Germany.

The shooting could not end soon enough for Petter, in this Germany where Hitler stormed and ranted, threatening to march into Czechoslovakia if his demands for the largely German-speaking Sudetenland were not met. Ingrid was sufficiently friendly to her hosts to be given a Nazi medal when the filming was over; it was still in her house at the end of World War II.

Before returning to Sweden, Ingrid and Petter took a trip through Western Europe.

No more than a month after their return to Sweden, on September 20, 1938, Ingrid gave birth to a daughter. Ingrid and Petter christened the baby Friedel Pia, the first name in honor of Ingrid's mother, the middle taken from the initials of Petter, Ingrid, and Aron, as well as being a fairly common name.

Ingrid had never lived in a home with a baby. She had entered into her pregnancy with nonchalance, not thinking that a baby might dramatically change her life. She was not particularly maternal. She herself later admitted she was not a good mother to Friedel Pia. Studio photographers took romanticized pictures of the star with her child, but Petter caught one shot that came closer to the reality of Ingrid the young mother. The star whom the cameras so adored stood there a bewildered young woman, appearing almost a child bride, the baby crooked awkwardly in her arms. It was as if she did not know what to do with this tiny bundle of vulnerability and fragility that was her firstborn.

Ingrid could always flee into her roles, exchanging the tawdry robes of reality for finer things. After the birth of Friedel Pia, she was planning to return to Germany for another film. She imagined that she could float between film capitals, above the clang of swords and the martial shouts. She could not see that early in 1939, a film made in Berlin was a political act.

Petter was obsessed with the idea that his wife not return to Nazi Germany. "I had told her not to go before she went the first time," Petter says. "This time I told her, If you go back to Berlin it's the end of our marriage." Petter understood Ingrid well enough to know that the one way to prevent her fulfilling the contract was to find better film prospects elsewhere. Thus without telling Ingrid he contacted Helmer Enwall, a leading theatrical booking agent, and asked him to find Ingrid roles in England or America.

Ingrid was already known in America, at least among those who searched the film world for talent worthy to be carried to the altar of Hollywood. When *Intermezzo* opened at the Cinema de Paris in New York in December 1937, the film and its female lead made a decided impression. "It is poignant, full of pathos, and above all, has shown, in Ingrid Bergman, a talented, beautiful actress," *Variety* noted. "Miss Bergman's star is destined for Hollywood."

Ingrid always credited Kay Brown with discovering her for America. In the late 1930s and early 1940s, Kay worked in New York as movie producer David O. Selznick's East Coast story editor. Ingrid loved to tell how Kay had first learned about *Intermezzo* from an enthusiastic Swedish elevator boy in her office building at 230 Park Avenue. Kay does not remember the episode, but it did not require the divine intervention of a young Swede for Selznick International to stumble across Ingrid Bergman. "As I recall it, David sent one of his famous memorandums to the office saying to look at foreign pictures for remake purposes," Kay says. "Elsa Neuberger, my assistant, and I went and saw *Intermezzo*. I didn't appreciate the story, but there was this wonderful girl in it.

"I reported on *Intermezzo* to David as story material, but I did not go overboard about it. But I went *madly* overboard about the girl. I thought she was the beginning and the end of all things wonderful."

If anyone can be credited with first discovering Ingrid for America, it is not Kay Brown at all but a woman whose role has been completely forgotten: Jenia Reissar. Jenia was Selznick's London representative, a position that she held into the 1950s. Kay wrote Selznick on July 26, 1938: "Miss Reissar has long been after me to look at a picture in which Ingrid Bergman appears. Today, I had the opportunity of seeing *Intermezzo*. . . . Quite frankly, I don't know what to say about Miss Bergman. She is absolutely enchanting in some parts of the picture and so terribly ugly in other parts. . . . The story of *Intermezzo* is very contrived but . . . if you are interested in Miss Bergman after seeing the picture, I have got all the data on her in the New York office."

Kay shipped a copy of the film west to Selznick the next day. In the movie industry, the term "genius" is an accolade that is bestowed with about the same frequency that the Boy Scouts award merit badges. But Selznick deserved the term as much as anyone. Still in his thirties, Selznick had already been a major producer, a top studio executive at RKO and MGM, and now, as head of his own new studio, Selznick International, he was in the midst of producing the most anticipated film in Hollywood history, *Gone With the Wind*.

The phrase "Produced by David O. Selznick" over a film's title was almost a guarantee of a quality production. Selznick was proud of his extraordinary attention to details, be they the publicity stills for *A Tale of Two Cities*, Marlene Dietrich's hair in *The Garden of Allah*, or the sound of the surf in *A Star Is Born*.

Selznick was enthusiastic about all the elements of *Intermezzo*: the script, the director, and Ingrid. "Keep it most confidential," he wrote in a memo on August 15, "but so that you can be guided, I want to make a deal to remake the picture; for the director; and for the girl."

Selznick considered it an enviable prospect to remake *Intermezzo* with its female star. The producer was so enthusiastic about Ingrid that he wired Kay Brown the next day that he "would still be interested [in Bergman] even if she does not start until next year." Selznick's personality was richly laced with paranoia, however, and he was already figuring out what could go wrong. Having noticed that the credits gave top billing to Gustav Molander and Gösta Stevens, Selznick wired that "a cold shudder has just run through me on the realization that maybe we are dealing for the wrong girl. Maybe the girl we are after is Gösta Stevens." That was the first and last time that Stevens, who shared a writing credit on *Intermezzo* with Molander, was ever mixed up with Ingrid.

When Selznick set his mind on something, he spewed out memos and directives and ideas with frenetic energy, forging ahead heedless of time or cost. Within three days he learned that Svensk Filmindustri wanted $25,000 for the rights to *Intermezzo*. He wasn't about to wait until he had formally bought the rights. Within the space of a few weeks he had thrown out the names of many possible actors and actresses for the film: Charles Boyer, Leslie Howard, William Powell, or Ronald Colman for the lead; Andrea Leeds for Ingrid's part; and Nazimova or Gloria Swanson for the wife; Lionel Barrymore for the violinist's manager; and Freddie Bartholomew for the son. A translator was hired at seventy-five dollars a week, and an English draft of the original screenplay written by September 24.

The Swedish film was shown to representatives of Joseph Breen, the industry censor, by Val Lewton, the West Coast story editor.* The Production Code administrator's main concern was that "the 'girl's punishment' will have to be made a little heavier."

---

* Lewton was a gentleman with a wry, literate wit. He delighted in the ironies and idiosyncrasies of the censors. Just the year before, during the making of *The Young in Heart*, he had cautioned Selznick about a scene in which Billie Burke allegedly "thrusts her head between the legs of a masculine statue, looks off and up, saying 'Aren't they sweet" or something similar. It is needless to point out to you that there is only one portion of the masculine anatomy that is referred to by the words 'they' or 'them.' In fact, I am reliably informed that Mr. Breen once cut the following dialogue from a western picture: 'Come on, boys, cut them off at Eagle Pass.' "

Ingrid heard about the *Intermezzo* offer through Jenia Reissar in London. Ingrid was eight months pregnant and Jenia cabled Kay in New York: "BERG-MAN NOT KEEN ANYWAY CANNOT WORK NEXT SIX MONTHS AS HAVING BABY AND MUST MAKE LAST PICTURE FOR UFA."

In late September, Reissar journeyed to Stockholm, hoping to sign Ingrid to star and Molander to direct *Intermezzo*, to finalize the deal for the film with Svensk Filmindustri, and to explore signing another young Swedish actress: Signe Hasso. The hotels were almost empty of foreigners. Placards in the streets announced that the British fleet was mobilizing. Newspaper headlines stated that Hitler wanted an answer from Prague by 2 P.M. In the middle of Reissar's meeting with Selznick's Swedish attorney, the lawyer received a call saying that he was to join his artillery unit in southern Sweden by the next day. Even neutral Sweden was mobilizing.

"This feeling of uneasiness is beginning to engulf even me!" Reissar wrote Kay. Nonetheless, she managed to buy the rights to *Intermezzo* for $12,500. She thought that Signe was a natural for America, but she had less luck with Ingrid. She met with Petter, who told her "it was pretty useless to talk business with her [Ingrid] at the moment, as she was not interested in pictures away from home, but that she did want to meet me. . . . He made me promise, though, not to worry her by insisting upon some answer or discussing terms."

In the afternoon Reissar went to the Lindstroms' residence. "It was as soon as she got home with the baby," Reissar remembers. "She was so proud and delighted with her baby. She brought it in to show me. She said she couldn't come to America or consider anything at the moment. She said the baby must be older. I told her they were thinking of casting Leslie Howard for *Intermezzo*. She was mad about him, and that was one of the things that I think made a great impression on her and she wanted to work with him. But she was still at the stage of not talking business."

"It is a very bad moment psychologically to talk to the girl," Reissar wrote Kay. Molander had been pressing Ingrid to sign, even though she was a new mother. He had told her that his deal to direct the American *Intermezzo* depended on her going with him. Although upset, Ingrid had resisted Molander's entreaties. Jenia assured Ingrid that the Molander negotiations were totally separate.

"Under no circumstances would she consider another picture engagement until 1940 except in Sweden," Reissar wrote Kay on October 4. "She was very flattered by Mr. Selznick's interest, and I think genuinely so. Though she seemed very scared of Hollywood she is anxious to go, but in a new role and preferably *not* *Intermezzo*. . . . I think the time to talk to that young woman would be after she has finished her UFA picture and got back into her working mood. At the moment she is quite satisfied with her home and her husband and her child."

Here once again was an Ingrid who could appear timid, yet was sure enough of her professional posture to scorn a role, and to ask the Selznick people to wait for her at least fifteen months.

Selznick was no longer interested in Hasso or Molander, but he still wanted to sign Ingrid, even if she couldn't co-star in *Intermezzo*. He had a superb eye for talent, and was not the only Hollywood producer interested in Ingrid: Hal Wallis of Warner Brothers had been in Stockholm recently and had seen *A Woman's Face*.

Selznick was having a devilish time casting his new movie. He had even thought of getting Jascha Heifetz, the great violinist, to play the lead. He tried to get Loretta Young, but that didn't work out, and by January he had reluctantly concluded that "there is seemingly no way of casting it properly, apart from showmanship, that would warrant the cost of the picture. I am commencing to feel that the way to handle this subject is to wait for Bergman, ballyhooing her debut in it."

Selznick was, by his own admission, getting "rather frantic . . . because we have no picture planned between *Wind* and *Rebecca* and *Intermezzo* seems much the most likely." Selznick was a high-stakes gambler. He didn't care about Ingrid's commitment to do Charlotte Corday for UFA. He decided to push her to come to Hollywood almost immediately, even if that risked losing her for good.

In London, Jenia Reissar was having an impossible time trying to deal with Ingrid by phone. She wrote Kay: "To almost every question I put to her she replied: 'Perhaps. I am not sure. I will write.' *And that is all*—except that she *doesn't* write." Reissar was persistent and she talked a reluctant Ingrid into doing *Intermezzo*.

The more Ingrid thought about the role, the more excited she became. The next time Reissar called Stockholm, Ingrid was enthusiastic. Ingrid was even more interested when, late in January 1939, she learned that her role in UFA's *Charlotte Corday* was canceled for political reasons. (In retrospect, it is hard to see how a sympathetic portrait of a demagogue's assassin could ever have been made in Nazi Germany.)

Ingrid immediately wrote Reissar that she was available either in the fall of 1939 or the following year to make a film for $3,000 a week with a six-week minimum. But Selznick wanted Bergman *now*. He sent Kay to Europe to try to close a deal. As Kay was braving the Atlantic in late winter, cables were going back and forth between London and Stockholm, further refining the details of Ingrid's contract. Reissar wired Ingrid, asking her to come to London to negotiate the final details. Ingrid was not amused. "I am very astonished—and not quite pleasantly astonished—about your sudden changing of dispositions," Ingrid wrote, flatly insisting that Kay come to Sweden.

The second week of February, Kay flew into Stockholm from London, through a Scandinavian snowstorm. If there was any doubt of the seriousness of Kay's quest, she had beside her a London lawyer, Joynson Hicks, to handle the legal details. Kay had girded herself against the winter winds in her inevitable fur coat, but she had become sick in the unpressurized airplane. Her neck glands had swollen, and she sat in a dressing gown in her suite at the Grand Hotel, hardly the image of the high-powered Hollywood representative.

Kay had received no call from Ingrid and Petter, but suddenly there was a knock at the door and there stood "these two lovely people. She looked absolutely beautiful. She had on a beaver coat and hat, and was carrying yellow and blue flowers for me."

"Welcome to Sweden," Ingrid said, and then apologized that she and Petter had a dinner engagement and would not be able to stay. If the Lindstroms were apprehensive about meeting the high-powered Hollywood representative, it was also a savvy negotiating technique not to be slavishly attentive to Kay. Before they left, however, Petter called a woman doctor and arranged for Kay to receive treatment.

When Kay first recalled her meeting with Ingrid, she admitted frankly that she had felt angry and frustrated, as would have been natural. The next day Petter laughingly admitted that they had had no dinner plans. They merely wanted to take Kay's measure.

Though she acted indifferent, Ingrid was very excited about the prospect of making films in Hollywood. Kay had promised her William Wyler as director and Leslie Howard as co-star, two names that she knew and admired. Petter was even more committed to getting Ingrid away from Germany and German films.

With Ingrid's cool Swedish demeanor and Petter's savvy, Kay had no idea how badly they wanted the negotiations to succeed; indeed, as she wrote the Selznick office, "when I arrived in Sweden I found Miss Bergman so utterly confused about our various requests, changes of dates, etc., that it looked as though there was no chance to make a deal whatsoever." Ingrid and Petter weren't sure how strong Kay's mandate was to bring Ingrid to Hollywood. And so for three days negotiations went on between Helmer Enwall, the Swedish booking agent contacted by Petter; Cyril Holm, Ingrid's attorney; and Kay and her London lawyer on the other side of the table. Ingrid sat watching, saying little.

Kay realized that "Ingrid wanted to go but under her own conditions." Kay wanted Ingrid to sign a standard seven-year contract, a gilded form of indentured servitude, which would give Selznick the right each year to drop her. Soon after the negotiations Kay wrote Daniel O'Shea, Selznick's top executive: "I suggested that her husband look over our draft contract." According to Kay, Petter would agree to no such thing as a seven-year contract. Petter, however, says that he was not present at the negotiations and had nothing to do with the contract. In later years, Ingrid and Kay both asserted that what Ingrid signed was a one-picture contract with an option for a second picture. Ingrid did, indeed, sign for *Intermezzo* at $20,000 ($2,500 a week for eight weeks). But the contract also gave Selznick the option to make one or two pictures a year with Ingrid for five more years, with the salary increasing finally to $40,000 a picture. At the same time, the contract gave Ingrid the right to make two outside pictures a year in a language other than English. Ingrid, then, had made a serious commitment to a life of international stardom, hoping to make at least two more films in Germany, films in Sweden, and of course films for the next five years in Hollywood.

Selznick didn't like Ingrid's name. He cabled Kay at the Grand Hotel that once the contract was signed, she might explain to Ingrid about the "SOME-WHAT UNATTRACTIVE AND EVEN SEMITIC SOUND OF NAME TO ANGLO-SAXON AUDIENCE." A week later, when Selznick still had not heard about a possible name change, he cabled Kay again: "I DO HOPE NOTHING WENT WRONG WITH THE CABLE."

"You can't conceive that childlike air of innocence which surrounded Ingrid," Kay said, remembering her visit to Stockholm. It was as if Ingrid and Petter were living in a land of gingerbread houses. In fact, at the age of twenty-three, Ingrid was already the veteran of eleven movies. In her circum-scribed world she was a sophisticated professional.

There were those in Sweden who said that Ingrid's aura of innocence was false, that she was a calculating, ambitious, self-centered young actress. But that aura was an elixir that Kay had caught whiffs of when she watched *Intermezzo*. This was what Selznick intended to package and sell to American audiences.

Kay could in fact catch glimpses of a more worldly Ingrid. In Stockholm, Kay had talked to Signe Hasso. "I was afraid that Bergman might find out that I had seen Hasso," Kay wrote Selznick, "and so casually brought her into the conversation to which Bergman replied that although she did not know her, she knew that she was an actress in Sweden. Bergman has a wonderful quality of arrogance about her which I personally like."

"You know you've got a lovely home and a lovely baby," Kay told Ingrid when they were alone. "You're happy here. If I were you I would think it over very carefully."

That was a curious remark for Selznick's representative to make. After all, Kay was not about to return to the States empty-handed to tell Selznick that she would not be a partner in subverting Ingrid's innocence. Kay's "terrible qualms about what I was doing to this wonderful young couple" were not so much disingenuous as paying proper obeisance to that "childlike air of inno-cence" that was the essence of Ingrid's appeal.

"Well if there are people as nice as you in America and in Hollywood, then I'm sure I shall like it, so I shall go, and take the risk," Ingrid responded, perfectly in character.

Before a month was up, Kay learned that when it came to her career, Ingrid was strong-willed and unyielding. Because of problems on Selznick's big film,

Gone With the Wind, Leslie Howard was no longer available to play the lead in *Intermezzo*. Charles Boyer was a possibility, if the starting date could be postponed until June. Ingrid cabled back that she was "utterly disappointed" that the agreement had been ruined. She insisted upon Howard or another star of his magnitude. She reminded the Selznick organization that she had "already sacrificed two pictures Europe" to do *Intermezzo*.

Ingrid was partially placated when Howard was reinstated as her co-star, but she was still full of quirks and requests. Petter says that at her request he wrote a long letter to Kay. Petter's English was far from fluent, but he made it clear how Ingrid should be greeted in America. Indeed, for all his concern, Petter could have been sending a patient for surgery.

Petter worried about people bothering Ingrid: "My wife, who since her childhood has been left to her own devices, avoids preferably foreign people and society life. . . . In Hollywood, she is afraid, that a similar crowd of Scandinavian people and nowadays even German people will disturb her, invite her etc." He wanted her to have proper lodgings: "This may be situated near the studio, if possible on a height and with some out look. No luxury apartment! More than 2 á 3 rooms might not be necessary. On a hotel she might be disturbed." Petter says that Ingrid wanted to do nothing anti-German: "She will, of course, not even in the future, work in film, which has any tendency or propaganda against a country, which has taken her services and showed her hospitality. . . . Of course, I will be very glad if we could inform the UFA that you have let us know, that Selznick Int. for inst. does not intend to give out German Hostile films."

Kay's approach was to try to soothe Ingrid, and not worry her over a possible later starting date for *Intermezzo*. Ingrid decided that she wanted to sail to New York on the boat with John Hay ("Jock") Whitney, the immensely wealthy socialite and vice-president of Selznick's new company. Whitney decided that he didn't want to spend time alone with Selznick's new discovery, and that was a problem too. "IF WE ARE GOING TO HAVE TO HANDLE HER WITH AS MUCH USE OF GLOVES AS THIS MAYBE WE SHOULD SEND HER BACK TO THE CUTGLASS FACTORY," Selznick cabled Kay.

But finally Ingrid set out from Stockholm, leaving her husband and six-month-old baby behind. Her plans were to complete the filming of *Intermezzo* by July. But her future in Germany still lay ahead of her as well.

CHAPTER FOUR

"A Figure to Take into Account"

*I*ngrid sailed on the *Queen Mary* from Southampton. The New York newspapers and columnists would have vied for a story about the arrival of the newest "Selznick star," but when the ship docked in New York City on April 20, 1939, only Kay Brown greeted Ingrid at the gangplank, and quickly shuttled her to the Chatham Hotel.

Selznick had told Kay that he wanted no publicity. He was still thinking of changing Ingrid's name. Moreover, he sensed that the public was satiated with the endless hyperbole about this new foreign star or that one. They came in an endless parade—Pola Negri, Anna Sten, Miliza Korjus, Luise Rainer, Luli Deste, Isa Miranda, Tilly Losch, Lya Lys—to be promoted, photographed, and in almost all cases forgotten. "I think that the best thing to do would be to import her quietly into the studio," Selznick wrote Kay, "go about our business of making the picture with only such publicity attendant upon her casting as would be the case with any unimportant leading woman and then feed an important and favorable public reception of her when the picture is finished."

Selznick had an indisputable genius for publicity. Even before meeting Ingrid, he had hit upon the essential ingredient that would make her unique. He would sell Ingrid by seeming not to sell her. He would tinker with her name, if need be let her be Ingrid Bergman in Europe and something catchier in the States, but he would nonetheless promote her "naturalness," hiding away anything gaudy or dark.

Ingrid knew nothing of this, and if she found it strange that there wasn't someone to interview her on her arrival, she didn't say anything. She had little time to worry, for Kay kept her very busy. At dinner parties Ingrid was a smash. Kay delighted in setting Ingrid up with what she called "eligibles," a service that Petter would have found less than amusing. One extremely wealthy escort was ready to hire a plane so that he and Ingrid could fly over New York. Ingrid said no to that offer, and to others as well.

In talking of her past, Ingrid usually emphasized the simpler aspects of her life, but what was striking was how she could go happily from the mundane to the exclusive, from beer to champagne, from hot dogs to caviar. Another European star might have opted only for chateaubriand at the Stork Club or a late supper at El Morocco. Ingrid's discovery was that emporium of the culinary arts known as Schrafft's. She had the appetite of a lumberjack, and her favorite new American food was the hot fudge sundae.

The Selznick people did not like their angelic property slurping down vanilla ice cream and fudge at Schrafft's. "I got in trouble taking her to Schrafft's," says Elsa Neuberger. "She liked it but they said that wasn't the place for Ingrid. She was a most unusual woman. She was simple in the way few actresses are. She wanted to know about America. She wanted to go on a bus, so I took her on a bus."

On her first Sunday, Ingrid met Joan Payson, Jock Whitney's sister; William S. Paley, the president of Columbia Broadcasting; and Mrs. Paley. She created what Joan Payson called "a sensation." Joan and the Paleys were so taken with Selznick's Swedish discovery that they offered to take her to the opening of the World's Fair.

Ingrid couldn't get enough of plays and movies. She went to the smash hit *Tobacco Road*, Erskine Caldwell's steamy excursion into the ways and byways of poor Southerners. Ingrid could not make out the hillbilly dialect, a handicap that she probably shared with some of the New Yorkers in the audience. The next night she went to see Raymond Massey playing *Abe Lincoln in Illinois*. The baroque nineteenth-century language was as foreign to her as Swahili.

With the starting date of *Intermezzo* less than a month away, Ingrid was less than sanguine. Kay wrote Selznick: "She asks me thousands of questions about you daily and is very afraid she is going to disappoint you."

Ingrid was a foreigner in America, speaking a strange tongue. In many respects she had been a foreigner all her life. She had been brought up half German in a Sweden that had very few foreigners. She had married not an urban Stockholm man but a man with all the strong values of small-town Sweden, where he lived his first eight years. She had just made a film in Germany, where she had often strained for the subtleties of language and gesture. Now she was in the United States, for her the strangest land of all.

Years later Ingrid wrote a relative that she was a *flyttfågel*—one of Sweden's migratory birds of passage. She was a bird, moreover, that wherever she landed, took on the protective coloration of her surroundings. At first, though, she became even more self-conscious. She found it strange the way so many Americans called one another by their first names and pretended everyone was a close friend. But she wanted so to be liked.

Ingrid had Kay to shepherd her around, traveling with her westward by train across the vast expanses of the continent. Kay draped herself in all the accoutrements of femininity—furs, silks, perfumes, and expensive heels—but she was a brassy, argumentative, shrewd woman with a brain that worked with the precision of a jewelry scale. A Wellesley graduate with a husband and two children, she was the classic "career woman" of her time. Born thirty years later, she would probably have become a producer. She had been the one who pestered Selznick to buy the rights to *Gone With the Wind*. Kay considered Ingrid her discovery and she watched over her with proprietary zeal, as well as with affection.

In Los Angeles the Selznicks had offered to take Ingrid into their house for a few days—an extraordinary gesture. David and Irene Selznick almost never had overnight guests at their new white brick house on Summit Drive, near the Beverly Hills Hotel. The whole household had enough to do simply to take care of the mercurial master of the house. Now in the midst of finishing *Gone With the Wind*, the most anticipated motion picture in Hollywood history, Selznick was strained and frayed. Mixing booze and Benzedrine, he sometimes greeted the dawn with sleepless eyes, and then outperformed men who had slept the sleep of the blessed.

The *Super Chief* arrived in Pasadena on Saturday, May 6, 1939. Ingrid was surprised when Selznick didn't meet her at the station, an offense more to her European sense of civility than to her ego. A publicity man drove her to the Selznicks' Georgian-style home with its tennis court and two-and-a-half-acre plot.

"How do you do," Ingrid said as she and Kay walked across the lawn to where Irene sat listening to a horse race on the radio.

"Sssssshh," Irene said loudly, as if Ingrid were a lowly retainer, and returned to the radio. At that moment Irene was less than delighted at having had Ingrid foisted upon her. Consciously or not, she had acted toward her husband's discovery as if she were socially inferior. The matron of Summit Drive was the daughter of Louis B. Mayer, the early film mogul. She had been brought up a Hollywood princess, amidst a royalty of moguls, financiers, directors, producers, and agents. A dark-haired young mother with sharp, narrow eyes that worked like cameras, Irene was a snob in a subtle and distinctly Hollywood way. This was a society based not on blood but on success. Out here success could come and go as mysteriously as the Santa Ana winds that blew down upon her new home. One never could be sure. Success might even come to this tall, big-boned woman who was squatting on her lawn.

Ingrid sat quietly, thinking that she had "come halfway round the world to listen to a horse race, and get shushed when I open my mouth."

"How do you do," Irene said when the race was over. "Would you like something to eat?" she asked, the Jewish hello.

As Ingrid went to her room to freshen up for lunch, her hostess noticed that she had only one suitcase. "Are your trunks coming later?" asked Irene, whose family traveled like Napoleon on his journey to Moscow, and whose husband believed that there were only two classes—first class and no class.

Ingrid did not understand the word "trunk." She finally made it clear to

Irene that this one suitcase comprised her entire luggage. She had come to Hollywood for three months to make a film, and on the set would be provided with a wardrobe.

Irene noticed that her husband's protégée was turning crimson. She changed the subject to a more pleasant matter: the dinner party the Selznicks were giving the following Saturday night in Ingrid's honor.

Ingrid explained that her suitcase even contained an evening dress that she would wear to the party. Irene told her that the party was "informal," one of the more unfathomable words in the bizarre lexicon of Hollywood. But as Ingrid appeared determined to wear her evening gown, an insistence based on necessity, Irene called the guests and told them to dress "formally."

That evening Ingrid made her first sally into the Hollywood world, at a dinner party at Don the Beachcomber's, a prominent restaurant that looked like a set for a Hawaiian musical. The dinner was hosted by Elsa Maxwell, a rotund party giver. Elsa was an inveterate celebrity seeker. She didn't know who Ingrid was, an ignorance she shared with practically everyone else in Hollywood.

Elsa did not corral the famous by supping with largely unknown Swedish actresses who could barely understand the phrase "Please pass the butter," much less witticisms and Hollywood gossip. While Irene tried to keep up a conversation with her guest, she painfully noted that Elsa hardly spoke to Ingrid, nor did Grace Moore, Miriam Hopkins, and Richard Barthelmess, the three stars who shared the table. Later, when Ingrid remembered that dinner, she did what she always did, splicing away the unpleasant and the nasty, remembering only the exotic coconut drinks and a few snippets of conversation.

After dinner, the group went to Miriam Hopkins's house for a screening of a yet unreleased film. Ingrid was still most anxious to meet the mysterious, unseen David O. Selznick, but as she sat on a cushion in the living room, she soon became lost in the performances on the screen.

A hand grasped Ingrid's shoulder: "Mr. Selznick has arrived and he's in the kitchen eating, and he'd like to see you."

Finally she was going to meet the man who would make her a star. In the kitchen, Selznick was seated at a table, devouring food like a man who could totally forget about meals for hours and then suddenly gorge himself. Selznick looked like a neurotic teddy bear who had been dressed on Savile Row.

"God, take your shoes off!" Selznick exclaimed. In comparison to his other great discoveries, a Vivien Leigh or a Joan Fontaine, this woman was an Amazon.

"It won't help. I'm wearing very flat-heeled shoes."

Selznick groaned.

"Do you mind if I sit down?"

"Of course not. How was your trip? . . . Of course you realize your name's impossible."

"It is? Why?"

"Well, the first name, to start with. We can't pronounce it. You'd be called Ein-grid, and Bergman is impossible too. Far too German. There's obviously trouble with Germany coming up, and we don't want anybody to think we've hired a German actress."

Two months before, Selznick had been concerned about the "Semitic" sound of Bergman. Now he found it too German. Ingrid's relationship with Germany and the German film industry was a legitimate concern, since Petter had written Kay for assurance that Selznick would not do anti-German films.

Selznick did not go into detail about the German situation. What was so striking about this first meeting, as remembered by Ingrid, was that it was devoid of social graces. The two got down to business immediately, as if they were agents discussing a client. Ingrid might have appeared shy, almost gawky, in social situations, but when she was discussing her career she was single-minded and unselfconscious. She insisted that Selznick not change her name, for she was an actress who saw herself as an international star, doing films in Sweden, Germany, and probably England.

According to Ingrid, Selznick complained about her teeth, and her thick eyebrows, but Ingrid insisted that she would not change them. She also remembered telling Selznick: "Let the movie come out, and then if people decide they like me, you can do the publicity and I'll give interviews. But let me try and creep into the affection of the American public." To this, Selznick purportedly meekly concurred.

Since, months before, Selznick had already decided not to publicize Ingrid, the words that Ingrid claimed were probably Selznick's. In later years the producer bitterly contested Ingrid's assertions that the wearing of simple makeup was her idea. In 1945 he wrote an angry letter reminding her of his "revolutionary instructions about your makeup and about leaving you alone in all your pristine beauty, eyebrows and all (although I now read in the press that you had a job with the studio to keep yourself intact)."

For the Saturday evening party much of Hollywood's elite had been chauffeured up to the Selznick home. The big stars: Gary Cooper. Katharine Hepburn. Tyrone Power. Greer Garson. Joan Fontaine. The big directors: King Vidor. Victor Fleming. Ernst Lubitsch. Almost everywhere Ingrid looked, there was a famous face.

If this had been a movie in which Ingrid played a European star arriving in Hollywood, she would have charmed her way through the evening, witty and gay. This was not a role, however, and for most of the evening Ingrid sat in the corner, wearing a dress she'd worn on the screen.

In most social circles it would have been considered not only polite but obligatory to talk to the honored guest. But in the Hollywood cosmos, life rotates around the established stars, and almost no one talked to Ingrid. The guests appraised her coldly as if the Selznicks had set down an exotic piece of artwork in their living room. The women, in particular, were less than charitable in their evaluation.

"We have enough trouble getting jobs as it is," Joan Bennett said. "Do they have to import kitchen maids?"

"She's such a big peasant," said Lubitsch.

It was a measure of Ingrid's uniqueness that her mere presence created such virulence. Most of the people in the room had their origins in the ghettos of Russia or Poland, the farms of the Plains states, the small towns of the Southwest. They reeked of insecurity and uncertainty themselves, and they delighted in throttling the aspirations of such as this Swedish interloper. If Selznick was right about his new discovery, then what would happen to their own worth and standing?

Ingrid was dazzled by the parade of celebrity that passed before her. She had no idea that she was being summarily ignored. After dinner, as she sat before the fireplace on a settee, Ernst Lubitsch sat down next to her. Most of the actresses in the room would have been delighted to have a tête-à-tête with the director of such films as *The Love Parade* and the current *Ninotchka*.

"Don't let this get you down," implored Lubitsch, who before dinner had been one of those roundly savaging Ingrid. "We all came to Hollywood for the first time, and it was hard for all of us."

"Get me down?" Ingrid replied. "I'm so happy I can't believe it. All these famous people, and I can sit here and see them all in real life."

Irene had been watching closely as the guests ignored Ingrid. She observed now as Ingrid worked her charm and Lubitsch seemed "beguiled." By the time the last expensive auto was wending its way down to Sunset Boulevard, Irene had decided that Ingrid had proved herself "a figure to be taken into account."

The studio rented a small house for Ingrid at 260 South Camden Drive in Beverly Hills. She didn't complain about the house or about the young woman hired to chauffeur her around. But her insistence on privacy was thwarted by a landlady who insisted on walking into the residence unannounced.

Ingrid had little time for squabbles with her landlady. Within ten days of arriving in Hollywood, she was already at work doing a screen test. The makeup people had been ready to rouge, pluck, fluff, and powder Ingrid until she looked like a Dresden doll. But Selznick would have none of that. "Understand this, you are not going to take one eyebrow or one hair away," Selznick yelled, as Ingrid remembered. "You are not going to do *anything*. If you alter anything at all I'll kill you. We're testing her tomorrow and we're testing her just like that, just like she is. Her name's going to be her *real* name. And above all, there are going to be no interviews . . . no *interviews*."

Ingrid had her screen test with her co-star, Leslie Howard. For all the gentlemanly demeanor, indeed nobility, of his onscreen image—an image that the world would soon see in *Gone With the Wind*—Howard was often impetuous, arrogant, and demanding. To placate him, Selznick had agreed to make

Howard associate producer on *Intermezzo,* and to pay him $10,000 a week, as against the $7,500 he had received for acting in *Gone With the Wind.* Furthermore, Howard had expressed himself adamantly opposed to Gregory Ratoff as director, and Selznick had signed William Wyler instead.

Selznick was intensely busy finishing *Gone With the Wind,* but he still found time to watch over the making of *Intermezzo.* Soon after the picture began shooting, Selznick fired Wyler and replaced him with the Russian-born Ratoff. Howard concurred with the change, leaving Ingrid confronted with a director whose accent was as thick as a porterhouse steak. After hearing Ratoff's unique rendering of the language of Shakespeare, one journalist described it as "a combination of Chaucer, Minsk, Pinsk and late Okmulgee, Oklahoma."

Ingrid would have had a difficult time understanding Ratoff if it had not been for her new English coach, Ruth Roberts, the sister of George Seaton, a writer and director. Ruth was bringing up three sons alone on the income she garnered teaching English to foreign-born stars, such as Hedy Lamarr. When she read that Ingrid was coming to Hollywood, she managed to be hired by Selznick. She knew that if Ingrid was to pick up English quickly, she had better not know that her teacher spoke Swedish.

On one of the first days of shooting, Ingrid had to speak the line "I am glad to meet you, Mr. Brand." It was hardly a line or a scene to stretch the limits of dramatic art, and Ingrid approached it with her usual professionalism.

"Yi! Yi!" Ratoff shouted. "Soch han hawkcent! Deez way say heet: 'I ham glad zu mit you, Meeser Brunt.' "

As an Englishman, Howard had to get in his twopence at this violation of his native tongue. Hearing this, Ruth came rushing over to intercede.

"Soch han hawkcent! Yi! Yi!" Ratoff repeated.

Ingrid learned to ignore Ratoff's accent, but it was difficult for her to understand him. Joe Finnochio, the soundman, took perverse pleasure in listening in on his earphones to the fractured exchanges, a veritable tower of babel. "I used to roll over in laughter," Finnochio remembers. "It was hilarious. It was a big laugh, the whole picture. There were all these arguments, getting her to do scenes. She had a hard time because she couldn't pick it up."

At one difficult juncture, Ruth broke into Swedish to explain Ratoff's meaning.

"My goodness, why didn't you tell me you could speak Swedish?" Ingrid said.

When Selznick saw the first rushes, he was unhappy at the way Ingrid was being filmed. The unspoiled naturalness that Ingrid projected on screen was neither unspoiled nor natural. Selznick admonished Harry Stradling, the director of photography, to do whatever he had to do, and to use whatever makeup and special shots were necessary, to give Ingrid "the combination of exciting beauty and fresh purity" she had evinced in the Swedish *Intermezzo.* Stradling couldn't do the job the way Selznick wanted it done. Selznick fired him.

Ingrid was momentarily distraught. She had been on the set only a few days and already the director and the chief cameraman had been fired. When Selznick told Ingrid about Stradling leaving, the producer noticed tears in her eyes. She asked whether the firing would hurt Stradling's career, and said that rather than hurt him, she didn't care if she photographed a little worse.

The first rushes under the new director of photography, Gregg Toland, didn't please Selznick either. "More than with any other girl that I know of in pictures, the difference between a great photographic beauty and an ordinary girl with Miss Bergman lies in proper photography of her," he lectured Toland. "This in turn depends not simply on avoiding the bad side of her face; keeping her head down as much as possible; giving her the proper headdress, giving her the proper mouth make-up, avoiding long shots, so as not to make her look too big, . . . but most important of all, on shading her face and in invariably going for effect lightings on her."

Selznick considered young Ingrid "the most completely conscientious actress" with whom he had ever worked. She was consumed with the film. She had already done *Intermezzo* once. She was full of ideas about how to film it. She knew the image of Ingrid Bergman that she wanted projected on the screens of America. She worked with compulsive energy. On the set during rehearsals for a dramatic scene with Howard, she insisted on complete silence. Every detail of her role had to be right. She was almost always on time, in vivid contrast to Howard, who was late twenty-six of the fifty days of production and retakes.

"Ingrid was here in the morning at six o'clock for makeup and she was shooting until six o'clock," recalls Reginald LeBorg, the second unit director. "Then I was supposed to work with her for an hour on a dummy piano for her piano-playing scenes. I had to explain that a pianist uses his head for special emphasis. After a week I thought she was fine. But she said, 'No, no, I want more.' By seven o'clock I was tired. I couldn't understand the energy of the girl. She wanted to succeed so much. She kept me there until nine or nine-thirty. She had this energy and this tremendous application."

During this period, LeBorg made a gentle pass at Ingrid, only to learn that "she was very much business." It was a lesson that other men were learning as well. All Ingrid cared about was her work. She would happily have stayed at the Selznick studios in Culver City until midnight. Indeed, at one point she asked Selznick about having her dressing room set up so that she could sleep in it, and never leave the studio at all.

Selznick was not beyond a little *shtup* on the casting couch, but with Ingrid there was none of that. In Ingrid, Selznick had come upon a person like himself, who found in pictures a life beyond life, one that could confer the gift of immortality. Selznick was not only a creator of Hollywood myths but a believer. He *believed* in Ingrid's pure, pristine image. He *believed* in the magic that Ingrid could project on the screen. If he hadn't, if Ingrid had been a cynical gambit, an exercise in Hollywood puffery, he would not have been so brilliantly effective at, and so almost maniacally devoted to, developing her as a star.

When Selznick asked Ingrid to sign a photograph to him, she wrote: "For David, I have no words." And indeed, what David meant to Ingrid was beyond words. "His judgment was very hard but it was just," she wrote in her diary after finishing *Intermezzo*. "To work for him is often terribly demanding and very hard on the nerves. But always there is the feeling that you have somebody to help with understanding, encouragement, and wisdom, and that is beyond price."

Ingrid consulted Selznick about everything. She called him out of meetings to discuss such monumental matters as a pair of shoes. She asked him about all the minutiae of publicity, and he guided and protected her. In most other societies Ingrid would have seemed almost pathological in her self-centeredness and apparent insecurity. But this was Hollywood, and Ingrid was an actress. And it was as if she were talking about someone else, a creation of hers and Selznick's.

Despite all Ingrid's effort, there was none of that inexplicable groundswell of rumor that in Hollywood is the first sign of a hit. Indeed, Selznick continued to be unhappy with the rushes on Ingrid, although he at least appeared confident in his Swedish protégée. But others were not so optimistic. "I don't hear particularly good reports about Ingrid in *Intermezzo*," Kay wrote Val Lewton, her counterpart on the West Coast, on July 17, 1939. "And I'm awfully sorry about this, as she's been so happy with us that I know she'll want to return."

Although Ingrid was not yet to be heavily promoted, Selznick's publicity department did make some efforts on her behalf. The publicists tried to get Ingrid an invitation to meet Garbo on the set of *Ninotchka*, but her legendary compatriot had no interest in greeting Ingrid. As an alternative the publicists were thinking about releasing a rumor "that Garbo herself has been trying to see this glamorous, new import from Sweden but Ingrid, by God, has been too busy to see her, because she is working day and night in *Intermezzo*."

One of the few interviews Ingrid gave was with Åke Sandler, a Swedish journalist who happened to be the son of Sweden's foreign minister. "I was told that I could not in the article report about Ingrid making films for UFA," Sandler said. "When I did mention it in articles published in Sweden, I was barred from the Selznick studios and from interviewing her again. I didn't say anything that negative, only that she was naive and didn't understand what was going on politically. But Selznick was very adamant about it. He didn't want any suspicion that she might be a German actress."

As the last weeks of shooting drew near, Ingrid's departure for Berlin was imminent. She was tentatively planning to sail on the *Bremen,* a German vessel. Then in early July, Daniel O'Shea told her that Selznick considered it potentially harmful. She agreed to sail on another ship.

Selznick had hoped that Ingrid's German commitment could be postponed until oblivion. He had contemplated buying out her contract, but he didn't want to do so until he knew how well *Intermezzo* would do. Thus now he was faced with a public relations problem so serious that it could ruin *Intermezzo.* In March, Germany had invaded Czechoslovakia, stilling the oracles of appeasement who the year before had lauded the Munich Pact as peace in our time. And Selznick had a new star on his hands who thought that she could go blithely from an American film to a German film to a Swedish film, totally unaffected by the political world in which she lived.

The Selznick people warned Ingrid that she was "to say nothing whatsoever about going to Germany or making a picture in Germany." Then, despite the precautions, on July 28 a story appeared in the *Hollywood Reporter,* headlined: "INGRID BERGMAN IN LEAD OF NAZI 'COMMANDANT.'" The article stated that as soon as Ingrid finished *Intermezzo* she would be off to Berlin to film a picture about a Tibetan expedition.

Selznick took the matter sufficiently seriously to decide that Ingrid should give no more interviews at all before she left the States, and in New York register in a hotel under another name.

"She was the most surprised person in the world to learn the extent of the anti-German feeling in this country, but she maintains, and I personally feel that she has every right to, that she has no grievance against the Germans," Selznick wrote Kay, the day the *Reporter* article appeared. "She is a characteristic Scandinavian isolationist and I think we might as well let it go at that."

In the last weeks of shooting, Ingrid's primary desire was to finish up in Hollywood and go on to make her German film, even though it meant traveling directly to Berlin without seeing Petter and the baby. At the end of July, as Ingrid was finishing retakes, Petter wired that her UFA film had been canceled because of problems getting Ingrid's fee paid in Sweden. Ingrid could have stayed a few extra days in Los Angeles, but now she was anxious to get back to Stockholm.

On August 3, her next-to-last day in Hollywood, Ingrid had her first color screen test on Stage 3, in Rhett's bedroom on the set of *Gone With the Wind.* A stagehand put a card in front of her face: "Ingrid Bergman—No Makeup— Test One." She had no part to play, but merely turned her head this way and that and said a few words. Ingrid loved the sheer act of being filmed, the camera exploring her with such intimacy yet never touching her. She looked embarrassed, shy, and utterly feminine, exuding a gentle fawnlike quality. Her translucent skin flushed with life and feeling, and her face appeared a kaleidoscope of beauty.

It was a remarkable piece of film, in good part because Selznick edited it, cutting out shots in which Ingrid appeared to have a mustache shadow, or harsh lines. *Intermezzo* had been photographed in black and white, but when Kay saw the test she understood: "Once she's photographed in Technicolor, then my darling's freedom is gone."

Even though Ingrid was leaving, Selznick was still not satisfied with all her shots in *Intermezzo*. He thought that she looked "dreadful" in slacks from the rear. He was obsessed with creating a brilliant new image. When Ingrid first entered onscreen, coming through the door, the American audience had to feel that they were seeing something they had never seen before.

"I've got to have the impact of a new face that has arrived on the American screen so that the audience will be suddenly aware and go 'Ahhh,' " Selznick said.

"But how do I do that?" Ingrid asked. "With what means? I'm just looking at a man and his daughter playing the violin and the piano."

"I don't know. Let's do it."

So they did it. And they did it again. And they did it until the very hour that Ingrid's train was to leave.

"But, David, I've got to pick up my luggage from the house."

"We'll send for it. Get Miss Bergman's luggage. Send a car. You'll catch the train, don't worry."

And then she was off at 8 P.M. on the *Super Chief*, arriving at the station just as the train was pulling out. As she rushed through the station, a little boy ran up to her and pressed a package into her hand, a gift from Selznick: a recording of the voices of the people with whom she had worked on *Intermezzo*. Tired as she was, Ingrid did not sleep very much that first night while the train headed eastward.

Ingrid knew that she was not supposed to talk to reporters when she reached New York, but she probably did not know to what lengths the Selznick organization had gone to isolate her. Although the summer film at UFA was canceled, Ingrid was scheduled to make another German film later in the year. Selznick wanted no mention of that to get out. At one time there had been plans for a large press luncheon in her honor in New York and photo sessions with *Harper's Bazaar* and *Vogue*. That had all been called off. To avoid even the possibility of reporters at Grand Central station, Selznick borrowed Jock Whitney's yacht and had it sailed up the Hudson.

At 5 A.M. on August 7, 1939, Kay quietly took Ingrid off the *20th Century Limited* in Albany. Ingrid sailed down the Hudson to New York City and left the country on the *Queen Mary* with hardly anyone knowing. From on board, Ingrid cabled Selznick that she was so sad she couldn't see America anymore: "THANKS FOR THE COLOUR FACE GOODBY INGRID."

CHAPTER FIVE

A Willful Ignorance

The first days that Ingrid was back in Stockholm, Pia cried and would not go to the mother she had not seen for over three months. But soon life was back to routine at the Lindstroms' rented yellow house by the water in Djurgården Park. Ingrid was sitting sewing hems for the living room curtains when, on September 1, 1939, she heard on the radio that the German blitzkrieg had entered Poland. World War II had begun.

A little more than a month before, Ingrid had been ready to go to Germany to make a film. If UFA had not canceled, she would have been in Berlin as the German armies marched on Warsaw. Ingrid would have become tainted merchandise to the French and British, who had now declared war on Germany. Most Americans would not have considered her much better. That would almost certainly have been the end of her contract with David O. Selznick. And with her career elsewhere thwarted, she might have felt compelled to make other films in Nazi Germany.

Ingrid's relationship with Germany was a continuing problem for the Selznick organization. In late September a dangerous item appeared in a column by Louella Parsons, who fancied herself Hollywood's moral arbiter, and whose power in the industry was almost unsurpassed. Parsons alleged that Ingrid had a relationship with a high Nazi official. Selznick was worried that "this thing could spread into a campaign against Bergman if we are not careful." Ingrid rebutted the charges in a cable to Selznick on September 29 in which she said that she had neither any political interest nor any "personal relations" among foreign officials.

Ingrid might have gone further and said that she would not make films in Nazi Germany, but she did not do that. Kay reported that Ingrid told her by telephone that UFA felt "they have a claim on her for one picture at the end of the war."

Kay was less than impressed with Ingrid's political sensitivities. "As regards the international situation, you know as well as I do that Ingrid's not too well informed," Kay wrote O'Shea. "I asked her if it was true that they were having black-outs in Stockholm as reported in the paper and she said that everything is fine there and that you'd never know a war was going on. It was an extremely stupid remark but knowing Ingrid, quite understandable."

Selznick realized that at any moment Ingrid's American image could explode, exposing his film and his studio to the shrapnel of bad publicity. If he had not been so sure that Ingrid would become "the greatest star in motion pictures," he might well have dropped her. He was so sure, in fact, and such a shrewd negotiator, that he had sought to tie Ingrid still more closely to him in a new contract even before the verdict on *Intermezzo* was fully in.

Selznick was consumed with perfecting every detail for the *Gone With the Wind* premiere, December 15, 1939, in Atlanta. Nonetheless, he gave to *Intermezzo* what for most other producers would have been a full-time effort. The film would open at Radio City Music Hall, the largest, most prestigious movie theater in America.

Ingrid had heard that the preview audiences for *Intermezzo* had been positive. Yet she waited apprehensively for the premiere. She wrote Selznick that she was not even going to start her English lessons until she had heard what the "frightening American critics" had to say. "Perhaps I don't need to be so interested in English lessons any more!!"

When *Intermezzo* opened in October, the critics were not totally taken with the film. Had they seen the Swedish version, they would have realized that much of the exquisite melancholy of the original had been lost. About Ingrid, however, the critics seemed to be not writing reviews but playing violins in her honor. Frank S. Nugent of the *New York Times* wrote that "there is that incandescence about Miss Bergman, that spiritual spark which makes us believe that Selznick has found another great lady of the screen." He found her "beautiful; not in any stylistic sense, through perfection of feature or the soft-focus lens, but in her freshness, serenity and (misused word) wholesomeness." Howard Barnes of the *New York Herald Tribune* called Ingrid "the most gifted and attractive recruit that the studios have enlisted from abroad for many moons." Wendy Hale wrote in the *New York Daily News*: "It is extremely unfair to call her a second Garbo, just because she hails from Sweden. She has a combination of rare beauty, freshness, vitality and ability that is as uncommon as a century plant in bloom."

Intermezzo was Ingrid's picture, Ingrid's triumph. When Selznick called to tell her the reaction, she cried. Ingrid's triumph was Selznick's triumph too, and he pressed forward to renegotiate their contract. He didn't care that outside the major cities *Intermezzo* did mediocre business at best. He wanted Ingrid back.

Selznick wrote to tell Ingrid confidentially that the film had been a disappointment outside New York, "but this does not . . . depress me, since I always planned that the principal purpose of the picture was to introduce you to American and English audiences." Like so many of Selznick's endeavors, that statement was gracious, even noble, and at the same time self-serving and manipulative. It was a wonderfully reassuring proclamation, particularly since Ingrid didn't know how many other actresses Selznick had sought for the part. It was also not a bad ploy, in the midst of difficult negotiations, to show Ingrid that she was indebted to Selznick even more than she knew.

Ingrid wanted to return to the United States. She was also interested in going to England to make a film with Leslie Howard. Under the terms of the contract, Selznick would not allow Ingrid to make an English-language film for someone else. To placate Ingrid, Selznick wired Gabriel Pascal, the Hungarian-born producer, about her playing George Bernard Shaw's Saint Joan, a role that she deeply coveted.

Although Ingrid appreciated Selznick's efforts, she was nonetheless a tough negotiator. Ingrid was proving, as Selznick wrote Kay, that "her angelic nature is not above being tarnished by matters of mere money." She was willing to add a third picture to the first fourteen months of their contract, but she was not about to make more than two pictures a year for Selznick. Nor would she unequivocally drop her work in Germany. She wrote Kay that "at present" she did not feel like making films in Germany but hoped for better times. She said that while UFA had not accepted the cancellation of her contract, she did not think they would be able to act upon it.

By October 1939 Ingrid was already back at work in Sweden, starring in *A Night in June*. She played a decent, well-meaning young woman who becomes involved with a young sailor. The part was full of romantic subtleties and received excellent reviews. For twenty-four-year-old Ingrid, though, *A Night in June* was a five-finger exercise. There was no challenge speaking Swedish. The crew and stage at Svensk Filmindustri seemed small and almost amateurish compared to what she had had in Hollywood.

During the contract negotiations, Ingrid told Kay on the phone that if she came before June 1940 she would be coming without Petter. Ingrid had been gone for over three months, leaving Petter with an empty house and a new baby, but he had such confidence in his wife and their relationship that he was willing to bid her adieu once again. "I wanted my wife and daughter safe," Petter says. "The Maginot Line was strong, but I was afraid that I was going to be called into the army."

On November 30, the Soviet Union invaded Finland. The net of war was closing tighter around Sweden. Even though the Selznick organization did not have a film for Ingrid yet, they pushed for her to come to the United States. Selznick was genuinely concerned for Ingrid; he offered her enough money to live on while she waited for work.

And so in that December of 1939, Ingrid, Petter, Pia, and a young Swedish nursemaid began the journey to the port of Genoa. They traveled by train through the blacked-out city of Berlin, through Germany and Austria, down the coast of Italy to Genoa, arriving in time for New Year's Eve.

"I think it was the saddest New Year's Eve ever," Ingrid remembered. "Petter and I sat downstairs in the dining room where they were having their

New Year's Eve dance. . . . And we danced and we were very sad, and we were too tired to pretend that we didn't know there was a blackout and bombers flying in the night . . . but we did know. And I thought, I'm leaving the next morning with Pia, and maybe I'll never see Petter again."

On January 2, 1940, Ingrid sailed on the *Rex* from Genoa to New York City. She was crying as she stood on deck, Pia in her arms, waving to Petter as he ran along the dockside, waving back.

Even on the high seas, the war was very much with the *Rex*. The ship docked unexpectedly at Lisbon and Horta, picking up ninety passengers whose plane flights had been canceled. The passenger list was full of those haunted by the war. Anne Morgan, the head of the American Friends of France, had been preparing to help the civilian population "if anything happened" to the French war effort. Dr. Chaim Weizmann, the Zionist leader, was sailing to New York to enlist aid in developing Palestine "as a haven and homeland for tens of thousands of Jews who have been uprooted and driven from their homes by the overwhelming wave of destruction now sweeping over Central Europe." Martha Gellhorn, a prominent journalist, was returning to the States after covering the Finnish-Soviet war. She was full of stories of horror, heroism, and tragedy. Gellhorn noticed Ingrid, "a woman with a baby on her back," and thought little more of it until months later.

While the *Rex* steamed through the winter seas, Selznick wired Ingrid that he was planning to star her in *Saint Joan* as her next film. Then Kay cabled to say that Ingrid could mention *Saint Joan* to reporters upon arrival, and that Kay had arranged to take Pia away before reporters saw that Ingrid had a daughter. Since her teenage years Ingrid had been obsessed with Joan and her martyrdom. She cabled back that she was ready for the press: "I AM BOLD. . . . INGRID."

Nine months earlier, Ingrid had sailed into New York unknown and unheralded. Now, on January 12, 1940, she was arriving with a full barrage of publicity. Among those scheduled to talk to her were representatives from the *New York Times*, the AP, the *New York Daily News*, *Screenland*, and *Harper's Bazaar*. Kay was there too, seeing to it that there would be no photographs of Ingrid with Pia in her arms.

"Don't talk too much about Joan of Arc—yes?" said Myer Beck, a Selznick publicist, before she met the reporters.

"What do you mean?"

"Well, we're not going to make it, not just yet anyway, but we'll tell you about that later. You just smile and say there's a movie coming up and you're going to California."

Ingrid had read about Joan of Arc when she was a little girl, and she had gotten down on her knees in the chapel on the ship to thank God for giving her *Saint Joan*. At the beginning of World War II, God may have had other things on his mind, for Ingrid learned upon arriving that the role was apparently just a publicity stunt. She was hardly in the mood to deal with the American press.

The reporters thronged around Ingrid. The cameramen got down on their knees, shooting up at her, getting as much leg as they could. The questions kept coming at her. Was she a jitterbug? Had she left her husband?

Ingrid burst into tears and ran out of the press conference.

Ingrid had been brought to America by the most celebrated, the most envied, the most admired producer in America. *Gone With the Wind* was ablaze on screens across America, the greatest triumph in Hollywood history, and one of the greatest Hollywood films ever made. In February 1940 it won the most Academy Awards ever given a single film. Selznick's new film, *Rebecca*, was not another *Gone With the Wind*, but with it he would win an unprecedented second Academy Award in a row for best film.

Ingrid imagined that Selznick was about to star her in his next great film, if not yet *Saint Joan*, then some other fine role. She was initially excited simply to be in New York, that great city she loved so much. It took hardly any time to settle into Kay's large apartment on Park Avenue, for, as Kay noticed, "her wardrobe resembles her make-up kit—a large-sized tube of toothpaste."

Soon Ingrid was distraught. Selznick had no work for her. To Ingrid, to be alive was to be busy. She couldn't understand. Her contract stated that she was to make one or two pictures for Selznick in the year starting April 1, 1940, and by then she was sure she *had* to be at work. Kay told her pointblank: the contract didn't mean the first picture had to *begin* April 1. As that sank in, Ingrid's mood collapsed like a deflated helium balloon.

On January 22, Ingrid took the train out to Los Angeles to perform *Intermezzo* on the *Lux Radio Theatre*, leaving Pia with the maid. Ingrid knew enough about Hollywood by now to realize how important it was for her to make her presence felt, to show herself at the proper parties, to meet the right producers and directors. After all, the year before, she had met Ernst Lubitsch at Selznick's house during her first week in Hollywood. And now, according to Selznick, Lubitsch was interested in working with her. Nonetheless, when Selznick attempted to take her around to parties, Ingrid would have nothing of it.

In her week in Hollywood, Ingrid did at least go to the Selznicks' house one evening for a screening. There she met Fredric March, who had played the has-been actor in Selznick's classic film *A Star Is Born*. March was so taken with Ingrid that he sought to have her star with him in his new film, *Victory*, based on the Joseph Conrad novel.

Selznick appreciated the qualities in Ingrid that allowed her to refuse to be hauled around to fancy parties. But he wondered whether he was in the early stages of creating a monster. He and Kay had filled Ingrid's head with sugar-plum dreams of glorious roles. In New York, Kay had squired Ingrid to one party after another, where Broadway directors and producers dangled before her impressionable eyes all kinds of theatrical offers.

The surprising thing, however, was that there was so little demand for Ingrid's services at the other film studios. Indeed, although Selznick gave the impression that Lubitsch was after Ingrid, it was Selznick who was courting Lubitsch to make a film with his Swedish discovery.

"I noticed a distinct difference in her attitude . . . from what it had been when she left for Sweden," Selznick wrote Kay after Ingrid returned to New York City. "I still think she is an angel . . . and I mention this only to indicate that there is the danger that we will succeed in accomplishing nothing except to create future trouble for ourselves if we get her thinking that everybody in the world wants her, and we are doing nothing with her. In fact, it may already be too late to correct this impression."

Ingrid at first considered Selznick her professional father in America, a man who could do no wrong. Selznick could speak with rude frankness in his memorandums about Ingrid, but to her face he was her courtly confidant and mentor, spinning dreams of glorious futures. When Ingrid arrived back in New York on February 4, she told Kay that she was to begin work on *Saint Joan* right away, studying the play and taking drama lessons.

Regardless of what Ingrid thought he had said, Selznick told Kay that he did not want Ingrid "spoiled or stylized" by drama coaches, and that *Saint Joan* was far from a certain thing. Kay was left with the unenviable task of trying to keep Ingrid's spirit aloft, bolstering her sagging morale, shepherding her around New York.

Kay would have made a fine criminal defense lawyer. She was full of plausible arguments why it wouldn't do for Ingrid to play *Saint Joan* until she had made another picture or two. She puffed Ingrid up with talk of English lessons, stage and radio work. She listened to Ingrid's endless chatter, and talked about the great future that lay ahead. But Kay was getting fed up—with Selznick, who complained that she was spoiling Ingrid, and even with Ingrid herself and her narrow interests.

Selznick lived by the memo and the letter, and Kay wrote Selznick frequently. "I can't see that I have spoiled Ingrid the slightest bit," Kay wrote Selznick on February 9, 1940. "I can't keep her cooped up in her apartment and not have her meet anybody, and she's not the slightest bit interested in meeting anyone outside of the theatre. . . . I have a great feeling of affection and friendship for Ingrid. On the other hand, it's like having four children to manage instead of two, and it's not all roses."

Ingrid was not the number one star at Selznick International; far from it. Kay took her to see an early television broadcast of a play about Charlotte Corday starring Vivien Leigh. Afterward, Ingrid talked enthusiastically about playing the part in a movie. As soon as the Selznick people heard that, they were worried about a "cat fight" between their Swedish acquisition and the star of *Gone With the Wind*. Selznick told Kay to inform Ingrid that *Charlotte*

Corday had first been Vivien Leigh's idea. That was true, but long before Vivien had become interested in the part, Ingrid had been scheduled to play Charlotte Corday for UFA in Germany.

What brought Ingrid out of the doldrums was the offer of a stage role in *Liliom*. The classic play by the Hungarian playwright Ferenc Molnár became even better known later as the basis for the Rodgers and Hammerstein musical *Carousel*. Molnár's play tells the story of Liliom, a barker for a merry-go-round, and his love for Julie, a housemaid. Liliom is a brutal, seemingly uncaring man who beats sweet Julie. Caught stealing, he kills himself, and then returns sixteen years later to seek atonement.

When Ingrid read the play, she said later, she assumed that she was to play not Julie but the second lead, Julie's friend Marie. Ingrid was not reluctant to attempt great parts such as Joan of Arc or Charlotte Corday on film, and it was a curious kind of professional modesty that Ingrid had suddenly developed. According to Kay Brown, Ingrid's story was pure mythmaking. The only question was whether Ingrid's English was up to a major stage role; indeed, two days after Ingrid returned to New York, Kay was already wiring Selznick about the role of Julie for Ingrid. Her English was still not good; she could speak adequately in a film, where she performed only a few lines of dialogue at a time. In a Broadway play her English and her acting would be put to a severe test.

Ingrid was game and Kay thought it would be a good idea, but Selznick at first opposed the project. The producer had no immediate offers for Ingrid, though he was boasting in Hollywood that he had. He worried that Ingrid's value in films would diminish if she received bad notices in *Liliom*. Few men, however, were a match for Ingrid when she was dealing with her career. She discussed the offer with him by telephone as if Selznick were her father, husband, lover, mentor, and friend. And she talked him into letting her play the part.

During rehearsals, Ingrid's apprehensions were increased when she learned that the producer had initially confused her with another Swedish newcomer, Signe Hasso, who had far more stage experience. If that were not bad omen enough, she was playing opposite a young actor, Burgess Meredith, whom she towered over. Nonetheless, like most of her co-stars, Burgess was taken with Ingrid, and their chemistry played out on stage during rehearsals.

Then came opening night, March 25, 1940. Some actors have only a few shivers of stage fright before the curtain opens. For others there is a moment of pure existential dread. As the audience began to enter the theater, Burgess sat in his dressing room while a group of gypsy musicians played, helping the young actor to get in the proper mood. Ingrid had no musicians, and though Kay felt that she was "not unduly nervous about the opening," Ingrid said later that she was petrified.

"Would my mouth even open, let alone utter a single word?" she wondered.

Then, suddenly, Ingrid was on stage. She was speaking. She was someone else. She was all right.

Many fine movie actors appear on stage like faded tintypes, or wax museum representations of themselves. They simply are not stage actors, and if they are smart, or if their career still allows it, they hurry back to the screen. Ingrid, however, was one of that rare breed who command the stage even before they say a line. It was not technique, for she was in some ways still amateurish. But as Brooks Atkinson wrote in the *New York Times*, she kept "the part wholly alive and lightens it from within with luminous beauty." She commanded the stage that evening. By the time she spoke her last lines, the audience was hers. She received as many curtain calls as the better-known Meredith.

Most of the reviews were positive, but there were several detractors, most vehemently John Mason Brown of the *New York Post*. Brown found the performance as a whole "shoddy." Although he admitted that Ingrid was "charming to look at" and could act well, he was the first American critic to sound the one theme of doubt that would follow her for years. "Miss Bergman fails to endow her love for Liliom and her power to treasure even his blows with the wan quality of abnegation for which the text calls and which is the source of much of its tenderness. . . . Her make-up does not help. She is so ruddy, well fed, and apple cheeked throughout that it is hard to believe in the passive proofs of Julie's devotion."

"Thank God it is all over and you don't need to be ashamed of me!" Ingrid wrote David in a short note after the opening. She had felt a burden not only for herself but for Selznick.

There are few excitements in the public arts to compare to a starring role in a hit play. For the first time in Ingrid's life there were fans surrounding her who saw a magic in her beyond the magic on the screen or stage. After some performances, as she sat in her small dressing room wearing a peasant dress and apron and high-top boots, she had to barricade the door from the onslaught of well-wishers.

"The theater was my mother and my father," she told an interviewer one evening after her performance, and it was indeed as if she had come home. Now for six weeks life was the routine of the play. There was nothing, or next to nothing, to worry about: No time for dinner parties, sitting next to New York gentlemen who burdened her with their charm and whose words she sometimes only half understood. No time to fret endlessly about her career, haunting the movie houses and theaters. No time to have to spend tedious days with Pia, but time simply to see her for a delightful hour or so, squeezed in between performances, English lessons, interviews, singing and dancing classes, and meetings. No time but for the exhilaration and challenge of each performance, the applause flowing over her.

Success in America was different, though. People thought they owned you. You were public property to be pawed over and whispered about. In stores strangers suddenly struck up conversations, not necessarily because they thought Ingrid a star, or beautiful; sometimes simply because such instant intimacy was the American way. The reporters were no better. They asked her if she had run out on Petter, and suggested the names of possible lovers. One evening a little boy pestered her for autographs. One signature wasn't enough. When she got in a cab, he jumped in after and began beseeching her for more autographs. The Selznick representative seated next to Ingrid picked the unruly tyke up by his neck and heaved him out the door.

"Oh, you've hurt him!" Ingrid cried out.

"Hurt him, nothing," said the representative, alert to the ways of New York. "I've killed him. So long as I didn't use a gun or crown him, it was legal. You're going to like America. It's a great country!"

Ingrid considered America a great country, but she was still worried about what her next role would be in Hollywood. She was at the mercy of whatever Selznick and Kay decided to tell her, and they treated her like an adolescent whom they were protecting from the rude realities of existence. Moreover, Selznick was still trying to renegotiate Ingrid's contract, and he was not about to give her information that would make her bargaining position stronger.

Selznick was at the top of his profession, and he might have devoted part of his creative energies to producing Ingrid's second film. But he wasn't doing that. He had done the ultimate with *Gone With the Wind*, and the Hollywood gossips said that he was burned out. His problem was larger than that. He was constantly coming up with new ideas for Ingrid and his other stars, squandering his money, time, and enthusiasms on scores of projects that never quite worked out. He was like a rich little boy in a room full of toys, so jaded by the array before him that he simply sat there unable to move.

As Selznick considered various projects for Ingrid, he treated her like a piece of property to be bought and sold and rented. It was like any other property in Los Angeles; as speculative fever took hold, it might increase geometrically in value, but it might fall to next to nothing too. The producer couldn't tell Ingrid about all the wheeling and dealing. He certainly didn't tell her that he had turned down the role in *Victory*, a decision that a few months later he regretted. He certainly didn't tell her that the problem in loaning her out for another role was that he had been offered only $50,000, not the $75,000 he wanted, and he wouldn't settle for a mere $25,000, or double what he paid her.

Ingrid did learn about some film projects. In May she read the script for *So Ends Our Night*, based on the novel *Flotsam* by Erich Maria Remarque, famous for his great antiwar novel, *All Quiet on the Western Front*. *So Ends Our Night* was an anti-Nazi film. Hitler's troops had invaded Denmark and Norway and were marching through the Netherlands, Belgium, and France, and the film was hardly full of revelations about the brutality of Nazism. But even at this late date O'Shea wrote Selznick that Ingrid expressed herself as having "reluctance about playing anything so decidedly anti-German." Kay, nonetheless, felt that she could be talked into accepting the part.

Ingrid's attitude toward Nazi Germany might once have been excused as mere ignorance, and a spilling over of her affections for her German relatives. But by now it was hard to be alive without being aware of the realities of Hitler. She had even sailed across the Atlantic in a ship that contained refugees and other witnesses to the horror of fascism. Her willful ignorance was no longer innocence.

Ingrid's one worry beyond her career was Petter, and the life and land she had left. She was emotionally halfway between Hollywood and Stockholm. When reporters talked to her, they found that when they asked of Sweden and Petter, her blue eyes filled with tears.

As sad as Ingrid was about the ending of the six-week run of *Liliom*, she was excited about Petter's arriving in June for a visit. She left Pia and the maid at Kay's summer place on Long Island, and took a room on the thirty-fourth floor of the Hotel Pierre, overlooking Central Park.

Petter forcefully assumed the role in Ingrid's career that his wife wanted him to play: the mentor and protector. In the few weeks that Petter was in the States, he and Ingrid had some crucial decisions to make. Selznick was trying to renegotiate Ingrid's contract, tying her up for more films, a longer period, and doing away with her right of cancellation. The producer succeeded in keeping Ingrid away from any agent who would seek to represent her. In this case, his shrewdness got the best of him.

Petter tended to be suspicious of the fast-talking, glad-handing Hollywood types who had brought his wife to the States to make movies but instead had plunked her down in Manhattan. Although Petter denies that he ever discussed contracts with O'Shea or Selznick, both Ingrid's recollection and communications within the Selznick organization suggest otherwise. Daniel O'Shea found him "stubborn as a mule—he has a whim of iron." O'Shea may have meant to say "will of iron," but it was indeed Petter's "whim of iron" that troubled the Selznick people, his refusal to do business as they did business.

Ingrid's contract gave her a right to make films in languages other than English in Europe. Although Denmark and Norway had been invaded by the Germans, Petter thought that Sweden would be able to remain neutral. And he wanted his wife back in Sweden by Christmas. After meeting Petter, O'Shea wrote Selznick: "He keeps harping on the fact that having brought her over here and not having made a picture with her for six months, and with a situation indicative of the fact that we will not be making one too shortly, we have cost her her German market and greatly interfered with and damaged her Swedish market. . . . I very frankly told him that the Hollywood and German situations were not reconcilable. That if she were going to be a star in Germany, she would not be a star in Hollywood."

When Selznick read O'Shea's letter he was infuriated. "It is outrageous that they should consider accepting the hospitality of civilized nations and want to work with the Nazis," Selznick wrote O'Shea. "I have no right to compel her or her husband to have any international morals—but I would like it to be made very clear that since they are always talking in terms of ethics and morality, I am shocked that they would even discuss working in Germany. . . . I think you ought to make it very clear to Ingrid and her husband that if the only terms they can understand are commercial terms, and they persist in talking in terms of money, they might as well face the fact that if she makes one more picture in Germany she will not make another picture in any of the few civilized nations still left. . . . They would probably stone the theatres in which her films played, and I wouldn't blame them."

One essential fact remained: Ingrid wanted to stay in the United States and to do what had to be done to become a major star. And Petter agreed to return to the United States to pursue his medical studies.

CHAPTER SIX

"The Bars of
My Cage Are Broken"

*P*etter was soon sailing back to Europe, leaving Ingrid to spend most of the summer of 1940 alone. What a strange, ironic time it was for her. Nine months ago her American film debut had seemed a harbinger of grand success. Just a month or so ago she had been heralded on Broadway. Yet here she was living an unsettled, uncertain life in hotels and other people's houses, from Kay's Windmill Cottage at Amagansett, Long Island, to the Hotel Volney in New York, to the Garden of Allah in Hollywood.

Ingrid felt so much an observer of the film world that one day in Hollywood she decided to hire a guide to the Hollywood homes. "You have heard about David Selznick, haven't you?" the guide asked his Swedish client, as they drove around the Hollywood hills.

"Slightly," Ingrid said, and winked toward Selznick's estate.

The one immediate film possibility for Ingrid was a loan-out to Columbia Pictures to do *Adam Had Four Sons*, directed by Gregory Ratoff. She read the book on which the film would be based. She and Kay found Ingrid's part as a governess too negative, and stars did not play negative parts. They assumed that the final script would be more positive.

Ingrid had no illusions that the film would be a box office triumph, but there was no immediate alternative. Her main problem was Ratoff. The director had no idea of what his Swedish star truly thought of him. To his face Ingrid cooed words of sweet appreciation. She flattered him so much that later he addressed her as "My Sweetest Swedish Baby." But privately she and Kay were bitterly disdainful of Ratoff and the performance he had gotten out of Ingrid in *Intermezzo*.

Ingrid was not sure she should do the film. At a party that summer at the William Paleys, she asked Selznick's advice. As Selznick remembered the conversation, he told Ingrid that he didn't think the part was good enough, and that he would prefer to pay her for remaining idle, waiting for the proper role.

Ingrid could not stand to be idle. She was eating compulsively, and had already gained five pounds. She felt that she had to work, even if it was in a film that would do her career little good. And so she headed west from New York once again to play a part in a movie that she knew wouldn't be very good, under a director in whom she had little faith.

To Europeans, Hollywood sometimes seemed one gigantic set. Stars were supposed to live like stars, even if their home was rented, their Rolls-Royce hired, their clothes on loan from the studio.

Ingrid felt that life should be lived with clean, simple lines, not cluttered with ostentation and pretense. She didn't rent a palace in the hills but took a two-bedroom apartment at Shirley Place, in the flats of Beverly Hills. It was a lovely place, with room for Pia and Mabel, the maid. But by Hollywood's standards her quarters were suspiciously modest. Moreover, she drove to the studio in a rented blue Ford coupe, a vehicle that her makeup man might have owned.

"At last something my teeth could bite into but it was not such a good apple," Ingrid wrote in her diary. She knew that *Adam Had Four Sons* would not be much of a movie, but she hadn't been prepared to find the production a shambles. Every day new dialogue was written. Ratoff had no idea how his film was going to end, and indeed, after the film was finished Selznick spent by his estimate "probably the equivalent of a solid week's work" editing a film that was in no way his responsibility. He did so solely so that *his* star would not appear in a debacle.

Ingrid liked—indeed, needed—her professional life to be as neat and orderly as her apartment, and she had some difficult times on the set. What helped immensely was that she had Ruth Roberts working with her again. Ingrid had written regularly to Ruth from the East Coast, primarily about her work and professional life. Ruth was becoming more than a mere language coach to Ingrid. She was her confidante, her friend. With Ruth Ingrid could discuss her career with utter frankness. She needed Ruth, and from then on she insisted that Ruth be written into the contract for each picture.

Ruth was becoming, in the words of her longtime housemate, Rae Pober, "addicted to Ingrid." Ruth was a talented woman, but she shackled her own aspirations to Ingrid's. She loved Ingrid and she would do anything for her. The two women were friends, and Ingrid often dropped by Ruth's home. There, sitting laughing on the sofa, or washing dinner dishes together, they did not seem like employer and employee, star and star's retainer. But on the set or in the gatherings of Hollywood, Ruth knew enough to pull away from Ingrid, and not to pretend that they were equals.

Ingrid finished work on *Adam Had Four Sons* one morning at three o'clock and began work on her next film, *Rage in Heaven*, seven hours later, on December 11, 1940. This time, Selznick had loaned Ingrid out to MGM for $34,000 to do a conventional, even hackneyed story, based on the James Hilton novel. Selznick was enough concerned about the quality of the production that before the film went into production he spent a Sunday going over the script and making suggestions.

Ingrid played a young woman who finds that she has married a man (Robert Montgomery) who is a borderline psychotic. Her husband's friend (George Sanders) attempts to help him, but he is too riddled with jealousy and self-hatred. He commits suicide, making it look as if his friend has killed him.

One of the people Ingrid met on the set was the co-screenwriter Christopher Isherwood, a brilliant young novelist who in Berlin had experienced a different Nazi Germany than Ingrid had seen at UFA. He went to the set every day to go over scenes with her.

"There are people who in the best sense of the word are amateurs, who due to their beauty and charm become stars," Isherwood says. "But she was a real pro. I feel at home with real pros the way Hemingway liked bullfighters. They're very tough and have a kind of glamour.

"She was absolutely charming. In some ways she was the most beautiful woman I ever met—not that women are my specialty. She wasn't a woman that you'd spend time with unless you were involved with her. She had a certain aspect of her that was almost masculine. She was so professional. When studio people would pinch her ass or something, she would give them a dry smile as if they were men in a locker room."

In her Swedish films Ingrid had played the suffering, innocent, misunderstood young woman often enough that *Rage in Heaven* should have been a mere exercise for her. But like *Adam Had Four Sons*, this new production was hobbled with one dispute or problem after another.

MGM fired the first two directors, finally bringing in W. S. Van Dyke II, whose most distinguished attribute as a director was his fancy name, and whose main claim to fame was that he got films finished, come hell, high water, or temperamental actors.

Van Dyke dressed like a martinet, in high leather boots and military breeches. He berated the actors as if they were recruits in boot camp. Ingrid felt that she could not work with such a man, and she went to Selznick to complain. Selznick had no control over MGM. Moreover, he didn't want *his* Ingrid to get a reputation as a temperamental actress. So he sent her back to the studio to complete the film.

When it came to her work, Ingrid was relentless. During the shooting she was not happy with a certain scene.

"I know I can do it better," Ingrid said, asking for another take.

"We're going to circle it," Van Dyke said, ready to move on.

"We're moving too fast," Ingrid insisted, making a scene in front of the crew.

One day Ingrid confronted Van Dyke in her dressing room. "Why didn't you stay with the army the way you go on marching and yelling?" she remembered telling the director. "You don't know anything about people's feelings. You certainly can't direct a woman."

*   *   *

Even while *Rage in Heaven* was in the first days of production in December 1940, Ingrid was looking for a better part for her fourth American film. She knew already that once again she was caught in an inferior, forgettable film. Once again she was playing under a director with whom she was far from comfortable. If she did not get into higher-quality productions soon, she would end up like so many other foreign stars, her career run aground upon the tricky shoals of Hollywood.

Ingrid had believed in Selznick, but he was shopping her around instead of starring her in "A David O. Selznick Production." Even Selznick could admit privately—though certainly not to Ingrid—that he had made at least two major mistakes: he had turned down *Victory*, and instead of purchasing the rights to *A Woman's Face* for Ingrid, he had let it become a vehicle for Joan Crawford.

Whatever Selznick was doing, he almost always had some other motive, some other scheme in mind. A year and a half earlier, when Selznick and Victor Fleming looked at the daily rushes of *Gone With the Wind*, he had the daily scenes of *Intermezzo* shown as well. Fleming was one of the most successful directors in Hollywood. As preoccupied as he was with *Gone With the Wind*, Fleming could not have found it terribly tedious looking at the footage of Ingrid. Selznick wanted him to see Ingrid "over and over again so that I would have the opportunity for my campaign."

Fleming was enough impressed with Selznick's Swedish protégée that he wanted her to co-star in his new film at MGM, *Dr. Jekyll and Mr. Hyde*, to begin shooting in February, a few weeks after *Rage in Heaven* was finished. Of course, Ingrid would play Beatrix Emery, the sweet, virtuous fiancée of Spencer Tracy as Dr. Harry Jekyll. As for the sensuous, low-life, amoral Ivy Peterson, that role was a natural for another new star, Lana Turner. But Ingrid wanted to play Ivy.

First, Ingrid had to convince Victor Fleming. The handsome, six-feet-two-inch-tall Fleming was, as Spencer Tracy called him, "the Clark Gable of directors." Fleming lived with his wife and family on a two-acre farm in Brentwood. Part Cherokee Indian, fifty-seven-year-old Fleming was a romantic figure who had traveled the world and piloted his own plane. As a director he was a consummate professional, who had made such diverse films as *Test Pilot*, *The Virginian*, and *Gone With the Wind*.

Ingrid went to Fleming and, as she remembered, said: "Couldn't we switch, and let Lana Turner play the fiancée, and I play the little tart in the bar, the naughty little Ivy?"

"That's impossible," Fleming supposedly answered. "How can you with your looks? It's not to be believed."

In her autobiography Ingrid wrote that she asked to do a screen test, but that Fleming told her Selznick would never put *his* star through the humiliation of trying out for a part. And so she and Fleming did the test secretly, and showed it to an incredulous Selznick.

Ingrid treated each man with whom she was involved as if the two of them were in a conspiracy against the rest of the world. That was the intimacy she offered a man, the sense that he and Ingrid were bonded together, against an uncaring, unfeeling universe. Selznick felt that he was Ingrid's great guide and mentor, leading her upward, gently wooing Fleming so that he would want to work with Ingrid. As for Fleming, he felt as if he and Ingrid were artists and lovers, creating beauty and fame and wealth.

At one point Fleming may have believed that he and Ingrid were working together almost against Selznick. But in fact, Selznick knew about the screen test from the beginning. He thought that Ingrid could indeed play a "sexy bitch." Early in December he even called Fleming to discuss being present for the screen test. Ingrid was the one worried about the onus of an unsuccessful test. Before shooting, she wanted to read for the part so that if it didn't work out, "we won't have any bad tests floating around."

Ingrid got the part of Ivy, a wonderful Christmas present, and a marvelous antidote to her experience on the set of *Rage in Heaven*. That Christmas of 1940 was special in another way. Petter had arrived from Sweden. He had not had a glamorous six-day sojourn on the *Queen Mary* but a six-week sail in a berth on a freighter from Portugal. A couple of weeks after he arrived, Petter and Ingrid flew to Sun Valley, Idaho, for skiing. Petter was a marvelous skier, who soared down the slopes, full of energy and enthusiasm. Ingrid was more interested in the ski lodge or sitting in the sun, but the vacation was a welcome respite between films.

Ingrid had other matters on her mind. There was not only her forthcoming role in *Dr. Jekyll and Mr. Hyde*, but the possibility of acting Maria in the film version of Ernest Hemingway's new novel, *For Whom the Bell Tolls*, which in a few months had already sold over half a million copies.

Hollywood was in the midst of the biggest hoopla over a book since the search for Scarlett in *Gone With the Wind*. When Selznick read *For Whom the Bell Tolls*, he thought that Ingrid was a natural for Maria, the young, emotionally anesthetized victim of Fascist rapists. So did Ingrid, who picked her way through the novel with the help of a Swedish-English dictionary. A few years before, Selznick might have bought the rights himself. Selznick had an entrée to Hemingway through his brother Myron, Hollywood's premier agent. Myron had sold the rights to the book to Paramount for $150,000, the highest amount yet paid for a novel, and Hemingway was grateful. Blood is blood and business is business, and Selznick commissioned his brother to help get the part for Ingrid.

Hemingway was as celebrated and publicized a figure as any movie star. And he was said to be mentioning Ingrid for the part. That was extraordinary, even if Ingrid and Selznick didn't think so. After all, in his novel, Hemingway had a very specific idea of his Maria. . . . "Her teeth were white in her brown face and her skin and eyes were the same golden tawny brown . . . Her hair was the golden brown of a grain field that has been burned dark in the sun but it was cut short all over her head so that it was but little longer than the fur on a beaver pelt." The description didn't sound quite like Ingrid Bergman, though it didn't sound like any other Hollywood star either. Moreover, Ingrid was not a major star. *Intermezzo* was her only American film yet to open.

Ingrid had one great stroke of luck. The year before, when she sailed on the *Rex* from Italy, the journalist Martha Gellhorn had been a passenger. Since then Gellhorn had married Hemingway, and the image of Ingrid on the ship had stayed with her. "I suggested Ingrid for *For Whom the Bell Tolls*," says Gellhorn. "I had seen her on the boat, a woman with a baby on her back. And then I saw her in a film. And then I made the suggestion to Hemingway."

Hemingway mentioned Ingrid as a possible Maria in an article in *Life*. That was enough for Selznick to try to set up a meeting for Ingrid with the novelist. Hemingway was about to sail for China from San Francisco. So on January 30, 1940, Ingrid and Petter cut short their vacation to meet the novelist. They drove through the night to Reno to catch the morning plane. The winter weather in the San Francisco area was treacherous. The airport was fogged in, and the plane landed at Oakland, across the bay.

Hemingway and Ingrid met on a street corner outside Jack's Restaurant, along with their respective spouses. The foursome then proceeded inside for a private tête-à-tête, the intimate moment duly immortalized by a reporter and a photographer for *Life*.

Twenty-five-year-old Ingrid was no longer an innocent at the Hollywood publicity games. To play at the highest level did not mean cheesecake pictures and interviews with the fan magazines. It meant lunches like this one, where calculated, public performances were made to seem like private moments, where *Life* was made to seem like life.

"If you don't act in the picture, Ingrid, I won't work on it," Hemingway told Ingrid, who, as reported by *Life*, was "shy" but "finally laughs."

Hemingway was in favor of Ingrid. But he did not tell her what he had told Selznick by phone earlier in the day: that among other things, Paramount considered Ingrid "dumb," "wooden," and "untalented."

During the flight to Los Angeles, Ingrid read the inscription on the copy of *For Whom the Bell Tolls* Hemingway had given her: "To Ingrid Bergman, who is the Maria of this story."

Hemingway had done all that could be expected to help Ingrid get the part. He had richly repaid his debt to Myron Selznick. Now it was up to David Selznick and Ingrid to make her choice as Maria inevitable. That would take some time, for Paramount was luxuriating in all its possibilities, relishing the windfall of publicity. Ingrid was mentioned as a possible Maria, but so were Paulette Goddard, Betty Field, Annabella, and others.

*   *   *

Petter was excited about Ingrid's career. He enjoyed skiing and tagging along on the visit with Ernest Hemingway. But he liked sitting around as little as did his wife. Petter was already in his mid-thirties. He was making a sacrifice that few men of his generation and professional position would have made. But he was not going to become Mr. Ingrid Bergman, hovering around the Hollywood set. He sat down and began applying to medical schools so that he could finish up his degree and become a doctor in the United States. "I could have stayed in Los Angeles and gone to USC, but I wouldn't be able to enter for a whole other year," Petter says. "I had an honorary fellowship with the American Scandinavian Foundation. They suggested that I visit and select one of three medical schools in the East. So I left California and traveled east, visiting medical schools at Yale and Rochester and Chicago."

Petter would be the one, this time, to establish himself for many months far from Ingrid and her work. A mark of Petter's confidence in himself and in his relationship to Ingrid, it was also a sad commentary on the nature of their marriage. Here was a man who believed in the sanctity of marriage and family. Yet he and his wife had lived apart for almost half of their three-and-a-half-year marriage. Theirs was a marriage of the special moment, of meetings in hotels or on vacation, or between films and projects. No matter what their marriage certificate said, they were still newlyweds who had not tested the mettle of their relationship in day-to-day living. These were the war years and millions of married couples were living separate lives; but it was not the army or the war that kept Ingrid and Petter so much apart.

Petter thought that Ingrid's contract would allow her months of freedom to live with him. But he knew, too, that she was a restless woman of boundless ambition.

Ingrid had what most women, even other stars, would have considered an enviable life: a starring role in an exciting new film, and a husband who adored her and was unquestionably faithful. But that was not enough.

"Ingrid told me often that she couldn't work well unless she was in love with either the leading man or the director," Petter says. Another husband would have asked his wife in no uncertain terms what "love" meant, and whom she was talking about. Petter did not ask. He seemed not to want to know, to learn too much about the woman who was his wife.

As an actress, Ingrid was always playing aspects of herself. She knew that when she made love to a man as the cameras rolled, she would give a better performance if she was making love to him offscreen as well. It was not a question of morality. Nor was it a matter of profound romantic love, a fact that it would take several men a good while to understand.

Ingrid was a woman of enormous professional cunning. That was nowhere more apparent than in her relationship with her new director, Victor Fleming, and her co-star, Spencer Tracy. *Dr. Jekyll and Mr. Hyde* began shooting on February 12, 1941. In it, she was playing a woman of wanton sexuality, who in one scene wallows in mud, in another rests voluptuously upon a bed of flowers. When she was acting in a part, her whole life was that part, and it was no wonder that she should become involved with both Fleming and Tracy.

On the set waiting to perform, she was, as Charles Schram, the makeup man, remembers, "shy and bashful and blushing a lot and very quiet and a little scared," but once the camera started, Ingrid appeared the personification of naughty, amoral Ivy.

Fleming got a stunning performance out of Ingrid, in part because she was playing the sensuous, hedonistic woman offscreen as well as on. Fleming had a long-standing reputation as a ladies' man. Indeed, in 1934 he had been accused by Paul A. Lockwood, a cameraman, in a $150,000 alienation of affection suit. Lockwood alleged that Fleming had promised his wife a career. She had agreed to go with the married director to Honolulu, but Fleming had left her in San Francisco, where she suffered a nervous breakdown.

Fleming was more than twice Ingrid's age, but in her presence all his youth and vitality seemed renewed. In the scene in which Spencer Tracy was to carry Ingrid up to the bedroom, Fleming showed his star what to do by sweeping Ingrid up into his arms, and carrying her upward as if the stairs were not part of a set but the entry to his private quarters. Tracy was not about to attempt to replicate the director's effort. He insisted that a sling be used to help hoist Ingrid's body aloft.

At times, Fleming could be almost sadistic. In a scene in which Ingrid was to cry hysterically, he slapped her across the face. If Van Dyke or Ratoff had tried such a stunt, Ingrid would have berated them endlessly. But as she admitted, she "was deeply in love with Victor Fleming," in love, too, with the performance he was coaxing out of her.

Ingrid was also involved with Spencer Tracy during the filming. "I watched her relationship with Spencer on *Dr. Jekyll and Mr. Hyde*," remembers John Houseman, the director and actor. "But that's not uncommon in this business." During the filming Tracy was extraordinarily enthusiastic about Ingrid. He came up to Selznick at a party and told him "that in all his career he had never seen her equal, either on stage or on screen . . . that she is clearly destined to be the greatest star in pictures." When Thornton Delehanty, a newspaper reporter, came to talk to Tracy on the set, the actor insisted that the reporter interview her as well.

Ingrid was exceptionally lucky on *Dr. Jekyll and Mr. Hyde*. She had both her director and her co-star slavishly devoted to her. They helped her to achieve a performance that brought more glory and acclaim to Ingrid than either of them achieved.

"Shall I ever be happier in my work?" she asked rhetorically in her diary. "I have never been happier. Never have I given myself so completely. For the first time I have broken out from the cage which encloses me. . . . It is as if I were flying. I feel no chains. I can fly higher and higher because the bars of my cage are broken."

Despite the imagery, Ingrid was not breathlessly describing erotic encounters with Fleming or Tracy. She was describing her work. To Ingrid, a good role was freedom and ecstasy.

On the set of the movie, Ingrid lived a whole life, and when the movie was finished, the affair with Fleming was finished as well. She said later that Fleming ended it because "he wasn't in love with me." However, a love letter that Fleming wrote Ingrid six years later suggests that the reasons were more complicated ("Six years is twice as long for me for what I've lost is lost for ever"). Ingrid apparently maintained a longer-term interest in Spencer Tracy. According to Petter, months later he prevented her from going off with the actor for two weeks in San Francisco to discuss "future roles."

After *Dr. Jekyll and Mr. Hyde*, Selznick had no new movie immediately on the horizon, but in August he was planning to star Ingrid in Eugene O'Neill's *Anna Christie* at the Lobero Theater in Santa Barbara. Before rehearsals, she had a chance to go east and spend time with Petter and her friends. Ingrid's long, restful days were made doubly tranquil because she had a challenging role ahead of her. She appeared to be happy, but she was full of her familiar insecurities. Selznick didn't comment quickly enough after seeing a screening of *Dr. Jekyll and Mr. Hyde*; Ingrid was sure that his silence meant that he didn't like the film.

In June, Petter, Ingrid, and Pia stayed a few days in upstate New York at a guesthouse on a property owned by Burgess Meredith. One of the other guests that weekend was Olivia de Havilland. She had met Ingrid only once before, at the Selznick studios during the making of *Gone With the Wind*. Olivia remembers Petter and Ingrid sitting in canvas chairs in front of the guesthouse. Petter read books, and Ingrid chatted and looked over scripts. "He adored her and I think she knew it, but I think every man adored her," de Havilland says. When it was time for lunch, Ingrid jumped up, walked over to the main house, and rummaged through the refrigerator. She was soon giving orders to Olivia and preparing a good simple repast.

Ingrid was soon traveling west once again, alone. Petter had been accepted at the University of Rochester Medical School, and he journeyed to upstate New York, where Ingrid would soon be joining him. Pia would stay with Kay Brown on Long Island, the first extended period that the child was without either parent.

Selznick took credit for getting Petter into Rochester through his acquaintance with Dr. Alan Valentine, the president of the university. Petter's credentials and training were first rate, and he states adamantly that he got into medical school on his own. Selznick may have helped facilitate matters, but in acting as if Petter was nothing without him, he was seeking to show Petter and Ingrid how much they needed him.

In *Anna Christie*, Ingrid was facing the most challenging theatrical role of her life. "Anna was a whore," said John Houseman, who directed the O'Neill play that two decades before had won a Pulitzer Prize. "And that was difficult for Ingrid. When she tried to be evil, it usually didn't work."

At the play's opening on July 30, 1941, there were far more stars in the audience than onstage. "Gimme a whiskey and make it a double!" Ingrid said to the barman as she stepped onstage, and the audience howled in laughter. It was hardly the reception a thespian would have wanted, but she was soon fully into the part. Four days later, when the play opened a short stand in San Francisco, the critic of the *Call-Bulletin* reported that he "hadn't heard [such applause] in a decade."

By the middle of August, Ingrid was on the train back to New York for yet another short run of *Anna Christie*, at the Maplewood Theater in New Jersey. *Dr. Jekyll and Mr. Hyde* had just opened, and as she traveled eastward, the first reviews were appearing in the papers. The common consensus, as the *New York Times* expressed it, was that "only Miss Bergman has emerged with some measure of honor."

Ingrid had hoped to enjoy Sunday at Amagansett with Pia, with whom she was spending so little time. But as her train arrived Sunday morning and she had to begin rehearsals Monday morning, she decided that wouldn't work out. Instead, Miss Olsen, the nanny, brought Pia into New York on the train.

Ingrid prepared diligently for the new summer stock production in a bare rehearsal room at 16 West 46th Street, but she had time one weekend afternoon to stand in line and see herself in *Dr. Jekyll and Mr. Hyde*. She saw other movies too and gave interviews to the local papers. New York reporters wore their cynicism like crowns; they were less than amused when they discovered that they had all been given "exclusive" interviews with the Swedish star. But as soon as they sat down with Ingrid they were taken with her. And the journalists proceeded to fill their columns with lyrical paeans to Ingrid.

Before Ingrid, there had been Garbo. Garbo the inaccessible, Garbo the mysterious, Garbo the incomparable, slinking in and out of the city in dark glasses. And here was Ingrid, another Swede, sitting apparently without makeup, looking "like the Ideal American Senior at Vassar, low-heeled edition complete with saddle oxfords." Here was Ingrid not only physically accessible but seemingly accessible emotionally, a star whose great mystery was her seeming lack of mystery, a star about whom there were no rumors of scandal, a star who was a happily married twenty-five-year-old mother, a star who when she wasn't working intended to live not in Paris, Palm Springs, or Hollywood, but with her medical student husband in, of all places, Rochester, New York. This, then, was the Bergman the reporters met, a Bergman who, as the *New York Post* headlined its article, was the "Garbo of the 40s."

For Ingrid, everything was going well, and she seemed to glow with well-being. The reporters adored her, but so did the public, and so did Selznick and Kay, and so did Petter, even more than the others. He came down from Rochester to see the Maplewood production, an even bigger hit than *Anna*

Christie had been in the West. Petter was enthusiastic about everything—his wife, the play, everything. He cabled Selznick:

> . . . EVERY EVENING HERE SOLD OUT IN ADVANCE AND ONLY FIRE DEPARTMENT WITH THEIR DIRTY TRUCK COULD STOP THE CROWD FIGHTING THEIR WAY IN . . . WE ARE SO GOOD AND WE ARE SO BEAUTI-FUL AND THE MORE WE THINK OF EUROPE AND COCA COLA THE MORE WE LIKE AMERICA.
>
> PETER

CHAPTER SEVEN

Money, Fame, and Power

After the close of *Anna Christie* in New Jersey, Ingrid traveled to Rochester. The move was a public-relations dream. The Manhattan reporters had been amazed. Ingrid Bergman, the Hollywood movie star, was going to live in Rochester, New York, a provincial city known primarily as the home of the Eastman Kodak company. The move seemed to confirm all the hype about Ingrid's naturalness, her disdain for the glamour and falseness of Hollywood.

After a couple days in the Lindstroms' rented house at 985 South Avenue, Ingrid pronounced herself "really happy." The house was "really sweet," almost a "dream house." As usually happened when Ingrid wasn't working, she was full of nervous tedium. And as she did throughout her life in such periods, she became a Swedish housewife, to whom life is eternal spring cleaning. The pail and scrub brush were Ingrid's Freud and Jung. She scrubbed away, exorcising the last heelmark on the kitchen floor, wiping out any recalcitrant streaks of dust.

There was only so much dirt, however, and Ingrid was soon discontent. Rochester was a farming center, and there was wonderful food—goat cheese, fresh apples, sausage. Petter had told her it was all right to eat, but she was gorging herself. The compulsive eating that frequently overcame her could have been viewed as a psychological problem requiring attention, but neither Ingrid nor Petter had such insight.

"I think I have tried everything to stop eating," she wrote Ruth. She was almost as fat as she had been in the spring in Hollywood. Next year how would she ever play the nun in *The Keys of the Kingdom*, the next role David had promised her? And what if after all this time she should get the role of Maria in *For Whom the Bell Tolls*?

No one like Ingrid had ever lived in Rochester, and articles about her arrival appeared in the local papers. One writer, Howard C. Hosmer, who had not interviewed Ingrid or Petter, described an extraordinary scene: crowds standing two deep in front of the Lindstroms' house; fans camped out on the front lawn; the curious peering through the windows. "The Lindstroms had been living in their house only two days when someone broke in, ransacked their bedroom, took lingerie . . . and several articles of value . . . little keepsakes for celebrity hunters," Hosmer wrote. "The next night, someone broke into the house again. The bedroom was turned upside down again. No money was taken, just small personal articles, souvenirs for someone of a screen actress' attempt to become a Rochester housewife." The article said the situation was so bad, Ingrid so badly badgered, that she was going to leave Rochester.

The two break-ins never took place, though Ingrid would tell the story repeatedly, including in her autobiography. To Selznick, however, on September 29, she sent the newspaper clipping with a note: "Don't get upset, because nobody actually got into the house and none of my 'dear precious things' disappeared." There had been one minor incident when a window was left open, but that was all. Nor were there crowds outside the house or swarms of relentless fans.

Ingrid had received occasional pestering phone calls, but Petter had installed an unlisted phone, and the calls were no longer a problem. If anything, the problem in Rochester was that life was too tranquil.

Ingrid didn't have to tolerate her life in Rochester very long. She had hardly been there a couple of weeks before she was off again to Hollywood for a screen test in *For Whom the Bell Tolls*. Ingrid had strong insights into her own ambition. In Hollywood, Dan O'Shea reported that Ingrid had said that she was "a very poor loser and when she undertakes a thing like this it is much worse for her to be turned down than if she never undertook it."

Ingrid was "frantic" about doing a poor test. Selznick understood his star's mentality. To get Ingrid to go along with the test at Paramount, Selznick insisted on all sorts of conditions. He wouldn't allow a full screen test, but a silent version, supposedly simply to show how Ingrid looked in a short wig. Only those producers and directors at Paramount directly involved with *For Whom the Bell Tolls* would be permitted to look at the film. Then the negative and all prints would have to be given to Selznick. O'Shea added a further precaution. Ingrid would do the test under an assumed name, Marie Devoe.

Ingrid waited for days while the Selznick and Paramount executives negotiated the specific conditions for the test. Finally, at the end of October, Selznick telephoned Sam Wood, the film's director, to learn what was holding up the test. Wood told Selznick that he thought Ingrid "was all wrong for the role. . . . He did not think she could wear trousers properly, that is without looking like a girl, and he thought she was too tall."

Ingrid got on the train and headed back to Rochester. She had heard Wood's excuses—her height, her look in slacks—but she realized that "another reason (perhaps the real one) would have hurt me more."

Ingrid had no agent and the Selznick people attempted to deal with Petter in renegotiating Ingrid's contract. In July, Petter had warned Kay that she had "better count on the possibility of an agent's voice loudly calling from Rochester in the future." He was a man of his word.

"I really feel a great responsibility," he wrote Kay Brown. "I have been fortunate to meet the finest character and one of the greatest actresses, both in the same person. We do not know very much about the future of that person, and actress, but . . . she probably will go on some years ahead. . . . If not, the reason most likely is that the people around her—including myself—failed and misled her."

Selznick wanted to tie Ingrid up in a longer-term contract, and add an extra movie each year. He had wanted to do it while *For Whom the Bell Tolls* hung in the balance. If she was offered the part of Maria, he had planned to refuse to lend her out until she signed a new contract. Although Ingrid knew about Selznick's plan, she found it useful to feign innocence and play the sweet ingenue. On November 7 she wrote him from Rochester: "With your wisdom and my intuition we should go far!"

Those were sentiments with which Selznick would not have disagreed. But he found her letter bewildering, disquieting. He was worried that Ingrid's English wasn't improving, because she was spending so much time with Petter, speaking Swedish. According to Petter, however, he and Ingrid always spoke English together. That was another extraordinary comment on the quality of their marriage. What they had in common above all else was that they were Swedish. To give up the language that they spoke with ease was to make even their most intimate moments a learning exercise, like not slouching.

Yet the ending of Ingrid's letter *was* incomprehensible enough to justify Selznick's concern. In her clear, large handwriting, Ingrid wrote: "It will please you to know that I understand, that my cabbage head should know you can't catch the larks by being in cahoot with hoodlums even for a C-note cash on the nail every day because there is always the danger of passing in your checks unexpectedly!"

Rochester was far from Sweden, but one could lead a very Swedish life in the upstate New York city. Petter, the boy from small-town Sweden, enjoyed much of his life in Rochester, and he thought that Ingrid could enjoy it as well. "She was working only eight weeks a year and I thought she would stay in Rochester," Petter says. "I thought she could be there just as well—we had skiing, swimming, and steam baths."

Petter had what he thought was quite a realistic vision of his marriage. "She was a healthy girl. I was a healthy boy. She had a sense of humor. As marriages go—and I saw a lot of young doctors and their wives—I was always hopeful. We always thought that she would work until she was about forty. That's when as a doctor I would really start to be at the top."

Back in Stockholm, Kay Brown had thought that Petter and Ingrid were naive innocents. There were, indeed, things about life that neither one understood. Ingrid breezed in and out of Rochester, in and out of her marriage, in and out of motherhood, as if this were just one of many roles. Ingrid didn't see that life is not a series of episodes but a continuum. If one was in endless motion, then one risked becoming nothing but memories, anecdotes, clippings, and reels of film.

Petter was abysmally unaware of the realities of his own marriage. A man of immense optimism, he projected that optimism far into the future. Medical students always dream of the day when they will have their own practice, their own life, but Petter dreamed not only of that day but of the day when Ingrid's career would be finished. He thought that she would change, and they would change, and he would be the head of the family, professionally and personally.

Ingrid had been back only a few weeks before she was off to New York early in December to do a radio program with Spencer Tracy. If anything, Ingrid was only looking for a divertissement, a little attention. When she saw an attractive man, she needed to know that he wanted her. It was like looking in a mirror, and if she sometimes ended up in bed it was proof of nothing more than her own desirability.

One evening when she returned, she went into Pia's bedroom. "Is it true, Mama, you are here tomorrow too!" her daughter asked.

Winter arrives early in upstate New York. By mid-December Ingrid and Petter had already gone skiing in Rochester. Petter was very busy, though, and for long hours Ingrid was by herself. Mabel, the maid, did the shopping, but occasionally Ingrid took Pia grocery shopping at Loblaw's on South Avenue. Sometimes they went ice skating on Riley Pond in Cobbs Hill Park or for a romp through the snow in Highland Park. Sometimes, too, Ingrid sat by the window looking out at the snow, listening to the radio, knitting sweaters for Pia's dolls, and thinking that she seemed "so very, very far away from a camera eye."

Petter decided to have a dinner party for the dean and a dozen or so of his colleagues at the school and their wives. "Ingrid stopped talking and just sat there," Petter remembers. "She said afterwards, 'Don't ever invite physicians again to our house. They don't know anything about film.' She refused to have anything to do with doctors from then on. I never had them in the house again. I was invited time and time again, and I could never invite people. I had to take people out or give gifts or flowers."

One of those Petter took out to dinner was Dr. Ella McCann, a biochemistry professor, who tutored him in scientific English. "We talked about his work," McCann said of her dinners with Petter and Ingrid at Rochester's Sagamore Hotel. "We didn't talk about her very much. He used to tell her she talked too much. He said, You have a good brain on you but you talk too much.

"I think that he thought a great deal of her. He was very proud of her career. I thought it was one of these European marriages that would never break up. They were unalike. There was no question. They were not alike."

Ingrid was profoundly restless to be back at work, but there were good moments in the house on South Avenue. She was so proud of three-year-old Pia, whom she considered an "extraordinary child." Ingrid didn't want her daughter to be spoiled. She told her that for Christmas they would give away all Pia's unwanted toys. Pia sorted through her possessions.

"Are you really going to keep that dirty old thing?" Ingrid asked, looking at a grubby worn doll.

"Yes, she is dirty," Pia answered, "but she really was a very good girl."

Selznick sent Ingrid expensive topaz jewelry for Christmas, but not the gift that she wanted above all others: a role in a new film. All she had in the offing for 1942 was the role of Sister Veronica in *The Keys of the Kingdom*. Even Selznick thought privately that the predicament was "a frightening one from the standpoint of her career."

Although, according to Petter, Ingrid rarely spent more than two weeks at a time in Rochester, she felt that she was "only half . . . alive. The other half is pressed down in a bag suffocated." She tried to keep herself busy. She noted her routine. "Letters and papers in the morning take so long. Walk in the park with Pia so long. Lunch. Answer letters. Play the piano. Paste my clippings. Coffee. English lesson. Dinner. Read. Sleep." She tried to anesthetize herself, to quell her fears and doubts.

Ingrid went to New York to do *The Kate Smith Show* on radio in January. Back in Rochester, she maintained her regimen of reading and writing and walking with Pia. Then in mid-February, for four days in a row, Ingrid sat in a corner by herself. She didn't care about anyone or anything, and she felt that Petter didn't even notice. She wouldn't even take Pia for her walk. She wouldn't exercise. She wrote Selznick that she was "down now, deep down."

Everything seemed to be going wrong. She was dying to make an American version of the British *Gaslight*, but Selznick was threatening not to buy the rights unless she signed a longer-term contract. She felt that Selznick and Kay had "lost all decency and they know they can press me now because I am so down I'm almost willing to scrub floors in David's office." She was losing all the parts she wanted. Ingrid had told Kay that "she would forgive [her] everything in the world, except the loss of *Strange Woman* to Bette Davis." And now Warner Brothers had announced that Bette Davis had the role.

Petter was the one person Ingrid could go to with her contract problems. Petter didn't consider himself truly to be Ingrid's agent. She had a long-term contract and, as he wrote Kay, "I should be very happy if you would discuss the present situation with me again ten years hereafter." Selznick, however, wanted to renegotiate the contract, and the Selznick organization found Petter impossible: proud, self-righteous, and unyielding.

Ingrid and Selznick had always exchanged sweet, adoring letters, no matter what brutal denunciations they might occasionally make in private. That facade collapsed now. When Ingrid met Kay in March, she had used "all the indecent words in [her] vocabulary. . . . I shouted so at least sixty floors could hear me that I hoped and prayed that David didn't take up the option for next year." According to Selznick documents, Petter and Kay spent a marathon seven straight hours in unsuccessful negotiations, a meeting Petter says he never attended. Kay was nonplussed at Petter's "genius of no-yessing everything." Petter did not renegotiate Ingrid's contract. Instead, Ingrid signed a nonexclusive contract with Charles Feldman, a top Hollywood agent, a solution that pleased both Ingrid and Selznick. It was, nonetheless, a mark of Petter's unfamiliarity with Hollywood that he didn't understand that an agent was paid out of his client's share; Petter wanted the agent to be paid by the studio.

On March 24, when Ingrid appeared on the Book-of-the-Month Club radio program, she managed a subtle dig at Selznick. "I've heard some curious accents come out of Hollywood," the interviewer said, "and from native-born actors and actresses, and I would say that they were further from the King's English than yours."

"I hope Mr. Selznick is listening," Ingrid replied.

A week later Ingrid played Jenny Lind on the *Cavalcade of America* program; Selznick was not listening. Afterward, he heard reports that Ingrid's accent was overwhelming. He wrote Kay: "I wish you would tell Ingrid . . . that she will be the prime sufferer from her laziness and indifference." Selznick was tired of Ingrid's "squawking about my not making pictures with her," when he was planning to star her in *The Keys of the Kingdom*, a movie that "from the standpoint of cast, exploitation and pretentiousness will be second only to *Gone With the Wind*."

Selznick wanted Ingrid to know that she wasn't the only actress in Hollywood. Rosalind Russell had read *The Keys of the Kingdom* and "was insane about it." Ingrid simply didn't appreciate Selznick. "But for the terrible way I have treated her, she might be happily now in Sweden waiting for the Germans. . . . I suppose it's time I grew up and learned that all actresses are alike whether they are born in Brooklyn or Stockholm."

Kay was getting tired of Selznick's outbursts. Still, she sat Ingrid down and conveyed Selznick's criticism. Ingrid couldn't understand. She had worked hard on the role of Jenny Lind. The New York critics had lauded her performance. The *New York Daily Mirror* called it "the greatest acting from a Hollywood star we have ever had on radio."

Kay also informed Ingrid that Rosalind Russell had called Selznick, seeking the lead in *The Keys of the Kingdom*. After hearing all this, Ingrid canceled her luncheon with Kay, saying that "she was so unhappy she wouldn't be fit company for anyone."

When Ingrid had arrived in America, she had thought that she and Selznick shared the same dreams. She had believed in him and had been almost giddy in her enthusiasm. But Selznick hadn't made a film since *Rebecca*. He was at times ranting, irrational, and megalomaniacal. One day he would be talking about "selling" Ingrid to another studio, with words that could have come from *Gone With the Wind*. The next day he was elaborating his glorious, golden dreams of films, spinning a web around Ingrid once again. "She [Ingrid] is bewildered by the constant beating I am forced to give her," Kay wrote Selznick. "I am a little bewildered too."

Selznick would have none of it. He railed against "that Swedish genius Lindstrom." He railed against Ingrid, whom he considered graceless and ungrateful. "Ingrid's devotion to me reminds me of Ronald Colman's friendship —both apparently give me the privilege of costing myself money," he replied to Kay. "I feel that from the outset all of us have failed to crash through that combination that Ingrid and Petter have shrewdly or innocently thrown together—a combination of stubbornness, irrational resistance to making the further development of her career easier, sweetness and light, and wounded animal cries."

Money, fame, and power were the only salves that could soothe these wounds. But none of Ingrid's potential roles were working out for her. There had been talk for a while of renewed interest in a screen test as Maria in *For Whom the Bell Tolls*, but that proved wrong. Moreover, Ingrid lost the other role that Selznick wanted strongly for her, starring with Spencer Tracy in *Keeper of the Flame*. George Cukor, the director, had wanted Ingrid, but MGM had opposed her. So had her old friend Spencer Tracy. He preferred Katharine Hepburn.

Ingrid had had so many disappointments, but finally, on April 20, 1942, she learned that she had a role in a new film. Ingrid was excited beyond excitement. She went to bed but she couldn't sleep. She tossed so next to Petter that he couldn't sleep either, and three times she had to go downstairs to sit by herself in the living room. For weeks she had not allowed herself to *feel* how much she missed the film world. Now she could admit it. In a few days she would be gone, back to Hollywood, back to her world. She knew nothing about the film except its name, *Casablanca*, but that hardly mattered.

Ingrid wired Selznick that she was "fainting crying screaming" and preparing to return to Hollywood.

For four months Hal Wallis, the Warner Brothers producer, had been seeking the proper female lead to play the beautiful, romantically tormented Ilsa Lund Laszlo opposite Humphrey Bogart as Rick, the cynical, world-weary saloon owner. In February, Ann Sheridan had been set for the part. Hedy Lamarr had been another possibility, but MGM wouldn't loan her out. On April 1, Wallis decided to go ahead with plans to test yet another actress, Michele Morgan, and to talk to Selznick about Ingrid.

Wallis now considered Ingrid his "first choice, ideal for the foreign girl with a slight accent." Wallis was the same kind of producer that Selznick once had been, with an almost compulsively detailed concern for his films. He was

disdainful of Selznick, whom he considered "an agent at heart," doubly disdainful of all Selznick's gambits and ploys to jack up the prices of the stars he
"seldom used under long-term contracts, . . . then farming them out at inflated
prices."

"Selznick was always very evasive," says Wallis. "I put up with Selznick
because when you're putting together a project of this kind, you're forced to
do a lot of things you don't want because he had the ace card." Selznick would
not return Wallis's phone calls. So during a trip to New York, Wallis called on
Selznick at the Carlyle Hotel, where both were staying. Selznick was interested, but he wanted to hear more about the script.

Julius and Philip Epstein, the two screenwriters on the project, were
assigned the unenviable task of telling Selznick the plot of an only partially
written script.

"What will we tell him?" Julius asked.

"Tell him anything, but get Bergman," Wallis replied. The Epstein twins
were a highly successful team. They were bobbing along in the swirling waters
of Hollywood, wit and quickness their only ballast. They could tear a screenplay apart in a few hours, turning characters and scenes upside down, and they
could wing it with David O. Selznick as well.

Julius talked while Selznick ate lunch at his desk, never looking up. Julius
had been in enough story conferences to know that he was losing it. He had
been there for a good while and he hadn't even talked about Ingrid's character. One device always worked in Hollywood: Say you were going to do a film
like the big hit of the day. So Julius mentioned *Algiers*, the Charles Boyer–
Hedy Lamarr hit. "I said *Casablanca* is going to have a lot of that *Algiers*
schmaltz—lots of atmosphere, cigarette smoke, guitar music," Julius remembers. "Selznick looked up and nodded. We knew then we had Bergman."

Now the deal had to be struck. Wallis had a touch of the agent in his soul
too. He also knew that he had some good cards. Warners had recently bought
the rights to Edna Ferber's novel *Saratoga Trunk*, a film that he had heard
Ingrid very much wanted to make. He knew, moreover, that for one of his
own pictures Selznick wanted Olivia de Havilland, then under contract to
Warner Brothers. Selznick, however, was not going to tie Ingrid up in a
two-picture contract. And so, for a promise of the lead in *Saratoga Trunk*, but
no signed commitment, the loan-out of Olivia de Havilland to Selznick, and
$25,000 in salary, Ingrid was signed for *Casablanca*.

According to Wallis, Selznick didn't even bother perusing the still-unfin-
ished script before signing the contract. One of the reasons Selznick was so
anxious to sign Ingrid to a film right away was that he had heard that Sweden
might soon be forced into joining the Axis; he had told O'Shea confidentially
that that made it "all the more important our bearing down on getting a
picture for her immediately."

With all his concerns, it didn't appear to matter to Selznick that by signing
Ingrid to do an anti-Nazi film, he was dumping upon Wallis and Warner

Brothers a public relations problem that could have been devastating to the success of *Casablanca*. Doubly ironic was the fact that a year before, Ingrid might well have rejected *Casablanca* as too anti-German.

Ingrid was delighted to be back in Hollywood in her new apartment at 413 South Spalding Drive in Beverly Hills. Each morning she tooled down Sunset Boulevard in her old coupe and through the white-columned gates of Warner Brothers. Ingrid had endured half a year of waiting, filled with lethargy and depression rather than restfulness and tranquillity. Now she surged with energy and anticipation. Her quarrels with Selznick seemed forgotten.

Michael Curtiz, her new director, had a background as clouded and mysterious as that of Rick Blaine, Humphrey Bogart's character in *Casablanca*. Curtiz had an abrupt Eastern European face, with high cheekbones and forehead, thick eyebrows set tightly against sharp, inquisitive eyes. A Hungarian Jew, Curtiz claimed to have worked in a traveling circus as a juggler, strongman, and trampoline artist before beginning work in the nascent Budapest film industry. In 1919, during the filming of Molnár's *Liliom*, Curtiz fled Béla Kun's short-lived Communist regime.

Curtiz was the most successful director at Warner Brothers. He had his own estate, where he played the country squire. Indeed, at the start of *Casablanca*, Curtiz's right hand was bandaged from a wound suffered on the polo field.

Curtiz might have his own polo field, but he could still remember hearing, as a boy on the street in Budapest, a policeman call out, "Long live the king and beat the Jew." His mother and two brothers were refugees who had fled Budapest. Curtiz had lived within modern history as few Americans had, and yet he had rejected that knowledge in Hollywood, making westerns like *Santa Fe Trail*, musicals like *Yankee Doodle Dandy*, films celebrating an idealized America, as if history were dirt that had been turfed over in America.

Curtiz understood that "we are not out here to preach with pictures, to take political sides or bring a great message. We are here to entertain." He knew, then, that he was not making a *Casablanca* that was Casablanca, peopled with Nazis that were Nazis. He was making an exotic romance, an *Algiers*, with a soupçon of reality thrown in.

Casablanca was shot sequentially. This was an unusual and expensive procedure, but since the script was not finished, Wallis had little choice. Most of the time the first day—May 25, 1942—was spent rehearsing and waiting while the lighting was set up. Then, as Curtiz began shooting the first scene, the sound mixer announced that he could hear the hum of the sun arc, and in the end nothing was filmed.

The first day was an unhappy harbinger of the entire filming. Ingrid did not make her initial appearance until well into *Casablanca*. Before that, she was busy with wardrobe tests. Ingrid was playing Hollywood's idea of a refugee, and it would not do for her to sit in Rick's Café dressed less than elegantly. Much of the original wardrobe was thrown out. She didn't look good in most of the hats; all but one large white hat were thrown out. So was an evening dress that made her look bulky. Ingrid heard Selznick's admonition that "the reason she has caught on is because of her lack of makeup and fresh appearance, so she should take the makeup off the eyebrows and stop using lipstick and go back to the way she was in *Intermezzo*." Ingrid promised to "be careful to use less" makeup, although as far as she could tell, she wasn't using any more than on her previous pictures.

Petter visited early in June, but most of his wife's time was taken up with preparation for *Casablanca*. Ingrid liked to prepare thoroughly for a role, but as she began work a full script didn't even exist. Films are almost by definition the most collegial of arts, but even given that, *Casablanca* was unusual for the number of people who made major contributions.

Casablanca is based on an unproduced play by Murray Burnett and Joan Alison, *Everybody Comes to Rick's*, a fact that Ingrid didn't even know. The Epstein twins and Howard Koch worked on the script. So did Casey Robinson, yet another Warner Brothers writer, who received no credit on the film, and who, according to Wallis, "along with the Epsteins probably did the major part of it."

Ingrid knew the broad outline of the story. In the film, Casablanca is a way station between the Nazis and the West, a dangerous, evil backwater. The hot spot in town is Rick's Café Américain, owned by Rick Blaine, a cynical American with a checkered past. Ingrid, as the Norwegian-born Ilsa Lund Laszlo, arrives in Casablanca on the arm of her husband, Victor Laszlo, a famous Czech anti-Nazi activist. They are seeking passage from the Vichy-controlled city to the West. To leave Casablanca on the plane to Lisbon, the Laszlos must obtain letters of transit. The nefarious Nazi officer, Major Heinrich Strasser, intends to prevent them from getting the documents.

At the Café Américain, Ingrid meets her old lover from her Paris days, Rick Blaine, whom she deserted the day the Germans arrived—the day, Rick reminds her, "the Germans wore gray and you wore blue." Rick is toasting his sorrow in champagne and cigarettes. Later, Ilsa tells Rick that when they were together in Paris she was already married to this "great and courageous activist who opened up for her a whole beautiful world full of knowledge and thoughts and ideals . . . and she looked up to him and worshipped him, with a feeling that she supposed was love." Ilsa says that in Paris she thought that her husband had died in a concentration camp. But when she learned that Laszlo was still alive, she fled from Rick, telling him nothing. Rick and Ilsa still passionately, profoundly love one another. Rick has obtained the coveted letters of transit, the key to freedom. The great romantic drama of *Casablanca* is whether Ilsa will choose her lover or her husband, personal happiness or responsibility.

Among Hollywood male stars there is only one commandment: the hero gets the girl. Both Bogart and Henreid insisted that they be the one to walk off with Ingrid. Henreid had just finished *Now, Voyager,* in which he made romantic film history by putting two cigarettes at once in his lips, lighting them, and passing one to Bette Davis. After such a strong role, he was worried that the part of the heroic Victor Laszlo conversing with Nazis in a North African nightclub was not only a comedown but a foolish role deserving of comic opera. At Warner Brothers, Henreid was considered "a bit of a ham." His part was built up enough so that he agreed to accept the role. It was, nonetheless, a role that could have seemed silly and naive against the brutal realities of Nazism. In real life *Casablanca* would have ended in the first reel: with Victor Laszlo's assassination.

Bogart was not much happier with his part than Henreid. An early reader of the play at the studio called the character "two parts Hemingway, one part Scott Fitzgerald, and a dash of café Christ." Bogart had snarled his way to stardom, as the bad guy in a series of Warner Brothers gangster films. Only in his latest role, as Dashiell Hammett's tough, cynical detective Sam Spade in *The Maltese Falcon,* had he played a sympathetic leading man. No romantic star had ever had a face like Bogart's. He did for ordinary-looking men what Perrier did for water. But he wondered whether in *Casablanca* the audience would believe that a woman as beautiful as Ingrid would fall for a man with a mug like his.

Bogart's problems with the unfinished script were larger than that. When all Europe was aflame, Bogart wasn't about to play a broken-down former lawyer crying into his beer about a lost love. Rick was too much of a "whiner." He wasn't tough enough. He hadn't done enough. Wallis agreed to strengthen Rick's character.

When Bogart made his first appearance, sitting at a table in his Café Américain, the audience had already learned about him from other characters. Bogart's acting resonated with all that knowledge. He owned the film. Yet when Ingrid arrived on the scene, he would have to make the audience believe that worldly, well-worn Rick could be so devastated by a mere love affair. Bogart, apprehensive about his female co-star, made a point of observing Ingrid's first scene.

Curtiz thought that Ingrid would be successful in *Casablanca* because she was playing *her* role. "From now on you should simply be Ingrid Bergman: do the same thing, play the same sort of role all the time, and you develop this one attractive side that the audience will love," the director told her. As Ilsa, Ingrid was, indeed, once again playing her archetypal role, but it was not a matter of developing "one attractive side." Instead, Ingrid was justifying, indeed making irresistible, behavior that much of her audience would have considered immoral.

Ilsa radiates goodness and vulnerability. Yet she is a woman who wants "no questions" asked about her past, whom Rick accuses of being little better than a whore. An early reader of the play at the studio pointed out that "the pre-action relationship between Rick and Lois [*sic*] . . . is one which does not seem permissible in a film." After all, Ilsa had been involved in either an adulterous affair with Rick or, if she is telling the truth, a torrid romance soon after the assumed death of her heroic husband. On one level the whole question of the movie is whether she will take up with Rick again, hardly a morally elevating plot, particularly in a World War II setting.

It would be no simple matter to make the character of Ilsa work so that the moral ambiguity and sensuousness become almost subliminal, deepening and broadening the part. The audience has to feel for Ilsa from the moment she appears onscreen.

If there is one definition of a great film star, it is that the world is different once he or she appears, different in a way that no one fully comprehends. Ingrid had much time to prepare her role before she made her first appearance, in the seventy-fifth shot of *Casablanca*. No other character had heralded the arrival of Ilsa Lund, telling of her beauty, vulnerability, or plight. Suddenly, Ingrid is there, dressed in white, walking with Henreid, in an off-white suit, into the shadowy world of Rick's Café. As she sits next to Henreid, Ingrid is not even the center of the scene. But it is as if a ray of light has entered Rick's Café.

Ilsa notices Rick's black piano player and alter ego, Sam (Dooley Wilson), and asks him to play "As Time Goes By." Sam reluctantly agrees and sings in a voice charged with poignancy:

> *You must remember this*
> *A kiss is just a kiss*
> *A sigh is just a sigh*
> *The fundamental things apply*
> *As time goes by.*

Rick rushes into the nightclub, tormented by the romantic strains of the song he has told Sam must never be played again. Rick sees Ilsa. On an emotional level, the rest of the film does little more than elucidate the look in Ingrid's eyes, a look that manages to convey yearning, courage, uncertainty, bewilderment, love, melancholy, and pain.

"I didn't do anything I've never done before," Bogart said afterward of his role in *Casablanca*. "But when the camera moves in on that Bergman face, and she's saying she loves you, it would make anybody look romantic." Seeing the extraordinary chemistry between Ingrid and Bogart, many moviegoers assumed that their relationship must have continued off the set. But when asked about this, Ingrid always said, "I kissed him but I never knew him."

An actor is a scavenger, picking up his ideas and techniques from his own life and the lives of others, from once-lived emotions, past lives, and lives merely brushed against. Despite his screen image, Bogart was full of insecurity and self-doubt. When his scenes were finished, he wasn't flirting with Ingrid, tossing off bons mots that could have been used in the film. He was usually off by himself in his small trailer, talking about his part to buddies such as Howard Koch, getting advice, or playing chess.

Bogart had no trouble looking world-weary on screen. He knew all about a tragic romance, and it wasn't crying in a café over a sentimental song. It was life with his third wife, Mayo Methot, at "Sluggy Hollow," his West Hollywood home. It was booze, blood, and brawls, a butcher knife in the back, a fistfight in the living room, pistol shots in the living room ceiling. It was a wife so jealous of Ingrid that he didn't dare get near his co-star. It was life as a forty-two-year-old balding actor with an alcoholic wife, a drinking problem of his own, and a co-star so beautiful, so irresistible, so shrewdly professional, that he was likely to lose the movie to her.

Ingrid didn't know much about Bogart's personal life. As part of her own preparation for *Casablanca* she had screened *The Maltese Falcon* over and over again. She could see that Bogart was a fine, strong screen actor. She could still be star struck herself, and she had been apprehensive about meeting Bogart. She discovered that he was nothing like his image. On the set he was very professional. She did not guess at his insecurities. He was too good an actor to display them to her. Nor did she have any idea of the lengths to which he was going to best her in their scenes together.

One of his advisers, Mel Baker, had told Bogart: "This is the first time you've ever played the romantic lead against a major star. You stand still, and always make her come to you. Mike probably won't notice it, and if she complains you can tell her it's tacit in the script. You've got something she wants, so she has to come to you."

Bogart did as he was told. It worked, not only for Bogart but for Ingrid too, as the emotionally vulnerable Ilsa drawn back and forth between the two men, the two focal points of her life. Here was Rick Blaine: romantic, sexual, irresponsible, untrustworthy, witty. And here was Victor Laszlo: trustworthy, conservative, responsible, paternal, solid. Blaine and Laszlo represented the two poles of male attractiveness, poles that would prove as far apart in Ingrid's personal life as in the film.

Ingrid worked best when she was in love with her leading man. A romance might have developed if Bogart's wife had not been watching so jealously. "I think Bogart was in love with Ingrid," says Bob William, Bogart's publicist on *Casablanca*. "He was kind of jealous if I would bring anyone on the set, another man, to see her. He would sulk. I had a feeling he was kind of smitten with her."

As for having an affair with Curtiz, Ingrid had affairs with directors, but that did not include fornicating with a man of Curtiz's reputation. She was perfectly aware that the Hungarian-born director almost always had at least one "starlet" on the set whose greatest performance took place in Curtiz's dressing room. Indeed, one day during the shooting, Peter Lorre secretly hooked up microphones in the director's love nest. "Oh, God! Oh, no, no, no . . ." Curtiz's impassioned voice came surging across the set. "Oh, yes, yes . . . Oh, God, yes . . ."

Ingrid's attitude toward the married Henreid was just as distant. In the film he was her loyal, caring partner. Henreid looked very much like Petter. Victor Laszlo had Petter's staid stability, his earnestness. In creating her emotional attitude toward her husband in *Casablanca*, she may well have drawn on her real marriage.

The set of *Casablanca* was a microcosm of the European world that seemed so distant from Ingrid now. To some of those on the set, a drama of refugees fleeing Nazism was as real as life. Henreid had fled Vienna after the Nazis marched in and had almost been interned in Britain as an enemy alien. Madeleine LeBeau, who had a featured role as a beautiful young refugee, had recently escaped from occupied France. The French technical director, Lieutenant Robert Aisner, had escaped from a German concentration camp and made his way to Hollywood via Casablanca. German-born Conrad Veidt, who played the villainous Major Strasser, was a prominent anti-Nazi.

Another famous German star in the film was Peter Lorre. Few Americans who saw Lorre as the sleazy Ugarte knew that the Jewish actor had only a few years before stood on a stage at a Berlin festival and daringly satirized the Nazis. S. Z. Sakall, who had a delightful cameo as a waiter at Rick's Café, was like Curtiz of Hungarian birth. One of the extras in a café scene, Trudy Berliner, had been a star at UFA in Berlin. Sitting next to Berliner was Dina Smirnova, once a great actress in her native Russia. In all, the Warners publicity office counted thirty-four nationalities among the cast of *Casablanca*.

Each one of these roles, then, was touched with a *vraisemblance* unusual in Hollywood films. It was as if in *Gone With the Wind* Vivien Leigh and Clark Gable had lived through the Civil War and the black actors had themselves once been slaves.

Ingrid liked her film life to be full of order, discipline, and certainty, but on the set of *Casablanca* she found herself often amid disorder, indiscipline, and uncertainty. She still was grieving over *For Whom the Bell Tolls*, a picture with a prestige and importance that *Casablanca* lacked. Not only had she lost the part, but she had lost it to Vera Zorina, a German-born Norwegian ballerina whom Ingrid dismissed as a "non-actress." Zorina did not have as many credits as Ingrid, but she had already made four films, and was a legitimate, even exciting, choice for the part.

Ingrid was as guilty as Bogart of retreating into her dressing room. "She was standoffish probably because she didn't know that many people," remembers Carl Schaeffer, a publicist on *Casablanca*.

Ingrid was more concerned with her career than anything so mundane as camaraderie. Even with a finished script, Curtiz was not an easy director with whom to work. *Casablanca* seemed in trouble, and Curtiz knew what could happen if the film failed. "In Europe, if an actor or director establish himself, he live forever," Curtiz said later. "Here, if he doesn't make dough, they kick him out. Hollywood is money, money, money.

"I work because I don't want to be kicked out. The only way you can stay on top is keep on smiling and show your teeth. You feeling lousy and they ask you how you feel. You say, 'Ok, fine, just fine. Everything is wonderful.' "

Curtiz conveyed his insecurity to everyone on the set. Nonetheless, he remained a courtly European who still clicked his heels when he met a lady. He was always civil to Ingrid. His English, though, was as difficult to understand as Ratoff's had been on *Intermezzo*. "Don't play it hard," he told her. "Act easy-go-lucky." During a café scene he directed: "Now we will hear mutters from the natives and visitors in the café. And in the background I will have the low throbbing music of the native tom-thumbs."

Even understanding Curtiz didn't always help. Ingrid had to know whom she was in love with: Henreid or Bogart. How could she play the part if she didn't know at least that? "We don't know yet," Curtiz told her. "Just play it . . . in-between."

Through most of the shooting, Ingrid didn't know which man had won. "No one knew where the picture was going and no one knew how it was going to end, which didn't help any of us with our characterizations," Ingrid said. "Every morning we said, 'Well, who are we? What are we doing here?' And Michael Curtiz would say, 'We're not quite sure, but let's get through this scene today and we'll let you know tomorrow.' It was ridiculous. Just awful."

Ingrid attempted to play the part down the middle. In doing so she became the emotional center of the film, moving between the two other main characters. Ingrid is successful because Bogart and Henreid are successful. Rick Blaine could have been a silly Hollywood invention, a tough guy who cries over a song. But Bogart's Rick Blaine is, indeed, a man worthy of Ilsa's love, a man struggling with his own personal isolation, a metaphor for America herself in the days before Pearl Harbor. As for Henreid, he had good reason to fear that his part could be no more than comic opera. But he played Laszlo with dignity, nobility, and the high naïveté of the idealist. He, too, was worthy of Ilsa's love.

In a typical Hollywood melodrama, Ingrid would have flown off with Bogart, after Henreid died heroically, a conclusion that was indeed contemplated. But in an ending as perfect as a poem, both men live and Ingrid does not have to choose between them. "I don't know what's right any longer," Ingrid says. "You have to think for both of us, for all of us." Bogart chooses for her, telling Ilsa that she must leave with Laszlo, as he and his sidekick, Captain Renault, go off to fight the Nazis.

In perhaps the most famous farewell scene in films, Bogart bids goodbye to

Ingrid on the gray tarmac on Stage 21, the fog machines blasting away with over a million cubic feet of vaporized oil. Standing in his rumpled trench coat and fedora, looking into Ingrid's tear-filled eyes, Bogart speaks: "Look, I'm no good at being noble, but it doesn't take much to see that the problems of three little people don't amount to a hill of beans in this crazy world. Someday you'll understand that. . . .

"Here's looking at you, kid."

CHAPTER EIGHT

A Tigress Who
Has Made a Kill

$\mathcal{D}$uring the last days of shooting *Casablanca*, Ingrid prepared to return to Rochester, to spend the rest of the summer with Petter and Pia. Then she heard incredible news. The first rushes of Vera Zorina in *For Whom the Bell Tolls* were so bad that Paramount wanted to test Ingrid for the part of Maria.

Paramount planned two full screen tests, one in the studio, the other on location. Hundreds of thousands of dollars were at stake, as well as the careers of several Paramount executives. There were rumors that if Ingrid didn't work out, Paramount might kill the film altogether.

Selznick felt that the idea of a screen test was "absolute nonsense." Hollywood was a sieve. Once word got out that Ingrid had tested for the part, Zorina was finished. If Paramount insisted on going ahead, though, the producer felt it was imperative to try to keep the whole business quiet. Ingrid's reputation was on the line.

Ambition is a rude imperative. Selznick wanted the test to take place on location in California's Sierra Nevada mountains, where *For Whom the Bell Tolls* was being filmed. That would give Ingrid her best opportunity. There she could play opposite the other star of the film, Gary Cooper, with Sam Wood directing, all presumably while Zorina rested unknowingly in her cabin.

Stars usually consider a screen test a humiliation, suggesting a lack of confidence in the performer. Ingrid always insisted that she was given only a makeup test. In fact, she was put through a major screen test at Paramount on Friday, July 31, 1942. By then everyone in Hollywood knew about the "secret" test. Two days before, the "Hollywood Rambler" column in the *Hollywood Reporter* had noted that "Buddy DeSylva [the executive producer] and Sam Wood are really battling. It seems the director still isn't reconciled to the way Maria was cast. . . . Ingrid Bergman is quietly testing, and if Zorina is replaced it'll be Ingrid."

The stakes, then, were even higher now. If Ingrid lost the part, her humiliation would indisputably be public. Zorina was almost certainly aware of what was going on. She was back down from location, having her teeth recapped and makeup altered for a separate screen test.

In *For Whom the Bell Tolls*, Maria is a long-limbed creature of the mountains. Ingrid had heard that in the early rushes Zorina had tiptoed through the rock-strewn passages of the Sierra Nevadas as if she were afraid that she might break her dancer's legs. For Ingrid, it was not her legs that she would always try to protect, but her face. And it was her face that would win her the part of Maria. Ingrid wanted to try one test with eyelashes, one without; one test without makeup but with her lips powdered down, and one with full makeup.

Maria's hair in *For Whom the Bell Tolls* has been cut off so that "it was but little longer than the fur on a beaver pelt." Vera's beautiful long hair had been so ungraciously cut that on film she looked like a freshly shorn lamb. Ingrid was not about to cut her hair until she definitely had the part. Nor, for the screen test, did she intend to wear a wig. She wanted Hazel Rogers, a prominent hairdresser, to be there to pin back her hair.

Sam Wood had complained about Ingrid's look in slacks, and as far back as *Intermezzo* Selznick had been unhappy with Ingrid's posterior. For the test Ingrid had the service of Miss Ray at Magnin's, a lady whom Selznick referred to inelegantly as "the best girdle woman."

Ingrid did the screen test on Friday. It would be Sunday, however, before Sam Wood, the director, returned from location and, together with Frank Freeman, a Paramount vice-president, and Buddy DeSylva, made his choice. They would presumably look at both Ingrid's and Zorina's tests.

On Sunday, Ingrid sat next to the phone, waiting for Wood's call. Finally it rang, and Petter's familiar voice came on. "What's the news? Have you heard anything yet?" It was a curious call, as if Petter wasn't sure that she would call him as soon as she learned. Abruptly, Ingrid told her husband that she would phone him when there was news. And then she waited. And the phone never rang.

The next morning Ingrid was at Warner Brothers making publicity shots for *Casablanca* with Henreid. During the filming Henreid had sometimes wondered how someone as sweet, unassuming, and vulnerable as Ingrid could have become a star. He assumed that there had to be someone behind Ingrid, an éminence grise pushing and prodding her upward.

Ingrid and Henreid stood posing together for the photographer, a not unpleasant chore for an actor. Yet Ingrid seemed ill at ease.

"Are you all right?" asked Henreid, ever the European gentleman. Ingrid appeared on the verge of tears.

"All right? I'm heartbroken."

Henreid was a man of the world. Though he knew about Ingrid's distant husband in Rochester, he assumed that she was involved in an unhappy love affair. He proceeded to try to cheer her up with a monologue on men, women, and love.

"No! No!" Ingrid interjected, as if nothing so common as *that* could be bothering her. "I'm talking about *For Whom the Bell Tolls.* . . . It's going to be a blockbuster of a movie, and I tested for it. It's a fantastic part."

"Well, maybe you'll get it," the actor replied, full of his profession's eternal optimism.

"Oh, Paul, I lost it. They gave it to Vera Zorina! I wanted that part so badly, you've no idea. Picking Vera Zorina of all people. She can't act, Paul. She just can't and I'm good. I'm really good! I just hope they find out how bad she is."

Ingrid talked with a conviction and energy unlike anything Henreid had ever heard. It was as if he was watching a great performance, though which was the act—the woman who stood before him now so proudly demeaning her successful competitor, or the modest woman he had known on the set?

The phone rang. Ingrid took the call.

Selznick's familiar voice was on the line.

"Yes, yes . . ." Ingrid said.

"Ingrid, you are Maria!"

Ingrid shrieked. To Henreid, the voice sounded like "a tigress who has made a kill, a yell of such joy and triumph."

"I got it, Paul. I got it. I got it."

"What happened?"

"I got the part of Maria. I just knew that if I fought hard enough they'd come to their senses and see that Zorina was wrong and couldn't act.

"Paul, we've got to celebrate."

Ingrid was her old self, but for an instant Henreid had seen the "triumphant vitality and strength," the great secret engine that propelled Ingrid upward.

Selznick settled quickly with Paramount, successful in his nearly two-year campaign to win the part for Ingrid. He first wanted between $100,000 and $125,000 for Ingrid's services, three to four times what he received for her on *Casablanca*. He settled on a contract that paid him $90,666.65, as against the $31,770.83 that he paid Ingrid. Selznick felt that he was settling for less than he might have, but still it was a neat bit of business. Ingrid didn't care. She simply wanted to get on with it. She had just finished a strenuous, enervating film, and Selznick had requested two weeks of rest for Ingrid. Ingrid didn't want to rest. To Ingrid, working was rest.

Ingrid had read *For Whom the Bell Tolls*. She carried it with her now as if it were her book of prayer, underlining and making notations. She knew the story of Robert Jordan and Maria so well that she could recite it like a catechism. Jordan is an American professor fighting in the Spanish Civil War for the leftist loyalist forces against the Spanish Fascists and their German allies. Jordan is assigned to blow up a crucial bridge in the mountains near Segovia before a Loyalist offensive. He enlists a group of guerrillas to help him. Among the scruffy peasants is Maria, a girl with no last name. Maria is emotionally disemboweled. Her parents have been killed. She has been gang raped by the Fascists, her head shaved in the prison at Valladolid.

Maria and Jordan fall in love. Their love is like a mountain flower, brilliant and short-lived. Jordan and the guerrillas blow the bridge, though the offensive has been betrayed. As they make their escape, Jordan is fatally wounded. He tells Maria that she must go forth and carry on the struggle. And so she leaves him to die on the mountainside.

Ingrid had just made a film in which at the end she left her lover to join the great struggle against fascism. But whereas *Casablanca* had been a patchwork of compromises that Ingrid considered simply a commercial venture, *For Whom the Bell Tolls* was literature. With a budget of close to three million dollars, it was the biggest production since *Gone With the Wind*, and it was being done with the same concern for the integrity of the original novel.

Ingrid's Hollywood movies had always required endless costume tests and fittings, hair stylings, and makeup tests, an aspect of making a film that Ingrid liked least. This time, though, there were only simple makeup tests that showed Ingrid glowing with vitality, her countenance radiant. There were costume fittings, but for *real* clothes: a pair of man's trousers tied at the waist with a piece of cord, a long-sleeved shirt, a brown jacket. For the test Edith Head, the costume designer, used men's clothing that she had found in the extras' wardrobe, but for the film Head had new clothes bleached and dyed.

On Wednesday, accompanied by David and Irene Selznick, Ingrid went to Paramount for her Maria haircut. Selznick was not about to have Ingrid disastrously shorn. The "Ingrid bob" that Sydney Guilaroff, the MGM hair stylist, devised was charming, fashionable enough to become a minor fad.

On Friday, August 7, only four days after she had learned she had the part, Ingrid left for the isolated highlands of the Sierra Nevadas. The location was 450 miles from Los Angeles, and two hours north of the nearest town, Sonora. Another actress might have been fretful and ambivalent about leaving the comforting confines of the studio, with its dressing rooms and endless solicitude, exchanging all that for primitive realities. Another wife and mother might have had her melancholy moments, realizing that it would be months before she would see her husband and daughter again. But Ruth Roberts, who was accompanying Ingrid and knew her so well, could see that her charge was "happy to [the] bursting point."

As soon as Ingrid arrived and saw the little cabin by the river where she and Ruth would live, she went to find the crew and actors. She had to drive a half hour more, then she took a horse farther up into the mountains, and when the horse could go no farther, she "climbed on all four [sic] up to the cliff where the actors were working."

When Ingrid met Gary Cooper, she blushed. "Hello, Maria," he said, and she blushed again. Up here one could almost believe that Ingrid was Maria and

Cooper was Robert Jordan, and that in the wild beauty of this place they were living out their lives and love. Cooper had a face that was not merely handsome but seemed to be making a statement about human courage. Ingrid looked at the tall, lanky forty-one-year-old actor and thought him a "beautiful man." Cooper was one of the great stars of Hollywood. He had just won an Academy Award for best actor in *Sergeant York*. He had starred in Hemingway's *A Farewell to Arms*, and went shooting and hunting with "Papa" himself in Sun Valley.

Ingrid was married and so was Cooper. He was immensely attractive to women, onscreen and offscreen, and the fact that Cooper was known as a womanizer did not hurt his reputation at all. Ingrid's image, though, was unsullied, and it would not do to have rumors in the gossip columns about her and Cooper. Luckily for Ingrid, the movie was being filmed away from the prying eyes of Hollywood.

Ingrid fell in love with Cooper, or was it that Maria fell in love with Jordan? Cooper and Ingrid spent much of their spare time together. They prepared their parts together, and in the evenings they often ate together. In Hollywood, when the Paramount executives saw the rushes of the love scenes, they surmised immediately that a romance had begun.

Ruth Roberts was endlessly solicitous of Ingrid, concerned for her professional and her personal life. "Really, Ingrid, you must stop looking at him like that," Ruth told her one day. "You sit there just looking! I know you are supposed to be in love with him in the pictures, but not too much in love with him!"

Although Ingrid did not fully confide in Ruth, her coach and companion knew more about her personal life than anyone else. Almost without realizing what was happening, Ruth had become part of a minor conspiracy, hiding the truth of Ingrid's love life, and hiding it particularly from Petter. The more Ruth knew, the more she had to hide. She mentioned nothing about Ingrid's personal life to anyone, not even to her dearest friend, Rae Pober.

Ingrid was mesmerized by Cooper's personality: "so enormous, so overpowering—and that expression in his eyes and his face . . . so delicate and so underplayed . . . the most underplaying and most natural actor I ever worked with."

"Tell him [Selznick] that I am so happy even in the most tragic scenes my eyes are dancing with joy," she wrote Dan O'Shea. "I am stunned at the patience, the preparation, and perfection Wood spends on the story," she wrote Irene Selznick. If Ingrid's eyes danced for joy even in the most tragic scenes, then the scenery danced as well, with too much life and color. Black paint was sprayed on the trees and the boulders, the fields, and the road, to suggest something of the somberness of the story, but even that didn't help.

Ingrid's legs and feet were black and blue and scratched, hidden under Maria's trousers. Her fingernails were broken. Her ears were full of dust. But she wrote Irene, "you don't hear any complaining from Maria," as if she and her fictional heroine had become one. After ten weeks on location most of the crew were overjoyed to go down the mountain for good. Ingrid would have stayed on and on.

Finally, early in September, everyone came down from the mountain, and the last twelve weeks of filming took place at the Paramount studios. Ingrid hoped that *For Whom the Bell Tolls* would prove the "turning point" of her career. She had the greatest faith in the quality of the film. But it would take months to prepare such a monumental picture for presentation.

As for *Casablanca*, a product of the Hollywood studio system, ground out and packaged like another link of sausage, it was already opening, November 26, 1942, at New York's Hollywood Theater. Allied troops had marched into Casablanca, and Wallis wanted to take advantage of the publicity. The film was an immediate popular success, playing to standing-room-only audiences.

For the purposes of the Academy Awards, *Casablanca* was considered a 1943 picture and received six nominations. The 1944 award ceremony would prove to be *Casablanca*'s night. The film received awards for best screenwriting from nonoriginal sources, best director, and, most coveted of all, best film of the year.

In one of the abiding ironies of Ingrid's career, *Casablanca* became the immortal film, not *For Whom the Bell Tolls*. *Casablanca*—the film that she had considered a sad alternative when she thought she had lost the part of Maria—was the film that helped make her the third-most-popular female star in America, according to the *Box Office Barometer* poll; it was the film that would be loved and admired and screened long after the reels of many of her other movies had been relegated to the vaults.

On the day before Ingrid left to go up to location for *For Whom the Bell Tolls*, Selznick dictated a long telegram to Petter, so brutal in its finality, so bitterly contemptuous, that if Ingrid had ever seen the document her relationship with the producer could never have been the same. All Selznick's attempts to sign Ingrid to a new contract had been foiled and he was fed up. "In a lifetime in the picture business I have never encountered such a stubborn resistance to common sense, such a persistent attempt to out-trade and out-smart me and my associates, such ingratitude for unselfish effort." If Ingrid did not sign a new, seven-year contract immediately, he would refuse to loan her out anymore, limiting her to one picture a year.

Selznick did not send that telegram, but his venomous anger remained the same. The situation was even worse because Kay Brown was no longer there to mediate between the Lindstroms and Selznick. She had left the producer in an acrimonious ending to their long relationship.

Selznick had been planning to force Ingrid to sign a new long-term contract before allowing her to do *For Whom the Bell Tolls*. But the producer had given up on that, in part because he thought that he and Charles Feldman, Ingrid's new agent and an old Hollywood hand, would be able to negotiate a contract. That had not worked out either, and Selznick blamed Petter.

Petter was involved with other aspects of Ingrid's career. He wrote a broadcast for her to deliver over the BBC's Swedish service. When he was unhappy with an Office of War Information essay that a Warner Brothers publicist had written for Ingrid's signature, he edited the manuscript himself. "I personally would have told Dr. Lindstrom to go fly a kite," Selznick told Whitney Bolton, his publicity director. "I think a little bludgeoning might do the good doctor some good."

At Strong Memorial Hospital in Rochester, where he was interning, Petter was proving himself to be an idealistic, dedicated doctor. He was concerned about patients as people and not just as receptacles for intriguing diseases. One day he had the unhappy duty of informing a middle-aged woman that her infected leg would have to be amputated. This was a task that many doctors would have dispatched as quickly as possible. Petter, however, performed the duty in such a way that over a quarter century later the woman's son still remembered. "The way in which your dad broke the news to all of us was done with such feeling and compassion that somehow it made the whole experience a much easier one to take, especially for my mother," Frank M. Kinsky wrote Pia Lindstrom in 1978. "But that wasn't all! Your dad made it a point to visit my mother every day. One day, he asked my mother if there was anything special that she wanted. She replied that she would like an ice cream cone. Would you believe your dad drove out of the hospital, up to a drugstore two blocks away that sold ice cream cones, and brought one back for my mother."

In late 1942 Ingrid returned to Rochester to spend some time with Petter and Pia. She loved her husband and daughter, but they were at times a disconcerting intrusion that had to be subtly manipulated. "I must handle my family with skill too," she told Selznick's publicity people, equating Petter and Pia with photo sessions, interviews, and other obligations.

Ingrid wouldn't let anyone do interviews in Rochester, and she shielded her husband and daughter from publicity. The reporters and columnists always wanted personal information that Ingrid did not like giving out. Petter did not think of himself as Mr. Ingrid Bergman. He wanted no publicity tied to the happenstance of his marriage. Nor did he and Ingrid want it for Pia.

Ingrid might look like a publicity-shy maiden, jolted by the flare of flash-bulbs, so embarrassed by intimate queries that her face flushed with mortification. But she was as canny and media wise as the most flamboyant star. In her free time she enjoyed harvesting the bounty of her publicity efforts, filling scrapbooks full of her clippings.

The articles about Ingrid manufactured in Hollywood had as little to do with journalism as professional wrestling has to do with competitive athletics.

Ingrid was part of a creative collaboration between herself, the studios, and the press in creating the image of Ingrid Bergman: great star, great mother, great wife, great person. In January, when she saw what she considered two "awful" interviews in the current *Silver Screen* and *Movies*, she knew that she was largely to blame. The Paramount publicity department had partially written the articles, and she had read and approved the final version. She could see now that she shouldn't have approved the publicist's having her talk about "good" and "bad" women, and about her family. She was even more worried about a forthcoming "life story" in *Photoplay*. She wrote Selznick, asking him to try to do something. The Selznick office was able to see the copy before it appeared in print, a privilege for which they wired Macfadden Publications their "deepest appreciation."

Ingrid put in time in Rochester. She enjoyed the snow and ice and the austere landscape of winter in upstate New York, as long as she knew that she would soon be leaving. She took Pia skating on the lily pond in the park. One young boy who saw her moving gracefully across the ice thought that what made her different was that she could get out of Rochester whenever she wanted to get out. She stayed awhile at home but then was off again, taking the train to New York.

For the holidays Ingrid was back in Rochester, arriving two days before Christmas. This was the third New Year's in a row that she had been away from Sweden. On New Year's Eve, thinking how happy she was that she had come to America, she sat down and wrote Selznick a note, as if he were her fatherly patron. "Dear Boss!" she began. "I hope that 1943 is a good year and that we stick together in spite of the big deals buzzing around us! . . . I'll promise, as I always do New Year's Eve, to be a very good girl."

Midnight was drawing near. Ingrid and Petter opened a bottle of champagne, and heralded a new year that seemed to promise a bounty of success and happiness. Ingrid had so much to look forward to. The summer before, up in the Sierra Nevadas, Ingrid, Sam Wood, and Cooper had all read Edna Ferber's new best-selling novel, *Saratoga Trunk*. They had decided that they wanted to do the film together.

All over America people were talking about who should play the romantic leads: sensuous, conniving Clio Dulaine, an illegitimate half-Creole adventuress; and her lover, Clint Maroon, a taciturn, handsome Texas gambler. Cooper and Vivien Leigh had led a *Cosmopolitan* poll for the parts. Ingrid was so unlike the dark-haired, fiery, French-speaking beauty that she received only three votes, tying for twenty-sixth place.

Ingrid could not stand to be second best, much less twenty-sixth best, to another female star, especially another Selznick favorite. "I never could, and never would, even try to play the part like Vivien," she wrote Ruth Roberts, when she learned that Selznick thought her wrong for the part. "I was not going to surprise only him [Selznick], but the whole nation if they were against me in this part."

At first, Selznick had not wanted Ingrid to play such an amoral character after her role as the saintly Maria. But Ingrid convinced him, in part perhaps because she was suddenly one of the hottest properties in Hollywood and he wanted to cash in. Warners ended up paying Selznick $253,802.08 for Ingrid's services, while he paid her $69,562.30. As part of the deal he also received the services of Olivia de Havilland from Warner Brothers for one film for $30,000; he quickly turned around and sold her to RKO for $130,000.

Selznick had been convinced that Cooper would turn down the smaller part of Clint Maroon, a role that would in no way do for his career what Clio might do for Ingrid's. It was, indeed, a measure of Ingrid's appeal to Cooper, and his desire for a renewal of their relationship, that he was so willing to take the part. "Cooper wanted to do it," remembers Hal Wallis, the producer. "I think there was a romance with Bergman that had started on *Bell* that carried over on our picture, which didn't hurt the chemistry on our film. It was a two-picture deal."

Petter remembers meeting and talking with Mrs. Rocky Cooper. "Mrs. Cooper talked about the two of them spending so much time together, and they're going to make another picture," Petter says.

As Ingrid anticipated returning to Hollywood, she was looking forward to more of the good times she had had with Cooper making the still unreleased *For Whom the Bell Tolls*. Pia and Mabel, the maid, would be going with her. In a few months Petter would be following them west, to take up his surgical internship at Stanford University Hospital in San Francisco.

In these last weeks in Rochester she packed her clothes and did more publicity chores, including another trip to New York early in January.

At the beginning of February, Ingrid left Rochester for the last time. On her way back to Hollywood she had agreed to make a side trip to Minnesota for the filming of a documentary film, *Swedes in America*, for the Office of War Information. Ingrid had at first appeared reluctant to make a week-long sojourn for which she would not be paid. Selznick had admonished her: "I feel rather strongly that up to date you have been asked to do very little in the general and common effort and that we all have to put up with a certain amount of inconveniences." Once it was made clear to her that her expenses would be paid, she was very willing to make the film.

Ingrid arrived the following evening in the winter-bound city of Minneapolis. Standing there waiting for her was Joseph Henry Steele, Selznick's new publicity director, a position that had the longevity of a front-line soldier in the battle of the Marne. Steele was a courtly, middle-aged gentleman. He had two crippling maladies for a movie publicist: too high principles and too big an ego. He was proud of the dignified image he had helped create for Ronald Colman, the British actor, before joining Selznick. But like most publicists, Steele had the feeling that his endeavors were not sufficiently appreciated.

Ingrid stepped off the train at Great Northern Station in a long mink, and a red-white-and-blue knitted hat. Behind her came the maid, carrying Pia in her arms.

Steele was absolutely taken with Ingrid. He was amazed at her "self-efface-ment" among the stern, gnarled Swedish-American farmers. He was struck by her exuberant spirit. She found him "tall, goodlooking." He loved her fresh beauty, which seemed almost eternal, beyond the craft of cosmetics. When she got ready for dinner with him in a mere fifteen minutes, he was astounded. "It's not true," he said as he helped her put on her mink. "You're entirely fictitious."

By the time they were back in Hollywood, Steele was probably in love with Ingrid. His was not a conventional love. Steele was seeking nothing so banal as a tryst in a hotel room. He was in love with Ingrid's golden image, with a Swedish goddess full of life and spirit.

From then on when he sat down to write articles for her or about her, when he advised her and trumpeted her praises, he did so with a passion, commitment, and concern that was rare among publicists. He believed in Ingrid, *his* Ingrid, and he wanted the world to know about her. Steele had been an occasional writer of fiction, and *his* Ingrid was an admixture of fact, fantasy, might-have-beens, conjecture. He saw in her glamour and glory a transcendent beauty that he could touch by knowing her. He had the arro-gance of a fan too, as if he knew and understood her better than she knew and understood herself. "Sometimes I think she's the most beautiful woman I have ever met," he wrote, in concluding one of many articles about Ingrid. "If what I have told you is not beauty, then my forty years and more have been meaningless and I have learned nothing."

By March 2, when Ingrid went to work on *Saratoga Trunk*, the censors had already softened the portrait of a Clio Dulaine whose amorality is justified in the novel by little more than lust, revenge, greed, and ambition. The censors and the studios were partners in producing films that would not grievously offend American filmgoers. The production code had created an organized hypocrisy whereby the studios adhered to the strictures yet did the films they wanted to do, largely the way they wanted to do them.

The censors were worried about a scene in which Clio, her black maid, Angelique, and her dwarf companion, Cupidon, were to be depicted in the famous New Orleans restaurant Beque. "People of the Southern states may very strongly resent the inference that colored people are permitted to com-mingle with white people in restaurants and public places," Mr. Obringer of the production code office wrote Jack Warner. And thus the scene was changed.

Ingrid had never appeared in such an elaborate film before. She had thirty-one costumes. She initialed the sketches as if clothes hardly mattered.

She didn't care about fittings either, telling Leah Rhodes, the designer, "What's the use, they always fit properly."

Ingrid looked sensational in the clothes, her body lush in the tightly bodiced outfits. When shooting began early in March, the chemistry between Ingrid and Cooper was still very much alive. In her dark wig and curious accent, Ingrid did not seem quite the French courtesan, but she exuded such wanton sensuality that it hardly mattered.

Ingrid and Cooper were full of high spirits. He called her "Frenchie" and she called him "Texas," as if they had become their characters. They were seen driving together down Sunset Boulevard, and there was considerable gossip about their relationship, gossip that may have reached the ears of Cooper's wife. But Ingrid was sacrosanct in the columns and movie magazines, and no conjecture about a romance appeared in print.

One day four-year-old Pia visited the set, the first time she had seen her mother at work. Ingrid was beautifully gowned for the ballroom scene. A score of elegantly dressed men and women swirled around the set while the camera focused on Ingrid and Cooper. "I can be an actress," Pia announced. "I want to be an actress."

Pia saw very little of her mother. Ingrid was off before Pia woke up in the mornings, and rarely back until late. Ingrid put in what the studio called "a modern screen record," working sixty-two days in a row excluding Sundays. Then on May 1 Ingrid arrived at the studio with a voice so husky that it couldn't be recorded. She took to bed with what was called "laryngitis and strained vocal cords," missing several full days of shooting before reporting back only two hours a day.

Saratoga Trunk was already weeks behind schedule, and Ingrid's illness was a serious handicap to the troubled production. A week later she was back on a regular schedule, but a month after that she was sick again. On June 1 a whole day's shooting had to be called off. "Miss Bergman was not up in her lines," the production manager wrote in his notes for June 12, 1943. Selznick blamed Ingrid's illness on Warners for "having overworked her in your frantic haste to finish your picture . . . and not due to any ordinary incapacity on her part."

Ingrid was under considerable emotional pressure as well. Petter had arrived on the West Coast to begin his surgical residency in San Francisco, only a short plane ride from Los Angeles. Up until now, she had had two lives: as Miss Ingrid Bergman, the star and actress, and as Mrs. Petter Lindstrom, the twenty-seven-year-old wife of a Swedish surgeon-in-the-making. She needed both those lives—the freedom and frivolity and adventure of her movie career, and the stability and strength and caring of her marriage.

When *Saratoga Trunk* finished, Ingrid was scheduled to go up to San Francisco to spend five weeks with Petter. "Ingrid Bergman, motion picture star, will bow out of existence," the Warner Brothers publicity department announced, "in favor of Mrs. Peter Lindstrom, housewife."

Ingrid's affair with Cooper was over. "In my whole life I never had a woman so much in love with me as Ingrid was," Cooper said years later. "The day after the picture ended, I couldn't get her on the phone."

Men often thought that Ingrid loved them with the very essence of her being. She seemed to be so completely with a man and then it was over, and he was left wondering what he had held in his arms, and who it was who had kissed and caressed him. The man didn't understand how Ingrid had played on his vanity, on his desire to possess her.

For Whom the Bell Tolls finally premiered on August 16, 1943, at Los Angeles's Cathay Circle Theater; it was the most star-studded opening since the beginning of the war. Ingrid arrived on the arm of Frank Freeman, vice-president of Paramount. She was on the cover of *Time* magazine as Maria ("Whatever Hollywood's bell tolled for, she rang it"), starring in what *Variety* called "one of the most important pictures of all time." Paramount had rolled out all the hoopla of publicity, and despite carping criticism in many papers, the film was, in *Variety*'s words, "a boxoffice bellringer."

The audience went to see the film, but *For Whom the Bell Tolls* was a great white whale of a movie, lying beached and lifeless. Up in the mountains Ingrid had been awed at Cooper's acting, but on celluloid his performance was so wooden that in kissing him it was a wonder that Ingrid hadn't ended up with a mouth full of splinters. Hemingway's novel was about people fighting for ideals, and about the victims of history. Yet controversial words such as Socialists, Communists, Nazis, Anarchists, Fascists had all been erased from the film. The politics was boiled out of the movie so it was like a soup so watered down that one could see the bottom of the pot.

Ingrid had the best moments in the film, the exquisite vulnerability, poised between ecstasy and tears. Her attention to Cooper had paid off; as James Agee wrote in his review, "his general support of Miss Bergman is nearly as good as the law will allow." Ingrid was nominated for an Academy Award as best actress. Yet the film had not really worked, not even for her.

"I enjoyed it all so much, particularly Gary Cooper," she wrote in her diary. "What was wrong was that my happiness showed on the screen. I was far too happy to honestly portray Maria's tragic figure."

Ingrid should have been extremely happy now. With the success of *For Whom the Bell Tolls* she was one of the biggest stars in Hollywood, who, as Agee wrote in his cover story in *Time*, "hit the *Bell* such a valiant and far-sounding clang that there had been nothing like it since her great compatriot Greta Garbo enchanted half the world." But unlike Garbo, Ingrid the person was being held up to the world as a beacon of light and virtue. "Ingrid Bergman [is] without an enemy in the whole [Hollywood] community," Agee wrote. "The individual herself . . . happens to be an uncommonly well-balanced and charming one."

While Ingrid was being eulogized and rhapsodized over, she was far from "uncommonly well-balanced." She was gorging herself again. Her face had broken out. Selznick set up a doctor's appointment, "with a view to watching her diet, and seeing to it that she gets the proper rest at the same time."

For her next film, Ingrid was scheduled to star in *Gaslight*, a remake of the British play and film. For several years she had wanted to play the part of Paula Alquist, a vulnerable, suggestible young woman whose husband, Gregory Anton, sets out to drive her mad. This was a new role for her, underneath its gothic veneer a tale of sexual subjugation. To do the film Ingrid was even willing to give top billing to Charles Boyer, the French-born star. Selznick was only too happy to loan Ingrid out to MGM, receiving $253,750 for her services as against the $75,156.25 that he eventually paid her. Selznick received even more money for the film, since he loaned out another of his stars, Joseph Cotten, to play Brian Cameron, the suave detective who saves Ingrid.

In playing Paula, Ingrid wouldn't be able to wear a wig as she had in *Saratoga Trunk*, fitting tightly over her still-short hair. For *Gaslight* she would have to be beautifully coiffed, her hair in cascading ringlets, romantic and feminine. That took time, as did her wardrobe. "Ingrid was a large woman overall," said Marion Keyes, the costume designer. "She was just a big girl. In *Gaslight* she was corseted. She didn't talk much. In those days people felt that Ingrid Bergman was rather remote."

On weekends Ingrid flew up to San Francisco, where she and Petter stayed in a hotel. It was not like a marriage but like a weekend affair, a distant romance, hours of sightseeing, eating in restaurants, walking the hills.

For Ingrid's twenty-eighth birthday, on August 29, 1943, Petter flew down from San Francisco for a party at the Selznicks' estate. Articles had appeared in magazines tallying up the moneys Selznick was making off her. And Ingrid had come to resent Selznick's hold over her. Yet the producer was often a man of grace and charm, and on an occasion such as this birthday celebration, Ingrid appeared admiring, even adoring, of David. In the evening, after Petter had departed, she sat alone wearing the pearls Selznick had given her, writing a thank you note. "I am going home to empty a bottle of your champagne in exclusive splendor and gratitude for a perfectly happy birthday," she wrote.

Ingrid and Selznick still had their moments of warmth and easy civility, but like partners in a doomed marriage, they maintained their relationship by avoiding discussing the unmentionable: the renewal of Ingrid's contract. They preferred discussing a happier topic: Ingrid's future roles for Selznick. Selznick still dreamed grand dreams, but he couldn't seem to get anything done any longer. Irene one day accused her husband of turning into a "flesh-peddler," selling his contract artists to the highest bidder.

Finding a David O. Selznick film for Ingrid, indeed finding a group of films, was the producer's top priority. He sent his underlings scurrying around, working on a myriad of projects. What about Ingrid and Gary Cooper in Somerset Maugham's *The Razor's Edge?* Maybe they should resurrect *Joan of Arc*—and the Selznick people filled boxes of material on that one. *Mary Magdalene:* that was another possibility. *Magnificent Obsession,* the novel by Lloyd Douglas: what a great idea that was for Ingrid! Du Maurier's *Trilby:* another idea. Or what about *Sister Beatrice?* Ideas and ideas and ideas, yet nothing happened.

While Selznick spun out his golden dreams to Ingrid, he applied subtle pressure on her to renegotiate her contract. Irene Selznick took Ingrid around looking for a house lot in Beverly Hills. Selznick told Ingrid that he intended to buy it for her; privately he worried that she might think he was planning to buy not only the lot but the house to go on it. A few weeks later, after his intended largess had sunk in, Selznick wrote Petter about renegotiating Ingrid's contract, a letter Petter says he never received.

Steele was spending a good deal of time with Ingrid. By now, in Selznick's words, "Miss Bergman mistrusted everybody in the Publicity Department except Joe Steele."

Steele was ready to guide Ingrid through all the shadowy labyrinths of Hollywood, seeking from her only a few scraps of attention. He didn't even always get that from her. Sometimes she treated him like merely another Selznick hireling.

Steele might fancy himself close to Ingrid, but there was a core of reserve, a mystery about her, that he could not enter. At one-thirty one morning he was driving through Beverly Hills in a drizzle, when he came upon Ingrid walking the streets alone, wearing a trench coat, flat-heeled shoes, and no hat. It was a strange spectacle, the woman whom *Reader's Digest* called "The First Lady of Hollywood" walking alone in the middle of the night. Ingrid would not accept Steele's offer to drive her to her car, three blocks away. So the publicist walked with her through deserted streets.

At the end of 1943 Steele resigned as publicity director and learned the melancholy truth about his dear relationships with the Selznick stars. Nobody called to thank him, to say they were sorry, to ask about him—nobody, not even Ingrid.

When *Gaslight* finished, Petter urged Ingrid to go off on a month-long visit to American soldiers in Alaska. Petter says that he signed up for the U.S. Army but was not called because he was a physician. He says that he felt America had given him and Ingrid so much, and that while he worked long hours in the hospital she should also do something in return. It was, nonetheless, as if he and Ingrid were avoiding the day when they would truly be living together, in the routine and ritual of married life.

Ingrid asked for only one day off before flying north on December 18, 1943. She would be spending Christmas away from her husband and daughter, but she was full of excitement and anticipation. Alaska was far from the front, but the frigid northland tasted and smelled of war: the bloodied and bandaged in the hospitals, the life of khaki-clad monotony, the loneliness, the camaraderie of men at war, the thousands of lonely American soldiers looking at a living pinup.

Until now largely ignorant of war and its wages, Ingrid on this trip felt the price of war and pain, and gained insights she had lacked before.

Ingrid wrote Selznick: "The worst part . . . is going around the wards talking. We don't give the whole show but one girl sings and sometimes I sing, sometimes I tell a story. I started to cry the first time. I felt so lost for words."

When she arrived, Ingrid had been taken in to meet a general, but she disliked him and decided to spend as much time as she could with the enlisted men. On Christmas Eve, she had not been at the officers club but among the troops. "Four hours without a pause I danced," she wrote Selznick, as she flew high above the silvery landscape to yet another base. "I wish you could have seen your reticent Swede in the middle of the room being taught to jitterbug by some nut with 500 boys standing around having the best time they ever had in Alaska."

Ingrid may have been half Swedish, but she couldn't stand running from the overheated huts into the frigid cold and back into the buildings again; she got pneumonia and had to be hospitalized. As she lay in bed, she realized that she probably had not really recovered from her "breakdown" during the filming of *Saratoga Trunk*. She found it curious that she, a sturdy Swede, should be the one to collapse first. She was not about to cut the tour short, however, and after a few days was up again.

Ingrid did meet at least one officer whose company she found appealing: Lieutenant General Simon Bolivar Buckner, Jr. "Buck" was a Patton-like character who refused to wear an overcoat in the subzero weather. He became infatuated and visited her in California. She had always kept her love affairs distant from Petter and Pia, distant from her life at home.

Buckner kept writing to Ingrid and she kept writing back until June 28, 1945, when he was killed by Japanese artillery shells on Okinawa.

CHAPTER NINE

A Hollywood Career

$f$rom the moment their car turned onto the long ascending driveway, Ingrid and Petter knew that it would be their home. The chiseled stone and redwood one-story house looked like a mountain lodge. It lay off Sunset Boulevard two miles up Benedict Canyon, protected by thick foliage in an area that was still largely rural. The house had an enormous vaulted living-dining room that Ingrid called "the barn." There was a copper bar-grill, a kitchen, a master bedroom with separate bathrooms for Ingrid and Petter, and a bedroom for Pia which had been the servant's room.

The unostentatious house appeared an omen of happiness, of good times and good cheer in front of the great stone fireplace, of long evenings and fine fellowship. A further good omen early in 1944 was that Petter had finished his internship and had started his neurosurgical residence at Los Angeles County Hospital.

For the first time in her life, Ingrid had her own house, and was a wife and mother living at home full-time with her husband. Ingrid and Petter had what only in Hollywood would be called a simple life. Ingrid was the number one actress in America, according to box office statistics. In the house there was a live-in housekeeper and a part-time secretary. Beyond those two Ingrid had another part-time secretary, Ellen Neuwald, and later a personal publicist.

Ingrid decided to give a housewarming party. She clicked off the names to Irene Selznick, an eclectic list that included producers, actors, cameramen, and writers. "This is impossible," Irene said, looking at the list. "Quite impossible. You can't mix producers with this little writer and you can't mix stars with this unknown actor."

"But it's just a party," Ingrid insisted, "just our first housewarming party."

"But you can't mix a feature player, a cameraman, and Miss Roberts, a language teacher, with the head of Columbia Studios, for example. No one will enjoy themselves. It simply isn't possible."

Ingrid gave her party for the top list, and considered the episode her "first lesson" in Hollywood social life. What she didn't comment on, and indeed didn't even think about, was that her original guest list was not so eclectic as to include anyone Petter might have enjoyed, doctors or medical people.

"Ingrid said, 'I'm only interested in two kinds of people, those who can entertain me and those who can advance my career,' " Petter says. In her first Hollywood party Ingrid was signaling to her world that her husband was not part of her professional life, the life that mattered to her. He was like her maid, her secretary, and even Pia, a diversion from the real work of her life. A party was *serious*, and though Ingrid might want to invite friends from all levels of her work, she was not about to invite any doctors. True, a mix of medical and theatrical people would never have worked, but there was *no one* from Petter's world.

Until now Ingrid could maintain the illusion that her marriage mattered profoundly to her. But with Petter living with her day after day, the reality of the marriage could not be hidden much longer, perhaps not even from Petter.

Petter, with his almost ascetic nature, did not view Ingrid as did the rest of the world. Selznick was awed by Ingrid's lack of concern for her looks. Indeed, Ingrid spent less time on her person and clothes than did practically any other star, but Petter thought his wife was full of vanity. He saw her spending half an hour in front of the mirror in the morning, primping and combing, applying makeup, and secretly shaving her hair back on her forehead. "Ingrid thought she would look more intelligent with a high forehead," Petter says. "So every morning she sat there and shaved one centimeter or so from her forehead. She didn't want anyone to know. Then she put on makeup, but did it in a way so it wouldn't look like makeup."

The reporters and columnists thought Ingrid didn't care much about publicity, and it was true that she did not exploit her family, as did many stars. But Petter saw and heard Ingrid, and watched her hover over her scrapbooks like a philatelist over his stamps. He thought she was consumed with publicity.

There were, indeed, good times in the house at 1220 Benedict Canyon Drive, good times when the guests sat in captain's chairs in front of the blazing hearth eating cheese and crackers, shrimp and lobster, good times when the house rang with laughter and fun.

Petter was an exuberant spirit. He loved his new home, his wife, his child, and his position. He was broadly enough interested in the world outside medicine to make a few friends in the movie community. Two of their closest friends, Jean and Dido Renoir, lived up the road in a house on a hill visible from the Lindstroms'. Ingrid had been one of the first people the French director and his wife had met when they arrived in Hollywood in 1941, fleeing Nazi-occupied France. The friendship had deepened and now included Petter. Sometimes in the afternoons when Petter couldn't be at home he would send little Pia up to the Renoirs' house, its walls lined with paintings by Jean's father, Auguste Renoir.

Other close friends who lived nearby were George and Phyllis Seaton. George was a writer and director who won Academy Awards for *The Country Girl* and *Miracle on 34th Street*. Pia and Mary Seaton both went to Hawthorne elementary school, a public school. Often Pia came to play. Later, when the Lindstroms built a swimming pool, Mary learned to swim there. Petter and George Seaton became close friends. Seaton was a good husband and a family man, and he and Petter respected and admired each other.

The Selznicks didn't live far away either, and though Ingrid could not be her employer's true friend, she did become close to Irene Selznick. Irene advised Ingrid on the niceties of Hollywood. Irene and Petter were friendly, too; indeed, later, Petter says that when the Selznick marriage was breaking up, Irene confided in him.

Ingrid took Petter along to a few Hollywood parties. She was no longer a foreigner to this world where professional and personal life have no boundaries, and deals are made on the tennis court or around the swimming pool as in the office. Ingrid had to go to fancy parties, seeing and being seen, receiving homage from producers and directors, discussing new deals, hearing the latest gossip.

When Ingrid talked with those who professionally courted and wooed and flattered her, Petter often talked to the wives. He could be a charming, gracious conversationalist who brought the same perceptions and insight to his social life as he did to counseling his patients. He enjoyed people as Ingrid often did not, in an innocent, frolicking way. More than anything, though, Petter liked to dance, and he danced as did few others in Hollywood.

Like many of his compatriots, Petter was usually sober, serious, self-controlled, but when he let go, he let go completely. If Petter knew there was going to be dancing, he carried an extra shirt to the party, for although he was a graceful dancer, he worked up a sweat.

Petter did not particularly like to dance with Ingrid. "She really was never a good dancer," Petter says. "She was a fair dancer, but she was terribly concerned with her appearance. She always had to look to see if others were watching."

"Peter was a fanatical dancer," remembers Gregory Peck. "He hopped around like crazy, a lot of leaping around. I don't think Ingrid was terribly taken with that, and she would shake her head."

As Petter whirled another actress, or the wife of a director or producer, around the floor, there were those who made fun of him. They thought that Petter was attempting to make Ingrid jealous, though he was only having a good time. Though Petter was a neurosurgeon, there were those who called him "the dentist," an appellation that would be considered an insult only in America.

Petter was in superb physical condition. He loved to challenge other men to arm-wrestling contests, particularly stars, whose manly images he almost always deflated with a quick twist of the arm. On weekends he took Pia on his back and ran up the hillside toward Mulholland Drive, a habit that in the epoch before jogging seemed peculiar indeed. He spent more time with Pia than did Ingrid. According to Petter, Ingrid never visited her daughter's school. If his schedule permitted, Petter liked to call for Pia. "I got out of school at two o'clock," Pia remembers. "I don't remember my mother picking me up."

Some of Ingrid's friends considered Petter miserly and domineering. He was not in fact a selfish man. He shipped several hundred packages to their relatives in Sweden and Germany during the war, an activity about which Ingrid could not be bothered. He was always helping people, be they relatives, poor patients, neighbors.

To Petter, simplicity was not merely a life-style but a moral value. As Ingrid and he grew wealthier beyond their Swedish-bred imaginations, Petter's very life standards risked being lost.

There were those in the movie business who admired Petter but believed that he felt superior to Ingrid and her world. "Lindstrom is an extraordinary doctor and humanitarian, but he had some old-fashioned European ideas," said Lewis Milestone, the director. "He had the attitude that he had bestowed his name on a poor orphan girl, and therefore she should be grateful to him for the rest of his life. He never let her forget it. But how long can you operate on gratitude?"

Visitors would be startled at Petter's domestic mastery. This was the same man who at Ingrid's direction had chastised her for her posture and eating habits in Sweden, only now Ingrid was a star.

Probably only other Swedes could understand this aspect of the Lindstroms' relationship. Petter often called Ingrid *kärringen*, a word that means "old lady." It is a term of endearment but one that could be a gentle put-down, suggesting an uneducated woman.

"Ingrid always wanted someone strong," says Alf Kjellin, a Swedish actor and director, who worked with Ingrid in her last Swedish film, *A Night in June*. "That's why Petter Aron was so good for her. He was what she wanted a man to be.

"When I came up to their house in Beverly Hills, I was surprised at the way he talked at her and treated her. He was the man of the house. And he was the man. He probably had to suffer from being what she wanted him to be. Petter is the only *Peer Gynt* character I've met in my life, strong and vulnerable.

"As for Ingrid, she was like a character in Swedish folklore. There are men who work all night making coke in the forests. They see these visions of a beautiful woman with red hair peeking out of the trees. They seek to go after her and they find that her other side is only a hollow tree with a fox tail.

"Ingrid had that beautiful side and the other side too. She was a smart woman and had a coldness about her. She could fend for herself and still need a man. One side was completely open, and the other completely steel."

In the first week of June 1944, Joe Steele drove up to the Lindstroms' new house in a chauffeur-driven limousine. A few days before, Ingrid had called Steele, talking to him with breezy familiarity, as if there had not been a half-year break in their relationship. She told him that she was going on a three-week war bond tour to nineteen cities, and she wanted him to go along as her personal publicist and companion. He readily agreed, beginning what he considered the most fulfilling part of his career.

"Isn't it wonderful!" Ingrid said as the limousine sped toward the railroad station to catch the Santa Fe *Chief.* "How I like to keep going. I hate to sit still."

And so Ingrid was off again, city after city, day after day, vignette after vignette. She seemed to personify goodness and nobility, and she sold thousands of dollars in bonds.

Back in Hollywood, Selznick was worried about *his* star. For the first time since *Intermezzo,* nearly five years before, he was about to star Ingrid in a David O. Selznick production. Shooting would begin soon after Ingrid returned, and he sent the script to her at the William Penn Hotel in Pittsburgh.

Spellbound would be a psychiatric thriller directed by Alfred Hitchcock and written by Ben Hecht. Selznick was in therapy himself, and perhaps that was why he was looking at Ingrid's emotional state in a different way. He knew her habit of "getting herself three or four ice cream sodas by way of extra dessert." He thought that his own analyst, Dr. May E. Romm, "might be helpful in getting a really good scientific dietician whose technique and psychology are such as to increase chances of whatever benefit can be secured being secured." Ingrid was willing to try a new diet, and when Selznick talked to Petter, he reported that Petter "accepted the idea although without enthusiasm."

Ingrid began filming *Spellbound* only a few days after returning from the bond tour. In the film she played Dr. Constance Peterson, a psychiatrist who falls in love with "J.B.," an amnesiac doctor played by Selznick's newest star, Gregory Peck. J.B. is convinced that he has killed the new head of the clinic, whom he has been impersonating. Dr. Peterson helps J.B. to reach down into his psyche. By learning the truths of his childhood, he frees himself of the delusion. And by analyzing one of J.B.'s dreams, she discovers the real killer.

Ingrid was not one to reflect on her own psyche. She could never understand why it was the rage in Hollywood to go through analysis. In most of America in the mid-forties, therapy for an adult was as unusual as braces on a child's teeth, and the film began with a self-conscious preface about the work of an analyst. The cast was told how to pronounce such esoteric terms as Freud ("Froyd") and therapy ("therr-ah-pee"). The script itself was full of hokey Freudianism. ("You got amnesia and you got a guilt complex and you don't know if you're coming or going from someplace. But Freud is hooey. This you know. A wise guy.")

The British-born Alfred Hitchcock was a brilliant director of psychological thrillers. Hitchcock wore the same gilded shackles as Ingrid. He, too, had arrived in Hollywood to make a film for Selznick in 1939. He had nearly been assigned to direct *Intermezzo*; instead, he had directed the classic *Rebecca*. Since then, like Ingrid, he had been loaned out to other studios, for half a dozen other films.

On July 10, 1944, the first day of shooting, and the seventh anniversary of her wedding, Ingrid wrote a note to Selznick on stationery labeled "The Green Manor," the name of the clinic in *Spellbound*. "You are so nice to come home to!" she told him, and she was indeed glad to be back at work. She was somewhat upset that for the first time she would be playing opposite a younger man, Gregory Peck.

Ingrid had at first wanted to turn down *Spellbound* because she "didn't believe the love story." Ingrid intended to have her say about how Dr. Constance Peterson should be portrayed. In her first shot she was supposed to walk across a room, photographed by a camera on a crane above her. Ingrid wanted to say her lines standing in one spot, and she told Hitchcock so.

Hitchcock would brook none of Ingrid's interference. Moviemaking for him was the preparation for moviemaking: the writing of the script and the detailing of each shot. During the shooting, Ingrid thought Hitchcock "regarded us [actors] as intruders to his fantasy."

Hitchcock was an obese man, who covered the director's chair like a shroud. Between scenes he often fell asleep, as if he could not be bothered with all this. He was full of as many private demons as any of the characters in *Spellbound*.

As far back as 1941, Hitchcock had had an idea for what Selznick considered a "rather erotic story" starring Ingrid. That had not worked out, but there was an erotic undertone to *Spellbound*, as the rigid, straitlaced psychiatrist falls in love, a seemingly obsessive love. Ingrid, however, played the part as if she were the heroine of a romantic thriller. From the moment she looked lovingly, yearningly at Gregory Peck for the first time, the audience knew that it was on familiar ground.

Even while *Spellbound* was shooting, Hitchcock was thinking about another film with Ingrid, in which the erotic, illicit quality would be to the fore, a film "about a man who forces a woman to go to bed with another man because it's his professional duty."

Hitchcock's quasi obsession with Ingrid was apparent on the set of *Spellbound*. "He liked to kid Ingrid a lot," Gregory Peck remembers. "He was always flirting with double entendres. He'd say things that would verge on the obscene but in a dry way. He could make her laugh with his slightly obscene remarks about her bosoms or legs. She'd say, 'Oh, Hitch, you're terrible.' "

Humor was Hitchcock's defense, art his solace, film his voyeurism, and there was never any gossip about Hitch and Ingrid. The gossip had to do with Ingrid and Gregory Peck, particularly on the day that, according to another cast member, "Ingrid and Peck came in late, all disheveled, and there was a lot of speculation." Peck says, "That's not the kind of thing I talk about."

In *Spellbound*, Ingrid played a psychiatrist who knows that the human psyche can be a dark magician, hiding away the truths of one's life, leading to endless obsessions and self-deceptions. Only through therapy or the most brutal shocks can the psychological sleight of hand be exposed, and the person enabled to live free.

Ingrid might have asked herself, Why was she compelled to fill every minute with activity? Why couldn't she spend some time at home with Petter and Pia? Why did Sunday seem such an endless, cursed day? Why once a film ended did she seek an excuse, any excuse, to be off somewhere, anywhere?

Ingrid did not ask herself such questions. Soon after production of *Spellbound* ended in mid-October, she was off on yet another lengthy journey, this time for a whole month, to sell bonds, to do a radio show, and to publicize her films on a sojourn that took her to Canada and New York City, as well as to Chicago and Minnesota.

Most actresses would have screamed loudly enough to be heard back in Hollywood if they had been asked to carry out Ingrid's schedule. But Ingrid didn't complain and she charmed her way through a month measured out in teas, official luncheons, banquets, cocktail parties, hospital visits, speeches, radio interviews, photography sessions with mayors and politicians.

In Toronto at the King Edward Hotel, Ingrid received from Selznick a package of "non-fattening foods and a pound of caviar." Ingrid sent Petter a wire that ended: "AND JOE WON'T LET ME EAT." Ingrid was like a schoolgirl on her holiday. As soon as she arrived in New York, where she was to appear on *The Kate Smith Show*, she went out to Hamburger Heaven to eat, and then had a chocolate sundae at Schrafft's. She was having so much fun that she wired Selznick for permission to stay a few extra days.

Then Ingrid was off for Minnesota. Traveling with her was not only Joe Steele but Bob William, the Warner Brothers publicist who had handled Bogart during *Casablanca*. William was a gregarious, unpretentious sort. Steele was not terribly taken with the idea of having another publicist along with *his* Ingrid. As for William, he found Steele "imperious, like a little Russian musical impresario, who was really enamored of her."

There was little glamour in this assignment, sleeping in what William remembers as "a crummy hotel, everything a sickly green," traveling to outlying regions on "a dinky train with parlor cars."

Then it was Thanksgiving Day. No rallies. No speeches. An empty hotel room. An empty day. The phone rang in Ingrid's room. William was calling with glad tidings. He had rounded up a rental car, not an easy thing to do on a holiday in wartime Minnesota.

"Thanks, Bobby, I was feeling sorry for myself," Ingrid said. She agreed to go with William and Steele for Thanksgiving dinner to the Lowell Inn in Stillwater.

When Ingrid arrived down in the lobby, William handed her a thermos with a red ribbon around it.

"There's martinis in here, Ingrid," William said. "And we're going to have a toast at every stop sign on the way to the inn."

The car, an ugly green 1938 Pontiac, stopped at twenty-six stop signs on the road to the Lowell Inn. By the time the threesome pulled up in the parking lot and toasted Winston Churchill and Franklin Delano Roosevelt, they were smashed. The proprietors knew a star when they saw one. They sat the party at a prime location, next to the indoor stone fish pond.

"What's that for?" Ingrid asked, in a half-drunken voice.

"Oh, that's how we choose the fish for dinner," the owner proudly told her.

"Oh," Ingrid said, and stuck her arm into the water up to her elbow, getting her sleeve totally soaked.

A flash went off. A second flash went off in William's head. If that picture got into the papers he would be fired.

But it was Thanksgiving and such worries were forgotten. There was cream of mushroom soup with almonds, and turkey, and more good cheer. On the drive back, William told joke after joke. Ingrid laughed so hard that she slid down beneath the dashboard.

"Stop, stop," she cried. "My ribs are hurting."

As soon as Ingrid got back to Beverly Hills, she and Selznick had to decide what her next picture would be. There were two possibilities: a Selznick film called *Daybreak*, which was still largely unwritten, or *The Bells of St. Mary's*, with Bing Crosby, directed by Leo McCarey at Rainbow Productions, and distributed by RKO. The film was a sequel to the extremely popular *Going My Way*, with Crosby and Barry Fitzgerald.

At first, Selznick did not want Ingrid to do the McCarey film. He thought "sequel" was synonymous with "second best." McCarey's films were extremely popular, but Selznick may have felt that a McCarey film was a little beneath a "Selznick star"; after all, McCarey had a reputation for making films so gooey and sweet that one risked tooth decay watching them.

According to Ingrid's recollections, she talked the reluctant producer into letting her play Sister Benedict. But the memo that Selznick dictated after their meeting states that "Ingrid is in doubt as to which she prefers to do, 'Daybreak' or the McCarey film . . . and I am reasonably sure that I can make her happy with whichever one I think she ought to do."

Selznick tested McCarey's devotion to Ingrid by negotiating one of the most lucrative loan-out agreements in the history of Hollywood filmmaking. Selznick received $175,000 in cash, the rights to the services of Gregory Peck for one film, and the remake rights to *Little Women*. RKO also assumed Selznick's obligation for outside studio space. This was all worth about $425,000, many times what the producer paid Ingrid. Nonetheless, Selznick was unhappy that he had to pay Ingrid an extra $25,000 because the film commenced after the starting date stipulated in her contract.

After the contracts were signed, Ingrid and McCarey scheduled a lunch together at Lucey's Restaurant, across from the RKO studios. Ingrid was so excited at the prospect of working again that she left for the one o'clock appointment a whole hour early. She practically crawled in her car down Benedict Canyon, but it was still only twenty to one when she arrived. Not wanting to sit alone in the restaurant for twenty minutes, she decided to walk around the block. There stood McCarey, who had been waiting since noon.

McCarey was a handsome forty-five-year-old Hollywood veteran. Of Irish ancestry, he had made his way in Hollywood directing comedies such as the Marx Brothers' *Duck Soup*, *My Favorite Wife*, and the Oscar-winning *The Awful Truth*. The director had discovered a rich vein of sentimentality and sheer good feeling that could be mined not only for critical success but for a fortune. In *The Bells of St. Mary's*, McCarey was attempting to mine it again.

Bing Crosby played Father O'Malley, a good priest ready to break into song at the hint of a sagging plot. Father O'Malley is assigned to head a traditional parochial school, which is in trouble. Sister Benedict, the school's mother superior, is an old-fashioned nun who believes in the value of simple prayer. With the help of God, a slew of child actors, and a miserly industrialist with a heart of gold, the school is saved.

In her nun's habit, Ingrid could eat her fill of sundaes without a worry. Her face was her fortune, and Ingrid almost levitated with saintliness.

On the evening of the Academy Awards, Ingrid worked on the set of *The Bells of St. Mary's* until six o'clock. Then, before going home to change for the awards ceremony, Ingrid, McCarey, and Crosby wished one another luck. All had been nominated, McCarey and Crosby for *Going My Way*, and Ingrid for *Gaslight*.

Petter arrived during intermission, and joined Ingrid and David Selznick in the auditorium. As she awaited the announcement of the best actress award, Ingrid held Petter's and Selznick's hands. McCarey had already won. Crosby had won too, for best actor.

The nominees for best actress were announced: Ingrid Bergman. Claudette Colbert. Bette Davis. Greer Garson. Barbara Stanwyck.

Ingrid couldn't hear.

"That's you, Ingrid!" Selznick shouted. "You've won! You've won!"

Ingrid turned to Petter. "Go get it," he said gently, and kissed her.

The next morning Ingrid was back on the set, being toasted in champagne and crying with happiness as she sat between McCarey and Crosby. In the sheer exhilaration of the moment, she felt that she would never reach such heights of happiness again. But it was a strange happiness, for all three of them. Here was Crosby playing good priests, gregarious, selfless men whose character spilled over into the public perception of Crosby himself. Yet he was a withdrawn, emotionally miserly man whom Ingrid could not get to know at all.

Here was McCarey, the most celebrated popular director of the day, lionized by the church, a man who would tell Louella Parsons that he could "never make a story that's in the least suggestive or vulgar." And this man was so deeply troubled that during the shooting of *The Bells of St. Mary's* he was arrested twice, once for creating a disturbance while drunk, then for suspicion of drunkenness as he drove out of control the wrong way down an incline to a highway.

And here was Ingrid, lauded across America as the perfect wife and mother. And as soon as the shooting was over she wanted to be off again, this time about as far from her house on Benedict Canyon as she could get, on a USO European tour. For years now she had maintained the illusion of her marriage by only rarely living a day-to-day married life. She pretended that she loved to cook at home, to play with Pia, but after a few days in the house she was climbing the walls. She was not a woman to say to her husband that things were not working out. She always tried to avoid conflicts and arguments, fleeing from them. Petter and Pia were all that she had from the past, all that remained of her life in Sweden. She felt that Petter had given her so much and was so strong, a rock upon which she could stand. But she wanted something new, something exciting—a party, a night of drinking, an assignation somewhere, anything but the silence of Benedict Canyon. Petter was almost never bored. He was always doing something—working in the yard, romping with Pia. But Ingrid was bored with life as most people lived it . . . bored with wifedom and motherhood . . . bored.

"Goodbye, goodbye, goodbye . . ." Ingrid wrote Selznick on June 13, 1945, as she sat in Compartment D on Car 182 of the Santa Fe *Chief*, heading eastward. "I am so thrilled and can hardly believe I am on my way. Where I fell short in Alaska won't happen on this tour. I can beat almost anyone with my jitterbug and I know samba, rumba, conga, swing, big apple and what have you!"

By the time Ingrid arrived in New York, she was down with sinus and ear infections, so sick she couldn't leave with the rest of the troupe. She missed the first few days of the tour, arriving finally on a "flying boxcar."

So much of the Europe Ingrid had known was gone. The Genoa from which she had sailed for America was now a city of the hungry and the maimed. Hamburg, her mother's city, was havoc, her once proud relatives dependent on the packages mailed by Petter from the States. And Berlin, where she had starred for UFA, was a city of hollow, burned-out buildings like the hollow, burned-out Berliners who haunted the ruins.

Ingrid arrived in Augsburg, an ancient city on the Lech River in Bavaria. As the Americans did throughout occupied Europe, they had appropriated the best houses for their officers. Ingrid was driven to the USO quarters, in a large private house. In the living room she found an intense, wiry little man playing the piano. She had never heard the music before.

"That is such beautiful music. Whenever you play, I will come to listen."

"It's just something I made up," the pianist said, shrugging off Ingrid's compliment.

The pianist was Larry Adler, another member of the USO troupe. Adler was the most famous harmonica player in the world. That was an accomplishment that might seem on par with fame achieved playing bongo drums, swallowing swords, or whistling, but only if one had not heard Adler play. He could do things on a harmonica that had not been done before. He was a virtuoso of the first rank.

Adler was no homespun Tom Sawyer who pulled his mouth organ out of tattered jeans. Neurotic, intellectually passionate, fiercely opinionated, egocentric, and a political leftist, he was not the kind of man who attracted Ingrid.

Ingrid loved to talk, though, and Adler was a talker too. She delighted in his personal revelations and told him of her own life. She thought him a man of brilliance, and on the two-show-a-day circuit, she had time to begin an involvement with him.

"Ingrid wasn't fascinating, but you were just dazzled by her beauty," Adler says. "You felt she'd never read a book. She had no interest in world affairs. The one thing I never got her to talk about was her filmmaking in Germany. I think if Ingrid could have made a good picture, she would have made it for the Nazis, for anybody. She was a very dedicated lady. She loved working. And I don't think any individual was as important as her work.

"I think she needed to show her power over men. She wasn't coquettish or a tease. Ingrid wasn't interested in sex all that much. She did it like a polite girl."

On one of their first evenings in Germany, Ingrid and the others were invited by an officers club to a dinner party in the former hunting lodge of Fritz Thyssen, a wealthy German. After dinner the group moved into the music room, a hall of baroque splendor. At one end of the room there stood a grand piano, in front of it a white bearskin rug.

Ingrid stood with Lieutenant Robert Orbach, who had fought his way across Europe with General Patton. A young pianist was introduced, a Hungarian refugee, one of the millions of nameless displaced persons who wandered the roads or huddled in camps behind barbed wire, the chattel of war.

The pianist had chosen a piece of great intricacy and difficulty, and she played it magnificently. It was hard to believe that after all that had happened, all the ugliness and pain, all the death and hatred, such sublime beauty could come from one who had suffered and lost so much.

As the young woman finished, Ingrid swept across the room, dropped to her knees beside the piano. And she thanked the woman in a few words of French, the only language they shared.

In the USO shows themselves, Ingrid's performance was rather limited. Ingrid did not have the humor of Jack Benny, the leader of the USO show. She couldn't sing like Martha Tilton, famous as Benny Goodman's vocalist. She couldn't play an instrument, like Adler. But she could play straight man to Jack Benny, recite something or other, and simply appear there, a beautiful image in front of the soldiers.

Ingrid decided to recite from Maxwell Anderson's *Joan of Lorraine*, a new play that she hoped to do in America. The soldiers had not fought the war to make the world safe for Joan of Arc recitals. They were restless while Ingrid performed, waiting for more music, some jokes, or another broad. In Kassel, Ingrid plunged onward, ignoring their indifference. When she saw that some of the soldiers were waving G.I.-issue prophylactics in the air, Ingrid ran offstage in tears. Adler wasn't going to let such behavior go unnoticed. "What a pity you haven't a better use for those," he told the GIs, a sentiment with which they surely agreed.

As Ingrid arrived at the Ritz Hotel in Paris, another great star was leaving: Marlene Dietrich. Dietrich had been a star in her native Germany and in Hollywood; during the war she sang before thousands of soldiers, and her famous "Lili Marlene" was beamed on the radio not only to the GIs but to homesick German soldiers too.

"Ah, now you're coming, when the war's over," Dietrich said. It was true. Now that the war was over, they were all coming: the actors and actresses, the singers and comedians, the politicians and businessmen, the rear-line officers in their front-line outfits, the columnists and reporters, decked out for war. The Ritz was full of them.

One afternoon Ingrid returned to her hotel room and found a note under the door. Two men were asking her to dinner. They said that they didn't have money enough to send flowers and take her to dinner as well, and "dinner won by a close margin." Ingrid didn't usually do such things, and she had no idea who Bob Capa and Irwin Shaw might be. "If we write much more we will have no conversation left, as our supply of charm is limited," the note concluded.

There was something so appealing about their little message, why not? She wanted to see Paris, and if they turned out to be dreary bores she would simply dump them.

When the phone rang in her room, Ingrid said that she would meet Capa and Shaw in the bar. She came downstairs at six-thirty wearing a red flower in her hair, and entered the dark Ritz bar.

Capa and Shaw had fueled their brashness on good liquor. Shaw had aspirations of becoming a great novelist; he would one day write *The Young Lions,* one of the best books about the war. Capa was the war's most celebrated photographer, but that didn't give one entrée to the likes of Ingrid Bergman. It was hard to believe that Bergman—that was how the world knew her now, like "Dietrich" or "Chaplin"—had actually come down to meet them.

The two men rushed to greet Ingrid. Capa saw the world through a camera's lens, a world of light and darkness, shadow and focus. Ingrid seemed to light up the dark room, "like the lobby of the Music Hall."

"You said you were going to take me to dinner," Ingrid said, sounding to Capa like "a school kid" taking a mischievous dare. "I hope you have enough money, because I'm very hungry."

The war in Europe was over, and Paris was once again the city of light. And so they were off in a cab to Fouquet's. And when they had eaten and drunk as much as they could, they went on to Maxim's, and had more to drink, and from there they went to yet another place, in Montmartre. They danced and they laughed and no one wanted the night to end, and when Capa and Shaw ran out of money, Ingrid paid, and when they said goodbye in the early morning, Ingrid and Capa knew that they would see each other again.

Ingrid knew nothing about Capa, but she was taken with the intense, darkly handsome photographer, who was two years her senior. In *For Whom the Bell Tolls,* Ingrid had made a film that was as much like war as glycerin is like a tear. Capa had been there during the Spanish Civil War. He had lost his lover, Gerda Pohorylles, crushed under a tank. And he had shot the most famous photograph of the war: a Republican volunteer at the instant he was machine gunned to death. The photograph was a stark, horrible testament that transcended journalism to become art.

Capa had been born Endre Friedmann, in Budapest, Hungary, a Jew. He lived like a citizen of nowhere. When he photographed happy families, babies, or buildings, he was a good photographer. But when he photographed war, he was the best there was and he knew that he was the best there was. It wasn't simply that he was brave, though he was as brave as they come. It was that he was always *there.* There watching Italians surrendering at Palermo. There riding an assault barge into Anzio. There in Naples seeing the funeral of Italian children who had died fighting the Germans. There wading in to Omaha Beach, D-day, June 6, 1944, the only photographer. There riding with Spanish Republicans in to liberate Paris. There during the Battle of the Bulge. There in Leipzig at the end, standing in a room as a last soldier dies, and lies in a pool of blood.

Capa was brave enough, had seen enough and done enough, to stand on the truths of his own life. But like Ingrid he was a man who was in some respects his own best creation. He treated his life story like a delicate portrait that had to be blown up into a gigantic poster of heroism. "The fabrication of his legend was no longer simply a matter of entertaining his friends," his biographer, Richard Whelan, writes. "It was also a matter of business."

A man of calculated self-deprecation, he'd had the inside of his helmet in Italy inscribed: "Property of Robert Capa, great war correspondent and lover." Of his reputation as a Don Juan, he joked: "I'm afraid I defend myself badly against the women."

Capa was a reckless man, who began drinking too early in the day, and drank too long, who gambled too much and too poorly. He made a good friend and a bad neighbor, a good lover and a bad fiancé.

Capa didn't know where he was going to go, and what was left that he wanted to photograph. Those first days, Ingrid had very little time with Capa. She had to be off again on the tour. The biggest event of the tour was the Fourth of July celebrations for the troops in Germany. Capa could be where he wanted to be, and when the USO troupe arrived in Berlin, the photographer was there in the ravaged city.

Adler was there as well. In his own way he was as taken with Ingrid as Capa was; his disadvantage was that he didn't know about Capa's interest in Ingrid. The threesome moved through the bombed-out streets of the city. In the middle of one street lay a bathtub, in which Capa photographed Ingrid and Adler. "The next day we asked him for the pictures and he said the negatives didn't come out," Adler says. "He smiled and said, 'I hate to take pictures of my friends.' "

On the Fourth of July, Ingrid stood beside Adler on the balcony of Hitler's ruined Reich Chancellery. She recited the Gettysburg Address and Adler played the harmonica. That same day the troupe flew to Nuremberg and gave an Independence Day performance for the soldiers there.

Capa didn't go along on the whole lengthy tour, and Ingrid and Adler continued their relationship. Adler was forever poking away at Ingrid, or beating on his own chest in recrimination or pride. He was a lively person, a truthmonger, who told Ingrid what and how he felt. One evening Adler and Ingrid saw *Saratoga Trunk* in a screening room in Nuremberg. She was especially interested in his opinion; although the film was being shown to GIs, it was still unreleased to general audiences in the States. Adler considered subtlety a euphemism for lying. He told Ingrid that he had seen few examples of miscasting to compare with a healthy Swedish maiden playing a black-haired New Orleans courtesan. For several days she would have nothing to do with Larry Adler.

One day Ingrid and Adler were driving through the German countryside in a Mercedes. When the chauffeur ignored a sentry and drove on, the soldier fired a pistol shot at the retreating Mercedes. Adler felt the bullet hit him in the back.

"I'm shot! I'm shot!" he screamed as he fell to his knees. Ingrid held him to her bosom. "Say goodbye to my wife and to my children."

"I will, I will, Larry, don't die."

Ingrid's aunt had died in her arms, and this tightly coiled, nervous bundle didn't seem quite ready to expire.

"Larry, Larry, I see no holes," Ingrid said. "And you're not bleeding or anything."

"I'm dying," Adler said mournfully.

"Sit up and stop moaning," Ingrid said. "You weren't shot at all."

"I am too shot," Adler insisted, death before dishonor.

The bullet had hit a spring in the seat. And the spring had hit the harmonica virtuoso in the back.

In Germany, Ingrid didn't like to look at what was ugly and mean. When Jack Benny, Adler, and the others went to see a concentration camp, she refused because she "didn't want to have it in my brain."

Ingrid and the troupe returned to Paris by mid-August, in time to celebrate V-J day in the city of light. For days there had been rumors about an end to the war. Jack Benny, Ingrid, and Adler broadcast live from Paris on August 14, 1945, almost at the very moment the word became official.

There were no recitals, harmonica playing, or jokes this day.

"I came overseas because I wanted to say a personal thank you to these boys," Ingrid said passionately, with just the trace of an accent. "Our boys and our allies for the job they have done. I hope that you too at home will get your chance to say thank you very soon."

"You're right, Ingrid," Jack Benny concluded. "And I hope the next time we travel around the world, any of us, it will be as civilian sightseers."

Paris had gone wild, the streets full of tens of thousands of celebrating Frenchmen united in joy and relief. Ingrid sat next to Capa in a jeep on the Champs Élysées. "I'm going to do that," Ingrid said, pointing to the French girls bestowing kisses on random soldiers. "I'm going to throw myself at somebody and kiss him."

"Which one?" Capa asked.

"Him—over there," Ingrid replied. And the biggest star in America jumped out of the jeep and kissed a soldier on the mouth. And the soldier kissed Ingrid back.

When the USO troupe had first arrived in Paris, Ingrid, Adler, and Capa had been a merry trio, the three musketeers exploring the great city. "One evening the three of us were in a nightclub at Montparnasse," Adler remembers. "Ingrid made it clear she wanted me to leave. The next morning she came into my room and said she was sorry. She felt she had let me down. I felt let down. After that, I felt a little different. But then Capa disappeared and I stayed with her in Paris.

"Ingrid, I think, feared going home at the end of the tour. She didn't want to go home. She suggested that we stay in Paris, and we did for a few days. But I was a coward. I knew that my wife and children would know that the tour was over, and Jack would be back. And I finally suggested that we go back. Ingrid didn't like that at all. She didn't want to go back to California. In New York she tried to get me to stay a few days. Then she wanted to take the slowest plane back to Los Angeles."

CHAPTER TEN

The Loneliness of a Bad Marriage

*I*ngrid's affairs were dangerous, not only to her marriage but to her magical image. But they were exciting, and she was getting away with them, without a word in a column or a whisper among her fans. And among those who knew about them, no one seemed to think her the worse for her behavior.

Ingrid often played roles in which her behavior would have offended conventional morality, but she made it seem permissible—indeed, almost romantic. As Alicia Huberman in Hitchcock's *Notorious* she did this to an unprecedented degree. Alicia's father has been convicted as a Nazi spy. She considers patriotism "waving the flag with one hand and picking pockets with the other." She is an alcoholic, promiscuous woman ("She's good at making friends with gentlemen"). In Miami she meets Devlin, a suave government agent, played by Cary Grant. Devlin asks her to go to Rio with him to help ferret out a Nazi group. Alicia agrees with a shrug of the shoulder, as if it hardly matters one way or another.

In Rio, Alicia and Devlin fall in love. Devlin asks Alicia to meet an old admirer, Alexander Sebastian, played by Claude Rains. In the name of duty, and to avoid his own feelings toward Alicia, Devlin acts as a pimp, setting Alicia up with the Nazi. Alicia sleeps with Sebastian ("You can add Sebastian's name to my list of playmates"). In order to learn the secrets of the group, Alicia agrees to marry Sebastian. She helps Devlin discover that the Nazis are mining uranium. When Sebastian and his mother discover Alicia's betrayal, they begin slowly to poison her. As Alicia lies dying, Devlin saves her and they escape together.

Alicia lives in a world where things never are what they seem to be. Devlin's kisses may only be meant to seduce her into counterespionage. Her own passionate embrace of Devlin outside the wine cellar where the uranium is hidden is not a sign of love but a ruse to fool her husband. The coffee and tea that her husband brings to nurture her are laced with poison.

In her personal and professional life, Ingrid was playing a role not unlike

Alicia's, where things were never what they seemed, where at her most innocent, vulnerable moments she was part of a higher game—and indeed, where what seemed most innocent about her was not innocent at all.

Ingrid continued her relationship with Larry Adler. When Petter was working they went to parties together, a dinner at the Hitchcocks', a Hollywood extravaganza at Jack and Mary Benny's. They were a curious duo, and a subject of considerable gossip.

"I hear you're having a wonderful affair with Ingrid," Mary Livingston Benny yelled at Adler out the window of her convertible.

Theirs was not a "wonderful affair" as Hollywood defined the term—passionate meetings at the Garden of Allah or a private bungalow. Ingrid, as Adler discovered, wasn't that interested in sex. But she took great pleasure in talking to him; she made fun of what she considered his childish sense of humor; she chastised him until he learned to read music.

They talked over lunch at Lucey's, or wherever they could grab a few hours together. Adler was in analysis, and he knew how to draw Ingrid out.

"She was unhappy with Petter," Adler says. "He was a very hard man to like. I remember once at a dinner party at Ingrid's. Jean Renoir and Alfred Hitchcock were there. Petter dominated the conversation and he didn't have much to say. Ingrid would say that she knew Petter was a difficult man. She said that he had done a lot for her. He had done a lot to make her grow up.

"Ingrid and I did talk about getting married. The thing that prevented me from getting closer to her was that I knew goddamn well I would be Mr. Ingrid Bergman, and I've got too much of an ego. I was serious about her, though, for a while. I was serious as long as she let me be serious. I thought I was in love with her, but I don't think she was ever in love with me. I think she was fond of me. She liked me."

Ingrid liked Capa too. He had come to Hollywood presumably to write his war memoirs for a possible film, but in part to continue their relationship. They met at parties or surreptitiously for lovemaking at Irwin Shaw's home in Malibu.

When Ingrid arrived home from the studio, parties, or meetings with Adler or Capa, Petter's affection and solicitude were like a slow poison. "I felt guilty for not being satisfied with all I had," Ingrid said. "Again and again I repeated to myself how fortunate I was, a faithful husband who loved me and did everything he could for me, a good child, a beautiful home. I had health and money and success in my work, but still I was in a constant struggle inside, looking for something I couldn't put my fingers on. Petter understood my restlessness, maybe better than I did. We had long talks about our lives, and I felt a great relief in leaning on him and letting him make the decisions."

Ingrid could not talk candidly to Petter about Capa and Adler and the others, but she could talk to him about her career. "Ingrid said that Petter managed her career," recalls Ellen Neuwald, her secretary. "I think it was something that she gave to Petter so that he could be part of her life. I recall her saying, I have to discuss this with Petter. She really did defer to him."

Ingrid's career was the greatest thing in her life. And when Ingrid and Petter talked business, there was still the mutual interest and concern that they had seemed to have during their days of courting so long ago. "She said that she hated Selznick," Petter says. "She really didn't hate him, but she disliked Selznick for several reasons. He kept her out of work when she wanted to work. He wanted to prolong her contract against her will. He refused to let her appear on radio. When he sold her services to other studios, he never gave her an increase in salary, though even despite the wartime labor law, he could have found a way to give her more money. She had firmly decided never to make another contract with him."

Almost nothing in Ingrid's life was what it seemed. Onscreen she and Cary Grant had extraordinary chemistry, but the British-born star had no sexual interest in her. One day Hitchcock filmed what would become one of the most famous kissing scenes in film. For over two and a half minutes Ingrid and Grant nuzzled one another, kissing on the lips, touching each other's neck and ears. "Hitchcock said discuss anything you want to discuss," Grant remembers. "We talked about who is going to wash the dishes. It's a very cuddly-looking scene. Noses are a difficult business in the kissing scene."

It was not Grant, the beau ideal of millions of women, who was infatuated with Ingrid, but the rotund, almost grotesquely unattractive Alfred Hitchcock. In *Notorious*, Hitchcock was directing his first true love story. The director had lost close to a hundred pounds, and by comparison his once three-hundred-pound frame looked positively wizened. Hitchcock was full of what his biographer Donald Spoto calls "unrealized and misshapen, adolescent romantic impulses of a lovesick middle-aged director toward an unapproachable goddess."

Ingrid and Petter were good social friends of Alfred and Alma Hitchcock. Sometimes the Lindstroms went to the Hitchcocks' home on Bellagio Road for dinner. One evening, according to Hitchcock, Ingrid approached him in the bedroom, insisting that he make love to her before they left. Hitchcock's biographer believes that the story was "a fiction, fresh at the time from the workshop of his [Hitchcock's] own fervid imagination."

Nonetheless, for Ingrid sex was not a big deal. She knew that Hitchcock adored her. She had heard his constant sexual banter. She was in love with the performances he was getting out of her. She may well have suggested an assignation, or teased Hitchcock, perhaps knowing that he would never act upon it.

Ingrid's relationship with Selznick was another kind of unfulfilled love and yearning. Selznick saw himself as the true, noble protector of *his* Ingrid. He felt that Ingrid and Petter were profoundly ungrateful for all that he had done.

125

The producer loved Ingrid as if he had molded her out of clay, breathed life into her, and taught her how to dance and sing and laugh.

Instead of putting Ingrid on film himself, parading his creation before the world, Selznick had sold her again and again. To Ingrid, that was a betrayal of their covenant. Such talk filled Selznick with rage. He would not be called a usurer, a peddler of talent. He called the roll of Ingrid's hits. He had chosen the parts with the same care as if he had been producing the films himself, and he had often helped with the writing and direction.

Ingrid's contract with Selznick was up at the end of 1945. She already was signaling her intention to have more freedom by negotiating a film on her own for 1946, *Arch of Triumph*, based on the Erich Maria Remarque novel. It was a formidable and exciting project, as good a choice for her new beginning as Ingrid could want.

Arch of Triumph would be the first film by a new company, Enterprise Pictures. It was a potential blockbuster: a big best-seller; a big-name novelist; a big co-star, Charles Boyer; a big director, Lewis Milestone, famous for *All Quiet on the Western Front*. And big money, for Ingrid alone $175,000 and 25 percent of the net profits.

Selznick knew all about Ingrid's prospects. In November, she was on the cover of *Life*. "BERGMAN'S YEAR" the magazine headlined, and Bergman's year it was. Already in 1945 *Saratoga Trunk* and *Spellbound* had opened to block-buster business. In a few weeks *The Bells of St. Mary's* would premiere as the Christmas attraction at Radio City Music Hall, and throughout America it would be viewed by more moviegoers than had seen *Gone With the Wind*. "Guess what?" went a popular joke of the time. "I just saw a movie without Ingrid Bergman."

It was not Selznick's year. The producer's life was in turmoil. He was leaving his wife, Irene, for Jennifer Jones, another "Selznick star." His produc-tion of films was down to practically nothing. Selznick had touched Ingrid and turned her career to gold. But Selznick was a Midas who did not dare touch anything any longer, for fear that he would turn objects not to gold but to dust. Ingrid was a symbol of Selznick's strength, his wisdom, his foresight. If she left him, his dreaded unspoken fear was probably not that she would fail but that she would succeed, rising to even greater heights.

Ingrid always needed a strong man. When she arrived in America for good, Selznick was, on Hollywood's scale, the strongest man of all. She called him "my father" and "my second husband." She listened to him. She laughed at his jokes. She teased him, but sweetly and graciously. The producer was never sure whether Ingrid was as unassuming, as spontaneous, as she seemed or whether she was a fount of disingenuousness. But if she was a Delilah, she cut this Samson's hair not while he slept, but while he sat in the barber's chair approving the new style.

Selznick blamed Petter for the nasty, protracted negotiations; Ingrid always remained sweetly conciliatory to Selznick. She wanted to placate him enough so that he would not rush to make an extra, mediocre picture before the contract ran out. In the midst of *Notorious*, Selznick suggested that Ingrid's last film under their old contract be *To Each His Own*, at Paramount. Ingrid talked Selznick out of it. (The role went instead to Olivia de Havilland, who in 1946 won an Academy Award for it.)

Ingrid and Selznick had a lunch to discuss their future together. Now Selznick wanted to do a film entitled *Katie for Congress*, as Ingrid's last picture. Selznick had purchased and developed the property especially for Ingrid. She didn't like the script. Selznick agreed not to do the film, which would have starred her as a Swedish maid in Minnesota. (The picture became *The Farmer's Daughter*, for which Loretta Young received an Academy Award.) Instead, according to Selznick, Ingrid agreed to make another film for him under the old contract in 1946.

Soon afterward, Petter wrote Ingrid's attorney a letter that suggested no such agreement had been made. Selznick was furious, accusing Petter of "fantastic distortion," and having "long been maneuvering . . . to break up the exceptionally cordial and mutually beneficial partnership between Miss Berg-man and ourselves."

Ingrid was perfectly aware of her own value and was not passively watching her future being decided. Ingrid's attorney told Selznick's negotiators that she "was extremely sold on her own importance in the industry, and that this was affecting her thinking to a marked degree."

In order to get another film under the current contract, Selznick had to begin production by December 29, 1945. In mid November he frantically wired Jenia Reissar in London, trying to obtain the rights to George Bernard Shaw's *Candida*. But it was madness to attempt such a project in so short a time. Finally, even Selznick understood that, and he realized that his only hope was to sign Ingrid to a new contract.

As the remaining days of Ingrid's contract grew to less than a month, Selznick tried to pretend that he still might start a new film with Ingrid by December 29. But Ingrid had so sweetly procrastinated that there was little likelihood of that.

Although Selznick had given up trying to sign Ingrid to a new long-term contract, he at least wanted to sign her for one new picture. The money that was on the negotiating table now was enormous compared to the sums Ingrid had been receiving under her old contract. He proposed to pay $150,000 plus 5 percent of the gross for one picture in 1946. O'Shea cabled Selznick that Petter had turned down that proposal "without moving an icicle of that frigid puss." The rejection would seem to support Petter's assertion that Ingrid had no intention of signing with Selznick again. There still might have been an agreement, but Selznick had no film ready for Ingrid that she wanted to do and she was too expensive a property on which to gamble.

It was all over. It was the end of the year, the end of an era. For Ingrid, there was the trepidation of a career on her own, but she had the prospect of earning within a few years enough money to become immensely wealthy.

To Selznick, it was as if he had lost a wife. He wrote Ingrid of his "sorrow over our divorce after so many years together of happy marriage. You once said that you had 'two husbands'; But Petter was the senior; and, of course, he knew all the time that his will would prevail. . . . So long Ingrid! May the New Year, and all New Years beyond, bring you everything of which you dream."

Selznick was not unwilling to seek a little revenge. He knew that for years Ingrid had been seeking to play Joan of Arc in a film. Selznick announced that he would be filming *Joan of Arc* himself in the summer and fall, starring Jennifer Jones.

Selznick was gone now, and Petter was the one strong man in Ingrid's everyday life. Now that Ingrid was on her own it might seem that their marriage would have come together. If Petter had been a producer or director, perhaps it might have happened. But they were each one-track workaholics, chained together by the bond of matrimony.

Ingrid and Petter were shadows passing across each other's lives. They were gone so often that they needed extra help. Elsa Neptune, who worked three or four days a week as their housekeeper, remembers "sometimes not coming home until two o'clock in the morning." Only then did either Petter or Ingrid walk in the door. "I am Swedish and I cooked special dishes that Ingrid liked to heat up," Neptune recalls. That, too, was part of the illusion, good wifely Ingrid whipping up Swedish delicacies, when her efforts were no more than turning on the stove.

Petter was the chief neurosurgical resident at Los Angeles County Hospital. With the wartime shortage of doctors, he was extraordinarily busy. He took the same narcotic Ingrid took: work, endless work.

"We were both very much preoccupied with our professions," Petter says. "Looking back, it was a marriage that looked good at the beginning, but when you really considered it, the personalities and how our lives developed, it was not a marriage based on good foundations. She became so preoccupied with herself from the age of eight or twelve."

Petter felt that he always did what Ingrid wanted him to do, always was what she wanted him to be. He continued to remind Ingrid about her slouching and eating. And he spent long days at the hospital. There Petter was a creative surgeon who in his extensive charity work insisted on only one reward: anonymity. To his colleagues he seemed to have everything: a brilliant career; a generous spirit; a lovely daughter; and as a wife, one of the most beautiful women in the world.

The fan magazines and movie columnists wrote that he had the perfect marriage. Once when Petter was driving home and thinking about his marriage, he became sick, and had to pull up along the roadside to throw up. He didn't know about his wife's affairs though the signs were everywhere, if only he could look. In his marriage he was plunged into an emotional world that was all grayness, shadow, and suspicion. He was from a good family with good values, and the idea of a divorce, of hurting his mother and father, was unthinkable. And he still loved Ingrid.

Late one night, Petter called Ruth Roberts's house and was told by Ruth that Ingrid was there. He drove to the house.

"She's in a room," Ruth said, as Petter remembers.

"I'd like to see her."

"She's not here," Ruth admitted finally.

"Where is she?"

"She has an appointment."

"With a man?"

"Yes."

"Where is she?"

"I don't know."

Ingrid came back at three o'clock in the morning, according to Petter. "That happened a second time. I went and she wasn't there. I didn't want to admit what was happening. I wanted to believe. That's how she got away with it."

Petter was deaf to certain sounds, blind to certain sights. He was as full of pride as ever, a pride that rankled certain people who waited for his fall.

It might seem that a man of such pride would not suffer a wife having a series of love affairs. But it was that pride that protected him from seeing and knowing and hearing what was happening.

There is no loneliness like a bad marriage, and sometimes Petter talked to Ingrid about what was wrong. "Why do we pretend that we have the perfect marriage, when you work all the time and I work all the time?" Petter remembers telling Ingrid once.

At times, Ingrid tried to show more interest in Petter's life. Early one morning she and Joe Steele visited the hospital to watch Petter remove a malignant brain tumor from a nine-year-old black boy. As Petter probed into the open skull, Ingrid appeared totally blasé, unaffected by the spectacle below. Steele searched for an answer, and decided that all her life Ingrid had hidden her emotions, releasing them only when alone in her bedroom. And now, after all those years, this "psychic subterfuge" had become part of her personality.

Almost everywhere Ingrid went now, she was recognized. She was comfortable among other celebrities, as if they were a species unto themselves. When she and Petter went skiing, it was not a weekend frolic in the snow, but a great ski trip to Sun Valley even before the resort was formally open, with Cooper and Gable and other stars.

Hemingway was up in Sun Valley too. He liked Ingrid, and she liked him, and the Lindstroms saw him occasionally. One day on a spring trip Petter went hunting with Cooper, Gable, and Hemingway. "We drove along the power lines in a jeep," Petter recalls, "and they shot eagles off the power lines using telescopic sights and rifles resting on tripods. Another day we went rabbit hunting. They engaged these farmers to ride in trucks chasing the rabbits toward them. I didn't shoot a single shot, either day. They killed maybe fifty rabbits. Nobody wanted them."

Life was different if you were Hemingway or Gable or Bergman, but sooner or later Ingrid had to return to life at 1220 Benedict Canyon Drive. Weekends were the worst. She hardly ever joined Petter on his jaunts with Pia up in the hills. She sat at home working on her scrapbooks, going over her fan mail, killing time. "What do you do with yourself on Sundays?" Ingrid asked the wife of a 20th Century-Fox executive. "I hate Sunday, I can't wait for Monday so I can go back to work again."

Now that *Notorious* was finished, Monday was just another Sunday. She enjoyed playing with Pia for a while, but that soon paled. She had to be off again.

One day Petter, Pia, and Ingrid spent the day at Sam Wood's beach house in Malibu. Ingrid walked into the water and began swimming. She swam farther and farther out into the surf.

"Should we signal the lifeguard station?" asked Laurence Stallings, a young writer who was working on a project with the director.

"Ingrid wouldn't like it," said Wood. "Someday Ingrid's going to start swimming and never come back."

"Why?" Stallings asked.

"I don't know," Wood replied. "But that's Ingrid."

In the spring, before she began work on *Arch of Triumph*, Ingrid left home for a visit to New York. There she spent a lot of time with Cary Grant, whom she considered a charming companion, if only a companion. One evening they went to a cocktail party at the Sherry Netherland Hotel. Neither of them enjoyed such parties very much, but Grant had arranged for Ingrid to meet Howard Hughes, the legendary multimillionaire owner of TWA, who collected stars and starlets as if they were Boehm figurines.

It was raining, and rain meant that Ingrid and Grant could walk through the streets unobserved, moseying along Fifth Avenue in old raincoats while New Yorkers scurried homeward under umbrellas. They looked in the shop-windows, knowing that any sweater, purse, or jewelry they coveted could be delivered to their hotel on approval.

Grant, always elegantly dressed, was properly attired to meet members of New York's social elite that evening. Ingrid wore a simple skirt and blouse, among these superbly turned out ladies with fashionable veiled hats and gold jewelry. People such as these considered it the height of politeness to appear studiously indifferent to the arrival of any mere celebrity. But when Ingrid and Cary entered the room, there was a momentary hush.

Hughes appeared and Grant made the introduction. For all his reputation as a ladies' man, the handsome, ruggedly built Hughes could be almost timid. While Ingrid talked to Hughes, one man after another approached Grant to ask for an introduction to her.

Later, Ingrid, Grant, Hughes, and Irene Selznick went out dancing at El Morocco. "I'm so lonely," Hughes told Ingrid. "I'm so terribly lonely. You know I have no friends."

"Then it must be your own fault," Ingrid said, "because you don't go out and look for friends. Anyway, I'm having a good time; you're not lonely tonight, are you?"

Hughes's friends and henchmen kept calling Ingrid, trying to get her to go out with him again. She remembered only that one evening with Hughes, but Steele had vivid recollections of another evening, at the Copacabana, where Hughes spent his time wooing not Ingrid but Lana Turner, another star at the table.

Ingrid could have no complaints, however, about the number of men who desired her. She felt comfortable in the warmth of masculine attention. When she was away from Petter, she had the perfect marriage: a loving husband, the security of home, and all the freedom she wanted. She didn't worry a moment about what others might think of her behavior. She simply intended to live her life as she wanted to live it.

In New York this meant that Ingrid generally saved her evenings for Capa, when the photographer was in the city. One morning they were seen nestled together at 4 A.M. in a Greenwich Village nightclub.

Ingrid kept her life in separate compartments. Petter was her husband and Capa was a lover. Joe Steele was a lover of Ingrid's golden image, and the guardian of that image.

In New York, Ingrid had to be free of Steele to live one of her lives. She instructed that her phone calls at the Drake Hotel go directly to her, and not through Steele. The publicist's whole sense of being, of self-worth, depended on his knowing and being closer to Ingrid than the others.

One evening, he asked Ingrid if she had a date with Capa. She became irritated and said that she was fed up with being watched over by the publicist.

The next day, May 26, 1946, Ingrid's schedule for the day appeared under Steele's door. She was intending to view paintings and have a drink with Grant, and go to the bathroom, and change her clothes for dinner. Then she would have "Dinner (not with Cary)" and lastly, "Home?" The question mark stood there like a taunt and a rebuke.

Ingrid did spend a good deal of time with Steele. They saw movies together. She went on a shopping spree and bought eight dresses at Bonwit

Teller and Bergdorf Goodman, spending $837.17, more than she had ever spent before on clothes.

Soon it was time to return to her house on Benedict Canyon Drive. Howard Hughes insisted on ferrying Ingrid back to Los Angeles in his private plane, a Lockheed Lodestar. Hughes was a collector of the famous, and Hitchcock and Grant would be on the plane as well.

On the morning that they were to fly out of La Guardia Airport, Hughes's plane developed minor engine trouble. He decided to fly another craft. Ingrid fell promptly asleep in the one berth; she did not intend to pay for her trip by chatting charmingly with the magnate. Hughes himself, a famous flier, holder of several records, may have felt more comfortable piloting Ingrid than talking with her. Behind him flew another plane, in case this craft developed engine trouble. Touching down in Kansas City for refueling, he was infuriated when a TWA Constellation revved up its engines: the noise might wake Ingrid. He ordered the engines shut down.

Hughes flew the craft hundreds of miles out of the way so that Ingrid could watch dawn come up over the Grand Canyon.

Steele shook Ingrid, who got up reluctantly and sat in the copilot's seat beside Hughes. She watched the Grand Canyon come alive, the pinks and browns and oranges so sublime in the half light of dawn. It was a sight few people had yet seen from the air.

"Thank you very much, that was marvelous," Ingrid said.

As her work on *Arch of Triumph* began, Ingrid was worried about her hair. Selznick's people had always been there to see that she looked her best, but she was on her own now, and her hair was a mess. If *Arch of Triumph* had been produced by a major studio, she would have had someone on the set whom she could trust. Enterprise Pictures was a new company, however, and she couldn't depend on anyone there to do her coiffure properly.

Ingrid made an evening appointment with Marcel Machu, a French hairdresser who tended to Ingrid's secretary and several of the stars. Arriving at Machu's Beverly Hills beauty shop, Ingrid asked tearfully what he could do with her unruly mop of hair, frizzy and kinky from a permanent. Machu washed her hair in mild soap, rinsed it in beer, and set it in a modern-looking bob. The next day he went to the studio, and with special permission from the union, began doing Ingrid's hair twice a day.

In *Arch of Triumph*, seemingly wanton, amoral Joan Madou loves an Austrian refugee and anti-Nazi underground leader, Dr. Ravic (Charles Boyer), and in loving him becomes a character worthy of empathy if not emulation.

That was an archetypal Ingrid Bergman role, but what followed was not. Joan's lover is deported from Paris, and she takes up with a ne'er-do-well playboy, Alex (Stephen Bekassy). Ravic kills the evil Nazi Haake (Charles Laughton) and seeks to renew his relationship with Joan. But Joan does not want to give up her new lover, who nevertheless, jealous, kills Joan, as World War II begins.

A great movie could have been made about refugees in prewar Paris, a motley breed carrying with them the truths of Nazism that most of the world was not yet ready to hear. But, as was painfully and expensively being learned, a great movie could not be made out of the Remarque novel.

Irwin Shaw, who knew Paris so well, had tried to write the screenplay, but his pages were rejected. Then Harry Brown, a Hollywood screenwriter, wrote a version. His script was at least a beginning, and most nights during the shooting, more pages were written. Even Bertolt Brecht, the German émigré playwright, was called in to try a couple of scenes.

Ingrid wanted *her* Joan Madou to be the center of the film. She and Ruth Roberts had underlined her part in the novel, and God help Lewis Milestone if he deviated, or cut down Joan Madou's role.

"Ingrid loved the idea of playing the part," remembers Norman Lloyd, who worked with the director on the film. "She saw the chance of a great romantic part with Boyer. She wanted all the aspects protected. There's a scene when Ingrid and Boyer go off to the south of France for a holiday. When Brecht saw those shots he said that no one who saw them on the Riviera living so beautifully would believe it. The scene should be taken out or reshot. Ingrid would have none of it because it was romantic and it showed her in a swimsuit. That's what the audience demanded, or so she thought. And the scene was kept."

Ingrid's character in *Arch of Triumph* was hardly virginal, but Ingrid insisted on playing Joan Madou with the maximum of decorum. In one scene in Boyer's hotel room, Milestone showed Ingrid how she should undress, flashing her thigh as she undid her garter belt.

"I'm sure the women of that time didn't wear garters," Ingrid said. "I want simply to roll my stockings down."

And that was the way the scene was done.

When she was on the set, Ingrid lived within the moment, her whole being consumed with her part. On *Arch of Triumph*, however, she often seemed to be somewhere else, concerned with other things, other parts. Her next role would be as Joan of Arc on Broadway. Several days a week, she ran across the street to the Western Costume Company for the fittings of her armor. After *Joan of Lorraine*, over a year from now, she would star in a period movie, *Under Capricorn*, for Hitchcock. She and Ruth Roberts were already working on her costumes, going through laces and linens in her dressing room.

In the evening Ingrid often did not go home but joined other cast members in the office of David Lewis, the producer. There was good talk, and good food, and good drink, and it was usually late before Ingrid returned to Benedict Canyon.

One morning Ingrid came on the set very disturbed. The night before, when she arrived home late, she had sat in front of the mirror taking off her makeup. Seven-year-old, golden-haired Pia had come into the room. "Why aren't you home more?" Pia asked.

Her hairdresser saw an Ingrid who had not prepared her public face. "She was a very unhappy woman most of the time," Marcel Machu says. "She would cry with no explanation. The subject she talked about most was her daughter. She was extremely proud of her daughter."

Ingrid had told Larry Adler another story about her relationship with Pia. "One day Ingrid told me that she was coming late from the studio and Pia came to meet her, rushed up to her to hug her and kiss her," Adler remembers. "And Ingrid slapped her. Ingrid said she was tired and she couldn't even say that she felt guilty about it. Ingrid was criticizing herself. She was saying, All I care about is my work and anybody who gets in my way, I take it out on them. She was ashamed of herself, but she never apologized, as far as I know."

Pia's childhood was, if anything, better than that of many stars' children. She did not have a series of "daddies" passing in and out of her mother's boudoir, and she was not shipped off to boarding school. She had not, however, spent her formative years in a family with mother and father both present day after day. She hungered for what, years later, she called a "normal" life, though she had no idea what that might be. " 'That's Ingrid Bergman's daughter,' is the way I was inevitably introduced at school and parties. Mama was a cinema queen, but I froze with shame whenever I saw gushing ladies beseeching her for autographs and making a fuss. She was so busy working that we had only minutes together from day to day. Visiting the movie sets, I was confused by the salaaming attention paid to Mama, the clutches of people chasing after her. . . . In the middle of all this stood Mama, an island in a dark sea. I was separated from her—and from the world. I ached to be 'normal' like everyone else."

Ingrid was usually so involved in her professional life that she could shove personal problems aside. But now she was working on her first independent production, a film that she sensed would be a failure. And she was living at home within the failure of her married life. The tensions had begun to show.

Ingrid started to smoke as part of her characterization in *Arch of Triumph*, and she soon started smoking heavily offscreen, a habit she would maintain for the rest of her life. She had always been a heavy drinker. Now she seemed to drink even more, enough to have ruined the constitution of a lesser woman. "She was so drunk one night that she fell and got a scar over her left eyebrow after the sutures came out," Petter says. "I was sleeping and I heard this fall. That was when I discovered a bottle under the bed."

Ingrid's personal life suddenly risked becoming as skewed, as much in danger of coming apart, as her film life. Capa was spending a great deal of time on the set. He stayed at the Garden of Allah and at least part of the time he lodged with Larry Adler. Capa had no real assignment from a newspaper or magazine, but he didn't seem to care. He was a man whose expertise was photographing war, but he loved to take pictures of Ingrid, and he shot roll after roll.

One day on the set, Ingrid sat on a stuffed chair, her head propped on her right hand. Nearby stood Lewis Milestone with a face that looked like a rumpled suit. The director gave the cue.

"I waited. Waited. And you never came," Ingrid said, as Boyer stood over her. "You've got to help me, Ravic!" As the cameras rolled on a poignant scene between Ingrid and Boyer, Capa shot his own still photos of what he called "the greatest love scene ever filmed."

Ingrid's life was like a wooden Russian doll that opens up to disclose yet another doll, and inside that another, and then another. In the film Ingrid was making love to Boyer. But it was Capa with whom she felt she was in love, Capa who stood photographing her. And Capa was staying with Adler, with whom Ingrid also was having an affair. And then there was Milestone, her director, whose feelings for her, unrequited, bordered on infatuation.

Capa squired Ingrid around, taking her at least once to Ruth Roberts's home for a party, as well as to her own home. At Ruth's home even her own companion had no idea that Ingrid and Capa were involved with one another. Ingrid found time to see Adler as well.

Men pursued her, and wooed her, and loved her, and she loved them back, or a small part of her did. She played them one against another. If the man was honest, he realized that Ingrid was not a woman of profound passion. She was not, moreover, a woman who could trust anyone completely, not even Petter, at least not anymore, with his growing suspicions. She was without a marriage that was a sanctuary of trust in what she considered largely a trustless world. All she had that was real was the unreality of her career, of her life on the stage and screen. She was full of tension. She was constantly on edge. Wherever she went, though, she maintained her placid public image.

In October, before Ingrid headed back to New York to begin rehearsals for *Joan of Lorraine*, she and Petter had a long discussion in front of the fireplace. According to Ingrid, she asked her husband for a divorce that evening. "I thought, I'll pull myself together and move out for some peace, go where I won't be frightened," Ingrid wrote later. "It was crazy to be married to the only person I was afraid of."

Petter's memories are very different. He denies that Ingrid asked him for a divorce or even hinted at such an idea. Moreover, he finds it absurd that Ingrid might have been afraid of him. What was there to be afraid of? After all, he was the one who managed the house and home and family while Ingrid ran off on her endless trips and evening sojourns.

Everywhere Petter went in the Hollywood world he met people who knew about Ingrid's affairs and talked behind his back. There was a great sense of betrayal within him, toward Ingrid and this life that was so unlike what he would have chosen. He was trying to hold on to his marriage, and on to his pride, and Ingrid may well have been afraid that one day he would let go.

CHAPTER ELEVEN

A Secular Saint

*I*ngrid had read about Joan of Arc as a teenager in Sweden and been mesmerized by her story. Joan is one of the great heroines of history, her life one of those stories familiar to almost everyone. During the Hundred Years' War, a seventeen-year-old, virginal peasant girl arrived at the court of the dauphin Charles of France and announced herself as France's God-anointed savior. Charles accepted Joan's vision, and she led his troops into battle at Orléans and defeated the English army. In May 1429, only nine months after she had first appeared before Charles, Joan was captured at Compiègne and sold to the British. Tried at Rouen, she was burned at the stake as a heretic in May 1431.

For years, Ingrid had wanted to play the martyred French girl. Selznick's promised film had not worked out, in part because during the war Selznick did not want to do a film that portrayed England as an invader of France.

Ingrid nurtured her dream of playing Joan. There was always the possibility of doing George Bernard Shaw's *Saint Joan*, but Ingrid found Shaw's Joan to be just that: Shaw's Joan, "a shrewd, plain pugnacious little girl, a sort of fifteenth century political agitator." Ingrid wanted to play Joan as she knew she had been, an unassuming, uneducated lass touched by God, a maiden of simple beauty and beautiful simplicity, a beacon of purity. Ingrid wanted to *become* Joan, lighting up stage or film with her martyrdom and perfection.

Ingrid's stardom had become a kind of secular sainthood. Moviegoers looked to Ingrid as a mythic figure, living beyond and above them. Her image in the movie magazines and newspapers was Joan-like, a simple, noble Swedish lass, unspoiled and selfless. Ingrid could not be portrayed as a sacred virgin, but articles about her almost always mentioned the many months she spent away from her loyal, loving Petter, as if she were celibate for long periods.

Ingrid had taken on the mantle of Joan, and she saw herself as having special affinities with the French saint and martyr. Joan of Arc was always alone. She was a woman among men, a peasant among nobles, a virgin among the knowing, a country woman among city dwellers, an illiterate among the literate. She was feminine but she was masculine. She was drawn to her martyrdom, and as the pyre was lit, her aloneness became transcendent, and in her aloneness she achieved sainthood, a woman unpossessed by anyone but God and her vision.

Like many religious figures, Ingrid was not beyond rewriting her own past to conform to her image. She said that she had come to America as part of a sacred quest to play Joan. "I knew I looked like Joan of Arc, who was a big peasant," she said. "I came here only because David Selznick said I could play Joan of Arc . . . and then he said, I can't do it now but someday I will, and so I waited and waited; and Ruth Roberts told me, have faith. And we read books about Joan and looked at paintings and statues and even wrote scripts ourselves. And soon I no longer thought of Joan as a role, I loved her so much. . . . I love the real Joan so much I want to be true to her."

Ingrid had not come upon a screenplay or play about *her* Joan. Maxwell Anderson, a New York playwright, had sent her his new play, *Joan of Lorraine*.

In Anderson's version, a group of actors are rehearsing a play about Joan of Arc. They have long discussions about such transcendent matters as "Why do you believe what you believe?" The main character, Mary Grey, is to play Joan. The actress disagrees with the director about how Joan should be played. She believes that Joan would never and could never compromise with evil. The director says that she would and did. When the actress plays Joan in a full rehearsal, she cries out: "I know now! She will not compromise when her own soul is in question. She'd rather die!"

For sheer intellectual pretension and longwindedness, Anderson's play made Shaw's *Saint Joan* seem like commedia dell'arte. But it was nonetheless Joan in the play within the play, and Ingrid decided to do the play on Broadway.

Everyone was waiting for Ingrid on October 5, 1946, when she walked into the Alvin Theater with her familiar entourage of Joe Steele and Ruth Roberts. Ingrid's presence in *Joan of Lorraine* almost guaranteed success. Tickets were already being sold for a twelve-week run. A group of fans waited outside to see Ingrid, and if they were lucky, to follow a few steps behind as she walked from the theater to her suite at the Hampshire House on Fifty-ninth Street. Not only those on the outside were in awe of Ingrid. For the first few days of rehearsals, Sam Wanamaker, the young Broadway actor who played Jimmy Masters, the director, couldn't even talk to her. He was too taken by what he called her "aura . . . partly her beauty, partly a spiritual quality, partly her dignity and reserve."

Ingrid knew how to use that aura, a weapon stronger than the bludgeon of threat or argument. Ingrid and Ruth had lunch with Maxwell Anderson almost every day. "Look, Max, at this nice thing Joan said here," Ingrid would say ever so pleasantly. "That's not in *your* play, Max. Don't you think that little bit would be wonderful in *your* play, Max?" Anderson was no match for Ingrid. By the time she and Ruth were through with him, the play had become, by her estimate, "seventy percent Joan, and thirty percent . . . talk . . . a complete reversal of how we started out."

Joan of Lorraine was scheduled for three weeks' tryout at Lisner Auditorium in Washington, D.C. Ingrid said later that when she arrived in the capital, she learned that the auditorium was segregated. She told Anderson, "Shame on you, coming with this play to Washington, knowing this would happen." She then decided, at "the press reception the day before the opening," to tell what she felt about segregated theaters: "I will not come back here again until black people, just like white people, can come to the theater. We play for everybody. Everybody!"

As Ingrid remembered the incident, her act had been Joan-like, a simple, profound moment of moral witnessing. Actually, she had not arrived suddenly on the scene in Washington, to denounce so daringly the iniquity of segregation. For several weeks in New York there had been an organized campaign by the American Veterans Committee, a liberal-leftist alternative to the American Legion, and the NAACP to end segregation in several important theaters across America. Several people worked on Ingrid to involve her in the effort, including Wanamaker and Steele.

Ingrid had never before expressed any great concern about racial injustice. When she stood up against segregated theater, she did it as part of a major campaign, and she did it not so dramatically, the night before the opening, but the day she arrived in Washington. With Steele as orchestrator, Ingrid made a statement in the capital on October 27. "If I had known of discrimination before I signed I wouldn't have come," she told a group of twenty-four reporters at the Carlton Hotel. "I heard in the midst of rehearsals a few days ago that no Negro can come into the theater. And in the capital city, too."

Ingrid's energies were committed to *Joan of Lorraine*. The rehearsals were not going well. Two nights before the Washington opening, the cast worked until after midnight. Ingrid had had no rest for months. Steele sat in the darkened auditorium, looking at Ingrid's troubled countenance. He knew Ingrid well enough to read the signs of stress and emotional crisis.

Petter flew in the next day, full of energy and advice. He had been in New York overnight during rehearsals, on his way home from a short trip to Sweden. On that trip he had just missed catching Ingrid with Capa; the night before, they had been out late at Café Society in the Village. Capa sent a white rose to Ingrid in Washington. Ingrid cabled: "My white rose is very near me." Steele noted that Petter was not himself. He wondered if Lindstrom had heard an item broadcast by Sheilah Graham, a Hollywood columnist, that his marriage was about over. He wondered how much Petter knew about Capa.

Joan of Lorraine's first performance received a standing ovation. Afterward, the cast and crew went to a big party at the 2400 Hotel. As the evening wore on, Kenneth Tobey, a young actor, shook Petter's hand in congratulation. Tobey found himself caught in the steely grip. In their tuxedos, the two men got down on the floor amid the dancers for a bout of Indian hand wrestling. They laughed and grunted, battling ferociously until Petter forced the actor's arm to the ground. Tobey demanded a rematch, and Petter beat him again.

The next morning Petter flew west to California. Soon afterward, Capa arrived, and as he sat in the first row, Ingrid gave what she considered "her all." The play still had problems. In the last week Sam Wanamaker took over as director in fact as well as role.

"How do you feel?" Steele asked Ingrid, as she waited to make her entrance before the opening night audience at Broadway's Alvin Theater on November 18, 1946.

"If they don't raise that curtain pretty soon, I'll break into little pieces."

Ingrid stood in the midst of Anderson's verbose, tedious play like a beacon of light, pure and transcendent. Wolcott Gibbs of *The New Yorker* wrote that her performance "may be incomparable in the theater of the day."

To many of those present, Ingrid *was* Joan, a saintly figure. "The cleanliness of her spirit is truly next to godliness," wrote John Mason Brown in the *Saturday Review*, as if he were talking of a religious figure and not an actress. "She contrives to make innocence exciting and virtue interesting."

Romney Brent, who played the Dauphin, said, "She has enormous charm and simplicity of manner . . . [is] genuine, self-effacing and considerate. Sometimes I think she really is Saint Joan." And Maxwell Anderson wrote that Ingrid was so successful as Joan because she was "so pure, so clean, so uncontaminated as a person." A *New York Times* feature asserted that "as Miss Bergman spoke she resembled more than ever the peasant maid from Domremy. One felt that faith had played a part in her success."

Joan of Lorraine was the greatest hit in New York. After each performance crowds waited to see Ingrid, Joan of Lorraine. On matinee days, some hundred and fifty people would gather outside the theater. Sometimes there were fans at Hampshire House too. One day a boy and a girl trailed Ingrid from the hotel for a dozen blocks. "Why are you following me?" Ingrid said, turning to face her two youthful shadows. "Because we love you," the boy said. "Well, I don't like being followed. It annoys me. So don't follow me anymore."

Warren Thomas and Adaire Curie were part of a large group of fans devoted to Ingrid, most of them teenagers still in school. They knew one another mainly by first names. When she asked Warren and Adaire not to follow her, they complied. All they asked was a glimpse, a smile maybe; that was enough.

Ingrid had a lovely suite on the twenty-sixth floor of the Hampshire House on Central Park South. She could look out the window and see all the way to the Brooklyn Bridge. What she loved best, however, was dusk, before she left for the theater, and lights came on all over the city. Then she would usually be driven to the Alvin Theater, often a half hour or an hour before she had to be there for makeup.

With hopes of getting Ingrid to extend the run, the Playwrights Company had knocked down two walls backstage to create a special oversize dressing room, with brightly colored wallpaper trimmed in pink and blue. Ingrid had lined the walls with pictures of Joan of Arc. Here she got dressed and afterward met the celebrity theatergoers who came to offer obeisances.

Through Michel Bernheim, the technical director on *Arch of Triumph*, Ingrid met family members living in New York, including Michel's widowed mother, and two brothers, Alain and Claude. Claude was the head of Coty Perfumes in America, and a charming, sophisticated companion. Ingrid was often attracted to European men, and she started an affair with the Frenchman.

Robert Capa was still Ingrid's favorite. One evening she and Capa were walking arm in arm along Central Park South, when they came upon Lewis Milestone and his associate, Norman Lloyd. Milestone had just finished editing *Arch of Triumph*. He was still infatuated with Ingrid. "Bob, let's have a drink," Milestone said, pulling Ingrid out of Capa's arms. Milestone appeared to Lloyd "a picture of a man totally frustrated."

Ingrid received more accolades for *Joan of Lorraine* than for any of her previous performances, stage or film. She received at least twenty-one awards, including the Drama League citation for "the most distinguished performance" of the year. Not only was Ingrid "Queen of the Broadway Season," as *Newsweek* called her in a cover story, but she was the best paid, receiving 15 percent of the grosses, or roughly $129,000 for the sold-out six-month run. George Gallup, the pollster, certified Ingrid as the most popular actress in America. The Associated Press named her "Woman of the Year" in movies.

Ingrid could do very much what she wanted now, and what she wanted was to do a film of *Joan of Arc*. Selznick's grandiose plans for a *Joan of Arc* with Jennifer Jones had gone awry, and Ingrid had the field to herself. Ingrid was hoping to do her *Joan of Arc* with Sam Briskin of Liberty Pictures, to be directed by William Wyler, whose credits included such classics as *Wuthering Heights* and *The Best Years of Our Lives*. Ingrid sought one third of the profits for her role as the saintly Joan. She stood outside the negotiations, as if such matters were beneath her, while Petter attended at least one meeting with Briskin.

One evening Victor Fleming arrived backstage at the Alvin, and pushed his way into her dressing room. The sixty-two-year-old director of *Dr. Jekyll and Mr. Hyde* had come to get Ingrid as star for his new film, to be produced independently by Walter Wanger. But as soon as he had seen Ingrid walk onto the stage he realized that his project was "junk," and that the woman he was seeing now was a far different Ingrid, a great actress, a great character. Fleming wanted to see *Joan of Lorraine* again and again.

The next day Ingrid, Fleming, and Steele had lunch at "21." Steele could tell that the aging director would do anything for Ingrid. The publicist suggested to Ingrid that Fleming direct a *Joan of Arc* produced by Walter Wanger.

Fleming became enormously excited by the project. He had had no major successes since *Gone With the Wind*. He was a near-alcoholic, a man who as he said later was "putting more trust in alcohol than in the Lord." A *Joan of Arc* was an extraordinary opportunity for him, an enormous film, a spectacle of war and peace, of blood and sacrifice, and at the center the noble simple peasant lass, his Ingrid. For Fleming, it would be more than a mere film. He had fallen irresistibly in love with Ingrid. *Joan of Arc* would be an offering to his love, to art, to ambition, to history. It would be his greatest film, *his* in the way *Gone With the Wind* had not been.

Ingrid had been attracted to Fleming once, but that was long ago, and she had gone on to other films, and other men. Listening to Fleming talk about *her* film rekindled the dead coals of infatuation. Ingrid had had affairs with directors before, but this relationship with Fleming went beyond that. They were partners in a great and noble project.

For Christmas, Petter sent Pia ahead of him, with her maid. One day Ingrid and Pia went walking with Claude Bernheim's mother. Suddenly, Pia ran ahead.

"Come back, Pia," Ingrid shouted.

Pia continued forging ahead.

"Pia, you shouldn't do that," Mrs. Bernheim gently scolded.

The child replied, "I hate to walk with my mother with all those people looking at her."

"It's not true that I didn't like to walk next to my mother," Pia says now. "It's that I was a small person, and it was difficult to be with her. I was shy in front of people staring at her. It made me feel conspicuous. I thought of her as my mother. I wanted not to be stared at. People always want to touch people who are well known. They put their hands on us. If you're smaller and you have to roll up the windows because they want to touch you, that's the thing that impressed."

A few days later Petter arrived. "A woman from the hotel came to me and said that Pia and the maid had been on a different floor until the day I arrived, the same day Fleming left," Petter recalls. "She said that Fleming had been in the room adjoining Ingrid's. I asked Ingrid, 'Why do you have two rooms?' She said, 'I can afford two rooms.'"

In those last days of the old year, Ingrid became sick. She lost her voice. Then her eye became swollen, and when that got better, she came down with a bad cold.

Petter left and Ingrid revived, but she still had complications beyond complications in her life. Capa was in Europe. He wrote Ingrid regularly, sometimes almost daily, letters drenched in alcohol and melancholy. He wrote her of the "850 bottles of wine" left over from the previous time that he did not "want to drink with anyone else."

From Paris he wrote that he would write her a "gay New Year letter" if she would only write him. On New Year's Eve he wrote again: "Pop, why is it so difficult to think, to write simply and say the things which cross my head in moments of . . . drunkenness." The next day he wrote her of his hangover. Then from Istanbul he complained that he could find no Champagne in Turkey and asked her to hurry and finish her film. . . . "*Please* listen to my voices."

Ingrid read Capa's letters and put them away. She talked to Petter regularly too. They chatted with the intimate camaraderie of a happily married couple. He advised her and took care of a myriad of little tasks. She told him of her plans to do *Joan of Arc* with Fleming and Wanger and asked him to extricate her from negotiations with Liberty Pictures.

Petter took on the burden. He wrote William Wyler, saying that Briskin had called the deal off because Ingrid wanted too much money. Petter concluded: "I would like to add that in no way is Ingrid responsible for the outcome of our negotiations."

"Lindstrom really was the patsy," said Wanger. "She was always going off half-cocked, making crazy financial commitments, and he was the one who had to extricate her. She had bum judgments, phony enthusiasm."

Fleming took a seventy-five-dollar-a-day suite at a reduced rate at the Hampshire House, and preparations began in earnest for *Joan of Arc*. Ingrid would be not merely a paid employee on the film but a partner in a production company that included Fleming and Wanger. Richard Day was named art director and joined the group at the hotel. Noel Howard, a young artist, was hired to go up to the medieval Cloisters in New York and make sketches.

A feeling of artistic fellowship and good times prevailed, aided by the director's heavy drinking. It wasn't all talk of *Joan of Arc* either. John Steinbeck visited Fleming's suite. So did Boyer, Remarque, and other friends and acquaintances. They talked and drank and gambled into the morning hours.

To set up the film, Fleming made regular trips back to Hollywood. Ingrid was upset by the endless business matters Fleming had to attend to, with "everyone trying to find out where and how to get the last dollar out of the picture." And yet Ingrid was one of those, negotiating a contract that paid her $175,000 plus 5 percent of the gross revenues once they equaled 2.6 times the negative costs.

Fleming could not stand being away from Ingrid for even a few days. Wherever he was—a compartment on the *Super Chief*, a studio office, a hotel room—he wrote Ingrid passionate letters, frightening in their intensity.

"Tears are just as wet and salty in my bed as in your own—and night is just as dark," he wrote, in mirthless reflection on their past affair. "For what I've lost is lost for ever. . . . I love you."

Soon Fleming was back at the Hampshire House. One evening Petter arrived unannounced on another visit. Ingrid was not in her suite and he waited in the hotel lobby. Early in the morning hours, Ingrid arrived from "21" on Fleming's arm and went upstairs.

Petter took the elevator to Ingrid's suite, but she was not there. He telephoned Fleming's suite. Ingrid said that she would be right down.

The next morning at around eight o'clock Fleming rang Steele's room, and told the publicist that the episode had been "damn embarrassing" and "pretty rough." That afternoon Petter came to see Steele, and didn't even mention the incident. He hurried off to catch a late-afternoon plane to Los Angeles.

There have been many cuckolded husbands too preoccupied or too vain to note the signs of their wives' affairs. Petter, however, had been confronted with the reality of Ingrid's relationship with Fleming. He had even seen the director's love letters in Ingrid's suite. But on one level he still refused to see and understand. He still hoped. It was an act of monumental will to hold in his anger and feelings of betrayal, and to return once again to the house on Benedict Canyon Drive, to live alone with Pia and the maid.

Ingrid was glad to see him go. He was a messenger bearing tidings that she did not want to acknowledge. Those days in New York, whenever he visited her she seemed to become sick, and when he left, the frenetic pace of her life picked up again. She appeared not to want Petter around, interrupting her career and her affairs.

As the last weeks of her run in *Joan of Lorraine* approached, Ingrid was full of a bewildering array of emotions. She felt that her performances weren't so good any longer. She could barely get to the theater each evening. As the most lauded actress in New York City, she was sought after for every benefit and gathering imaginable. She was tired, simply tired.

For her new film Ingrid had an array of responsibilities that she had never had before. Capa told her one thing. Someone else had other suggestions to make about the script. She didn't know whom to believe, what to do. Maxwell Anderson had been hired to write the movie script, but he couldn't catch on to Ingrid's simple Joan. Ingrid was exhausted. Too much drinking. Too much food. Too many late nights.

Ingrid would soon be home with Petter, who had written her that "the boy that made sure you had flowers at Oscar's Theater—he is still longing for you." She told Steele, "Petter is so lonesome." Yet as tired as she was, as much as Petter wanted her, as many weeks as it had been since she had seen Pia, she dreaded, as she wrote Ruth, that in three weeks she would "go back into the cage, sit in the sun, obey Petter and be sober and look eighteen years old."

That was the horror of it. The very things that Petter had to offer—and they were good things: love and concern and devotion and stability and family—she didn't want anymore, at least not from him, and perhaps she didn't want them at all. Fleming was working indefatigably on the project, but his love was a burden of time and emotion too. "Don't think for a moment I believe I can turn Victor round my little finger," Ingrid wrote Roberts, "but I'll try to talk like an angel, be strong like a god, and dangerous like the devil. Forward my friends. Now starts the battle for Joan!"

Fleming left the Hampshire House for the last time, to return to Hollywood and begin production of *Joan of Arc*. The *Super Chief* streaked westward, and Fleming wrote Ingrid that he couldn't sleep or eat. When he arrived at the station in Los Angeles, he was crying, saying, "There's no fool like an old fool."

Petter arrived in New York a few days before the final performance of *Joan of Lorraine*. Ingrid developed a cold serious enough to force cancellation of the last Wednesday matinee, but by Saturday, May 10, she was well. After the last matinee, about three hundred people were waiting outside the Alvin to see Ingrid emerge.

Ingrid had decided not to leave the theater for dinner. She asked if the throng might be allowed inside, so that she could address them. Ingrid's fans trooped in. As the word passed along Broadway, more and more people came, filling the orchestra. Ingrid stood onstage in a wine-colored dressing gown, thanking her fans.

In the evening, the formally dressed audience was far different from the motley fans who had crowded into the theater a few hours before. For the final curtain, fifteen or so of her most fervent fans entered the theater and trooped down the center aisle. One of them, thirteen-year-old Frank Edwards, worked part-time in a florist's in the Bronx. He had brought an armful of daffodils, and as Ingrid stood before the curtain in Joan's simple robe, Frank and his friends threw the flowers at her feet.

The next day Ingrid and Petter flew to Los Angeles. At the airport Petter pushed aside the fans who had come to say goodbye to Ingrid. As the skyscrapers of Manhattan disappeared into the haze, Petter sat reading *Time* magazine. Beside him, Ingrid put her head on his shoulder and closed her eyes.

Ingrid had had great roles before, but never had she starred in a film in which she was so much the center as *Joan of Arc*. Never had she spent so long on one project. Although she began work on the movie as soon as she got back to Los Angeles, *Joan of Arc* didn't begin filming until September 17, 1948, continuing for ninety-two shooting days, with major filming completed by Christmas.

The Joan of Arc that Ingrid wanted to portray was not the historic figure playing out her life in the blood-drenched, morally ambiguous world of fifteenth-century Europe. It was not a Joan who made of humility a circular virtue, carrying it to the point where it became high arrogance. Ingrid wanted to play the mythic Joan, the Joan of her school chapbook. Her challenge was to embody that spiritual miracle, to make Joan's sainthood believable, to make the audience feel that they, too, were burning, that innocence and goodness were burning.

Ingrid was *serious* about playing Joan of Arc, and everyone in Hollywood knew it. Charades were all the rage at Hollywood parties in the early postwar years. At one gathering, the guests agreed that they would have Ingrid act out Joan of Arc and pretend not to understand whom she was playing. Ingrid opened the slip of paper. She got down on her knees and began praying. She led imaginary armies against the battlements of Orléans. She grimaced as if she were burning at the stake. No matter what she did, all that greeted her were blank, bewildered stares. Finally, when she had tried everything except setting herself on fire, she was told of the joke. Everyone laughed, everyone but Ingrid.

On *Joan of Arc* Ingrid was not only the star but a partner in the film company, the director's lover, and the screenwriter's favorite actress. She insisted that it be *her* Joan on the screen. Ingrid loved the business of filming, the life within a life that was a movie. In preparing the film, everyone involved spread money on the project like children spreading jelly on crusts of bread. The company set up business at the old Hal Roach studios in Culver City. Ingrid's four-room bungalow was refurbished into a modern suite and dressing room at a cost of $5,000. Ingrid felt at home. "That little studio was full of friendship," Ingrid remembered of her months doing *Joan of Arc*. "We worked together, and when the work was over, we laughed together. I was very hungry for laughter in those days."

Ingrid was possessed of special cunning in her relationship with Petter. He never knew for sure about Adler, Capa, or Fleming, in part because Ingrid gave no better performance than when she and Petter met one of her lovers socially.

"Ingrid was supposed to go up to San Francisco for some kind of promotion and she wanted me to come with her and afterwards to Honolulu," Adler says. "This was the only time my analyst took an active part. He said, As long as you're a patient and still married, I think it would be disastrous for you to do something as dramatic as that. I don't know whether he was right or not, but considering that the romance with Capa was in full bloom at the time, I could never figure it out: why would she do that?"

Ingrid's contradictions and moral complexities remained unexamined, as did her failing marriage with Petter. Neither of them wanted a confrontation. Ingrid's way was always to avoid the unpleasant, to turn her face away from emotional ugliness, to go on, to forget. As for Petter, that man of strong, almost rigid principle and high moral standards, it was unthinkable that he would be married to an adulterous woman, a woman whom he still loved.

Now that Ingrid was no longer a Selznick star, many people thought that Petter was the man to see if you wanted to sign Ingrid Bergman. One of those who sought Petter out was Howard Hughes. Hughes had taken more than a casual fancy to Ingrid. At Steele's urging, she had set up a meeting with Hughes at her bungalow. Shortly before the four o'clock meeting, Ingrid told Steele that Petter insisted she cancel the appointment.

Hughes told Ingrid that he would make her the great star of RKO Pictures, his newest acquisition. He wanted to take her on a three-month "promotional" tour of South America. Ingrid told Petter that Steele was behind the idea and would be the chaperon. Petter says that Steele told him years later that he had had nothing to do with the proposed trip.

"Ingrid wanted to go," Petter remembers. "Five times Hughes came out to see me, driving his worn-out little Dodge car. He always checked that nobody was in the house. I enjoyed talking to this very strange man. He was trying to buy me. He offered me some money if I cooperated. He couldn't understand me, why I gave him a flat no."

Everything possible had been done in preparing the $4.6 million *Joan of Arc*. Researchers had documented the smallest detail for historical accuracy. When the king drank wine, a servant would hold a saucer under his chin, as it had been done in the European courts. The music he listened to would be authentic fifteenth-century music played on instruments copied from museum originals. Draft horses were brought from Iowa and trained by cowboys wearing armor. A craftsman prepared Ingrid's armor of exquisitely wrought, lightweight aluminum, shining silver bright.

Everything was ready. Everything was right. Everything except the story.

There is nothing in art quite so complicated as simplicity. There is nothing more difficult to portray on film than the spiritual. Fleming was the least spiritual of directors. When he had begun work on *Gone With the Wind* he had told Selznick, "David, your fucking script is no fucking good." This time the original script was no good either, but Fleming didn't know what to do about it, and he didn't have a Selznick to work out the problems. There was a sheer silliness about part of the script. That was true even in the final version. In one scene the Dauphin greets the saintly peasant maid with the immortal line: "My dear Joan, you look radiant."

Fleming spent hours in his office trying to figure the film out. Time and time again he screened *Gone With the Wind*, as if there he would find some guidance. He complained that the problem was that everyone knew the ending of this film. He sat in his office late at night with a bottle of Scotch, muttering, "She's a girl. Her parents were poor."

Fleming tried anything to get a hold on the picture. One evening the director, Ingrid, and Laurence Stallings sat watching *Great Expectations*. In the film, a small boy is shown walking up a staircase and along the hall of an English mansion. Ingrid and Fleming knew how the scene helped set the whole tone for the film. They knew, too, that the shot had required a crane and was very expensive. Stallings compared it to the famous scene on Rhett Butler's stairway in *Gone With the Wind*.

"But the cost," Ingrid interjected, no longer simply an actress but a co-producer, a financial partner. "Think of the cost."

"Vic Fleming wore himself out on the picture," Ingrid said years later. "I think the pressures got to [him]. He was so anxious to make this a great success because he knew I was in love with Joan and her story."

Unable to get a hold on the story, Fleming poured his energy into the sheer spectacle of the film. There was no burning of Atlanta in *Joan of Arc*, but there was the battle of Orléans, a dinner at the palace of the Dauphin, the coronation, and the burning of Joan. So much money had already been spent, however, that the great battle scene had to be filmed on a sound stage.

Sierra Films had taken what was then considered to be the largest bank loan ever on a film, $3,500,000. Nonetheless, to complete the film Fleming deferred payment on $120,000 of his $175,000 salary. Wanger not only deferred payment on his entire $50,000 salary but invested an additional $100,000. Ingrid, whose idea the film had been, took her full $175,000 salary. She did, however, defer about $70,000 in overtime payments.

Fleming wanted Ingrid to be the radiant center of the film. In her aluminum armor she shone in the arc lights like a silvered prism. At thirty-two, she was almost twice as old as Joan, and at times she looked almost Amazonian, but Fleming was consumed with making her performance shine as brightly as her armor.

For the battle scene at Orléans, Fleming wanted Ingrid to raise her arm and, holding her sword high, lead the charge against the French. Alas, it was impossible in fifteenth-century armor—or even a lightweight replica—to raise an arm above one's head. Fleming was so upset that, in Howard's words, he went "berserk." The armor was modified with rubber so that Ingrid could do the scene the way Fleming insisted it be done. The director watched over the tiniest detail. He helped Ingrid to adjust her armor, and daubed her countenance with mineral oil, to resemble perspiration.

"I remember that in one scene Ingrid had to be out of breath," recalls José Ferrer, who played the Dauphin. "And she started running, and running. For a stage actor that was funny."

Despite the high-minded aspirations, at some moments Ingrid seemed to be playing not *Joan of Arc* but the tin man in *The Wizard of Oz*. She spent hours resting against a tilted board in full armor. A special-effects crew of four or five men was devoted to her armor. When she signaled, they would oil her joints, or help lift her onto her worthy steed.

The horse was another problem. Ingrid had had directors and co-stars attracted to her, but this was the first time she had to deal with an infatuated horse. Whenever the horse saw Ingrid, he greeted her with an enormous erection. For their big scene together, the horse was sedated with tranquilizers and Ingrid got up on a wooden platform and attempted to mount. The horse started walking away. As Ingrid fell to earth Howard caught her, one hand around her shoulder, the other hand firmly grasping her crotch. The photographer who caught this unsaintly scene had his film confiscated and destroyed.

While Fleming watched *Gone With the Wind* in his office, Ingrid screened Carl Dreyer's 1927 *Joan of Arc* in her office. The silent film classic dealt with the trial and burning. Watching it, Ingrid sought new inspiration. She had little sense that things were not going right, and adored every moment of the filming. She asked friends and colleagues to come onto the set to see her as Joan. She invited Pia once as well. She had scores of pictures taken for her own use.

"Every actress wants to play Joan of Arc," says Ferrer. "Actors identify with a noble character and they feel they have a real deep handle on it. Their professional lives are full of corruption, and yet they're idealized beyond their contribution. I think that Ingrid began to believe her own mythology. She was a strange woman."

The greatest moment in *Joan of Arc*, and what boded to be the most transcendent moment of Ingrid's film career thus far, was Joan's burning at the stake. The crew referred to the scene as "the barbecue," but Ingrid was not so irreverent. Indeed, for Christmas she distributed, to crew members and helpers, replicas of the simple robes that Joan wore for the burning, a gift that the recipients found extremely bizarre.

On the day of the burning, the set was full of spectators. Ingrid stood on the pile of fagots, tied to the stake. Soon she was led down, and a double took her place. Ingrid took her own photographs of the spectacular scene as the stand-in stood on the burning pyre. As the flames leaped upward, the double left, to be replaced by a dummy. Within minutes the flames had engulfed the stake, and there was nothing left but fire and smoke, and an actor dressed as a priest holding a cross above the inferno.

Soon after Ingrid finished filming *Joan of Arc*, she and Petter went off skiing to Mount Rose and Heavenly Valley ski resorts near Reno, Nevada. Always before, vacations were Petter's time, days of skiing and outdoor activity. Maybe there would be stars and Hollywood people around, but it was still a good time for Petter. But now Ingrid seemed not to want to be alone with her husband. Addicted to the attention and energy of a star's life, she lived ever more on edge, gambling with her saintly image, gambling with what was left of her marriage, gambling with personal scandal.

Nothing dramatized this as much as the fact that Capa had traveled to the resort to be with Ingrid. What act of will did it take for Petter to pretend that Ingrid was still his loyal and loving wife? What could she think of this man, her husband, to taunt him with her infidelity? Or did she want Petter to confront her? Did she hope that now he would make the final break? Did she want Petter to act as she could not act? Or did she not know what she wanted Petter to do?

There was still a childish quality to Petter that was one of the most endearing things about him. He was proud of his physical prowess, and when Capa offered to teach him to ski, Petter found the proposal amusing, a foolhardy attempt at ingratiation. Capa fancied himself quite the skier, but when they got on the slopes it was clear that Petter could have given master classes to the photographer. Petter took his skiing seriously, and he was a joy to watch, schussing down the powdery slopes, cutting back and forth with geometric precision.

Ingrid wasn't watching. She had twisted her ankle and spent her time in the lodge, much of it with Capa. Petter fancied himself a rational man, a man of science, and he knew that he was better than Capa, a better skier, a more disciplined man. While Ingrid stayed in the lodge, Petter skied and skied some more.

One evening Capa went down to the casino to gamble. The photographer gambled the way he did everything else, as if he were waging his life itself, risking everything on the toss of the dice or the turn of a wheel. It was his night, and after a while Capa brought his chips up to show Ingrid, as if the chips symbolized the photographer's luck in life and love.

Later, Petter went down to the gaming room. Petter knew the odds, and he was not a gambler. He watched Capa and saw the photographer's luck change. Petter took no pleasure in watching a man throwing his money or his life away. He went upstairs to tell Ingrid what was happening: "He's just going mad down there."

"Well, that's the way gambling is," Ingrid said. "You win some and you lose some."

Petter went back to the casino, but he couldn't stand watching Capa. "Capa is just foolish," Petter told Ingrid. "The money he's losing! Someone really should stop him."

"All right. I'll go down and see what I can do."

Ingrid hobbled down to the gaming tables, but she could not stop him. He intended to stand there until he had either won back or lost his entire two thousand dollars in savings.

The next morning Ingrid saw Capa. One look at his face and she knew he had lost everything. "What difference does it make?" he said. "It's very good for me. Now I have to work harder."

"Capa was gambling and wanted her to be there," Petter remembers. "During that ski trip I saw them staying up and drinking together. I went skiing and they went together. Then just one day to the next I said we're going to go home, we're not going to stay here."

Ingrid said later that if Capa had asked to marry her, she probably would have assented. But Capa didn't ask, in part probably because, in Adler's words, "Bob Capa couldn't take being Mr. Ingrid Bergman."

Running off with Capa was a notion better to contemplate than to act upon. Capa was a marvelous man with whom to spend a few evenings, an interlude. His constant wanderings, his drinking, his gambling, all were wonderfully romantic, if one didn't have to clean up after his life. Ingrid had seen how Capa didn't care about money, passing out his last dollar to a friend, blowing a check on an evening, nonchalantly gambling away his savings. She had seen him laughing and gay on evenings that lasted till dawn, but she had seen him, too, in the cold dawn of hangovers, nicotine-stained fingers, and empty accounts. Despite her own wanderings, her ceaseless affairs, Ingrid demanded a certain order and discipline in her life. If she had ever run off with Capa, the results almost certainly would have been disastrous.

Soon after the ski trip, one of the most extraordinary evenings in their married life took place, according to Petter. "Both Adler and Capa had come to the house before, but rarely together," Petter recalls. "When one was there, the other wasn't. Both were friendly with me. Capa had wanted to teach me to ski. Adler gave me a harmonica.

"Then each one came to tell me about his affair with Ingrid and to complain about the affair the other one was having. They were sure that I knew about it. It was obvious to me that they thought I had a kind of marriage where that sort of thing was acceptable. They said it can't go on like this. It was as if they wanted me to select between them.

"Ingrid admitted it. I told her that I was going to get a divorce. I said get the hell out of my house, though I didn't have a right to say that. Then she started to put on a show and started to cry. She said I was the only one she loved. She put on such a show the next weeks that I gradually believed her. I dropped the idea."

Ingrid never talked about this incident, but she was what might charitably be called reticent in talking about her love affairs. "The part was not easy," Ingrid wrote years later of her relationship with Capa, "not easy at all, because I was so moral, so prudish you might say." She would admit to one affair during her married life, but not to more, and not, certainly, to two or three at a time.

Larry Adler, however, who is anything but a man of reticence, asserts that he never talked to Petter about Capa. "I would not have betrayed in any way," Adler says. He points out that in 1949, at the beginning of the blacklist period, he left the United States instead of betraying political friends. He does say, however, that his relationship with Ingrid continued at a diminished pace until he left for Europe.

Petter remains just as strong in his recollections. It seems impossible to know absolutely what happened in the house in Benedict Canyon. But soon after the time that Petter says Ingrid promised to reform, she wrote a letter to Ruth Roberts: "I know the Hungarian influence. I'll always be grateful for it. . . . We are drinking our last bottles of champagne. I am tearing a very dear piece away from my life, but we are learning and also making a clean operation so that both patients will live happily ever after."

CHAPTER TWELVE

"Ti Amo"

*I*ngrid loved to tell the story of the evening in the spring of 1948 when she and Petter went to a theater on La Cienega Boulevard in Los Angeles to see Roberto Rossellini's *Open City*. When Hollywood made movies about Nazism, they were usually like *Casablanca*: romantic adventures. This was different. The searing documentary-like film told the story of a group of Romans in the last days of the Nazi occupation. To Ingrid, "the realism and simplicity . . . was heart-shocking. There was darkness and shadows, and sometimes you couldn't hear, and sometimes you couldn't even see it." This neorealistic Italian film was a lens opened upon life itself. As Ingrid left the theater, she remembered telling her husband: "Petter, we must get this director's name straight. If there is such a man who can put *this* on the screen, he must be an absolutely heavenly human being!"

A few months later Ingrid was in New York to do a radio program. "And I was walking on Broadway and suddenly—suddenly—I saw that name Rossellini outside a cinema again: some tiny cinema on Broadway. A film called *Paisan*. I went in alone, and I sat there once more riveted to my seat."

"I want to write him," she says that she told Irene Selznick that evening. "I've had ten years of doing the same kind of beautiful, romantic movies. Now I want to do something realistic. I want to do something like *Paisan*." According to Ingrid, her friend's first reaction was to tell her that Rossellini would "misunderstand," but that perhaps Ingrid was "the only one who can write the sort of letter which will *not* be misunderstood."

And so Ingrid wrote a short, simple note to Rossellini. And many lives were changed.

Ingrid's story of first seeing Rossellini's films is a scene out of a romantic novel, the great star mesmerized by the art of a great director, while her husband sits beside her. In her account of writing to Rossellini, there is all the purity of impulsiveness. She has acted with noble intent, on her own, not for sordid careerism but for the nobility of art.

The truth, however, is far more complicated. Ingrid did not see *Open City* in the spring of 1948 with Petter. The film was not even showing in Los Angeles then. She saw it two years before, when it opened in the United States at the World Theater on Forty-ninth Street in New York. She saw it that spring of 1946 not with Petter but with Steele. Ingrid was impressed with *Open City*, but she did not think about the film until two years later when she saw *Paisan* in New York, and was worried about her career.

It was not Ingrid but Irene Selznick who suggested that she write to the Italian director. Indeed, Irene says that Rossellini was only one of five directors whose work intrigued Ingrid. "She told me she didn't care about money," Irene Selznick remembers. "She wanted opportunity. She was prepared to take a real cut for the chance to work with any one of five directors; she named William Wyler, Billy Wilder, George Stevens, Roberto Rossellini, and I believe, John Huston. She wondered what to do about it. I came up with a plan that was as simple and direct as Ingrid herself. The thing to do was to write each one, in her own charming style, asking him to bear her in mind in case the right story came along."

In some ways it was extraordinary that Ingrid should have even considered seeking work. Her three films released in 1946 had grossed $17,500,000, an enormous sum, as much as that grossed by some studios in a year, and she had been the number one female star in America, the biggest box office draw of them all. However, no Ingrid Bergman films had been released for over a year, and there were rumors that the forthcoming *Arch of Triumph* was a disaster.

Ingrid had plenty of offers, nonetheless, and she could have contacted the American directors by picking up the phone. As for Rossellini, the letter itself may have seemed like one of the madly impulsive gestures of which she was capable. But it was equally the result of calculation and forethought, a scheme generated by Irene Selznick, who understood Ingrid very well.

Ingrid wrote: "If you need a Swedish actress . . . who, in Italian knows only 'ti amo' I am ready to come and make a film with you."

By writing "ti amo"—I love you—Ingrid was not trying to entice Rossellini into thinking that his rewards from employing her would be more than professional. Ingrid had learned the two Italian words from her role in *Arch of Triumph*; the year before, she had even signed a letter to Lewis Milestone "ti amo."

Ingrid mailed the Rossellini letter to Minerva Films in Rome. It was found when the studio was burning old correspondence. Mr. Potsius of Minerva Films, the very man who had bought the rights to *Open City* for a pittance, opened Ingrid's letter by mistake, and made the not astounding deduction that Roberto was being handed a "beautiful present." According to Ingrid, when Roberto read the letter, he remembered that he had first seen Ingrid in the American *Intermezzo* three times during a bombing raid.

And so on May 8, Roberto's birthday, he cabled Ingrid:

I JUST RECEIVED WITH GREAT EMOTION YOUR LETTER WHICH HAP-
PENS TO ARRIVE ON THE ANNIVERSARY OF MY BIRTHDAY AS THE MOST
PRECIOUS GIFT. IT IS ABSOLUTELY TRUE THAT I DREAMED TO MAKE A
FILM WITH YOU. . . .

Rossellini promised to send her a long letter, with his ideas for a movie
spelled out in detail.

Rossellini's telegram was the opening aria in his relationship to Ingrid.
Roberto conceived life as an opera, of which he was the composer and con-
ductor. He did not let the discordances and banalities of facts distort the grand
themes of his life.

Roberto had in fact received Ingrid's letter not with "great emotion" but
with the zeal of an entrepreneur on to a good thing. He hadn't considered the
letter "the most precious gift." It was not "absolutely true" that he had been
dreaming of making a film with Ingrid. It was absolutely not true.

Oh, it was romantic to think of Roberto watching *Intermezzo* three times
during what must have been one of the longest air raids in history. It was not
so romantic to think that his sister Marcella was the one who had first
mentioned Ingrid's name, after seeing *The Bells of St. Mary's.* As Marcella
remembers it, Roberto had shrugged his shoulders and said, Who cares?

Roberto was the least punctual of men, but soon after his telegram, a letter
came. Roberto told Ingrid that he had been journeying by car north of Rome
when he saw a high barbed-wire fence enclosing a field full of refugee women
"turning round just like mild lambs in a pasture." Roberto stopped his car,
and although the guards called him off, he walked up to the fence. There he
saw a Latvian woman who grabbed his arm "just like a ship-wrecked person
would clutch at a floating board." Haunted by the woman's image, Roberto
returned to the camp, to find that she had run off with a soldier.

"Shall we go together and look for her?" Rossellini asked rhetorically.
"Shall we together visualize her life in the little village near Stromboli, where
the soldier took her? . . . I feel, that with you near me, I could give life to a
human creature who, following hard and bitter experiences, finds peace at last
and complete freedom from all selfishness. That being the only true happiness
which has ever been conceded to mankind, making life more simple and
nearer to creation."

Ingrid had never received a film idea anything like this. Roberto was not
asking Ingrid to come to Europe to make something so banal as a movie. He
was asking her to join him in a glorious journey. He was inviting her to share
with him in an artistic quest. Ingrid was full of ideas about her roles, but always
before she had had to insinuate her ideas, to push and struggle with her

various directors. Now from the outset she would be a partner in the making of a noble film.

Ingrid may have been a woman of instant enthusiasms, but she did not in a moment see Roberto as an antidote for all that was wrong with her life in Hollywood. She saw promise in the project, though. She knew that she needed to do something new, something dramatic. After all, she was thirty-two years old, an age when an actress knows that her days as a young romantic lead are numbered. She was on her own now, without the security and judgment and public relations savvy that Selznick and his organization had provided. She had made her first two independent films, and she was aware that they were both potential failures. She was flattered by Roberto's long letter, struck by his passionate commitment to art.

Ingrid would have been less enthusiastic about Roberto, and perhaps would never have made a film with him, if she had known what he was up to in Rome. For when Roberto was sending his impassioned letter to Ingrid, he was professionally courting Jennifer Jones, Selznick's lover and soon-to-be wife, and Ingrid's rival for the part of Joan of Arc. Indeed, Roberto was supposed to be signing a contract with Selznick, with whom Ingrid was hardly speaking.

The very week that Roberto received his letter from Ingrid, he had dinner with Jenia Reissar to discuss his contract with Selznick. He pulled out the letter from Ingrid, and asked the woman who had discovered Ingrid for Selznick to translate it into French. "From the time I read the letter, the whole dinner was spent talking and asking about Ingrid Bergman," recalls Reissar. "He knew about her. He was like a child with it. He kept asking questions about it. He kept taking the letter out."

It never occurred to Reissar that Roberto already knew the contents of the letter, and was using Ingrid's note as a negotiating ploy.

As Roberto was penning his effusive reply to Ingrid, he also was writing one to Selznick about Jennifer Jones. He said that he was particularly thrilled with the prospect of making a film with Jones. This time the master was once again driving through northern Italy, among the Lombardy lakes. "I was thinking about Miss Jones, and I immediately felt it to be the ideal setting for her character and qualities."

Roberto sketched a story of an unhealthy, selfish American businessman and his wife. Jones would be "a symbol of redeeming love . . . the message that all are waiting for."

Selznick was all for making Jennifer Jones the symbol of "redeeming love." He thought that he had a contract with Rossellini and that Jennifer would make the film during the year, and possibly make two films. Rossellini kept changing conditions, though, and Selznick was afraid that he would lose him. "This danger is aggravated by the fact that Ingrid Bergman and others who are after Rossellini may talk him into changing his mind," Selznick wrote Reissar. "However, Bergman knows that Rossellini is tied exclusively to us."

Ingrid did not know that Rossellini was tied exclusively to Selznick, for he was not. She did know now that she had competition for Rossellini's services from her former employer.

Ingrid had even greater interest in working with Rossellini after *Arch of Triumph* proved a commercial calamity. The four-million-dollar film lost most of its money, reputedly the largest loss in Hollywood history. The film was not the noble beginning but the ignominious end of Enterprise Pictures. Ingrid was to have shared in 25 percent of the profits of the film, and she felt this failure as she had never felt one before. And the reviews had a tenor that she had never experienced. "How that role cried for Dietrich and the quality she would have brought to it!" wrote one critic—an odious comparison for a star of Ingrid's stature. "Too much of a good thing—even of Bergman and Boyer —is too much," wrote Bosley Crowther in the *New York Times*.

Ingrid had little time to contemplate her losses. In June she flew to England to make a film directed by Alfred Hitchcock, produced by Sidney Bernstein for their new Transatlantic Pictures. "Ingrid was upset that Hitchcock was getting 30 percent of the profits and she was getting only 25 percent," Petter remembers. "She said, 'I have a bigger name than his. You must go and tell them and say what you want.' I went to Bernstein. He said he'd talk to Hitchcock. He came back and said they'd both have 30 percent."

The production costs were so large that the fledgling company had to borrow $2.5 million to make the film. For her third time in a row, Ingrid was starring in an expensive film produced by a new company, with a director who was infatuated with her.

Hitchcock had chosen a project that was not a natural for him, but one that he thought would appeal to her. In *Under Capricorn* Ingrid would play the withdrawn, tragic figure of Lady Henrietta Considine, an alcoholic English lady married to the baseborn Sam Flusky, played by Joseph Cotten.

Ingrid saw the film as a chance to get away from the enclosed sound stages and routines of Hollywood. "Now look, it's set in Australia," Ingrid told Hitchcock. "Let's go to Australia and do it there."

London was not Australia, but Ingrid had freedom to do as she pleased. During her first weeks in London, Ingrid wrote letters to friends in the States about visiting nightclubs and having a great time. Despite avowals to Petter, one of those Ingrid saw in London as well as in Paris for weekends was Capa. Their affair had decidedly cooled, but Ingrid still enjoyed Capa's company and being near what she called his "gay gypsy shoulders." Ingrid was not about to sit around. She was restless and high-strung, and seemed not to know what she wanted. She might laugh and joke with Capa, or sit in a nightclub with other friends, but then she would go back to the hotel and write a letter to Petter. She said later that her marriage was already dead, but there was still part of her that needed and wanted Petter, as long as she could manipulate him to be what she needed him to be.

Ingrid wrote Petter, asking him to write her every day. Petter himself suggested afterward that his love for Ingrid was dying, but here he was writing so often to her that in two days she received five letters from Petter and three from Pia. He sent her packages of food and tea as well.

"What a wonderful family," Ingrid wrote Petter on the evening of July 19, after the first day of shooting. She thanked him for sending pictures, asked for more, and then discussed Petter and Pia's trip to England. She wanted him to come by ship so that Pia would experience a transatlantic crossing. "You don't have to bother with her. You can find some little girl, like Mrs. Lindstrom 10 years ago on her trip back. You can dance and read."

Petter, with his doubts about his marriage, still had faith in marriage, and he prepared for his European trip with anticipation.

In getting away from the stifling world of the Hollywood studios, Ingrid discovered that she had given up more than she had intended. The crew was unbelievably slow.

Then there was the problem with Hitchcock. The director had decided to experiment with long takes, some of them six or eight minutes in duration. To Ingrid it was a child's game, like running with an egg in a spoon, a game the audience didn't care about or understand.

Given the way *Under Capricorn* was proceeding, it might have seemed that Ingrid would have been counting the days until Petter and Pia arrived. She was counting the days, but with mounting dread. She had gained weight. She was smoking one cigarette after another. "I'm going to be in trouble," she wrote Ruth. "I smoke all the time. I drink more than ever. I have put on at least 10 pounds." She added ironically: "I am just ready for Petter!"

Ingrid continued working on *Under Capricorn*, but more than anything she was looking forward to seeing Rossellini. To arrange their meeting in Paris, she sent a telegram to Amalfi near Naples, where the director was working on *The Machine That Kills Bad People*.

Roberto was known as not only a great filmmaker but a great lover. No casting director, not even the most fervent believer in neorealism, would ever have chosen Roberto for such a role. Here was this plump Italian burgher with tiny feet and hands, narrow mouth, beaked nose, and thinning black hair, smelling of perfume and talc. And to some women he was a man of almost infinite seductiveness, enveloping them in such attention, such romantic fantasy, such drama, that for a while they forgot everything.

"He creates a dream atmosphere about him," said his sometime friend and collaborator, Sergio Amidei. "The women around him live in a dream world. He is very tender but at the same time can be brutal and vulgar. He is the true man of today. The rest of us are silly romanticists with foolish notions about how gently women should be treated."

In his attitude toward women, Roberto was not unlike many Roman gentlemen of his time, only he was more successful. And as was true of many of his compatriots, his charms were not nearly as appreciated by women of his own class and country as by foreigners. In the past decade Roberto had had affairs with women of several nationalities.

The life of "the true man of today" was in constant turmoil. He had so many women in his life that he was like a short-order cook with a dozen differing orders frying and steaming away. There was Marcella de Marchis, his wife, the mother of his young son, Renzo; she was a compassionate, rather simple woman, of good blood and infinite understanding. He had left her years before, but they remained good friends, and he kept Marcella on a back burner, bubbling peacefully along, to be stirred only occasionally. Then there was Miss America of 1946, whom he met on one of his jaunts to Paris and brought back to Amalfi, where he wrote her into the movie. She was a choice delicacy, to be eaten and forgotten. There were other dishes as well, and Roberto was not beyond some steak tartare from the bordello. But sitting in the middle of Roberto's stove was an enormous boiling caldron: Anna Magnani.

Anna and Ingrid were as different as sun from earth, and steam from snow. When men fell in love with Ingrid, they fell in love with her beauty, with her apparent neediness, her vulnerability. No one fell in love with Anna for her beauty; she had a face as variegated as Italy. Nor did anyone fall in love with Anna wanting to protect her.

Anna and Roberto had a relationship that the late Father Antonio Lisandrini, their close friend, calls "a phenomenon of nature, incredible in love and anger." Anna tried to seal off Roberto from other women, but it was futile, like trying to close off the Mexican border.

One day Roberto and Anna were sitting in an outdoor café in Amalfi with Bill Tubbs, an American actor, and his wife, Helen. Near them sat a young Italian beauty in a bare midriff. The woman had aspirations to a movie career, or at least to a matinee performance with the master himself. In her hand she held a glass with a frothy pink concoction that she was using not to quell her thirst but to increase Roberto's. She stroked the glass, running her fingers up and down, occasionally glancing over at the director. Anna tried to ignore this, but suddenly she exploded with the wrath of Vesuvius. "I was a whore before you were born," she screamed, a statement with which no one saw fit to quarrel, and that effectively quashed the performance at the next table.

Long before, Roberto had learned that he must go to extraordinary lengths to avoid Anna's jealousy. He was worried that Anna would learn about Ingrid and the fact that he was suggesting for her a film he had originally intended for Anna.

At the Albergo Luna Convento in Amalfi, where Roberto and Anna were staying, Roberto had given orders that foreign mail should be delivered to him discreetly. The head porter considered Anna to be practically family. He brought Ingrid's telegram to their luncheon table.

If Anna was one of the greatest actresses in the world, at that moment Roberto was trying to be the greatest actor. With a languid, disinterested air, he stuffed the unopened telegram in his pocket. Anna continued mixing a plate of spaghetti.

"Is this all right—eh, Roberto?" Anna said as she swirled the spaghetti in the bowl. It was terrifying to know a person the way Anna knew Roberto. She could smell the truth. She could see their future together, their lack of future, written on his face.

"Ah, yes, yes," Roberto said.

"Good."

Anna picked up the serving bowl and threw the spaghetti in Roberto's face.

If more of Robert's machinations had been known, Anna might not have been the only one to want to crown him with spaghetti. At the same time that Roberto was setting up his meeting with Ingrid, he was cabling Jennifer Jones, whose film *Duel in the Sun* had recently been released, congratulating her for her "wonderful performance" and hoping to do a film with her in the near future.

Selznick didn't know what to make of the cable. He thought his negotiations with Roberto had fallen apart for good, and now this cable had arrived. Selznick was still ready to go ahead, though, and Roberto agreed to meet Reissar in Paris between September 23 and 27 to sign the contract.

On Thursday, September 23, Selznick's representative called the Hotel Raphaël, to be told that Rossellini had already departed, leaving no address. Reissar called again on Friday, but there was still no message. "Personally, I don't believe any penalties, however severe, would make any difference to Rossellini," Reissar wrote Selznick. "He is temperamental and irresponsible."

While Reissar fumed in London, Rossellini was preparing for his Sunday meeting with Ingrid at the Georges V Hotel. Ingrid was met by the director; Rudolph Solmsen, a producer and his European representative; and Ilya Lopert, a foreign film distributor in the United States.

Roberto kissed Ingrid's hand. "We were introduced and Petter said something to me, and I didn't hear him," Ingrid remembered. "I was looking at those dark eyes of Roberto's. . . . He was very shy, and he didn't look like a movie man—not the sort I was used to anyway."

Roberto talked about the film he and Ingrid would make together. He didn't care what language she spoke in the film, or what clothes she wore. None of that mattered, only the searing reality of the story, of the art they would create together. Ingrid listened to this story of love on the barren island of Stromboli, and it was as if he were presenting her with a great treasure, a golden work of art.

Petter has no memories of meeting Rossellini in Paris, only of sitting with three Italians who chatted with Ingrid while he listened. In a 1952 interview

Ingrid and Roberto said that Petter had not, in fact, been present for the initial meeting, but joined the group later. No contract was signed that day, but it was agreed to go ahead once Roberto sent Ingrid a full synopsis of the story. Back in Rome, Roberto could not restrain himself from commenting on his impressions of Petter. "Swedish women are the easiest in the world to impress because they have such cold husbands," he said. "The love they get is an analgesic balm instead of a tonic."

In November, Ingrid finally received a letter from Rossellini. The story he outlined promised her anything but an analgesic balm. "I am sure you will find many parts of the story quite rugged, and that your personality will be hurt and offended by some reactions of the personage," Roberto said, as if Ingrid had lived her life in a nunnery. "But I can't deny in the deepness of my soul there is a secret envy for those who love so passionately, so wildly, as to forget any tenderness, any pity for their beloved ones. They are guided only by a deep desire of possession of the body and soul of the woman they love. Civilization has smoothed the strength of feelings; undoubtedly it's more comfortable to reach the top of a mountain by funicular, but perhaps the joy was greater when men climbed dangerously to the top."

Roberto didn't have a script or even a detailed story for her. He didn't work that way. He was infusing into Ingrid's film life a whole new level of danger, of risk. For years, she had sought danger in her personal life, risking exposure and betrayal of her saintly image. She had fled the security and sanctity of her home, of Petter and Pia, of routine and order, of her earthbound soul. Reading Roberto's letter, Ingrid wanted more than ever to make their film on Stromboli. Before she signed any contract, however, she would have to wait until early in 1949, when Roberto was coming to California.

Ingrid had another reason for being excited about making a film with Roberto. The same month that his letter arrived, *Joan of Arc* was opening in New York City. No role had meant more to her than this one. No film ever monitored by George Gallup's polls had ever been so anticipated. Three hundred thousand dollars had been spent on comics and magazine advertising alone. There was a paperback book in drugstores, with Ingrid's picture on the cover. She was on the cover of *Life* in armor, riding a horse. High above Times Square stood an eight-story-high figure of Ingrid in white plastic armor, which had cost $75,000. A few blocks north, the Victoria Theater had been remodeled, the walls sheathed in aluminum mail.

The premiere was a glorious evening, but Ingrid had never received such mixed reviews. Some critics ridiculed her whole persona, the glorious image that had taken a decade to grow to its present eminence. "Possibly Ingrid Bergman may be partly held to blame for this lack of the deeper human feelings and comprehensions in this film," wrote Bosley Crowther in the *New York Times*, "for Miss Bergman, while handsome to look on, has no great spiritual quality." Wrote C. A. Lejune in London's *The Observer*: "Miss

Bergman, in fact, makes an important principal boy, and Hollywood's Joan of Arc . . . is a triumph of matter over mind and spirit."

Joan of Arc was a disaster of the magnitude of *Arch of Triumph*. The film took in only a little over two million dollars. Nothing was left of Sierra Films except endless legal squabbles. Fleming was suddenly an old man. On January 6, 1949, he died of a heart attack, brought on, many people felt, by his work on *Joan of Arc*. Joe Valentine, the cameraman, and Casey Roberts, the set decorator, also died soon afterward, just as unexpectedly.

Although Ingrid continued to see Capa in Europe, she was taking an interest in her family unlike any she had ever shown. She was thirty-three years old, and with the failure of two pictures in a row, she might have settled down into a slowly declining career and the blessings of family life. But instead she embarked upon a fantasy. She decided to have a son—not simply a child, but a son, whom she would call Pelle—as if she and Petter had that much control over their destiny. She began to renovate their house, putting in a nursery and a maid's room. Ingrid worked with the architect, and according to Petter told him that these were the happiest days of their married life. Dr. Peter Veger, a refugee doctor who was living in the guesthouse, noticed the dramatic change in Ingrid as well. "Ingrid was the matriarch of the home and I am witness to the fact that she was building the nursery," Veger says. "It cost her terrific money, and she wanted very much the baby."

But Ingrid did not become pregnant. "I was reluctant to have another child since our marriage seemed so shaky," Petter says.

Nothing seemed to be working out right for Ingrid—not her plans for a new baby, and not her career. "She was obsessed by her failures," Petter remembers. "She kept saying, 'I have to get out of Hollywood. I hate Hollywood.' "

Petter worried about Ingrid's heavy drinking and her depression. But he was in no condition to nurture and to soothe her. He had suffered a serious case of food poisoning over the Christmas holidays. For the first time in their marriage, Petter was sick, and he had the feeling that Ingrid didn't care.

Ingrid seemed to be clearing away all the brush and brambles of her professional life. Even years later Steele could remember every detail of the day in January that Petter called him and told him that he was fired. Steele insisted on a meeting, and at three o'clock in the afternoon arrived at the Benedict Canyon home. He found Ingrid and Petter seated in the grass next to the pool. Ingrid didn't even grant Steele a hello. Petter explained that Ingrid would no longer be needing Steele's services. Ingrid sat silently, eyes down, as her longtime aide and confidant defended his efforts to Petter.

Petter claims that he was only doing what Ingrid had asked him to do. "She said, 'I want to get rid of Joe because he knows too much about me and is checking up on everything I do.' " Once again, Petter's great public strength was based on private weakness, whereas Ingrid's seeming weakness and reticence was a mask for her strength. Steele should have remembered that when he had left Selznick, his beloved Ingrid had acted no better than any of the other Selznick stars. She hadn't even called him until months later, when she needed him. But he forgot things like that because he wanted to forget them. And he blamed Petter solely and absolutely, and hated him with a passion almost as great as his love for Ingrid.

In 1946 Ingrid had gone out on her own willfully, proudly, sure that her career, her fortunes, would prosper as never before. *Arch of Triumph* and *Joan of Arc* had started as grand, glorious, ambitious projects and they had ended up humiliating failures, two of the biggest debacles in Hollywood history. She could not know how *Under Capricorn* would fare, but there had been major problems on the set, harbingers of more doom and failure.

"Ingrid was desperate," Petter says. "She said, 'In Hollywood, you're never any better than your last picture. I have to do an artistic feature in Europe.' "

Ingrid's career had begun an ominous trend, and she knew how fast a star's career could plummet. Going to Italy did not signify a jettisoning of her Hollywood future. Rather, in one daring move she was hoping to achieve an unprecedented position in world cinema. Roberto would bring to Ingrid a level of art, of reality, of meaning almost unknown in Hollywood. She would bring to him an audience as large as the world. If the Bergman-Rossellini collaboration succeeded, if they produced a film on the level of *Open City* and *Paisan*, then Ingrid would have a success undreamed of even in Hollywood.

It was perfect. Not only did Roberto make art out of everyday life, he made life into art. Ingrid's whole life would be infused with adventure. She had wanted to go to Australia to make *Under Capricorn*, to get that far away from Petter and Hollywood. Now she would be going to Stromboli, off the coast of Italy.

To Ingrid, Roberto was everything Petter was not. He was romance. He was daring. He was adventure. He was creative genius. He was exotic. "Probably, subconsciously, he offered a way out from both my problems: my marriage and my life in Hollywood," she said later. "But it wasn't clear to me at that time."

Ingrid thought that she and Roberto were kindred spirits. Alas, Roberto was not only a kindred spirit in the nobler parts of Ingrid's personality. Like Ingrid, he was self-absorbed, though he seemed to be totally involved with his woman of the moment. He was a man of impulse and whim, who created a universe of people around him who would serve him. He was a man incapable of a relationship in which he was less than the center.

Ingrid's primary interest in Roberto was still the furtherance of her career. Roberto, however, did not think in such linear terms. He did not spend time contemplating standing together with Ingrid at the heights of cinematic world success. He thought about himself and Ingrid together in quite another position. "I'm going to put the horns on Mr. Bergman," he announced to his friends. There was nothing of lyrical, romantic musings in Roberto's desires.

He talked so often of cuckolding Dr. Petter Lindstrom and he bragged so to his male friends about his intentions toward this American star that Ingrid Bergman, the person, seemed hardly more than an object to enhance his ego.

First, Roberto had to divest himself of Anna. One evening at the Excelsior Hotel in Rome, where he and Anna stayed, he told her that he was going to walk the dog. He left the animal with the concierge and then ran down the street, off for America. Anna spent the evening accompanied by Bill Tubbs, going from restaurant to restaurant trying to find him.

In New York, Roberto accepted the New York Film Critics award for *Paisan* as best foreign film of the year. He cabled Ingrid: I JUST ARRIVE FRIENDLY. Ingrid replied: WAITING FOR YOU IN THE WILD WEST. The smell of an affair was already in the air. While Roberto rode the train westward to Los Angeles, Walter Winchell, the radio gossip columnist, announced: "Ingrid Bergman's one and only love is coming to Hollywood to see her!"

Roberto would think of staying nowhere but the exclusive Beverly Hills Hotel (the bill paid by Ilya Lopert, the producer). Soon after arriving, Roberto visited the Lindstroms' house in Benedict Canyon. Ingrid had prepared for this momentous event by laying down a thirty-foot runner of red carpeting into the house. Roberto had had some curious greetings, but never one quite like this, a welcome as befitted a king of cinema. To Dr. Veger, Roberto's entrance seemed "like the arrival of Agamemnon."

"I was uncontrollably nervous," Ingrid remembered. "When he walked in, I couldn't talk. I tried to light a cigarette, but my hand trembled so much that the flame died out."

Ingrid did not remain nervous long. Roberto told her about his childhood and life in Rome. Although she complained later that Petter had been too old for her, Roberto was one year older than her first husband. He was born on May 8, 1906, the eldest son of a wealthy architect. Roberto had been brought up in a great Roman house in the best part of the city, with nannies and tutors and indulgence. Money was for spending, and he had squandered his inheritance pridefully, disdainfully, as if he thought the notes might dirty his hands. He had not bothered with a university education, but had got into film work for the Fascists.

In Los Angeles, Roberto had nothing but time: time to discuss art and life and love with Ingrid in French, time to meet with Hollywood producers and moneymen, discussing films and ideas in phrases that made no sense to the Americans.

Roberto and Ingrid approached Sam Goldwyn. The legendary producer was famed for his cynical wit. He spoke fractured English, but he was a shrewd, observant man. He saw possibility in this union of America's great star and Europe's great director.

At a dinner party, Goldwyn screened Rossellini's *Germany Year Zero*, filmed in bombed-out, ravaged Berlin. The film was not a facile attack on

Nazism but the bleak account of a Germany where the spiritual rubble lay deeper than the physical. When the lights went up in Goldwyn's screening room, there was an uneasy silence.

Ingrid got up, walked over to Roberto, threw an arm around him, and kissed him on the cheek. She meant her embrace to symbolize artistic camaraderie. The other guests read more personal meanings into her gesture.

Ingrid and Roberto were the center of the evening. Petter stood to the side, confiding to Hedy Lamarr that "he went to these functions with his wife because he knew it was good for her career."

"As time wore on, Ingrid was standing with Roberto in a corner, twisting a button on his brocade vest and looking into his eyes with a tiny, inviting smile," Lamarr remembered. "She was beautiful and it was clear her charm was being appreciated. When I saw Ingrid and Roberto, hand in hand, stroll over to Petter, who was still standing alone trying to look happy, I was drawn closer, to hear what would be said. A dramatic moment was definitely coming.

"Ingrid very coolly said to Petter (while Roberto looked on smiling), 'Mr. Rossellini is going to take me home. May I have the key, please?'

"I could see Petter was terribly embarrassed yet reluctant to make a scene. Hesitantly he brought out his key chain, opened it and slid a key off. Without one word he handed her the key and she didn't say one word in return. Then Ingrid and Roberto walked out."

The next day Goldwyn discussed with his son Sam junior his decision to turn down the project. "I can't understand a guy who says, 'I want to make up the scenes when I see the actors,' " Goldwyn said. "I'm crazy about Ingrid. Everyone in town is offering her scripts. Why does she want to get into a story without a script? There's got to be something else going on. They're either having an affair or about to have one."

Roberto insisted on living within the luxury and ambience of the *haute bourgeoisie*, but he could not be bothered with such petty middle-class concerns as checkbooks, contracts, deal memos. Goldwyn backed out of the deal. Lopert felt that Roberto had double-crossed him by seeking another producer, and he stopped paying Rossellini's bills. According to Petter, Roberto didn't give a second thought to borrowing two thousand dollars from Petter, as well as money from Ingrid's agent and her insurance salesman.

Roberto didn't have enough money to remain at the Beverly Hills Hotel. Ingrid invited him to stay in their guesthouse. Petter greeted the director and went to his office.

Ingrid and Roberto went off too. They experienced Los Angeles in a way that, in all her years in the city, Ingrid had never experienced it. They drove up the coast. They drove into the mountains. They went to lunch at the Farmer's Market and Don the Beachcomber's, where Ingrid had first dined when she arrived in Hollywood. They went to drive-ins. They had dinner with Billy Wilder, the director and writer. They had meetings and lunches with many other leading Hollywood people. They went everywhere together, talking in Ingrid's poor French or Roberto's fledgling English.

"Roberto was so warm and outgoing," Ingrid said of those first days. "When I was with him, I didn't feel shy or awkward or lonely—perhaps for the first time in my life. He was easy to talk to and interesting to listen to. Most of all, he was alive, and he made me feel alive."

Roberto infused each day with warmth and color, bringing to their relationship a vitality that he seemed certain to bring to their film life together. Only two months before, Ingrid had wanted a new child and a remodeled house, but now, "every time a workman hit the roof with a hammer, it was like a nail going into my head."

Ingrid was a woman of impulse. Nothing Roberto did seemed to bother her or to raise questions. She took him to Howard Hughes, and he agreed to finance their film for RKO, his new studio. Here she did not let her adulation of Roberto stand in the way of business. She would receive $175,000, the same basic salary she had earned on *Arch of Triumph* and *Joan of Arc*. She also would receive 40 percent of the net profits, against a salary and 20 percent of the net profits for Roberto. As an American star making a film in Italy, Ingrid would also receive a subsidy from the Italian government worth at least $50,000.

Rarely has idealism paid so well. For her adventure into the world of Italian neorealism, Ingrid would earn by far the most she had ever earned. If the film was a major success, she would have wealth far beyond anything she had yet known.

Ingrid and Roberto went out to a nightclub on the Sunset Strip to celebrate. Petter made a belated appearance and spoke to his wife in Swedish. Soon afterward, a Hollywood column retailed gossip about a certain famous star's public spat with her doctor husband.

One evening Celeste Holm invited Ingrid and Petter to a party, in part to celebrate Ingrid's forthcoming movie in Italy. The two of them arrived and found all their friends. Petter danced with abandon, changing his shirt at least once.

Ingrid was more interested in talking about the film she and Roberto would be making on Stromboli.

"Oh, it's going to be so marvelous to get out of this predictable society!" Ingrid said emphatically.

"Is it a good script?" asked George Seaton.

"Oh, there's no script," Ingrid said, as if she had to instruct these novices about the new cinema. "We get there to a place and we do it."

"I always thought a good script is a good idea," said Charlie Brackett, the actor, with wry understatement.

When it came time for Roberto to depart for Italy, he wanted to buy a gift for his son, Renzo. In the toy store he bought cowboy boots, a cowboy hat, and an Indian headdress. Then Roberto spied an enormous stuffed cow, wearing an apron. It was about as big as a real calf and cost seventy-five dollars. Roberto charged the cow to Petter's account and took it home to a delighted Pia.

On February 27, 1949, the evening before Roberto left, he and Petter sat down for a long talk. Roberto remembered Petter telling him that "Ingrid is easily enthusiastic, sensible but not intelligent, and that she has a temperament that makes her thoughtless." Petter denies talking about Ingrid. He says that Roberto said that he cared for him "as his own brother." He was a man Petter could trust with his wife. He would take care of Ingrid in Italy, protecting her from gossip. He would introduce Ingrid to Anna. Also, according to Petter, Roberto promised that he and Ingrid would take separate boats to Stromboli, a tacit admission of the rumors.

The next day Roberto left for Italy, and Petter and Ingrid went to Aspen, Colorado, for a skiing vacation. Ingrid was supposed to begin work in Italy on April 1, but she couldn't wait to be with Roberto. "I'd like to be in Rome," she said to Petter. "I'd like to learn the language. I'd like to be with those people. . . . I think it's better if I get there a bit early."

Ingrid told Petter that Roberto had promised to take her to Capri, Amalfi, and Messina before beginning the film. Petter did not like the idea of his wife traveling around Italy with Roberto and he told her so.

"I'd like to come now," Ingrid wrote Roberto from Aspen. "I try to be careful so I can come to you in one piece." She wrote letters childlike in their trust and feeling, as if she and Roberto were in a conspiracy against the world. She wasn't worried about complications. She didn't think about bad publicity. She didn't give Pia a mention. She simply wanted to be with Roberto. And she wanted to work. She wanted desperately to work. "If I don't work soon, I'll go crazy," she told Roberto.

On March 9, Ingrid said goodbye to the household help and to Pia as she had said goodbye so many times before. Ingrid looked back and waved at Pia. At the airport, seeing Petter standing there, "so lonely and silent," Ingrid felt, for the first time, "sentimental."

Ingrid had had other affairs. She had had these great rushes of emotion before, but she had always returned to Petter, and Petter had always been there. He was her past. He was her country. He was her language. He was the soil from which she had sprung.

What a burden of yearning and caring, memory and remorse, their marriage carried. So much had not been said. So much could not be said. There had been so many times when their marriage had torn apart, to be sutured up again, leaving new scars. If she abandoned Petter, she would abandon herself, her history, her memories.

Ingrid was not one to weigh alternatives, to think of consequences. She didn't think about Petter or Pia. She didn't think about the past. She didn't think that this time she might be headed into an affair that she could not control. She thought about Roberto. She thought about Italy. She thought about the film. She thought about herself.

Petter returned to the half-empty house in Benedict Canyon, with its new nursery. Petter's strategy had been to wait Ingrid out. Until the arrival of Roberto, his plan had worked.

Petter went into Ingrid's dressing room, adjoining their bedroom. Standing there, he knew that this time was different. Ingrid had cleaned out many of her possessions. Gone were two fur coats, two fur jackets, many of her dresses, and all the jewelry that she kept in the house. Gone were her clipping books, personal letters, and photo albums. Gone, too, were Ingrid's promises, their years together. Everything was gone.

CHAPTER THIRTEEN

The Prince of Disorder

For the whole week in New York, Ingrid had been frantic with anticipation and excitement. As soon as she had arrived, Roberto telephoned her at the Hampshire House. She could have talked to him ten times a day, but she was worried about the gossip. "There has already been so much written about us, I discovered when I came back from the mountain," she wrote Roberto. "I am very unhappy about it and don't want to add any daily telephone calls."

There was only a week to wait anyway. She went to see several plays. Visiting with José Ferrer, who was starring in *The Silver Whistle*, she sat in his dressing room until the morning hours, drinking Scotch and talking about Roberto and movies.

Ingrid was impolite to autograph seekers. "I gave you one five years ago," she yelled at one fan. "What do you want with another?"

On her last evening in America, she went to see Irene Selznick in her new apartment at the Pierre. Irene's divorce had become final three months before. Ingrid didn't want to talk about Irene and her new life as a Broadway producer. She wanted to talk about herself. Listening to Ingrid's endless monologue, Irene thought that she "was not so much exhilarated as fevered."

Irene, who lived life as if discretion were the highest virtue, didn't want to know about Roberto. She undressed for bed, but even that didn't stop her guest. Finally Ingrid picked up the phone and called Roberto in Rome. It was so late now that Ingrid didn't want to go back to the Hampshire House alone. She asked Irene if she might stay and sleep next to her.

For hours Ingrid had been drinking and smoking and talking. As she walked to the bathroom, she slipped and struck her head on the side of the air conditioner. "She fell so heavily I thought she was a goner," Irene remembered. "An eighth of an inch in a different direction and she wouldn't have gone to Rome."

In the week that Ingrid had been on the East Coast, she had not called Petter or Pia, and she had no idea what had happened after she left her husband at the Los Angeles airport. If she had called, and if Petter had been candid with her, he would have told her that he'd had a visit from Lopert, the disgruntled producer. "Lopert didn't get any share from Rossellini and RKO," Petter recalls. "He said to me, 'Rossellini is a liar and a cheater and now he has fooled me again. There is one thing I want you to know. Before we arrived in Los Angeles, he said to me, 'I will have Bergman in bed within two weeks.' "

As the plane droned eastward, Ingrid was fairly relaxed, remembers Ellen Neuwald. "We talked and slept a lot. I didn't know anything. And she knew that I knew she wasn't going to say anything."

At Rome's Ciampino airport a great welcoming crowd started to gather well before the scheduled arrival of the plane at midnight on Sunday, March 20. They waited for the woman they viewed as the madonna of films, an angelic figure descending on them from the distant land called Hollywood.

In the years before World War II, Hollywood had captured the hearts of Italians; in early 1939 the most popular film in Italy was *Snow White and the Seven Dwarfs*. Now the American films were back, capturing over 70 percent of the audiences. The American presence was everywhere, even in several of the best neorealistic films themselves, like Vittorio De Sica's *Shoeshine*, where Papa has his bicycle stolen while working at pasting up posters for a Rita Hayworth movie. The Italians didn't want to see a mirror held to the scars left by the war. They wanted to see, in the magical mirror of Hollywood, a life that was bigger and more beautiful, if only for an hour or two. They wanted to see Ingrid Bergman.

The Italians *believed* in Ingrid, in this pure, transcendent being who was blessing them and their land with her presence. And she was not coming merely to use Italy as a setting for a Hollywood film. She would be starring in a film directed by the master of the modern Italian cinema.

Searchlights played on the plane as it touched down. All the other passengers filed out. As Roberto entered the airplane with an enormous bouquet of long-stemmed roses, Ingrid kissed him and whispered, "*Je t'aime.*" Then, in her fur coat, and holding the flowers in her arms, she stepped out into the cool Roman air. Spread out below was a great crowd, welcoming her, she said later, as if "it was a queen arriving."

Roberto thrust a way for them through the crowd. Ingrid had pushed her way through adoring fans before, but there was a celebratory fury here unlike anything she had ever experienced. Roberto merrily grabbed one photographer, ripping his coat down the back. Then he rammed his way to the door. The crowd pursued him, but Roberto finally pushed Ingrid into his red Cisitalia sports car, and accelerated off into the night.

In front of the elegant Excelsior Hotel on Via Veneto, another crowd stood waiting to catch a glimpse of Ingrid. Roberto led her through the throng into the grand lobby. Roberto had a permanent room at the Excelsior, for the director was a man who always had to make *la bella figura*. Few people realized that it was a tiny, dark, inside room, more appropriate for pails and mops than for love affairs. For Ingrid, though, Roberto had taken a suite, to be paid for by RKO.

Roberto planned the mise-en-scène of his love affairs with a precision and concern for detail that he didn't always bring to his films. Although it was nearly three o'clock in the morning, his friends were waiting to greet Ingrid. There was champagne and little gifts and what Ingrid considered Roberto's wondrous, magical presence. Everything went well until Roberto introduced Ingrid to Helen Tubbs, whose husband was acting in Roberto's films.

"Here is the correspondent from *Variety*," Roberto said. Ingrid looked at Tubbs with eyes that the American reporter thought full of terror.

"Don't worry," Roberto said.

"I'm not writing gossip," said Mrs. Tubbs, the Italian correspondent for America's leading entertainment-trade newspaper. "I won't put in what you don't want."

Ingrid looked relieved, as if she still had control over her image in the newspapers and magazines.

Roberto had planned this moment, even to the extent of making sure that Anna Magnani would be out of the country, unable to stage one of her operatic scenes. Anna still loved Roberto, and she understood him as well as she loved him. From London she called her friend Suso Cecchi d'Amicos, a prominent screenwriter.

"Did Ingrid arrive?" Anna asked.

"Yes."

"Did Roberto go to the airport?"

"Yes."

"At the airport, which road did they take?"

D'Amicos thought a moment. Two roads led to Rome. The new modern highway, a direct swath cut through the countryside. That was the road everyone took. Then there was the Via Appia Antica, the ancient route, tree-lined, meandering, romantic, a road that had been there since the Romans. This was the road on which Roberto had often driven Anna, mesmerizing her with his tales of ancient Rome.

"I think the old road."

Anna hung up the phone.

On Ingrid's first day in Rome, Roberto scheduled a press conference in one of the mirrored salons of the Excelsior. A crowd of about three hundred reporters, photographers, publicists, and hangers-on were jammed into the room. Roberto pushed his way to the front of the room, pulling Ingrid along with him. Some of the crowd were not about to settle down to the mundane business of asking questions, when Ingrid's autograph could be captured. Scores of people pushed forward while the photographers took hundreds of pictures, the flash guns lighting up the room like a firefight.

Ingrid tried to smile, but she had never been in such a scene before. Her face froze into grimness, and then looked pursed with fear. "Give her air!" Roberto shouted. He had had enough. "Let's go," he shouted, and tried to force his way out of the room. The crowd would not let Ingrid out. Roberto gave no quarter. He and Ingrid finally popped out of the room. "*Maleducati!*" he screamed, as he and Ingrid made for the elevator.

Afterward, Ingrid was blasé, almost blissful. "I always knew Italians were very passionate people," she said, as if the crowd had been making love to her. "But I didn't know they were that passionate."

Ingrid was totally mesmerized by Roberto and Roberto's Rome. He had told her about his family's summer home at Ladispoli, just north of Rome on the coast. In broad strokes Roberto had sketched an image of an idyllic retreat, something out of Chekhov, and Ingrid insisted on driving out to see it. Vittorio De Sica and Sergio Amidei joined them.

Whatever the town had been before the war, it was now little more than a wart on the land. But as Ingrid and Roberto walked hand in hand through the cluttered, dirty streets, Ingrid was in ecstasy. She saw only the glorious images Roberto had created for her, not the squalor beneath her feet. De Sica returned to Rome to tell his friends, "Ingrid's completely crazy. It's a bidonville and she was enchanted." The director coined a new term to describe Ingrid: "*la grande ignora.*"

Ingrid was enchanted not only with one Italian, but with all Italians, and with the sun-drenched land itself. Like so many other new arrivals, she felt that the simple tonic of happiness was in the very water and the wine. She was exuberant, living as she did in a movie, without past or future, feeling each moment.

The Frenchman may fancy that he speaks the language of civilization, and that if God does not speak only French it is because he saves the language for state occasions. The Italian feels that his is the language of life, and better to speak it poorly than not at all. He believes that laughs and sighs are all in Italian, and that if God lives in heaven, he takes his vacations in Tuscany. Roberto was the most Italian of Italians. He was just as prideful a man as Petter. But whereas Petter's was a moral pride, Roberto's pride was that he knew how to live, how to feel, how to love.

Roberto was charming, but even his sister admits that "people would say he was charming like a snake, like a snake with little birds." Love has no rules, at least as Roberto played the game. He wanted to make Ingrid irrevocably his. To win her, he first wanted to show her his Italy on their journey to the island of Stromboli. So after a few days in Rome, Roberto and Ingrid took the Appian Way out of Rome. The red Cisitalia convertible sped southward, the wind blowing Ingrid's hair.

To Ingrid, each twist in the road, each new village, each new town, brought more moments with neither past nor future. Robert knew and loved his Italy, and as they sped onward, he spun his web of anecdotes and history. Roberto led Ingrid to Capri, but he neglected to tell her about his personal romantic history on that most romantic of islands. Indeed, one of his previous lovers, Roswita Schmidt, a German actress, was living on the island.

At Amalfi, seventy miles south of Naples, Ingrid and Roberto stayed at the Albergo Luna Convento. The former Capuchin monastery was a favorite stopping place for Roberto. It was here that Anna Magnani had thrown a plateful of spaghetti in Roberto's face. And it was here that Ingrid sat down to write a letter to Petter, asking for a divorce.

Roberto had purportedly promised Petter that he would treat Ingrid with decorum, not even allowing a scent of scandal. Yet he seemed positively chummy with the paparazzi. As for Ingrid, she had always guarded her own public image, and when she had been careless, Steele or Selznick had watched out for her. She was alone now with Roberto, and she didn't see that it wasn't simply the two of them in a romantic idyll. And so the photographers took pictures of Roberto and Ingrid holding hands as they walked in the ruins of an ancient tower, and sent them to their newspapers.

Petter had been writing. Though he knew that Ingrid and Roberto were lovers—as much as he could know it without discovering them in bed to-gether—his letters were resolutely innocent, full of advice and goodwill, as if even now he could not face the reality of his life without her.

Sitting in her hotel room before a blank paper emblazoned with the hotel's name, Ingrid could no longer ignore Petter and her past. She tried several times, before she said what she wanted to say. What she had to say was poignant, and deeply felt, but it did not include even a single word about her daughter.*

> *Petter lilla [little]—*
> *It will be very difficult for you to read this letter and it is difficult for me to write it. But I believe it is the only way. I would like to explain everything from the beginning, but you already know enough. And I would like to ask forgiveness, but that seems ridiculous.*
>
> *It is not altogether my fault, and how can you forgive that I want to stay with Roberto?*
>
> *It was not my intention to fall in love and go to Italy forever. After all our plans and dreams, you know that is true. But how can I help it or change it? You saw in Hollywood how my enthusiasm for Roberto grew and how much alike we are, with the same desire for the same kind of work and the same understanding of life.*
>
> *I thought maybe I could conquer the feeling I had for him when I saw him in his own milieu, so different from mine. But it turned out just the opposite. The people, the life, the country is not strange. It is what I always*

* Years later, in Ingrid's autobiography, the name Pelle was changed to Pia, so it appeared that she mentioned her daughter.

*wanted. I had not the courage to talk more about him at home than I did
with you as it all seemed so incredible, like an adventure, and at the time
I didn't realize the depth of his feelings.*

*Min [my] Petter, I know how this letter falls like a bomb on our house,
our Pelle, our future, our past so filled with sacrifice and help on your
part.*

*And now you stand alone in the ruins and I am unable to help you.
Stackars lilla pappa men also stackars lilla mama [Poor little papa, but
also poor little mama].*

Mama

Ingrid believed that it was Petter who stood "alone in the ruins" while she
had moved on. She would suffer her moments of sadness, but nothing of the
burden that her husband carried. With Roberto she might even outrace fate.

Before the great onslaught of publicity had begun, Ingrid and Roberto
were speeding southward again. For ten days they journeyed south, unaware
of the tidal wave of turmoil that pursued them. In Rome, Roberto's friends
and relatives were already worried that the affair might engulf him and his
work.

Roberto had had his affairs before, but they had always been sideshows to
his real work. His relationship with Ingrid, however, risked becoming a circus
that would dominate his life. "I was worried about what Ingrid would mean to
my brother's life," remembers Marcella, his sister. "I worried because Ingrid's
coming here would bring all these awful things—not her, of course—the
paparazzi, all of that, so we couldn't live anymore."

Roberto's cousin Renzo Avanzo felt much the same. "Sure, we disapproved," he said, "but not from a moral point of view. Nobody gave a damn
about that. We disapproved because we knew that, with her, he was through
making the kind of pictures he should be making. She came out of a proper,
serious, commercial world of filmmaking. He didn't fit in with that. They were
enamored with the idea of what they could do together artistically—and it was
a lousy idea."

Roberto was under the same illusion as Ingrid: that he had control over his
art and his life. To Ingrid he was this god of the cinema who created greatness
out of nothing. He needed no script; the dialogue and scenes would spring
full-blown out of his genius. He needed no professional actors; he would
anoint his cast, plucking them off the street, choosing a face, a figure. On the
beach at Salerno, he told Ingrid, he would find her leading man. Twenty
minutes later he returned, to tell her that he had found two men, and one of
them, Mario Vitale, a handsome twenty-one-year-old fisherman, became the
romantic lead for the munificent pay of seventy-five dollars a week.

The farther south Ingrid and Roberto traveled, the poorer the land became. In southern Italy poverty had drawn its sharp marks as much on the
lined and harrowed faces of the people as on the land. Roberto sped along

narrow roads bordered by windowless huts where peasants worked the soil with spades and sweat, spending nine of every ten lire they earned on food.

In this forgotten land, movies were the main, and sometimes only, contact with the urban world. Ingrid appeared almost as well known here in southern Italy as in Dayton or Des Moines. In the town of Catanzaro, the main street was lined with well-wishers, waiting to see Hollywood's golden queen. Ingrid and Roberto had the finest room in the hotel, but even the finest room did not have a private toilet. When Ingrid had to go to the bathroom, the local dignitaries were still standing in the hallway. She was applauded on her way into the bathroom, and on her way out, though her audience allowed her to perform her ablutions in silence.

For their bed at the hotel, the mayor of Cantanzaro donated his silk wedding sheets, asking that they kindly sign the sheets in the morning. He would keep them like a relic of the church.

By the terms of their contract, Ingrid and Roberto were supposed to begin work on the film April 1, 1949. It was already the fourth of April, however, before they sailed from Messina, Sicily, on the *San Lorenzo*. Since the only regular passage to Stromboli was a weekly mail boat from Naples, for the filming of *Stromboli*, as the movie was eventually titled, an old forty-foot fishing schooner had been leased. The *San Lorenzo* was hardly the luxury cruiser that a Hollywood star might have expected. There were no staterooms or private compartments at all, nor even a deck awning to protect the passengers from the unyielding Mediterranean sun.

Ingrid was still protected by the euphoria of her great adventure. The boat stank of dead fish, but she smelled only the fresh sea. She hadn't complained of the hardships during the filming of *For Whom the Bell Tolls*, and she did not complain now as the boat lumbered along, the motor coughing and spitting. On their way they spied the island where Anna Magnani was having her artistic revenge, making a film entitled *Volcano*.

For four hours the boat chugged toward Stromboli, the most northerly and remote of the Lipari Islands. Suddenly, there rising out of the ocean stood the great steaming three-thousand-foot-high cone of the volcano, then the black bulk of the mountain, and finally the island itself, little more than a pedestal for the volcano. The volcano was one of the most active in the world. Only recently it had erupted, spewing forth a mass of lava and smoke and flames, the lava spilling down its side to the sea. Some days the smoke blocked out the very sun. Anyone who lived on this island could have few illusions about man's control over his destiny.

The boat nosed around the farther side to the tiny village. Above the black sands stood a group of whitewashed Moorish-style homes huddled together. Once there had been five thousand people living here, but now there were only about five hundred, and the empty homes were the tombstones of lost lives. The daring and the young had gone, leaving Stromboli to the old, the lame, and the inert, an island shrouded in the black of widows, and in the gray of the volcano.

The arrival of Ingrid and Roberto was the greatest event in the history of Stromboli, and almost the whole village stood on the black sands, waiting. As Ingrid looked on the island for the first time, she thought that it was "a spectacular setting for a movie." She did not think that it would be difficult to make a film here that would capture the world's imagination.

Unquestionably, Stromboli was a spectacular setting for a love affair. For the first week or so, that was Roberto's main concern, even if it was on RKO's time and money. Roberto was an expert diver and spearfisherman. The waters around the island are rich with fish, and time and again he dove into the sea, surfacing long seconds later, with a fish to deposit before Ingrid's feet.

Ingrid and Roberto lived together in the schoolmaster's home, the best house on the island. Each had a bedroom. The island had no running water. For Ingrid a bathroom was specially built onto the end of the house. It included a makeshift shower, consisting of an old oil drum on the roof that the maid filled with water heated on the stove. There was a little courtyard as well where Ingrid and Roberto could at least not be overheard.

"I have seen her sit on a low wall outside the house—the Love House as it came to be called—for hours on end without saying a word," said Michael Wilson, the British public relations man assigned by RKO to the film. "Just nodding her head, while Rossellini talked."

On April 7 Roberto began filming in his languid, desultory way. Ingrid wrote in her dairy: "Start of film." Two days later she noted once again in her diary: "Try start film." Sunday she wrote: "Start film."

Ingrid knew filmmaking was the most collegial of arts, combining a dozen abilities and crafts. With Roberto she anticipated that she would share in the artistic process, in a marriage of art and artist. Roberto, however, was a man of monumental hubris, along with an insecurity that he masked with bravado. He was unwilling to share the creative process. He was the screenwriter, but he had no screenplay to be picked over and criticized by producers, actors, and others. He had only his ideas, and by writing the dialogue and the scenes almost as he filmed them, he controlled the daily production of the film.

Ingrid had a grandiose conception of her life as an actress with Roberto. Here finally she would begin exploring roles with all the depth and subtlety of a Magnani. But Roberto had cast *Stromboli* with the islanders not simply because they looked authentic, but because he didn't want "actors" and was disdainful of them and their narcissistic craft. Roberto treated actors as little more than puppets, dumb creatures who mouthed whatever words he told them. On *Stromboli*, Roberto even tied string to their big toes, which he pulled when he wanted an "actor" to speak.

Ingrid had no string, and she tried to act with depth and subtlety in a part she didn't understand, in a plot that hardly existed. In the evenings, while, if she was lucky, Ingrid had some lines to memorize, Ellen Neuwald worked as a dialogue coach with the other cast members. "The actors could hardly speak Italian, only their dialect Italian," Neuwald says. "At night I had to hammer the Italian words into them. Rossellini said, 'Don't you dare tell them what the lines mean. Just drill the lines into them. I'll supply the meaning.' "

Ingrid tried to pretend that all was well with Roberto. Finally, one day, she exploded.

"You can have these realistic pictures," she screamed. "To hell with them! These people don't even know what dialogue is, they don't know where to stand; they don't even care what they're doing. I can't bear to work another day with you."

Roberto listened to Ingrid's outburst in silence, but he did not change. In Ingrid, as in most of Roberto's women, there was a vein of masochism, which he mined with great skill. He had Ingrid doubly under his sway. As her lover and as her director, he dominated her, forcing her to do his bidding, at times almost humiliating her.

Despite Ingrid's many affairs, there was still a deep Victorian strain in her. She had never posed for revealing cheesecake pictures. She had always refused to reveal much of her legs.

In one scene Roberto asked Ingrid to raise her skirts, before the crew and the camera.

Ingrid pulled her skirt up a few inches.

"A little higher, *carissima mia*," Roberto said. "A little higher."

Ingrid pulled her skirt up slightly above her knees.

"No," Roberto said, as he walked over to her. "Not like that—like this."

Roberto yanked her skirt up so that her white thighs appeared naked before the camera.

If Ingrid had reflected on all that she knew about Hollywood and publicity, about men and love and marriage, she would have realized that her idyllic moments could not last much longer. But she treated her life as if it were a series of films, of episodes and characters, that one lived and then forgot, or relegated to a few snapshots of memory.

On April 9 and 12 Petter cabled Ingrid on Stromboli, asking her to telephone him. He had no idea that the island was so remote that there was no telephone or electricity. Pia was anticipating her mother's call, and she spent all Easter Sunday inside a bungalow in Palm Springs, waiting for the phone to ring.

On April 13 an item appeared in Cholly Knickerbocker's column in the New York *Journal American* about "rumors" of a romance between Ingrid and Roberto. "I had to be pretty careful," remembers Igor Cassini, who wrote the column. "I had to be pretty sure. I knew that the story was going to break. I wrote it very carefully. You had to be more careful because scandal in a person's personal life was taboo. I knew that she was in love with that man." Within days of the New York column, the story was appearing almost everywhere. The most sensational evidence of Ingrid's new love was a picture in *Life* of her and Roberto holding hands.

After writing her letter to Petter in Amalfi, Ingrid apparently had been afraid to take the irreconcilable step of mailing it. Roberto, infuriated, had taken it from her. Before mailing the letter he displayed it to his friends like a Sicilian newlywed hanging out bloody wedding sheets. And thus the news found its way into Italian and American newspapers.

All his life, Petter had tried to avoid the glare of publicity. Now he found himself pursued and hounded. He had wanted Pia to be brought up like any other little girl, but now even her name was bandied about in the columns. He sent Pia off to stay with Lydia Vernon, the wife of their business manager. When summer came, Pia went to Minnesota to live with friends on a farm.

Petter was a man who tried to act well and good. In his reply to Ingrid's letter he did not attempt to woo Ingrid back to him ("A wife that does not want to stay with me is no good to me"). He focused on the morality of the situation. He clearly thought of Roberto as a Latin Svengali. He could rarely bring himself to write Roberto's name. He referred to him as "your Italian." Petter pointed out that Roberto was married, living in a Catholic country. Ingrid would end up as merely his mistress.

This man to whom Petter had taken breakfast in the mornings, to whom he had loaned money, was betraying not only his wife but Petter. He swore on his mother's memory that when "the Italian" left Hollywood he had promised Petter that he would take care of Ingrid and protect her. This was not the kind of man, the kind of relationship, for a woman who was "originally good and fair."

Petter told Ingrid it was "about time you grew up." He called up the litany of all that he had done for her, all his sacrifices, all that he had done to protect her. Job-like, Petter called out in anguish and disbelief that this woman, his wife, would drag their years together into the filth of publicity. If she wanted a divorce, he insisted that she not hide away in Italy but return to America and get it there.

Ingrid cried when she read the letter.

"I think probably Ingrid felt like Charlie Chaplin, with one eye laughing, the other crying," says Ellen Neuwald. "We were both thirty-three years old, a good age for a woman to be. And I suppose when you aren't that happy in your life, it can be a wonderful thing to be in love. And I think the combination that they could work together, and the liberation that she felt, was all positive. And at the same time it was a very hard period. I said, Whatever you do now is going to be incredibly painful for you, and I think especially for Pia. She cared for Petter and couldn't understand.

"After the first week or so the whole thing broke. We spent half our time answering cables. It could only be done at certain times. Suddenly the whole world had converged on Stromboli. It was the most important thing."

Ingrid and Roberto were making their film on one of the most inaccessible islands in Europe. At first he thought that he could keep the journalists away. When the first two American reporters descended on Messina, he generously offered them the use of the *San Lorenzo*, to bring them to Stromboli. Alas, the boat developed mysterious "engine trouble." Several days later, when the journalists rented their own vessel, they found themselves under house arrest, accused of the nefarious crime of seeking to interview a Sicilian bandit. "Sometime afterward, I learned that it was Rossellini, with a fine Machiavellian touch, who had tipped off the police," wrote Michael Stern, one of the reporters.

Even Roberto could not hold back the tide of reporters and photographers. Soon the tiny harbor of Stromboli was full of boats. The whole western world seemed to have an insatiable appetite for news of the scandal. Editors printed column after column of speculative stories.

One day a larger ship anchored offshore. Several hundred excited, gesticulating Italians from Naples descended on the island. The tourists had signed up for a one-day excursion, and they bounded merrily up toward Ingrid and Roberto's house. Roberto was outraged, but he had the good priest of Stromboli hold the crowd back while Roberto and Ingrid ascended to the balcony of the priest's house. Here they stood while the visitors took snapshots and appraised Italy's newest tourist attraction.

If there was an element of amusement in the tourists' arrival, there was not in the message brought by another series of emissaries. Ingrid's affair had begun to affect a commodity that the world takes more seriously than love: money. In Los Angeles and New York lived moguls, moneymen, agents, columnists, and publicists who felt betrayed by this new Ingrid.

RKO had the most to lose or gain from the film. Ed Killy, the corporate production manager, was on Stromboli when the filming began, to push the film along. Killy had never seen such a haphazard, leisurely approach to filmmaking as Roberto's. Not only time but RKO's money was being squandered. Killy could do little to speed Roberto up, and he lasted scarcely a month before being replaced.

RKO was not spending hundreds of thousands of dollars to finance a romance. Killy's replacement was Harold Lewis, a six-foot-four-inch-tall movie "troubleshooter." Lewis was paid, not to care about art and nuance, but to get films finished quickly and cheaply.

Even if the film went way over budget, *Stromboli* had received so much free publicity that it was bound to be a great *succès de scandale*. It was doubtful, however, if audiences were going to line up to see Ingrid play a virgin saint in *Joan of Arc*. Walter Wanger cabled Ingrid to accuse her of "endangering my future and that of my family . . . if you do not behave in a way which will disprove these ugly rumors. . . . Do not fool yourself by thinking that what you're doing is of such courageous proportions or so artistic to excuse what ordinary people believe."

The industry that had brought Ingrid wealth and celebrity was now in deep trouble. Television was not yet major competition, but the studio system of long-term contracts was beginning to end. The House Un-American Activities Committee had begun its investigations into Communist and leftist influence in Hollywood. Actors, writers, directors, and others were being blacklisted. Larry Adler was among those who left the country, never to return; Robert Capa felt threatened as well.

Hollywood stood accused of cultural as well as political betrayal. Newspaper columns were full of scandalous tales, but nothing to equal the sensation of the liaison between Rossellini and the star who played Sister Benedict and Joan of Arc. Joseph Breen, director of the Production Code Administration, was ready to censor not only Ingrid's films but her very life. "Such stories will not only *not* react favorably to your picture, but may very well *destroy your career as a motion picture artist,*" Breen wrote. "I am constrained to suggest that you find occasion, *at the earliest possible moment,* to issue a denial of these rumors—to state, quite frankly, that they are not true, that you have no intention to desert your child or to divorce your husband, and that you have no plans to marry anyone."

Like almost everyone who had known Ingrid in America, Kay Brown had a vested interest in the "old" Ingrid. Kay's career had been based in part on her only partially deserved reputation for having discovered Ingrid. She was now an agent at MCA, the giant entertainment company. Her biggest coup had been signing Ingrid as a client. Kay's concern, however, was not simply the 10 percent that Ingrid represented to MCA. Kay knew Ingrid. She knew Petter and Pia. She knew Ingrid's impulsiveness, her impressionability, her simplicity, and where they might lead her.

Kay was soon flying over to Italy, as MCA's representative. She arrived on Stromboli at six one morning in a fishing boat, attired in a mink coat and high heels; she was carried ashore on a sailor's back. Roberto was waiting on the beach to greet Kay, but he was not happy to see her. Even if she had been a different sort of emissary, Roberto would not have liked her. He had no use for agents. He considered them parasites sucking the blood of creators. Moreover, Kay's personality was not appreciated by either Rossellini or his sister, Marcella, now in residence on Stromboli. Marcella expressed the family sentiment succinctly: "Kay is so American. It's terrible."

Ingrid might have been expected to express some pleasure at finally seeing an old, trusted friend, but that was not so. "The whole thing is crazy and depressing," Kay commented. "When I see Ingrid she's not the girl I know. She's very remote, she's not happy to see me. . . . I didn't realize at this time that RKO and MCA, in fact all things American, were taking over as 'the enemies' as far as Roberto and therefore Ingrid were concerned. . . . Our conversations were so useless. I would say, 'Ingrid, this is ridiculous, you'll lose your husband and your daughter and your career and everything'; and Ingrid would simply reply, 'Yes, I know.' To me she looked so lost and wan and bewildered."

Kay remembered: "At Stromboli Ingrid looked shell-shocked, defeated."

Ingrid's life of grand, glorious romance had lasted no more than three weeks. Now she stood at the center of a world of intrigue, suspicion, and calculation. Wherever she looked, someone was pulling at her, yanking her this way or that. Roberto and Petter were both men capable of emotional cunning. Petter was six thousand miles away, but his letter had been a cry in the night. For a husband who felt that he had given his wife so much, his demands were deceptively small. Petter asked only that Ingrid stop behaving so scandalously, and return to the United States to discuss a divorce.

Roberto would have nothing of it. God's little joke on the devious is that they are forever doomed to imagine that others may be just as untrustworthy as they are. Roberto didn't trust Ingrid to go off to California alone to settle things with Petter. He certainly didn't trust Petter alone with Ingrid, not even for a moment. He swore to Ingrid that if she left him and returned to Petter he would blow his brains out with a revolver.

A marriage does not die overnight, and beyond the legal questions, Ingrid and Petter had much to say to one another. Petter was not willing to sail blithely into the adulterous lair of Stromboli. He wanted Ingrid to fly to London or somewhere else in Europe. Roberto would not allow that. And so it was decided that the meeting would take place the first days in May in Messina, the Sicilian city from which less than a month ago Ingrid had embarked so excitedly. Petter agreed with only one stipulation: that Roberto not be present.

A century earlier, Messina had had a famous architectural seafront, lined with palaces whose balconies were protected by exquisite wrought iron. Only remnants of that remained now, and Messina was a bustling provincial city, whose premier hotel, the Albergo Reale, had a splendid entrance, and a grand and elegant double staircase leading to a series of dark, nondescript little rooms.

Ingrid arrived with the entourage of an Italian prima donna. Of course there was Roberto, who would not think of allowing Ingrid to meet alone with a man whom he considered cold and dominating, and who he feared might manipulate Ingrid. Then there was Kay Brown; Art Cohn, a writer working on the English-language version of *Stromboli*, and his wife, Marta; and others of Roberto's entourage, including an attorney.

Unknown to Petter, Roberto was the grand maestro of the occasion, shuffling the others in and out of their rooms, displaying a talent for secretiveness worthy of a Medici courtier. Outside in the streets there was a great May Day parade, the streets awash in red flags, the Communist slogans reverberating down ancient streets, a scene that to the Americans looked like a harbinger of revolution.

Petter wanted to meet his wife alone, to discuss matters in a way that he could not among these jabbering strangers, gesticulating and arguing in Italian and English. In the evening Kay was led through a labyrinth of back alleys and corridors until finally she stood before Ingrid's door. Kay took Ingrid to Petter's room, and left the two of them alone.

Petter locked the door. As soon as Roberto learned that Ingrid and Petter were together, he was filled with rage and jealousy. Ingrid was *his* now, and she was locked up with a man whom Roberto considered an icy tyrant, who might once again lay his steely grasp on Ingrid's body and soul.

Roberto probably had another worry. On Stromboli he could see that Ingrid was no longer full of joy. He may have been trying to make Ingrid inexorably his by impregnating her. And he may have feared what for him would be the most horrible of fates: that if Ingrid did have his child, Petter might now be able to claim it as his own.

Roberto called the police. The police decided that the dreadful crime taking place was that a man and his wife were together in a hotel room. If the police would not do their sovereign duty, then Roberto would have to act on his own. He stationed three of his worthy underlings at the entrances to the Albergo Reale so that Petter would not be able to spirit Ingrid out of the hotel. Then he jumped into his sports car and began racing around the hotel.

"Petter and I were in the room and Roberto was circling around and around every thirty seconds—vroom—vroom—vroom—with me saying 'Here he comes again . . . here he comes again!' " Ingrid remembered. "He never stopped all night long, hour after hour, and I just sat at the window and stared out and listened to Petter talking until the dawn came up. It was a nightmare."

Petter insisted that Ingrid tell Pia herself. Ingrid must return, meet Pia, and tell her of the wreckage of their marriage. Only thus could she feel and see what she had done, whom she had hurt. And only in Ingrid's act of contrition could he win moral vindication, and go on with his life, alone with Pia. Until that time, Petter asked only that Ingrid act with a modicum of discretion, and not stir up further publicity.

Ingrid talked later of the five or ten hours "of insults that were hurled at me by Dr. Lindstrom in the room where he had locked himself with me."

"I didn't insult her," Petter says. "There was no argument and no car running. She was pleased I decided on a divorce. She promised to see Pia in London if I waited a couple of weeks. She said she would cooperate in a final, simple divorce. We didn't stay together all night either. After our talk she went out."

Before everyone left Messina, Petter met with Ingrid and her advisers. "Kay Brown sat there," Petter remembers, "and this writer [Art Cohn] and the writer's wife. I stood up and made a little speech. I said, I'm going to arrange for a divorce no matter what happens. I insisted that Ingrid talk to Pia before the divorce. I said I'd bring Pia to London or Ingrid could come to the United States. I said she should tell the child. That was the end for me."

Petter made his position clear, but there were more meetings and discussions among the others. To Kay Brown, the whole event seemed like not a grand opera but "an Italian farce." The others agreed that on Stromboli Ingrid and Roberto would live separately and make no public appearances together except those involving the film. In Rome or on location they would also live apart and not socialize publicly together.

Ingrid's advisers decided that some kind of statement had to be issued. Ingrid said later that she wanted to announce the divorce, but that the others were far more concerned about completing the picture, and maintaining her reputation, than they were about either the truth or her happiness. The group argued over the language, producing a document that even diplomats might consider a classic in obstructiveness. "I have met my husband here and have clarified our situation," the statement said. "I am returning to Stromboli . . . to continue work on my picture. On its conclusion I will leave Italy and meet my husband either in Sweden or the United States."

Messina had shown no more interest in the proceedings than in a fisherman and his wife squabbling in the street. Roberto was sure that that would not last and that by now the reporters and photographers would be onto them, and that when the group departed the hotel at two o'clock, the streets would be full of autograph seekers, photographers, and hordes of the curious. To avoid all this, Roberto had planted a series of white paper flags to guide his party from their rooms, down lengthy corridors, and out a back door of the hotel.

Petter insisted that he walk out the front door of the hotel. Roberto had no choice but to signal his coconspirators that the cars should be brought around front. When Ingrid marched out of the Albergo Reale, the entire horde that greeted her consisted of a young boy with a Leica camera.

Roberto and Ingrid jumped into his sports car, and he accelerated madly. Kay and the Italian lawyer followed in a tiny Fiat. A mile down the road, Roberto's car broke down. Roberto and Ingrid piled into the Fiat and the solicitor drove on. "How I managed to keep a straight face, I'll never know," Kay remembers, "but of course, at that moment Ingrid was far too unhappy to see the funny side of anything."

The two women said goodbye in Messina, and Ingrid and Roberto sailed back to Stromboli. A crowd was waiting there to greet them. "She looked tired and haggard," said a photographer who was there that day. "Roberto practically danced off the boat, hugging everyone who was close to him. She stood there white-faced for a moment, and then she said sharply, 'Roberto, come on!' He followed immediately. You could tell he had won and she was still in a great quandary."

Petter was supposed to fly from Rome to Paris on May 4 but he did not show up. Not until May 6 did he leave.

The French reporters were waiting for him. Until now his mere refusal to give interviews had been enough to make the press leave Petter alone, but he was now fair game to photographers and reporters, his comings and goings chronicled for the public. "All I want to do is to sleep and eat and see friends here," he said now. "I am very tired and all I want is to be left alone."

Petter remained in Paris a few days and then flew to London to wait for *Stromboli* to finish shooting, in what he had been told would be two weeks. Then Ingrid was supposed to fly to him and they would have the talk he so desperately desired. Petter stayed in Kent with Sidney Bernstein, the producer of *Under Capricorn*, then took private accommodations.

Petter had been suffering from gastritis. His stomach pain worsened. He lay in bed for some days. Although Petter was working on a research paper and visiting the Neurological Institute, he had nothing but time now, time to stir the dying coals of his marriage. Days passed, and then weeks, and still the filming continued, and Ingrid's promise to see him seemed more distant still.

With his illness, Petter didn't even have the balm of alcohol. He appeared to some to be living in a tomb of memory. He wrote Ingrid that he was writing on the anniversary of their engagement, a date that now meant nothing to her. He apologized that for some weeks he had not been able to help her. Clinging to the last vestiges of their life together, he said that whatever happened they must remain friends.

"Petter called me like someone drowning," recalls Britt Engstrom, Ingrid's Swedish cousin. "I left my baby and I went to London. He was quite sick. Petter said I was the only person, the last chance. He knew if I begged Ingrid, she would do as I said. He wanted to see her again, to talk to her. I think he thought she would come back to him."

Britt had seen and known Petter as a young man in Stockholm, carrying rocks in his knapsack, dancing till dawn, a young man who could climb anything, do anything. She had seen him go off to America and succeed in his way, as Ingrid had succeeded in hers. She had seen and known Petter, his pride and his goodwill and his generosity and his hope for the future.

The man Britt saw in London was someone else. "I've never seen anything like that," Britt says. "He was like a little boy."

According to Petter, he had had no contact with Britt for years. He says that she had refused to see him on three visits to Sweden and that he had not asked her to come to London. He says that he was in no way emotionally sick.

Britt made the journey down to Stromboli. She told Ingrid that Petter had lost much weight and seemed like a broken man. "Ingrid didn't want to see Petter, but I convinced her," Britt says. "Roberto didn't want her to see him. He thought Petter would kidnap her. Roberto said he would commit suicide if she went."

Ingrid acted as if she had fled from a tyrant who had controlled her every moment and built a great moat around her emotional life. She didn't see that she was the one who had largely manipulated each of her relationships, be it a marriage or an affair. Now, however, she was with a man who played these games of love with weapons that she had not thought even existed. She had always fled from emotional strife. She was no match for a man who threatened to kill himself, at least not now, when Roberto's threats were almost as fresh as his avowals of love. Roberto was more feminine in his guile than Ingrid, more masculine in his ego, and he played upon Ingrid's emotions as upon a fine instrument.

Ingrid had dreamed of a partnership of art and love. And here she was living with an artistic oligarch who dominated everyone and everything. He had no room for Ingrid's ideas or feelings. Ingrid had left Beverly Hills to soar free, to live a life of artistic and emotional freedom, and here she was trapped, chained down. On some deep level she couldn't even think about what had happened to her. She had given up to Roberto. She couldn't struggle against him. She couldn't fight anymore.

Ingrid decided to renege on her agreement to see Petter before going ahead with the divorce. She wrote him that she was sending a lawyer to London to seek a legal separation. "I don't know why you stay so long in London," she wrote. "I am afraid I don't have the strength for more arguments. I am afraid of more tears, and I am afraid of going crazy."

Petter, that man of emotional tenacity, was tried beyond even his endurance. "I was waiting in London for the film to finish," says Petter. "She was going to take the plane to London. Two months was a long time to wait. Every week I thought she'd come. She didn't come. She said, I'm sending an attorney. She never sent an attorney."

Petter might have given up now, but he wrote Ingrid another letter from England on June 23, saying that he wanted to see her once again, "alone and at peace and then leave you as a friend," without "hard words or reproaches," but with his memory of Ingrid "as the little girl in the gray collar."

Ingrid told Petter that he should go ahead and tell Pia that her parents were getting a divorce and that her mother would not be returning immediately from Italy. Although Ingrid refused to see Petter she sent an emissary to meet him in Paris.

"My mission was to ask him to please give Miss Bergman a divorce," Marta Cohn testified later. "He was very tense and angry at first, but he had consented to meet me, so I pressed the issue. I told him the divorce matter was important and urgent and that Miss Bergman was going to marry Mr. Rossellini as soon as she could get a divorce.

"Dr. Lindstrom laughed. He said it was entirely out of the question. He said he would not give her a divorce. . . . Dr. Lindstrom wanted Ingrid to tell Pia herself. . . . I also told him that Ingrid loved him sincerely and loved Pia. . . . He said, 'By the time I get through with Ingrid, she will never be able to see Pia again and I will blacken her name.' "

Petter denies threatening to destroy Ingrid's reputation, and says that he asked only that Pia's mother be the one to tell the child about the divorce. He never, in fact, publicly attacked Ingrid. Nor did he seek to prevent her seeing Pia outside Italy. "I said I'd meet Ingrid anywhere, except Russia, of course," Petter testified two years later. "She [Mrs. Cohn] said he [Rossellini] was threatening to shoot himself if Ingrid ever saw me again. And she said she had to take the revolver away from him. I told her, 'This sounds like nonsense. If he would wave a pistol and let a woman take it away from him, there is not much substance to the man.' "

Finally, Petter returned to the States.

When Ingrid returned from Messina, Roberto lived up to the verbal agreement by moving out of the house he had shared with Ingrid and Marcella. For a while Ingrid and Roberto pretended that their relationship was strictly professional. Roberto, however, was the prince of disorder. Both his art and his life demanded turmoil. It was time, Roberto decided, for his entourage to leave the languid clime of Stromboli for Rome.

Hollywood directors do not whimsically drop their cameras and crews in the middle of a production. The day-to-day costs are simply too great. Roberto didn't care about those who had accountants' souls. Nor did he concern himself with the humdrum, tedious demands of public relations.

On the boat from Stromboli to Messina, Michael Wilson, the RKO public relations man, tried to talk Roberto into turning back. "Ingrid took no part in the discussions, though they became pretty violent," Wilson wrote later. "She just lay quite still on an old grey canvas sail. I don't think she moved once on the whole of the eight hours' journey. It was impossible even to guess at her thoughts. Through a pair of dark sunglasses her eyes gave nothing away."

Ingrid, who had fled to Italy for its color, light, and freedom, now was penned up within her fate, impotent to act. The emotional logic of Ingrid's life had always been to avoid pain and conflict for herself. Now whichever direction she took brought recriminations and threats. In Rome only two months before she had been at the center of a glorious romance and adventure. Now Roberto shuttled her off to a small apartment with his sister. Here she sat away from reporters and observers, while for much of the week Roberto moved freely around the city.

On their return to Stromboli, Ingrid and Roberto brought with them a little black dog that they named Stromboli. The dog became a symbol of their romance and love.

Ingrid had no one on the island in whom she could confide. Kay was gone, and even when she was on Stromboli she had seemed less than sympathetic. Although Petter denies it, Ellen says that she was acting as an intermediary with Petter, receiving and answering letters about events on Stromboli. She showed Ingrid all the letters. Despite that, Ellen had the feeling that Roberto no longer trusted her. That was true enough, for on Stromboli Roberto trusted no one not of his blood and race. As for Ruth Roberts, she had become so upset over the scandal that she left Hollywood to work for many months with the Quakers in Europe.

Ingrid felt that she needed someone who cared and thought indisputably for and about her. When Joe Steele wrote she responded quickly. The last

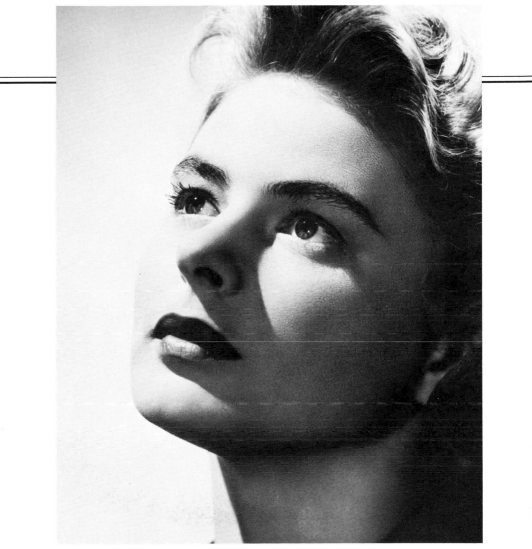

The transcendent beauty of Ingrid Bergman.

Above: Ingrid and Petter Lindstrom standing at the altar at the Lutheran church in Stode, Sweden.

Left: Ingrid and Petter as man and wife.

Opposite page:
Top: Ingrid and her father.

Middle: Ingrid as an extra. Despite being placed in the far left of the back row, Ingrid made sure her full face appeared.

Bottom: Ingrid (front left) studied only a year at the Swedish Royal Dramatic School.

Left: Ingrid's first film role was in *The Count of the Monk's Bridge*, co-starring Edvin Adolphson.

Below: The Swedish *Intermezzo*, with Ingrid's idol, Gösta Ekman.

Right: A personal picture of Ingrid taken around 1937.

Below, left: A pregnant Ingrid making a film in Nazi Germany in 1938.

Below, right: At times, Ingrid looked as if she didn't know what to do with her infant daughter, Pia.

Above: Ingrid traveled to Nazi Germany to make *The Four Companions.*

Right: Ingrid takes direction from Gregory Ratoff in the American *Intermezzo.*

Above: Ingrid in Hollywood in 1939.

Left: One of the many unused Selznick publicity shots taken in 1939.

Above: Ingrid and Leslie Howard in Selznick's *Intermezzo.*

Left: Ingrid and Burgess Meredith in *Liliom,* her American stage debut.

Opposite page:
Top: Ingrid, Humphrey Bogart, and Dooley Wilson at Rick's Café in *Casablanca.*

Bottom: Casablanca: The most famous goodbye of all.

Sam Wood directs Ingrid and Gary Cooper in the famous sleeping bag scene in *For Whom the Bell Tolls.*

Cooper, Ruth Roberts, and Ingrid during the making of *For Whom the Bell Tolls.*

Petter and Pia.

Behind Alfred Hitchcock's back, Ingrid jokes for the camera.

Above: Ingrid, Cooper, and Clark Gable on the ski slopes.

Right: Gable proudly displays an eagle shot off a Sun Valley power line while on a trip with Ingrid and Petter.

Ingrid and Pia in the living room of the house on Benedict Canyon.

Ingrid and Petter's bedroom.

Below: Pia, Petter, and Ingrid.

Ingrid, Leo McCarey, and Bing Crosby on the set of *The Bells of St. Mary's* the day after they each received an Academy Award in 1945.

A very rare publicity shot.

A costume test for *Saratoga Trunk*.

Ingrid reunited with Cooper in *Saratoga Trunk*.

Right: Ingrid and Gregory Peck in *Spellbound.*

Below: Ingrid and Cary Grant in *Notorious.*

time she had seen the publicist was the day Petter told him he was fired. She didn't mention that day. Nor did she come right out and try to hire Steele, but simply asked what his plans were at the end of June.

Steele left for Italy, not even thinking about a contract or expense money. He was a man of great decency and honesty, professional failings that were now catching up with him. He believed that doing what was morally correct on Stromboli would be correct public relations as well. He thought that it was morally right for Ingrid to see Petter again, as she had promised. He told Ingrid, and once again Roberto threatened to kill himself.

Roberto was covetous of Ingrid's every moment. He was like a child with a cherished doll that he would not let out of his sight, night or day. He didn't even care if the film was partially sacrificed on the altar of his jealousy. In *Stromboli*, Ingrid was supposed to be married to her co-star, Mario Vitale. Roberto, however, wouldn't let Ingrid kiss the fisherman; their scenes together had as much excitement as the mating of insects.

In Hollywood, Steele had spent days alone with Ingrid. On Stromboli, he saw her primarily over meals, where the air reeked of mistrust and paranoia. Ingrid and the other English-speakers spoke *their* language and had *their* conversations. Roberto and the other Italians spoke *their* language and had *their* conversations.

One day Steele found Ingrid alone for a few seconds. He told her that things couldn't go on the way they were, that she would have to see Petter another time. Ingrid did not disagree, but said that Roberto had threatened to kill himself if she went.

As soon as Roberto saw Ingrid talking to Steele, he came over and asked what they were discussing. Ingrid told him that both she and Steele agreed: she had to see Petter.

"Okay," Roberto said, and turned away. He had weapons other than bombast and suicide threats. He walked to the dock and took the *San Lorenzo* to Messina. When he returned the subject was dead, at least for a few days.

Sometime late in May or early in June, an event occurred on Stromboli that made the discussions about meeting Petter totally moot. Ingrid revealed that she was pregnant. For several weeks on Stromboli she must have known that she was carrying Roberto's child, known that whatever had passed as a scandal before was a minor irritation compared to the wrath and condemnation that would fall on her now.

Ingrid never talked about when she first suspected she was pregnant, or how she told the father of her child-to-be. Roberto told his story of the day he learned to the late Father Antonio Lisandrini. Roberto often confessed to the priest in the sanctity of friendship, not of the Church.

"When they began work on their first film they had an intimate relationship," says Father Lisandrini. "Ingrid came into the room and told Roberto, 'Roberto, I feel I am pregnant.'

"A moment of silence. 'Ingrid, this is a very important moment. I know what will happen when the public learns. You are Jeanne D'Arc. You can imagine. Ingrid, do as you like.'

"Ingrid stood up. 'You don't mean this thing. This is my child. Even if the whole world should fall down upon me, I don't care. This is my child, and I want him.' "

Roberto's version of Ingrid's reaction to her pregnancy has all the marks of a great director's mise-en-scène. Later in the year Ingrid wrote a letter to Steele about her pregnancy that almost certainly comes closer to the truth. "In the beginning I did not have the courage to go through with it, to face worse scandal, more insults, more dirty talk, more stones thrown," she wrote. "But slowly, through Roberto, I gained the strength and the courage. . . . It would have been possible, when I had regained my health after Stromboli, to do something about it. But, after all, what a poor, miserable way out."

Ingrid, then, had contemplated getting an abortion as soon as she left Stromboli. During their last weeks on the island, Roberto apparently talked her out of ending her pregnancy. Roberto was not a practicing Catholic, but he would not have made the films he did if he had not had a profound sense of the sanctity of life. He had lost one of his two sons, and he wanted more children.

There were other reasons. What greater sign of his possession of Ingrid could there be than her bearing his child? He wouldn't have to worry about Petter any longer, or about Ingrid leaving him even for a day. He cared little for her career or her fame, except as a symbol of his high conquest. Her ambition, her celebrity, could drop from her now, like scales before her eyes. He thought little enough of actors and actresses. He wanted Ingrid to give up her career, to be his wife, the mother of his children.

Roberto almost certainly knew that Ingrid was pregnant when he filmed the last climactic scenes of *Stromboli*, wherein the husband is so jealous that he nails up the windows and doors of the house, imprisoning his wife. When she discovers that she is pregnant, she escapes up to the volcano. There, in Roberto's words, "in the midst of hostile nature, broken by fatigue, bowed down by a primitive terror, in animal despair, she unconsciously calls upon God."

On the morning that they began shooting up on the volcano, a team of eight mules stopped in front of Ingrid's door. There had never been any mules on the island before the filmmakers arrived. It was only 3:30 A.M. She was wearing pants and boots. She looked haggard and worn, as if she belonged on the island now.

Ingrid got on one mule, and she and Roberto and the film crew set off for the volcano. The mules struggled upward, jumping across the smaller gullies, scratching for a foothold on the black gravelly surface.

Roberto had the camera set up near the cone of the volcano. For her scene walking up to the volcano, Ingrid wore thin sandals, scant protection against the black lava sands, as hot as a tar roof on a summer afternoon. Ingrid was never one to complain about the rigors of filming. She began her walk under the unyielding sun.

Roberto was usually in favor of quick takes, but he rehearsed this scene over and over. Repeatedly Ingrid struggled upward, through the fumes and the stench of sulfur. She was soaked with sweat. Michael Wilson noticed that Ingrid "was trembling. From time to time her mouth twitched in painful spasms."

When Ingrid and the others returned to the village at noon, they were on foot. To save time, they had slid two thousand feet down the mountain on their behinds. Their faces were black and sweat-streaked. They looked as if they had suffered a terrible defeat up on the volcano. Steele waited for them. He thought they looked like newsreels of rescued coal miners after a disaster.

Ingrid and the others returned to the volcano again and again. One day Lodovici Muratori, a production executive, was overcome by the fumes and died of a heart attack.

The shooting continued.

In Hollywood, RKO did not know about the rigors of the shooting. The studio knew only that the film was supposed to be shot in six weeks and the crew had been on Stromboli over twice that long. Ingrid was paid $17,500 a week, and financially, at least, she was onto a good thing.

On Stromboli, Harold Lewis issued Roberto an ultimatum: either finish filming immediately or RKO would take drastic action, possibly even shutting the production down. Roberto, Steele, and a few others wrote a cable to be sent by Ingrid to her lawyer, Mendel Silverberg, protesting Lewis's action. By now Steele was as much a part of this Italian melodrama as anyone else, and the cable was excessive not only in length but in hyperbole. Ingrid, Roberto, and the others were involved not in anything so routine as a mere movie but in a dangerous, dramatic artistic quest.

"NO ONE REALIZES WHAT SACRIFICES WE MADE EXCEPT THOSE WHO HAVE HAD TO LIVE ON THIS ISLAND." Alas, it was equally true that no one except those on the island knew about the weeks that Roberto had run off to Rome, or Sicily, or merely to go spearfishing.

"ONE OF OUR MEN DIED OF SULPHUR FUMES ON VOLCANO. ROSSELLINI SUFFERED SEVERE INJURIES IN FALL AT CRATER AND IS NOW WORKING DE-SPITE DOCTOR'S ORDERS TO REST FOR TEN DAYS." Muratori had, indeed, died on the volcano, as much a victim of Roberto's penchant for "realism" as of his own weakened heart. Roberto had not fallen on the crater and been injured and there was no doctor on the island.

"THIS IS THE MOST IMPORTANT PICTURE I HAVE EVER MADE." For all that Ingrid had gone through, all the professional and personal sacrifices she had made, that had better be the truth.

Silverberg cabled back that Roberto could have a few more days to complete *Stromboli*. Even during the last days of shooting, the question of Ingrid and Roberto's future had to be faced. Roberto's attorney, Signor Verdozzi, arrived from Rome. He said that Roberto's request for an annulment rested in the Italian court, and advised that both legally and strategically, Ingrid should make a last visit to Petter.

The attorney did not know that he was involved in an elaborate charade; his client had told him everything about the situation except for the one essential fact: Ingrid was now two and a half months pregnant. Ingrid told Steele nothing about the pregnancy either. Ingrid and Roberto had a double reason to be quiet. As long as there was a possibility that Ingrid might seek an abortion, they could afford to tell no one. Public knowledge that Ingrid had ended her pregnancy would wreak such havoc on their personal and professional lives that what had come already would seem as nothing.

Ingrid, then, had only one person who knew the secret of her life. Everything else was acting and pretense and facade. In many respects Steele was the saddest of all those deceived. He saw himself as the impresario of Ingrid's image. He had come to her as soon as she had called. And now he was engaged in a frantic, foolish, misguided, misinformed attempt to salvage Ingrid's reputation.

Steele stayed up much of the night on July 27 writing a letter to Ingrid and Roberto. He did not think of this as a story of love and lust, of jealousy and ambition, but as a grand historical drama starring a woman who despite her threats to give up her career would soon desire to rescue the career that God had intended for her, and a man who like Ingrid lived in a world full of duties and tasks that he could not deny. Steele argued that Ingrid should see Petter again because it was morally wrong to deny him. He feared that Petter might issue a statement full of bitterness and hate. The publicist was not merely proffering advice. He was writing a scenario. He envisioned the very day that they would meet. Ingrid would cry and that would be the end.

Ingrid and Roberto said nothing to Steele about his interminable letter. Instead, under the supervision of Roberto's lawyer, Steele was instructed to prepare a dramatic statement to be released a few days later in Rome.

CHAPTER FOURTEEN

The Edge of a Volcano

On August 2, Ingrid and Roberto left Stromboli for good. On their way back to Rome, they stopped in Amalfi for two days. Ingrid and Roberto stayed in the small suite in Albergo Luna Convento where Henrik Ibsen had lived while writing *A Doll's House*, his great study of a woman's subjugation.

Regarding Amalfi, Ingrid already had her own sense of personal history. Four months before, she had come here flush with romance, excited by the prospect of making a great film. Ingrid remembered so well the day she and Roberto had taken a walk together, a day of unfettered happiness, Roberto telling stories as if all Italy was his to know and to relate. He had seemed to hold the key to everything she had ever wanted.

Ingrid remembered how the photographers had photographed them walking hand in hand in the ruins of an ancient tower. The photograph was published in *Life*, and helped to set off the whole furor, a picture worth not merely a thousand words, but a marriage, an adopted homeland, perhaps even a daughter, or even a career.

So much had changed that now that photograph might as well have been an ancient tintype, faded and yellow. What Ingrid had lost was bad enough, but now Roberto and his advisers were asking Ingrid to make what for her was the ultimate sacrifice: to end her career in films.

Steele was the one person left in Italy to whom she could turn. Although Ingrid was still deceiving the publicist about her pregnancy, she asked him to journey to Amalfi from Rome so that she might seek his advice. She told the publicist that she would not consider retiring unless forced to take such drastic action. Steele pointed out how much she needed the money from *Stromboli*, and if she announced her retirement, the film was less likely to be boycotted. Moreover, she could resume her career later.

The following day, August 5, Steele issued a press release in Ingrid's name to reporters in Rome:

It was not my desire to make any statement until the conclusion of the picture I am now making. But persistent malicious gossip that has even reached the point where I am made to appear as a prisoner has obliged me to break my silence and demonstrate my free will. I have instructed my lawyer to start divorce proceedings immediately. Also, with the conclusion of the picture it is my intention to retire into private life.

The very day after Ingrid's announcement, the even more dramatic news of Ingrid's pregnancy was splashed across a page of *Corriere Della Sera*. The Roman newspaper presumably had learned of it from one of Roberto's friends or advisers.

Ingrid had decided to have the child, but she and Roberto needed time before announcing her pregnancy. If the story got out now it would create a firestorm of new controversy, probably causing the banning of *Stromboli* in the United States, and complicating the divorce proceedings even further. Their concern over *Stromboli* was far from one of mere artistic vanity. Roberto was in his usual financial straits. It took the simplest of arithmetic to see that *Stromboli* was the way out. Between them Ingrid and Roberto would get 60 percent of *Stromboli*'s net profits, a windfall such as few stars and directors had ever received. If the film was a major success, Ingrid could easily expect to earn more than a million dollars.

Steele was Ingrid's best weapon in killing the story. The publicist was outraged at such sordid lies and wanted Roberto to file a libel suit. He saw the arrival of Hedda Hopper in Rome on August 9 as fortuitous. Roberto and Ingrid were not quite so sanguine. The famous Hollywood columnist was not one of Roberto's reporter friends, who could be trusted to shape the story to fit his demands.

Hopper was a great arbiter of power in the film business. There was a beautiful simplicity to her use of power. For her column she wanted news. If you were a star and you or your publicist gave her news, then you were generally written about positively. If you did not, then you were ignored. Once, at a party in Hollywood, Ingrid had been seated next to Gene Tierney and seen Hedda exercise that power. The actress had not informed Hopper that she was expecting a baby. "Wait till your next picture comes out," Hopper threatened. "Don't think you can expect anything good about it from me."

There was one other subtlety to Hedda Hopper's equation of power. She was not about to approve of public scandal. This stately lady in flowered hats was the Savonarola of Hollywood, a fierce moralist who ranted and raved against what she considered the moral decay and decadence of the new Hollywood. Scandals threatened her professionally, for she told her millions of readers that there was a different Hollywood, Hedda's Hollywood, a studio upon a hill where stars like Ingrid lived good American lives, raised their families, and went to church.

Ingrid understood the workings of publicity as well as Steele did. In agreeing to see Hopper she was playing a dangerous game, chipping away at one of the pillars of her own career. Ingrid was going to have to deceive the gossip columnist. The truth would not stay hidden forever, and when the news came out, the columnist's reputation for accuracy would be as sullied as Ingrid's image. For now, though, Ingrid would have to give a great performance.

Steele escorted Hopper to the interview in Roberto's chauffeur-driven car. Hopper usually set the time and circumstances of her interviews. Now she was in the midst of an Italian melodrama, being escorted to a secret rendezvous. The car stopped in a residential area where Enrico Donati, Marcella's lover, waited to lead Hopper to his apartment. There Ingrid sat waiting for the interview.

Ingrid rushed forward to greet Hedda as if she were her oldest friend. As they chatted, Hopper cast a practiced eye on Ingrid, looking for telltale signs of pregnancy. Ingrid had dressed with particular flair today, all in red, from her dotted blouse, and her skirt, to red slippers. Alas for Hedda, if a woman's body had ever been constructed to hide a pregnancy, Ingrid had that body. Not only was she tall and big-boned, but she was often ten or fifteen pounds over-weight, as plump as a Swiss milkmaid. If she looked pregnant, then every robust, healthy-looking woman in the world looked pregnant.

Hopper asked her questions for an hour or so. Ingrid frequently punc-tuated her conversation with the word "hell," a profanity that had previously never passed her pristine lips in Hopper's presence. In some quarters in America, the use of such language was by itself a sign of moral depravity, and Hopper made note of Ingrid's language.

Ingrid spoke like a woman who had been hemmed in, cooped up with people to whom she could not easily talk. She shed her usual professional modesty and talked to Hopper with a pride that was bound to rankle the columnist's readers. "I took a beating on the island of Stromboli," she said. "I am sure no other actress could have stood physically the things I did willingly because I felt we were getting a great picture. . . . I would like to see another actress work on the edge of a volcano with sulphur fumes choking her almost to death and the wind trying to blow her into the crater. Well, I did it. . . .

"People don't seem to understand. Never before in my life had I been tired, but on Stromboli I have been so tired I cried from exhaustion, and when I realized that I was a prisoner—I never received my mail, my messages—I cried from rage. . . . I have been the victim of a lot of lies. . . . Now I just want to go away and hide."

"But, Ingrid," Hopper countered, "there is no place in the world you can hide. You can rest for three or four months and then the longing for work will return and you will be right back in harness."

Finally Hopper asked the one question she had come to ask.

"What's all this about you being pregnant?" she asked.

"Oh, my goodness, Hedda, do I look it?" Ingrid laughed.

"That's all I wanted to know," said the columnist, content that virtue and her column had been well served. Ingrid, however, had the actor's vice of always wanting strong exit lines. She went on to give Hopper the impression that she was about to sue *Corriere Della Sera* for their disgusting, dishonest story.

Hopper left to write her column. "A more bewildered girl I never talked with," she wrote, hardly the impression that Ingrid had tried to convey. The columnist thumbed her nose at the rumors of pregnancy by relegating that part of the story to the last paragraph. "Ingrid declares she will bring suit against the Italian papers which said she was going to have a baby.

"I don't blame her; there is not a word of truth in it."

Ingrid did not have the sort of bohemian spirit that considers a child born out of wedlock a child of love. One of the paradoxes of Ingrid's life is why, once she decided to have Roberto's child, she didn't immediately and insistently pursue a divorce, if not in the United States, then in Sweden.

Ingrid hid not illogically but partially because she and Roberto feared that if her pregnancy became known, *Stromboli* would be banned in the United States and she might lose a fortune.

According to Steele, Ingrid tried to file for a Swedish divorce, but the technical difficulties made it impossible. According to Petter, he is the one who contacted a Swedish attorney about a divorce for Ingrid. Ingrid and Petter were Swedish citizens. They were living in different countries, thousands of miles from their native land. The technicalities were, indeed, large, but it is doubtful that Ingrid went as far as she might have in exploring a Swedish divorce.

Ingrid was an actress, and as with most actors and actresses, there was at her center a core of passivity. She waited for roles to fill her up. When she could not flee from unpleasantness, she waited for something to happen to her.

Roberto was a man of great occasion, and August 29, 1949, should have been a memorable day, the celebration of a triumphant romance as much as Ingrid's thirty-fourth birthday. Roberto did his best, giving Ingrid a diamond scorpion brooch. Ingrid, however, was full of bourgeois strictures about buying only what you can afford. She could not have been unaware that Roberto was as pursued by bill collectors as by reporters, and that in marrying him she was marrying his debts as well. Roberto did his best to make the evening gay and lighthearted, but the conversation fell like the dull beat of broken drums. He had been feuding with RKO, seeking to cut, edit, and score *Stromboli* in Rome, not Hollywood. For a while he had even refused to give up the last shots of *Stromboli* to the studio.

Ingrid was trapped in their rented apartment on Via Antonelli, unable to go out by herself. At times she thought the unthinkable: if only she could be back in Beverly Hills, if only she could have Petter and Pia back. On September 3, 1949, she wrote Petter's sister, Anna-Britta, in Stöde:

> You know, if I woke up tomorrow and found that I was in Beverly Hills, California, and I had dreamed this, all these months of soul agony, tears, scandal, etc., I would probably be satisfied and continue my life as before. I am always thinking of Petter and Pia, but at the same time I tell myself that it is impossible to go back. Petter is a settled, good man, I really know that, and I am flyttfågel [bird of passage]. I have always, ever since I was a little girl, looked for something new, new. I had longed for the big adventure, as much as I had, saw and lived through, it was never enough. I tried to get through the daily tristesse and find happiness and satisfaction. But I didn't know what gave me happiness and peace.
>
> How do I know, dear Anna-Britta, if this is the real happiness? I understand well that I have taken the big step. But who knows the end?

Ingrid may have had her doubts, but she was pregnant, and she had little choice but to pursue the divorce. There were many Rossellini family discussions, some of them overheard by Roberto's cousin, ten-year-old Franco Rossellini. "From what I heard, a lot was based on the fact that she had made a lot of money in America," Franco remembers. "A lot of things were based on feelings but also on cash, cash and carry."

Roberto's attorney, Signor Verdozzi, hired forty-year-old Monroe E. MacDonald, an American lawyer living in Rome. He traveled to New York and Los Angeles as Ingrid's emissary, to find legal representation on the West Coast, and to push the proceedings along.

MacDonald carried to the States Ingrid's three-thousand-word autobiography of her years with Petter. The confidential document had none of the heartfelt perspective of Ingrid's letter to Anna-Britta, but was a tough, one-sided legal brief. It would be a useful weapon as her case was prepared, as well as an explosive missile if it ever found its way into the newspapers.

As soon as MacDonald landed in New York, he met with the columnist Igor Cassini—"Cholly Knickerbocker." The next day, September 21, 1949, the first-page banner headline in the New York *Journal American* read: "NOW FOR THE FIRST TIME: INGRID'S REAL LOVE STORY." Cassini's article was a devastating attack on Petter, based on both MacDonald's and Ingrid's statements, and full of errors:

> Since her marriage . . . Ingrid has been a faithful and devoted wife. The doctor dominated her completely. Eleven years her senior, he had complete ascendency over her, and never let her make a decision by herself. Every contract Ingrid has ever signed always had to be first okayed by Peter. He controlled all the money . . . Although they had a splendid home

and lived luxuriously, Ingrid never owned a single piece of jewelry except her wedding ring since they were married. When she left for Europe last March he gave her $300, and that's all she has received from home since.

Sooner or later all the pettiness, the ancient grievances, the endless recriminations, surface in a divorce, like maggots from the earth. They do not, however, usually find their way to the front page of newspapers. Even if Cassini had written the full truth, it served no one—not Petter, not Ingrid, not Pia—to have the stories told in the press. It demeaned Petter, but it demeaned Ingrid too, and demeaned the years of their marriage together. Moreover, the story had appeared the day after Pia's eleventh birthday, a curious gift indeed.

Ingrid expressed herself as appalled that MacDonald would give an interview and hand out her statement to a gossip columnist. It is unlikely, however, that the attorney would so brazenly, so dramatically, so immediately violate his mandate. He could be disbarred or censured for violating his pledge of confidentiality.

In Rome, MacDonald had talked not only with Ingrid but with Roberto and other members of the Rossellini family. Indeed, Cassini reported in his article that MacDonald had come to America with full power of attorney "to negotiate with Dr. Lindstrom for Ingrid's freedom and *to present before the American public the real facts behind the great love story.*"

Cassini was of Italian descent. He had, as he points out, "friends in Italy and was the best informed columnist on Europe." The columnist says that he does not remember how MacDonald contacted him, but it may well have been through Rossellini's intrusion, either directly or by means of intermediaries.

That possibility is reinforced by the fact that Steele found Rossellini strangely unaffected by the turmoil over the disclosures. Roberto had taken a profound visceral dislike to Petter. He would have enjoyed making a public spectacle of him, ripping apart the good doctor's reputation as Roberto felt that his own reputation had been torn at and dirtied.

As soon as MacDonald arrived in Los Angeles, he hired Gregson Bautzer as Ingrid's California attorney. Ingrid had met the lawyer when he had come to Rome on Howard Hughes's behalf to try to buy Ingrid and Roberto's rights to the profits of *Stromboli* for a lump sum. In Hollywood, Bautzer was as well known for his techniques in the boudoir as in the courtroom. He was squiring about Joan Crawford, Lana Turner, and other stars and starlets, but he was also a tough, ambitious attorney. He immediately let it be known that he was offering Petter a queen's ransom for Ingrid's freedom.

"INGRID OFFERING FORTUNE TO GAIN MARITAL LIBERTY," read the banner headline in the *Los Angeles Examiner* on September 23. The story, by Louella Parsons, said that Ingrid was "prepared to offer Dr. Peter Lindstrom half of their community property—the remaining half to be put in trust for the use and benefit of their daughter, Pia. Miss Bergman will ask for part-time custody of their daughter. All she wants from Dr. Lindstrom is an oil painting of her little girl." Bautzer was a virtuoso at playing the press, and he had struck a dramatic opening note. Ingrid appeared a generous free spirit willing to give up everything for love, while Petter seemed a miserly soul hoarding the gold of Ingrid's earnings.

Until now, Petter had maintained a semblance of a relationship with Ingrid. He had even talked to her recently on the phone. But as soon as he saw this new onslaught of publicity, he lost whatever residue of goodwill and trust he had left.

Nonetheless, Petter still refused to talk to reporters. In Hollywood, silence is fool's gold, and George Seaton wanted to set up a press conference where his friend could tell his side of the story. Åke Sandler, another friend and a fellow Swede, wrote an article for *Collier's*. But Petter decided not to have it published. He did not want to create even more scandal, whose consequences Pia would have to deal with.

Petter refused interviews, but two days after the Cholly Knickerbocker column, his rebuttal found its way into the newspapers. John Vernon, Ingrid's former business manager, issued a lengthy statement in which he was described as a "spokesman for Dr. Peter Lindstrom." It was Vernon and his wife who had kept Pia awhile during Petter's lengthy sojourn in Europe, and Mrs. Vernon who had taken her to Minnesota.

The most interesting part of Vernon's statement dealt with financial matters. Vernon said that Ingrid "did not go to Europe with $300" but went with an unnamed larger sum. He said, moreover, that Ingrid had "always had full access to all of her funds" and had "transferred to Italy quite a few thousand dollars and could have more for the asking." He added that "aside from their home, their joint assets are very nominal."

Petter was so upset by the publicity that he wrote Ingrid to complain. "You say my lawyers have offered you a fortune for my liberty," she replied. "And in headlines. It is not their fault what the paper makes headlines of. Probably the paper people were as surprised as the lawyers. It is not usual for a woman not to ask for anything. Probably they think I am a fool to give you all I have. Half of what I have earned is mine. But I want to leave it for you and Pia."

Ingrid was anything but a fool. California has a community property law, a marital Marxism that divides assets equally between husbands and wives. Ingrid and Petter's declared joint assets in the United States were amazingly small, given the over half-million dollars she had earned on her last three films, as well as Petter's income as a surgeon.

Tangible assets consisted of the house in Benedict Canyon, valued at around $70,000, savings accounts of approximately $30,000, savings bonds worth about $19,690 in cash, substantial life and health insurance policies, three automobiles (a 1947 Chrysler Windsor, a 1948 Pontiac convertible coupe, and a 1949 Chevrolet), a small farm in Sweden worth a few thousand dollars, plus jewelry, furs, household furnishings, and personal effects. These assets were worth over $200,000, her share being half of that, or something over $100,000.

Ingrid's own assets in Italy were already larger than the total assets in America. For her earnings on *Stromboli* Ingrid had received $205,000 from RKO, paid in a country where avoiding taxation is considered one of the creative arts. That did not include the large Italian subsidy or anticipated profits on the film. As Steele learned later from Bautzer, Howard Hughes had offered Ingrid and Roberto $600,000 for their share of the American and European rights. That was an enormous sum, but Ingrid and Roberto rejected it in anticipation of even larger earnings.

If Ingrid and Petter's total assets were equally divided, she would have had to pay a share of her *Stromboli* earnings to him. That may have been unfair, particularly when Petter was at the beginning of a lucrative medical career and Ingrid's future earnings were so uncertain. But that indeed was the law. Petter says that he never sought nor would he have accepted what he considered the tainted money of *Stromboli*. According to Ingrid, however, Petter asked for 50 percent of the film money, first for himself, then for Pia, while offering her only a third of their assets in the United States, presumably with Petter and Pia dividing the rest.

Whatever the truth, the divorce negotiations were a nasty bit of business, fought not over right and wrong, love and emotion, but over money and property.

"I feel really like Don Quixote fighting against the windmill," Ingrid wrote Petter. "You are my windmill and probably you are hoping to hit me one day with a big blade and kill me."

Petter saw no reason to hurry the divorce along, especially when Ingrid's minions pilloried him in the press. He felt that he had acted well and asked for little—only a meeting between Ingrid and Pia. And he had been abused and tricked. He sought what his supporters called "justice" and his foes deemed "revenge." He had no truck with those who tried to be "objective" or "philosophical" and wished to discuss "Ingrid's side of the story," as well. If you were Petter's friend you were *his* friend.

Petter had a hard time knowing just whom he could trust. During his years with Ingrid, the men who had clasped his hands most fervently in comradeship had often been Ingrid's lovers. The hospitality and friendship in the film community had been for Ingrid, and not really friendship at all. He found it impossible to maintain relationships with friends who thought they could be Ingrid's friends as well.

In Rome, Ingrid heard almost nothing but bad news.
Under Capricorn had opened in Radio City Music Hall, the great theater

where so many of her movies had been spectacularly successful. But not *Under Capricorn*. The movie was Ingrid's third bomb in a row, the third that destroyed a new film company. The exhibitors in Chicago exploited Ingrid's current plight in their newspaper ads: "STRANGE THINGS KEEP HAPPENING TO INGRID BERGMAN. YOU'LL SEE THE HEIGHTS—AND THE DEPTHS TO WHICH A WOMAN CAN GO." Even that didn't help.

The bird of passage was now a caged bird, plumed and pampered, encased in the apartment on Via Antonelli. Roberto bought her furs and jewels, the money conjured out of somewhere—a distributor, a banker, probably Ingrid's own accounts. When, rarely, Ingrid went outside, her shoulders were graced with mink and her fingers sparkled with diamonds, but her eyes were red and raw.

Ingrid's only old friend in Rome was Joe Steele. He kept trying to talk to her, but Roberto put him off. Finally the publicist decided that it was time he returned to America. Full of sorrow, he came to tell Ingrid that he was planning to go. Roberto sat beside her touching her, stroking her cheek, whispering to her. Steele thought that all the blue of Ingrid's eyes appeared washed out. Her cheeks sagged. Her voice was nothing but a whisper. She appeared sick and alone.

On the evening of Steele's departure, he came again, to say goodbye to Ingrid over dinner. She had thought they would be alone, but Roberto had invited other guests. After dinner, Ingrid motioned Steele to another room. Roberto entered, and admonished Ingrid to get back to her guests.

Later, Ingrid went with Steele to the door. Her lips quivered. Steele wondered what her message would have been. Ingrid hugged Steele, and they cried, and then the publicist left, without saying goodbye.

Soon after, Ingrid took sick, suffering from a serious cough that she attributed to her sadness. She had no sense of place any longer, and in the midst of her new illness she was rooted up once again and moved into a new apartment at 49 Via Bruno Buozzi, in the suburb of Rome known as Parioli.

The apartment was a large place decorated with antiques, but to Ingrid these were cold lodgings indeed, barren of the homey touches that had made the house on Benedict Canyon Drive so friendly and inviting. She had never been a woman who cried very often or very long, but she kept sobbing.

Roberto was used to a woman like Anna, who cried in great cathartic outbursts, thunderous torrents of tears that lasted no longer than a summer storm. Ingrid's tears came from somewhere deeper inside. Roberto, appearing helpless, sat in the poorly heated apartment playing solitaire.

Ingrid kept trying to call Pia. Finally, she reached her daughter in Los Angeles. Pia asked when the picture would be finished and Ingrid would come home.

For a good while Ingrid had been planning to tell Pia that she had left her father for good and would be marrying Roberto, but she never could quite say it. When she had first written Petter that he was "alone in the ruins," she seemed to believe that it was Petter who would have to reassemble the broken shards of their life together, and sweep away the painful memories. Petter, in trying to force Ingrid to be the one to tell Pia about the divorce, was meting out his own exquisite revenge, forcing her to act with what he considered responsibility.

Pia had read about her mother and Roberto, and probably had heard about them from schoolmates or others. "The experience of having my mother go from being a saint to a tramp in a few days was traumatic," Pia says. "Both my father and I suffered a tremendous sense of loss. The publicity was monstrous. It happened to be my mother. She happened just a week before to be my mother. I think she went through the rest of her life carrying a profound guilt."

Pia wrote Ingrid that she refused to look at the map in her schoolroom because she couldn't stand seeing Italy. She asked her mother why she hadn't come to Hollywood for the dubbing of *Stromboli*. She said that none of her mother's pictures had ever gone on so long.

Ingrid was suspicious that the fine hand of Petter stood behind Pia's letter. Inevitably, though, Pia's initial sympathies were for a father who was there, not for a mother who had rarely been there and one day departed, leaving her with a father and memories. Like many children of separation and divorce, Pia had spun a cocoon around her emotions, seeking to protect herself from news she did not want to hear. Pia was only eleven years old, but she was mature for her age, even by Hollywood standards, a pubescent child-woman who sat at the head of the table, playing the mistress of the house.

Finally, as the Christmas season drew near, Ingrid wrote to Pia, telling her of the divorce.

Sitting alone in the apartment, Ingrid wrote many letters. On November 26, she composed a long, gossipy letter to Steele that sounded like the old Ingrid. She wanted the publicist to know that no matter what he read, she loved Roberto and Roberto loved her. The next day, before she sealed the envelope, Ingrid added a second message:

"There is only one thing I have to warn you about . . . if again somebody prints that I am pregnant, don't sue them, because you will be sure to lose your case . . . that's all in a nutshell."

The impact of the letter numbed Steele. He believed that he knew and understood Ingrid better than anyone, and was sure she trusted him in ways that she could not trust Roberto. He needed to believe that, or what was he but a poorly paid retainer, a flack whose integrity was for sale by the hour?

Steele might have raged against an Ingrid who had dropped him once with no more ceremony than if she were returning an overdue library book; then had picked him up again, and rewarded his loyalty and devotion by having him unknowingly spread the seeds of falsehood. But Steele still loved Ingrid. He considered her life a great epic in which he wanted to play a part. He wrote back the next day, offering not recriminations but advice. He told Ingrid to be wary of everyone, and he warned her that if the newspapers learned the truth, it would finish *Stromboli* in the United States, a threat of which she and Roberto were only too aware.

Steele had hold of the greatest secret in American popular culture, and he wanted to tell someone, wanted to help. He decided to tell Howard Hughes, and to ask him to release *Stromboli* immediately, a move that would benefit not only Ingrid and Roberto but the coffers of RKO as well.

On December 11 Steele went to see Hughes in his bungalow at the Beverly Hills Hotel, not more than a mile from Ingrid's house in Benedict Canyon. When Ingrid had first known Hughes he had been debonair, handsome, and adventurous enough to have won his share of stars and starlets even without his immense wealth. But already he was showing signs of the quirkiness and irrationality that would lead to a pathetic, hermetic decline.

Greeting Steele in sloppy, unpressed pants and a white shirt, Hughes beckoned for the publicist to sit down on a sofa. Steele said that his comments had to remain confidential. Hughes nodded his assent.

Hughes did not appear excited about the dramatic news. He listened sympathetically as Steele outlined his plan to book *Stromboli* immediately in as many as five hundred theaters. Before the two men parted, Hughes gave Steele the impression that he would go along with the plan.

The next morning, the *Los Angeles Examiner* headlined:

INGRID BERGMAN BABY DUE
IN THREE MONTHS AT ROME

Louella Parsons's story played on front pages across America. Parsons made historical comparisons as if she were not a gossip columnist but Gibbon or Michelet. "Few women in history, or men either, have made the sacrifice the Swedish star has made for love," she wrote. "Mary Queen of Scots gave up her throne because of her love for the Earl of Bothwell. Lady Hamilton, beautiful English queen of society, gave up her position in the London social world to bear a child out of wedlock to Lord Nelson. King Edward VIII . . . renounced his throne to marry the woman he loved."

Parsons did not have to beat her little drum any louder. The story had a stunning impact across America, driving such matters as President Truman's announcement of the development of the hydrogen bomb off the front page. It touched a raw nerve end, creating a great, dramatic controversy.

The United States of the late 1940s was the strongest power in the world, but the country had the sexual maturity of a gawky adolescent, fascinated by sex yet afraid of it. Teenagers were told that masturbation leads to insanity, a statement that, if true, would have created a generation of lunatics. America was a land so consumed by sexual questions that if a person asked, "What are your morals?" he meant primarily, "What are your sexual attitudes?" America was a country of hidden sexuality as well. The late President Franklin D. Roosevelt had had mistresses. For years there was a whorehouse a few blocks from the Capitol, which some lawmakers frequented with the same regularity that they went to church or gave speeches about the sanctity of marriage and the family. All this was *understood*, not to be written about by journalists, or brought to the attention of constituents, as long as everything was discreet.

Hollywood was much the same. As Gregory Peck points out, the film community was not surprised by Ingrid's affair with Rossellini because Hollywood knew about Ingrid's affairs. Hedda Hopper, Louella Parsons, and the other movie reporters were as certain to know about Ingrid's relationships as White House reporters were to know about Roosevelt's affairs. In Hollywood, there was plenty of wenching and whoring, adultery and abortions, though perhaps not any more than in Grosse Pointe or Scarsdale. Almost anything was permissible as long as it didn't get in the papers, and there were battalions of highly paid publicists to see that such news didn't make the press.

Ingrid had left her daughter and husband to run off to Italy with a married man. It was an act that most people would find morally objectionable, but that did not account for the enormity of the scandal. But it was Ingrid Bergman who had done this, not Rita Hayworth, or Lana Turner. Ingrid had refused to be what America thought her to be and, indeed, she had wanted America to think her to be. She had flaunted her relationship with Roberto, had thumbed her nose at the mores of the country that had made her a great star, and a symbol of the moral system that she was so thoroughly violating. Worse yet, she was committing her sin at the very moment that America's system of sexual mores was beginning to crack at its foundations of hypocrisy and cant.

The psyche of fundamentalist America feared Europe as the home of communism and free love. Communism was seen not as a system of power but as a seductive mechanism that could enslave the minds of good Americans. A man like Roberto was viewed as an enslaver of the minds and wills of women, a dark Don Juan against whom God-fearing American men could hardly compete, a man who, in the words of Senator Edwin C. Johnson, was "vile and unspeakable."

As soon as the news reached Rome, the reporters began their watch in front of Ingrid's home. Inside, the phones rang; family members ran in and out; Roberto added his own level of melodrama to the events. Ingrid was the one island of calm. She could even be dispassionate enough to find Roberto funny-looking, as he ran around, hair on end, his clothes disheveled.

Roberto ran back and forth like the Mad Hatter, and screamed, "I beg you, take something for your nerves. You are driving me crazy. I can't stand to see you hysterical. Do you hear what I'm telling you?" Finally he fell asleep, only to wake up and chase around the apartment in his bathrobe. Then he dropped back in bed, to be served his food on a tray as if he, not Ingrid, were seven months pregnant.

Roberto finally got up and dressed and decided that he and Ingrid should give their only press interview to Camille M. Cianfarra, of the *New York Times*. Roberto dominated the discussion. The scholarly reporter usually covered the Vatican—an appropriate background for deciphering the meaning of Roberto's comments.

"Whether she is or is not [pregnant] is nobody's affair," Roberto said, as he sipped espresso in the living room. "I think that report deserves neither denial nor confirmation because it is an attempt to pry into the private life of a woman who, to assert her right to her own life, has given up her career—which is what an artist regards as the most important thing in life. Isn't that enough?"

Of the famous meeting in Messina, Roberto told the reporter: "Our situation was fully discussed. And I want to make clear that at that time the relationship between Ingrid and myself was absolutely correct." If Roberto were telling the truth, Ingrid had been impregnated by immaculate conception—the greatest story a Vatican reporter could want!

Ingrid was denied the tranquillity and rest needed by any woman in the last weeks of pregnancy. She hardly dared to leave the apartment. The best she could do was to sit on the terrace, in wry moments spitting over the railing, aiming at the photographers keeping their watch on the street. Over the holidays a story appeared that Ingrid had had a nervous breakdown. Early in January Roberto told the Rome *Daily American* that he had "planted" the story so that "we could be left in peace over the Christmas and New Year holidays."

On January 22, 1950, a sunny day, Ingrid decided to leave the apartment for the first time in a month, and go for a drive with Roberto. She went downstairs in a long fur coat and ankle-high boots, and she looked decidedly pregnant. As she stood waiting for Roberto to pick her up, a photographer jumped out of nowhere like a big-game hunter who has cornered his prey. Ingrid hurried for the protection of a newspaper kiosk. By now she should have known some choice Italian expletives, but she relied on her English: "Stop it, you devil." The photographer ran around the other side of the kiosk and got another full shot as Ingrid broke into tears.

If Ingrid and Roberto had merely let the photographers get their pictures, they would have been left alone, and the drama would have been partially dissipated. But they were all part of this gigantic melodrama, and Ingrid, who had been photographed thousands of times, considered each photo a violation of her being.

Ingrid and Roberto felt buffeted and attacked from many directions. RKO had taken away the final editing of the American version of *Stromboli*, tearing

Roberto's child from the womb. Not a man to sit moping about the past, however, Roberto was already off in the mountains outside Rome, shooting *Francis, Jester of God*. For Roberto that was decidedly healthier than worrying and waiting over *Stromboli*, but it meant that Ingrid was alone with servants much of the time.

It was a strange life. Not only was Ingrid without her old friends; she was now often even without Roberto. He was as mercurial as ever, telling a reporter late in January that "he had 'contemplated suicide' because of the international publicity." Ingrid could still only half understand Italian. She was frequently grasping for comprehension of words and phrases that were beyond her. Had she been an introspective woman, she might indeed have become half mad puzzling over the ironies and uncertainties of her life.

Ingrid's good news was that Roberto was awarded an Austrian annulment of his first marriage. On January 23 he registered the document. Only Ingrid's delayed divorce now prevented a marriage that would allow the baby to be born in wedlock. For weeks proposals and counterproposals were exchanged between Rome and Los Angeles, with Petter continuing to insist that Ingrid tell Pia about the divorce.

Ingrid's attorneys decided that the only way to obtain an immediate divorce was to get one in Mexico.

Ingrid was waiting for the final decree from Mexico when at noon on February 2, 1950, the telephone rang. It was Lydia Vernon, and Ingrid at first feared that Pia might be hurt or sick. She was shocked that Mrs. Vernon had her number, because that meant that Petter had it too.

"What's the matter with you?" Mrs. Vernon scolded. "You really must pull yourself together and come back and see Pia. Do you understand that?"

Having read that Ingrid was going to Mexico to get a divorce, Mrs. Vernon was willing to escort Pia there to see her mother. She told Ingrid that her eleven-year-old daughter cried because of the bad things she read about her father in the newspaper.

Ingrid promised to see Pia soon. As she set down the phone, she felt the first of her birth contractions. She knew that she had a good while to wait before she would have to go to the hospital. She would have time, she thought, to write a letter to Pia. She had a "terrible presentiment" that she was "going into the hospital to have this baby and perhaps I wouldn't come out of it alive."

It was so much like Ingrid to hide away unpleasantness in the cellar of her life until forced to retrieve it. Ingrid was writing to Pia for the first time in many days. She was finally telling her daughter that she was "expecting another baby" and that she "couldn't come home and have the baby" but would stay in Italy, where Pia would come and Ingrid would visit her. This difficult news would not be received by Pia until well after the baby was born.

Some of the first letters that Ingrid wrote from Italy surged with the passion of truth. The words seemed to have flowed from her heart to the page without forethought or calculation. There is, nonetheless, a staged, mannered quality to many of her supposedly candid letters, more so as time went on. Ingrid kept copies of almost all her letters, as if she were living an autobiography, not a life.

This letter to Pia, which Ingrid thought might be the last letter she would ever write, is not a document of the heart. It is an apologia, a letter that seems at least as directed at posterity as at Pia. Ingrid spends more time trying to elicit Pia's sympathy than commenting on the child's difficulties. She tells Pia of her problems with the press, how newspapers printed things that were only negative, and that she was not able to travel freely ("I have not left the apartment for five weeks"). She gives her daughter a little of her own philosophy—to forget the past, to hide it away, and to go on:

> *I am going to have a little house here and I am going to have a little room called Pia's room, and whenever you come, it is there ready for you, with your things, and you will see that after a while it won't seem so strange to you to have two homes, one with Papa and one with Mama. And we will make trips together. . . .*
>
> *I am so sorry that you have to go through all this. But Life is long and this is only a short period in the shadow. The sun will shine again and we will all be happy.*
>
> With all my love and kisses,
> Mama

By the time Ingrid finished the two-and-a-half-page typewritten letter, the birth contractions were coming less than every three minutes. It was already after three o'clock. She called Dr. Pier Luigi Guidotti, who arrived at the apartment on Via Bruno Buozzi at four o'clock to take Ingrid to the exclusive Villa Margherita Clinic on Via di Villa Massimo. As Ingrid left in the doctor's small car, there were no photographers or reporters outside. That evening, at seven o'clock, Ingrid gave birth to a seven-pound-fourteen-ounce boy.

Ingrid rarely talked about her labor or the joy of her first son. She spoke of the publicity, the circus of her life. "The guards at the gates directed the crowds like a Hollywood premiere," she wrote Steele later.

Robertino's "premiere" had in fact ruined the premiere of Anna Magnani's *Volcano*. When Magnani learned that Ingrid had chosen *her* moment to give birth, the actress reportedly said that this was Roberto's ultimate sabotage. It was indeed a bad night for Magnani. During the middle of the showing at the Fiamma Cinema, the projector bulb broke. That was perhaps God's grace, for the film was terrible. The reporters and photographers, learning that Ingrid had given birth, took off to witness a different melodrama.

Over thirty American reporters and photographers were in Rome, and scores of Italian and European correspondents. For the next few days it seemed that all of them congregated in front of the newly locked iron gates of the clinic. The western world had an insatiable appetite for news about Ingrid, Roberto, and the baby. Robertino, named after his father, was a beautiful, blue-eyed baby.

The photographers salivated at the thought of what an exclusive picture of the new baby might bring: five million lire was offered—roughly eight thousand dollars. The reporters knew that an interview with the new mother would bring accolades and bonuses galore.

As Roberto rushed into the hospital, he viewed the press with disdain. It was a cold night and the journalists built a fire, snapping off branches from stately old oak trees. In her suite Ingrid could hear the raucous clamor as the media representatives pounded on the gates and tried to climb over the wall.

By the following afternoon the reporters and photographers were a more mannerly bunch, their good behavior fostered no doubt by the timely arrival of the Celere, the Roman riot police. Civility is often a journalist's last subterfuge, and several of the reporters convinced the clinic director to let the press inside to inspect the new reception room.

Once within, the photographers, who had hidden their cameras under their coats, took off down the corridors in search of their five-million-lire prize. The reporters ran after them, pursued by nuns into the kitchens and the sickrooms. A photographer for *Life* scurried up a back stairway and made it all the way to the locked door of Ingrid's suite before he was accosted. Then, with the help of the carabinieri, the clinic was cleansed of the scourge.

The inventiveness of the press was endless. Photographers shimmied up rainpipes, danced along the tops of the clinic walls, and tried to bribe a nun to open Ingrid's door. A photographer fell off the wall and broke his arm, his only solace being that he did not have to go far for medical treatment.

One reporter had the good luck to have a pregnant wife, whom he enlisted in the cause. She took a room in the clinic. When the good nuns who opened the woman's valise found that she intended to garb her new child in a collection of cameras, she was asked to leave.

Alas, Ingrid gave no interviews and permitted no photographs. Neither did Roberto, though he kept his impeccable reputation with the press by punching an American photographer in the stomach. All Ingrid and Roberto had had to do was invite the journalists in for a few minutes, and they would have been free. But this was a contest that took two teams of players, and if all the journalists succeeded then none of them did, and the story became little better than a press release.

Roberto had a small moment of revenge when after twelve days Ingrid and Robertino left the clinic. Roberto immensely enjoyed the prospect of outwitting the press, and he planned the getaway with the detail and surprise of a bank heist.

"Let's go," he said dramatically at 4 A.M. Ingrid grabbed Robertino and hurried after Roberto. Patients weren't allowed to go running off in the middle of the night, and nuns pursued the fleeing couple. Ingrid jumped with the baby into Roberto's car. He accelerated away, followed by a friend in a second car and by the now wide-awake photographers and reporters.

The press cars might have caught up and photographed Ingrid and the baby as they entered the apartment, but Roberto had planned a parting gesture. Suddenly, his friend spun his car around in the road, blocking off the press cars from further pursuit.

CHAPTER FIFTEEN

A Child of Love

*I*ngrid was happy with her new baby, but her emotions were nothing compared to Roberto's. He was a proud Italian father, ready to show off his son to his friends if not to the world. One of the first outsiders to see Robertino was Father Lisandrini, Roberto's close friend and a collaborator on his new film on St. Francis.

The intense, intellectual Franciscan father looked at the tiny blue-eyed baby. Robertino had a rare beauty that was appreciated even by a priest who had seen hundreds of newborns.

"How nice is this baby of sin," Lisandrini said as he made the benediction over the baby.

"What do you mean, a son of sin?" Roberto said angrily. "This is a child of love."

Ingrid and Roberto wanted their child of love to be considered legitimate. Unfortunately, by February 9, 1950, when Ingrid's Mexican divorce was granted, it was too late, and according to Italian law Ingrid could not be called the child's legal mother. In Rome's city hall, Renato Roberto Giusto Giuseppe Rossellini was registered: "Father, Roberto Rossellini; mother unknown."

Unsurprisingly, Robertino's birth augmented the criticism. Monsignor Dino Staffa of the Vatican's Supreme Tribunal accused Ingrid and Roberto of "living publicly in adultery" if they went ahead with a civil marriage. In the United States, *The Pilot*, the Boston Catholic paper, was hardly more welcoming to the infant, saying that "while thousands of pious people milled about the Eternal City with the glow of holy pilgrimage in their eyes, a simpering Swedish actress and an Italian director become the parents of a little boy. And the whole world is informed of the progress of illicit love."

Variety announced the results of a survey of movie owners asked whether they would show *Stromboli*. The theater proprietors took a position of rare moral subtlety: they would ban *Stromboli* if after its first days' showing it did not make money. In Indianapolis, the owner of a group of theaters called for a boycott of Ingrid's movies. In Annapolis, a legislator tried unsuccessfully to push through the Maryland state assembly a resolution condemning *Stromboli*.

On March 14, Senator Edwin C. Johnson of Colorado took to the U.S. Senate floor to denounce Ingrid and Roberto. Speaking in the Senate, the Honorable Mr. Johnson did not have to worry about suits accusing him of slander or defamation of character. He savaged Ingrid and Roberto without subtlety or grace: "Mr. President, even in this modern age of surprise it is upsetting to have our most popular but pregnant Hollywood movie queen, her condition the result of an illicit affair, play the part of a cheap chiseling female to add spice to a silly story which lacks appeal on its own. . . . The disgusting publicity campaign . . . the nauseating commercial opportunism . . . the vile and unspeakable Rossellini who sets an all-time low in shameless exploitation and disregard for good public morals . . ." The senator went on to call Ingrid "one of the most powerful women on earth today—I regret to say, a powerful influence for evil."

To counteract this "evil," Johnson was going to introduce a bill that "demands the licensing of actresses, producers and films by a division of the Department of Commerce." The law would have been nothing but veiled censorship. It was a mark of the moral climate of America in 1950 that a senator could make such a speech and not be condemned as vigorously as he condemned Ingrid and Roberto. Johnson was adept at the craft of publicity and he reaped his own rich bounty of attention. Indeed, thirty years later his attack on Ingrid Bergman would be the best-remembered aspect of Johnson's political career.

The marketplace condemned Ingrid and Roberto and their film *Stromboli* with a finality and brutal quickness beyond even Senator Johnson's words. The American version of the film opened February 15, 1950, in 300 theaters across the country, including 102 in the New York City area. "This is it!" the handbills and advertisements screamed. One might have expected to see nuns and priests and ministers picketing the theaters while outraged mothers pulled their impressionable daughters away from the lines in front of the box offices. However, on Broadway that first morning there were only ten people in line, fewer moviegoers than reporters and photographers. The film was a commercial disaster both in America and in Europe. Ingrid and Roberto would make no more money from *Stromboli*.

Although the film received several awards in Europe, it was generally considered, as Bosley Crowther wrote in the *New York Times*, "incredibly feeble, inarticulate, uninspiring and painfully banal."

Roberto raged against the desecration of his work, condemning the brutal editing and the American narration, which suggested a happy reconciliation at the end. He renounced his American earnings on the film, a gesture that would have been a mite more noble if it had come before the film's disastrous opening. In the Communist weekly *Vie Nuove*, Roberto attacked the "low level of culture and intelligence of Hollywood. The setting has been redone and I have discovered at my expense what the brutal and uncivilized methods of Hollywood are."

In Rome, Ingrid was leading the most private, the most restricted of lives, yet she was as deeply fascinated by her publicity as she had ever been. When Janet Flanner, a writer for *The New Yorker*, visited Ingrid's apartment, she reported that "in the vast, rather empty salon of her apartment, her clippings . . . form a sort of cheap, extra upholstery laid out over the divans and chairs."

In the past months Ingrid had received thousands of letters from all over the world: Birth congratulation cards from America, whose uplifting sentimental messages hardly fit the case of a married woman giving birth to another man's child. Sacred medals which their senders hoped might drive away the criticism. Congratulatory notes from Italian-Americans, as if Roberto had impregnated Ingrid in the name of all Italians. Letters condemning Italians, one of which included a picture of Roberto over which two pithy words had been scrawled: "Wop wolf." Letters and cables in support from Cary Grant, Ernest Hemingway, Helen Hayes, Georges Simenon, John Steinbeck, and other celebrities. Letters that mentioned Hawthorne's *The Scarlet Letter* and condemned not Ingrid but puritanism. Letters savagely rebuking her for leaving her husband and child. A letter in French from "Un homme Nordique" in Alsace, who threatened to kill her.

Always before, Ingrid had been appalled by negative publicity. Now, as much as she disliked the criticism, she appreciated the sheer volume of attention. Slowly, though, the world—or at least the world of the newspapers and gossip columnists—began to look elsewhere for headlines and drama. By the end of March Ingrid could look out the windows in the apartment on Via Bruno Buozzi and see no reporters.

In Stöde fourteen years before, Ingrid had wed Petter in a ceremony of such beauty and elegance that it seemed their marriage would last forever. Now she would marry Roberto in a ceremony that was elegant only in its manipulation of the law.

Steele had implored Ingrid to come to Mexico to be wed and there to see Pia, but she could not face that. Instead, she and Roberto decided to marry by proxy. Roberto's friend and attorney, Marcello Girosi, flew to Mexico City to represent Ingrid, while a Mexican attorney represented Roberto.

Ingrid considered her marriage to Roberto not a mere formality but a sanctification of their relationship in the eyes of God and society. Many is the unhappy bride who looks back on her wedding day and reads omens there that she once pretended did not exist. Ingrid wanted her wedding to be more than a rude legal formality. On May 24, 1950, at 10:30 A.M., while the vows were being said by attorneys in Mexico City, Ingrid planned to exchange her own sacred vows with Roberto in Rome.

It would be early evening in Rome, and Ingrid picked out a lovely little church for the ceremony. She dressed in a blue and white silk dress with white cuffs and collar. Then she waited for her husband-to-be to return from his day of filming. And she waited. And she became almost hysterical.

When Roberto finally arrived home, the church had already shut its doors for the night. Ingrid could not be angry at Roberto, on this of all days. Roberto found another church, the Chiesa della Navicella, near the Colosseum. There they knelt and held hands and repeated their vows. Afterward, a dozen of their friends saluted them in Roberto's champagne, and Ingrid displayed her husband's wedding gift: a gold charm bracelet with a tiny police whistle.

Roberto had promised Ingrid that they would go to Paris for their honeymoon and stay at the Raphaël, his favorite hotel. Ingrid had bought a new wardrobe for the trip. Just before they left, Roberto told her that Anna Magnani was planning to be at the Raphaël at the same time, and had asked that the newlyweds stay elsewhere. Another bride would have suggested that her husband's ex-lover take herself elsewhere, but Ingrid said nothing. Roberto was so devastated at being unable to stay at the Raphaël, where Ingrid said he was treated "like a little king," that the Parisian trip was called off.

Instead, the honeymooners journeyed to Capri. Roberto was not about to spend his honeymoon on the island as he had his visit with Ingrid the year before, simply holding hands and musing romantically. Instead, he decided to partake in one of his favorite sports: spearfishing. He swam too deeply for his forty-three-year-old ears. He became temporarily deaf and lost his equilibrium, forcing a return to Rome.

Ingrid tried to settle into the life of a Roman matron. She was infinitely more comfortable as the mistress of a hotel room or a dressing room, where she could ring for food and drink, laundry and sundry services. Here she was forced to rule over a small battalion of servants: Helena, the maid; the nurse; the wet nurse; Pietro, the chauffeur; the other maid; and the cook. The maid and the nurse fought with one another, and Ingrid tried to mediate. She applied her own Swedish standards of cleanliness, dusting what had already been dusted, but she had little to do. "Most of the time I stare out the window, and smoke and smoke and smoke," she wrote Steele in one of her more despondent moods, shortly before her wedding.

Ingrid might complain, but she did not lead the homebound life of most new mothers. For the summer, Robertino had been sent up to Fiuggi with his nurse and grandmother. After their return from Capri, Ingrid and Roberto drove to the mountain resort to see their son. They did not stay very long, however, and they were soon off to Florence, Pisa, and Portofino.

Roberto was everything to Ingrid now, and much of her life was spent waiting on him, or waiting for him. In Rome she planned a dinner party, with Artur Rubinstein and his wife as the honored guests. The Rubinsteins had been Ingrid's next-door neighbors in Beverly Hills. On the appointed hour they arrived, to find that their host was still working. Ingrid called the studio. Roberto didn't care that one of the world's greatest pianists was sitting in his living room nursing his third drink. He was busy cutting his film. As the party sat down to dinner, Ingrid called again. Roberto was still busy.

After dinner, Ingrid went to the back of the apartment and found Roberto in bed with a "headache," unwilling to meet Rubinstein. Ingrid dutifully tromped out to the living room, where she proceeded to make her limp excuses.

"*Maestro!*"

The double doors to the living room burst open. There stood Roberto, his arms outstretched. The two men embraced and talked until well into the morning hours.

Roberto had infinite charm, which he drew on at will, buying his way out of almost any problem or unpleasantness by the sheer force of his personality. He was, however, a magician with only so many tricks, and there was a distressing similarity to his performances.

On another occasion David Lean, the director, and his actress wife-to-be, Ann Todd, were dinner guests at the Rossellinis'. Lean was already a prominent figure in the world of film, and Roberto might have been expected to want to meet him, or at least to show up for dinner. But as Todd remembers the evening, Roberto was in bed asleep, not to be bothered. Ingrid did her best to be a considerate hostess over dinner, and afterward to keep the conversation moving ahead.

"*David!*"

Suddenly, there in the doorway stood Roberto, in his pajamas. The two men embraced. . . .

Roberto was a hospitable sort when the guests were *his* friends, visiting his house on *his* terms. He was most comfortable with Italians, and at their parties and gatherings Ingrid was usually the only foreigner in attendance. "I saw her the first time in their house," remembers Federico Fellini, the director, who was working for Roberto then. "She was the way she always was in films, a queen, serene and pacific and saintly."

Ingrid was indeed like a fairy queen who did not quite comprehend the world around her. "She had this necessity of always trying to understand," says Fellini. "She couldn't understand why we were laughing sometimes. When we were at the table once, someone compared a woman to a monkey and said that she was cute. Ingrid couldn't understand why we would call her cute. I remember Ingrid's innocence. She was very naive. For those of us who knew Roberto well, it was amazing to see them together, always surprising."

When an amusing story was told, everyone would laugh, everyone except Ingrid. Then Roberto or another guest would repeat the story for Ingrid, and she would laugh alone. Ingrid had the gift of mimicry, and she picked up Italian rapidly, albeit with grammatical errors that the Rossellini family joyfully mimicked. Even when she understood the conversations, though, there was a dullness about her, an inability to grasp the nuances and subtleties of Italy and its culture.

"Ingrid's reaction was always late," recalls Giulietta Masina, Fellini's wife, who would gain international fame as the waif in her husband's film *La Strada*. "She would always discover things with a delay. It wasn't only language."

In later years, when Roberto wanted to put Ingrid down he would say that she was "a Swede." Roberto had no particular quarrel with Scandinavians, but Ingrid was not one of those foreigners who are born with the music of Italy sounding in their ears and often seem more Italian than the Italians. That did not mean that Ingrid did not love Italy, for she surely did. But she had a distance from Italy and Italians.

Ingrid's most trusted friend and confidante during those early years in Italy was Fiorella Mariani, the teenage daughter of Roberto's sister, Marcella. She was a young woman doubly sensitive, for she possessed an artistic temperament and was a child of a broken marriage.

Ingrid first became close to Fiorella in August 1950, when she returned to Fiuggi to spend more time with Robertino. Ingrid taught Fiorella English and talked to her for hours about Pia. Fiorella was a young woman of fierce loyalty, with a passionate concern for Ingrid. One day when photographers tried to take pictures of Ingrid, Fiorella threw stones at them.

"We were like sisters," Fiorella says. "We called each other sister. I was sixteen but I was like twenty-one because sorrow brings you maturity. She was childish in a way, and the difference between us was completely gone. I had suffered because of my mother and father, and maybe I was a help to Ingrid to understand Pia's feelings. I was always severe about that. She never understood why Pia was so angry. I said, You went away. There is no excuse for a child. She was always very upset when I was telling her that. I said what my experience was. I had suffered and I said there was no reason why Pia shouldn't have suffered.

"I became Ingrid's best friend. With my uncle it was not so easy because he had this intellectual life that was a hole between them. She was not a cultivated woman. If he was reading about something that had nothing to do with Ingrid, they could not talk. She was not the kind of woman who could help him intellectually. She realized that but she didn't care.

"You could never see what she really felt. She could be bursting with laughter and holding a tragedy within. She was afraid of suffering. She was afraid of evil. She couldn't stand discussion of it. She was afraid of violence, of things that maybe she couldn't say."

Already in the late spring of 1950, when Robertino was only three months old, Ingrid had begun to think seriously about ending her "retirement." David Selznick visited Ingrid in Rome and found her, as he wrote Jenia Reissar, "with a very definite nostalgia for her contractual past with us . . . completely finished with Rossellini type of pictures." Selznick had heard rumors that Ingrid was already talking with Sam Goldwyn, who was very interested in signing her to a new contract.

Ingrid expressed a certain bitterness at the way her professional life had been handled. "Kay Brown has apparently lost all of her influence with Ingrid as a consequence of some advice she gave to Ingrid which Ingrid thought very bad, at a critical moment," Selznick reported. "She is thoroughly aware that Joe Steele and all the others, with whom she surrounded herself, helped to do her in, not of course deliberately but through bad judgment."

Ingrid might rail against Steele to Selznick, but she continued to write the publicist long, chatty, intimate letters. She admitted to Steele that she had in fact had discussions about new pictures with various individuals. She said that she hardly ever saw Roberto, and that it seemed foolish that she should sit at home while he carried "the enormous load."

Even epic romances do not maintain themselves at a fever pitch, but Ingrid was a newlywed and she was already making the familiar complaint of long-time-married middle-class housewives everywhere: she hardly ever saw her husband. Ingrid was incapable of perceiving the irony of her plight. In the States, she had been the one to fly off for filming, bond tours, assignations, and meetings. That had not been enough for her. She had run off in search of freedom and she had ended up in an apartment in Rome, a lady on call to the will and whims of Roberto Rossellini.

Roberto had not remained the adoring loyal husband for very long. One night he was walking down the street when he spied an old friend, a prominent director who had once worked with Rossellini.

"Let's go to a bordello," Roberto said.

The man was aghast. Roman gentlemen didn't go to brothels the way many of them had before the war. If *any* of his friends had suggested such an evening, he would have been taken aback. But Rossellini!

"You are living with one of the most beautiful women in the world," the director reminded him.

"Ah, yes," Roberto said. "But she doesn't do the things that a whore does."

Roberto, like many men, saw oral sex not only as a symbol of intimacy but as a mark of submission, subjection, even humiliation. Ingrid had refused him, but Roberto subjected her to an even greater humiliation, though one that she was almost certainly unaware of. He told his friends and colleagues about her sexual inadequacies. "If you someday want to get married, don't get married to an actress," he told a confidant, "because they're actresses also in bed." Years later he commented to his assistant Francesca Rodolfi that Ingrid was "a woman without passion."

Though Roberto may have found his new love passionless, Ingrid felt differently. "While she was not a good woman for him, he was a good man for her," says Father Lisandrini. "One time she told me confidentially, 'Father Lisandrini, I am happy. This man of Rome has gotten me upside down, turned my world upside down. I know what's love in Rome. This man has been unbelievably beautiful.' "

Ingrid might have been happy for a while had she lived a pampered existence, savoring the luxuries and pleasures of Roman life and her hours alone with Roberto. But she couldn't even do that, for almost every day, she was confronted with severe money problems.

Roberto was, indeed, carrying an "enormous load" of expenses, but so were the banks, the shopkeepers, his friends, and other creditors. In films and in conversation, Roberto criticized the selfish, spiritually empty world of the Italian bourgeoisie, a life based in part on purchasing endless new possessions and showing off. But Roberto understood that world so well because he was part of it. Roberto was capable of grand and generous gestures, and when he had money he had it for many of those around him. But he was a prisoner of his life-style, sacrificing if not his artistic freedom, then at least his artistic tranquillity on the altar of acquisitiveness.

Even since Ingrid had come to Italy, Roberto had spent a small fortune. It wasn't just the furs and jewelry for Ingrid, or the costs of lawyers and transatlantic telephone calls. Nor was it simply the parties, the dinners, the vacations, where everything had to be the best. That was only the beginning. Roberto had purchased a summer home on the Mediterranean at Santa Marinella, fifty-nine kilometers from Rome. The seven-acre estate consisted of an eight-room house, a caretaker's cottage, and another large, dilapidated two-story house.

Roberto could not be the *grande signore* without a worthy retinue of household retainers. Even in the garage there was a retinue of automobiles— Roberto's new red racing Ferrari, an Alfa-Romeo sedan, a Fiat coupe, a Fiat station wagon, and later a Rolls-Royce.

Roberto parted company with the bourgeoisie when it came to paying for his acquisitions. He had learned one of the great secrets of modern finance: if you owe enough money, if your debts are positively horrendous, there is very little your creditors can do except give you more money or wait helplessly.

This is a system that requires great charm and chutzpah, both of which Roberto had in ample supply. He could go in to talk to a banker who was determined to call in a loan, and walk out with twice as much money for a new project. He was forever selling this piece of a movie or divvying up some future project that somehow never became a reality. Roberto was the most democratic of borrowers, taking from both the biggest banks and the smallest neighborhood storekeepers, from his friends and his enemies.

Ingrid came from a land where historically people survived by hoarding food and supplies for the long, dark months. She had never been comfortable with extravagance and waste. She was far from comfortable with Roberto's debts and endless expenses. After all, they were now her debts and expenses too.

Ingrid had come to enjoy much of Roberto's luxurious life-style, and she was perfectly willing to help pay for it. Working was no burden but a joy to Ingrid, and she wanted to help Roberto "carry the enormous load." Indeed, if she worked for Selznick, Goldwyn, or another American producer, she would earn far more than her husband. Nonetheless, as she wrote Steele, she "would not do anything without Roberto."

Roberto would not let Ingrid work with any other director. His friends see this as a mark of Roberto's virtue: despite all his debts he was unwilling to hire his wife out. In fact, Roberto was unwilling to let his wife out of his sight, and unable to face the melancholy fact that she was still a bigger international success than he.

Ingrid's other problem was Pia and the American divorce. Petter could not tolerate the idea of his young daughter going to Italy to be in the presence of Roberto. He was not, however, trying to shut off Ingrid from Pia totally. In the early part of 1950, he arranged to have Phyllis Seaton take Pia to see her mother. According to Mrs. Seaton's sworn deposition, she telephoned Ingrid to "express to her my hope that she would allow me to bring Pia to her, either in England or in any other place of her choosing except Italy. . . . Miss Bergman appeared to be pleased that I called but she declined my offer to arrange such a meeting between her and Pia."

Ingrid believed, as she said later, that one of the keys to happiness is a bad memory. She did not want to feel bad inside, to feel guilt, remorse, and pain. Pia was a witness, who brought with her all the memories, and much of the pain.

Ingrid wanted to see her daughter, but she was seemingly unwilling to risk the unpleasantness of a trip, or other discomfort. She had the forlorn hope that in the summer, when Petter journeyed to Sweden, he would leave Pia with her for a visit. She didn't understand that Petter thought of Roberto as a moral cancer that at all costs must be prevented from infecting his daughter, thought that Roberto might in fact kidnap Pia.

In Los Angeles, Petter was proving a remarkably tenacious opponent in the divorce proceedings. Ingrid was hardly an easy mark. She no longer was offering Petter and Pia all her property in America while seeking to hold on to the rights of *Stromboli*; the film rights were almost worthless. Now Ingrid asked for *all* the community property, including the house, cars, and furniture, on the grounds that she was the one who had earned the money to pay for their life-style; $154,000 that she claimed Petter was holding from *Stromboli*; plus complete custody of Pia.

The negotiations over a property settlement were complicated even more when John Vernon mysteriously disappeared, carrying some of the pertinent documents with him. Several days later Ingrid's former business manager was discovered suffering from amnesia, unable to talk coherently. The accountant was found to have embezzled some of Ingrid and Petter's money. Ingrid's attorney, Greg Bautzer, reported finding $80,000 in Vernon's name in a Los Angeles bank, plus a cashier's check made out to Petter for $10,000. According to Petter, Vernon had actually stolen about $15,000. On October 26, 1951, Vernon died by swallowing an overdose of sleeping pills. His suicide note concluded: "I no longer blame Ingrid and Petter for my breakdown. Lydia must take the responsibility. . . ."

By late April, Ingrid's and Petter's attorneys had largely worked out the property and divorce settlements. On April 19, 1950, Petter signed a property settlement that supports his assertion that he had never received any money from *Stromboli*. The agreement makes no mention of Petter having the money, but gives him the house and furniture in Benedict Canyon, plus one half of their savings bonds, his life insurance policies, one half of their savings, their three automobiles, and their Swedish property. Ingrid received the other half of the savings and savings bonds, her life insurance policies, plus all interest and money from *Stromboli*, *Under Capricorn*, and *Joan of Arc*.

Two years later, in court proceedings, Petter's attorney, Isaac Pacht, detailed the moneys he said Ingrid actually received from the property settlement. Pacht told the court that Ingrid had received over $140,000. This included $15,000 in savings, $19,690 in cash from savings bonds, $43,000 in cash from life insurance policies, a $30,000 tax refund, a $50,000 Italian government subsidy for *Stromboli*, her furs and jewelry. That did not include the film money from *Stromboli*, which brought in close to $200,000 more.

Ingrid gave up seeking complete custody of Pia, a point that was largely a negotiating ploy anyway. She settled for seeing her daughter during vacation, but the question was where and how.

Because she was living outside the United States, Ingrid resigned as coguardian of Pia's estate. The estate had been started with $10,000 that during the war Ingrid and Petter had contributed to a bank account in Los Angeles. Ingrid agreed to pay $10,000 more into Pia's estate, a fund to be drawn upon each year to help pay Pia's living expenses.

On August 17, Petter's attorney wrote a letter to Bautzer responding to his letter "of August 9, 1950, requesting that $10,000 be paid to Mrs. Lindstrom out of the guardianship of their daughter Pia." Ingrid may have felt that she had done enough. Petter was financially in excellent condition, while she was already in the midst of severe money problems. Moreover, she apparently felt that the money would go to Petter. This $10,000 was nevertheless her one direct contribution to Pia's day-to-day upbringing.

The exchanges between Ingrid and Petter were now only barely civil. He had agreed to send Pia to Europe chaperoned by Phyllis Seaton, but Ingrid had turned that down. Petter felt that he had taken full responsibility for their daughter, and Ingrid had even forsworn her minimal financial obligation, giving nothing for Pia's upbringing and education. Ingrid wanted Pia to visit her in Italy, but more than ever, Petter felt that he had to protect his young daughter.

Ingrid did not understand Petter's intransigence. "I think you can just as well know that however you try to explain what are or are not my rights to Pia, I know as well as you that I cannot lose her," Ingrid wrote Petter October 6, 1950, in a letter that Petter asserts he never received. "In the long run you will only lose the child you try to take. It has been proved again and again."

On November 1, 1950, the divorce finally reached Judge Thurmond Clarke at Los Angeles Superior Court. Petter had been coached by his attorney, Isaac Pacht. His testimony was full of the same sort of disingenuousness of which he often accused Ingrid. Contrary to his statements later, he claimed that he had gone to Messina to dissuade Ingrid from staying in Italy with Rossellini. "She said she would have to change, that she would stop," Petter said, as his attorney gently nudged him along. "She also promised that she would discontinue the relationship she had started—that she would have nothing more to do with the Italian director outside their professional relations. . . ."

"Do you have any bitterness in your heart as far as Mrs. Lindstrom is concerned?"

"No, I have no bitterness," Petter said calmly. "I feel sorry for the awkward predicament she has placed herself in. I think she has many good qualities besides being very beautiful."

Ingrid's attorney wanted Petter to agree to allow Pia to visit her mother. Petter pointed out that boats sailed both ways across the Atlantic and nothing prevented Ingrid from visiting her daughter. "I would be glad to take Pia to see her mother," he said. "But I have no intention of taking my daughter to Italy."

Ingrid did not contest the proceedings, and after an hour Judge Clarke granted the divorce. He did not specify the grounds, "to avoid legal difficulties later." He gave Ingrid and Petter joint legal custody of Pia. Petter was to have physical custody, but Ingrid could have Pia during one half of her school vacation in the United States. Ingrid's attorney filed a stipulation for Petter to take Pia to Europe to visit Ingrid within a year, barring any restrictions on travel or their daughter's illness.

And thus the thirteen-year marriage was over.

On November 10, nine days after the divorce, twelve-year-old Pia appeared at Federal Court in Los Angeles to become an American citizen. She wore a checkered jumper and had ribbons in her hair, and looked very grown up as she stood with 250 others. On this day she changed not only her nationality but her name. She had come to hate the name Pia, and all the word connoted. She had hated the way children had made fun of her. She had hated the way the name was supposed to be derived from Petter and Ingrid and Aron, as if she were a hybrid creature. Now she would be Jenny Ann, a name of her own choosing for a new life.

On this day Petter was even cooperative with the press, taking Pia to another room for pictures. He, too, was seeking a new life, apart from Ingrid, selling the house and moving on. A few days later he received a letter from his attorney in New York, Lawrence E. Brinn, that reinforced his intention to keep Pia away from Italy. "Mr. Borre from my Italian office was in New York recently and he stated that you should not take the child to Italy," the prominent international attorney wrote. "He also stated to make sure to remind you again that under no conditions would the child ever visit Italy."

Ingrid tried to keep up contact with Pia, but it was haphazard and unsatisfactory—a telephone call, a gift, a letter. She wrote Steele that if she hadn't telephoned occasionally, she wouldn't even know if Pia and Petter were "still alive." Ingrid sent money to Steele to buy a stuffed monkey and some books. Petter wrote Ingrid that one of the books Pia—or Jenny, as she was now known—received was entitled *Jenny, or The Abandoned.* He told her that when no Christmas gift for Pia arrived, he gave their daughter two dolls "from Ingrid."

Ingrid finally gave up hope that Petter would bring Pia to Italy. Indeed, on March 20, 1951, Petter wrote that she would be able to see Pia in England the fourth week in July. Ingrid had agreed not to publicize any mention of the impending visit. Petter warned her that "you and your spokesmen have repeatedly . . . discussed the probability of Pia's . . . meeting with you and under such circumstances I must inform you that if that is repeated I might without further notice cancel all plans of taking Pia to England where she could visit with you."

Court permission had to be obtained for Pia to go to Europe, and to have $2,000 of her $22,084 estate used for the trip. Superior Judge Newcomb Condee only allowed the trip after he was assured that Pia "would be certain to return to Los Angeles" and that Petter would take "special precautions . . . to prevent anything happening."

As the summer approached, Ingrid and Petter had several telephone conversations. They still knew how to probe each other's vulnerabilities. Ingrid was not about to allow Petter to dominate *her* visit with Pia. She insisted that she had the right to take Pia wherever she wanted in Europe. Not only did Petter disagree with that, but he now suggested that Ingrid see Pia in Sweden. When Ingrid became more conciliatory, Petter wrote: "I have decided that the best place for Pia to meet you and where she would be the least exposed to complications and planned publicity, would be in Stöde, Sweden."

Petter felt that Pia would be safe in Stöde. That was true, but he would be forcing Ingrid to return to the scene of her first wedding, in a village among Petter's people. Petter's attorney announced on July 10 that Ingrid would see

Pia in Sweden for "an extended visit" under conditions "where she would not be involved in any contact with Roberto Rossellini."

Petter finally relented and agreed to let Ingrid see Pia in London. Late in July, Ingrid set out for London, where Petter and Pia were staying with Sidney Bernstein, who was Ingrid's friend as well as Petter's.

Petter suspected that Ingrid would make a publicity spectacle of her first visit with her daughter in a year and a half, but she wanted nothing of that. Ingrid remembered how she traveled by train from Italy to France and on a ship across the English Channel, all that time managing not to attract the attention of reporters and photographers. Fiorella Mariani traveled with Ingrid to begin school in England. She remembers Roberto accompanying them as far as the Italian border.

Petter was fearful that Roberto would journey to England to be with Ingrid. "I had requested that Ingrid come to London but without Rossellini," Petter says. "However, the day that Ingrid arrived in London, Sidney Bernstein informed me that he—that same day—had paid for Rossellini's transportation from Calais to Dover. Rossellini had gotten as far as Calais with his expensive sports car but did not have the money to get over the Channel. Amazingly, Ingrid told me that she did not know anything about Rossellini's traveling to London at the same time. Due to his presence in London, I became more concerned about the protection of Pia."

Roberto did, indeed, arrive in London, at least in time to pick Ingrid up. Petter was consumed by the idea that Roberto might somehow spirit Pia away. He took precautions to protect his daughter. Petter and Pia met Ingrid at the home of David Lean and Ann Todd. Here Ingrid and Pia were to spend their first night together. Ingrid was highly emotional when she first saw Pia. Her daughter was cold and withdrawn. Ingrid later claimed that this was due to the fact that "her father had given her a sleeping pill, just before she came. This Pia told me herself," a statement that Petter denies.

Petter stayed in the house for several hours. "Dr. Lindstrom told me that his chief worry was that if he left the house he might not be admitted again," Lean said in an affidavit given the following year. "In order to alleviate his fears I asked him whether he would be willing to leave our house for the night if I gave him the key to the front door. Dr. Lindstrom accepted the key. . . . Some time after we had gone to bed . . . Dr. Lindstrom re-entered the house and at seven o'clock in the morning the cook found him sitting in the hall which has a view of the stairs and the front door."

"I had a lovely bedroom suite in that house," Ann Todd remembers. "Ingrid had permission for Pia to stay in our house. Petter arrived and he stayed that night. Ingrid cried. It was the only time she cried."

Petter denies that he had a key to Lean's house and says that he arrived at nine o'clock in the morning to take Pia to Bernstein's estate, where she spent about five days with her mother. "She kept repeating in front of the child that she had a right to take the child wherever she wished," Petter said in an affidavit. Ingrid "insisted on bringing up our past in front of the child and in berating me. She unfairly reprimanded me in front of the child saying 'Why did you save money and why did you buy all that insurance? We could have spent the money and had fun with it.' I found it necessary to answer her that we had lived well and that she had never been denied anything she wanted. She retorted 'we live much better on debts. We have more cars and servants than you and I ever had but we have nothing but debts.' "

Ingrid's memory of those days is totally different—Petter threatening to take Pia away to Sweden, condemning her within earshot of Pia, and harassing her emotionally. "I recall when Dr. Lindstrom grabbed me by my arms and stared into my eyes, swearing that he didn't love me any more and that he wouldn't want to have me back, even if I tried," Ingrid said in a sworn deposition the following year. "At another moment, he told me he was delighted to see me cry and suffer, as it would make me understand how much he had suffered in turn. . . .

"As I happened to mention the name Pietro, Pia asked who he was. I said our chauffeur. . . . 'Oh, you have a chauffeur,' she said with her eyes sparkling. Dr. Lindstrom saw this and saw that after all his blackpainting of Italy and my life there, I might have *something* that attracted a 12 year old girl, were it only a chauffeur. So he said immediately: 'Sure they have a chauffeur, lots of servants, lots of cars and lots of debts.' . . .

"Once and only once, it was I who spoke in front of Pia . . . of my right to have the girl with me. It was at the Bernsteins' country place, the very last morning. . . . I sorted out, in front of both, my lawyer's letters reporting the text of the Court's order. . . . All I wanted was Pia to realize that her father was exaggerating, especially in his accusations that I was not to be trusted and I would try to steal her. I was happy that Pia herself smiled during those silly kidnapping stories."

Ingrid's last memory was of Pia "trying to be so nice and light as if nothing had happened, trying to cover up what she really felt." That was, indeed, the daughter who was the legacy of the divorce.

Ingrid went back to Italy with Roberto. She believed now that Pia was not an emotionally torn child of divorce but, as she wrote Irene Selznick, "calm," "serene," and "sweet," a child-woman who "loves maybe her father more because she has to take care of him."

"We both suffered tremendously," Pia says. "I want to correct the impression that there is someone to blame. He was mother and father to me. He tried as much as he could to make up for the loss. Everyone tried to do the best they could. There has been a great deal of suffering through the years."

On their way back to Los Angeles, Petter and Pia stopped in New York. An Associated Press reporter asked him if he had any romantic interests.

Petter smiled and looked at Pia. "Yes, this is the one," he said.

As much as Pia cared for her father, she was learning to hide her emotions. Petter saw only a smiling, happy child, but others saw a different Pia. "I remember going on a six-hour auto trip with Pia in 1951," said David Lewis, the producer. "She talked all the way, almost as if the wind would tear her words away and no one would hear them. She told me how much she missed her mother, but that she didn't want to hurt her father."

When Ingrid was at home in Hollywood, she and Petter were home-bodies. In Italy, she and Roberto went out frequently. Sometimes they went to a small fish restaurant near Santa Marinella for dinner with Fellini and Giu-lietta Masina. Sometimes it was one of Roberto's favorite restaurants in Rome. Roberto was usually well groomed and perfumed, and Ingrid had begun to dress with greater flair, achieving a more dramatic look.

Roberto always wanted the best table in the house, to go with the best bottle of wine. One evening in June 1951, the best table was in full view of the avenue. A passerby noticed Ingrid and soon a crowd gathered. It was the hottest night of the year, and Ingrid was wearing a low-cut dress, provocation enough for the young boulevardiers. They began shouting comments that were spicier than any of the dishes set before Ingrid. Roberto took offense. He marched boldly out on the street and asked the revelers to disperse. This brought on more comments, boos, and shouting, drawing even more specta-tors. Before long the crowd's amusement turned to anger, and it took riot police to disperse the large group.

Another evening Roberto took Ingrid dancing at the Excelsior, where they had spent their first evening together in Italy. As Roberto swirled Ingrid around the crowded room, he noticed that Anna Magnani was also on the dance floor.

"How are you with that *woman?*" Anna asked as she and her partner danced nearby.

"Do you mean my *wife?*" Roberto asked as he led Ingrid away.

"Oh, chicken shit," Anna said.

For Ingrid, life had meant her work, but now when she did work it was only for Roberto, a mere prop for his vision. She was embedded in a life of endless small private dramas. She and Roberto lived like royalty and fled from their creditors like gypsies. She had few real friends, no one like Ruth or Steele, Kay or Irene. She was at peace, if boredom is peace. She didn't think about her life, though. She didn't think about the might-have-beens, the ironies of fate. She had blocked it all off.

Ingrid's life wasn't all eating out, shopping, and waiting. In the fall she began work on her second film with Roberto, *Europa '51.* Roberto's screen-play told the story of Irene Girard, a self-satisfied, self-absorbed, self-indulgent Roman lady, not unlike some of those in the circle in which Ingrid and Roberto often traveled. Her life is without focus, full of little but a terrible busyness. Irene, played by Ingrid, is shocked into awareness of the world around her when her young son, the same age as Pia, commits suicide.

In the wake of tragedy, Irene travels into the bowels of society seeking to do good work, and to meet others doing good work. She befriends a prostitute, and an unmarried mother (played brilliantly by Masina). She is disillusioned everywhere, as much by the Communist organizer who purports to exalt the poor, as by the disenfranchised themselves, dumb to their plight, and irresponsible. She says, "If I thought I had great spiritual powers, I would be insane. My love for them is born out of hate, hate for myself." She is a "fool of God," and when she helps a young man escape the police, she is institutionalized in a mental hospital.

Ingrid tried her best to play the part, but she simply couldn't understand how a woman of that class and background would make such a journey. Even if she had better understood the role, working with Roberto was for her an endless exercise in frustration. Shooting was supposed to begin at 1 P.M., but that was Italian time, Rossellini time. The crew and cast began arriving at two, and work wasn't finished until eight or ten at night.

Although Ingrid talked warmly about her husband in public, there were already rumors that their marriage was failing.

"Ingrid was like the sun, clear like light," says Masina. "She was cut in a direct manner. Roberto was completely different, from his education, to his temperament, to his tradition. It was very difficult to reconcile these two manners of living. I liked Roberto very much as a friend, but I wouldn't want to have a life with him. It was impossible to have confidence in him. He gave a lot and then he was off somewhere. He was unstable in a way. He was a man who spoke well, who liked to listen to you, and to talk, an extrovert. But he was a man who was born to be alone."

Roberto was not a man but a mosaic of men. He was an intuitive genius. He was a fraud. He was a soothsayer. He was a charmer. He was a liar. He was an adventurer. He was a crook. He was a man of saintly generosity. He was a cheat. He loved humanity. He manipulated humans. He was an egomaniac. He reeked of insecurity.

One day on the set of *Europa '51*, Roberto talked to an interviewer from *Bianco e Nero*:

> The world is more and more divided in two, between those who want to kill fantasy and those who want to save it, those who want to die and those who want to live. This is the problem I confront in Europa '51. . . . The ability to see both sides of man, to look at him charitably, seems to me to be a supremely Latin and Italian attitude. It results from a degree of civility which has been our custom from very ancient times—the habit of seeing every side of man. For me it is very important to have been born into such a civilization. I believe that what saved us . . . was this view of life we have, which is unmistakably Catholic. Christianity does not pre-

*tend that everything is good and perfect: it recognizes sin and error, but it
also admits the possibility of salvation. . . . The only possibility I see for
getting nearer to the truth is to try to understand sin and be tolerant of it.*

Roberto's film, his way of getting nearer to the truth, was greeted as a
miserable commercial failure both in Italy and in the United States. In the
New York Times, Bosley Crowther called *Europa '51* "dismal and dolorous,"
an opinion shared by most of the critics.

Roberto's themes of alienation and loneliness and isolation are now such
clichés that the great originality and daring of *Europa '51* is almost as lost now
as it was in 1952. Roberto had not strayed as much from neorealism as his
critics charged. He had filmed the rubble and blood of the war in Italy, and the
devastation of Berlin. Now his camera turned to the spiritual ruins of Europe,
to the psychological devastation.

It wasn't easy to make what Roberto called "a cinema of the Reconstruc-
tion," and he admitted later that he perhaps "wasn't capable of producing it."
Nonetheless, *Europa '51* made Roberto a hero and mentor to a generation of
filmmakers, including Antonioni and Godard.

In her role, Ingrid, in the words of Bosley Crowther, "does what she's
asked to do fitly, with a maximum of confusion and dismay revealed in her
lovely eyes and features as she represents her thwarted woman's grief." If
Roberto had tried to help Ingrid understand her part better, the film might
have been better. That was not his way, however, not with mere actors. And
even if he had tried, Ingrid might not have understood.

During the filming of *Europa '51* Ingrid was pregnant again, this time with
twins. She became so enormous, and the pregnancy was so difficult, that on
May 28, 1952, she entered Salvatore Mundi nursing home. There, during the
last weeks of her pregnancy, Ingrid would lumber back and forth on the roof,
and try to relax, while accustoming herself to intravenous feeding. She worried not only about the two children she was carrying but about her firstborn.

In those June days a sad, dramatic spectacle was playing out in a Los
Angeles courtroom. In April, Ingrid had filed suit in superior court asking that
Pia be permitted to visit her in Italy in the summer, accompanied by an escort
other than Petter. He had already lost one professional opportunity because of
the notoriety over the divorce. Yet he still felt so strongly that he was willing
to fight Ingrid in public battle. This time, however, it was Pia who was the one
and only focus.

Petter did not want his daughter to testify. Nonetheless, his claim that Pia
did not wish to go to Italy in the summer was the center of his case, along with
his assertion that Pia should not be in Rossellini's presence. In retrospect, it is
unlikely that a U.S. court would order a father, an American citizen, to send
his daughter, also a citizen, overseas to visit a mother who was not a citizen.
But Petter was so determined to win that he put in evidence the passionately

felt letter that Ingrid had written him from Amalfi, telling him of her love for Roberto.

Bautzer had the unenviable task of making a case with a client unwilling to testify in person. Since the divorce, Bautzer had visited Rome. "I don't think I've ever seen a woman as ravaged with feelings of guilt, love, and remorse," Bautzer says. "Ingrid was a tremendous woman. But who knows what happens to a woman hopelessly in love. Rossellini was a Svengali. She was like a prisoner. I pleaded with her and Rossellini to come back. I said, You're condemned. You've got to come back. Rossellini wouldn't let her go. He was afraid that Petter would prevent her from returning. He was the most jealous man that I've ever known."

During the first days in court, character witnesses attested to Ingrid's and Roberto's virtues, while Pacht, Petter's attorney, slashed away at their reputations in savage counterattacks. He read from Senator Johnson's attack on Roberto, calling him a "narcotics addict," as well as immoral, and a wartime Nazi collaborator. "I don't want the child to be exposed to Mr. Rossellini," Petter told the court. "He has a bad reputation in this country and abroad. He ran away with the mother of this child. He has a reputation as a drug addict and a habit of living with mistresses who are married to other men."

When Roberto learned of Petter's charges he vowed to fly to Los Angeles to defend his reputation. He cabled Bautzer, asking that he be "afforded time and the opportunity to make myself heard." Judge Mildred D. Lillie was unwilling to postpone or unduly delay the trial. Roberto ended up sending the judge a long, impassioned letter that years later she still had in her files.

The crucial person in the trial was neither Petter nor Roberto. It was Pia. A few months before, during her Easter vacation at Squaw Valley, Pia had written an autobiography, as was done by all graduating students at the Hawthorne School. Pia was an excellent student, and the essay was well written. Extraordinarily, in all the pages Pia did not mention Ingrid even once.

Before having her testify about her mother, Judge Lillie wanted to speak to Pia privately. As Phyllis Seaton drove Pia to the judge's house, the girl asked, "Will the judge talk about my mother?"

"I'm sure she will, dear, but I don't know," Mrs. Seaton replied, as she remembered later. "It's not appropriate to ask a judge what she's going to say."

"If she asks me, what shall I tell?" Pia asked.

"Pia, you and I must not even talk about this. When the judge talks to you it will be private. And when she asks you, tell the truth."

Judge Lillie was a sympathetic figure, a woman young enough to be Pia's mother. After talking to the girl, the judge decided to allow Bautzer to question Pia in court chambers closed from spectators and press.

On June 13, Pia, on her father's arm, walked into chambers cleared of journalists and reporters. She wore a blue, high-collared dress and looked as if she had dressed with great care for the occasion, brushing her shoulder-length blond hair until it glowed. From certain angles she resembled Ingrid amazingly.

"Friday the thirteenth!" Pia exclaimed as she noticed a wall calendar. "This is supposed to be a very unlucky day."

"Some of my luckiest days have been the thirteenth," Petter reassured his daughter, as he led her inside.

In the court chambers the questioning began.

"Have you ever written your mother letters in which you told her that you loved her?" Bautzer asked.

"I always sign them 'Love Pia.' "

"And does that express the way you feel about her?"

"No, it's just the way I end the letter."

"Now I take it when you signed your letter 'Love Pia' you didn't actually love her?"

"I don't love my mother. I like her."

"And you don't miss her?"

"No."

"And you don't have any desire to see her?"

"No. I would rather live with my father."

"Do you feel that your mother doesn't care about you now?" Judge Lillie asked.

"Well, I don't think she cares about me too much."

"Why do you say that?" the judge asked.

"Well, she didn't seem very interested in me when she left. It was only after she left and got married and had children that she suddenly decided she wanted me."

Bautzer seemed determined not to quit until Pia showed some sign of deep affection for Ingrid. "Miss Lindstrom, whether or not you know your mother very well or whether you will have the opportunity in the future to know her well, do you love your mother?" the attorney asked.

"No, not very much," Pia answered in a thin, emotionless voice. "I mean I have seen her enough, and I know I have met her, but I haven't seen her enough to really love her. My father has mostly been taking care of me. I lived with my father mostly."

For Petter, it was a pure moment of vindication, spoiled for him only when others suggested that he had coached Pia. To Bautzer, Pia's repudiation of her mother would always be "one of the most extraordinary moments of my career." He had the unpleasant duty to call Ingrid and Roberto and tell them of Pia's testimony.

For Ingrid, there was a dual shame: the public humiliation of a public figure and a mother's private humiliation. As she sat in her hospital room sobbing over Pia's words, she did not blame her daughter. She blamed Petter. She conjectured that "perhaps she had to say things like that because she is living with her father." She remembered how just a few weeks before she had talked to Pia on the phone and her daughter had said, "Oh, are the twins coming soon? You must cable me as soon as they arrive." It did not occur to Ingrid that Pia might be able to be different things to different people.

Ingrid's babies were overdue, and in the heat of Rome, the wait was agonizing. On the eighteenth of June, her doctor induced the birth of two hefty baby girls, Isabella Fiorella Elettra Giovanna, weighing seven pounds, three ounces, and Isotta Ingrid Frieda Giuliana, weighing eight pounds, five ounces. Roberto was doubly delighted. The healthy, wailing fraternal twins seemed testimony to the father's manhood and the mother's maternal gifts.

The superior court in Los Angeles had a different verdict on Ingrid's maternal gifts. For a week Judge Lillie had listened to charges and counter-charges, not about fraud, or murder, or embezzlement, but about love and loyalty and caring. Although Ingrid was not paying child support, Bautzer had argued that she had "bargained for and bought" the right to have Pia, as if she were a puppy or a vacation home.

On June 24, Judge Lillie ruled that it was not in Pia's interest that she go off to Italy. Pia was not chattel to be "passed back and forth between parents to satisfy their pride, convenience and desires." The judge said that "whether Miss Bergman wishes to admit it or not, the responsibility rests with her."

Judge Lillie did not blame only Ingrid for the fact that Ingrid and Petter's love for Pia had led them to this pathetic end. The judge criticized both father and mother, as being "more interested in what each deserved or was entitled to under the law than what would be to the best interest of the child." She warned that "unless both of you put aside pride and selfishness, this child will never have the normal affection and love she is entitled to from both parents."

By the time Judge Lillie gave her verdict, Ingrid's catharsis of grief was over, and her emotions had frozen into hard anger. She was not going to accept the verdict passively, but would appeal, this time attacking Petter without reserve. Bautzer had failed her, and she asked him to contact Jerry Giesler, a prominent celebrity attorney whose involvement would mean publicity and more publicity.

Ingrid then called reporters into her hospital room, and raged against Petter and the verdict. In her blue dressing gown, Ingrid looked positively maternal, but she was full of fury, pledging no longer to hold "back from saying things that would hurt my ex-husband," and "now I will have to let my hair down." Her one solace was Roberto, the "best and kindest man I ever met. . . . I punished myself plenty for falling in love with this man."

Ingrid vowed she would come to the United States to "fight like a tigress" for custody of Pia, even though she was "practically broke." Ingrid raged against Petter. "[I] kept up our home with my salary, but I don't regret it," she said. "However, I am bitter against him."

"I gave up most of my financial substance . . . just to have Pia with me during the summer," she claimed. "You can say that I am practically broke and my husband is providing for me." If that was true, in less than three years Roberto and Ingrid had spent over $300,000 of Ingrid's money, expenditures that she could not justly blame on her former husband. But Petter had become the great symbol of all Ingrid's frustrations, and there was little wrong in her life that she didn't trace back to him.

Even when Ingrid wrote to Pia telling her of the birth of the twins, her anger spilled out on the page. "What you said to the judge couldn't hurt me deep down in my heart, it hurts just on the surface for a time," she wrote. "Because a child can't hurt its mother, for that love is too big and protecting. But I must continue to fight for my right to have you in my home. There is nothing I hate so much as injustice and I'll fight until my last drop of strength."

Soon after the court verdict, Petter and Pia moved to Pittsburgh, where he became head of the Department of Neurosurgery at Aspinwall Veterans Hospital as well as director of a research project on brain disorders at the University of Pittsburgh's Addison H. Gibson Laboratory. Three years later he married Dr. Agnes Rovnanek, a lovely twenty-six-year-old pediatrician, twenty years his junior. They began a family of their own, and Petter tried to forget Ingrid. The scandal was so notorious that he subsequently lost positions offered at two prominent universities before being hired as Chairman and Professor of neurosurgery at the University of Utah and head of neurosurgery at the Veterans Administration Hospital in Salt Lake City.

CHAPTER SIXTEEN

The Donna of Santa Marinella

On a grand summer day, Ingrid and Fiorella drove out to Santa Marinella. Ingrid was just as happy driving her little Fiat, and not being chauffeured in the Rolls. She cherished moments like this one, away from the servants and the telephones, the money problems and the guests, away from the constant melodrama of life with Roberto.

Suddenly, in the rearview mirror, she saw the familiar red of Roberto's racing Ferrari zooming up behind. Roberto maneuvered alongside Ingrid's car, waved gaily, and pulled in behind. Ingrid laughed. It was boring always driving the same stretch. Roberto wanted to liven things up by having a little race.

Ingrid floored the accelerator. The Fiat shot ahead. Roberto let Ingrid lead for a while. Then he moved up beside her again, the Ferrari roaring like an enraged lion. He waved again and eventually dropped back behind. She sped onward, occasionally watching Roberto in the mirror. Once again Roberto moved to pass Ingrid. Once again he waved and waved some more, and dropped back. Ingrid sped onward, noticing that the Ferrari had dropped out of sight.

When Ingrid and Fiorella arrived at Santa Marinella, they were still laughing about their little race. Fifteen minutes went by and Roberto didn't arrive. Then a half hour. Ingrid began to worry. She jumped into the Fiat and drove back toward Rome.

A few miles down the road, Ingrid found Roberto on the shoulder. He had run out of gas when he had been unable to get Ingrid to stop. "Don't laugh," he cried out. "Don't laugh. It's not funny."

Ingrid had many wonderful, joyous moments with Roberto, and in the scrapbook of her mind those were what she remembered. She had dreadful, painful times too, and these memories she tried to turn into benign anecdotes, commentaries on Roberto's idiosyncrasies.

Roberto had a fierce, violent temper that rose up like a Kansas tornado, a black force appearing out of the quiet sky. Ralph Serpe, a producer long associated with Dino De Laurentiis, remembers "how Roberto mistreated her.

I was once walking behind them on Via Veneto when he slapped her. His reputation was hurt by the way he treated Ingrid."

Ingrid and Roberto's fights were such regular and dramatic occurrences that when the skirmishes began, they would routinely send their dog, Stromboli, upstairs to Roberto's sister's apartment. For a while Ingrid tried the same approach, simply disappearing, hiding away from Roberto, but that didn't work. She decided that she would have to do something about Roberto's dark rages.

Ingrid asked her husband's advice. Roberto suggested that the next time he exploded, she boldly rush up to him and embrace him. Ingrid did not have to wait very long. As Roberto spouted and fumed, she threw her arms around him. Roberto broke her grasp, hurling her from him. Ingrid made a joke of the incident.

It sometimes seemed to Ingrid that Roberto didn't even let her share fully in the parenting of their three children. He treated his children the way he did his lovers, showering them with affection and concern, and then rushing off. "Father would say he was the big pig and we were the piglets," Isabella remembers. "He was always in bed, and we would get in bed with him. He said the thing he regretted most in life was not being able to nurse us. I remember him telling a reporter once why it was so important being a father. He said he was like a Jewish mother."

One evening when the twins were beginning to talk, Ingrid and Roberto gave a small dinner party. "Children, it's late," Ingrid said at eight o'clock, clapping her hands. "Go to bed."

"Oh, no, my children," Roberto said, drawing Isotta, Isabella, and Robertino to him, shepherding them in his arms. "Oh, stay a little longer with your father, my good children whom I love so much."

When the children finally went to bed, Ingrid turned to Roberto. "You rob my children of my heart," she said coldly. "You take away my children from my heart."

Ingrid was always present for Roberto's friends and gatherings, but he was often not there for hers. For visiting stars from Hollywood and celebrities from all over, Ingrid's home became almost as much a stopping place as the Sistine Chapel or the Colosseum. Joseph Cotten. Eddie Albert. William Wyler. John Steinbeck. Ernest Hemingway. The Swedish sculptor Carl Milles. They all came and as often as not Roberto treated the Hollywood guests with cold disdain or simply ignored them.

"I was filming *Roman Holiday* and I was invited out to Santa Marinella with Billy Wilder," Gregory Peck remembers. "Ingrid had gone to some pain to prepare a Hollywood lunch. She kept apologizing for Roberto not being there. She was very hurt at his nonappearance. He finally showed up. He didn't sit down. He leaned on a chaise, yawning and stretching. He was rather indifferent to the Hollywood crowd. I thought he was acting like a spoiled kid."

Roberto didn't like Ingrid's friends in part because he feared that they were trying to talk Ingrid into going back to Hollywood films. Her movie friends did, indeed, consider Ingrid's return, often in films they would either star in or direct.

Despite the scandal and the debacle of *Stromboli*, it was remarkable how much interest Hollywood still had in Ingrid. The producer Sam Spiegel had flown to Rome in June to discuss a film also to star Marlon Brando. Walter Wanger was sending her scripts. Graham Greene thought Ingrid the perfect choice to star in the film of his novel *The End of the Affair*. Even Howard Hughes, who had lost hundreds of thousands of dollars on *Stromboli*, had not given up on Ingrid. "I was in Hollywood with Howard Hughes," remembers Gina Lollobrigida. "He was mad at Rossellini because he had succeeded in taking away Ingrid from him. He really wanted to get her back. I never saw a person so angry."

Ingrid was not yet ready to step out artistically on her own. She was more interested in putting on a show of domestic bliss than in other sorts of public performances.

Hers was indeed a peculiar fate, to be ensconced at Santa Marinella, with Roberto often off somewhere, or arriving home in the middle of the night, the throbbing motor of the Ferrari signaling his arrival. A railroad line ran past the villa, and when the train went by, the passengers looked out the window, waving at Italy's newest national monument, the *donna* of Santa Marinella. When Ingrid was in a certain mood, she waved back.

Evenings were often the best times now, evenings when Roberto wasn't there, and it was Ingrid and Fiorella, and perhaps Roberto's son Renzo. "We would talk for hours and hours and hours," Fiorella remembers. "We'd talk on and on until four o'clock in the morning. When we started talking about God, that meant that we had drunk too much. Ah, the *bel vino*. In Roberto's films God is always the solution."

Renzo recalls, "She told wonderful stories in her moments of loneliness, . . . some love stories, very open, all in great detail." Ingrid was like an old lady recounting her life. She usually started talking to Renzo after dinner, telling him that it would only be for a drink or two. Soon it would be midnight, and then, of course, they would have to wait until one so they could see the mouse that every night at that hour raced across the railing of the terrace on its way to bed. Ah, but after the mouse made its nightly dash, it was close to two, and they might as well wait to see the fishermen in their boats. And by now it was dawn, and the sun was rising up out of the sea.

Ingrid was getting offers from Hollywood, but Roberto would have nothing of it. His wife would work with him or she would not work at all. It did not matter that so far their collaboration seemed to have benefited neither one of them. He would try again. Ingrid listened to her husband and did what he wanted her to do. She did not like the films that they were making, but it was as if she had no energy left to throw off the artistic yoke that Roberto had placed over her, no energy to begin again.

In the summer of 1952 Roberto directed Ingrid in *The Chicken*, a short humorous film, one of five segments in *We, the Women*.

Ingrid's next major role was in *Journey to Italy*. It is the most autobiographical of Roberto's films. *Journey to Italy* does not exploit the drama of Roberto and Ingrid's life together, but traces much of Roberto's spiritual journey with Ingrid, through the story of a wealthy British couple, Alexander and Katherine Joyce. After ten years of marriage, they travel to Italy to visit a house they have inherited, and to get away from the mind rot and boredom of their deteriorating marriage. In the vapid, tedious exchanges between the couple, there is all the existential horror of a love gone bad, of courtesies and routines that have no meaning, except to hide the truth.

There is a stench of death in *Journey to Italy*, not of the skulls and ruins that the couple visit in Pompeii, but of lives that are entombed. Alexander seeks out a prostitute and travels by himself to Capri. Slowly, though, in the warmth and depth of Italy, Alexander and Katherine discover themselves and their feelings. During a religious festival, a small miracle takes place: the resurrection of Alexander and Katherine's own love. The film ends with the couple determined to try again, to keep their marriage alive.

Roberto's reputation had reached the point where in order to raise money, he needed an international star to play opposite Ingrid. He chose George Sanders, whom Ingrid had worked with years before in *Rage in Heaven*. Sanders had made a career out of playing charming men of questionable character. A dour, self-absorbed, melancholic man, he was an actor of large, if unappreciated, skills, who needed a director who directed, a script that was a script, and a working day full of order and discipline. He needed anything but Roberto Rossellini.

Sanders arrived in Italy convinced of Roberto's greatness. Before long he had decided that Roberto had every attribute of a genius except genius. By the time the film began shooting in Naples, Sanders wanted out. To Sanders, the back of an envelope was for writing a return address, not for jotting down a movie script. He didn't understand what Roberto wanted or was doing—the aimless shooting, the jumbled dialogue, the nonexistent plot. He couldn't believe that Roberto would go off skin diving in the middle of the film, or take the whole crew to Capri for a regimen heavy in spearfishing and light on moviemaking.

One day Sanders started crying in front of Ingrid: "I can't go on, I can't do this commedia dell'arte and invent and get the lines at the last minute." He began calling his psychiatrist in Hollywood, worried not only about his role but about his very sanity.

Roberto's film was *his* spiritual autobiography, not Ingrid's or Sanders's. The actor could have told the character he was playing a thing or two about bad marriages. Sanders had the not uncommon honor of being married to Zsa

Zsa Gabor. Sanders's marriage was about over. His wife was having an affair with Don Porfirio Rubirosa, the Dominican ambassador to the Republic of France.

When Zsa Zsa visited her husband, Sanders took her with him when the film went on location in Ravello. A Hollywood film was also shooting there: *Beat the Devil*, directed by John Huston, starring Humphrey Bogart, Jennifer Jones, and Gina Lollobrigida. The whole group was sitting on the hotel terrace when Ingrid sauntered up.

"I want to meet George's wife," Ingrid said, stretching out her hand to Zsa Zsa in greeting.

"And I also would like to meet Mrs. Rossellini," replied Zsa Zsa.

Zsa Zsa appraised Ingrid's clothes like a jeweler looking over a handful of glass baubles. She felt that Ingrid left almost immediately because "she did not want to appear as she appeared completely without makeup, in a shapeless sweater and slacks." Whether or not Ingrid was so easily put off, she probably realized that *she* could have been the one starring with Bogart, and not Jennifer Jones, sitting there demurely in her tailored black slacks and white blouse. It could not have been easy, moreover, to have Bogart, her co-star in *Casablanca*, tell her bluntly that "he disliked everything Roberto does—even without looking at it." Still, Ingrid enjoyed being with these Hollywood people with whom a few years ago she had pronounced herself bored. There she heard laughter, for, as she wrote Steele, there was not much laughter on her film.

More and more, whatever joy and gaiety Ingrid had in her life was lived offscreen from her marriage with Roberto. She was once again practicing the gentle arts of subterfuge, a craft she had practiced so well on Petter. It wasn't new lovers she was looking for, but life, moments of laughter and fun and flirtatiousness.

Helen Tubbs was doing public relations for the film, a job she had taken on after her husband died. Ingrid noticed Helen drinking with some American naval officers in the bar. One evening Tubbs telephoned Ingrid in her suite at the Continentale, telling her that the officers were calling. "Go down to them," Ingrid said quietly. "Then call me and say I must go down. Make a reason."

Another evening Roberto called Tubbs to tell her that he had to drive to Rome. He wanted her to keep Ingrid company by having dinner in their suite. When Tubbs arrived she found herself in the midst of a typical Rossellini melodrama.

"Ah, the children have a fever," Roberto moaned, as if it were time to call a priest for the last rites. "I don't want to leave."

"Oh, come on, all children have fevers," Ingrid said, in exasperation.

"Oh, all right," Roberto replied uncertainly, running to hug and kiss the children once again. "*Cari miei, cari miei.*"

Ingrid waved goodbye to Roberto from the balcony and then turned back into the suite. "Now for martinis," Ingrid said, suddenly alive. "I'm the great Bergman, so you mix the first one for me."

Tubbs mixed her best martini. "It's fine," Ingrid said, as she emptied her glass. "But I'll do better."

The two women proceeded with their competition. After a while Ingrid started to do imitations, mimicking one celebrity after another.

Suddenly, the door was flung open. There stood an incredulous Roberto. "I leave my poor children with you and look!"

"I looked in." Ingrid shrugged.

"I've come back to take their temperatures and you're in an alcoholic stupor!"

The telephone rang and Tubbs answered. "It's Captain Hal," she said brightly.

"Oh, I was supposed to have dinner with him," Ingrid said.

"You're not going anywhere at all."

Roberto took the children's temperatures, tucked them in, and set off once again for Rome. Ingrid waved him adieu. As soon as he was out of sight, she and Tubbs started drinking again.

During the filming of *Journey to Italy*, Ingrid announced that she was "through with films" and would work onstage "only if I could be near my husband." Her "retirement" from films may have been rather providential; she wrote Steele that she didn't think her new film was very good. When the film opened in Italy there was even more tedium and boredom in the audiences than on the screen, and Ingrid and Roberto had racked up another dramatic failure. As much as the public ignored *Journey to Italy*, the film was viewed with respect, even awe, by many young filmmakers and critics. In 1958 *Cahiers du Cinéma* named it one of the twelve greatest films of all time. In 1964 Bernardo Bertolucci, who would one day win notoriety for *Last Tango in Paris*, paid homage to Roberto in *Before the Revolution*, in which a character says: "I saw *Journey to Italy* fifteen times.... Remember you cannot live without Rossellini."

The tragedy of Ingrid's professional life with Roberto was not that they made bad films together. It was that although Ingrid knew that some people still admired Roberto's work, she didn't have any sense what it was they admired in his recent films. She didn't understand her husband's artistic sentiment and daring—the best thing about Rossellini.

In late April, after the film was finished, the family moved into a large modern apartment at 62 Via Bruno Buozzi. The residence would have been stunning if there had been more furniture. Although there was little money, one day Ingrid had gone shopping for a new living room set and purchased one for 200,000 lire. As soon as she got home the store called to say that there had been a mistake. The furniture was 400,000 lire. Ingrid knew that it was only because she was Ingrid Bergman, the wife of Roberto Rossellini, and she canceled the order.

In the fall Roberto would direct the Paul Claudel–Arthur Honegger oratorio *Joan at the Stake*, with Ingrid playing the one speaking part, but that was months off. Meanwhile Roberto had time to take part in a hundred-mile road race. Halfway through, his car broke down, but Roberto took pride in the fact that he had been averaging one hundred miles an hour, and his assistant had passed out beside him.

Roberto did not limit his road racing to scheduled events. In June he and Ingrid drove to Stockholm to attend a Saturday evening party in her honor. For Roberto, the great unfairness of most races was that if you did not arrive on time, you could not compete. Driving to Stockholm was different, and Roberto was not ready to leave Rome until Friday morning for the more than fifteen-hundred-mile journey, giving the roads a sporting break.

Ingrid sat alongside Roberto as he sped northward, stopping only for gas. He drove a day and a night to the Hamburg dock. He had made extraordinary time but missed the Denmark ferry by a few minutes.

Ingrid began to cry.

"This is part of the fun of traveling," Roberto laughed, ever the philosopher.

Ingrid and Roberto finally arrived in Stockholm at 3 A.M. Sunday morning. The party was still going on.

In December, Roberto staged *Joan at the Stake* at the Teatro San Carlo in Naples. Ingrid wore her by now familiar long sackcloth and spoke her lines firmly. The performance received generally good reviews.

Roberto took the oratorio on to La Scala in Milan. One evening Ernest Hemingway and his friend A. E. Hotchner came to visit Ingrid in her hotel suite. Ingrid hugged the novelist and took him into the living room full of red roses an admirer had sent.

"How do things go?" Hemingway asked. "How do they really go?"

"Oh, when I think how it was a few years ago and how it is now! If only in a crisis one could learn to have patience, everything would be fine."

Hotchner asked if Ingrid had any movie roles in the offing.

"No, none," she said. "But I really don't care. The way things are now I could just concentrate on being a housewife and be perfectly happy, because I have a husband who is in the theater and talks movies, and artists are around all the time."

"Listen, daughter," Hemingway said. "I have looked into Dr. Hemingstein's crystal ball, and a housewife is one thing you ain't gonna be. When they are starved enough for your talent, they will come to get you. In the meantime anything I can do with my checkbook or my sixteen-gauge Winchester or maybe just to cream a couple of characters who need creaming, you have only to say the word."

Roberto insisted on filming the oratorio, though there was no real audience for such a film. Roberto was having no easy time finding backers for his film ventures, and he and Ingrid needed money. So they took the oratorio to Barcelona, Paris, London, and finally Stockholm.

Roberto was proud that he had refused to replicate his early success, never seeking to make another *Open City*. Here he was, though, traveling through Europe with his wife and three children, the nanny, and the Rolls-Royce, endlessly repeating himself. Before Rossellini, Ingrid would never have gone on tour with a play, becoming a traveling theatrical sideshow. Yet now she was being burned at the stake nightly, in five different countries.

Ingrid and Roberto were a spectacle that transcended any drama on the stage. When they arrived in Stockholm the streets were lined with the curious. If there were those who thought that Ingrid was a blot on the Swedish flag, there were many others who admired her immensely. The opening of *Joan at the Stake* on February 17, 1955, was one of the events of the season at the Stockholm Opera House. The list of dignitaries was headed by the prime minister himself, and included most of the leading social and theatrical figures in Sweden.

The next morning the *Swedish Daily News*'s critic wrote that "the Joan of Ingrid Bergman seems comparatively vague and cool, basically lacking the right charisma. What's all right in this interpretation is the actress's clear voice that carried the text clearly and steadily through the play and is never artificial."

The reviews were far from the best Ingrid had ever received, but not the worst. What stung her more than anything ever written about her was a piece by Stig Ahlgren in the *Weekly Journal*. At times Ahlgren appeared as mild as the third cup of tea on a teabag. But he wrote satirical columns full of spite and bitterness. He might have been ignored if he had not been so amusing, and often just enough on target to raise welts on his victims. Ahlgren wrote:

> The criticism both here and abroad has been acid against Ingrid Bergman. Her register is too narrow. Her tone of voice is too trivial. She doesn't know what passion is, etc. What she earned when she acted as Joan of Arc was not small change. . . . Ingrid Bergman is not an actress in the usual meaning. Her career has been on a completely different level. To compare her with professional actresses is both mean and unjust. She travels around and is shown for money. The promoter is Roberto Rossellini, with whom she has three children and one Rolls-Royce. With art this traveling company has nothing to do. . . . But why criticize? . . . Ingrid Bergman is not an actress but a clever businesswoman. Coolly and soberly she has assessed the chances of making money out of her special attraction. . . . Ingrid Bergman is a commodity, so far a desirable commodity which is offered in the free market. She is paid according to the same pricing mechanism that is valid for herring and pig iron.

It was at this same time, Ingrid reported, that a reporter and a photographer "tried to break into my hotel suite early one morning to take pictures of Roberto and me in our bedroom . . . they went from door to door listening for the sound of children's voices. When they heard Robertino playing with Little Isabella and Ingrid, they forced their way in and began snapping pictures of the children. It was only because the nurse threw herself in front of our door that they did not burst into our bedroom."

Roberto called the police and sued the reporter, but Ingrid decided to mount her own attack against her detractors. In her years in Italy she had become inured to criticism in the press, but somehow Sweden was different. She felt that her native land was a small country full of small minds that attacked anyone who went abroad and became successful. There was an intimacy to attacks in her own language, too, as if she were among kin, people who took advantage of knowing her better than others. Her profound bitterness toward Swedes and Sweden stayed with her for years.

On Sunday evening Ingrid was supposed to make a few remarks at a charity benefit for the Swedish polio fund. "I summoned all my courage and got up and told them of the attempt to break into my hotel room," she said. "I said, 'The entire Swedish press emphasizes lies and insults. This is my only chance to fight back, and that's why I'm doing it, because they cannot say anything worse about me than they have.' The lights went on, and I could see men and women crying. They kept calling me back to the stage. When I finally left, I was weeping, too."

Ingrid was crying out in self-conscious martyrdom. The truth was that though she was not greeted by the critics in Stockholm as if she were bestowing a great gift on her native land, the opera house was filled to overflowing every night. Her performance had not been lauded in the press, but almost all the reviews were legitimate, serious criticism. She raged against the press, but Stig Ahlgren had been the only writer to make a personal attack, and he even poked fun at King Gustaf.

Sussie Bjuvstedt, the reporter who dared to violate the inner sanctum of Ingrid's family life, paid a fifteen-dollar fine and suffered rebuke in the press. Her story was different than Ingrid's:

> *My editor understood there was to be a press conference the morning after the opera opened, and a photographer and I went to the Grand Hotel, where the Rossellinis were staying. It was 10 A.M., not early in the morning. . . . The desk clerk said he wasn't aware of any press conference. Since I knew the number of the suite, we went up and knocked on the door. A nurse opened the door. She spoke only Italian. I gestured toward our camera to signify we wanted to take pictures. She called another nurse, who asked us, in French, to come in. The photographer took one picture of the boy and one of the three children together. The nurse helped and even wrote down the names of the children and the way*

they were standing. The whole thing took about five minutes. As the
photographs show, everyone was friendly and smiling and pleasant.

If it was indeed 10 A.M. when Bjuvstedt and her photographer arrived,
Ingrid would have had time to read the reviews of *Joan at the Stake*. She would
not have been in a terribly gracious mood.

Ingrid had played Joan of Arc so many times, so many ways, that people
thought she was like the Maid of Orléans. One evening at Santa Marinella, she
was sitting out on the terrace with Masina, Fiorella, and a priest friend of
Roberto's.

"When you did Joan of Arc, you felt you had to do such a saint?" the priest
said, as much telling Ingrid as asking her.

"No," Ingrid said, shrugging. "I loved to do the role and I thought I could
understand it."

"And you, Giulietta?" the father asked. Masina had just had a brilliant
success starring in Fellini's *La Strada*.

"I was really inside the character," the actress said. "I felt I was part
of her."

"I was not," Ingrid said. "I was Joan of Arc like a shoemaker doing his
shoe."

Ingrid was proud that she did not inhabit her roles, but it was her inability
to reach deep within herself that limited her as an actress. And now the
shoemaker was working on a splintered last, producing shoes that no one
wanted to wear. She and Roberto had made yet another movie together, *Fear*,
filmed in Germany. She played a bored wealthy housewife who is blackmailed
when she takes a lover. The film received the now familiar complement of bad
reviews that often had a few kind, if slightly patronizing, words about Ingrid's
performance. Ingrid could ignore most of the criticism, but one review, by
Angelo Solmi in *Oggi*, had the deadly resonance of truth:

> [Miss Bergman and Mr. Rossellini] *will either have to change their style of*
> *work radically—or retire into dignified silence. The abyss into which*
> *Bergman and Rossellini have plunged can be measured by* Fear. *This is*
> *not because this film is any worse than their other recent motion pictures*
> *together, but because after half a dozen tries with negative results it proves*
> *the inability of the couple to create anything accepted by the public or the*
> *critics. Once the world's unquestioned number one star and successor to*
> *Greta Garbo, Miss Bergman in her latest pictures has been only a*
> *shadow of herself.*

Ingrid's films were such financial failures, and Roberto's extravagances so
monumental, that talk of shoes and shoemakers was not only an artistic

metaphor. "If a good picture comes up, it might be better to do that so as to buy the children new shoes," she wrote Steele.

Roberto could not be bothered with such banal worries as children's clothing, but even he knew that things could not go on as they were. He decided that he would allow Ingrid to work with another director—not just with anyone, but with Jean Renoir, the great French director of *Grand Illusion*.

For years Ingrid had dreamed of working with her friend from her early days in Beverly Hills. In Paris, Roberto and Ingrid went to the building where Renoir was working, and waited for him outside. Ingrid became tired and sat on the curb.

Suddenly, the rotund, cherubic Renoir appeared, accompanied by Mrs. Renoir.

"I give you Ingrid," Roberto said, as if he were making a grand bequest. "She is very unhappy."

In June, Ingrid announced from Santa Marinella that she and Roberto were "splitting artistically" and that she would be making a film with Renoir in Paris. Three weeks later Ingrid sent the Rolls-Royce to bring Hedda Hopper out to the villa for an interview. The last time Ingrid had seen Hedda was in Rome, when she had led the columnist to believe that she was not pregnant, and had used her as a vehicle for spreading that untruth. If Ingrid was going to renew her film career, she needed Hedda on her side. She didn't tell Roberto quite that, only that Hedda "could stop the papers from writing how unhappy I am." Roberto agreed to behave with civility.

As soon as Roberto saw the aging columnist, he took a profound dislike to her, an emotion not lost on Hopper. Roberto sat over the lobster, squash, figs and loquats, fruit and cheese, eating in disdainful silence. Ingrid and Hedda talked about Ingrid's future movie and stage projects. There was the Renoir film. Then there was the stage play of the American hit *Tea and Sympathy* that she was planning to do in Paris. And Hedda mentioned that she had heard about a possible role in *Anastasia*, a 20th Century–Fox film.

The conversation could have taken place ten years before in Hollywood. Looking at Ingrid, it was hard to believe that in two months she would be forty years old, an age when most actresses are playing mothers and middle-aged wives, not romantic leads. Hedda had "never seen her looking better." There was a definition to her face, a depth that she had not had before. This was a face that had known joy and pain, a face that might grace a woman who would play great parts in great plays and great movies.

Ingrid was still a star, and as she laughed and charmed Hedda, it was as if Roberto weren't there, and had never been there. She talked about Selznick and Kay Brown. She talked about America and Hollywood. She talked about everything but her husband.

Roberto seemed not even to be listening. And who could blame him if he had stopped his ears up with cotton? He was the grand cuckold now, cheated not by another man but by the seductions of a career. He was the one left in the ruins, unable to get backing for his own films, left with debts and with movies that few people wanted to watch.

Hedda was not about to be fooled by Ingrid again. As she left she thought to herself that Ingrid's "love idyll is over." She wrote in her column, "how sad careerwise it's become."

Ingrid waved goodbye as the Rolls glided onto the highway. Then she began to berate Roberto.

"I don't talk to women like that," he said. "I didn't know she was such a bitch."

"I did warn you, didn't I?"

"I don't care. What do I care what she thinks or what she writes?"

There was so much about Ingrid that Roberto didn't care about any longer. He didn't care enough even to pretend. Ingrid didn't care that much either, but she had had enough of scandal and controversy. She would do her own work now, pretending to the world that her life with Roberto was the same as always, though the heart of their marriage was dead.

"From the beginning Ingrid's union with Rossellini seemed a bit strange," Fellini says. "But it seemed like the same kind of relationship that Pinocchio had with the blue-haired fairy. Through Ingrid, Rossellini could be transformed into a good boy, though perhaps it was the blue-haired fairy who risked becoming a female Pinocchio. But before Pinocchio could become a good boy, the fairy left. The miracle never happened."

CHAPTER SEVENTEEN

"Welcome Home, Miss Bergman"

The Parisian winter of 1955–56 was the coldest in decades, but Ingrid acted as if it were spring. As Albert, her French chauffeur, drove back and forth from the film studio, she insisted that the car windows be rolled down and the heat be turned off. She rode with her beaver coat open, without a hat, either napping contentedly or chatting amiably to her shivering companions.

Ingrid did not have the finest dressing room, and her co-star, Mel Ferrer, tried to watch out for her. "Why are you sitting here with a shawl around you in a dressing room with no heat, waiting to be called to go on in a picture that probably will never be released in the United States?" Ferrer asked her one day. "I mean, it's not a great picture. Jean is failing now. It's not great Renoir. Why are you sitting here freezing to death?"

"Mel, I work because I like to work," Ingrid said. "I'll work until I'm an old lady and I'll play grandma parts."

Ingrid was doing the one thing in life that gave her complete fulfillment. In Jean Renoir's comedy *Paris Does Strange Things*, Ingrid played Elena, a poor Polish princess, who uses her considerable charm to enchant, inspire, and then dismiss various suitors, including General Rolan (Jean Marais) and Count Henri (Ferrer).

Paris Does Strange Things was filmed simultaneously in French and English, a double burden. Ingrid was so enthralled with acting in a full-fledged, professionally scripted movie that even when she wasn't working in a scene, she occasionally showed up at the studio in Joinville, outside Paris, to watch. On Sunday, when the studio was closed, she haunted the movie houses of Paris, watching two or three films in a day. She frequented not simply the great first-run theaters, but the dank, musty art theaters of Montmartre. There she sat among the students and the movie buffs, watching *Carnet du Bal*, *Les Enfants du Paradis*, and other classics.

Good news rarely travels alone, and every knock of the door seemed to bring Ingrid more professional good tidings. For months Kay Brown had been looking for a suitable film to reintroduce Ingrid to the American public. Kay was now an agent for ICM, a prominent entertainment company, and Ingrid was her biggest client. At ICM, Kay saw the cream of Hollywood projects. She decided that Ingrid should star in *Anastasia*, a 20th Century–Fox film about the woman who claimed to be Grand Duchess Anastasia, the youngest daughter of Czar Nicholas II, and the only member of the royal family not to have been murdered. Kay had never been enchanted with Ingrid's Italian life, Italian husband, and Italian career. She saw *Anastasia* as a way for Ingrid to enter what Kay considered the "real" movie world. "I think it was terribly difficult," Kay says. "You can't say, 'I think you should do it to rehabilitate yourself.' "

Ingrid thought that there was nothing to rehabilitate. She was, nonetheless, still so much a figure of controversy in the United States that Fox decided to poll theater owners before offering her the part. The results were decidedly mixed, and both Spyros P. Skouras, the president, and the sales force preferred Jennifer Jones. But Darryl F. Zanuck, the executive producer, and Anatole Litvak, the director, insisted so strongly on Ingrid that she was offered the part for a reported $200,000, alongside Helen Hayes, as the grand duchess, and Yul Brynner, as Bounine, a White Russian general and her Svengali.

"I had to tell Roberto that not only did I want to do *Anastasia*, but that it was going to be made in England," Ingrid remembered. "Roberto didn't like that. So a big fight started and as usual he threatened to drive the Ferrari into a tree. In the past he had always frightened me with this suicide threat: he was going to commit suicide and it would be on my conscience. And I had enough on my conscience as it was. But I was determined to do *Anastasia*. I just didn't believe his suicide threat any more. I said, 'We must think of the children. We must have more money. We must pay our bills. I must get back to the kind of work I can do successfully.' "

Ingrid had her career again, and her career was real as her life and love with Roberto never had been. She was tired of Roberto, tired of his words, tired of his histrionics, tired of his excesses, tired of their failed films. But she cared about the image she and her husband presented.

Bad news travels in company too, and Roberto's existence in Paris was at times a pathetic remnant of a career. Everywhere he looked he saw signs of Ingrid's success. Wherever he tried to walk on his own, he fell stumbling over his own gigantic pride. In Paris he was supposed to direct a play about Judas at the Théâtre de Paris, but he had his ideas and the cast had theirs and he was fired. Then he was hired by Skouras to go to Jamaica to direct *Sea Wife*, starring Richard Burton and Joan Collins.

Five years before Roberto would have laughed at the idea of directing a commercial Hollywood film. Now not only was he accepting the job, but he was being given it by Skouras as a favor to Ingrid, a kind of artistic alms. Roberto flew to Jamaica, but he had his ideas and the producers had theirs and he soon left the film.

In January, Roberto had stormed out of the Raphaël, telling Ingrid that he would never come back. If once, for a few short weeks, their life had seemed a romantic saga, it was now full of scenes grand only in their ugliness. No matter what Roberto said, no matter how mean his words, how terrible his threats, he could never get through to Ingrid. He never had and he never would. She was emotionally impenetrable, be it to his passion or to his fury. Roberto threatened Ingrid with scandal, throwing her back into the emotional gulag from which she had only just escaped. He coerced her and berated her. She was no match for him. He wore her down until she signed a letter of separation, stating that the children could live only in Italy or France.

"I tried tonight, after I had signed the letter, to plead with him, to laugh, to be angry," Ingrid wrote a Roman friend. "He went and lay on the bed. I went to him and put my head on his chest and I cried. And cried. And cried. Then I suppose I got my sense of humor back at the whole sad situation and began to laugh." Roberto raced off to Italy in his new Ferrari. He was soon back, and their tormented relationship continued.

Since September 1955, Roberto had been vowing to travel overland to India to make a documentary film. He had been saying it so long and had put the trip off so many times that "Roberto's India trip" had become a standing joke in the family. Roberto needed the creature comforts of his class and city; his idea of roughing it was a bad room at the Excelsior. The betting among the other Rossellinis was that Roberto would never leave, and would give up his cockamamy scheme as soon as he had a new film project.

It was a mark of her renewed ambition that for the first time since marrying Roberto, Ingrid was not living in the same house as her three children. She had shipped them to Santa Marinella for the summer and well into the fall. She was separated from the children for close to half a year.

In the summer of 1956, when Ingrid was working on *Anastasia*, Roberto came to see his wife only once at the Savoy Hotel in London. A film set is a fraternity that has little time for outsiders, and it was just as well that Roberto stayed away.

Ingrid threw herself into the part as she could not in a Rossellini film. Often she sat in her dressing room reading a book about Anastasia given her by Felix Aylmer, who played the cynical old court chamberlain. Ingrid tried to understand the nuances of the character. She had decided to wear her hair in a bun in the early scenes, then in a swept-back style similar to her own coiffure. Looking at the pictures in the book, she saw that instinctively she had chosen hairstyles like those of the character whom she was playing.

Anastasia is a grand romantic saga, unlike anything Ingrid had attempted since *Saragota Trunk*. The name Anastasia is derived from a Greek word meaning "of the resurrection." In the film Ingrid's character goes through a stunning resurrection, changing from a mousy, frightened, half-starved refugee into a regal princess, glowing with beauty. If in the early scenes Ingrid looked too well-fed and radiant, the fault lay as much in her forty-one-year-old beauty as in the relentless glamorizing of Hollywood.

Helen Hayes had no trouble looking the aged duchess. When she lost her teenage daughter to polio, her main solace was not her career but her strong marriage to the playwright Charles MacArthur. But now he had died too. She had not even wanted to take the role, but to stay at home alone with her grief and her memories. When she came on the set the first day, Ingrid "almost burst out crying . . . all the suffering she had gone through just breaks my heart."

"I think that Ingrid was at home only in one place in the world: working," Hayes says. "As for me, I was always a shadow in my professional life, yearning for my personal life."

Ingrid had never before acted in a movie where she played her greatest scene with the other female lead—the dramatic meeting where the grand duchess must decide whether Anastasia is an impostor.

"We had a fierce experience together doing that scene," Hayes remembers. "We played that confrontation scene for nearly two weeks with all the different cuts and takes. She had been working with Rossellini and she said, 'I don't understand these takes.' He didn't do any of that, and she couldn't get herself back.

"It was a nightmare. Keeping the emotion low and then at the end they said we had to loop it. So each of us in turn had to go into a darkened room speaking out lines of high emotion. That was just slow death. I think in my heart it finished my career in pictures."

For Ingrid, however, *Anastasia* was part of a professional resurrection. Already in September, with the opening of *Paris Does Strange Things* in Paris (with the French title *Elena et les Hommes*), that resurrection had begun. The lines outside the theater on the Champs Élysées were a block long.

Even while she was shooting *Anastasia*, Ingrid was busy on the weekends studying her role in *Tea and Sympathy*. At one point Roberto had been asked to direct the play, but he took a visceral dislike to the drama, pronouncing it "trash." *Tea and Sympathy* is a very American play of the 1950s, with a subject matter and sensibility that might seem totally alien to a sophisticated European audience. It is the story of a boarding school boy who is thought to be homosexual. He is teased by his classmates because of such clearly deviant behavior as playing tennis and enjoying poetry. Ingrid, as the headmaster's wife, grows close to the young man. In the climactic scene, she makes the ultimate sacrifice, initiating the young man into the wonders of sex. In the Broadway play, Deborah Kerr merely unbuttoned the top button of her blouse. But this was Paris, after all, and Ingrid stripped down to her bra, a black one at that.

By the time the play had its first Parisian opening, on December 1, 1956, Ingrid had been preparing the role for over a year. And for over a year Roberto had been mocking her, denigrating the play, belittling her attempt at drama.

He was sure that after opening night, Ingrid would be the one needing tea and sympathy.

By now *Elena et les Hommes* was a great hit in Paris, and every indication was that *Tea and Sympathy* would be even bigger. Opening night, the theater was full of Parisians eager to see Ingrid Bergman and to hear her speak French.

Roberto was still planning to leave for India, but he was there in the dressing room at the Théâtre de Paris. He had lived among actors and actresses, and he knew that these last moments before the curtain opened were sacrosanct. It was particularly difficult for Ingrid, who was recovering from an appendectomy and was going to have to go onstage speaking a language she still only half understood. Roberto knew all this and yet he chatted with her in Italian. "You won't be on very long," she remembered him saying. "Be prepared when the first intermission comes for half of them to walk out."

They did not walk out after the first intermission. They did not walk out after the second intermission. And when the play ended they applauded until their hands were red. They shouted bravo in a chorus of praise. They gave the cast fifteen curtain calls. As the great waves of applause rolled over Ingrid, like a warm, enveloping sea, Roberto stood offstage. One of the other actresses, Simone Paris, saw Roberto standing there: "I looked toward him and his face was red with fury."

Ingrid saw him too, as the audience continued its applause. "They were standing up and screaming, standing up and applauding, and the 'bravos' never stopped," Ingrid remembered. "Then I took my solo bow in the center of the stage, and as I bent over I turned my head and I looked at Roberto. Our eyes met. We looked straight at each other. I knew then my marriage was over even though we might stay together."

The next day Roberto packed his bags. Ingrid went with him to the railroad station to see him off. He was finally leaving for India.

Tea and Sympathy was a smash hit. The French consider the mispronunciation of their language practically a felony, but no one seemed to mind that Ingrid spoke French as if she had put it through a blender. The crowds were coming to the Théâtre de Paris to see Ingrid, not to hear the language of Racine.

In Paris a play has a public opening and a critics' opening. For the second opening, two weeks later, Ingrid had a special guest, Robert Anderson, the author of *Tea and Sympathy*. Anderson's wife, Phyllis, a literary agent and producer, had died a few days before, after a five-year struggle with cancer. The playwright was buried in remorse and melancholy, hardly able to perform the basic rituals of daily living, much less attempt writing again.

Anderson was tall and handsome enough to have been a leading man. Much like his youthful hero in *Tea and Sympathy*, thirty-nine-year-old Anderson was so open in his emotions that his more macho brethren wondered why he had such a way with the ladies. He was the kind of man whose best friends were almost always women. He would cry at the drop of a sentiment, and was the archetypal "sensitive" man that in the age of women's liberation would become an emotional cliché.

Anderson remembers: "Phyllis and I had met Ingrid in Rome, when she said she liked the play and wanted to do it. Then I came to Paris. I wouldn't dare write the story. It's so corny that nobody would believe it. Ingrid had been writing me, saying, You have to come over for the opening. I told her Phyllis was ill and I said I don't think I'll be able to make it. Ingrid would get quite angry at me. She would say it will be a great opening. And then Phyllis died and I just wanted to die too.

"Ingrid said, You belong here. I packed up all these letters of condolence, a thousand, Phyllis was so popular, and Kay Brown took me out to the airport. It was winter and the plane was delayed and over Boston we lost a propeller. Then we couldn't come down in Paris.

"When I finally walked into her suite, Ingrid said, 'You should be older.' I said, 'I'm sorry I'm not.' She was extraordinary. She really took me in hand and I think I took her in hand. It was one of those weird times when people need each other. At the theater I would be in a little stage box, and she would occasionally look up when I was there. We'd either go out for drinks or supper or go back to her place. She lived right across the hall. She was marvelous.

"She had such energy. She never wanted to go to bed. She was drinking a great deal. She would polish off a big bottle of champagne or Scotch, and it would mean nothing to her. She'd want to stay up and talk and chatter.

"She was self-centered. Sometimes it would drive you crazy. It would seem that all she could talk about was herself. But she was very caring. She nurtured me for weeks and this was a very selfless act. Of course, she needed me too. She didn't have patience for people who were sad too long. She said, 'If you had children you'd have to shape up sooner than this.'

"She took me everyplace. She didn't accept an invitation without including me. In the morning I would sit over the letters, crying, thanking people for all the wonderful things they said about Phyllis, and in the evening I'd go out with Ingrid. She was the toast of Paris."

Ingrid was courting her own scandal with Anderson, whose room was just across the hall from her suite at the Raphaël. But she wasn't thinking about her husband and was not reflecting much on her marriage. Roberto was gone now, gone from her bed, gone from her life. She was half a world away from the man for whom she had given up a husband, a child, and a career. She wanted to get on with her career and her life.

It was no simple matter to say when Ingrid's marriage died. In the modern world it is often as difficult to define the end of a marriage as to determine the end of a human life. For a long time the heart and brain of Roberto and

Ingrid's marriage had been dead, kept alive by such mechanical rationales as routine and convenience. Did it begin to die when Ingrid and Roberto came to understand each other's languages? Did it die when Ingrid became pregnant and could no longer soar free? Did it die when their films died and there was no money? Or did the pebbles and stones of the press bruise their romance with fatal impact? Perhaps it expired that opening night of *Tea and Sympathy*. Or perhaps there had never been that immense love. Perhaps Ingrid and Roberto's marriage had always been a mechanical contrivance, powered by the electricity of ambition and pride and illusion and money.

The heart is no historian, and Ingrid saw the truths of her relationship with Roberto as truths of the moment, to be interpreted according to her mood and situation. Ingrid had been through enough controversy for five lives. She had no intention of ending her marriage to Roberto, creating another scandal and a struggle over children. She was not about to put Robertino, Isabella, and Isotta through a divorce.

As it was, the children had been shuttled in and out of their mother's life like boxcars on the side rail. Robertino didn't come home to find that his mother had prepared a glass of milk and sandwich for his lunch. He would often walk into an expensive restaurant to meet his mother for their midday meal. To the twins, food was something that arrived on linen tablecloths; all you had to do was dial a phone.

As a mother, Ingrid was a woman of the great occasion. For Robertino's seventh birthday she hired two clowns and a large private room for the party. The children loved such events, but they didn't grow up seeing life as a matter of connections, of bread growing from seed, cut flowers from the earth, and a mother's love from the rich soil of constant nourishing. Ingrid was too distracted, too absorbed in her career, for the day-to-day business of mothering. To her children, though, Ingrid was their mother, and they had no idea that it might have been different.

"When I look back on my childhood, it's very difficult because of the confusion over real remembrances and film, whether it's something I saw on film or something that happened," says Robertino. "Mother was filming from the time I was born, and we saw the film all the time. It's a little bit of confusion. We were moving so much and changing apartments because we were going around Europe. Even when they were married, my parents weren't living together that much. I remember living with my sisters. We were used to being very much alone. I don't remember the typical family home. For me our life was normality. It's still like that. I think that people living very quietly are not normal."

Soon after the opening of *Tea and Sympathy* in Paris, *Anastasia* opened in the United States. Ingrid's professional resurrection was complete. The movie was her first international hit in a decade, and a critical success as well. In the *New York Times*, Bosley Crowther called her "nothing short of superb . . . a beautifully molded performance worthy of an Academy Award." At year's end, the New York Film Critics voted Ingrid the best actress of the year, and invited her to New York City to accept the award.

The previous July, Ed Sullivan had announced on his popular variety show that he was considering showing a film clip of Ingrid and Helen Hayes in *Anastasia*. "Now I know that she's a controversial figure, so it's entirely up to you," the dour-faced columnist said. "If you want her on our show, I wish you'd drop me a note and let me know . . . and if you don't . . . you also let me know that too because it's your decision."

In the world's greatest democracy, the citizenry voted not only on governorships and mayoralty contests but on such transcendent matters as all-star baseball teams and favorite movie stars. But never before had the populace voted on the moral propriety of allowing a soiled movie star to appear in living black and white in homes across America. Sullivan usually took such matters into his own hands. With Elvis Presley, the scandalous new rock-and-roll singer, Sullivan had made the Solomonic decision of showing the gyrating musician from the waist up, a video castration that made him morally tolerable.

The results after a week were hardly gratifying to Ingrid's fans: 6,433 respondents didn't want to see her, while 5,826 did. No matter what the figures, Ingrid had no intention of being exploited on *The Ed Sullivan Show*. And neither did 20th Century-Fox. What Sullivan accomplished, however, was to generate sympathy for Ingrid, and editorials in her favor, while underscoring the fact that almost eight years after she left America she was still a figure of controversy.

So that Ingrid could go to New York to receive the Film Critics Award, Fox bought up three performances of *Tea and Sympathy*. Her arrival would be nearly as dramatic a moment as her arrival in Rome, and Ingrid prepared for her two-day visit with apprehension and care. She still had her own gift for public relations, and she knew that she must arrive alone, without entourage, without spokesman, without protectors. As the day approached, she decided that she would not have the time to see Pia, who was a freshman at the University of Colorado.

Ingrid remembered seeing her eldest daughter only once since leaving the United States in 1951. Petter, however, says that he took Pia to Europe not only in 1951 but in 1953 and 1955 as well, and on all these occasions Ingrid met Pia in England. For her part, Pia says that she remembers going to Europe twice, and recalls visiting Ingrid in London in 1951 and 1953. But there is a vagueness about Pia's recollections that seems as much a shroud of sadness as a lack of memory, and a devastating comment on the relationship between mother and daughter. Pia does, however, vividly remember her mother's trip to New York. "I was very sad that she would make a trip to the United States and she wouldn't see me," Pia says. "I offered to come to New York and she said, 'Don't do it.' She had her own reasons."

According to Petter, Ingrid had already made a secret trip to New York, two years before. At that time, he says, he bought a new coat for Pia to wear while visiting her mother, but Ingrid said that she had no time. Pia says that she cannot recall if her mother made such a trip.

Though Ingrid said that she did not have enough time in New York to see Pia properly, the hard fact was that she was not about to clutter up her return to America with the emotional baggage that came with Pia. She looked at the bright side of it, anticipating calling Pia from New York. She wrote Steele that she looked forward to talking to her daughter by phone. "Then we'll have no trouble hearing each other and we can have a nice, long, quiet talk," she continued. "It'll be wonderful to hear her real voice and not that awful sound that comes over the radiophone."

Saturday morning, January 19, 1957, was frigid and overcast, and the TWA plane from Paris was already a good two hours late. Some of the journalists awaiting Ingrid's arrival at Idlewild Airport were cynical about the whole matter. They were particularly cynical about a motley group of "fans" camped out in the arrivals lounge, carrying signs of welcome ("DEAR INGRID: THANK YOU FOR RETURNING—THE ALVIN GANG"; "WELCOME HOME, MISS BERG-MAN—THE ALVIN GANG"). The reporters were connoisseurs of publicity stunts. They would have bet a lukewarm cup of coffee that the whole bunch had been hired by 20th Century-Fox to hype *Anastasia*. One of the reporters was intrepid enough to go up to the "fans" and ask them some impertinent questions, hoping to add a sardonic paragraph or two to his story.

The "fans" were indeed fans and they viewed the reporters as the murderers of Ingrid's image, out to assassinate her anew. The group included four members of the group that a decade ago had stood outside the Alvin Theater when Ingrid played in *Joan of Lorraine*. Warren Thomas was the most loyal of the loyal, who saw in the woman he called "my lady" a moral and spiritual perfection rarely found on this earth. He loved her with a fidelity and concern that none of Ingrid's lovers had ever shown her. He was sixteen when all Ingrid's public trouble had begun; he had written her in Italy but received no response. He tried to pass messages on through columnists and others flying to Rome, but that hadn't worked either. To them he was only a fan. He had entered the army in hope of being assigned to Europe, near his idol. He was sent to Korea instead.

To welcome Ingrid back, Warren had made a few signs. Along with Adaire and Frank of the old Alvin Gang and a few other friends, Warren had come out to the airport in the middle of the night. On the subway they had pulled down advertising placards and on the back written some more welcoming messsages in lipstick. When the reporter accused the group of being mere hirelings, Warren exploded with wrath, as if journalists were the architects of all the abuse his lady had suffered.

The plane finally glided down out of the leaden skies and taxied toward the terminal. The passengers quickly descended, everyone except for Ingrid. Five minutes. Ten minutes. Still, no Ingrid. Finally she appeared, standing there in a full-length mink and a white kerchief, waving toward the hundred or so photographers, reporters, and fans.

The photographers and cameramen surged forward. Whatever doubts the journalists might have had about Ingrid were all over now. There was no other star in America with such a radiant glow. It was not simply beauty. It was the sheer incandescence of the woman, a great warm light that the photographers and cameramen vied with one another to capture on film, and the reporters wrote about in lyrical phrases. It was a light that shone in good movies and bad movies alike, and put criticism in its eternal shadow. It was a glow that seemed a higher truth, that made journalism with its revelations seem a mundane business, a craft that captured everything but what mattered.

"Miss Bergman, do you have any criticisms of the way the press in general handled the story of your life?" a reporter asked, almost gently, at the airport press conference.

"Oh, sure I had some criticism," Ingrid said, her mouth in a half smile. "I think a person has to have a private life. But I also know that if you choose being an actress, you have to take both sides of the coin. So there it is." As she spoke, Ingrid seemed both a sophisticated European woman and a wistful child.

"Looking back on it, do you have any regrets about anything that you've done in the last few years, Miss Bergman?" a reporter asked.

"No, I have no regrets at all," she said, suddenly serious. "I regret the things I didn't do, not what I did." Ingrid threw her head back and laughed, a laugh full of promise and secret thoughts.

"No, I think my life has been wonderful," she continued, speaking with the intensity she often showed when talking of her past. "I have done what I felt like. I was given courage and I was given adventure and that has carried me along. And then also a sense of humor and a little bit of common sense. It has been a very rich life."

Ingrid was driven to the Pierre Hotel, where she was to stay with Irene Selznick. She had scarcely time to chat a little with Irene and change clothes before she was off to the exclusive Colony Restaurant for lunch with Buddy Adler, the 20th Century–Fox production chief. This was supposed to be a private luncheon, but Adler reported that within minutes there were "at least 50 photographers from every wire service, syndicate and magazine surrounding us. She posed for their pictures throughout lunch."

Adler could smell the fragrant blossoms of celebrity and adulation once again blooming around Ingrid. He was willing to take full credit for signing her to do *Anastasia*. Now he was attempting to sign her to a long-term contract.

It was not just the producers and publicists and photographers and other professional admirers who hovered around Ingrid like hummingbirds, sucking

Above: At Hampshire House
during *Joan of Lorraine.*

Right: Ingrid and Sam
Wanamaker in *Joan of Lorraine.*

Director Victor Fleming adjusts Ingrid's armor for *Joan of Arc*.

Joan burns at the stake.

Above: Arch of Triumph's director Lewis Milestone was infatuated with Ingrid.

Right: A romantic scene with Charles Boyer from *Arch of Triumph.*

Above: Ingrid and Roberto as she arrives in Rome.

Left: Ingrid and Roberto at the Excelsior Hotel.

Above: Shooting *Stromboli.*

Right: In *Stromboli.*

Right: When a pregnant Ingrid
left her apartment, a
photographer captured her
picture.

Below: With Giulietta Masina
in *Europa '51*.

In the Honegger-Claudel
oratorio *Joan at the Stake*.

With Pia at airport, 1957.

Ingrid with Oscar, 1957.

Reunited with her three children Isabella, Isotta, and Robertino.

New York press conference, 1957.

The dramatic confrontation between Helen Hayes and Ingrid in *Anastasia*.

Right: With Lars Schmidt, 1958.

Below: With Lars at the Théâtre des Nations in Paris, 1959.

Above left: Dancing with Goldie Hawn in *Cactus Flower*.

Above right: In *A Walk in the Spring Rain*, the chemistry was gone between Ingrid and Anthony Quinn.

Below: With Isabella, Pia, and film producer Edgar Lansbury, at the New York premiere of Lansbury's film *Godspell*, in 1973.

Opposite page:

Top: Accompanying her three children back to Italy from Easter holiday in Paris.

Middle: With Lars.

Bottom: Ingrid with Pia and Hugh O'Brian at the Beverly Hilton.

With Lauren Bacall in *Murder on the Orient Express*. This cameo appearance won Ingrid her third Academy Award.

In his last years, Rossellini looked like a languid cat.

Above: Ingrid and Lars's island off the coast of Sweden.

Right: The view from Danholmen's living room.

Below: Directed by Ingmar Bergman in *Autumn Sonata*

With director Alan Gibson during the screen test for *A Woman Called Golda*.

On a sunny day in April 1982, Ingrid came out of her London town house and let the photographers take her picture. The shawl completely covered her swollen arm.

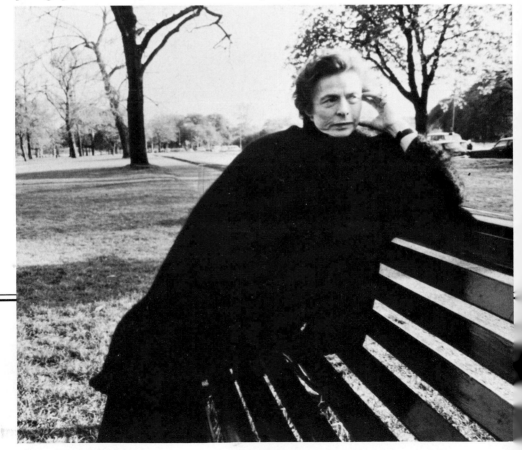

on the sweet nectar of celebrity. As she left the Colony, a crowd of perhaps a thousand fans stood in the street.

With the help of eight policemen, Adler led Ingrid to her next stop: a matinee performance of My Fair Lady, the biggest hit in New York. Saturday matinees on Broadway are as glamorous as jars of cold cream, but as soon as the audience saw Ingrid slip silently into her orchestra seat, there was a tremor of excitement and applause. As the musical ended, Ingrid applauded like everyone else and then left to go backstage. The audience gave her a standing ovation as great as the one they had given Rex Harrison, Julie Andrews, and the rest of the cast.

Wherever Ingrid went that day there were crowds to greet her. Two thousand fans waited in the street when she stopped at the Roxy Theater, where Anastasia was playing with such success. There were crowds in the evening outside "21" when she arrived for dinner, and crowds when she left. There were crowds outside Sardi's, where she went to appear on television's Steve Allen Show and then to receive the New York Film Critics Award. And there were crowds when she departed.

Ingrid had won not only the fans but New York's proudly cynical journalists, whose stories Newsweek called "well-nigh rhapsodic." She could have spent much of Sunday merely reading the press accounts. Instead, she went off to see Robert Anderson, who had returned to the United States January 5. It was a visit that could have embroiled her in a new romantic controversy.

"I had given her a big gold bracelet," Anderson remembers. "She said that at the airport the bracelet created a big stir. 'Who gave it to you?' they asked. She wouldn't say. The next day she came over to my apartment and was well chaperoned by Irene Selznick. She was taking a big risk as it was. I thought it was pretty brave of her to have the car drive up in front of my place. I said to Ingrid, 'When I come back and take a place on the Left Bank, may I see you?' And she was always a little hesitant. She said, 'Come, but don't come now.' I think she felt the relationship had gone its course."

Ingrid had found time on Saturday to call Hedda Hopper in Hollywood, ensuring that she would be the subject of Hopper's Sunday column. She did not find time to call Pia until Sunday, before she left. "I tried to tell her that I didn't know how to fit in what was the most important thing in my life on this journey: to see her," Ingrid remembered, a bit of logic that would have befuddled Aristotle. "I tried to explain that I couldn't handle it because I was afraid I would absolutely go to pieces emotionally. . . . But poor Pia didn't understand that. She thought I didn't want to see her; she thought my career was more important to me."

Pia tried to live her own life, but she was haunted by Ingrid's legacy. She told reporters that she had had a "nice" conversation, but Pia's attempt at diplomacy was not completely successful; she said that she could not remember the last time she had talked to her mother.

For Ingrid, the phone conversation with Pia was the one unpleasant interlude in a triumphant return. When she left New York at five o'clock that
Sunday afternoon, she was once again a figure to be idolized and praised in
America, a woman whose picture sold magazines and whose name perked up
the celebrity columns, a woman who to her fans was not a woman at all but a
goddess, part of the mythology of stardom.

As the plane took off, she wrote a letter to Anderson on pages in a small
notebook:

> *Dear Bob,*
> *I can't wait to write! I cried. I turned my face out the window, so no one*
> *would see it. I am so tired, Bob, but I was also moved by all the people that*
> *were there . . . I was just on the verge of breaking down and cry in front of*
> *them. . . .*

Monday evening Ingrid was back once again on the stage of the Théâtre
de Paris, back alone at the Raphaël, half a world away from her husband. In
many respects she had the best life she had known in years. She was the star of
one of the biggest hits in Paris, and she was being wooed by producers and
studios. Ingrid's dream house was not some great estate in Tuscany, a mansion
in the Hollywood hills, a duplex on Manhattan's East Side. It was what she had
now—a suite of rooms in a first-class hotel, with maids and meals at beckoning
call.

Ingrid had already won the New York Film Critics Award, but she was up
for the Academy Award as well. The night of the award ceremony, March 27,
1957, Ingrid took a sleeping pill so that she would not toss and turn all night.
In Hollywood, Cary Grant had agreed to accept the award for her, if she won.
"I seldom went to the ceremony unless I had been nominated, and even then
reluctantly," Grant remembers. "But I turned up that night so that no other
person could get up and say, 'Dear Ingrid, we forgive you.' All that crap. I
didn't want to risk anyone else getting up."

When Ingrid's name was called, Grant stepped forward: "Dear Ingrid,
wherever you are in the world, we, your friends, want to congratulate you, and
I have your Oscar here for your marvelous performance, and may you be as
happy as we are for you." Ingrid was sitting in the bathtub when the 20th
Century-Fox publicist called to tell her that she had won.

Late in April, Anderson visited Ingrid, to spend his fortieth birthday with
her. Like so many men before him, Anderson sought to break through to
Ingrid, to share a profound intimacy with her. They had come together in a
moment of mutual need and pain. For Ingrid, though, what was past was past.

When the playwright returned in June from the Congo, where he was working on *The Nun's Story*, Ingrid had a new suitor, introduced to her by Kay Brown. The agent had come to Paris to discuss a new movie deal. She had another client to see as well, Lars Schmidt, a theatrical producer, also living in the Raphaël. Kay didn't consider matchmaking part of her profession, but she thought two Swedes working in Paris—indeed, living in the same hotel—should meet.

Lars took Ingrid to the Coq d'Or for dinner. Ingrid stared at her Swedish compatriot.

"Isn't it strange, us not meeting before," Ingrid said.

"But we have met before," Lars insisted.

"Have we?" Ingrid asked. "Where?"

"You came to see my production of *Cat on a Hot Tin Roof*."

"Oh, is that your production?" Ingrid said, remembering the evening in December when she and Anderson had seen the Tennessee Williams play. "But I didn't meet you."

"Yes, you did. You had champagne at the intermission. I poured it for you."

"You poured it! Oh, dear, I thought you were the waiter."

Lars did, indeed, have the manner of a headwaiter. He carried simple matters of eating, drinking, socializing, to such perfection that it seemed a livelihood by itself.

The next time Lars called Ingrid, to invite her to lunch, Anderson was back in town. She told Lars, "Oh, I am so sorry. I have to take care of my children."

Anderson and Ingrid drove out to the Bois de Boulogne to have lunch in a romantic outdoor restaurant. Among the other guests was Lars Schmidt. After eating, he walked up to Ingrid's table: "Ah, Miss Bergman, so this is the way you take care of your children."

"And she looked up at me and she blushed," Lars remembers. "I'd never seen anyone blush like it. Then she looked at me with this most divine smile. And that night I called her again. And that broke the ice completely."

Ingrid's marital life might have developed in the predictable pattern of so many professional marriages. She would have her affairs, and Roberto would have his, and they would meet at the accountant's and at family gatherings, and have occasional interludes of cohabitation.

But that was not Roberto's way. On May 17, 1957, at 3:27 A.M., Ingrid was wakened by a half-hysterical husband. He said that she must not believe anything she heard, that it was all nothing but blackmail.

Roberto was having a torrid affair with a very wellborn, and very married, Indian woman. Indian women simply did not have affairs, and certainly not with married Italian film directors. Although Ingrid could not be expected to appreciate the sheer audacity of Roberto's act, it was akin to setting up a pork barbecue on the streets of Mecca.

Much as he had in Beverly Hills, Roberto had befriended the husband. The man this time was Hari Das Gupta, an ambitious young film producer who met Rossellini in December. Das Gupta loaned and eventually sold Roberto his American station wagon, invited him to dinner, and introduced him to his beautiful twenty-seven-year-old wife, Sonali, the mother of their two small children. Roberto was almost immediately infatuated with the doe-eyed, silken beauty.

Sonali was not the only Indian woman to whom he was attracted. Later, an Indian film starlet told reporters that she had dated Roberto soon after his arrival in Bombay. She had gone to his room at the Taj Mahal Hotel in Bombay to discuss movie projects but had left when he took off his shoes and "the atmosphere was too intimate."

Roberto's companion and cameraman, Aldo Tonti, says, "There was another woman he tried with too. She also was married. But Rossellini loved Sonali. . . . With women Rossellini was an enchanter. He talked and talked and talked."

Sonali was not only a great beauty but a woman of strong intellectual interests. Roberto could talk to her the way he could not talk to Ingrid. By the time Roberto called Ingrid, however, there was little time for intellectual discussions. The story of Roberto's latest romance was about to break and Sonali was ensconced in the Taj Mahal Hotel, in a suite adjoining Roberto's, protected by hotel guards from her husband and his relatives. Sonali came from a prominent Indian family, and when Prime Minister Nehru learned of the love nest he reportedly called Roberto a "scoundrel."

Even here, in the midst of his own international scandal, Roberto could not escape Ingrid's presence. Her picture was all over the city, on posters advertising *Anastasia*, and the film was a great success.

The reporters asked Roberto almost as much about Ingrid as about Sonali. "My wife and I have much understanding," Roberto told a reporter in his less than impeccable English. The reporter said that if he hurt Ingrid, the women of the world would consider him a Dracula. "Tell the women of the world they have nothing to worry about," Roberto replied nobly. "I know my wife. She is a strong woman, stronger than I in many ways. She is very independent. Believe me, I know what I have done to her life, how she has suffered. But remember, she did what she wanted to. I did not kidnap her, and we have had a good life together. What else about me worries the women of the world?"

Roberto was told that the women of the world were interested in knowing why he was such a success with their sex.

"I don't know the secret of my influence over women," Roberto said. "But I'll say women are very human, easily touched by a humble, simple, honest man, and I do pride myself on being absolutely honest about my work and myself."

"And your women?"

"And my women."

*   *   *

On May 29 the Italian embassy announced that Roberto had promised to stay away from Sonali, a promise that would have sounded familiar to anyone who had been in Messina, Sicily, in early May 1949. Within a few weeks Roberto was in deepest trouble again. He was planning to leave India, but because of tax and other legalities he was not being allowed to take his film with him. He soon had a further, more familiar problem: Sonali was pregnant.

In Paris, Ingrid gave some of her most skillful performances. "There were nights when Ingrid would arrive at the theater barely able to hold back her tears," said Simone Paris, her fellow actress in *Tea and Sympathy*. "When she heard about Roberto and that Indian girl, she sobbed hysterically backstage. She said, 'How am I going to play?' But somehow, at the last minute, she pulled herself together and did it."

Roberto had had lovers before during their marriage, but never had there been the shame of public disclosure. Ingrid knew that her saintly persona had long been superseded by the image of a passionate, daring woman who sacrificed everything for love. What did it say about *that* Ingrid if Roberto could debase their marriage in open scandal? She wrote Steele that it was all false, created by a reporter upset with Roberto.

Roberto and Sonali were indeed in great trouble in a land where the traditional wives' manual states: "Be her husband deformed, aged, infirm, offensive . . . debauched, immoral . . . a wife should always look upon him as her god." Sonali had been denied a passport to leave India, but that was resolved. Now Roberto's most immediate problem was to get his film out of India.

Early in July, Roberto called Paris once again in the middle of the night. According to Ingrid, he told her: "Now it's all nothing—it's stupid—this woman I'm supposed to be in love with. I don't understand what they're talking about. . . . But the only man who can help me with the film is the Prime Minister of India, Nehru. He's in London. You know lots of people in London. Can you get to him and see to it that I'm allowed to bring my film out of India?"

As Roberto so frequently said, Ingrid was not a woman of passion, and it was that very lack of passion, that matter-of-factness, that let's-get-on-with-it attitude, that allowed her to call her friend Ann Todd in London to try to help Roberto. Ingrid knew that Ann and her husband, David Lean, were friendly with Vijaya Lakshi Pandit, the Indian ambassador in London, and Nehru's sister.

"Ingrid rang me from Paris," Todd recalls. "She said, 'I know your sunburned friend. I'd like to meet her.' "

Todd set up a dinner for the following evening, July 5, 1957. *Tea and Sympathy* was in summer recess, and the children had already been sent to Italy. Ingrid flew over for the meeting. At the ambassador's residence, Ingrid also met Nehru, who was in London for the Commonwealth Ministers Conference.

"My husband, Roberto Rossellini, is in trouble over in your country," Ingrid remembered saying.

"So I have heard," Nehru replied, with the inscrutability that was as much the product of his British education as of his Oriental heritage. Nehru made no promises, but Roberto's problems in India ended almost immediately.

Ingrid flew back to Paris and on to Rome, where five-year-old Isabella had gone through an emergency appendectomy. Isabella was fine, but Ingrid's life was still one of crisis and drama. The papers were full of stories of Roberto's new romance. While, in India, Roberto publicly denied that he was coming back to spend the summer with his wife, Ingrid told reporters: "We will spend the summer together at our Santa Marinella villa as we always have since our marriage."

Ingrid had still another great drama on her hands: Pia's arrival in Paris to spend the summer with her. Almost as soon as Ingrid arrived in Rome, she had to turn around and fly back to Paris. The press was chronicling Pia's journey toward her mother as if it were a historic event. On July 5, the *Los Angeles Times* had a front-page photo of Petter and Pia at the airport. On July 6, the papers noted that Pia was in Stockholm, on her way to see Ingrid.

The daughter whom Ingrid had not seen for several years was now a nineteen-year-old college student. Her hair was blond, not the light blondish brown of her mother's. She had blue eyes—deep blue, not the blue gray of her mother's. She was pretty, tall, and slightly plump, appearing not voluptuous but as if she were still carrying baby fat. She was charming but some observers felt a coldness in Pia, and a mistrustfulness.

Pia's arrival at Paris's Le Bourget airport, July 8, 1957, was the most dramatic moment in her life since she had told Judge Lillie that she did not love Ingrid. Some seventy-five reporters and photographers waited, about the same number that had covered Queen Elizabeth's recent state visit to France.

The other passengers left the plane first. Then Ingrid entered to see Pia in private before running the gauntlet of reporters. As mother and daughter stood before one another, with a look as much wary as loving, a flashbulb illuminated their first greeting. The photographer, who had been hiding on the plane, had the exclusive photo for which *Paris Match* was paying him.

Later that day Ingrid and Pia left the Hotel Raphaël to dine in a café in Montmartre. "Mama ordered a bottle of champagne," Pia remembers. "We drank to our meeting again, to happiness and the best of days." Pia spent over a month with her mother, traveling to Rome, Santa Marinella, and Capri, visiting with Robertino, Isabella, Isotta, and the other Rossellinis. Pia had never been to Italy before, and her mother, the paparazzi, the daily drama of Ingrid's life, all blended together in a cacophony of images and memories.

"That summer I fell in love with Italy," Pia said later. "The family camara-

derie in Italy, the buoyant expression of feeling, the loving care and considera-
tion for others—all this provided an armor against loneliness."

Pia says now that the trip was a "media circus." It was indeed that, but
much of the time Ingrid was the ringmaster. She was the one who invited a
photographer into her suite at the Raphaël to take intimate "candid" shots of
mother and daughter. She seemed always to understand what the journalists
wanted.

Ingrid complained frequently about the press, yet she was like a man who,
arrested for exposing himself, did penance by spending time in a nudist colony. It was thrilling to have photographers and reporters constantly about,
especially for Pia. "As I look back on it, I found that Paris meeting very
exciting," she says. "All that attention was very exciting; there were hundreds
and hundreds of people at the airport just to see my mother and me."

Who could blame Pia if she found life with Ingrid more exciting than her
life in America? And who could blame Ingrid if for a few weeks she found a
solace and happiness with her daughter that was gone forever from her
marriage.

One evening Ingrid sat at Santa Marinella listening to Pia and her new
friends dancing on the terrace. "Of course everybody is trying to make each
day a feast," she wrote Irene Selznick. "Each day we do different things, but
what is nice is that when we come alone or stay alone here at Santa Marinella
she thinks that is wonderful too. She is so much more than I ever hoped for. I
can't tell you how happy I am these days. I long for the moments we talk, but I
won't force myself on her."

During her summer in Italy Ingrid acted unconcerned about her career,
but she was always thinking what her next project would be. One day Stanley
Donen, the young director of Cary Grant's new picture, flew into Rome to try
to convince Ingrid to take the female lead.

"I've brought you this treatment, and I'd like so much for you to do this,"
the thirty-three-year-old Donen said, as the children scurried through the
apartment. He was in awe of her.

"I know you're frightened and nervous," Ingrid said. "I want to put you at
your ease. I'm going to do the movie no matter what it is."

On August 18, Ingrid and Pia flew from Rome to Copenhagen. Ingrid said
goodbye to Pia, who immediately got on another plane to join her father in
Stockholm. The photographers noticed that whereas Ingrid always smiled for
them, today she looked downcast.

Roberto flew into Paris on October 21, after an absence of ten months. As
soon as he got off the plane, he was deluged by reporters and photographers
asking about Sonali, who was rumored to be in Paris already. "It is rubbish—
how you say rubbish," Roberto said emphatically. "This girl means nothing to
me. I love my wife."

In the midst of this, Ingrid appeared, running toward Roberto across the crowded arrivals lounge. She hugged her husband, and they kissed on the cheeks in the Italian manner. "I am very happy," she said, her eyes glistening with tears. It was a touching scene. And at the request of the photographers, she kissed Roberto a few more times, repeating the greeting. As a director, Roberto believed in one take, but he kissed Ingrid back. "That's enough," Ingrid said finally, and she and Roberto left in a waiting car.

In the privacy of her hotel suite, Ingrid vented her anger. But she and Roberto knew that it was all over. Roberto was a magician whose tricks no longer fooled Ingrid nor even particularly amused her. She had already met Sonali, who says that she went to see Ingrid in Paris to deliver a letter.

Ingrid and Roberto discussed terms of divorce. According to Ingrid, Roberto agreed that she should have the children, but asked that they never go to the United States, a demand that echoed Petter's feelings about Pia and Italy.

"So what's the second thing?" she asked.

"That you'll never marry again."

"I'm not going to promise you that," Ingrid remembered saying, and then she "began to laugh. It was all very funny, I couldn't help laughing. That was Roberto."

Tea and Sympathy had finally closed. Early in November, Ingrid returned to Rome to finalize the divorce and end her life in Italy. On November 7, 1957, she and Roberto appeared secretly before Rome Civil Court President Mario Elia to sign a separation agreement. As they had agreed in Paris, Ingrid was given custody of the three children; they would be educated in Europe in the Italian language. Roberto agreed to pay $976 a month for their support.

On the day they signed the agreement, they went to the apartment on Bruno Buozzi. And there in the bathroom was the dog they had named Stromboli and taken to the island back in the summer of 1949. The dog was dead.

As the time for Ingrid's departure approached, she finished packing the last few things she would take from the apartment that she and Roberto had shared. Roberto watched her, as she methodically and neatly put the belongings into her suitcase.

The apartment was bare now of almost everything but memories. There was only one painting left on the wall, a painting that Ingrid had never liked.

"Ingrid, take also that painting," Roberto said.

"It's not good," Ingrid said firmly. "I don't like it."

"But it's a very important painting," Roberto said, always the teacher.

"Who is the painter?" Ingrid asked, suddenly curious.

"It's a Guttuso," Roberto said, naming a prominent contemporary Italian artist.

"How much does it cost?"

"Oh, very much."

"Then I'll take it away."

Ingrid got up on a chair and took down the painting by Renato Guttuso. Soon afterward, she was gone, leaving Roberto sitting in the empty apartment, alone with Father Lisandrini.

The priest kept thinking about Ingrid taking the painting down. "You have no money," Father Lisandrini scolded. "You could have sold it to somebody and made enough to live on for a month."

Roberto looked at the priest, full of rage. "You . . . you . . . you Franciscan father!" Roberto shouted. "You son of St. Francis of the Poor. You! You tell me this thing."

CHAPTER EIGHTEEN

A Man of Perfect Manners

*I*ngrid flew out of Rome like a star, with a sable coat, fifteen pieces of baggage, and no children. When the plane landed in London, where she was to begin work on *Indiscreet*, Grant and Donen were waiting for her. So were the photographers and reporters.

Ingrid tried to sound as upbeat as possible, saying that the first thing she was going to do was to find "a home big enough for all my children." The reporters were not as interested in her immediate future as in her immediate past.

"Why don't you leave me alone?" she implored in a sad, weary voice, as they asked about Roberto. She had had enough of journalists for the day. "I will say no more."

"Come on, boys," Grant said finally, gently shepherding Ingrid toward his waiting silver-and-white Rolls-Royce. "You've had enough."

Like Grant, Ingrid was as bankable as a pound note. She was a modern, independent Hollywood star now, a creature as much of commerce as of art. Indeed, the most creative aspect of *Indiscreet* was not what would appear on the screen but the deal itself. The primary owners of the film were not a studio but Grant and Donen's corporations. Grant's deal even included the Rolls-Royce, which would be used in the film and then become his property. Ingrid's deal included 2,327,000 francs for her wardrobe, $75,000 as an "employment contract," plus 10 percent of the gross above $4,000,000 and the payment of any excess taxes because the picture was shot outside Italy.

This was a great deal of money. But when Ingrid arrived at the Connaught Hotel, a bastion of decorum and discretion, she had less money than the porters who carried in her fifteen bags. "Mother had to borrow a hundred dollars from the hotel," says Isotta, her daughter. "She said, 'You know me and I'm going to work.'"

Steele wrote, concerned about Ingrid's financial situation. She reassured him that she had finally decided to become wealthy. "By the time I have finished these pictures, we will have 'champagne and caviar' every day." Ingrid approached her renewed film activity with a gambler's eternal optimism, as if it were a bet on a horse race, or a pull on a slot machine. Only, with this kind of gambling, if you were the star, and the contract was right, the game was indeed a sure thing.

Indiscreet represented a coming out for Ingrid as a romantic comedienne and as a sophisticated, elegant lady of the screen. In this endeavor, Grant was a perfect partner. He may have been fifty-five years old, but he was still a role model for many young men, as well as the romantic ideal of women half his age. Since the days when he and Ingrid had worked together on *Notorious*, Grant had developed a persona of lighthearted sophistication; he was a man who showed his feelings to about the same degree that he showed his cuffs.

The publicists promoted the film as if it had three stars: Ingrid, Grant, and Ingrid's wardrobe. That was just as well, for *Indiscreet* had an anorexic plot. The story was little more than a device that allowed Ingrid and Cary to be relentlessly amusing and gay, wear elegant clothes and go elegant places. The story, such as it was, concerned Ann Kalman, a wealthy, world-weary actress, with just enough similarities to Ingrid to allow the audience to think that they were watching life itself, if only they could get there. She meets a NATO official, Philip Adams, a confirmed bachelor who tells Ann that he is married to a woman who refuses to grant him a divorce. In the end, he admits the truth and proposes marriage.

Indiscreet was an hour and half of pleasant diversion provided by two actors who enjoyed the sheer craft of making a film. "She was so good on camera because she had a completely rooted quality," Donen says. "She was completely at ease. She never seized up while acting. Her concentration was complete. She was in her element."

Ingrid was glad to be out of the daily realities of her second marriage, and she talked often of the sheer magic of filmmaking, in an "atmosphere of make-believe. The people who work in them are like children creating an illusion." It was a world infinitely preferable to the world she lived in, or in which almost anyone lived.

"We had a wonderful time making the film," Grant recalls. "I found her a joy to be with. One day she said, 'Do you realize the two of us make a hundred years together?' "

Ingrid was off by a couple of years, but *Indiscreet* seemed to prove that romance is wasted on the young. So did Ingrid's personal life. Anderson wrote saying that he was coming to London to live, and asking if he still had his toe in the door. Ingrid answered that although he might still have a toe in, Lars Schmidt had his whole foot inside.

Since that day she had seen Lars Schmidt so unexpectedly in the Bois de Boulogne, Ingrid's romance with her compatriot had blossomed. Lars looked very Swedish, so much so that he could have been Petter's brother. He was tall and blond and handsome, and wore horn-rimmed glasses that gave him a vaguely intellectual look. A man of perfect manners and grace, Lars was an ideal companion for a woman coming out of a bad marriage.

Lars had certain similarities to Cary Grant's character in *Indiscreet*. Not only did he intend to remain single, but at his best he was full of gracious repartee that could have been lifted from the film's dialogue. He was a producer, not a wildly romantic, irresponsible director. Nor was he an ambitious surgeon. He was a man who could advise Ingrid on matters large and small, a man who listened for hours as she talked about movies, the theater, and herself.

Ingrid's life in London was all so wonderfully civil. The city. The English. *Indiscreet*. Cary. Lars. Everything. She had planned to bring the children to London. After all, she had custody, and Roberto was spending much of his time in Paris and elsewhere. But she decided that wasn't quite what she wanted to do. Roberto was proving difficult. The London winter was dreary and cold, and she preferred to leave the children a bit longer in Rome, with the nanny and Marcella, her former sister-in-law. She would bring them back with her after Christmas.

As the holidays approached, though, Ingrid decided that that wouldn't do either. She blamed Roberto and she was involved in a legal dispute over final custody. But she appeared more interested in her film career than in her children. Moreover, in February she would be off to Formosa on location for her new film, *The Inn of the Sixth Happiness*. Even during the periods when Ingrid could have spent more time with her children, she did not. She flew to Rome December 23, 1957, and spent only a week with her family before the children were sent to Switzerland for a longer vacation.

Ingrid was back in London in time to spend New Year's Eve with Lars. Lars always knew the perfect touch. They greeted the new year in front of Big Ben, toasting each other with champagne. Then they went off to the Milroy Club for Donen's party, and danced and drank till dawn.

Ingrid had not wanted to become seriously involved again so soon, but she was not a woman who could get along without a man for very long. There were still vast aspects of life that she felt incapable of dealing with on her own; and she didn't like solitude. Lars took care of her the way no man ever had. He was willing to organize her life, to be everything for her from banker to valet, publicist to lover. He had a producer's ego, reveling not in publicity but in creating publicity. He enjoyed not applause for himself but knowing that without him there would be no applause.

Lars had been born into a wealthy shipping family in Göteborg, Sweden's second-largest city. As a young man he traveled to Wales to learn firsthand about the shipping business. He spent part of the Second World War in New York, where he was introduced to Broadway theater life. He bought the foreign rights to the hit *Arsenic and Old Lace*, and began a lucrative career, primarily taking Broadway plays and producing them in Scandinavia and elsewhere in Europe. This was the work of a connoisseur of theater, not a creator.

Lars was a man who was always seeking ultimates. He sought these ultimates not in religion or in art but in the details of life. He could not write plays himself, but watched over every facet of their production, meticulous and demanding to a fault. In his personal life, every meal had to be right, every towel in place, every flower arrangement exquisite, every ashtray clean. Life is full of dirty ashtrays, and hardly a day went by when Lars didn't experience endless petty frustrations, demands not met or half fulfilled, and people who did not measure up.

The great sadness of Lars's life was not the failure of his first marriage but the death of his son, electrocuted when he put his fingers in a power socket. It was not something that he talked about, but he had been as much affected by it as Roberto had been by the death of *his* son.

There was a spiritual aspect to Lars, and in March Ingrid traveled with him to Sweden to see that part of the man whom she was considering marrying. The area on the southwest coast of Sweden where Lars was taking Ingrid could have been in Japan. The Swedes are, in fact, in certain ways like the Japanese. They are both people of almost rigid decorum, who suddenly explode in reverie, or drunkenness, in excess joy or sadness. They have a similar aesthetic sense too, seeing profundity and great beauty in things simple and pure, seeing everything in nothing.

The fishing boat from the village of Fjällbacka cut its way through the ice toward the island that Lars had recently purchased. As the boat approached, Ingrid could see that Danholmen was little more than a rock in the water: a hectare of land, and two large, plain wooden houses. The ice age had smoothed the rocky surface until it was like glass. There was nothing there. No electricity. No telephone. No neighbors. Nothing but the sea and the sky and the rocks and the two wooden houses.

"The house was upside down," Lars remembers. "It became her place as much as mine."

"I love your island," Ingrid said, as they sat outside.

"Right," Lars said. "Let's get married."

Ingrid was not willing quite yet to say publicly that she would marry Lars. But when they returned to his large family estate in Göteborg, the reporters asked Lars about a marriage. "We can neither deny nor confirm that," Lars said. "That says a lot, doesn't it?"

Ingrid and Lars were both in their early forties, entering a graceful middle age. They were in the same profession. If it was not a mad passion, so what. Ingrid knew where mad, impulsive gestures led.

"Ingrid said, 'You want to get married to me and I want to get married to you,'" Lars remembers. "She said, 'But no man will ever be able to play the second fiddle.' Ingrid knew her strength. She knew a man would always blame her for being first. I said, 'You have a big ego. And I may have a big ego too. I'm fairly successful and you're successful too.' "

Ingrid was almost devoid of insight into the kind of man she needed; nor was she perceptive about her future husband. She believed that Lars was not only extremely honest but highly uncomplicated, though Lars was an immensely complicated man capable of deviousness. She believed, as she wrote Steele, that for the first time in her life she had a lover without a large ego. Ingrid would have ridden roughshod over a man with a normal-sized ego; she might like to pretend that Lars had a modest ego, but he was ambitious and selfinvolved.

Ingrid could not get a divorce in Catholic Italy. Before Ingrid and Lars could get married, her marriage to Roberto had to be annulled. This was done by arguing that their Mexican marriage had not been legal in the first place. In June 1958 the courts voided the eight-year marriage, creating considerable controversy. A high Vatican official told UPI: "We reach this enormity—two persons first go through all legal strategy and tactics to justify their concubinage, and when the experience is over they themselves admit that the so-called marriage was null and void."

The annulment was scandalous enough to Italian conservatives that in August the Roman prosecutor filed an appeal, preventing Ingrid from marrying legally for a number of months.

Because of problems with the Chinese Nationalists, *The Inn of the Sixth Happiness* was filmed not in Taiwan but in Wales. Ingrid played Gladys Aylward, a British servant who decides to go to China to do missionary work, converting the Chinese to Christianity. In *Europa '51*, Ingrid had played a bourgeois Roman lady who sets out to help the poor, and discovers that in the modern world there are few things as difficult as truly to help another person.

In the Hollywood of the 1950s everything was possible, however, everything except casting Chinese as Chinese. Better, by far, to have a dying Robert Donat play the cynical mandarin, with a cynical mandarin's beard and eyebrows, and to have Curt Jurgens play the Nationalist general. After all, he was German, exotic enough. The movie reeked of goodness, as good Gladys leads a hundred singing orphans over the mountain, the screen awash in Technicolor. *Time* said that the film contained "more sheer treacle than anybody has seen since the Great Boston Molasses Flood . . . the woman's simple story comes to seem rather like a Cecil B. DeMille version of 'Now I Lay Me Down to Sleep.' "

Isotta and Isabella came to visit their mother in Wales. They traveled like rich gypsies, from place to place, from parent to parent. UPI noted: "The children have divided their time between father and mother in Rome, Paris, London, Wales and the resort coast of central Italy."

In Wales, Ingrid decided that it was time to tell the six-year-old twins that their mother was planning to remarry. What would have been a difficult moment for any mother was infinitely more difficult for a wife of Roberto.

"How would you like it if Mama got married again?" Ingrid asked, as she recalled.

"That would be great. Have you found somebody?"

"Yes, you remember that nice person, Lars, who came to visit us here in Wales?"

"Oh, yes, we liked him; when can you marry him?"

Isotta and Isabella lived in their own world, above such traumas as divorce or remarriage. Robertino was not as enthusiastic about Ingrid's remarrying, but even he tolerated the idea of his mother living with Lars. "I was maybe a little jealous," Robertino says. "My father was so furious. Maybe he pushed us a little."

In Paris, Lars drove Ingrid and her children to Choisel, an hour outside the city. Here he had purchased an estate, where he hoped they would make their home.

"Mama? Does Lars know that you want to marry him?" Isotta asked.

Lars was not used to such candor from the mouths of babes, and he drove silently on.

"What did he say?" Isotta asked.

"He didn't say anything."

"Oh? Lars, my mother is still young."

"Well, if you want me to marry your mother, maybe I will."

"Yes," Isabella chimed in. "We would like very much if you would marry our mother. And don't worry about Robertino because we will talk to him and make him understand."

Roberto was spending much time in Paris where Sonali was hidden away. He was bitterly disdainful of Lars. "Rossellini never knew my name," Lars says. "He was so violent. It wasn't that Ingrid left him. I think he disliked the idea of Sweden, and the idea that another man might marry her."

Roberto did not want Ingrid to remarry, but it was doubly painful that it would be a man like the Swedish producer, a businessman of the arts. He was suspicious of a man who would buy an estate at Choisel together with his future wife, and yet have the papers only in his name. Ingrid said that this was done simply to hide the matter from the press, but it was the beginning of Lars's careful management of Ingrid's finances. Almost the entire Rossellini family felt that Ingrid was making a terrible mistake. "Some of them felt that Lars was not a creative person and was after Ingrid for the prestige of her name and for her money," says Franco Rossellini, Roberto's cousin. "Roberto was fuming."

Roberto was a man of overweening pride. He might complain and condemn Lars until eternity, but one fact remained: In a failed marriage, the best revenge is no revenge at all, to go on and love again, and to forget the pains of the past. Ingrid had done just that, leaving Roberto mired in his problems. He even had to see Ingrid's new romance celebrated in the press, a smiling picture of the couple on the cover of *Paris Match*.

Roberto was in such desperate financial and professional straits now that even he could not ignore the problems. Isabella, Isotta, and Robertino served as human antidepressants, pulling him up out of his despair. He began to fight with Ingrid, increasingly seeking custody of the children. It didn't matter that his life, his livelihood, was collapsing from all directions and it would be hard for him to give the children the home they needed. He wanted them, and more than that, he needed them.

In October, Ingrid went to a railroad station in Paris to pick up her children and the maid. Roberto was at the railroad station as well, for after he put them on the train in Rome, he had flown to Paris. Roberto insisted that the children come with him to stay at his hotel. They argued until Roberto put Robertino in the car and Ingrid drove off with the twins. The children had been divided like chattel.

One of those present that day to witness Ingrid's anger was Joe Steele. Steele was living through hard times. Ingrid had been the greatest thing in the publicist's life, and he had nothing to show for it but clippings and letters and memories. He had saved no money, and in Hollywood he was reduced to taking piecemeal jobs as the unit publicist on quickie, ten-day pictures—he, Joe Steele, former head of publicity for David O. Selznick, confidant and adviser of the great Ingrid Bergman. Another man might have figured that Ingrid owed him something. Not Steele. Instead, he decided that he would write a book about Ingrid. Steele was in his early sixties. He had lived a peripatetic publicist's life. He had never experienced the solitary confinement of writing a book. For months he sat over the typewriter that Ingrid had given him fifteen years before, not taking a full day off for close to two years, going ever deeper into debt.

His was a work of love, and Steele filled the pages with Ingrid's letters, and private conversations, and thoughts. He knew that he would have to get Ingrid's permission, and when he was finished, he borrowed five hundred dollars and flew to Paris. Ingrid read the manuscript and said that it was fine and true, and eventually *Ingrid Bergman: An Intimate Portrait* was published. Steele made some money, though not nearly as much as he had hoped, and while Ingrid stayed friendly with him, privately she condemned her old publicist for making money off her life.

Ingrid wanted to rid herself of Roberto and his problems. She wished to formalize her marriage as soon as it was legally feasible. In Rome, however, the appeal dragged on and on, and Lars took action. "I met an English barrister," Lars says. "He said, 'Do you want to get married or not?' He said that we shouldn't worry about the legal situation. Ingrid can never be a bigamist. And so we decided to go ahead. This was at a time when we were followed everywhere. *Paris Match* said they'd be at our wedding. I said let's make a bet."

Ingrid's wedding to Lars was a perfect symbol of her marriage, just as her previous two weddings had been. Lars won his bet, and he managed the wedding with the same sense of timing and detail that he gave to his theatrical productions. The ceremony took place at 11:15 A.M., December 21, 1958, at musty old Caxton Hall, near Westminster Abbey, in London. Caxton Hall was a favorite wedding spot for celebrities, but not on a Sunday morning, when the building was empty except for watchmen, and the street outside bare of traffic and onlookers. To ensure privacy, Lars had told practically no one except the guests: Lars's old friends Göran and Marianne von Essen; his attorney, Ambrose Appelbe; and the Sidney Bernsteins.

After a champagne luncheon at the Connaught, the newlyweds flew to Paris with the von Essens. By the time the group reached Choisel, Bernstein had announced the wedding on Granada Television, and they were soon under siege. Reporters pushed and jostled outside the gates, climbed up on the walls, and tried to force their way into the house.

Lars was not going to be held hostage inside his house, and he called the police. French gendarmes are not usually called out to shoo away photographers. They could not understand why Lars and Ingrid didn't simply let the journalists get their pictures and go back to Paris. Lars was not about to face photographers and reporters on his wedding day. It was not until the next morning that pictures were taken of the smiling, happy couple.

Ingrid was sure that this time her marriage would last. Lars might look a little like Petter, but he was tolerant and understanding in a way that Ingrid felt her first husband was not. Lars wasn't like Roberto either, burdening her with his melodrama, his debts, and his artistic dreams. This time, Ingrid had thought the whole thing through. She was settling for something realistic; she was sure that she would obtain it.

At first glance, Choisel appeared very much Ingrid's home. Lars had filled the rooms with souvenirs of Ingrid's career and life. On the walls were two paintings by Ingrid's father: a self-portrait and an oil of her mother. There was a three-foot painting of Ingrid in *Joan of Arc* that once had been a lobby display, and a bronze of her as Joan from her days in *Joan of Lorraine*. On a desk there was yet another souvenir of her career as Joan: autographed photographs of Arthur Honegger and Paul Claudel, the composer and librettist of *Joan at the Stake*. There were also autographed photographs of Ernest Hemingway and Maurice Chevalier.

Despite all the remembrances of Ingrid's career throughout the house, Choisel represented Lars's taste far more than it did Ingrid's. He was the master of Choisel. Ingrid thought that she cared about neatness and cleanliness as much as anyone, but she was practically slovenly compared to Lars.

For a while Ingrid enjoyed playing the mistress of Choisel and having Lars totally managing her investments and business. Indeed, if one symbol of their marriage was Choisel, the other was a small, seventh-floor walk-up apartment in Geneva that allowed Ingrid Swiss tax status.

Once, Dora Jane Hamblin, a writer for *Life*, spent the weekend at Choisel. "My sense was that it was clearly an adult love affair," she remembers. "If they were put in separate beds for the night, they wouldn't have been upset. They weren't demonstrative in their affection, but they amused one another. The children were there too, and Lars was dealing with the kids. She treated the children as if they were adults, very cool, while he was indulgent."

Lars was the grand host, offering "a tour of Scandinavia by aquavit," serving glasses of the fiery Scandinavian liquor, to the occasional accompaniment of a Swedish drinking song. Then it was time for another Scandinavian custom, a nude jump in the sauna.

Though their marriage began well enough, Lars and Ingrid were not the kindred spirits that they appeared to be. As her two previous husbands had discovered, there was an impenetrable quality to Ingrid, and large aspects of life in which she had absolutely no interest. Lars was a man of deep intelligence, and though Ingrid was highly perceptive about the plays Lars produced, there were many things that she could not talk about. Lars was not beyond putting Ingrid down, even in the presence of guests. Though he found having Ingrid as a wife helpful professionally, he was far from comfortable with all the publicity.

"We were too much in the limelight, but I think Ingrid liked publicity in a way," Lars says. Ingrid could never admit that; she always played the coy maiden startled by the burst of attention. But what greater sign of Ingrid's fame could there be than that each summer a certain Belgian lady spent her vacation camped outside Choisel? And hadn't the press sanctified the marriage anew in articles about the adoring couple?

Sometimes the press was an irritant, but it was no more a problem to Ingrid than a rough sea is to a sailor. Even her children, particularly Robertino and Isabella, were slowly learning to experience the photographers and reporters as a natural part of life. "I may be more honest than the others, but I think Mother and Father both hated and enjoyed the publicity," Isabella says. "I sensed that myself. When they are not there it's frightening. You lose your social status. All of a sudden you get frightened to go to a restaurant. You sort of fear that now you're not going to be spoiled anymore. And it's a very frightening feeling. And I think that all the family had that."

At Choisel, Ingrid was too far from the bustle of photographers, the happy nods of recognition, the life of streets and people, the laughter and energy of the boulevard. Choisel was boring. Lars treated Ingrid like a precious objet d'art that he had accumulated on his travels, to be appraised, catalogued, and set down in its appropriate place. He was often off on trips. "Separation is not good," Lars says. "She had that enormous personality to handle with her private and public life. At Choisel she'd come back after a picture and say, 'I've been sitting here for ten days. I can't sit out here.' I had a lot to do. I should have been there more. She should have been there."

Ingrid enjoyed their grand forays into Paris, to attend the opera, theatrical openings, dinner parties. Unfortunately, though Choisel was only an hour from Paris, it was a world away from the excitements and energy of the city. Ingrid could not walk here, as she loved to walk, strolling rapidly along concrete sidewalks, looking into shopwindows, gazing into the anonymous faces. She had no friends with whom she could on a moment's notice go out for lunch. As much as she enjoyed Choisel for short intervals, she enjoyed setting off from it even more. And slowly, very slowly, she became a wife of the special occasion, as she was already a mother of the special occasion.

Ingrid would have been better off living in Paris for other reasons as well. In January 1959 she won a provisional ruling by a French court, giving her custody of the three children. The court ruled, however, that they must attend an Italian school in Paris. The court ruled also that their father would have weekend visitation rights. To ensure that the children did not leave France, their passports were surrendered to the judge.

"In many ways those years of the late fifties and early sixties were tough years for Ingrid," Lars says. "With her honesty she would talk to Roberto about absolutely everything, and she was so determined that her children's upbringing should be right. On the other hand, she didn't want to disturb the newfound happiness we had discovered."

The dilemma facing Ingrid was common among divorced parents: how to be true both to a new spouse and to one's children from the previous marriage. Roberto made it particularly difficult. He could hardly bring himself to mention Lars's name. He couldn't stand the idea that the children were with Lars. In a letter to Ingrid, he wrote that when the children were in Rome, "they don't see this stranger and they are happier and they are always more comfortable with me."

It was inevitable that Roberto would be jealous of Lars, and worried that he might steal the children's loyalty and affection. What was striking, however, was how petty and vindictive he was toward Ingrid and Lars. Nothing delighted him more than hearing Roberto, Isabella, or Isotta tell him some little trick they had played on Lars, or some argument they had had.

Ingrid fought for legal custody of her children, but not for emotional custody. She was not willing to make the emotional and professional sacrifices. The children could not possibly live at Choisel and commute an hour and a half to the Italian school. Another mother would have insisted that her new husband move with her to Paris so that the family could live together. Instead, Ingrid took a suite for the children at the Raphaël, where they lived with

Elena, the maid. Since Roberto frequently visited the children on weekends, and they were in school all day, Ingrid saw relatively little of her children. And when she did see them, she was incapable of nurturing them with a strong, disciplining love.

The children did not feel that they were suffering. "We lived in a hotel and we changed rooms sometimes to a cheaper hotel," Isabella remembers. "I looked forward to visiting Choisel. We could go to the farm next door and play with the cows. I would come home smelling like shit. Mother wouldn't say no. She would just wash us.

"It wasn't an emotionally difficult time. I thought that Father was coming every weekend just to visit us. But father also had Sonali in Paris. Sonali was pregnant and hiding in Paris. Father didn't say right away that he had another relationship. I think that he and Mother were in an emotional stress. The only time I sensed that was when Father had to tell us that he had another woman and family. I really got frightened, because I didn't know what he was going to tell us. He was trembling, looking for words. Father had a much more difficult time expressing himself than Mother. Mother could control herself. I don't think she felt guilty marrying Lars. Maybe my father did feel guilty."

Roberto's guilt did not reach such heights that he felt he should make his child-support payments. He continued a legal fight for full custody and confined his largess to extravagant presents. One weekend he arrived with a little monkey for his daughters. The management of the Raphaël was running a hotel, not a menagerie, and the monkey was shipped out to Choisel, where Lars had the pleasant task of caring for Roberto's gift. On another visit Roberto arrived with a live kangaroo. This was too much even for Choisel, and the animal was shipped by rail to a zoo in Rome.

The children had no idea that their father's gifts were wildly impractical, as much a product of thoughtlessness as thoughtfulness. They knew only that they had a father as extraordinary as any of his gifts, a magician who brought joy and excitement, and left as suddenly as he appeared. Of course they didn't realize how much he was struggling in his own professional life.

In April 1959 Ingrid and Lars flew to Hollywood to attend the Academy Award ceremonies and several parties. With the worldwide success of *Anastasia* and now *The Inn of the Sixth Happiness*, Ingrid was once again a box office attraction of the first magnitude. There were a hundred reporters and photographers waiting to greet her as she arrived, on April 3, almost exactly ten years from the day she left Hollywood. That times had changed was signalized by the big news the reporters were after: Was she pregnant? Ingrid said that she hoped to have the child that Lars wanted, but "That's something between God, my husband and myself. And anyway, I don't think I should tell the newspapers before I tell my husband."

Ingrid was enjoying the whole spectacle of celebrity in Hollywood, seeing old friends, accepting accolades. She had left bitterly disdainful of Hollywood and its life-style, but she loved the attention, the adoration.

Pia flew down from Mills College in northern California, where she was completing her education. When Pia saw her mother it seemed always to be like this: moments of drama and special attention. Pia was a stunning blonde now, so grown up that her mother's representative didn't recognize her when he met her at the airport. He took Pia to Ingrid and Lars's cottage at the Beverly Hills Hotel.

"We will be going to parties, parties," Ingrid said, "and Jenny will be with us." Pia insisted that everyone call her Jenny. She attended the Academy Awards ceremony, where Ingrid presented the award for the best movie of 1958 to Arthur Freed, producer of *Gigi*.

"It is so heart-warming to receive such a welcome," Ingrid said as the applause for her finally ebbed. "I feel that I am home. I am so deeply grateful."

There was a party afterward, and a splendid dinner for two hundred in Ingrid's honor given by Buddy Adler of 20th Century-Fox. And then Ingrid and Lars were off, and Pia was back to school. She spent her holidays with her father's family in their new home in San Francisco, where Petter was chief of neurosurgery at both Presbyterian Medical Center and Children's and Adult Medical Center, with an international reputation for his work with ultrasonic surgery.

Back in Paris, Ingrid continued her struggle with Roberto over the children. In April she petitioned the Italian court to make Roberto pay 9,000,000 lire ($14,500) in back child support and start regularly making the 600,000-lire (about $1,000) monthly payments. In September she flew to Rome, where the children were spending the summer with their father at Santa Marinella. There outside the civil court she saw Roberto for the first time since her third marriage. "Why can't we be friends as we always were?" Roberto asked, as they stepped into the courtroom. Ingrid smiled slightly and put out her hand.

Inside, Roberto told the judge that Ingrid was a "bigamist" for having remarried while her annulment was still in question. When Ingrid left the courtroom two hours later, her eyes were red from weeping. She walked down the long corridor alone, and could not even find her way out without the help of a policeman. She had won, turning back Roberto's attempt to win full custody, but at the price of confrontation and pain.

Soon after winning the case, Ingrid flew out of Rome, on her way to New York with Lars to appear in her first television production, Henry James's *The Turn of the Screw*. Ingrid played a British governess teaching English to her two young charges while she seeks to save their souls. "Imagine me being hired as a governess to teach English!" she said, as she rehearsed at the Hotel Edison. Ingrid worked hard with John Frankenheimer, the director, but she loved her free time in Manhattan. She went up and down Broadway, searching for joke gifts for the children: fake flies, wind-up teeth, fake horns that stick on one's forehead. The production was taped one long frustrating evening that lasted well into the morning hours. "It's no good!" Ingrid shouted after the fourth take. When the program was shown on NBC, the critics thought otherwise, and Ingrid would win an Emmy for the year's best dramatic performance by an actress.

By the second week in October, Ingrid was back in Rome, to take the children to Paris. When she called to make the final arrangements, she learned that Roberto had spirited the children away from Santa Marinella and was refusing to give them up. It might seem that the children would suffer profoundly from being used as emotional chattel, and the lecture that Judge Lillie had given Ingrid and Petter in Los Angeles was even more appropriate now. But the children had grown up in the hot light of publicity, and they acted as if this spectacle were a part of everyday life.

"I don't see why I should be forced to return my children to Ingrid, who is living with a man they cannot stand," Roberto told a reporter. If Roberto did not surrender custody, he could be sent to jail for three months. Under a court order, he was told to give up the children by 5:00 P.M., October 15. At 4:55 he called Ingrid and gave her an address on Bruno Buozzi, across the street from the apartment where she had once lived. While a UPI photographer with a telephoto lens recorded the exchange, and their mutual attorneys observed, Roberto handed over Robertino, Isabella, and Isotta to their mother.

Roberto was not quite ready to give up. He adored his children. He wanted them brought up as Italians. In his mind he had surrendered everything to Ingrid, and had only his children left. He sent a telegram to the police, objecting to the fact that Robertino's passport had been handed over to Ingrid. This was improper, he complained, because Ingrid's name was not mentioned on the boy's birth certificate as his mother. This final gesture was one of extraordinary disdain for a woman who had borne him a son out of wedlock. Roberto was not able to separate his son from his daughters, however, and Ingrid and the three children flew out of Rome on October 16, 1959.

Roberto continued his court fight. Ingrid fought back, matching Roberto revelation by revelation, accusing him of being the father of Sonali's two-year-old daughter. Her attorneys submitted to the court a letter that Roberto had written from India admitting his relationship with Sonali.

In June 1960, as the struggle for final custody continued, the court formally annulled the Rossellini marriage.

During the summer Ingrid and Lars took the children to their island for the first time. At first, it was hard for Ingrid to go back to Sweden. Ingrid was bitter as one only can be toward a blood relative. Her memory of her reception in Stockholm during the *Joan of Arc* oratorio was still painful, exaggerated in her memory into a time of brutal rejection and stunning impoliteness. But the longer she lived with Lars, and the more often she came to Danholmen, the more she made peace with her native land.

The favorite month for a summer vacation in Sweden is July, and that was when they came to Danholmen. Roberto had filled the children's minds with tales of the bizarre rites of the Swedes, and as much as they enjoyed having their own island, they were wary around Lars.

"Everyone swam naked," Isabella remembers. "But Lars went behind a rock to take off his trunks. I crept up and watched. The next time I saw my father, in order to please him I told him that Lars had a penis like a pig's tail. He laughed and laughed and every time guests would come he would make me tell the story again."

When the children told Roberto of Lars's new boat, he decided to buy *his* boat for *his* children. But it was a sad old boat, and when Roberto took his children out on the water, the boat sputtered and coughed and broke down.

Although Ingrid had legal custody of Robertino, Isabella, and Isotta, in the fall she sent the children back to Italy to live with their father. In Paris she was at work again, on the film version of Françoise Sagan's *Aimez-vous Brahms?*, called *Goodbye Again* in the United States. "I would have little time with them since we start at noon, work until 7, then look at rushes," she told Hedda Hopper.

That was true enough, but it was clear that Ingrid was more interested in custody of the children as a symbol than as a nurturing day-after-day obligation. Motherhood was only a role to her, a part-time appearance to be fit in between her major roles on film and stage.

In *Goodbye Again* Ingrid played Paula Tessier, a middle-aged interior decorator. Her love life centers on Roger Demarest, an aging roué played by Yves Montand. She takes up with Philip Van der Besh, fifteen years her junior. Left without either man, she ends up staring at her aging, lonely face in the mirror.

Yves Montand was famous in France as a singer, but he was struggling with English and acting. Anthony Perkins would later become a major star in films such as *Friendly Persuasion* and *Psycho*, but he was already considered one of the most promising young stage and screen actors in America. Ingrid was an astute judge of actors and she knew that Perkins was so strong that "he could steal it." As for Perkins, although he called Ingrid his "idol," he went into the picture like a boxer going into the ring with a champion. "I wanted to remain on my feet," he said.

Actors compete not like boxers but like dancers, wedded to one another's steps and moves. Soon after completing the film, Perkins told a reporter that when he arrived in Paris, Ingrid had said, "So you're Tony Perkins. I hear you're pretty good. I guess maybe I better watch out for you."

Perkins remembers that "Ingrid started talking about how as an actor she always kept her ego out of it. She said how she'd done a play and she went up to someone and said, 'I understand you can be very hard to work with and are very competitive and I don't work that way.' I was grateful to her for her frankness and having the first salvo—how wonderfully air-clearing."

Ingrid's story was possibly apocryphal, but it ensured that their dance in *Aimez-vous Brahms?* would be as much to Ingrid's music as to Perkins's. Soon afterward, before their first kissing scene in the film, Ingrid called Perkins into her dressing room.

"It'll take time, the kissing," Ingrid said in her most professional voice. "We'll get it wrong. Let's practice kissing."

Years later, in a lengthy interview with a reporter from *People*, Perkins remembered how Ingrid had attempted to seduce him. "She would have welcomed an affair," he was quoted as saying. "Every day she invited me to her dressing room to practice a love scene. I insisted on standing near the door, which I kept open." Perkins now, however, asserts that the quotation was "a presumably undeliberate distortion of me."

One day Anatole Litvak, the director, stopped work to wait for evening, to shoot an outdoor scene on the streets of Paris. Ingrid and Perkins went to a small bistro for dinner. Afterward, they walked slowly back toward the shooting. Turning the corner, they could see the cameras and the crew and the lights up the street. In the dark it was like a glowing hearth in the distance.

Ingrid started walking quickly toward the set.

"What's the matter?" Perkins asked urgently.

"Look at that," Ingrid said, pointing toward the scene. "This is all for me."

The film was as big a success in Europe as it was a failure in the United States. For every reviewer who talked of Ingrid's "indestructible inner grace" or "compassion and dignity," there was another reviewer who spoke glowingly of Perkins. "No one, of course, can completely cast Miss Bergman into shadow," noted the *Saturday Review*, "and she pulls out a few organ stops of her own (always in a minor key, though) in an attempt to compete with the astonishing Mr. Perkins."

Ingrid and Lars were both extremely busy. Lars had won the European rights to *My Fair Lady,* as good a source of wealth as an oil well in Kuwait. He had time, however, to be the executive producer of Ingrid's second American television production, *Twenty-four Hours in a Woman's Life.* Ingrid played Clare, a grandmother, recounting her sad amorous past.

If *Twenty-four Hours in a Woman's Life* was a fair indication, Lars was far better at refurbishing American musicals than at producing projects for his wife. The hour-long drama received almost universally dreadful reviews. *Variety* reported the rumor that close to half a million dollars had been squandered on the project.

As boring as the drama was, the audience knew that it was watching something that was supposed to be serious. Indeed, Ingrid's career in America had reached the elevated status where her name no longer meant "scandal" but meant "culture." She signed an agreement with American and British television to do plays produced by Lars and David Susskind.

Under this agreement Ingrid's first role was Ibsen's *Hedda Gabler*. The production was shown first on the BBC in England and then on CBS in the United States. Ingrid starred in the drama with a brilliant British cast including Michael Redgrave, Ralph Richardson, and Trevor Howard. She also played the role in 1962 at the Théâtre Montparnasse in Paris, with a cast of equally outstanding French actors (Claude Dauphin, Jean Servais, and Jacques Dacomine).

Ingrid had never been attracted to the dark plays of her compatriots, Ibsen and Strindberg. But *Hedda Gabler* is one of the great female roles in modern theater.

Hedda Gabler is a contemporary Lady Macbeth trapped in a wifely role. In her manipulations she seeks not great kingdoms but only to alleviate her boredom and ennui. To have been a great Hedda, Ingrid would have had to open the trapdoor into herself, grasping among the shadows and the darkness for self-knowledge. But she was one who fled her own past as if the darkness might cover her over, making her disappear. And her Hedda was light and unbelievable, lacking energy, daring, and depth.

A French critic wrote that Ingrid was "too obviously a nice person to play a wicked woman." And Jack Gould asked rhetorically in the *New York Times*: "But what of Hedda, the embodiment of evil and destruction, who generates an ascending tension that should be almost unbearable? On television Hedda was too much the suffering heroine of the cinema and not enough the Ibsen animal of cold cunning and temperament who savors her evil acts."

Ingrid was reaching an age when many actresses go through a professional menopause. She was a great movie star, after all, not a dramatic actress with years of training, apprenticeship, and performance in the theater. Audiences were used to seeing her in romantic roles, looking stunningly youthful and beautiful. She became more aware of her appearance than before, and John O'Gorman, a talented makeup artist, eventually became an indispensable part of her artistic entourage.

It was Anthony Quinn who came to Ingrid with her next role. Ingrid had known Quinn since the old Hollywood days. Then, when he was a struggling actor, she had met him one day when she was having a malted milk at a drugstore. They had seen more of each other in Rome when Quinn had such a brilliant success in *La Strada* opposite Ingrid's other old friend, Giulietta Masina.

Now Quinn was a big star. He still admired Ingrid immensely, though he knew that she was at an age and a stage in her career when she was not getting many choice film roles. He was delighted that after several years of negotiation and discussion over the script, Ingrid agreed to star with him in *The Visit*, based on the play by Friedrich Duerrenmatt. It was a role that any middle-aged actress would die for. Ingrid would play Karla Zachanassian, a role that offered almost as much potential as *Hedda Gabler.*

In the stage version Lynn Fontanne had had a stunning success, creating a memorable portrait of evil and vengeance. Seduced and pushed into prostitution by a youthful rake, Karla returns to her small town seeking vengeance. Her seducer, Serge Miller, is the town's leading merchant, and Karla is one of the wealthiest women in the world. "The world made me into a whore," she declares. "Now I will turn the world into a brothel." She agrees to give the townspeople a fortune if they will prosecute Serge, legally condemn him to death, and execute him. As Duerrenmatt sees it, prostitution, legal or otherwise, is a matter of price, and the people condemn the town's leading citizen to death.

The Visit could have made a stunning movie, every bit as memorable and unusual as *La Strada.* Unfortunately, by the time Ingrid was through with Quinn, *The Visit* was not *The Visit* any longer.

"Ingrid begged me not to make her an old lady," Quinn remembers. "But I thought that this most beautiful woman playing the most ugly woman in the world would be a credit to her as an actress. I said, 'Beauty is not only face. A woman can be very beautiful and be very ugly because the ugliness comes out of the soul.' But she chose to play the part sympathetically and I would have done anything to do the picture with her. So we did the picture and it wasn't the play anymore. It became something else."

Ingrid used the same technique on Quinn that she had used on many co-stars and directors. She became romantically involved with him. And soon Anthony Quinn wasn't Anthony Quinn. That was the higher irony. Here, after all, was the actor who seemed to personify animal vitality and rude energy, a man that no woman could ever push around—until Bergman.

"When you like someone too much, it's like a horse riding you, and you not riding the horse," says Quinn. "I liked Ingrid Bergman so much that I seemed to lose my identity. I wasn't fighting for my identity. She was so dominant. She was too strong for the average man. She was even too strong for Mr. Lars Schmidt.

"I don't think Ingrid wanted to dominate, but she was such an enormous personality that she dominated everything around her. The only people that survived working with her were people where you know there can't be any romance. They could dominate because they didn't care. Anybody that cared, she took over. I would say that falling in love with Ingrid Bergman would have been a tragedy of my life, because not being able to control a woman, or at least not having equal dominance, is an impossible situation."

During the making of *The Visit* at Cinecittà on the edge of Rome, others on the set noticed the romantic chemistry between the two stars. "Somehow in the course of the film, when the love scene comes they went out and had dinner and one gathers they spent a lot of time together," says Mark Nichols, the publicist who went on location with the film. "It was more like method acting, building up to the scene."

*   *   *

With *The Visit* Ingrid had what might have been a classic part; instead, she had one of the worst failures of her career. "At the Cannes film festival the critics criticized her performance and the audience shuddered over the film," wrote Leonard Mosley in London's *Daily Express*. "Can the once-golden name of Bergman touch filmgoers once more? Or is this the moment of truth for her too—as it once was for Greta Garbo, Joan Crawford, Bette Davis? They lost the Midas touch and got out—Garbo for good, Crawford and Davis until they found new roles as ageing horror-film actresses. I can hardly see Bergman as a murderous old lady, can you?"

Even before the release of *The Visit* Ingrid was in London making another film, *The Yellow Rolls-Royce*. The film consisted of three episodes, each with different stars. Ingrid was in the final segment, playing a lovely American widow who meets up with a Yugoslavian partisan (Omar Sharif) in early 1941. Ingrid still looked delectable on screen, and it did not seem entirely ludicrous that the youthful guerrilla would forget the Germans long enough to wage a struggle to bed down the widow in the back seat of the Rolls.

As the *London Sunday Telegraph* critic noted, *The Yellow Rolls-Royce* "looked less like a film than an investment, laden with everything that money can buy." In that marketplace, Ingrid was still top of the line, earning $275,000. That was more than was received by Jeanne Moreau ($67,660.23), George C. Scott ($75,000), Rex Harrison ($240,000), Omar Sharif ($75,000), or Alain Delon ($99,000). It was the newest star, Shirley MacLaine, who earned $560,500, more than double Ingrid's salary. Ingrid magnanimously agreed that the billing for the female stars should be alphabetical, "but on understanding that she will actually be in top position on that column." She might have better asked that her name be buried, for the film was a complete failure, "terrible" in the words of *The New Yorker*. The producers had made an expensive commercial film. They had paid Ingrid $275,000 for a month's work. It would be a while before anyone would pay her that kind of money again.

When Ingrid returned to Choisel, it was to an empty house. Back in May 1961, Ingrid and Roberto had ended their lengthy custody fight. The decision gave the children to each parent a year at a time, starting with Roberto during 1961–62. Of her own volition, however, Ingrid gave over complete custody of Robertino, Isabella, and Isotta, limiting herself to visits such as during the making of *The Visit*, vacations, and other trips.

In interviews, Ingrid always pictured her action as a generous one, ending three years of nasty emotional struggle. In private, she was more candid. "She said to me that she was not as good a parent as her former husband because she was more interested in having actress written on her tombstone than wife or mother," says Mark Nichols, remembering a discussion during the making of

The Visit. "She saw the children when she could, but her devotion to the children wasn't as good as Rossellini's."

For all Roberto's struggle over his "Italian" children, he didn't even live with them in Rome. He had his own new family with Sonali. Robertino, Isabella, and Isotta lived in a separate apartment with their new housekeeper, Argenide, and a governess. Roberto would come rushing in, kissing and hugging his children, telling them of his work, and then, when the whole house seemed ready to burst with his personality, he would be off somewhere else.

"My uncle would call many times a day, but the children were not listening to him because he was not following their everyday life," says Fiorella. "That's why it was so difficult. I remember saying to him, 'You can't pretend that you want them, because you are not living with them.' You can't be severe with someone you are not with. Ingrid was in Paris or London. They went to her with their little problems. For their big problems they took care of themselves."

Roberto continued to outdistance his creditors, though the rich brocade of his life had grown threadbare. Isabella remembers the times their furniture was repossessed, and friends bought it back at auction. For Sonali there are memories not only of bare rooms but of bare cupboards, of the days she wondered where she would get the money to put dinner on the table.

"Roberto was a spoiled child," she says. "He was a child who couldn't choose between the cake and the lollipop. But he always gave. There was no selfishness. People came to him to take, to take not only tangible things. It was such fun to be with him. But after they left they were full and he was empty. I told him once, 'You have no friends.' He said, 'Don't I know it.'

"I don't know if it was possible to be his friend. He needed converts. Whether he made a confusion between that and friendship, I don't know. Whether in a difficult dramatic moment and without complexity at two in the morning he could call a friend and say, 'I need you,' I don't know.

"I happened to live the difficult years, but he was still so full of enthusiasm. We were always studying. He'd wake me up at two o'clock in the morning. He was always in bed reading. He used to say this is a sign of great civilization. It only looks like laziness."

The extraordinary thing about Ingrid's visits to Rome now was that she could see her entire family. In what no one would have ever predicted, Pia had moved to Italy and was living with Robertino, Isabella, and Isotta.

Adulthood had meted out some harsh lessons to Ingrid's eldest daughter. In 1960 she ran off to Nevada and married twenty-eight-year-old Fuller E. Callaway III, a divorcé, the heir to a Georgia fortune. Pia's marriage received wide publicity, including a two-page spread in *Life.* The following year her divorce received even more publicity. She charged that Callaway had called her a "parasite" and hit her, pushing her down a flight of stairs.

Pia announced her intention of becoming an actress, and studied drama at

Stanford University. After a year she traveled to France. She lived at first at Choisel. Pia sought to develop a deep daughter-mother relationship with Ingrid. But after six months she took her own apartment in Paris and went to work for UNESCO as a secretary. From there she moved to London to study acting.

Ingrid's daughter had decided to take her old name again. She was Pia now. It was an intelligent decision in terms of her career to take the name that her mother and father had given her, the name that had been so widely publicized. Moreover, the change symbolized Pia's identification with her mother's career and life.

Ingrid, however, was not a mother to inspire confidence in her daughter that she, too, could be a successful actress. If anything, Pia left her months in Paris full of even more self-doubt. In London she said that she didn't even dare to take lessons at the Royal Academy of Dramatic Arts because at the age of twenty-five she felt that she would be among "hordes of bright teenagers." She did dare to admit publicly that she wanted to act. "I was a coward," she said then. "I didn't want to be compared to her. But I've had some offers, and one of these days, when I feel ready, I'll accept one."

There was an isolated quality to Pia's life. She had received the money in her guardianship account, and she lived extremely well for a would-be actress. She spent much of her money and much of her energy and she got nowhere.

Ingrid could have helped Pia with her career. But when she called her daughter in London, it was with a different sort of offer. "My mother asked me to go to Rome and take care of the children," Pia says. "Their grandmother had died. My mother didn't want to live with them or bring them to France. I had been living in England for a year. I had been lonely. And so I went. I managed the accounts. I took care of things. I tried to be an adult in the family—such as it was."

According to Petter, Ingrid had also promised to help Pia find movie roles in Italy. However, it was not Ingrid but Roberto who helped Pia win her first movie part. He called his old friend Vittorio De Sica, who was directing *Divorce Italian Style*. Pia was given a small part as a cashier. In her one scene she kissed Marcello Mastroianni. It was only a tiny moment, but Pia was so excited that she called Ingrid in London to tell her about it. When Mastroianni's co-star in the film, Sophia Loren, saw the rushes, she said, "Her beauty is astonishing."

Pia's second role, as a peasant girl in *Zorba*, was much bigger. Anthony Quinn, the film's star, was a man of considerable charm and fascination. Pia became good friends with Quinn. "Pia was marvelous in our scenes," Quinn says. "In many ways she was almost more beautiful than her mother. But she took second place to Ingrid. She couldn't stand up on her own. The mother controlled her."

Ingrid was reported to be "no doubt . . . interested in Pia's career . . . but not pushing her, and has sent word to Sophia Loren and Quinn that she must not be pampered." There were some friends and observers who thought that

Ingrid was even jealous of her lovely young actress daughter, and did not want the world to know that she was old enough to have a daughter playing roles Ingrid once had played. Ingrid told friends that she doubted her daughter's acting ability.

Pia did not have Ingrid's ambition and drive, but she knew that if she was to become a star, this was her moment. She worried that her first two film performances would be compared not with her mother's first two Swedish films but with later films. On one hand, she expressed herself embarrassed and frightened by the "undue publicity my tiny roles may get because of Mamma." On the other hand, she used that relationship to get publicity and promote herself. Indeed, a publicist working on *Divorce Italian Style* contacted George Christy, a successful freelance writer, about doing a piece on Pia. The article, under Pia's byline, appeared in *Good Housekeeping*. It was titled "My Mother, Ingrid Bergman." She said that in her early years she was "estranged, lonely and withdrawn," living in a house "surrounded with an electrically-wired fence" in which she dreamed "we were imprisoned like convicts. . . . I was disillusioned in childhood, but now the cockleburrs are gone from my heart. At last Mamma and I are together, yet we have learned to be apart." Pia made no mention of how Ingrid had left her without a word, only that "unswerving in her honesty, Mama admitted her feelings, and the world whipped her with stinging words."

In later years, indeed even in Ingrid's own autobiography, Pia's judgment of her mother was far more complicated and ambivalent. In 1964, however, Pia appeared to be identifying with her mother partially in a self-conscious, calculating way. She did not yet understand what it would be like to be cast between her mother and her father, asked by journalists and others to become the arbiter of their pasts. "I don't want to be the one to defend, to judge one way or another," she says now. "I've always been put in that role and I must go on." She felt that she never said quite what she meant to say, or perhaps she didn't know what to say.

Petter read the magazine article and was profoundly hurt. For his own and Pia's edification, he wrote a seven-page, single-spaced document refuting the article almost paragraph by paragraph. He pointed out that there had not been an "electrically-wired fence" on the Benedict Canyon house, only a gate with an electric buzzer, and a five-foot-tall wire fence "as required by law because of our pool." He talked about all that he had done for Pia, teaching her "to dance, to swim, to ski," taking her on trips to Lake Placid, New York, to Puerto Rico and the Virgin Islands. "I would like to know what disillusion in childhood Pia had suffered that required ventilation in public," he concluded, comforting himself by believing that "Pia had very little to do with this whole interview."

Petter sought the truth in details. He could not see that in Pia's memory there indeed had been a great fence around the house in Benedict Canyon. Nor could he understand that despite all he had done for his daughter, all the sacrifices that he had made to be both mother and father to her, all the playmates and friends she had had, Pia nonetheless was a child of divorce, who perceived her childhood as full of loneliness and sadness. He could not yet see that he had a daughter who seemed to have learned not to trust people, a woman who to make her way in the world would on occasion appear to pillage her past for what was useful.

Even if she was not a major talent, Pia might have gone a way in films as the beautiful daughter of Ingrid Bergman. But her scene in *Divorce Italian Style* was cut out. And then when *Zorba* proved to be too long, her entire role was left out. Pia had wanted to be compared with her mother's first Swedish films, but Ingrid had never been left on the cutting room floor. After all the publicity about her new movie career, it was a humiliating beginning.

"I thought that maybe my movie career would work out," Pia says. "But it didn't come from the depths of my being. I wasn't the one to push it. I wasn't driven the way so many people in films are driven. It occurred to me when I was cut out of my two first films that I wasn't going to succeed. If your mother is Ingrid Bergman, I thought this is too much to compete against."

Left without even one brief moment on film as a memorial to her film career, Pia was living a role stranger than any she might have played onscreen. She was living in the land and among the people her father had kept her from so long. And she was playing surrogate mother for a mother who had once left her, though not quite the way Ingrid left her three younger children.

When Ingrid made her periodic forays to Rome, she found it more and more difficult to deal with the problems and questions that her children asked. "Many things Ingrid didn't know about life and didn't want to know about life," Marcella Mariani says. "The children were brilliant and she was a little lost. She didn't have the patience to understand their problems. As the children got older, she'd say, 'Please come with me because sometimes I really don't know what to say.' "

Pia stayed on and on, without a real life of her own. In the spring of 1966 she tested for yet another part, in a film entitled *The Devil in Love*. Once again, all she got out of it was publicity, including a bathing suit picture in *Time*.

Pia decided she had had enough of Rome and her Italian "movie" career for a while. After three years in Italy, she returned to the United States for what was supposed to be a summer visit. "I felt I couldn't stay there and take care of her children any longer," Pia says. "I realized that the years were going by. The children were getting older. I had been there long enough."

There was still great value in being Ingrid Bergman's daughter. Pia received an offer from Fiat to make a fourteen-thousand-mile promotional tour of the United States, driving the company's new Fiat 1100. She traveled with ten pieces of luggage, and designer outfits by Fontana.

When Pia arrived in Hollywood, she told a *Modern Screen* reporter, "I am sincerely ambitious for a career." But she found no roles in Hollywood either, and when she reached her family in San Francisco, she got a job on a morning television show and began a very different career.

CHAPTER NINETEEN

An Elegant Facade

*I*t was Christmas and Lars was away. So much of Ingrid's life had become an elegant facade. Lars was good at the rituals of living—the parties, the holidays, the vacations on the island—but it was all ritual now, duly formalized in pictures of their happiness. Choisel was more a stage setting for parties, photo sessions, and occasional children's visits than a real home.

It was a marriage of inconvenience. Lars was always jetting off somewhere —New York, Paris, Stockholm—and they met sometimes as if they were not husband and wife but members of the board flying in for the semiannual meeting. Lars took care of Ingrid, though, managing her money, drawing a good return.

Ingrid could tolerate Lars's absences, but no one wanted to spend Christmas alone. She had Isabella and Fiorella and the servants there with her, but that was not the same. She called Lars's secretary, and the secretary called Raymond Gérôme, an actor and director who was one of Ingrid's few friends in Paris, and a close friend and associate of Lars's.

"Do you know that Ingrid is all alone at Choisel?" the secretary asked.

"No," Gérôme responded. He was surprised that they wouldn't spend Christmas together.

"And she doesn't know what to do."

Gérôme changed his plans. He took Ingrid and Fiorella to the theater that evening, and afterward arranged a dinner party. To the other guests Ingrid was a blessed, beautiful person, whose laughter rang in the Christmas day. They had no idea of the irony of it all, and they never imagined that Ingrid could be so alone, so emotionally passive.

She sat now at Choisel, doing practically nothing. She knew that she was good for Lars's career. He was already successful when she had met him, but now he had developed into perhaps the most successful producer in Europe. His take on *My Fair Lady* alone was enough to make him a rich man; by 1964 he had already grossed over twelve million dollars on the various European productions.

The world still considered her the lovely, youthful Ingrid Bergman, but she could feel her age. She knew how badly Lars wanted a child, and she could not give it to him. Worse yet, she was beginning to look older than Lars. He was in his prime.

Ingrid might have felt better if she had become enveloped in a new life, a new society, new friends. But although Lars chose to live in France, he had no particular affinity for the French, and cultivated few friends there. As for Ingrid, she was at an age when learning languages becomes more difficult. It was too much effort to strain to speak French as well as she spoke Italian, especially since she spoke Swedish at home.

"Sometimes it was very lonely there," Isabella remembers. "We took walks. We'd clean up everything. I had the feeling that you always had to do something."

When Ingrid was alone at Choisel, and Lars was off somewhere, the phone didn't ring very often, and she was indeed lonely. "For three or four years people were even surprised that Ingrid was living here," Gérôme says. "I think she was surprised by the way she was living in Paris. Ingrid was very humorous about all the Swedish entertaining, these parties of forty people. She said, 'Our habit is to have speeches.' But she'd do it.

"She could get out of temper with a tiny matter. I remember once at Choisel she got nervous, her hands got red, and she took tiny steps. I could see she was so upset. She said, 'We're out of white wine.'

"I was so surprised at her marriage that I said once or twice, 'I don't understand it.' She said, 'There's nothing to understand. You just live it.' Both Ingrid and Lars would make a point that was very Swedish; they would say, 'Love is ridiculous at our age.' She said, 'Me with grown-up children.'

"Ingrid couldn't stand to be alone anymore. One day in Paris I said, 'You're lonely. You're a lonely lady in a luxurious estate. Why don't you go to Paris?' She said, 'There comes an age when you want to speak your language at night.'

"Lars is sort of brilliant, full of references, a good reader, and very enthusiastic about his work in the theater. He's a very enjoyable companion for a couple of hours. Then he becomes gloomy and grouchy. Lars can be a bully and cruel.

"Ingrid was going through a sort of bad moment in her career. I told Lars, 'It's crazy to have Ingrid Bergman sitting at Choisel.' He said, 'What can I do?' He argued that it was all over for Ingrid. She was left at Choisel fixing sauce béarnaise."

Ingrid might, indeed, have measured out her days in sauce béarnaise. She knew that her career as a romantic lead in films was over. She could laugh about sixty-year-old Cary Grant making love to women a third his age. "Audrey [Hepburn] is now too old for him and in his next picture he will be making love to someone like Jane Fonda," she said. But she did not want to end her film days like so many aging stars, the final performances filmed with the light of the camera softened in gauze, and then, like Greta Garbo or Loretta Young, their whole life a gauze of illusion.

In the summer of 1965 Ingrid had an offer to play in Ivan Turgenev's *A Month in the Country* at the Yvonne Arnaud Memorial Theatre in Guildford, England. At first, she thought that she shouldn't take the part, not only for Lars's sake but for that of the children, who were looking forward to visiting their mother as they did each summer. But Lars told her that she should accept the offer, and it took very little persuading to make her agree.

At Guildford she met Dirk Bogarde, the British actor, who lived outside the city. Bogarde invited Ingrid to stay with him in his country house so that she might not constantly be in the public eye.

Ingrid called the weeks in Guildford "one of the happiest times of my life." Ingrid played Natalia Petrovna, a lovely, spiritually deprived matron, her life growing dry and untended. Bored with her husband, Yslaev (Geoffrey Chater), she flirts with his friend Mikhail Rakitin (Michael Redgrave) and then with a young tutor, Alexei Belaev (Daniel Massey). Natalia is a jealous, passionate woman. In the end, both Alexei and Mikhail depart. Natalia is left alone with her memories and her husband.

Ingrid stalked the stage in long silk dresses, dominating the production. *A Month in the Country* was such a success at Guildford that in September it was taken to the Cambridge Theatre in London. There it played for eight months and was one of the biggest hits of the season. According to *The Times*, "The production would hardly have exerted this special appeal without the presence of Ingrid Bergman, an actress impervious to changes of fashion and whose star quality as an ice goddess with warm human sympathies remains intact after a quarter century in the public eye." The playgoers were not coming in such droves to see vintage Turgenev. They were coming to see Bergman. They didn't care about the occasional petulant critic who carped that Ingrid's "performance hardly goes beyond the pictorial." They didn't care that unlike her British colleagues, Ingrid was not a disciplined creature of the stage. She was a presence. She was Ilsa and Maria and Sister Benedict and Dr. Constance Peterson and Alicia Huberman and Anastasia. She was a quarter century of memories.

In the tiny universe of the theater, Ingrid found an order and routine that were absent in the real world. Everyone knew what had to be done and when to do it. The only problems she had with her husband were the ones on the stage, and they were the same every night. If she had children at all, they were stage children, knowing their lines and getting off. And when her work was over, there was a warm shower of applause.

Queen Elizabeth came to the theater one evening with her lady-in-waiting, leaving as quietly as she arrived. *A Month in the Country* was indeed a play a queen might enjoy, elegant and refined and courtly. It was the kind of play Ingrid herself enjoyed, not the brutal realism of John Osborne and the other angry young men of the theater whose plays were the new sensation of the British stage. Ingrid looked neither backward nor forward in anger. She couldn't understand playwrights who wrote such things, and playgoers who enjoyed them. She preferred Turgenev, "where nobody was brutally hurt."

There were times now when Ingrid questioned the meaning of her life and work. One evening she had dinner with Maximilian Schell, who was starring in John Osborne's stunning play *A Patriot for Me*.

"Where does it all go?" Ingrid asked rhetorically.

"Think what an actor's life used to be," the Austrian-born actor said. "All that remained was memories and photos. Now, with film, the art of acting remains."

"Yes, but what am I doing it for?" she asked. "I just don't know."

Schell stared at Ingrid. "I grew up with you. You put on my mind the stamp of a woman, the ideal woman. In my thoughts, you belong to me."

Lars had become little more than an occasional weekend guest, and their relationship risked becoming an arrangement more than a marriage. Ingrid's children were growing up, with questions and problems, and with a mother they rarely saw.

Robertino now had perfectly coiffed blond hair and matinee idol eyes, an aesthetically pleasing blend of Scandinavia and Italy. He was shy among strangers, masking his apprehension with perfect manners. He was a young man of great charm, who like his father enjoyed fast cars and fine clothes. Unlike Roberto, though, Robertino was not fascinated by the world outside his purview; if he did not develop interests beyond his flashy, well-born Roman friends, he risked becoming a perfect snob.

Isabella and Isotta were only thirteen years old, but they appeared much older. They were five feet seven inches tall, and were knowledgeable about what many teenagers think is the adult world: travel, restaurants, famous acquaintances. Indeed, they towered so much over boys their own age, in height and experience, that sometimes to their peers they seemed a different generation. That was particularly true of Isabella. She was a vivacious, extro-verted, irrepressible child-woman with big warm eyes that saw life as endless possibilities. Almost since birth Isabella had been the dominant twin, and that was even more true as the two girls entered their teen years. Isotta was attractive too, but she did not have the same glowing personality. She was as shy and timid as her sister was outgoing, a studious girl whose papers at Santa Giuliana Falconeri, a Catholic girls' school, were always neat and well done, but who hardly ever raised her hand to talk in class.

The twins were growing so fast that when Isabella started complaining about back pain, no one had any idea how serious the condition might be, not even Roberto, king of the hypochondriacs. Roberto took his daughter to a well-known bone specialist, who told him that the condition was serious indeed. Isabella had scoliosis, lateral curvature of the spine.

A Month in the Country had completed its long run and Ingrid flew to Rome, and then, with Roberto and Isabella, traveled to Florence, where a specialist told them that Isabella would require surgery. She would have to wear a body cast for many months, both before and after the operation. Surgery could not be performed for six months, until Isabella's spine was pulled as straight as possible. The machine on which this was done reminded Ingrid of a medieval torture rack. The doctor used his patient's pain as a measure of how far to pull the spine, and thus did not use an anesthetic.

During the first stretching treatment, Ingrid waited in the hall. She could hear Isabella screaming. When Ingrid finally saw her daughter again, she was encased in a plaster cast from hip to neck.

Within a few days Isabella was walking in her cast, and she and her mother went back to Rome. A few weeks later Roberto drove Ingrid and Isabella back to Florence for another stretching. With her body cast, Isabella had to kneel in the car during the long drive. They made another trip to Florence, for a third stretching of the spine.

Finally they traveled to Florence for the operation itself. The evening before Isabella entered the hospital, Ingrid went with her daughter to a church to light a candle and to pray. She held tightly to Isabella's hand, as if by that gesture she could infuse her with strength and courage. Ingrid was crying as she left the church. She tried to ignore the beggar who accosted her. The beggar saw her tears and her vulnerability, and he followed, whining in supplication, his hand out. As he walked onward, Isabella remained calm, hurrying along beside her mother. The beggar continued moving along next to Ingrid.

Suddenly, she turned to the man. "Here! Here! Take it! Take it!" Ingrid screamed hysterically, her words like a terrible curse. She opened her purse and threw all her money at the beggar, every bill, every coin.

The operation took almost seven hours. When it was time for Isabella to be wakened, the nurse slapped her face.

"How can you do that!" Ingrid yelled. "Stop slapping her face!"

"Ingrid, please don't get angry with the nurse," Roberto said. "This is routine."

Ingrid passed out in her ex-husband's arms.

In some ways Isabella accepted the illness and dealt with it better than her mother. When Ingrid talked of the illness years later, she remembered her daughter's courage, but she did not remember that Isabella was sometimes testy and irritable, as is part of any equation of courage.

Ingrid loved to tell the story of the boy who drove all the way from Rome to see Isabella. "I turned to Isa and asked if she wanted the boy to come in," Ingrid recalled. "Her whole face lit up. I didn't need to wait for an answer. I said, 'Come in, boy. She'll be happy to see you.' Her happiness was boundless. So was his. I left them alone."

Isabella remembers the visit differently: "He came all the way from Rome. He was one of my brother's friends. He had decided to fall in love with a sick girl. I was in the worst mood. I hated him. I didn't want to be with anyone."

For the year and a half of Isabella's illness, Ingrid took only one professional assignment, an hour-long television version of Jean Cocteau's one-character play *The Human Voice*. But after a few weeks in London in the fall of 1966, she was back in Italy with Isabella. Her daughter did not let the cast limit her life. She wore special dresses that masked the body cast. She walked with a straight posture that seemed to express pride and upbringing, not the dictates of the neck-high cast. She even went out dancing with her cast, while, as often as not, Isotta stayed home with her mother and the maid.

"That period changed my perception of her," Isabella says. "Until then I was very much my father's daughter. But it established the relationship that we had afterwards. I don't know if she regretted that she hadn't spent more time with us. She did always come and visit."

Ingrid was immensely proud of the time she spent in Italy. Years later, for her autobiography, this was the one episode in her life about which she wrote herself. Isabella's illness had come at a relatively low point in Ingrid's career. Moreover, it came at a point when distance was the best way to maintain her marriage. But Ingrid had other alternatives and she had indeed sacrificed her personal and professional life for her daughter.

After Isabella's cast was cut off, Ingrid was ready to get back to work. She was about to sign for the lead in a French production of *Anna Karenina*. Instead, she decided to go to Los Angeles and then to Broadway to play Deborah Harford in Eugene O'Neill's final play, *More Stately Mansions*. Ingrid had been away from Choisel and Lars for over a year.

Ingrid flew into Los Angeles alone on August 3, 1967, to begin rehearsals. The next morning she arrived at the Ahmanson Theater for the first readthrough. The Ahmanson was Los Angeles's new cultural mausoleum. There had never been a play performance in the cavernous new theater. There were none of the echoes of old plays and old players, none of the memories and the ghosts.

Ingrid walked onto the great stage, where the cast members and director José Quintero sat in orange plastic chairs. Ingrid knew the others only by reputation. Colleen Dewhurst, the other female lead, was one of the great actresses on the American stage. A woman of animal intensity, she had a deep, throaty voice that could carry effortlessly to the farthest reaches of the two-thousand-seat theater. The male lead, Arthur Hill, had co-starred with Dewhurst in the Pulitzer Prize–winning play *All the Way Home*. He looked as if he belonged on a university campus, with a pipe clenched in his teeth, and indeed had brilliantly played a college professor in Edward Albee's *Who's Afraid of Virginia Woolf?*

"Why is everyone here before me?" Ingrid asked. "Am I late. I'm not late. You're all early."

When Ingrid was nervous she often talked in non sequiturs. "It's simply astonishing, nine hours' difference in time from Paris, yet I feel fine, I feel all right."

Ingrid sat in the one empty chair.

As a director, Quintero was the greatest contemporary English-language interpreter of O'Neill. He approached his task not only with passion but with a scholarly reverence for a great playwright. This would be the first American production of *More Stately Mansions*, and it honored Ingrid's reputation that she should be asked to play in such a company.

For the next month, Ingrid spent her days and nights thinking about *More Stately Mansions*. Deborah Harford is a role for a mature actress of the highest ambition and ability. Deborah is a tough-willed matriarch who believes that her son Arthur's bride, Sara, is below his station. The dramatic fulcrum of the play is the relationship between mother and daughter-in-law, between the refined, cold, brutally realistic, conniving Deborah and earthy, lusty, ambitious, greedy Sara, and their struggle over the heart and soul of Arthur.

In her first scene, Deborah meets her son in the forest after a long absence.

"You come running in and you stop—dead still—and stand there transfixed," Quintero said, as Ingrid remembered.

"But I'm a mother who hasn't seen her son for four long years," Ingrid said. "She's going to meet him at this little deserted cottage in the forest. Surely she'll creep in hesitating and worried, frightened to see him, fearful that she's aged."

Ingrid was forever mixing up the truths of the stage with the truths of her personal life. When she saw her children after a long period, she made herself up and dressed with particular care. And she indeed crept in hesitating and worried, frightened to see them, fearful that she had aged. She knew that she was not like most mothers, a constant presence to her children. When she did see them, it was as if she felt her aura of beauty would make up for her infrequent visits. And so, she imagined, would Deborah's in *More Stately Mansions*.

Beyond the stage would sit two thousand spectators who had not seen Ingrid for years; for them, too, she felt like creeping into the spotlight, frightened to see them after so many years.

"Next you come right downstage to the footlights. Right down to the steps there, and you sit on the steps there," the director said.

"But they'll hear my heart going bang-bang-bang," Ingrid insisted. "In those very first moments I'm frightened of the audience. . . . I'm terrified of the audience. You're close enough to say hello to them. You can hear them talking about you. 'She still looks pretty good for her age. How old do you think she is?' "

Ingrid argued with Quintero almost daily, winning some of the arguments, losing others. On the first scene they compromised. Ingrid agreed to walk dramatically onstage; but she would stop before walking forward to the footlights. "I drove poor José crazy," she wrote Lars. "I confess that. He blew his top and bawled me out and told me off. I thought at first he was talking to someone else. You know how sure I am of myself."

Opening night, September 3, 1967, finally arrived. This would be not only the first American performance of *More Stately Mansions* and Ingrid's first dramatic performance in America in twenty-one years. It would be a great day in the cultural history of Los Angeles, the opening of a theater with dimensions beyond anything the city had known. The audience was as star-studded as any that had ever attended a play in Los Angeles. And Lars had flown in for the opening.

Ingrid stood in the wings, waiting to go on. Quintero stood beside her, holding her hand. "Do it for him!" the director said, and Ingrid rushed forward to the center of the stage. As she stood there motionless, the audience applauded. It might have been expected that there would be some applause, but not this great salvo. It went on and on, for two minutes, but here, in the early moments of the play, it seemed far longer. Ingrid thought: "You mustn't cry, you mustn't cry, you'll lose your eyelashes and the mascara will run, you mustn't cry."

The applause finally ended, and Ingrid stood speechless. She couldn't remember her first line. As always, Ruth Roberts was backstage, waiting, and she whispered the first line. But Ingrid did not hear, and finally the stage manager shouted her line and Ingrid began:

"What can you expect, Deborah? At your age, a woman must become resigned to wait upon every man's pleasure, even her son's."

Ingrid did her worthy best as Deborah. There were few actresses in America, however, who could hold an audience the way Dewhurst could. When the play was over, the applause for Dewhurst roared through the great new theater. Ingrid's reception seemed only an echo, a polite welcome to a hometown favorite, after the applause at her entrance.

Dewhurst was the star of the play, but Ingrid was the star of the evening, and at the party afterward she was deluged by reporters. Ingrid sat holding Dewhurst's hand, answering questions. For every reporter interested in the arts, there was another needing a good thirty seconds for the 11 P.M. news.

"If you had your life to lead over again, would you?" asked a television reporter. This was a question she'd been asked a thousand times before.

"Yes, yes, I would," Ingrid said, as Lars stood nearby. "Wouldn't you?"

"No," the journalist said. "I think your conduct was outrageous."

"Gentlemen, that is enough," Lars interjected, leading Ingrid away from the pack of journalists.

Ingrid was far more comfortable on a stage before two thousand playgoers than here in this hot, crowded room. There were so many things she had to deal with, so many people needing attention, recognition, a word. She was besieged not only by reporters but by well-wishers, by vaguely familiar faces that looked at her as if she should recognize them. She was approached, too, by faces from long ago, faces that had aged so that it was like looking into the mirror after many years.

"I hope you understood my card today," said Alfred Hitchcock, who rarely came out for such evenings. "Did you?"

Ingrid looked down at the man who had directed more of her movies than anyone else. Hitchcock appeared far more comfortable with the glare of lights and attention this evening than she was.

"Thank you, I haven't the time to thank you for anything," Ingrid said. Then she laughed, as if she could make that her transition away from this whole matter.

"Do you know what it is?" Hitchcock insisted, his gaze fixed on Ingrid. " 'Best wishes for a faulty stocking.' "

"You know . . ." Ingrid laughed.

"Do you know what that is?" Hitchcock would not let her go.

"No."

"Long run," Hitchcock said triumphantly.

More Stately Mansions was among the least of O'Neill, but the play received generally respectful reviews. When the play opened on Broadway a month later, it proved as popular with New York theatergoers as it had with those in Los Angeles.

The New York critics sounded themes that were familiar since Ingrid had opened in *Liliom* almost three decades before. They questioned her ability to play a character of such cunning and evil. But they praised Ingrid's "beauty" and "presence," as if she now transcended any role that she might play. "Ingrid Bergman . . . is herself a work of art," wrote Clive Barnes in the *New York Times*. "She trades heavily on her natural charm and in a sense, her very real inner goodness . . . but makes less of the strangely disparate character of Deborah Harford than you might have hoped."

Critics like Barnes were not talking about an actress but about a mythological being. They knew nothing, or next to nothing, about her life offstage, but that didn't matter. To them, she had transcended art and its judgments, as much as she had transcended the judgments of biography.

One of those who for years had worshiped at the temple of the mythic Ingrid was Warren Thomas, who had loved her and lived through her since the days of the Alvin Gang and *Joan of Lorraine*. Warren's mother had died at his birth, and he had lived with his father in a room in a house full of prostitutes. His friends said that Ingrid was his mother fixation, and he had taken "a vow that one day My Lady would be my friend." For years, he had sent her flowers and pictures, kept a scrapbook, and whenever she was in town stood waiting to catch a glimpse of his lady. During the New York run of *More Stately Mansions*, he asked to come backstage to take her picture.

"I showed her the scrapbook," Thomas says. "She said, 'All those years.' I said, 'I haven't reached my goal yet.' I reached out my hand in friendship and she kissed my face. That was it. It started a friendship that grew and grew."

Ingrid had another guest during much of the run of *More Stately Mansions* in Los Angeles and New York. She felt that her daughter Isotta had been neglected during her sister's illness. Ingrid noticed a bitter cast to her mouth. Isotta insists that she had not felt the least bit jealous of Isabella, only a certain awe at how well her twin sister could maneuver in her body cast. But for Isotta it was a special time, indeed, to be deposited in Ingrid's dressing room in Los Angeles one evening by her father, to live at the Hampshire House in New York, to have a private tutor and endless adventures. Isotta loved Ingrid, not as a home-loving mother, but as a whirlwind that passed in and out of her life, full of endless vitality.

Ingrid had tasted the glory and glamour of stardom once again, a flavor decidedly more to her taste than sauce béarnaise at Choisel. While she was in America, Lars had written letters asking her to return and be with him. He was not a forthright man, however, and when he wrote Ingrid, "you are always away from me and it's no fun to sit here alone and I can't wait for you to come back," she had no idea that this was a letter of intention.

Soon after Ingrid returned to France, she and Lars went to visit their island. Danholmen was almost a sacred place for Lars, a respite from the world of theater and telephoning and dealmaking. The island had become famous, and when an occasional small passenger boat passed by, the guide pointed it out. On at least one such occasion, Ingrid stood on a rock and waved at the passengers, much as she had done to the trains that passed Santa Marinella.

This summer Ingrid invited Stirling Silliphant, a screenwriter, to come to the island to talk about a film based on the novel *A Walk in the Spring Rain* by Rachel Maddux. Silliphant, who had won an Oscar for his screenplay for *In the Heat of the Night*, had a writing-producing contract with Columbia. From the moment he read the Maddux novel he had wanted to star Ingrid.

Silliphant met Ingrid for the first time at the small wooden dock on Danholmen, as he arrived in Lars's speedboat. The screenwriter thought it like a scene out of an Ingmar Bergman movie, and his candlelit dinner with Ingrid and Lars as "the most urbane, delightful evening I think I've ever spent in my life." Ingrid served fresh bread on a wooden plank, and Lars poured fine French wine, and they ate fish that Lars had caught.

Lars was the kind of man who could never look at a painting without wondering if it could be better framed. This evening he complained about a radio antenna ten miles inland; the top of the mast could be seen from Danholmen on a fair day. To Lars, the antenna was the beginning of the end, and Silliphant was impressed by his aesthetic perfectionism.

Ingrid listened to the two men talk of the world and sailing, but all she wanted to discuss was *her* film.

"Would you like to go out sailing with me tomorrow?" Lars asked.

"Damn it," Ingrid interrupted. "You came here and what about the script?"

"Yes, I've brought the script," the screenwriter said, suddenly remembering why he had come to the island. "But I've only done about a third of it."

"That's terrible," Ingrid said.

When Ingrid read what he had brought, she decided to play the part, and Silliphant spent several days on the island. "I'm going to take you somewhere I've never taken anyone," Lars said one day. And he sailed the screenwriter to a small rock that rose directly out of the water and looked like the back of a giant turtle or a small whale. "Very few men I know would have the sensitivity to react to this," Lars said as if he were testing Silliphant. "And I hope I'm not going to be disappointed."

Silliphant took off his shoes and jumped out onto the rock, and experienced an extraordinary sensation. It was as if he were on the back of a sea creature.

"What do you feel?" Lars asked.

"I feel as if I'm like Jonah, but not in the mouth of the whale but on the back."

"I love you for saying this. This is where I come. This is my rock."

Ingrid would not have understood the pleasure Lars took in his rock. And though Silliphant saw Ingrid and Lars's marriage at its best, even here there were things that divided them.

As Ingrid talked about the film, she was insistent that Anthony Quinn should co-star, as the Tennessee mountain man. The Mexican-born Quinn was a fine actor, but he usually played Latin types. The casting made no sense unless one knew that Quinn and Ingrid had been romantically involved. As Ingrid had done with Gary Cooper years before, she wanted to continue her relationship in a second film. And she talked Silliphant into the casting.

After her return to Choisel, Ingrid received a phone call from Mike Frankovich, a Hollywood producer, asking her to star in a film version of the Broadway comedy *Cactus Flower*. Ingrid was supposed to play a dental assistant in her mid-thirties, attracted to her philandering boss, Walter Matthau, who has his eyes on a very young woman, Goldie Hawn.

Ingrid had long since declared her intention of no longer playing romantic roles. She was fifty-three years old, almost double Hawn's age. Matthau might look like an aging bloodhound, but the idea that he would ever choose Ingrid over Goldie could end up the biggest laugh in the film. The producer flew to Paris to convince Ingrid to accept the part.

Ingrid had two choice roles, back to back. One of those with whom she discussed her plans was Ann Todd, her old friend. "Ingrid said she was leaving to go to the States and she didn't care about her husband or her children," recalls Todd. "She said they were secondary."

In Italy in the old days, the Rossellinis had called Ingrid *bocca da verità*, "mouth of truth." She was indeed a truthmonger, thinking what most others did not dare to think, and saying what only a few thought. Yet people were always seeking some greater truth in her words, some greater passion that was not there. She had said what she thought about her marriage, and about her family. It was not that she did not care. She cared, but in her own terms, her own way. She understood the odds against the survival of her marriage, but they were odds she was willing to risk.

In Hollywood, Ingrid took pleasure in the sheer business of making a film; it was "Goldie" this and "Walter" that, all kissing and hugging. The public imagined that a film like *Cactus Flower* was a fraternal business, weeks of camaraderie and good times.

But careers were to be made or lost on the movie set, and the stars had no time and little interest in developing long-term friendships. Ingrid argued with the director over her lines, seeing that she was not bested by Hawn, in the young television star's film debut. She didn't socialize with Matthau either. "We weren't close," Matthau says now. "I don't think you ever get a chance to get close to anyone you're working with."

Ingrid's closeness to her male co-stars had usually been based on sexual intimacy and romance. Without that, she had little to say to Matthau. It was quite enough to have lunch together.

One day Ingrid, Matthau, and the director, Gene Saks, sat over lunch in the executive dining room at Columbia Pictures, observing a play in which she knew neither the characters nor their parts.

"What movie is he in?" she asked, looking at a young man whose long blond hair was neatly pulled back by a barrette.

"He's not in a movie," Matthau said. "He's writing one."

In Ingrid's day writers had looked like writers. She saw another hippie-like young man, and made the logical conclusion. "Ah, then that one must be a writer," she said.

"No," said Saks. "That's Peter Fonda, the actor."

"And that little man?" Ingrid said, not venturing a guess at the occupation of the chubby man wearing what appeared to be zipperless pants.

"A vice-president of Columbia Pictures."

"Hollywood has changed dramatically since I left."

Soon after she finished *Cactus Flower*, Ingrid was off to the mountains of Tennessee to film *A Walk in the Spring Rain*. Ingrid had convinced Anthony Quinn to accept the role of a mountain man, as bizarre a bit of casting as Woody Allen playing Zorba. "I knew it was wrong for me, but she wanted me for the part and I did it," says Quinn, who in the film spoke in a peculiar accent more appropriate to the mountains of Shangri-la than to the Great Smokies.

Ingrid and Quinn's last film had been shot in an ancient city of eternal fascination, where making a bad film hardly seemed the end of the world. The

Gatlinburg, Tennessee, that Ingrid flew into was a city of motels, fast-food emporiums, and souvenir shops stocked with all the wealth of Taiwan and places east, surrounded by the magnificent mountains.

Ingrid discovered soon enough how far Silliphant had gone to provide for her creature comforts. Tennessee was dry and the producer-writer knew that that would not do for Ingrid. So he set up a private cocktail lounge in the rather seedy motel that was to be their home. He imported a Filipino bartender from the Beachcomber restaurant in Los Angeles, along with a myriad of fruit juices, and enough of Ingrid's favorite rum to keep her floating in rum toddies, Mai Tais, and other exotic drinks even if the filming ran for a year. He envisioned days of passionate, happy filmmaking and evenings of happy drinking with Ingrid, Quinn, and other members of the first team.

Almost from the moment Ingrid met Quinn again, it was obvious that their relationship had as much fizzle as a Coke left open overnight. "They were like dead lovers," Silliphant says. "You could sense the separation. I had banked hopefully that there may have been a resumption of the affair and some of the passion would rub off."

Ingrid was cast as a professor's wife who with her husband, played by Fritz Weaver, is spending his sabbatical year in the Smoky Mountains. She falls in love with the earthy mountain man. As the rehearsals began, the transcendent question was whether the professor's wife would physically surrender to the charms of the mountain man. Ingrid had had affairs during all three of her marriages, but she was not about to have one onscreen. She said that she was striking out for her own generation in "the 'love bag' as against the 'pornographic bag.'" She was convinced that *her* character would never commit adultery.

"Look at me," Quinn argued, as Silliphant remembers the scene. "I'm an animal. Look at me! You mean to tell me this woman wouldn't succumb to my warmth and my love and my sexual allure?"

"Tony, of course not," Ingrid said, as if she had never been involved with the actor. "She would not."

"You're wrong," Quinn insisted.

Silliphant had to please both his stars, and he kept the script ambiguous. Ingrid could play her part as a virtuous wife, indulging in a mild and innocent flirtation, while Quinn could play it as if the hills were alive with the sound of rutting.

Even during rehearsals Silliphant realized that before this production was over, he might be needing his share of Mai Tais and rum toddies. On the evening before the first day's shooting, he worked until 3 A.M., rewriting the script. Soon after he woke up he began to hear news from the location that sounded like battle reports. The more the day wore on, the worse the reports became. When the assistant director got back to the motel, he told Silliphant that he was "in deep shit" and that "Ingrid is really pissed."

There is no guilt like the guilt of the innocent, and Silliphant was terrified at the thought of what was happening to his film and his star. When he was told Ingrid wanted to talk to him, he called her room and invited her down to the closed bar for a private discussion.

"You failed me today," Ingrid said, not bothering to embellish her feelings in pleasantries.

"What do you mean?" Silliphant asked.

"I thought you understood how important it is for an actress to have the writer-producer, the person she started the project with, there for the first shot," Ingrid lectured. "The fact that you weren't there, that you didn't watch me, has caused me to worry how good a producer you really are."

"Boy, that's a heavy charge," Silliphant said. "I could try to say I was exhausted after being up until three, but I can see that's not going to change your mind."

"Not at all," Ingrid said, with all the wrath of an Old Testament prophet. "Had you been up all night, you should have come to the set just long enough to come to me and put your arms around me and say Ingrid you're brilliant, I love you, I know you're going to be great; then you could have gone to sleep."

By now Ingrid was crying. "I only tell you this because I really care for you, but you have to understand these things. And you'll never learn them unless someone tells you."

"I'm very grateful to you," Silliphant said, vowing never to miss an opening shot again.

Ingrid had not always had the treatment from a producer that she insisted was the norm. But she had been in enough films to know that this would be a long, tedious production, and she vented her frustration on the most obvious candidate.

By the time the first rushes reached Hollywood, Columbia knew that the basic chemistry between the two stars was gone. "The romance was finished," says John Veitch, the executive supervising the production for Columbia. "There was nothing really left between them, on the screen or on the set."

Quinn was so fed up with Ingrid and the production that he rented a house to get away. He could not get away from the film itself. Silliphant kept hoping that Ingrid would give in and allow her character to have an affair, but she did not, and the film had as much drama as a Sunday school picnic.

"One of my great tragedies is that I wish I had done a successful picture with Ingrid, because we had such faith in each other," Quinn says. "But sometimes in motion pictures you love someone so much, but it doesn't work on the screen. And you don't like somebody and you're wonderful on the screen. The two greatest talents I worked with were Ingrid and Anna Magnani. But I would prefer to work with Anna Magnani, whom I didn't like, than Ingrid, whom I loved."

On the set Quinn had isolated himself emotionally and physically from Ingrid. He had not given in to her ideas for the film, as he had given in on *The Visit*. Whatever she had intended when she coaxed the actor into taking the part had not worked out. She had not had a renewed relationship with Quinn, and now after over half a year in America she was ready to return to Lars and to her marriage.

"I have calmed down a bit," she wrote Lars. "I can understand now that I can be very tiresome. . . . My little old man, I'm much kinder now, you wait and see."

CHAPTER TWENTY

"Darling,
That Is You Crying"

*I*ngrid loved to talk to her husband about her work and, back with Lars, she was full of tales of her half year in America.

Ingrid pretended that she was a woman of perfect candor, but if that were true, her honesty would have begun with her husbands. As in her previous two marriages, Ingrid had had adulterous relationships. Her marriage was full of large and small deceits, but to her husband and to the world she acted the loyal and loving wife.

The elegant charade of their marriage extended to Lars too. He was involved in an affair with a beautiful, wellborn young Swedish woman. According to Gérôme, months before at a dinner party one of the guests, a Swedish director, had nonchalantly said, "I was talking to Kristina and . . ." The director assumed that Ingrid must have known about her husband's relationship with Kristina Belfrage. Ingrid did not, and she did not believe in Old Testament justice: an affair for an affair. She felt betrayed, but she had decided to be quiet, and to wait Lars out.

On the evening of her return from the States, Lars told Ingrid about Kristina. Lars's great error was not his betrayal but his admission of betrayal. "At first I didn't take it calmly or peacefully," Ingrid said later. "I realized I had given myself this blow. I knew I couldn't blame Lars, but at first I didn't accept it with much patience. I was angry with him. We discussed divorce, but it was only discussion. I thought I would leave. I would go away. Then I thought, maybe this other relationship will end. There was so much that Lars and I had between us. Perhaps we could make up and go on as we had before—which of course is not possible. You make up, but it's not the same as it was before."

So Ingrid Bergman, whom much of the world considered the great symbol of romantic love and courage, settled down into a life of compromise and mistrust rather than face life alone. With Roberto, too, she had been willing to settle for a marriage that was little more than a legal arrangement until public scandal intervened. With Lars, such an arrangement might go on indefinitely, for he was a man of infinite discretion.

There is no loneliness like that of a failing marriage, but Ingrid stayed at Choisel, hunkered down into the remnants of her marriage. So many years ago she had written Petter, telling him that she was leaving him alone in the ruins. She had left Roberto too, lost among the broken fragments of his early career, while she went on to great new stardom. This time, she was the one alone in the ruins. She felt that she was too old to start again. Life had few roles for aging actresses, either on stage or off. She had no one but Lars, and she would take even a part of him rather than be alone.

"It was a very strange destiny," reflected Father Lisandrini. "She was the queen of the world and she had no one to love. Ingrid said once, 'I am an unfortunate woman. I have no husband in my life. Roberto was just a little while, and I have gone from bad to worse.' The solitude of this universal actress was extraordinary. She was the most alone woman, but she had no time to reflect on her solitude, and no one noticed she was alone."

Ingrid didn't work during the last half of 1969 and all of 1970. Gérôme tried to talk her into taking an apartment in Paris, but she wouldn't even do that. Lacking insight, she didn't realize how depressed she had become. She was living with the hope of Lars's return to a marriage that she had never really cared profoundly about. Now she cared. She needed Lars.

Fiorella Mariani was one of the few people to whom Ingrid could talk openly. Fiorella admired Ingrid immensely; without her aunt by marriage, she never would have dared to start her own career as a theatrical designer. One evening they talked until four in the morning, as they had done so often years before at Santa Marinella.

"Lars is a weak man," Fiorella remembers saying. "He's never happy, never satisfied with himself. He's always reaching for something, but without passion. I really feel sorry for him. I like him because I understand his weaknesses."

"How can you say that?" Ingrid interjected. "How can you say you like him because of his weaknesses?"

"There's something wrong in his strength, Ingrid. Don't you see?"

Robert Anderson paid a visit in late April 1970. The playwright's feelings for Ingrid had mellowed into friendship. "Ingrid and Lars were having a bad time," Anderson says. "Lars would either not come back or come back and leave in the morning before I was up. I would sit and listen to her stories. She said, 'It happens to every middle-aged French housewife.' I said, 'Do you think of yourself as a middle-aged French housewife?' And she did."

Lars might have tried to instill confidence in his wife, but instead he acted as if her career had ended, and she had become an appendage to his life.

When finally Ingrid did work again, it was 1971. A British producer, Binkie Beaumont, offered her the part of Lady Cecily Waynflete in George Bernard Shaw's *Captain Brassbound's Conversion*. Ingrid found the play "boring" and "unbelievable"—a charitable assessment—but the role delicious. Lady Cecily is an intrepid, highborn British lady. She sets off for Morocco, accompanied by Captain Brassbound. No one is immune to Lady Cecily's charms, not anyone of the twenty-three members of the all-male supporting cast—not anyone but lovers of a good play.

What an opportunity it was, though, for a fifty-five-year-old actress whose husband has taken up with a woman half her age, and who feels that her charm and desirability are history. Ingrid and twenty-three men. It was hardly a play, but a vehicle for the mythological Ingrid Bergman, who had so little to do with the woman sitting at Choisel, drinking and smoking and thinking about old times.

Once Beaumont had signed Ingrid, the producer called Frith Banbury to ask him to direct.

"Well, Lady Cecily Waynflete is a *British* aristocrat," Banbury said, taken aback by the casting.

"It doesn't matter," Beaumont insisted.

"You're going to get a certain amount of criticism."

"I know."

"Well, what do you want, a real *Captain Brassbound* or a showcase for Ingrid Bergman?"

"A showcase for Ingrid Bergman."

For the first day's rehearsals, Griffith James, the company manager, had arranged chairs for the cast on the stage of the Brighton Theatre. Everyone was there except for Ingrid, and James went to the stage door to await her.

If Ingrid was late, it was usually simply long enough to signal the entrance of a major figure. Today, no more than ten minutes after the scheduled beginning, she arrived.

"You're late," James said. He was going to run the company the way it had to be run. When he was younger, the stage manager had done some acting, but he was far more comfortable backstage, handling the myriad details of a production. He loved the theater as much as any actor or playwright or director, and he did his job as well as any of them did theirs.

Captain Brassbound's Conversion opened in Brighton before moving to London, where it opened February 18, 1971. The play was a resounding popular success, though the most creative aspect of the evening was Ingrid's British accent. The rest of the cast knew that the audience was coming to see not a play but Ingrid.

"She would only play a role if she could identify with the character, that she could see something of herself," says Joss Ackland, who played Captain Brassbound, and became a good friend. "Technically, she was hopeless. I would say, 'For God's sake, stand still.' She was playing a nineteenth-century English woman, which she could never do. But she had such enthusiasm. In this and her other plays she worked with wonderful stage actors. With people like Redgrave, when they talked of her acting, they would just smile."

Ingrid was the great new star of the season. She was full of life. All the troubles with Lars seemed to be gone. She talked to him on the phone, about the play and about movies she had seen, about other actors and dinner parties. She laughed and gossiped with him, and took comfort in the fact that he was her husband. It was better this way, and Ingrid appreciated Lars's guidance and professional concern.

Life was good again. Ingrid would arrive early for the performance, two hours before curtain time. There in her dressing room, everything was right. Her dresser, Louie Hollis, saw to it. Louie was from London's East End. She was as short and stout as a cruller, and spoke with a cockney accent that Ingrid could sometimes not understand. Louie watched out for the woman she called "my lady." It wouldn't do to have her lady drying her hands on towels that others had used, so Louie brought in her own linen towels. She knew how much her lady liked things tidy and clean, and when Ingrid was onstage Louie was always busy, making the little dressing room as neat as a pin.

The Cambridge Theatre wasn't air-conditioned. On hot summer evenings the backstage area felt like an adjunct to the tropics. Every time Ingrid came offstage, Griff James or someone else would be there to lead her to the scenery door, where she stepped outside to breathe some real air before hurrying back to catch her next cue.

During the run of *Captain Brassbound's Conversion* Ingrid became very close to Griff. The tall, bespectacled stage manager was not interested in a romantic relationship with Ingrid, but wanted merely to be her friend. He may have looked like a mournful basset hound, but he was a man of quick, subtle wit. He was a man of great feeling too, and he cared for Ingrid immensely. He was of Ingrid's generation, without wife or family. He loved the theater as she did, and had little life beyond it.

After the performance, Griff usually stopped in, while Louie finished her daily routine. Ingrid was not like some of the young actors, rushing out the stage door, with the echoes of the applause still vibrating, hurrying off for a date, or a drink with friends. Louie claimed "she could go out any night, but she preferred to go home alone." Actually, her life was here, not only on the stage but in this dressing room too, in the narrow corridors and the darkened theater. She loved the smell and bustle and warmth of the theatrical life. She loved the extravagant words of affection among the actors, and yet that they kept their distance.

To her old friends she was loyal and thoughtful, never forgetting a birthday, forever sending picture postcards. She was terribly well organized, but she sometimes became irritated at the endless rituals of remembrance and caring.

When she met new people, she couldn't be bothered remembering names, or even faces. They all became a blur to her, even sometimes people with whom she had worked. One day she was at Burberry's buying a trench coat for Lars when she saw Walter Matthau, her co-star in *Cactus Flower*.

"Walter, it's me, Ingrid," she said, rushing up to the actor.

"Ingrid *who?*" asked Matthau, who was as notorious as Ingrid for forgetting people's names.

"Ingrid *Bergman,*" Ingrid said, not realizing that Matthau was having his little joke.

Captain Brassbound's Conversion was such a success that early in 1972 the play was taken to the States, with an American supporting cast. It was even less appropriate for modern-day America than for London, but no one seemed to notice, especially not the full houses in Wilmington, Washington, Toronto, and New York.

There was no star like Ingrid, no one who still glowed with the magic of the old Hollywood, and had had a life more dramatic than any of her films. To the American public she was a cultural icon, to be treasured and paraded past, like a precious work of art.

Ingrid was such a draw that in Washington *Captain Brassbound* was booked into the 2,300-seat opera house, which usually played only musicals. On the day that Ingrid addressed a luncheon audience at the National Press Club, the room was jammed with tables and guests. Those turned back made up the largest waiting list for tickets in the club's history. During the luncheon Ingrid sat on a raised platform with other notables. At their tables, the journalists, publicists, and lobbyists filled out questions that were passed forward.

So much had gone on in the two and a half decades since Ingrid had last appeared in Washington. Nineteen forty-six was an ancient epoch, and Ingrid was a miraculous survivor of a time and a place that most of those in the audience knew only from yellowed news clips. Indeed, the question written on almost half the cards was how Ingrid at the age of fifty-six continued to look so radiant.

Ingrid laughed and said that she could tell them that she had a good plastic surgeon in Sweden, but that, really, she had always looked young.

As usual, people were seeking in Ingrid concerns and feelings that she didn't have. She told the audience that she had no real interest in politics: "I have been an entertainer. . . . I try to live in a way that I am of help to other people, but that's not politics." She wasn't about to pretend that she had an intellectual approach to acting: "I haven't read many of those books about acting. Stanislavsky, I tried to plow through. I think, instinctively, even the first time I read a script I know exactly how the woman is. That is why I turn down many things I don't understand."

"We are told that the golden age of Hollywood has gone forever," a questioner said. "Is this a great loss or a good thing?"

"I think it is in a sense a loss," Ingrid said. "But time marches on. I suppose everything has to change. Everything became very glossy and unrealistic, and that was one of the reasons why I left. . . . I have to say that when I left for Italy there was a senator in Washington who made a speech against me, and he ended by saying that out of Hollywood's ashes will grow a better Hollywood. . . ."

Ingrid had meant to say "out of Ingrid Bergman's ashes," but the Hollywood she'd known had, indeed, gone up in flames the day she left. A new Hollywood and a new Washington had grown up, and the new Washington was ready to make its own atonement for the half-forgotten words of Senator Johnson of Colorado.

Charles Percy of Illinois, a politician astutely aware of the value of publicity, stood up on the floor of the Senate and said: "Mr. President, one of the world's loveliest, most gracious, and most talented women was made the victim of a bitter attack in this chamber twenty-two years ago. Today I would like to pay long overdue tribute to Ingrid Bergman, a true star in every sense of the word. Our culture would be poorer indeed without her artistry. To the American public she will always hold a place in our hearts as one of the greatest performing artists of our time. . . . Miss Bergman is not only welcome in America; we are deeply honored by her visits here."

One evening, Ingrid attended a special showing of *Casablanca* by the American Film Institute. She couldn't stand seeing the whole thing again. "She said, 'When I die I hope they won't show it again,' " Griff remembers. Ingrid arrived in time for the last reel and sat in the last row of the balcony.

People watched the film not because it was a dusty cultural artifact, or simply one of the great American films; they watched it as an act of homage. There were Rick's Bars everywhere from Jamaica to Germany. There were people who had seen the film dozens of times, and could recite the dialogue like a catechism. There was hardly a day, hardly an hour, when *Casablanca* wasn't showing somewhere, and Ingrid wasn't wearing her blue in Paris, her white in Rick's, her trench coat at the airport, standing on the tarmac saying goodbye to Rick, goodbye forever.

As Rick turned to Louis and said, "I think this is the beginning of a beautiful friendship," the audience laughed in appreciation, and Ingrid laughed with them. She had given up trying to understand why people loved the film so. The audience rose to greet her, and she walked to the front of the crowded theater.

She had talked about *Casablanca* so many times. She had answered the same questions about Bogie and Henreid and the others more times than she could possibly remember. But she loved to talk about the past, her past, and her responses sounded as fresh as *Casablanca*.

Ingrid went to New York for the run of *Captain Brassbound's Conversion*. Remaining in New York, she played the title role in a children's film, *From the Mixed-up Files of Mrs. Basil E. Frankweiler*. She spent considerable time with Pia, who lived in the city and was making her career as a television journalist.

One evening Ingrid visited Joseph Daly at Pia's apartment. Daly was a feisty, fast-talking Irish-American who had started out as a salesman for Siren Lingerie. Now he was in real estate, on the make. When Ingrid arrived, Joe told her that a late-breaking news story had detained Pia. Ingrid marched into the living room in her Chanel suit and stood there a moment. As she always did when she was nervous, she talked too rapidly.

A look of absolute horror crossed Daly's face. "Miss Bergman, there's something I must tell you. We've got a new puppy, and . . ."

Ingrid looked down at the rug. Her designer shoe was standing on puppy excrement.

Ingrid laughed. She was soon down on her knees, scrubbing the rug, telling her future son-in-law stories about her life.

In December 1971 Ingrid attended the couple's wedding. At the wedding dinner dance at the Hotel Carlyle, Ingrid saw Petter for the first time since meeting him with Pia in England. Petter's youthfulness was as striking as Ingrid's. He looked at least a decade younger than his sixty-four years. His wife, Agnes, was twenty years younger than Petter, and they made a handsome couple, alongside their nine-year-old daughter, Brita, one of their four children.

Petter was a prominent neurosurgeon in the United States. In Europe he was a consultant to the Swedish government. Still suspicious of his ex-wife's motives and publicity seeking, he made sure that no pictures were taken of the two of them together.

Ingrid spent time with Pia and her new husband, but she was a woman of the special occasion, not a home-loving mother who looked forward to becoming a grandmother.

In June 1973 Ingrid took Robertino with her to the Cannes Film Festival, where she served as president of the jury. She was taken out and paraded around at gatherings and dinners and then set back down in her room, treated the way Mexican peasants carry their favorite saints through the streets of their village before storing them away. Often she was left alone in her suite. She would have liked more invitations, but no one seemed to know that she wanted company or that she might be lonely.

Ingrid had her children, but she didn't know quite how to deal with them. They had been brought up like hothouse flowers. None of them finished their higher education. "From an early age the children learned to be free, to do what they wanted," says Fiorella. "They were free but they had no responsibility. Robertino told me when he was taking the matriculation exam, 'I hope I fail. If I don't fail, I will have to assume responsibility.' "

So often Isotta had lived in the shadow of her more flamboyant sister. Now she took up with Alberto Acciarito, a son of the working class. Although Isotta at first considered him a prince of the people, some of the family thought him ill-tempered and argumentative. Ingrid was willing to have her daughter live with the young man, and she would even help out, but the last thing she wanted was a marriage.

"This was the only time when I had tension with Father and Mama," Isotta says. "They knew that we were fighting a lot and didn't see the point. For a few months I was on my own, not talking to them. We didn't see one another very much because it was embarrassing. I remember Mama sending me a very nice picture of the two of us holding hands in the country. There was a little note saying that we should always be like that, holding hands."

When Isotta went ahead and married Acciarito, for a time her parents didn't see her. Roberto was even less forgiving than Ingrid, but eventually both of them made a tenuous peace with their new son-in-law.

Ingrid didn't know what to do with her children. "She gave Robertino cars, sports cars," says Ann Todd. "I said, 'Ingrid, you shouldn't do that.' She said, 'How else will they love me?' "

For her next role Ingrid accepted the part of Constance in W. Somerset Maugham's *The Constant Wife.* Constance is an infinitely more intriguing character than Lady Cecily, her previous role. Constance discovers that her husband is having an affair with her best friend. Instead of raging in rebuke, she sweetly asks him if she might accept a position as an interior decorator. She is immediately successful in her new job. A year later she leaves for an Italian vacation, taking with her an old beau, who may or may not become her lover.

The Constant Wife is a witty, amusing play. The London production had an excellent supporting cast and, as director, John Gielgud, one of the great names of British theater.

Gielgud knew that Ingrid was hardly the beau ideal of an aristocratic British lady. In rehearsals, Ingrid spoke the line: "I wonder what my mother would say about it?"

"Wouldn't it be possible," Gielgud said wryly, "to change it to 'my *Scandinavian* mother'?"

When the play opened at the Albery Theatre in London's West End, the audiences hardly noticed Ingrid's curious accent, and neither did most of the critics. *The Constant Wife* was one of the biggest hits of the season. Audiences loved the idea of a delightfully civilized revenge.

Lars visited London occasionally, and the meanest aspect of his stay was not the talk of his relationship with Kristina but his attitude toward Ingrid's newest and dearest friend, Griff James. From their first meeting Lars had little use for Griff. Lars was a meticulous, elegant dresser, while Griff was a man of backstage, even in his attire. Lars didn't appreciate—or didn't care to appreciate—the qualities that made Griff such good company. It reached the point where Griff disappeared when Ingrid's husband was in town.

One evening in late November, Ingrid returned after the performance to her lovely flat on Mount Street in Mayfair. She could never go to sleep right away, and usually she had a few drinks to help her along. She lay in bed leafing through a magazine. She noticed an article about breast cancer, an affliction that seemed almost an epidemic now, affecting Betty Ford, the President's wife, and other famous women. As she read about how women should check their breasts for lumps, she touched her own breasts, and in a desultory way examined herself. Suddenly, on the underside of her left breast, she felt something. A small lump. There was no mistaking it. A small, hard lump. She'd always been perfectly healthy. She thought: No, it can't happen to me.

It was late. But as she always did when she had a problem, she called Lars in France.

"You must go to the doctor," Lars said firmly. "Go tomorrow. At once."

"But I'm in the play, and we've got a long run ahead," Ingrid insisted. "I can't do anything for the moment."

Ingrid attempted to forget the lump in her breast. The critics might sing hosannas to her youthful beauty, but Ingrid knew that she was a fifty-eight-year-old woman whose husband had taken a lover half her age. Yet she was still a desirable woman, of that she was sure. The idea that she might lose her breast was unthinkable.

The following evening Ingrid sat before her mirror at the Albery, making up. Griff was in the dressing room, chatting away amiably.

"Am I insured in case I can't go on with the play?" Ingrid asked casually.

"Insured?" Griff said, in the chiding manner that Ingrid found so endearing. "Why? Are you sick? You don't look sick to me."

Ingrid laughed. "All right. So I'm not insured. That's all I was asking."

"Of course you're not insured. Without Ingrid Bergman, there's no play. If you leave the play, the play's off."

Better by far to think of yourself as a heroic trouper, saving the jobs of a score of actors, than as a frightened, lonely, aging lady facing the prospect of losing your breast. Ingrid finally went to see a specialist on Harley Street, that most exclusive of addresses for London doctors. "You must do something about it," he told her.

But very often people hear the kind of medical advice they want to hear. According to Ingrid, her doctor told her, "Yes, you must do something about it, but there's not all that much of a hurry." Ingrid could wait to get a biopsy that would reveal if the lump was malignant.

That was the reprieve she wanted. She threw herself into the role of Constance. Each evening was an adventure for the actors who played with her. They never could tell just how she would speak her lines, or where she would stand. A critic who attended a performance in January 1974 reported: "Miss Bergman's technical performance . . . was way off. Several of her lines went clear out of her head, and many others emerged as sound without sense." One evening Ingrid was standing in the wings talking to Griff, and she missed her entrance; she swept blithely onstage and said, "I'm sorry I'm late. I was talking to Griff." Another evening, she was standing onstage alone at the end of an act when the curtain didn't come down. She simply stood there and laughed and said, "The curtain should have come down." Another actress would have come stomping backstage, infuriated, raging at the stage manager. To Ingrid it was simply an amusing story, and to the audience it was something special, an added memory of their evening with Ingrid Bergman.

The play continued to do spectacular business, and the producer wanted to extend the run well into 1974. When Laurence Evans, Ingrid's agent at ICM's London office, told her this, she confided to him about her illness. It was unthinkable that Ingrid should extend the run, and put off the operation any longer. But she did. It was doubly unthinkable that she should also accept a role in a new film, even if it was something as choice as *Murder on the Orient Express.* "Do you think this is wise?" Evans asked her, and she said that it was.

In the evenings Ingrid played in *The Constant Wife.* During the day she played in *Murder on the Orient Express.* Sidney Lumet, the director, cast the film with an extraordinary collection of stars, everyone from Albert Finney to Anthony Perkins, Richard Widmark to Sean Connery, Lauren Bacall to Vanessa Redgrave, and half a dozen others. Lumet wanted Ingrid to play an aging Russian princess, the natural role for her after *Anastasia.* When Ingrid saw the script she preferred a smaller part as a dowdy Swedish missionary, nothing more than a cameo, with twenty-five lines of dialogue. It was unusual for a star of Ingrid's stature and age to make such a choice, and it led to a brilliant comic performance.

In the late spring, when the run of *The Constant Wife* ended, Dr. David Handley wanted Ingrid to go into the hospital for the biopsy. But Ingrid decided that she would fly to New York to see her first grandson, Justin, born to Pia and Joe Daly. And there, six months since the original diagnosis, she sought a second opinion from an American doctor.

It did not take the New York specialist very long to realize that Ingrid had already taken incalculable risks with her health and life. He was the kind of doctor who thought that a bedside manner was for the bedside. He told Ingrid bluntly and categorically, "You've got to have an operation right away."

"Well, I've got Lars's birthday party on June 11," Ingrid said. "And I want to see the chalet we've bought in Switzerland. Then there's a party for . . ." Ingrid was treating the whole matter as if it were a problem between the doctor and the disease, and had nothing to do with her at all. She acted as if she were doing the doctor an enormous favor allowing him to examine her when she had so many more important things to do.

"How in the world can you drag on like this?" the doctor said in exasperation. "This is ridiculous. Right into the hospital—tonight."

"No-o-o-o," Ingrid insisted. "I'm here in New York and I've lots of plans."

To impress upon Ingrid the seriousness of what he was saying, the American doctor called Dr. Handley in London. The two specialists talked awhile. Then the New York doctor handed the phone to Ingrid. "Yes, I must agree with my colleague that you are pushing it very far," Dr. Handley said. "You should come back to London immediately."

"I can't come back now because I'm going bicycling tomorrow in Central Park with Pia and my grandson and—"

The American doctor had heard quite enough. It takes time for many patients to face up to their situation, but he would not allow self-deception to go on indefinitely. "Which is more important to you?" the doctor asked. "Your husband's birthday party or your life?"

"My husband's birthday party."

The American doctor could say no more.

Ingrid flew to Europe for Lars's birthday. She called her children and told them about the operation. "I have to go into the hospital," she told Isotta, who had recently visited her in London and had no idea about the illness. "I have a little lump and I have to check what it is." Isotta thought that her mother was so healthy that the problem couldn't be anything.

After the party at Choisel, Ingrid returned to London, and on June 15, 1974, entered the London Clinic as Mrs. Schmidt.

All four of her children and Lars flew to London, together in her sickness as they had rarely been in her health. They waited for Ingrid to come out of the anesthesia. "Oh, how tiresome this woman is, crying all the time," Ingrid said, as if she were watching someone else. "Please ask her not to cry anymore. She is just crying and crying."

Ingrid heard a voice through the haze of half sleep: "Darling, that is you crying."

Ingrid held her arms locked so tightly against her chest that no one could possibly move them. She looked up and saw Dr. Handley staring down at her. She could tell without a word that he had removed her breast.

Ingrid called Laurence Evans. "It's all over," she said, as if she were talking about a film that had been wrapped.

Soon afterward, Lars appeared in Evans's office to tell him that it was not all over at all; the tumor was malignant. "Is it the worst?" Evans asked. "No, I don't think so," Lars said calmly. "We should be optimistic."

To her children, Ingrid had always appeared a woman of formidable strength, with the kind of energy that was almost unbelievable. They had grown up with an image of her always off somewhere doing something marvelous and exciting. It was almost inconceivable that she should be sick. Ingrid herself acted as if the discovery that the tumor was malignant was no great matter, of little more importance than a theater curtain that wouldn't close, or a bad review.

Immediately after the operation Ingrid and her children flew to Paris to spend two weeks at Choisel. Ingrid was wheeled into Heathrow Airport in a wheelchair. Nothing went right. The twins' tickets had to be changed so that they could fly to Paris before going on to Rome. And Pia needed a new ticket too. Isabella and Isotta ran in one direction; Pia rushed off toward another ticket counter.

"We have our tickets!" the twins shouted.

Ingrid jumped out of the wheelchair and chased after Pia. "Get on the next plane! We'll take this one because Lars is waiting with the car at Orly."

Ingrid and the three Rossellinis hurried down the corridor and caught the bus to the airplane.

"Well, Mama, what about the wheelchair?" Robertino asked.

"I didn't have time for it, did I?" As the bus started to pull out, Pia's face appeared in the doorway. And everyone left for Choisel together.

Ingrid said often that Lars was a better friend than a husband. In her pain and doubt, Ingrid turned to Lars as she had not turned to him in love and marriage. He saw her as no one else did, the anger, the bitterness, the fear. Lars, the manager of play productions, of accounts, of investments, of houses, took control of Ingrid's illness.

Ingrid had heard terrible things about radiation treatment, and she returned to London for it with foreboding. The doctors told her that she might get tired and depressed and want to die. She always had Isabella or Isotta with her, and they were there when she came out of the radiation room, to nurse and guide her. Her dresses were remade so that no one had to know that she had been "mutilated," as she called it. And slowly, very slowly, she realized that it was not so terrible, that the suffering of the treatments did not last, and that life was still out there in the streets and the stores and the restaurants, there as it always had been.

Early in 1975 Ingrid set out once again, to tour America in *The Constant Wife*, traveling to Los Angeles, Denver, Washington, Boston, and New York. She had never particularly liked Los Angeles, and a place like Century City, site of the Shubert Theater, was one of the reasons she still disliked it. The cluster of tall office buildings hovers over the flatlands of Beverly Hills and West Los Angeles. It is as if a forlorn attempt to make a city had been abandoned leaving an enclave of commerce and culture accessible only by cars that are parked mainly in immense subterranean garages.

When Ingrid was onstage, everything was fine, but an actress, even when she is working, has endless time. One Sunday afternoon Ingrid went to a multiscreen movie theater. "I've been to four movie houses," she told Griff later.

"That must have cost you lots of money," Griff said jokingly.

"Oh, no," Ingrid replied. "Three dollars."

"Oh, Ingrid, you're supposed to pay in each one."

Ingrid took Griff to see her old haunts. Los Angeles had changed so much that most of the restaurants were gone, or didn't look the same, and Hollywood housed as many derelicts as memories.

She went to see Jean Renoir. Benedict Canyon had grown. There were houses all the way to the top of Mulholland Drive, and the winding road sometimes was backed up with traffic. She used to be able to see Jean and Dido Renoir's house from her own home. But the foliage had grown up. The

Renoir home was in a little cul-de-sac. The house had not changed, with its living room as warm and friendly as a French country house, the walls lined with masterpieces painted by Jean's father. Jean lay dying, only half aware of the world around him. Ingrid held his hand, and talked to him of good films and old times.

To Ingrid, it sometimes seemed that everybody was sick or dying or dead. Jean. Lewis Milestone. Leo McCarey. And thanks to a bond of silence, almost, no one even knew that she was sick.

Alf Kjellin, the Swedish actor and director, came to see her. There was no one left, no living actor, who went back as far with her as Kjellin. He had appeared with her in her last Swedish film. He went back further than that, back when she was fresh as dawn, arriving at the studio in Stockholm. "She was at a desperate stage," Kjellin says. "She was at a desperate stage also sensually. She wanted just to be with someone."

The play was still the thing, though, and the audiences made her forget. And Ingrid was a walker, even in Los Angeles, where a pedestrian is as rare a spectacle as a natural blonde. After a Saturday matinee in mid-March, Ingrid decided that she and her friends would walk to a French restaurant for dinner.

She had not got very far before she stumbled over a stone, twisting her ankle. Her friends helped her limp back to the theater. A Beverly Hills doctor told Ingrid that she had broken a bone in her left foot. He proceeded to put the foot in a cast.

Ingrid's role did not call for a plaster cast on her leg. Griff phoned the theater manager to tell him that he would have to cancel the sold-out performance. The manager envisioned a thousand irate playgoers assaulting the box office for refunds. Ingrid decided that broken foot or not, the show must go on.

The stage manager stepped in front of the curtain and began to speak. At such moments audiences have a sense of dread, knowing that in all likelihood they will be told that one understudy or another will be performing. The stage manager, however, told the audience that because Miss Bergman had just broken her foot, the play would start an hour late, giving the cast time to harden. The playgoers took the announcement like troupers, part of a special evening with Ingrid Bergman.

Ingrid was always playing Ingrid anyway; this evening she played Ingrid with a broken foot playing Constance. Since the rest of the cast was used to her being the center of attention, flubbing the lines, and moving unaccountably around the stage, they had good training in following Ingrid as the butler pushed her around the stage in a gray swivel chair appropriated from one of the offices. The audience relished every delicious faux pas, every inside joke, that was being played on old Mr. Maugham and his ancient play.

Playgoers soon heard about Ingrid's broken foot; it was a double delight. Ingrid loved the sheer showmanship of the whole business, propelling herself back and forth in her wheelchair. Even when a doctor told her that she could walk, she continued playing from the wheelchair awhile. And when finally she played standing up, she took her bows from the wheelchair.

Ingrid received an Academy Award nomination for her supporting role as the Swedish missionary in *Murder on the Orient Express*. She was sure that the award would go to Valentina Cortese for her performance in François Truffaut's film about making a film, *Day for Night*. That was a real part, and Ingrid's role in *Murder on the Orient Express* was so tiny that it didn't seem possible that she might win.

Ingrid went to the Academy Awards ceremony primarily for another reason: to accept a special honorary award given to Jean Renoir. Ingrid cared deeply for the aged director. She always visited him when she came to Los Angeles. And she wrote him notes from all over the world, little remembrances that many stars would not have bothered with.

When Ingrid walked onstage she was given a standing ovation. She wore a long, silky dress with wide, long sleeves that made her look rather matronly. But she still exuded that shimmering glow.

"He has left behind him a body of masterpieces on film, just as his father did on canvas," Ingrid said. She had written the words herself, and she spoke them as firmly as if she were imprinting them on time. "In the cinema universe, he is a living god. In gratitude, thank you, we love you, Jean."

When the winner of the best supporting actress award for 1974 was announced, Ingrid heard her name being called. At the Academy Award ceremonies, actors are always saying that they can't believe they won, when they truly feel that any other outcome would have been an outrageous miscarriage of justice. This time, Ingrid truly believed that she should not have won.

"Thank you very much indeed," she said, accepting her third Academy Award. "It's always very nice to get an Oscar. . . . In the past, Oscar has shown that he's very forgetful and also has the wrong timing because last year when *Day for Night* won [for best foreign film], I couldn't believe that Valentina Cortese was not nominated because she gave the most beautiful performance. . . . Therefore . . . it's so ironic that this year she's nominated when the picture won last year.

"I don't quite understand that, but here I am and I'm her rival and I don't like it at all. Please forgive me, Valentina. I didn't mean to. . . ."

As Ingrid spoke, Cortese blew a kiss at Ingrid, and Ingrid blew it back. The two other nominees seated in the auditorium, Diane Ladd and Talia Shire, blew no kisses. And Ingrid discovered that an act of graciousness toward one can be considered an act of ungraciousness toward others. "I realized later I had acted—as usual—too impulsively," she said. "It would have been better if I'd kept my mouth shut altogether."

*　　*　　*

"Oh, we are going to do the crying scene now," Ingrid said, as she sat regally on a divan. She summoned the makeup man.

It was the fall of 1975 and Ingrid was at work again in Rome, making *A Matter of Time* with Liza Minnelli and Charles Boyer. She played an aged contessa who had nothing left in the world but memories and a room in a cheap hotel. She was doing her first big dramatic scene with Liza, who played a chambermaid.

Liza was off in a corner. She was going to have to cry too. She stood there thinking of all the bad memories in her life, an expedient that would have made Buddha cry. But then she caught sight of Ingrid, and stopped. Ingrid, who Liza believed cried more beautifully than any actress in films, was having glycerin applied to her eyes!

Liza walked over to the divan. "What are you doing?" Liza asked incredulously, as the makeup man continued blowing glycerin until Ingrid's eyes began to sting and run.

"The crying scene," Ingrid said.

Liza turned back toward her corner. She had only just met Ingrid, and she didn't know what to say.

"Liza, what are *you* doing?" Ingrid asked, calling her back.

"Well, I'm trying to cry," Liza said.

"*Really* cry?"

"Yes," Liza said sheepishly.

"Well, use the glycerin."

Liza thought a moment. "Ingrid, but don't you *really* cry?"

"No," Ingrid said matter-of-factly. "If I really cried, I'd be unhappy."

Liza laughed, as if she had made a great discovery. "When you looked at Humphrey Bogart and had tears in your eyes, that . . ."

"Glycerin."

"Ingrid, we can't tell this to the world."

"No, of course we can't. But I'll tell you a secret, and it's something you should remember as an actress. It's not whether you really cry. It's whether the audience thinks you are crying."

Ingrid and Liza did the scene together, with only Ingrid using glycerin. That evening Liza hurried to see the rushes. Ingrid looked as if she had just been told that her entire family had been wiped out by a mass murderer. And Liza looked as if she had a slight head cold.

Ingrid was glad to be back in Rome making a film, though from the beginning *A Matter of Time* smelled of disaster. Vincente Minnelli had been a fine director once, but that was long ago, and he had this assignment in part because he was Liza's father. And seventy-six-year-old Boyer was in far from a good mood.

Ingrid's twin daughters were working on the film and she saw them every day. Isabella was making her film debut in a tiny role as a nun and Isotta was working in makeup. Ingrid spent long hours at the studio, though the stages were being heated with portable gas burners that sucked the oxygen from the air, and left some of those on the set with headaches.

It almost always took several takes for Ingrid to get a scene right, but she had particular difficulty on *A Matter of Time*. One morning after she had blown a long scene several times, she had lunch with Joel E. Siegel, a young film scholar. "It's really not my business," he said, "but I think there's a typo. There's a word missing. That's why it doesn't make sense."

Ingrid leaned over toward Siegel: "It's all rubbish."

Even if it was all rubbish, there was a human quality to filmmaking in Italy that was totally unlike making movies in Hollywood. Over lunch, Ingrid might sit down with actors, actresses, directors, and producers of half a dozen other films being made at the studio. They discussed all their movies, half a dozen plots and a dozen characters, and exchanged anecdotes. It was as if they were cheating death, living a dozen lives, a dozen lifetimes within the parentheses of a moment. They discussed the past too, and that was another lifetime, a lifetime that Ingrid could not help thinking about, and that in blessed memory had lost all its pain.

CHAPTER TWENTY-ONE

Ingrid's
Great Performance

*I*ngrid and Roberto were friends once again, and in Rome Ingrid saw her former husband fairly often. She could understand Roberto's stunning intellectual soliloquies no more now than she could a quarter century before, but she cared for him. Since the divorce, Roberto had not had the great international success that Ingrid had enjoyed. But he was lionized by a new generation of filmmakers, and several of his films for television were almost as unique and innovative as *Open City* and *Paisan*. He was more in debt than ever, and his relationship with Sonali had finally ended, inevitably over a younger woman, Silvia d'Amicos, a film writer.

Roberto looked like a fat, languid cat. He would lounge in his bed or on a sofa for hours on end, would steam himself in the bath, and then perfume his body. He flew to the United States for conferences, talking of human society as if he, Roberto Rossellini, was living within history, affecting the events and ideas of his time.

On the morning of his seventieth birthday, May 8, 1976, the Roman papers were full of stories about Roberto. Ingrid was in Rome, but she pretended that she was leaving for Paris that day. In the evening Isabella and Isotta took Roberto to his favorite restaurant for a quiet dinner. And there, seated around a U-shaped table covered with fake dollars and lire, sat everyone—Ingrid; Roberto's first wife; his sister; his eldest son; his nieces; the grandchildren—everyone except Robertino, who was in Paris working for Lars.

Roberto took the menu from the white-coated waiter. This was a matter of importance, and he concentrated on the lengthy bill of fare.

"Papa! It's me," the waiter shouted finally. "Papa! It's me, Robertino."

They had always been a family of the great moments—Ingrid jetting in for a few days, Roberto descending on the home like a traveling circus in town for a one-night stand. If that life had often served the children poorly, it served the family well now that they were adults, and their visits together were so often a time of memorializing.

The past was always with Ingrid now. She decided to let Alan Burgess write her authorized biography, sharing the royalties with him. She had known the BBC journalist since she starred in *The Inn of the Sixth Happiness*, based on his book. He was a witty raconteur and she enjoyed her hours with him. Burgess, however, was not the only one who thought he was going to write Ingrid's book. Joe Steele had received a promise from Ingrid as well. As Steele looked forward to the project, he did not know that on the other side of the Atlantic, work on Ingrid's official biography had begun. Ingrid was good at forgetting, and besides, she felt that Joe was getting old and quirky, and was in no condition to write a book.

First, Ingrid had to go through all the papers and clippings and copies of letters that she had kept all these years, and were stored at Choisel. To help her she had Pavo Turtiainen, a young Finn who had worked on and off for her and Lars since 1970. Lars had plucked Pavo out of a restaurant in Helsinki when he served their table impeccably one day. Pavo was a meticulous, infinitely discreet young man, and he worked alongside Ingrid all day.

Ingrid decided to start with the pictures. That would be easiest. Then they began going through the letters, and other material. After two months it became too much for Ingrid—too many memories, too many faded, yellow yesterdays. "I can't look at it anymore," Ingrid said. She left Pavo alone, to spend two more months organizing the files.

"I'll give you a tape recorder and when you wake up at night you can speak into it," Burgess told Ingrid.

"What, Alan, without an audience?" Ingrid laughed. She enjoyed talking about her past, and if she was going to do it in a book, she wanted Burgess there, listening, asking questions. And so they began spending many hours and many days together, as Ingrid reminisced.

In the fall of 1976, Ingrid flew to New York for a visit. Isabella was living there now, working for Italian television as a journalist. One evening Ingrid and Isabella went to Warren Thomas's apartment on the upper West Side to attend a thirtieth-anniversary party for the Alvin Gang. Warren's apartment was a shrine to Ingrid. And Ingrid's greatest fan considered it a miracle that she would come to his home. He was the anointed, chosen out of the ranks of fandom, and he was aghast that some of the others did not know how to behave. One of the old Alvin Gang members kept taking Ingrid's picture. Another member, Eleanor, was too shy even to appear, as if to see Ingrid in the flesh might destroy her image. Warren was a kind man, and he arranged for Eleanor to shake Ingrid's hand in her limousine one evening, but as Eleanor was saying hello, other fans arrived, and Eleanor never did get her chance.

Ingrid spent much of her time pretending—that she hadn't had a mastectomy, that she was happy, that she still had a marriage. Choisel was not a home any longer, but a tomb of memories. She was still hoping that somehow things might work out, and even if they didn't, she intended living this life of illusion until the end of her days.

But now, in the spring of 1977, Kristina was pregnant. Ingrid needed Lars, and even now Lars did not want to admit that they could not go on together any longer, that it was all over.

Ingrid couldn't stand sitting at Choisel. She moved into the Raphaël, where she had lived during the days of *Tea and Sympathy*. Soon after she arrived, Roberto called her. He happened to be in Paris for a few days. When he checked into his favorite Paris hotel, the doorman had told him that Ingrid was staying there too.

Roberto was a good friend in bad times. The mere fact that Ingrid was alone in Paris told him something was wrong. He took Ingrid to dinner that evening, and he put her to bed with a hot-water bottle and aspirins. And then he took her to lunch the next day.

Roberto was strangely reticent in discussing private lives. He had been married to Ingrid. He knew her, if anything, too well. Yet he did not ask her what was wrong, why she was so depressed. And she did not tell him. He did not talk of the past or the pain of the present, but of the future, of the life that lay ahead. "Ingrid, don't ever look back," he said. "You're a nervous wreck trying to figure out what to do with the past. To hell with the past. Look ahead—go forward."

Roberto kissed Ingrid on the cheek and flew back to Italy. "Does Ingrid have any problems?" he asked Isabella, in Rome, not admitting to his daughter that he had just seen Ingrid.

"Yes, I think Lars is going to have a baby," Isabella said.

Roberto looked very sad.

"He said that Ingrid was like his daughter," says Francesca Rodolfi, Rossellini's assistant during his last years. "For Ingrid, Rossellini was the only family. The relationship was tender, like a brother and a sister. He would talk about her like a young girl."

Roberto was learning his own lessons in loneliness. He had a great hunger still for people, for noise, for discourse, for all the crying, wailing, laughing, arguing sounds of people. But for the first time in years he was without a real family. He had moved into an apartment in Parioli, across the street from Marcella, his first wife. And Marcella took care of Roberto in his last years, as she had so many years before.

Roberto asked his niece Fiorella if he could meet a group of her women friends. "Women can understand," he said. And so they arrived one evening and they talked and they laughed, Roberto and the young women, and the room was alive with voices.

Ingrid could not bear to sit around in Paris or anywhere else. She accepted the part of rich, eccentric middle-aged Helen Lancaster in N. C. Hunter's *Waters of the Moon* at the Chichester Theatre in England. The play had been a formidable West End success in the early 1950s. If it was a bit dated, there was a double draw to the summer production, for the other female lead was Wendy Hiller, one of the great actresses of the British stage.

Ingrid stayed with Ruth Roberts in a charming cottage outside town, bicycling around the countryside. After all these years, Ruth was as devoted as ever to Ingrid, but it was hard sometimes when Ingrid pretended that she was as healthy as when Ruth had first met her.

"What's the matter with her?" Hiller asked during rehearsals, when Ingrid looked terribly tired.

"She's not well, and she won't ask John Clements [the director] if she can go home."

Dame Wendy was a formidable lady who had played great roles in films and on stage. "What's the matter, Ingrid?" she asked.

"I think I have shingles," Ingrid said. "But I don't want to ask John Clements . . ."

Dame Wendy marched up to the director. "If you don't let Ingrid go home, and right now, we'll be in a right mess."

Ingrid went home to the cottage and took two days off. Roberto called one day to say he had been chosen as president of the jury of the Cannes Film Festival, an honor that Ingrid had held four years before. On Friday, June 3, 1977, when Ingrid and Ruth returned to their cottage from lunch, there was a phone message from Fiorella: "Please call Rome urgently. Children are okay."

Ingrid called Rome. Fiorella told her that Roberto had died of a heart attack. He had been in his apartment getting dressed for an appointment with the head of RAI television when he felt pain in his heart. He telephoned Marcella, and had died in her arms.

Ingrid could not face going on that evening. She could not make others laugh. She telephoned Griff in London and asked him to come down, but he said that he could not.

"I don't know how I can get on the stage, Griff," Ingrid said.

"Well, you will," he said gruffly, as if he were lecturing a young aspirant. "You have to. They don't have understudies."

Griff's great gift to Ingrid was knowing that in a time like this, a feigned lack of sympathy was the highest sympathy. The more he felt, the more he cared, the more he acted as if he didn't feel and he didn't care.

At the theater Dame Wendy didn't sense Ingrid's overwhelming distress. That was Ingrid's great performance that evening.

The next day Lars telephoned to tell her that Kristina had given birth to a baby boy. For Ingrid, the two events, the birth and the death, were linked in her mind, symbols of her aloneness.

Soon after Roberto's death, she saw a Swedish newspaper with the head-line "CONGRATULATIONS MR. SCHMIDT." As she read the words, she became angry. Ingrid had had a son born out of wedlock too. None of the papers had saluted the birth of Robertino.

Roberto left nothing but films, memories, and debts. He had 200,000 lire

($200) in the bank, not enough to bury him, and over a million dollars in debts, a monument to his golden tongue. Roberto's funeral was a great cathartic outburst that matched the drama of his life. They carried the body through the streets of the city, and they were all there—the young and the old, the Christian Democrats and the Communists, the rich and the poor, the famous and the unknown. And when they laid him to rest, they buried not only Roberto Rossellini but a whole era.

After the funeral, Isabella flew to England to be with her mother. Driving from the airport, Ingrid asked, "Do you think Father knew about Lars?"

"Yes, I told him a year ago," Isabella said.

The last time Ingrid had seen Roberto, she told him that Ingmar Bergman, the Swedish director, was planning to do a film with her. "How perfect, how right," Roberto said. "And you must make it in Swedish."

For years people had talked about Ingmar Bergman directing his compatriot in a film. They were the best-known Swedish artists in the world. They were of the same generation, from a country so small that it sometimes seemed like one great village. Indeed, Ingmar's father, Erik Bergman, a prominent Lutheran minister, had confirmed Ingrid when she was a little girl, and baptized Pia. He was a minister who in his sermons could invoke terrifying images of damnation and salvation in a phrase.

There was a demoniac quality to Ingmar Bergman. He brought to the screen the dark magic that the theater arts had once known, when the public feared actors, suspecting them of witchcraft. He could invoke terrifying images of damnation and salvation on a reel of film. In 1960, when Ingrid first saw Ingmar's *The Virgin Spring*, she found it "beautiful in the beginning but at the end . . . heavy and brutal. But as always his films stay in your mind for days, while others are gone the minute the picture ends."

As a young director Ingmar had known all about the legendary Ingrid Bergman, Hollywood's great star. He had seen her films and been "fascinated by her face . . . the skin, the eyes, the mouth—especially the mouth—there was this very strange radiance and an enormous erotic attraction." He had seen her in person in the early days of her marriage to Lars, one winter in a hotel suite in Stockholm. "She came in loaded with packages and with a high coloring," he remembered, "and I had exactly the same feeling from the first moment: a very strong erotic attraction and she was very beautiful."

If most directors had met such an actress they would have wanted to work with her right away. But Ingmar worked only with what he considered real actors. "There are an awful lot of people going around playing in films and the theater in the absolutely worst sense of the word," he said. "They haven't the least talent for acting, but they get by on the strength of their personalities and some special radiation which is extremely hard to define—a form of sensuality, I think, that makes the camera marry them and the audience love them."

In the years since Ingmar met Ingrid in Stockholm, he saw her only once in a play. "She was not very good," he says. "She performed like an enthusiastic amateur."

This was the Ingrid Bergman whom Ingmar asked to be in his film *Autumn Sonata*, playing Charlotte, a world-famous pianist, returning to visit her daughter after a long absence. Many of the others in the cast had appeared with Bergman before. They were part of an ensemble company unique in filmmaking. Liv Ullmann played Charlotte's daughter, Eva. Liv and Ingmar's own daughter, Linn, born during their long relationship, played Eva as a child. Among those with small roles were Gunnar Björnstrand, who had been a classmate of Ingrid's at the Swedish Royal Dramatic School; she had acted with Björnstrand before in a short episode based on the Guy de Maupassant story "The Necklace" in the eight-part film *Stimulantia* in 1967. There was also Mimi Pollak, who had been a good friend of Ingrid's since the days of her marriage to Lars.

The production manager, whose name also happened to be Ingrid Bergman, was Ingmar's wife. His former wife, Käbi Laretei, a concert pianist, played the Chopin prelude that Charlotte and Eva play in the film.

When Ingrid first saw the script for *Autumn Sonata*, she was less than impressed. She met Mimi Pollak soon after reading it, and turned her thumb down.

Charlotte is a totally self-absorbed artist, whose art has crowded out everything else in her life. A woman of monumental hubris, she has sought perfection in her art that she cannot find in daily life. Years before, she left her chronically ill child in a home. And she has not visited even her other healthy daughter for seven years.

"Look, the script is terribly depressing," Ingrid told Ingmar when they discussed the project. "In life I have three real daughters, and we do have our little *discussions* from time to time—but this! Can't we have a little joke here and there?"

"No. No jokes. We're not doing *your* story. Her name is Charlotte, the world-famous pianist."

"But seven years without seeing her daughters? I mean! And one of them is paralyzed and almost dying. It's unbelievable."

There are those close to both Ingrid and Ingmar who claim that he wrote Charlotte with Ingrid's life in mind. There is something of Ingrid in Charlotte, but the knowledge of a musician's life comes in part from Käbi Laretei. In Charlotte's affair, there is a hint of his own mother, who was profoundly attracted to a man outside her marriage. And there is surely something of Ingmar himself, an artistic egotist like Charlotte, molding actors to his purpose and will as if he were writing a novel.

Though there is much of Ingrid in Charlotte, Charlotte is not Ingrid. Ingrid did not have Charlotte's self-knowledge. Nor did she have her strength of will. And never in her life was she confronted with the reality of her being, as Charlotte was in *Autumn Sonata*.

Charlotte struck closer to Ingrid's emotional center than any character she had ever played. The role was the greatest challenge in Ingrid's acting career, not only emotionally but physically. She would be acting the part of a strong, willful woman in the full bloom of health, at a time when her own doctor had discovered a mysterious enlarged gland under her right arm. She would be acting in Swedish, without even the shield of an acquired language between herself and the character. She would be acting with a proud, disciplined group of actors who knew one another as well as they knew their lines. And she would be directed by Ingmar Bergman, a man who she had been told was "diabolical to work with."

Ingrid had spent most of her career entertaining people. With Roberto she had tried to make a different sort of film, but he treated actors like puppets with wooden hearts and sawdust souls. She had never had to reach down into herself.

In early September, Ingrid flew to Stockholm to begin rehearsals at the Swedish Film Institute. The year before, Ingmar had felt humiliated by Swedish tax authorities, who removed him from the Royal Dramatic Theater and temporarily withdrew his passport. He had vowed never to make a film in Sweden again. And so, while the film was being rehearsed for two weeks in Sweden, the shooting would be at Norsk film studios in Oslo.

On the day Ingrid arrived for the first rehearsal, the rest of the cast of *Autumn Sonata* was already there, looking as theatrical as a school board meeting. Ingmar was seated at the long conference table in a blue sweater vest, with paunch, balding pate, and horn-rimmed glasses. Liv Ullmann, the best-known of the actors, had the face of a woman who spilled punch at her junior prom, and years later still remembered the ignominy of that evening. Ingrid appeared an almost dowdy, matronly woman, looking all of her sixty-two years. There was a manliness to her now, a largeness in her body and gesture and step. She had a deep, cigarette smoker's voice, as if her vocal cords had been seared by flames.

Ingmar had decided to add a dimension: to film the filming, make a documentary film about the making of *Autumn Sonata*, a Bergman film within the Bergman film. And thus the actors were playing themselves, acting when they were not acting.

Ingrid waited hardly an hour before she did what she usually did at the beginning of a film. She began to test her director. This time, though, she did it with a civilized fierceness, as if she were protecting more than her role.

"In a way, she didn't understand," Ingmar says. "She didn't have that much imagination. She had this idea that 'I am Ingrid Bergman.' The first days were horrible. She had planned the whole performance. She had planned it in detail. So when I told her, You can't do it this way, she was furious.

"It frightened her. All actors are frightened, all good actors, and Ingrid was really a good actor. Good actors know that they have to go deep inside to find the real emotions and feelings. It's the only way. She found it impossible. She went to a limit and objected to go beyond the limit. I had to take her with me by hand and by violence. We were fighting all the time. Sometimes it was very tiring. She knew what she wanted and I knew what I wanted. I had to tell her, This is not you. This is the pianist."

At the end of the first reading that first day, Liv Ullmann went into the next room and cried. She was sure that the film would not work out. Ingmar knew Liv as well as one artist can know another, and he came into the room too. "I don't know what to do," he said. "Is the script bad?"

"No, it's not bad," Liv said, trying to comfort him. "And I'm sure Ingrid doesn't feel it is bad either. She's not used to your language, and you're not used to hers. But maybe you will get used to each other."

The life and blood and fury of the film is the relationship between Charlotte and Eva. Most of the rehearsal days were spent working with Ingrid and Liv. In their great climactic scene, the daughter confronts the mother with the realities of her life. Charlotte is devastated. Complaining of her back, she lies down on the floor, and there begins her soliloquy.

"If I lie down on the floor the audience will laugh," Ingrid said, as if it were Ingrid Bergman on the floor, not Charlotte.

"A pianist when he has a pain lies on the floor," Ingmar said.

"We were talking about life and death and now I'm supposed to lie down. I feel very awkward."

"That's exactly how you're supposed to feel."

Ingmar did not let up. "You lie down on the floor and you take your stuff with you."

"And then, 'I remember hardly anything from my childhood,' Ingrid said, reading the script. "I wonder about that part. Doesn't anyone remember something from their childhood? Couldn't I just say I remember very little from my childhood. It seems a little better."

"Yes, you can say that," Ingmar said. "I think it differs a lot with different people. It's very common that people block it."

"I don't remember anything before eight or nine," Liv said.

"I remember very well from childhood," Ingrid said proudly. "I remember everything."

"What she means is from three or four years," Ingmar said, returning to the script.

"But it's still better to say, 'I remember very little,' " Ingrid insisted.

Lying on the floor, Ingrid spoke her lines:

"Nay, I remember so little about my childhood. Neither parent could express affection. Touching was forbidden either as a punishment or as a caress. I was very ignorant about anything that might pertain to love, intimacy, contact, nearness, warmth.

"I found my outlet in music. There was no other place for emotions to show. At times when I lie awake at night, I wonder whether I have really lived. . . . I'm older, face and body both aged. I've memories and I've acquired experience and inside all that is just a void."

On the day of the wardrobe tests, there was another camera in the room. This was the real camera, not the documentary camera, the interloper that had been there since the day Ingrid arrived. And when the new camera focused on her, she seemed to burst into life and color. She looked like a movie star, or a world-famous pianist off to visit her daughter.

Finally they traveled to Oslo and another scene familiar to Ingrid: a press conference. Ingrid, Ingmar, Liv, and Sven Nykvist, the cameraman, sat on the platform before fifty or so reporters. Ingrid had almost always been the center of attention at such gatherings, but it was Ingmar who was asked most of the questions. Ingrid sat smoking Gauloises, her hands betraying her nervousness.

The reporters were soon gone, and Ingrid and the others settled down on the set, alone with the camera and the script. There were only fifteen people in the whole production company, two thirds of them women. They hurried around quietly, efficiently, while Ingmar went to work. The set was closed, not only to visitors, but to life outside its confines.

For forty days the cast and crew were together, like mountaineers in a tent during a great storm. Ingrid became friendly with several of the women in the crew, but still she was somehow isolated from the others.

She had never had a part that demanded so much of her. Ingmar coaxed, wooed, led her into herself, using the camera as an instrument of violation. In one scene Ingrid lay on crumpled sheets in bed. Next to her lay Lena Nyman, playing her catatonic daughter, Helena. If people were sick in Ingrid Bergman films, they were sick as she had been in *The Bells of St. Mary's*, with tuberculosis, a few coughs on the screen; or maybe some picturesque alcoholism, as in *Notorious* and *Under Capricorn*.

But this was the kind of disease that Ingrid had never faced on screen or in life, messy and ugly. It was a disease that confronted Charlotte's own humanity as a mean and terrible challenge, God's dark joke. Nyman's performance was so strong, so terrifying in its realism, that it did not seem that she was an actress at all. Lying there on the rumpled sheets was this horrifying, hopeless creature who reached out to life in blathering, salivating, half-human sounds.

Ingrid was sweating. Above, the camera pressed upon her. Above that camera stood the documentary camera. She lay there, trying to control her emotions, as if she could not stand to be touched. Suddenly, she heard a sharp, clanging sound. Someone had dropped something. Ingrid jumped up, her nerves half shattered.

Ingrid and Ingmar sat on a sofa, talking.
"I live on borrowed time," she said.
Ingrid had never mentioned her illness before. Ingmar knew that it was

hard for Ingrid, especially at night. Lars had called and said that it was very bad, and asked him please to hurry; Ingrid needed another operation.

Ingmar pared the script down. He cut three weeks out of the shooting. He decided that they would use a double for the outside shooting, so that Ingrid wouldn't have to go on location. But he could not cut down on the emotions of the film itself. He could not cut down on what he was demanding of Ingrid.

Now it was time finally to shoot the climactic confrontation scene between mother and daughter. It is after midnight, the hour of truth. In the dark of night, the two women confront each other. Mousy little Eva rises in a paroxysm of wrath, and with brutal words strikes down her prideful, self-possessed mother, battering her with the truths of their relationship. Ingrid tried the scene again and again, but she couldn't quite grasp it. She didn't understand such confrontation, such brutal truth. She didn't understand her own reaction as Charlotte, begging her daughter for forgiveness and love, totally exposed. She had never pleaded for love or forgiveness. When she accepted blame, she usually did it proudly, as a burden that she could lift without thought or worry.

"Now, Ingmar, you have to explain this scene to me!" she said, her voice rising in anger. "You can't let me down like this. You must explain it to me. I can't do this scene. You must give me a reason."

Ingmar stood up and walked toward Ingrid. "If you had been in a concentration camp, you'd say *anything* for help!" the director said angrily.

Ingrid, finally, understood "the hopelessness and depths of my defeat and despair."

Ingmar shot the scene.

"People like you are a menace," Liv said, in her role as Eva. "You should be locked away so you can't do any harm."

As Liv spoke, accusing her mother of abandoning Helena in a nursing home, Ingrid's face was red, as if shame were a color. "Look at me, Mama," Liv said. "There can only be a single truth and a single lie. There can be no forgiveness."

"You can't say I'm entirely to blame," Ingrid said.

"You want exclusive rights. Concessions are ruses for you. You've managed to set up a discount system of life. One day you're bound to find out that your agreement is all on your side. You must come to realize you've been harboring guilt like everyone else."

"What . . . what guilt?" Ingrid said. Her eyes were wet with tears, and her face was as damp as if tears were flowing out of her very skin. "Dearest Eva, can you find it in your heart to show forgiveness. I'll try to change myself. You'll teach me. We'll take time with each other. But help me. I can't go on any longer. Your hatred is so terrible. I haven't realized how—how selfish and childish I've been. Can't you hug me? Or if you would touch me at least. Help me!"

*   *   *

"Ingrid was an anarchist, an erratic anarchist," says Ingmar. "When she took away any makeup and showed her naked face in the midnight scene, that was the anarchist. That was the anarchist who doesn't think of seeing her past face.

"I remember one day Liv and Ingrid standing in front of a mirror, staring at themselves. It was a time when they were both looking terrible. Ingrid said, 'I don't think Liv and I will have any more engagements, but you and Sven will have your awards.' "

CHAPTER TWENTY-TWO

"Oh, Wendy,
It's Only a Play"

*I*mmediately after her last scene in *Autumn Sonata*, Ingrid flew to London. In a few weeks the lump under her arm had grown as big as an egg. She was put in the hospital, where she remained only three days, long enough to have the growth removed, and to learn that it was malignant.

Each morning Griff took her in a taxi to Middlesex for a nine o'clock appointment. "She'd enter through this door that said 'Nuclear Medicine' and she'd emerge a half hour later," Griff says. Inside, Ingrid lay under a supervoltage X-ray machine that generated 22 million electron volts. Then Griff took her by another taxi to the ten-thirty rehearsals at the Phoenix Theatre for the West End revival of N. C. Hunter's *Waters of the Moon*. Ingrid played Helen Lancaster, a rich, spoiled woman whose Rolls-Royce becomes stuck in a snowdrift, marooning her, along with her husband and daughter.

Griff never asked what happened behind the door marked "Nuclear Medicine" and Ingrid never told him. If anything, Griff joked even more mercilessly with Ingrid, chiding her, putting her down. Griff could not imagine *his* Ingrid ever faltering, ever being dreadfully sick, ever dying. But he watched over her during the long hours of rehearsals, never letting her know how closely.

Actors can be merciless in their self-absorption, and when Ingrid grew terribly fatigued, the others hardly noticed. Ingrid said nothing, but continued as best she could. It was Griff who walked quietly over to Patrick Garland, the director. "Patrick, I think you should finish now, for Ingrid is getting rather tired."

Though Ingrid was alone now, she still had Lars. She had made up with him, and had met Kristine and the baby. Lars still managed her money and property, and took care of all the details she had never been able to manage. She talked to him practically every day. Once, from Los Angeles, she called him in Paris to ask how much she should tip at her hotel. Lars pointed out that Ingrid's phone call would cost more than any tip, but Ingrid wanted to leave knowing that she had done the right thing.

Ingrid did have a new man in her life, John Van Eyssen, an American film executive living in London. Van Eyssen was a civilized, solicitous divorcé who made few demands on Ingrid. "Obviously, I loved her," Van Eyssen says. "We had a wonderful relationship. We laughed a great deal. I thought of her as a great marvelous person. The big laugh. She bore no grudges. She bore no ill will. If people didn't like her, *tant pis*. If things were really bad she would laugh."

The opening night tryout at Brighton was one of those dreadful evenings that make actors such a superstitious breed. Everything went wrong. At the end of the first act, Wendy Hiller was supposed to play the piano while Ingrid and the rest of the cast danced. Hiller plunked her fingers on the piano keys, setting off a deafening silence. She started again, but still the tape machine didn't supply the music. The audience began whispering.

"I'm terribly sorry, but the piano does not seem to work," Ingrid said. "Please forgive us, but we have to bring the curtain down for a moment."

The next day Garland and the cast went through a postmortem discussion. Wendy Hiller was three years older than Ingrid, but even at sixty-five she was the eternal perfectionist. She, too, had portrayed Joan of Arc, but it had been Shaw's Saint Joan, the old playwright himself having chosen her. She had played O'Neill, Shakespeare, and Ibsen, played them brilliantly, and she was not about to be embarrassed in front of a Brighton audience. She fumed with anger.

"Oh, Wendy," Ingrid said quietly. "It's only a play."

When *Waters of the Moon* opened at the Haymarket Theatre on January 26, 1978, the tape recorder was working, and the play became the great new hit of the season. Wendy received better notices than Ingrid, but it was for Ingrid that there were lines at the box office. The two actresses were forever joking about Wendy's notices and Ingrid's fans. One day early in the run, Wendy came up to Ingrid in her dressing room. "If anyone stops me in the street again and says, 'Ah, Miss Hiller, isn't it a lovely play and isn't Miss Bergman beautiful,' I shall say Miss Bergman is not beautiful. She's a dreadful woman and terrible to play with." The next day Ingrid handed her co-star an azalea, from "the dreadful Bergman woman."

Ingrid went to the front of the Haymarket, where the management had posted quotes from critics celebrating Wendy's performance. She had herself photographed sneering as broadly as a villain in a silent film, and distributed the picture to Wendy and other members of the company.

Like most actors in London, Ingrid had always wanted to play the Haymarket, a historic 1820 building. With its exquisite portico, crystal chandeliers, gold leaf, and blue upholstery, the Haymarket is the most elegant dramatic theater in all London. Backstage, however, is a very different sort of relic of the nineteenth century, quarters so threadbare and cramped that they seem to propel the actors on stage to their relief. For her dressing room Ingrid had chosen not the star's quarter, number 10, upstairs, but number 1, downstairs, a rectangular room the size of a small bedroom. The austere white and cream-colored dressing room was lit by two lamps hanging on cords from old gas fixtures. Outside her door, the bare wooden staircase looked almost worn through.

On matinee days, Ingrid and Griff went to dinner together at a little Italian pizza restaurant that they had discovered. Usually, before the performance, she sat in her dressing room, writing letters, chatting with Griff or members of the company.

Louie was seventy years old and retired. But she had come back to serve "my lady." As her dresser, Louie knew about Ingrid's illness, but she never said anything, and tried to be as chipper and gay as always. She had been there the day Ruth Roberts had come, and after Ruth left, seen Ingrid sitting on the floor crying, looking at her pictures in their silver frames: her mother, her father, her aunt.

"Louie, they're all dead," Ingrid said.

"What was wrong with them?" Louie asked.

"Cancer."

"I do hope that you dodge it," Louie said. "We don't want that."

Although Ingrid and Wendy kept up their good-natured repartee, the British actress found it frustrating to work with Ingrid. Wendy had no star persona. When she trundled off to Buckinghamshire after a performance, pushing her way through the fans waiting primarily to see Ingrid, it might have been the nice old lady who ran the teashop on the corner. Hiller was her role. When she was at her best, in a great role in a great play, the audience knew that it was seeing something that was born and lived and died within the time span of a performance.

Hiller needed the disciplining confines of a script. She needed a director who had shaped the play. She needed to work with actors who knew their lines and followed the director's biddings. Now, on this great stage where she had appeared five times before, with some of the greatest actors in the British theater, she was acting with Ingrid, out of whose mouth came the most peculiar words and phrases, and who wandered the stage like Ahab.

"It was a bit of a dicey situation," Wendy says, "telling an international star for God's sake keep still."

It was Griff, the company manager and Ingrid's dear friend, to whom Wendy confided. Griff spoke to Ingrid, but his admonitions only seemed to make it worse.

After one performance in which Ingrid had uttered several lines of gibberish, Wendy called Patrick Garland. "You must come in," the actress said. "She's speaking Chinese again."

The director came to the Haymarket to talk to his star. Ingrid only laughed. "I had a chat with Lars in the morning and spoke Swedish. The children came in the afternoon and I spoke Italian. And my French friends came in the early evening. I just got quickly through the play and went to bed."

Garland had directed enough plays in his day to know that even if Ingrid forgot half her lines, the audience hardly cared. After one performance, an American director came to congratulate Garland. "It was a beautiful play," he said. "And what a wonderful idea to have that pin spotlight on Ingrid during the entire play. This one figure always emblazed by a tiny spotlight."

"But there wasn't any spotlight," Garland said.

Garland had learned from Griff that Ingrid had cancer. "If she has a period of fatigue, understand," Griff said. Garland knew all the jokes about Ingrid forgetting her lines during *The Constant Wife*, and he could hardly believe that she was sick. She had such vitality.

A few days before the played closed, Louie was helping Ingrid into her last-act costume. As she always did, Ingrid took hold of her dresser's shoulder, to steady herself. Louie saw that Ingrid's face was clenched in a grimace.

"Whatever is the matter?" Louie asked.

"It's started again," Ingrid said, feeling the pain that she had hoped was gone forever. This time, however, she felt it somewhere new in her body, in her right breast.

Ingrid had always experienced the end of a play or a film like a death in the family. *Waters of the Moon* could truly be her last play. On Saturday evening, July 1, 1978, the house was full, as it had been full from the first night. At the end the audience applauded as if by the sheer force of their appreciation they could make the evening last forever. But the applause finally died down, and the curtain closed for good, and Ingrid walked back to her dressing room.

Louie was busy packing things away. She could see that Ingrid "seemed out of it, she was in such a state." Louie folded the hand towels that she had brought in for Ingrid to use.

"Don't do that, Louie," Ingrid said. "Don't do that, little Lou."

Louie stopped working. Ingrid took off her makeup and dressed. Ingrid said goodbye to the rest of the cast, embracing them and wishing them well. Finally they were gone too.

"Why don't you go home?" Louie said.

"No, I don't want to."

The car that was supposed to take Ingrid home did not arrive. She walked back into the theater to see the Haymarket a last time. She expected to see the stage all dark and quiet, but there was a flurry of activity, as the stagehands struck the sets. In her whole life in the theater, she had never seen this. In a few hours, all the props and fixtures that had defined her life for months would be carted off. The new sets would go up, and Monday evening there would be a whole new world on the stage.

"I didn't know all this went on," she told Griff.

Anthony Peek, the deputy theater manager, came out and sat with Ingrid for a while. Peek talked about how successful the play had been, six months without an empty seat. He told her of the Japanese tourists who had attended, to see her and hear her voice, though they could not understand a word. Ingrid stored such compliments in her memory the way she pasted clippings in scrapbooks. But memories are memories, even those as fresh as this evening's performance. Soon the stage was bare. The stagehands were gone. It was time to dim the lights.

Soon after the play closed, Ingrid entered the Harley Street Clinic. When Dr. William Slack opened her right breast, he found that it was malignant and he performed a mastectomy. Once again Ingrid made her daily journeys to the Middlesex Hospital for radiotherapy. She felt better. Nevertheless, the doctors made her cancel her American tour of *Waters of the Moon*, and the news of her illness was out.

Ingrid had nothing but time now, and perhaps not very much time at all. For the first period of her life, Ingrid had her own place. "She was very happy to be alone," says Fiorella. "She said, 'Now I understand.' "

Ingrid had bought a red-brick town house, at No. 9 Cheney Gardens in Chelsea. Her duplex was reached by a small private elevator. The apartment itself was pleasantly, if rather plainly, furnished, with Ingrid's three Oscars the most notable adornment in the living room.

Like Greenwich Village in New York City, Chelsea is both a classy, up-scale residential neighborhood and a bohemian hangout. Down the street, Ingrid had a dressmaker, a greengrocer, the Beehive Pub, and the Bow Tie Café, an establishment whose only distinction was its name. She was a block from a walk along the Thames. Kings Road was only two blocks away. That's where the bus came, and where she loved to walk, looking at the outrageous clothes in store windows, and at the outrageous young people, with their purple hair and chains.

In October, Ingrid flew to New York to dub *Autumn Sonata* into English. She spent time with Pia, who was a theater and film critic for NBC-TV. Ingrid's visit with her eldest daughter in her spacious apartment on Central Park West was not quite like a scene from *Autumn Sonata*. But the pain and memories were still terribly alive.

"Mother thought she was going to live in New York for a while," says Isabella. "Pia said, 'You can always stay here.' But Pia said that Mother complained that the children didn't eat with a knife and fork or didn't eat vegetables. Apparently there was some sort of tension. Pia said that next time you come maybe you should stay at a hotel.

"In order to help Pia with the furnishings, Mother bought her a sofa bed. Pia felt she did it because she wanted to be there. Mother was hurt when it was sent back. Mother cried, saying that she made a mistake. And then she got a letter saying, 'I don't want you.' I called Pia. I was open with her. Pia said, 'I sent it back because it was like I was greedy. It wasn't meant to be a slap in the face.'

"But it was a big commotion and Mother cried. Everyone cried."

The children knew that their mother was dying, and the great unspeakable was not cancer but their inheritance. There was apprehension that the assets, valued finally at more than four million dollars, might end up unfairly distributed.

Even since Ingrid's divorce, Lars had continued to manage his ex-wife's business affairs. He had a shrewd awareness of tax and investment law, and Ingrid's moneys were kept in sheltered corporations and Swiss banks. She owned nothing personally, not even her London town house. There were others, including Ann Todd, who talked to Ingrid about putting her financial affairs in good order so that her children would receive their due. In the end, the children inherited about a million dollars apiece.

For her role in *Autumn Sonata*, Ingrid received a level and intensity of praise unique in her career. The critics rhapsodized not over her persona on the screen but over her performance. Ingrid was nominated for an Academy Award as best actress; had she won, she would have been the only person ever to have received four Academy Awards for acting. She had plenty of solace, including the New York Film Critics Award as best actress and the Donatello, Italy's version of the Oscar.

In the spring of 1979, Ingrid flew to Hollywood. Jean Renoir had died a few weeks earlier, and she was driven up to Benedict Canyon to see his widow. She went out to the Motion Picture Home and visited Joe Steele, sneaking him some whiskey.

Steele's great final dream had been to redo his biography of Ingrid, leaving a financial and literary legacy. He thought he had Ingrid's approval and cooperation, but she had gone on with her own project. And Steele and his collaborator, Bill Davidson, lost their publisher. Although Ingrid reportedly helped Steele financially, he felt betrayed, and without the project to sustain him he deteriorated rapidly and died.

In Los Angeles, Ingrid participated in an evening in which the American Film Institute gave Alfred Hitchcock its Lifetime Achievement Award. She had expected to say a few words, introduce a few people, and sit down, but the day before, George Stevens, Jr., the director, told her that she would be mistress of ceremonies. It was not the kind of thing she liked to do, especially at the last moment. But it was Hitch, and they pushed and pushed, and she agreed.

On the evening of the tribute, Ben Benjamin, an ICM agent who handled Ingrid's affairs in Hollywood, drove to the Beverly Wilshire Hotel to pick Ingrid up. Benjamin called Ingrid's suite, and she said that she needed some help from his wife, Carla, who was waiting in the car. So Carla Benjamin went to Ingrid's suite and found her there unable to finish hooking her dress. Carla knew now that Ingrid was sicker than anyone in Hollywood imagined. Ingrid finished dressing, spread a shawl over her shoulders, and walked with stately cadence through the lobby.

They were all there that evening at the Beverly Hilton Hotel. The old stars and the new stars. Cary Grant. James Stewart. Jane Wyman. Olivia de Havilland. Christopher Reeve. Walter Matthau. Michael Caine. Barbra Streisand. And Hitchcock. Seventy-nine-year-old Hitchcock had a pacemaker, arthritis, a drinking problem, and was more than a hundred pounds overweight. He waddled into the International Ballroom in tiny mincing steps, like a child just learning to walk, his scowl lost in the jowls of his face. It seemed a merciless act to have brought him here. He sat down between Alma, his invalid wife, and Cary Grant at a dinner table that included Ingrid, James Stewart, Sidney Bernstein, and Lew Wasserman of ICM. They were all old friends, but Hitchcock sat as if alone, his face devoid of emotion.

As mistress of ceremonies, Ingrid was an ebullient, radiant presence. Looking at her and then looking at Hitchcock, it was like looking at life and death, youth and age. Through most of the evening Hitchcock rarely stirred out of his somnolence. At the end, when he had received his award and made his little speech, Ingrid spoke a last time.

"We must leave you now, but thanks to film, Hitch's work never will," she said. "Now there's just one little thing I want to add before we finish this evening."

Ingrid looked down at Hitch.

"You remember that agonizing shot when you had built some kind of elevator. It was a basket or something with you and the cameraman. And you were shooting this vast party in *Notorious*. And you came zooming down with your elevator and all the way down into my hand, where you saw the key in a close-up.

"Now, well, you know that Cary stole that key after the scene. Yes. And he kept it. He kept it for about ten years. And one day he put it in my hand. And he said, 'I've kept this long enough. Now it's for you. For good luck.' I've kept it for twenty years. And in this very same hand there is the key."

As Ingrid held the key up, the audience applauded. Even Hitchcock struck his hands together. Then Ingrid had a terrible realization. She was holding up the wrong key.

"It has given me a lot of good luck and quite a few good movies too. And now I'm going to give it to you with a prayer that it will open some very good doors for you too. God bless you, dear Hitch. I'm coming to give you the key."

Ingrid swept down and across the room as she had in so many movies. She hugged Hitchcock and as she gave him the key, the old man smiled.

Afterward, Ingrid mailed Hitchcock the right key, along with an apology. In his earlier days Hitchcock would have found the mix-up richly amusing, an anecdote to be told and retold. But he did not answer the letter. She wrote him a second letter, and a third. Finally he replied with a one-line message: "I got the key."

A few months later, when Ingrid returned to Hollywood, she went once again to visit Hitchcock. "He took my hands," she said, "and tears streamed down his face and he said, 'Ingrid I'm going to die,' and I said, 'But of course you are going to die sometime, Hitch—we are all going to die.' And then I told him that I, too, had recently been very ill, and that I had thought about it too. And for a moment the logic of that seemed to make him more peaceful."

In July 1979, Ingrid had a visit from Petter. He was cooperating with Alan Burgess on Ingrid's biography, giving him material, letters, and countless interviews. Burgess had come highly recommended by George and Phyllis Seaton, and the British journalist had, in Petter's words, "somehow become a sort of 'father confessor' for both sides."

"As soon as Petter knew I was writing a book about Ingrid Bergman, he was interested in meeting her," Burgess says. "I said to Ingrid, 'Would you like to meet him?' She said, 'I don't know. I suppose so.' "

According to Petter, Burgess had asked him to meet with Ingrid, at her request. He says, "I knew that if I said no it would be in the papers that Dr. Lindstrom refused to see his former wife who is ill with cancer."

At times, Petter could be hopelessly naive about human relationships, trusting people without restraint or full understanding, then coming to distrust them. He had already heard rumors that Ingrid had editorial control over the book, but Burgess kept insisting that Petter would have *his* say. And he continued to give the author information and assistance, seeking his vindication in what in fact was Ingrid's authorized biography.

Ingrid was not alone when Petter entered her London town house one July afternoon. Burgess was there as well, because Ingrid feared that it might be an unpleasant reunion, filled with accusations and recriminations. Ingrid and Petter seemed to hit it off so well that Burgess soon made his exit.

Petter was seated alone with Ingrid in her living room. In his briefcase he carried two bottles of wine, some special sandwiches that he had brought for their lunch, and an old newspaper clipping. He insisted to Ingrid that she had met Pia in 1953 and 1955 as well as 1951, but Ingrid insisted that she had not. Ingrid listened to Petter though she was not interested in what she considered old battles and ancient wounds.

They got along well enough. Indeed, Ingrid invited him to return a second afternoon. The second day, Petter looked at Ingrid's swollen arm and suggested that she wear a stockinette. After his visit he wrote her, enclosing samples of stockinettes, and recent photos of Stöde, where they had married so many years before. He addressed her as "Dear Grandma" and offered her more medical information: "The swelling and edema of an arm after the kind of treatment you have had is caused by obstruction or coagulation of veins and lymph vessels and therefore the swelling might come and go."

Petter wrote about their past together as well, confronting Ingrid once again with matters such as the Capa and Adler affairs, Pia's trips to London, and the details of the Messina meeting. "It is understandable if some of the details and dates of the past are not so clear to us," he wrote. "In the past I never published anything to correct the abundant interviews published to make me look rather despicable. However, it seemed best to clarify a few issues that came up at our recent meetings in London."

Ingrid answered Petter's letter immediately, writing in longhand on airmail paper. She did not view their mutual past as if she were a historian, arguing data, facts, and detail. She regarded her past as her lover, to be enjoyed, reminisced about. As she always did with what was unpleasant and tedious, Ingrid pushed it aside, and got on with better matters. She didn't even mention Petter's questions. She thanked him for sending recent photos of Stöde, where they had married so many years before; "Stöde is just as I remember it when we drove up there the first time."

Ingrid filled that summer with travel so that, as she wrote Petter, she had no time for illness. In August she went to Sweden and traveled by train, bus, and ferryboat, and not only to Danholmen but to Stockholm.

Her children's lives were moving on, and that gave her more occasions, more places to travel. Isotta was pregnant. Then Isabella called to say that she was planning to marry Martin Scorsese, the Italian-American film director. Isabella had met Scorsese when she interviewed him in New York City, as part of her work for Italian television. Scorsese was a great admirer of Isabella's father, and the two of them quickly became involved.

"Does he move you?" Ingrid asked.

"What do you mean?" Isabella asked.

"Does he *move* you?" Ingrid asked again.

"Yes, Mother, he moves me completely."

"I told you, I think, that Isabella is getting married Sept. 30," Ingrid wrote Petter. "So are all my three girls out of the nest—well, three wasn't much of a nest."

When the newlyweds flew into London, they met Ingrid at her town house. Scorsese's director friends Steven Spielberg and George Lucas happened to be in town too. Scorsese invited them to come along to meet the woman he described only as "my wife's mother." When the men walked into the living room, they were stunned to discover that Isabella's mother was Ingrid Bergman. After being introduced to Ingrid and her friend Ann Todd, they sat down and said very little.

Neither Ingrid nor Ann realized that these silent bearded young men were among the biggest talents in the new Hollywood, responsible for *Jaws*, *Star Wars*, and other films. After all, they didn't look the way directors were supposed to look. Spielberg was in cowboy boots, and might have been a grip, a prop man, or a gofer.

Scorsese had grown up in New York's Little Italy, and he affected the rude demeanor of mean streets. But not today. He was playing the good son-in-law this afternoon, trying to make small talk with Ann Todd while attempting to bring his silent friends into the conversation.

Ann Todd was Ingrid's closest female friend in London. The two actresses had a good deal in common. Both were divorced now. And each had had troubles with their children. In some respects, though, Todd was a peculiar companion. The British actress believed that "the only reality is in the World of Spirit," and was forever talking about mysticism. But the two women laughed together and spent good weekends at Todd's cottage in Suffolk. And as Ingrid became more ill, Todd felt that she had to watch out for her.

Ann was a talker herself, but she listened quietly to Scorsese's monologue, which was accelerating and crescendoing. Isabella took this as a sign that Marty was scared, terrified of Ingrid, petrified at being thrown into this tea-time socializing.

As for Todd, she had had quite enough of this Martin Scorsese and his bearded friends. She was sure that he was putting Ingrid down, treating his mother-in-law as if she were an old lady.

"Don't you give anyone a chance to talk?" Ann said angrily, interrupting a soliloquy that sounded like a machine gun attack. "Do you talk all the time, young man?"

Scorsese quieted down, and the afternoon concluded on a congenial note. But it was clear to Ingrid that her world had changed so much that sometimes she didn't understand just what was happening.

In November, Ingrid flew to Los Angeles for a tribute in her honor put on by the Variety Clubs of America to raise money for a new hospital wing. These tributes had become a minor growth industry in Hollywood, a predictable formula that was at least as calculating as it was sentimental. On the evening that Ingrid walked onto Sound Stage 9 at Warner Brothers, a formally dressed group had assembled on the old Rick's Café set.

Ingrid wore a long-sleeved, neck-high, floor-length white gown. Around her neck was a diamond-and-emerald-studded necklace worth as much as half a million dollars, a gift from Lars. This was the first time she was wearing it in public, at her former husband's insistence. Midway into the program, she received an award from the Swedish consul. He pinned the ribbon around her neck, totally covering the jewels.

"Ingrid worked very hard on her speech for the tribute," said her cousin Britt, who had flown in for the evening. "She wanted to make one big performance. During the tribute she said, 'Why is Goldie Hawn talking? I hardly talked to her during the filming of *Cactus Flower*.'"

At least Goldie Hawn had worked with Ingrid. Most of those eulogizing Ingrid knew her hardly at all. Jack Albertson was not her friend, though she had tears in her eyes as he sang to her "You Ought to Be in Pictures." Besides being Scandinavian, Victor Borge, the Danish comedian, had no relationship with Ingrid, though he performed too. Peter Falk's only connection was that he had announced the Academy Award for supporting actress the night she had won. Signe Hasso had changed the remarks prepared for her, rather than claim a closer relationship than there had been between the two Swedish actresses. Cary Grant had deep feelings for Ingrid, but he didn't even see her when he was in London.

Beyond her family there were only a few present who truly knew Ingrid. Lewis Milestone sat in a wheelchair in a corner, unable even to rise to salute her. Ruth Roberts was there, but she, too, was sickly and old.

It was forty years since Ingrid had first arrived in California, thirty years since she had left. Hollywood had changed, and the people Ingrid had known in the 1940s were for the most part dead or dying. It was not Ingrid being eulogized this evening, but a golden glorious image that even now she could step back and examine as if it were another person, her finest creation.

At the end of the evening, Ingrid got up to make her speech. "I thought I should give you a surprise," she said. "You don't know how long I have been in the film industry. You see, when my father had discovered that something new had happened and that was motion pictures, he was so enthusiastic that he went on my birthday and rented a camera that he cranked by hand."

A tiny baby in her mother's arms. A little girl on her second birthday pushing a wheelbarrow. A young mother holding her daughter. A little girl at a graveside.

"I was always polite, at least on the screen," Ingrid said. "I am three years old, coming to my mother's grave. That's why I was so happy to have those shots, so at least I can see her move."

The images flickered on. A little girl greeting her relatives from Germany. A bigger girl with her cousin Britt. Ingrid and Greta, her father's lover. A teenager getting off a small boat near her vacation home.

Ingrid spoke as proudly as if these were images from her famous movies, and she was the creator of the character on the screen. There was, indeed, a truth in these home movies beyond anything that had been said at the tribute. There had been such a feeling of warmth and family and security in the first pictures. But then the mother is dead, and the camera draws back. There are relatives and friends in the pictures, Ingrid not the center any longer. Then finally a child-woman alone in a heavy coat getting off a small boat.

"I came off a quite small boat," Ingrid said, "and ten years later I came off a much bigger boat to the harbor of New York."

While Ingrid was in Los Angeles, she and Griff went to visit the Farmer's Market. It was one of the places she had always liked in Los Angeles, one of the places she had taken Roberto. The market had become something of a tourist trap, but Ingrid ignored that, and enjoyed her lunch. During the meal Griff jumped up and ran over to a nearby newsstand. In the racks were piles of

National Enquirers with the headline "INGRID BERGMAN HAS CANCER." Griff turned the papers over and returned to the table, hoping Ingrid hadn't noticed.

On the day that Ingrid was leaving Los Angeles, she stood in front of the Beverly Wilshire. A parade of limousines and exotic cars moved up the long winding driveway to the canopied entrance of the hotel.

"Waiting for your limousine, Miss Bergman?" the doorman asked.

"I don't think it will be quite a limousine," Ingrid said.

As she spoke, a rented Ford Fiesta with a loose exhaust pipe clanked up the drive. Ingrid hopped in beside Alan Burgess, while her luggage was stored away in back, and they set off for San Diego to visit Petter.

"Where's the necklace?" Burgess asked as they drove southward on the freeway.

"I've got it with me."

Burgess gulped. "You've got it with you! A half-million-dollar necklace!"

Burgess did not feel safe until Ingrid and he had checked into the Coronado Hotel in San Diego and the Bulgari piece was in a safety-deposit box.

Ingrid had never really been invited to San Diego. A few months before, Petter had talked to Kay Brown in New York. "Kay mentioned that she and Ingrid would visit me in San Diego," Petter wrote Burgess later. "That was quite a surprise, since I had not extended any such invitation to them. Kay got a cold and couldn't come to California, but by then you telephoned me [the day before] saying that you and Ingrid were coming to visit me in San Diego. This seemed strange indeed. However, I could hardly refuse to see Ingrid if she indeed came to visit, just as I could not say no when you told me last June in London that Ingrid wanted to see me there. How would that have come out in Ingrid's interviews that her former husband, a physician and a Professor of Surgery, refused to see her when she was suffering from cancer, and when she was in his vicinity. After your arrival here with Ingrid last November, I frankly asked you why Ingrid had come to visit me. Equally frankly you answered that Ingrid wanted to see my children and wanted to include a report about her visit here in your forthcoming book. In other words, that trip of hers to San Diego was mainly for publicity reasons."

Burgess's version is that Petter had invited Ingrid's longtime agent down to San Diego after the Variety Club tribute, and Kay had assumed that Ingrid was invited as well. Burgess, moreover, says that his book was finished and he was going to San Diego to give Petter part of the manuscript to read. "I had no intention of writing about the trip," he says.

Burgess had not yet written the conclusion of the book, though. It would have been an almost irresistible bit of drama to end not with the Variety Club tribute, as he did, but with Ingrid's sentimental journey southward to Petter, and a reconciliation with her former husband. "It was my idea of getting these two people together," says Burgess. "They were both decent characters. Petter didn't object to it. He was overjoyed when she got here."

Petter was not interested in sentimental reconciliations. If he gave the impression of being "overjoyed" at seeing his ex-wife, he was disturbed at her visit. Since their divorce he had achieved what by any measure was the American dream. His second wife offered him a kind of companionship and concern that Ingrid had never given him. Not only did he have a lovely fellow doctor as a wife, three healthy, well-mannered sons and a daughter, and a home with a pool and sauna, but he was still a vital man, a practicing physician with an international reputation. He looked a good fifteen years younger than his seventy-two years, this man whom Ingrid had once considered too old for her.

An observer might think that Petter had it all. Yet when he spoke of events of thirty years before, it was as if they had just happened. Although Petter felt that he was almost totally unemotional and dispassionate about Ingrid, there were those who thought that he was obsessed with his former wife. Some of those who had heard Petter's stories, such as Alan Burgess, believed that Petter had never loved Ingrid, that it had all been pride and possession. Others who had heard the same stories thought that he had never stopped loving her.

Even after all these years, Petter was still on occasion being reminded of his first marriage. Earlier in the year, a two-part article in a leading Swedish magazine, *Husmodern*, had been full of errors and half truths that he felt slandered him and his life. There were also articles that quoted Pia about her hard times as a child. His eldest daughter insisted that she had been misquoted, but her remarks were painful to Petter and complicated their relationship. If he ever planned to tell his side of the story, to right what he considered thirty years of wrongs, to show how an actress's image can be so distorted that it has little to do with the truth, that time was now.

Ingrid and Burgess settled into rooms at the Coronado. The next day they arrived at Petter's house, on a bluff overlooking the Pacific Ocean. It was Thanksgiving. Though Petter had pointedly not asked them to share the holiday repast, he now invited Ingrid and Burgess for dinner.

Ingrid was drinking a great deal. Petter could see that she was in some pain. He knew that there was a special kind of sling that would help. The next day he took her to a medical supply house to have it made for her.

Ingrid wrote Petter and Agnes a warm thank-you note from the Hotel Pierre in New York. She said that it had been a "joy" to visit Petter's family. "I miss the delicious air in San Diego!"

Whatever hope Ingrid might have had for a reconciliation with Petter ended the moment he read the pages that Burgess had left with him. Although there was a lengthy interview with Petter, on most of the major points Burgess had sided with Ingrid's version.

Burgess wrote Petter that he was sorry Petter was upset about the material he had read. "I know you have given me a lot of material which in my hurry to get this first draft on paper I have not yet examined very closely. But I will go through it like a detective . . . and incorporate it in the book."

Ingrid tried to smooth things over with Petter by simply ignoring the problem of the book. On March 26, 1980, she wrote him a gay little note addressed to "Dear Grandpa," thanking him for more photos of his family and wishing him a happy Easter. On that same day, Petter wrote a long letter to Ingrid addressed to "Dear Grandma."

"The past thirty years you yourself and your representatives have never stopped publishing some very bad reports about me, some pure lies, other gross distortions," he began in the five-page, single-spaced communication. "I never responded, never gave an interview regarding you or our relationship in spite of all the invitations and pressures. . . . Time has changed. Someone recently reminded me of the old saying that if a lie is repeated often enough it becomes truth. . . . I have submitted extensive records and comments to Alan and I suggest that you read them all."

Petter learned soon afterward that what Burgess had told him was an objective biography would be published in the fall of 1980 as Ingrid's autobiography. He felt doubly deceived, and he and Pia both asked that their letters be removed. Although Petter could not be expected to believe such an unlikely tale, it was the publisher, Delacorte Press, that convinced Ingrid that she should expand her first-person interviews and put her name on the book as an autobiography.

The curious form of the book allowed Ingrid, in Burgess's words, "to say what she wanted to say in the first person and have me, the narrator, say what she didn't want to say or couldn't really say." It was even less likely, now, that Ingrid was going to allow *her* book to become a running debate with Petter, giving him the right to reply to anything he felt was "inaccurate or distorted," as Burgess had promised him in writing in 1978.

"Dear Alan Burgess, who I thought I knew," Petter wrote Burgess on July 29, 1980.

> *I have difficulty admitting that I might have made a mistake when I relied on you and trusted all your verbal and written promises regarding your book. . . . I have received a copy of a letter of yours where you talk about slander to which you feel you have been exposed and where you imply some possible legal action from your side. It might be of some interest to you to see how you and your "heroine," as you call her, would appear in court under cross-examinations. Since I.B. recently telephoned from London to the Husmodern Magazine in Stockholm that she never had felt better in her whole life, I assure that she will be in good condition to appear in court, and not only in the many public appearances which evidently have been scheduled for promotion of your book.*

By this time you too have probably seen enough of the contradictions and the fairy tales I.B. is capable of during her neverending play acting. As I have explained to you, it was my impression over several years that I.B. was basically an honest and kind person, and with a good sense of humor, although totally obsessed with her career and her publicity. Nothing else really concerned her.

Petter and Pia both separately contacted Harriet Pilpel, a prominent New York literary attorney, who in turn contacted Delacorte Press about removing their letters and interviews. Petter was on strong moral if not legal grounds. Ingrid did not see it that way, and she took the restrained legal letters as personal attacks.

"Ingrid said that she was so stunned at the anger and rage still boiling in Petter after all these years that she almost abandoned the book," says Ross Claiborne, then the editorial director of Delacorte.

"We were writing the book in galleys," remembers Jeanne Bernkopf, the editor. "She would work every day. One day she came in tears and said, 'I can't go on with this. It's tearing me apart. It's too much.' She was extremely unhappy over the problems with Pia and Petter.

"I was deluged with legal problems. Our answer was to paraphrase the letters. But on the interviews with Petter, I finally said just remove them, just remove all the things that Petter had told, all the pro-Petter stories. Ingrid didn't like them anyway, and didn't particularly want them in the book. I called Alan and said, "Every single piece of information, take it out.' "

Ingrid thought that with Petter out of the way, everyone would be happy with the book. But she soon discovered the mixed joys of authorship. Irene Selznick was upset at Ingrid's portrayal of her in the book and equally bothered by Ingrid's treatment of Sidney Bernstein. "So your two best friends ended up on the cutting room floor," Ingrid wrote in her trip diary before setting off on her book tour to Chicago. She realized that she had upset most of the people mentioned in the book, and those not mentioned as well.

To promote *My Story*, Ingrid traveled extensively in both the United States and Europe in the last months of 1980, and she was received not as another celebrity plugging a best-seller, but as a great star, a great dying star. When she could, she watched her taped interviews on television. She was as self-critical as she had ever been. But she viewed an interview a success when there was no mention of Petter, whom she called in her diary "Dr. L," and no ugly intrusion into her illness.

In Paris one sunny afternoon she noticed a poster with her name on it advertising a newspaper story about "La dernière lutte contre la morte" [the last fight against death]. She bought the paper and sat down at a sidewalk café to read about herself and her illness.

Afterward, she wrote in her diary:

> The theme of the story inside was condamnnee. A full page of photographs of me in bed (from movies) everything in the story was false.

CHAPTER TWENTY-THREE

"I Don't Want the Film to Be Over"

In November 1980, Harve Bennett, a Paramount producer, got together a group of people in his office to discuss the casting of his new project, a television miniseries based on the life of Golda Meir, the late Israeli prime minister. It was a great part, but for the life of them, Bennett and the others couldn't seem to come up with the right name. Liz Taylor? Faye Dunaway? Bette Midler? Jane Alexander? Barbra Streisand?

As Bennett's secretary, Silvia Rubinstein, listened to the suggestions, she thought that this was becoming ludicrous. She had trouble picturing Liz Taylor as Golda. Then she remembered the televised tribute to Ingrid Bergman, and her surprise at how old Ingrid had looked.

"I have a suggestion," Silvia said. "How about Ingrid Bergman?"

"She's retired," Bennett said.

"I don't think there's an actress who's retired," Silvia said.

Bennett reflected on that a moment. "It's a great idea." The more he thought about it, the better it sounded. "A *great* idea, Silvia."

Before contacting Ingrid, Bennett checked things out as best he could. Golda was a sacred name to most Jews. There had been a terrible brouhaha over Vanessa Redgrave, an avowed supporter of the Palestinian Arabs, playing a Jewish concentration camp inmate in the television film *Playing for Time*. He didn't want any of that. He learned that "some people thought the Jewish community would be offended by Ingrid playing the part." But people in Hollywood always run scared.

Bennett had Marilyn Hall on his side. She had been involved with the project from the beginning, and she had as good contacts with the Jewish community as anyone. She was married to Monty Hall, a TV game show host, and was a formidable fund-raiser for Jewish organizations.

Marilyn seemed to know everyone. She phoned Mike Frankovich, the producer of *Cactus Flower*, and asked him to call Ingrid in London.

When Frankovich called from Hollywood, Ingrid gave him an immediate and emphatic no. Golda was not Ingrid's new Joan of Arc, a role she identified with and had dreamed of playing. Ingrid knew very little about Golda except that she was tiny, Jewish, and recently deceased, in 1978. People remembered every nuance of her personality. They would not accept a Golda who was tall, Protestant, and spoke with a Swedish accent. That was the end of that.

Though Ingrid's arm had become increasingly swollen, she couldn't stand the idea of simply sitting around waiting for visits from the children and friends. Early in 1981 she set off on her first trip to Israel with her cousin Britt.

Although this was purely a tourist trip, Ingrid couldn't help but think sometimes of Golda Meir. Beyond that, she was being wooed, sometimes in ways she didn't quite realize. Marilyn Hall had called Teddy Kollek, the mayor of Jerusalem. Although Kollek had been less than a full-fledged admirer of the prime minister, he spent several hours showing Ingrid films of Golda, and talking about the early years of Israel.

Ingrid received a call from Gene Corman, the on-location producer of *A Woman Called Golda*, who was in Israel making another film but had time to woo Ingrid. "Apart from being a motion picture producer, I'm a movie fan, and I'd love to have dinner with you."

"That's very thoughtful, Gene," Ingrid said. "Why don't you call me the day after tomorrow."

Corman called and left a message, but Ingrid didn't call back. The producer called again and arranged to see her the following evening.

Corman was indeed a movie fan, and when he saw Ingrid walk into the lobby of the King David Hotel in Tel Aviv, he was stunned. If he hadn't known she was coming downstairs he would not have recognized her. The illness had eaten away her beauty. Then, as they sat in the candlelight of the hotel bar, an extraordinary thing happened. Through the flickering light he saw Ingrid again, the Ingrid of *Casablanca* and *Saratoga Trunk* and *Anastasia*, the Ingrid of his youth.

"I want to talk to you about Golda," the producer said.

"I'm not Jewish."

"That doesn't matter."

"She was tiny. I'm five nine. I'm two of Golda."

"Golda never measured herself in inches."

Corman told Ingrid all that he knew about Golda. This was no simple Hollywood heroine he was talking about. Here was a Golda Meir who had left her husband and children to pursue her career; who had lovers while she was married; who had struggled not only for Israel but for herself, for her own recognition and success. Yet here was a Golda Meir who when she was prime minister might be found in the kitchen cooking dinner. Here, finally, was a Golda Meir who died after a long struggle with leukemia.

As Corman sketched the outline of Golda's life, the producer could see Ingrid become more and more responsive. He could see tears in Ingrid's eyes. And when he was finished, when it was time for them to part, Ingrid asked Corman for some books about Golda.

It was a measure of Ingrid's ambition as an actress that she would consider playing such a homely woman, a role that many aging, once beautiful stars would summarily have rejected. Politicians and movie stars have a great deal in common, and the more Ingrid read about Golda, the more the character resonated within her. Here was this world figure, a creator not only of Israel but of her own image. And here was this little lady who somehow had the ego and ambition to crawl out of her marriage and family life and rise to international heights that few women had ever reached. And here was a woman who knew guilt, knew it as a wife and mother.

In deciding whether to play Golda, Ingrid was not unlike a politician deciding whether to run again. She talked to practically everyone about Golda. Laurence Evans, her British agent, thought that she was wrong for the part. Sidney Bernstein was opposed too, as worried about dangers in Israel as about the role itself. Initially, Kay Brown had not been enthusiastic either, but she knew Ingrid so well that she realized that anything that would get her working again was good.

When Ingrid returned to London, the script for *A Woman Called Golda* was waiting for her. Although she had been very interested in the film, she decided to turn it down. Ingrid wrote Bennett on April 9, 1981: "From what I have learned and seen, I have deep respect and admiration for Golda Meir and I simply cannot *act* her."

A month later Ingrid attended a large dinner given by the International Variety Clubs, the charity that the year before had given her a tribute. Seated next to her was Marilyn Hall, whose husband, Monty, was the honorary chairman. Marilyn spent the evening trying to get Ingrid to change her mind about playing Golda.

"The main reason she gave was how could the Israelis accept her when her mother was German," Marilyn says. There were other questions in Ingrid's past that were far larger. No one has a memory like the Jews, and there were surely those in Israel who knew a good deal about Ingrid's short-lived career for UFA, and the film she made in Nazi Germany in 1938.

Ingrid also had reason to be worried that Petter would make some statement. He was upset enough over the pages of her autobiography to have suggested that he might end his years of silence. He had written her: "You really had a poor understanding of Nazism and you could not understand my anti-Nazistic attitude. Your aunt and her boyfriend, a very wealthy manufacturer, who sold uniforms to the German SS, were fanatic Nazists. With their help you were determined to make a second picture with UFA, and you were all enthusiastic about it and you stated that you would become a greater star than the Swedish Sarah Leander, who at the time was UFA's greatest singer and actress."

That evening in the ballroom at the Grosvenor House, Ingrid made other excuses. "The life of Golda is too fresh in people's minds," Ingrid said. "If it was someone like Isadora Duncan I would take a chance." And she admitted, "You know, I know nothing about Israel. I'm not political."

At the end of the evening, Marilyn agreed to send a driver to pick up the script. When no one showed up at Ingrid's town house, she called Marilyn at the hotel.

"Oh, I'm very sorry about the driver. . . ."

"That doesn't matter," Ingrid said brusquely. "If for my purpose I wanted to play Golda Meir and felt that I could, I would be willing to play the part. Why don't you come over to my flat and we'll talk about it."

Marilyn came and Ingrid talked eagerly about the role. On the table sat the script that she had wanted to return. There were marks all over it, and pages turned down. "You know you can't insure me," Ingrid said. "And I'll have to have a screen test."

The last time Ingrid had made a real screen test was for *For Whom the Bell Tolls,* but she wanted one this time.

"But why?" Bennett asked, as they talked on a transatlantic connection.

"I don't want to make a mockery of Golda or myself." Ingrid made reference to the heavy makeup she would wear as Golda. "I have never played underneath a mask in my life. I want to see if I can do it."

Bennett made plans to fly to London for the test. The executive producer had seen recent photos of Ingrid, and he felt that it would not be that difficult to make her look like Golda. "It occurred to me that the problem was her own self-perception," Bennett says. "She did not see the changes in herself any more than any of us do who think of ourselves at an earlier age. She would not perceive herself as resembling Golda Meir."

To help prepare her, Ingrid was sent voice and video tapes, including a lengthy BBC interview. Golda's voice alone contained the story of her life. One could hear the expanses of Russia, where she was born; the irony and humor of Yiddish; the brashness of big-city, beer-making, tough-talking Milwaukee, where she lived as a young woman; and the struggles of life in Palestine, to which she came as a Zionist.

In her career, Ingrid had played in five languages—Swedish, German, English, Italian, and French—but always with *her* accent. Yet if Ingrid couldn't get Golda's voice right, she could get nothing of the role right. She practiced in the shower, and in the kitchen. She played the tapes, pacing back and forth in her living room. She practiced over and over again.

Pia came to visit from New York, and one day heard her mother reciting in the shower. Pia knocked on the door. "Is that you in there or is it Golda?" Pia said.

"Is it that good?" Ingrid asked.

On the day of the screen test, Ingrid arrived at the small studio. She went into the makeup room, where Wally Schneiderman began his work. When Alan Gibson, the Canadian-born director, saw Ingrid sitting there beside a large picture of Golda, his heart sank. He thought to himself: "There's no way she's going to look like Golda Meir."

Schneiderman had been in the business for almost forty years, and was one of the finest makeup men in films. He had saved pictures of Golda in his files, with hopes that one day he would have this assignment. With modern film stock, he didn't need the heavy makeup he once would have used. Highlights and shadows would be enough, alone with a gray wig. As Ingrid watched critically, he brushed her face with makeup, and applied a small bridge on her nose.

When Ingrid walked back into the studio, there was a momentary hush. It was no longer Ingrid Bergman but a woman who had the feel and walk and look of Golda Meir. A fine actress can look fat when she is thin, and short when she is tall, and what was most amazing was that Ingrid didn't even seem big any longer, but appeared to be a tiny, dumpy old lady. Ingrid looked at Frederick Young standing there behind the camera. She walked up to Young and embraced him. Freddy had shot *Indiscreet* and *The Inn of the Sixth Happiness,* and they talked awhile about old times. Ingrid felt comfortable working with people she knew; Freddy was the only person here with whom she had worked before, hired for this one day. Most of the others treated her with overwhelming deference and caution, as if a harsh word might shatter her.

While Gibson, the director, was blocking the shots with a stand-in, Ingrid sat in a chair, chain-smoking. Corman noticed that her hands were shaking. The producer thought: "What have we done?" He walked up to Ingrid, knelt beside her, and attempted some soothing, aimless conversation.

"You know I'm nervous," Ingrid said.

"Ingrid, we are all very excited to have you, and you are so dedicated that you want a screen test."

As Corman talked, the camera was dollied in closer and closer. Ingrid looked past the producer, to the camera.

"Oh, you know I see an old friend," she said.

"If you're ready we'll begin now, Ingrid," Gibson said in his gentle voice.

Ingrid did four scenes that day, showing Golda at different stages in her life. Another actress would play Golda as a young woman, but sixty-six-year-old Ingrid would have to play Golda from middle age to almost eighty. There was no one there that day who was not impressed. But as always, the proof was in the film, and it was not until the following afternoon that Ingrid arrived at the Paramount offices to see the test.

The lights went off, and the first scene played upon the small screen. The camera had always loved Ingrid, loved her when she blushed and glowed with youthful loveliness in her first color test for Selznick forty-two years before, loved her as Sister Benedict and as Anastasia. And as the camera moved in, framing her face, it loved her still as homely old Golda, loved the nuances and lines in her face, loved the sadness and depth.

There was no sound in the room except for an occasional nervous cough.

When the footage ended, Ingrid asked that it be screened once more. And when she had seen the test again, and the lights came on, she turned in her seat, tears glistening in her eyes. "If you want me, I'm yours," she said, and then Corman and Bennett and Gibson had tears in their eyes too.

Ingrid invited everyone over to her flat to celebrate and drink champagne. She kept playing the screen test over and over again in her mind, and she had begun to pick it apart.

"Maybe I don't need much of a mask," she said, as if she were getting used to the idea. "No, I don't really need all that makeup, do I?"

Ingrid had only one bottle of champagne in the apartment, but the others had brought several bottles more. Ingrid drank glass after glass, and the others matched her as best they could.

"Do you have any comments?" Ingrid asked, half drunk on the champagne.

Bennett had a comment, but if it hadn't been for the champagne he would not have made it. When he watched the screen test, he had thought back to his boyhood days, going to the synagogue and hearing the cantor sing with a sob in his voice. Ingrid had a sob in her voice, a way of talking that made one want to cry. It had made him want to cry watching *Casablanca* and *For Whom the Bell Tolls*. It made him want to cry in the screening room, but he had had the feeling that if Golda had heard it, she would have said, "I'm not so sentimental."

"I have only one thing to say."

"Yes," Ingrid said, suddenly sober.

"Watch the self-pity."

"You noticed?"

"Yeah."

"Yes, yes, yes, I can control that," she said.

Ingrid wasn't about to let anything stand in the way of her performance. When Nastassja Kinski was suggested for the part of the young Golda, Ingrid felt that a lesser-known actress would be preferable. The suggestion was made that Isabella play the young Golda, but Ingrid dismissed that as well. Instead, the fine Australian actress Judy Davis was hired for the part.

On September 4, 1981, Ingrid flew from London to Tel Aviv, accompanied by Margaret Johnstone, who from now on would spend more time with her than anyone else. Margaret was a tall, big-boned woman who looked more like a Swedish farmer's wife than the British-born masseuse and expert cook that she was.

Ingrid had called on Margaret to give her a massage when she returned to England after the American run of *The Constant Wife*. Ingrid could not hide her illness from a masseuse, and the two women talked about the disease. "I've gone through woes and so have you," Margaret said, and showed Ingrid a scar from a nonmalignant growth. In the months that followed, Ingrid had become more dependent on Margaret, not only for massages but for cooking and companionship and errands. For Margaret, it was an exciting new world, and she was delighted to be asked to go to Israel with Ingrid.

Ingrid knew that the film would be made under the most punishing of schedules. This was not a theatrical picture, after all, but a four-hour television miniseries, filmed at three times the pace of a Hollywood feature. Moreover, it was not even network television, but a syndicated program, with a decidedly smaller budget.

In Israel, *A Woman Called Golda* was an event of major cultural and political importance. Everyone in the country had an opinion about Golda Meir. Making the film in Israel was like a portrait painter attempting to sketch a likeness while family members, neighbors, enemies, and assorted kibitzers stood criticizing every brush stroke. In this case, however, the producers allowed the onlookers to pick up a brush and paint a few lines. Moshe Dayan, the former defense minister and war hero, was worried about how he would be portrayed. He was shown his lines, and he tinkered with them until he felt he came out well.

Golda's children wanted nothing to do with the film. They had expressed their concerns that Golda's love life would be graphically and openly portrayed. That was taken care of in the script by giving Golda a relationship with only one, composite figure, Ariel, and making a veiled suggestion that he and Golda might have been lovers. The producers had the full cooperation of the Israeli government, and the script was far from a balanced portrait of the Zionists' fight for the birth of Israel. Although there was much in the film about Arab terrorists, nothing was said about the terrorism of the Irgun and the Stern gang or about the life of the Palestinians.

The film, then, was not about the brutal business of history. Nor was it about the human price of power. Philip Gillon wrote in the *Jerusalem Post* that Golda, along with Ben-Gurion, "was a good hater. . . . We saw nothing of their capacity to hate in the film. . . . Golda emerges as that ambitious young girl who marries the wrong man but goes on to become an implacable, strong Momma plying the kiddies with ghastly Jewish delicacies."

Ingrid saved the film. "I have a feeling that what I perceived, as the producer, and Harold Gast, as the writer, and Alan Gibson, as the director, was a romanticized version of Golda, our ideal," says Bennett. "But I think Ingrid reached beyond that."

In her first few days in Israel, Ingrid immersed herself even further in Golda's life. She spent a day at the Rad Film Archives and another at United Studios, looking at an Israeli version of *This Is Your Life* about Golda. She went to Jerusalem to watch a three-hour documentary at a television station. She spent an afternoon with Lou Kaddar, Golda's longtime secretary and confidante. She met Moshe Dayan a few days before he died.

Ingrid did not complain when she was shown the small, nondescript trailer that would be her dressing room. Here every morning Schneiderman spent an hour and a quarter making Ingrid up, before letting the hairdresser come in to fit on one of the four wigs. Schneiderman used less makeup than he had for the screen test, and no longer employed a bridge for the nose. Ingrid had lost a lot of weight, and she wore special padding around her legs.

Ingrid had to play Golda as a fortyish mother and as a nearly eighty-year-old grandmother dying of leukemia. That would have been challenge enough, but she had to play the role with a right arm that had become grotesquely swollen. When her right breast was removed, the lymph glands had been affected, and now large amounts of body fluid flowed into her arm. When she was not being filmed, she rested her arm on a telescoping stand that she called "the gun." At night she slept with her arm strapped above her head.

For Alan Greenberg, the Israeli cameraman, the challenge was extraordinary. He could see how the heat of the lights bothered Ingrid, and he tried to keep the lights to a minimum. The costuming department had fitted Ingrid with long-sleeved dresses, but Greenberg had to make the audience unaware that Ingrid had an enormous, almost immovable arm. Worse yet, in some of the early scenes he had to make an ill sixty-six-year-old actress look like a vibrant, healthy woman in her forties.

One evening early in the shooting, Greenberg sat watching the rushes along with Ingrid and other members of the production. "She was supposed to be young, but she looked very old," Greenberg remembers. "Her attitude was very bad when she saw how she looked. I didn't sleep all that night. But from that I learned how to work with her."

When the filming began, Ingrid got up in the morning at five forty-five. She left the hotel an hour later and was dressed and made up, on the set ready to shoot by eight-thirty. Even on an air-conditioned set, her rubberized padding would have been unpleasant, but in the heat and sun of Israel, it was like sitting all day in a sauna. In the morning she was usually vivacious, full of energy, but when Schneiderman touched up her makeup in the afternoon, he could see the fatigue written all over her face.

Margaret was staying with Ingrid in her suite in Tel Aviv. She knew better than anyone how tired Ingrid was becoming. "Let's switch to a later start," Margaret suggested.

"Oh, no, they're on a tight budget and schedule," Ingrid said, unwilling to complicate the filming.

When Sidney Bernstein came for a visit, he became upset that Ingrid was having to get up practically at dawn. Margaret called Corman and from then on Ingrid started several hours later each morning.

Kvetshing is the national sport of Israel, and when Ingrid arrived there were those who thought that she could never play Golda. But almost from the moment she appeared on the set, such talk was heard no longer. Everyone knew that she was sick, and what she was going through to play the part. Because of Ingrid's illness, the producers had been unable to insure the film.

The great unspoken worry was that she could not complete the film, and everything would be lost. "There was concern whether she could get the job done," says Leonard Nimoy, who played Golda's husband, Morris. "I saw a very talented lady going through these stages of self-doubt, and seeing her confidence grow. It was a daring thing that she did, quite subtle and powerful."

Ingrid understood her own value, and she worried that Paramount did not understand it. One evening she called Corman into her suite. "I think I made a very bad financial deal," she said.

"Honestly, Ingrid, I hadn't really gotten myself involved in that," the producer said.

"I would like my deal to be better," she said.

This was not a situation that Corman wanted to handle. "I took the responsibility once I saw this project was going to go to tell my attorney what I wanted," he said.

"Yes, but my situation is different," Ingrid insisted. "Since you're so involved in this film, don't you think you should have helped?"

"Ingrid, but that's why you have agents and attorneys! All I can say is that there's not enough money to pay you for what you're doing."

This was the same Ingrid Bergman who had to be chided to review her legacy to her children. And yet, even after signing her contract, she was worried about *this* money, the symbol of her value as an actress and a star.

Late in the afternoon of October 6, 1981, Ingrid arrived in Bialik Square in Tel Aviv. Here stood the first municipality building in the city, in an area constructed by early Jewish immigrants. But for today it was Independence Square, the setting for the nighttime shooting of the celebration of Israel's declaration of independence in 1948. Several hundred extras were there too, to spend the night dancing and singing in the streets, in a joyous recreation of one of the great moments in the country's short history.

Then the news began to filter through the crowd: Anwar Sadat, the Egyptian president, had been shot in Egypt. Overhead, F-15s roared through the night. In Israel history is omnipresent, and newspaper headlines are read as if they are the diary of one's own life. Some of those on the set feared that there might be war by morning, and no one there was without a shiver of apprehension.

For Ingrid, though, history was an intrusion. The movie was always the thing, and she acted almost bewildered that she, too, was living within history. "Impossible!" she said. "Why don't people appreciate life? The whole world is going crazy; look at what happened to the Pope."

The heat was insufferable and Ingrid was growing weaker by the day. Though she did not complain, she had rarely had to put up with such conditions, and never with such a schedule. She tried to rest in the trailer, but the air-conditioning kept going off, and it heated up like an oven.

Israel was usually cooler than this by October, but the sun scorched the earth, and it was tough for the healthiest members of the cast. One day when it was close to one hundred degrees, and a dog left in a closed car would die in a few hours, Ingrid shot a scene in a car in Jerusalem. The car was jammed with a driver, the cameraman, and lights, and by the time Ingrid returned from the drive on a road parallel to the Knesset, she was exceedingly tired and irritable. She took out her anger on the one person not involved with the film, Margaret.

The next shot that day was in a café overlooking the Wailing Wall.

"I don't know if I can make it," Ingrid told Corman.

Ingrid sat in a chair with a coat around her, while the scene was set up. Mayor Teddy Kollek happened to be visiting the set that afternoon, but Corman asked him not to talk to Ingrid.

The shot was made, and Ingrid finally arrived back at the Solomon Sheraton Hotel. When Margaret entered the suite she found Ingrid out on the balcony.

"Darling, I'm sorry if things have been a little difficult for you today, but I know you understand that I want to die with my boots on."

Despite the rigors of her role, Ingrid found time to do interviews and accept invitations. One evening she was the honored guest at the opening of the Israeli film archives. Ingrid made a few remarks before a showing of *For Whom the Bell Tolls*, and then sat down next to Monty Hall. *For Whom the Bell Tolls* was Ingrid's first color film, and her youthful beauty is astounding. She glows with health and well-being, and her suntanned, tawny skin seems the color of life itself. Ingrid watched for a few minutes, and then turned to Hall: "You'll have to forgive me. I can't stand it."

One day when they were filming a scene at a hospital, Ingrid took time to visit some of the sick and elderly. "It was like the little old ladies had gone to heaven," Margaret remembers. "The little old ladies thought it was her, Golda had returned to see them."

Ingrid was seeing too much of hospitals, though, especially on the days that Margaret and Marilyn Hall took her in for chemotherapy. She kept losing more weight, and the padding she wore covered a shriveled frame.

Golda had leukemia for the last fourteen years of her life. In one scene a doctor tells her of the disease. Ingrid was the same age as Golda in the scene, sixty-six years old, and the scene resonated with meanings within meanings.

"How much longer do I have?" Ingrid asked, playing with such understatement and poignancy that a mere whisper had more power than a scream.

"I'd say you have a good few years ahead of you."

"Well, I'm sixty-six. How long can I expect to live anyway?"

As Ingrid spoke the lines, Greenberg turned his head away from the scene he was filming. "I just can't watch her," he said softly to Gibson.

In the following scene, Golda tells Lou Kaddar that she is ill, but does not tell her that she has leukemia. "But I don't understand why she would do that," Ingrid said, arguing with Gibson.

"Because she realizes its impact on other people," the director said.

Ingrid thought a moment. "That's right," she said, and went ahead with the scene.

Ingrid was concerned about every nuance of her performance. She had seen the famous picture of Golda when she hears herself named prime minister and puts both her hands over her face in a gesture of amazement. The edema of Ingrid's right arm and hand seemed to mandate a double. She insisted that the double's hands be old and weathered.

On the morning of the shooting, Corman had lined up a middle-aged woman whose hands would be shot. The night before, however, Ingrid had strapped her right arm up high above her head, trying to drain the fluid. She slept very little, but when she got up, the hand appeared almost normal.

Corman shot the scene as soon as Ingrid emerged from her trailer. She had to say nothing, only to raise her hands to her face, and when it was over and Corman said "Print," Ingrid exclaimed, "I did it!"

Ingrid was weakening so fast that by the time Lars and Isabella arrived for a visit, it was impossible to hide the physical deterioration. Several times in the last months Lars had thought Ingrid was about to die. But she had reservoirs of sheer strength that amazed him.

Lars was the one person to whom Ingrid confided all her complaints. One day Ingrid, Lars, and Isabella visited the Wailing Wall in Jerusalem. "See, you're standing between two wailing walls," Ingrid said.

Lars laughed, but he was profoundly worried. As soon as the shooting finished in Israel, Ingrid was supposed to fly to Los Angeles to shoot the American scenes. But Lars doubted if she was up to such a long trip. "Lars was rather extreme in what he said her condition was," Marilyn Hall remembers. "He said her death was imminent. His words floored me."

"I don't look forward to that flight to L.A.," Ingrid told Corman. Less than two weeks before the end of the shooting in Israel, Corman and Gibson decided that they would have to finish the film in London.

On the eve of Ingrid's return to England, a grand party was held at the Tel Aviv Hilton. There were belly dancers, and live music, and mounds of food, and even a camel, and Ingrid stayed on and on. The next morning the El Al flight to London was delayed four hours. When Ingrid, Margaret, Gibson, and Schneiderman finally arrived at the airport, they learned that the airline had gone on strike.

That evening they flew out of Tel Aviv on the only connection available, an Air France airbus. Ingrid refused the one first-class seat available, and stayed with her colleagues instead. By the time the plane reached Nice, she was very tired. She wanted to get off and go to sleep, but the baggage had been checked to Paris. It was after one o'clock by the time the group checked into a Paris hotel, and the restaurant was closed. Ingrid was exhausted, but she still could laugh that because of a broken shoe strap Margaret had walked into the hotel in her bare feet.

The journey to London was tiring in itself, but given Ingrid's disease, it was a wonder that it didn't drain the last lifeblood of energy and health she had left.

There was still work to be done, though, a film to be finished. The last scene to be shot takes place in 1948. Golda, who has gone to the United States to raise money for arms, learns that war has already begun in the Middle East, while she is thousands of miles away.

Ingrid arrived for the scene in White's Hotel at Lancaster Gate, near Hyde Park. As the camera tracked slowly in on her face, Ingrid was to speak the line: "In another seventy-two hours it will all be over."

The camera moved in and stopped, focusing on Ingrid's face. She sat there. Silence. The camera rolled on.

"My God," Ingrid said. "I forgot it. . . . I don't want the film to be over."

CHAPTER TWENTY-FOUR

"I'm Alone"

*A*s long as the lights of the camera remained on her, no shadow of death played across Ingrid's countenance. But as soon as the film was wrapped, and the cameras were put away, Ingrid appeared to shrivel up. She retreated into her house in Cheney Gardens and into herself, venturing out as little as possible.

When Lars came to visit, he was sure once again that this was the beginning of the end. He told Ingrid that she must call Margaret to say that she wasn't feeling well, and needed her help. He phoned Margaret from the airport at seven o'clock in the morning to see if Ingrid had called.

On his next visit, a few days later, Lars phoned Margaret once again. As soon as Margaret heard Lars's voice on the telephone, she knew that he was going to ask her to take care of Ingrid full-time. And she knew that her answer would be yes. "She was such a strong personality that I never thought of her not being there," Margaret says. "She was quite amusing about it. She said, 'You don't know what you've taken on. Old ladies can be quite difficult.' "

Often terminally ill people are brutally frank, while those around them retreat into a world of euphemism and half truths. Ingrid had often been blunt. Now her truths were like clubs. At Christmas she flew to Choisel to spend the holidays with Lars and members of her family. "She was very sad," Isabella remembers. "I could tell she felt it was the last time. . . . I knew she was very lost, talking about death at the party. She couldn't go to sleep. She said, 'What is the best way to go?' I felt she was talking about suicide. She showed me articles about euthanasia."

When Ingrid returned to London, Margaret moved into the town house. Margaret was endlessly solicitous, but Ingrid did not find it easy having her in the house twenty-four hours a day. She didn't do things the way Ingrid did them. She tried to manage Ingrid's life. But Ingrid needed someone willing and able to be there.

The rich are not allowed merely to die. They are examined and medicated, poked and probed, to the last measure of their patience and stamina. Although Dr. Edward MacLellan was dubious about chemotherapy in Ingrid's case, she went to St. Thomas's Hospital in Lambeth for five week-long visits during the next four months. To prevent the loss of her hair, ice packs were placed on her scalp before each treatment, freezing the roots.

Chemotherapy is war on the body, and Ingrid suffered greatly from her treatments, experiencing acute nausea and extremes of temperature. For all the agony, the therapy did no good, and after each session Ingrid seemed to sink more into herself. Rae Pober says she wrote Ingrid that Ruth Roberts needed money to help with her rent, and Ingrid sent a curt note saying that she had her own troubles.

"The terrible thing for Ingrid was that she had that arm," Fiorella says. "It was like a sausage. It was so awful, I couldn't even think about it. She had three mirrors in the apartment and she was sitting looking into the mirror."

Ingrid would spend long hours before the television screen. When she wrote letters, she did not let on how she felt. She was sometimes full of bravado, as if she were a character in somebody's play. On March 14 she wrote Oriana Fallaci, the Italian journalist, about her arm: "I call him my dog, I joke with him: 'You are a dog, a nasty sick dog. Come on, let's go walking.'"

Lars instructed Margaret to get Ingrid out of the house. "I would use Lars's name," Margaret says. "She never complained, but she must have thought I was awfully hard. Sometimes we'd go to the movies. We used to go in my little car. She used to say that we got along well because we had this routine." Ingrid loved the movies, but she couldn't stand what she considered the foul-mouthed, vulgar realism of many new films, and if she didn't like what she was seeing after a few minutes, she would march right back up the aisle.

Ingrid did not have many friends, but the friends she had were good ones, and Griff was the best of them all. Ingrid didn't have to play "Ingrid Bergman" with Griff. She would call him and usually he came over right away. And they would talk and laugh, and he would scold her, or make fun.

Once, they talked about dying. "You'll come to my funeral," Griff said. "I'm going to the greatest prop corner in the sky."

"I want Prokofiev's *Romeo and Juliet* played at my funeral," Ingrid said.

"I want the music from *Gone With the Wind* at mine."

"You shall have it," Ingrid said, and feigned anger, "even though it's not from an Ingrid Bergman movie."

Ingrid and Griff laughed and then talked of something else.

Lars called every day, wherever he was. Ingrid waited for his call like a teenager with a new beau. There were those who said that Lars felt guilty about Ingrid, but guilt was perhaps too small a word for all that he felt. He had his son now, but his relationship with Kristina had not worked out. He was at an age when most men would have slowed down, particularly one of Lars's wealth, but he continued his restless sojourns, as if he knew that he no longer belonged anywhere.

One day early in April, Lars called from Stockholm. Britt was visiting and Ingrid was in bed.

"Isn't there anything you would like?" Lars asked.

"I would like a *fastlagsbullar*," Ingrid said, naming the marzipan bun that in Sweden is served with warm milk for Easter.

Lars arranged for four buns to be sent express to London, with a chauffeur waiting in London to deliver them to Ingrid. The buns missed the plane, however, and arrived the following day. Britt warmed them up, and Ingrid ate two immediately, and two more the next morning.

When she went to the theater, Ingrid always took a seat on the aisle, so nothing would touch her arm. "She was so happy at the theater," Ann Todd says. "I think she liked hearing clapping."

Ingrid could not stand to have people take notice of her, now that she looked as she did. One evening she and Ann arrived at a theater, to find a contingent of photographers waiting under the marquee. Ingrid ordered the chauffeur to turn around and go back to Chelsea.

"Come on, what does it matter?" Ann said. "We can get through this."

The two actresses ran the gauntlet of photographers, but Ingrid was furious as the theater manager led them to their seats. "Who told the press I was coming?" Ingrid asked accusingly.

"No one," the man said mildly. "They're waiting for Princess Margaret."

Ingrid and Ann laughed at that story again and again. But there came a day when there were indeed photographers waiting for Ingrid. In mid-April, when she decided that she was not strong enough to go to New York for the first screening of *Golda*, the tabloids announced that Ingrid was fighting for her life. "INGRID BERGMAN BATTLES FOR LIFE," announced the *Daily Mirror* on its front page. "STAR INGRID IN FIGHT FOR LIFE," said the *Express*.

Outside on the sidewalk in Cheney Gardens, the photographers began their watch. They had telephoto lenses and Ingrid didn't even dare go near the front window. She had experienced nothing like this since her days in the clinic in Rome, when the paparazzi were waiting for a birth, not a death. "They wait there to see my body," she told Fiorella, who was visiting.

One lovely April morning, Shirley Green, a British friend of Marilyn Hall's, arrived to deliver a gift of Ingrid's favorite perfume, L'Air du Temps. When Griff opened the door the photographers pressed forward.

"Go away, you vultures," Griff said. "Go take photos of Elizabeth Taylor."

"She's too boring," one of the photographers yelled.

If Ingrid did not intend to spend her days blockaded in her town house, she would have to go outside and let the photographers have all the photos they wanted. And so that day she called Ann Todd and had her come over to help make her up. She wore a wool cape that masked her enlarged arm, and she sat on a bench near the Thames and let the photographers have their way. "I am not as young as I used to be," she said. "But my health is fine. I am not dying."

Finally Ingrid had something to look forward to: Isabella and Isotta's thirtieth birthday party in New York, on June 18, 1982.

Isabella was starting a new career, as a model. Ingrid couldn't get over the money Isabella could earn simply by posing, not having to memorize a line. Isotta was living in New York too, her marriage at an end. She was afraid of her estranged husband; to protect herself and her son, Isotta had moved to America.

Ingrid prepared for the trip as she would for a great performance. She wanted to look as good as possible for the children. She went to Franka, her designer, and had new outfits made. She had the days all thought out, and the clothes she would need, from what Franka calls "her little day luncheon outfits" to more formal wear.

On June 15, Ingrid flew to New York on the Concorde, accompanied by Robertino. "She was very tired," Robertino remembers. "She was really skinny. But always a sense of humor." All three of her daughters were living in New York now, but she stayed by herself at the Wyndham Hotel. One day Ingrid and Isotta were in an elevator with two elderly ladies, who inspected her as if she were a disreputable forgery. "Is that her?" one lady whispered. "It can't be her," the second lady whispered back. "She's so old."

One of those who saw Ingrid in New York was Steven Weiss, an investment banker, who was close to Lars and had once dated Pia. "We talked about her death," Weiss says. "Death was part of her. She said she could deal with it. She'd overwhelm you with her honesty, but I'm not sure that she realized the inner parts of her life. I think if you really analyzed it, you could say that she never felt comfortable with anything but her career. She was not entirely emotionally involved with her three husbands. She was so honest and candid, and yet she seemed to be shielding herself from things. Even with her children she didn't have time for the little things. Ingrid was Ingrid. She was almost an island unto herself."

The birthday party was Ingrid's party, and she helped plan the evening. She had learned that Pavo, the young Finn who had worked at Choisel, was in town. She hired him to prepare a smorgasbord. A Salvation Army choir would come and sing "Happy Birthday."

That evening Ingrid made up with particular care. She wore a long-sleeved, high-necked dress, with a sling the same color. She had a hard time even sitting in the limousine, but she smiled out at the faces that peered in the windows. When she arrived at Pia's apartment on Central Park West, photographers waited outside. And Warren Thomas was there too, waiting outside for her this day as he had been waiting for her for more than three decades.

The relatives and friends had gathered in the spacious living room overlooking the park. Ingrid tried to appear completely relaxed, but her arm was a constant irritation, affected by the least touch or jostling.

Ingrid had an exquisite sense of the proper gift. She gave the twins two old pearl necklaces that had been her mother's. And she also gave her daughters a picture of their Swedish grandmother wearing the pearls.

Ingrid was still a Swede with a speech to give. Even here among her family, she was not comfortable speaking extemporaneously, but read remarks she said she had found, written by Peter Ustinov. Ingrid began to speak, and the room grew absolutely quiet.

"Youth is not a time of life—it is a state of mind," she said. "So long as your heart receives messages of beauty, cheer, courage, grandeur, and power from the earth, from man, and from the Infinite, so long you are young. When the wires are all down and your heart is covered with the snows of pessimism, then you are old and may God have mercy on your soul."

It was a memorable party, and its prospect had sustained Ingrid for many weeks. Even at such a gloriously sentimental gathering, she still had bitter thoughts of Petter. "A lot of Rossellinis were in New York from Italy," she wrote Bang Alving in Sweden. "I wonder what Petter would have said if he had seen them all invade his daughter's home."

Ingrid stayed on in New York longer than she had planned, for her days were alive with reminiscing and gentle gatherings. On July 3 she finally flew back to London, to be met by Griff and Margaret.

Ingrid had always loved the summers. The days of July and August had been a time for the island and the children, for champagne and laughter, a short respite from work. Now the summer was a time of heat and long days, of a life that stretched out before her without work or purpose.

One day Fiorella visited and, receiving a phone call, was informed that a friend had committed suicide.

"He died the way he wanted to live," Fiorella said.

"What courage," Ingrid said, and Fiorella thought that Ingrid was thinking of killing herself.

Fiorella was not the only one worried that Ingrid might be contemplating suicide. "Ingrid had some mild sleeping problems," Margaret says. "Lars used to bring these pills that came from Switzerland. Lars said when he brought them, 'We must hide these because she has said if she ever has enough pills . . .' "

"At the end she was very sad, you know," Isabella says. "She felt extremely depressed. I think she would have killed herself. I think that made Griff and Margaret be there all the time. I think she didn't do it because she didn't want to have another scandal. I think she would have been very happy if there had been an accident, if she fell down the stairs or something. But they were afraid that she would create a situation.

"Mother didn't want to have people there who had pity for her. That's why I went every three weeks, but not for longer, because if she just perceived I was there for that she would have been outraged. She would have been so violent if I was there just for that. If you just sat around watching TV, she would get angry. 'What are you doing watching TV! Why don't you do something! I hate you just looking at me!' "

Isotta made visits to London too. "For Mama it was a constant struggle. I'd see her very depressed. Sometimes I'd go to London and she wanted to die. Sometimes. She'd say, 'I can't go on. I have no strength.' What do you say? What do you tell? She didn't want us. As a mother she didn't want me there bored sitting. After a week she would say, 'Go home.' We knew that we would be scolded. Very often she said, 'If I become very sick so I'm helpless, I'm going to jump out of the window.' But I knew that it wasn't true. She was touched with life. She said, 'I don't want to leave, but I can't go on.' Mama loved life."

Ingrid's children had their own reasons for not staying with their mother for longer periods, and for rushing in and out of the town house. Robertino, in Paris or Monaco, was nearer physically than his sisters, but he was endlessly flitting from place to place, gathering to gathering. To some, he had a life-style that was enviable at twenty, amusing at thirty, and would be sad at forty. But he did not see it that way. He seemed to float above the mundane pursuits of society, living a life full of amusement and pleasure. He had become close to Princess Caroline, and he spent his time with her and other friends.

Ingrid wanted to spare her children as much of the pain as she could. And yet to her cousin Britt she expressed a different opinion. "When the girls were visiting her, she said they always had something to do," Britt said. "I have a feeling she felt a little lonely."

Margaret and Griff believed that they had been delegated a burden that members of the family should have shared more fully. The most difficult aspect of the family life were the phone calls to Ingrid from Isotta's estranged husband, allegedly threatening Ingrid.

One day Marilyn Hall called Ingrid in London. *Golda* had been a spectacular success on American television, but Hall was calling her as a friend.

"Margaret has the flu," Ingrid said. "My cousin Britt was here, but she had to fly back to Sweden."

"You're not alone?" Hall asked.

"Yes, I'm alone. And it's hot as hell."

"Why don't you have an air-conditioner?"

"I won't need it next year."

"Where are your children?"

"They're not here. I'm alone."

She was alone, but she had always been alone. And it was out of her aloneness that everything had come. She had risen out of the aloneness of her room at Aunt Hulda's to begin her career in the theater. She had been alone in America, with people that she only partially understood. She had been alone with Petter, and she had fled from him. She had fled into roles, and into the arms of lovers, into other marriages and other lands. She had fled from the aloneness of Choisel, the aloneness of inactivity. She lived within aloneness now, though she did not even know how alone she was.

Ingrid spent hours talking and thinking of her past. She was not reflecting back on her life to justify it or draw meaning from it, as much as to sanctify it.

Ingrid's friends talked about the future the way a nurse fluffs up a pillow. They talked about a visit to Martha Gellhorn's cottage in Wales, though Ingrid could not possibly travel so far. They talked about attending the Edinburgh International Festival in September, though no one was sure that she would live that long.

"How are you feeling, darling?" Ann Todd asked one summer evening, on what turned out to be their last outing together.

"I'm fine," Ingrid said. "It's just this pain in my back that troubles me."

"Perhaps you've been sitting in a draft."

"Yes, I expect that's what it is."

For a Swede, July is high summer, and for Ingrid, the summer had always meant the island of Danholmen. July was over now, and the crowds had thinned at Fjällbacka, but the sun was almost as high, and the sea was still warm. As weak as she was, Ingrid wanted to visit the island. And so on Monday, August 10, she flew to Stockholm, moving through the airports in a wheelchair. Britt was there in Stockholm, waiting for Ingrid.

For Lars, Danholmen was a magical antidote. He kept Ingrid's clothes and possessions in a bedroom there, as if he and Ingrid were still married. He said that anyone got right on the island, and he could see how good the sun and the sky were for Ingrid. At first, she was not strong enough to make her daily walk around the island, but her skin freshened with color and she grew stronger. "She started sitting in the sun," Lars remembers. "We took the first little walk. She started to walk. With that weight of her arm, she managed to walk around the island. Even that she managed."

Ingrid said that her life had been good and full, and she would have changed nothing. She said it again and again, as a litany. She permitted herself not even one regret. But sitting on the island watching the windsurfers sailing the sea as if sail and sailor were one, she said that she wished she had done that at least once, she wished she had sailed around Danholmen the way Lars and his friends did so often.

There had been so many lovely times on the island, so much good fellowship, so many good friends and good evenings. Whenever there were guests for dinner, Lars planned the evening as if it were a dinner at Choisel, preparing an elegant centerpiece.

Lars called Lasse Lundberg, a good friend who ran a sailing school in Fjällbacka, and said, "Ingrid's bad, but let's have a party Saturday night." They came, Lasse and his wife, Ingela, bringing the crayfish that Ingrid loved so much. Ingrid felt comfortable with the Lundbergs, and they were the only guests besides Britt and Lars, and Pavo.

For a while Ingrid had seemed to be growing stronger, but she needed help this evening to walk to the main house from her quarters. In the dining room, she sat in one of the padded yellow chairs and looked out at the sea. On the wall was painted a mural of the sea and wherever Ingrid looked she saw the deep blue of the water.

There are few sunsets in the world like those along the coast of Sweden on a summer day. For a while the horizon seems to be in flames, and then the skyline glows, and nighttime arrives not as blackness but as a soft half light. Scores of times Ingrid had sat here at this table watching the sun go down, as if she and Lars and their guests were the only people in the world. And watch it she did this day, and talked of the past, of moments that were as gone as the sun.

"When he was little I would always tell Robertino bedtime stories," Ingrid said, laughing to herself. "One time I said, 'Please tell *me* one.' He said, 'Well, there was this poor little boy. He lived with his poor parents in a poor house. He was so poor he had to leave home. He took his Rolls-Royce and drove away.'"

Ingrid had told that story before, but everyone laughed.

"This reminds me of the Last Supper in the Bible," Ingrid said. Everyone laughed again.

Lars left the island the day before Ingrid. Pavo and Britt would close down Danholmen. It was not like Lars, and Pavo felt that his employer could not stand to be there when Ingrid sailed away for the last time.

Ingrid was planning to spend a few days in Stockholm before returning to London. She was so weak now, and her condition was so painful, that it was clear that she should fly to the Swedish capital, but she would hear nothing of that. She didn't want any photographers to take pictures of her the way she looked now. She insisted that she be driven.

On the day that they left Danholmen for the last time, Pavo closed the two houses for the season. Then, as the sky grew gray and threatening, Britt and Pavo helped Ingrid down to the small fishing boat. Ingrid and Britt sat in the stern of the boat, protected by a blue awning. Pavo looked up at the black clouds and thought that perhaps he should wait. But he decided to leave, and as they sailed toward the mainland, the storm fell upon the sea.

In Fjällbacka, Ingrid said goodbye to Lasse and Ingela and got in the back seat of Lars's Citroën. Pavo could see that every jolt, every bump resonated through Ingrid, and he drove as quickly and smoothly toward the capital as he could, stopping only for a picnic lunch.

In Stockholm, Ingrid stayed in Britt's small apartment, only a few blocks from the apartment where they had lived as teenagers. "She often stayed with me," Britt says. "But this time she didn't like anything; the bed was wrong, anything."

As sick as she was, Ingrid went out to visit old friends, to remember old times. In this district she had walked as a young girl, looking up at the marquees of the theaters.

On her last evening in Stockholm, Sunday, August 23, Ingrid and Britt traveled to Mälarstrand, overlooking the water, not far from the town hall. There, in a large apartment high above the street, lived Greta Danielsson and her husband. All that remained of the beauty that had captivated Ingrid's father over half a century before were two sparkling eyes, and a kindness and warmth that time had only enhanced.

When Ingrid arrived, Greta thought that unlike all that she had heard, Ingrid was still beautiful, unmarked by the illness. They talked of old times, and Greta remembered the visit Ingrid had made to Örebro, in the lake country, when Greta was living there with her young doctor husband. They lived in an apartment overlooking the marketplace, and the townspeople had stood in the street, crying for Ingrid to come out on the balcony. And Ingrid had said, "I'm not a royal person," but she had gone out on the balcony and the townspeople had cheered.

Greta realized now that Ingrid had come to say goodbye.

"I am not afraid to die," Ingrid said. "I've had a rich life. I am content."

Ingrid told Griff, "I said goodbye to everyone," as if she had everything in order, just the way she tucked her stockings in her shoes at night.

Ingrid's sixty-seventh birthday would be on Sunday, August 29, 1982, less than a week away. On Saturday morning, as she was getting out of the bath, she felt a pain unlike anything she had felt before. The cancer had advanced to her spine, collapsing her twelfth vertebra.

To ease her pain, Dr. MacLellan gave her injections of diamorphine, a form of heroin. For the first time in the seven years of her illness, Ingrid was bedridden, with little prospect of ever rising to her feet again.

All week there had been phone calls back and forth between Ingrid and her children. And Ingrid had kept insisting that they not bother coming to London. But it was still strange, knowing Ingrid and her sense of occasion, that none of her children were there for her birthday.

"I'm so tired, darling," she told Ann Todd on the phone. "I'm so tired."

"How lovely, Ingrid, how lovely. You just go to sleep."

On Sunday morning there were several calls, calls from friends who did not know how sick Ingrid had become, calls wishing her a happy birthday, but Ingrid flitted in and out of consciousness. Dr. MacLellan visited and discovered that her right lung was not working any longer, and only the upper third of her left lung had not collapsed. The doctor told them that the end was near.

Ingrid knew that Griff was coming to wish her a happy birthday. "Do I look all right?" she asked Margaret. "Give me my brush and makeup."

Griff arrived at the town house and so did Lars, carrying a box of flowers. They stood over Ingrid's bed, Lars and Griff, Margaret and Britt, and they toasted her in champagne. They brushed her lips with champagne too, and she smiled, and then they left her and the room was quiet.

Griff and Lars left, and in the evening, when Britt and Margaret went to bed, the only sound was Ingrid's labored breathing.

Britt was in the next room, sleeping fitfully. At three-thirty, she realized that she could no longer hear Ingrid's breathing. She went into the bedroom and saw that there were tiny beads of blood on Ingrid's lips. She took a mirror and placed it upon Ingrid's lips, although she knew already that she was dead.

CHAPTER TWENTY-FIVE

The Endless Sea

In October they came to Saint Martin's-in-the-Fields Church in London to say goodbye to Ingrid, twelve hundred of them in all. The children were there: Pia, Robertino, Isabella, and Isotta. Lars was there, and so were the Rossellinis, Fiorella and Marcella and Franco and others. Britt was there, as were many others from Sweden. Gérôme had come over from Paris. Liv Ullmann was there too, and Sir John Gielgud and Dame Wendy Hiller and Joss Ackland. Warren Thomas was one of them now, one of the family and friends. And some of Ingrid's other fans came, those who had seen many of her forty-five films, her plays, and her television performances.

Words of Shakespeare and Saint-Exupéry were read in her honor. Birgit Nilsson sang a Beethoven song. A children's choir marched down the aisle of the great church and sang "This Old Man" from *The Inn of the Sixth Happiness*. But there was nothing that was as touching as the moment when, from a distant corner of the church, a violin played the strains of "As Time Goes By."

Ingrid had ascended into myth. The woman who had lived, the woman of bone and blood, of ambition and self-absorption, of courage and cunning, was no more. That person lived on, however, in the lives of those she had known. There was no one, though, who had shared all of her joy and emotion, all of her solitude and fear. For some, like Griff or Margaret or Warren, her loss was as deep as if they had lost part of their own body, and they mourned her as if she were their own blood. For Pia, her mother was as ambiguous a legacy in death as in life, and she seemed to live in an emotional no-man's-land between the memory of her mother and the living presence of her father. When she accepted her mother's Emmy for *Golda*, no one who heard her that evening would have imagined how complex her feelings were toward Ingrid. For Ingrid's other children, the memory of their mother was far sweeter, and they did what they could to serve her memory.

Ingrid's death did not free Petter of his regret that years before he had not spoken out to tell of an Ingrid Bergman the world did not know. As for Lars, he lived on his own island, an island more isolated than Danholmen. He had become the curator of Ingrid's image, and he loved her in memory as he had not loved her in the flesh.

In June, Lars invited a small group of relatives and friends to Danholmen. They walked to a tiny bay, carrying baskets of flowers that they had collected on the island. They stood on the gray rocks, looking out to sea.

Lars and Isotta sailed out into the water in a small boat, with Lasse and a Swedish priest. There they cast Ingrid's ashes into the water, while those on shore threw their baskets into the surf.

The sea was calm and the baskets slowly drifted out. They finally reached a fisherman tending his lobster pots. The fisherman did not know why the water was full of flowers, but he did not touch the baskets, and the flowers drifted farther out and disappeared in the endless sea.

The Films, Plays, and
Television Performances of
Ingrid Bergman

The Count of the Monk's Bridge/*Munkbrogreven*
Svensk Filmindustri, 1934
Produced by AB Fribergs Filmbyra
Directed by Edvin Adolphson and Sigurd Wallen
Screenplay by Gösta Stevens, from the play *Greven fran Gamla Sta'n* by
  Arthur and Siegfried Fischer
Cast: Valdemar Dahlquist, Sigurd Wallen, Eric Abrahamson, Weyler Hilde-
  brand, Artur Cederborg, Edvin Adolphson, Ingrid Bergman, Tollie Zell-
  man, Julia Caesar, Arthur Fischer, Emil Fjellstrom, Viktor Andersson

Ocean Breakers/*Branningar*
Svensk Filmindustri, 1935
Produced by Film AB Skandinavien
Directed by Ivar Johansson
Screenplay by Ivar Johansson, from an idea by Henning Ohlsson
Cast: Tore Svennberg, Sten Lindgren, Carl Strom, Ingrid Bergman, Brof
  Ohlsson, Knut Frankman, Karin Swenson, Weyler Hildebrand, Georg
  Skarstedt, Henning Ohlsson, Vera Lindby, Viktor Ost, Emmy Albiin,
  Viktor Andersson, Helga Brofeldt, Carl Browallius, Olle Grenberg, Holger
  Lowenadler, E. Rosen

The Family Swedenheilms/*Swedenhielms*
Svensk Filmindustri, 1935
Produced by AB Svensk Filmindustri
Directed by Gustav Molander
Screenplay by Stina Bergman, from the play by Hjalmar Bergman
Cast: Ingrid Bergman, Gösta Ekman, Karin Swanström, Häkan Westergren,
  Björn Berglund, Tutta Rolf, Sigurd Wallen, Nils Ericsson, Adèle Söder-
  holm, Mona Geijer-Falkner, Hjalmar Peters, Sven Jerring

Walpurgis Night/*Valborgsmassoafton*
Svensk Filmindustri, 1935
Produced by AB Svenskfilmindustri
Directed by Gustaf Edgren
Screenplay by Oscar Rydquist and Gustav Edgren
Cast: Lars Hanson, Karin Carlsson, Victor Sjöström, Ingrid Bergman, Erik
 Berglund, Sture Lagerwall, Georg Blickingberg, Stig Järrel, Richard Lund,
 Linnéa Hillberg, Marie-Louise Sorbon

On the Sunny Side/*Pa Solsidan*
Svensk Filmindustri, 1936
Produced by Aktiebolaget Wivefilm
Directed by Gustav Molander
Screenplay by Oscar Hemberg and Gösta Stevens, from the play by Helge
 Krog
Cast: Lars Hanson, Ingrid Bergman, Karin Swanström, Edvin Adolphson,
 Einar Axelson, Marianne Lofgren, Carl Browallius, Bullen Berglund, Eddie
 Figge, Olga Andersson, Viktor Andersson, Eric Gustafsson

Intermezzo
Svensk Filmindustri, 1936
Produced by AB Svenskfilmindustri
Directed by Gustav Molander
Screenplay by Gustav Molander and Gösta Stevens, from an original story by
 Gustav Molander
Cast: Gösta Ekman, Ingrid Bergman, Inga Tidblad, Hasse Ekman, Erik Berg-
 lund, Hugo Björne, Emma Meissner, Britt Hagman, Anders Henrikson,
 George Fant, Folke Helleberg, Millan Bolander, Carl Ström

Dollar
Svensk Filmindustri, 1938
Produced by AB Svenskfilmindustri
Directed by Gustav Molander
Screenplay by Stina Bergman and Gustav Molander, from the comedy by
 Hjalmar Bergman
Cast: Georg Rydeberg, Ingrid Bergman, Kotti Chave, Häkan Westergren,
 Birgit Tengroth, Elsa Burnett, Edvin Adolphson, Gösta Cederlund, Erik
 Rosén, Carl Ström, Axel Högel, Millan Bolander

A Woman's Face/*En Kvinnas Ansikte*
Svensk Filmindustri, 1938
Produced by AB Svensk Filmindustri

Directed by Gustav Molander
Screenplay by Gösta Stevens, from the screenplay *Il Était une Fois* by François de Croisset
Cast: Ingrid Bergman, Anders Henriksson, Karin Kavli, Magnus Kesster, Erik Berglund, Gösta Cederlund, Georg Rydeberg, Bror Bügler, Tore Svennberg, Göran Bernhard, Gunnar Sjöberg, Hilda Borgström, Sigurd Wallen

The Four Companions/*Die Vier Gellen*
UFA, 1938
Produced by UFA in Germany
Directed by Carl Fröhlich
Screenplay by Jochen Huth, from his play
Cast: Ingrid Bergman, Sabine Peters, Carlsta Löck, Hans Söhnker, Ursula Herking, Leo Slezak, Erich Ponto, Heinz Welzel, Willi Rose, Karl Haubenreisser, Wilhelm P. Krüger, Lotte Braun

Only One Night/*En Enda Natta*
Svensk Filmindustri, 1939
Produced by AB Svensk Filmindustri
Directed by Gustav Molander
Screenplay by Gösta Stevens, from the story "En Eneste Natt" by Harold Tandrup
Cast: Ingrid Bergman, Edvin Adolphson, Aino Taube, Olof Sandborg, Erik Berglund, Marianne Löfgren, Magnus Kesster, Sophus Dahl, Ragna Breda, John Eklöf, Tor Borong, Viktor Andersson, Ka Nerell

Intermezzo: A Love Story
Selznick International–United Artists, 1939
Produced by David O. Selznick
Directed by Gregory Ratoff
Screenplay by George O'Neil, based on the Swedish scenario by Gustav Molander and Gösta Stevens
Cast: Leslie Howard, Ingrid Bergman, Edna Best, John Halliday, Cecil Kellaway, Enid Bennett, Ann Todd, Douglas Scott, Eleanor Wesselhoeft, Moira Flynn

A Night in June/*Juninatten*
Svensk Filmindustri, 1940
Produced by AB Svensk Filmindustri
Directed by Per Lindberg
Screenplay by Ragnar Hyltén-Cavaallius and Per Lindbert, from a story by Tora Nordström-Bonnier
Cast: Ingrid Bergman, Edvin Adolphson, Aino Taube, Olof Sandburg, Erik Berglund, Marianne Löfgren, Maghus Kesster, Sophus Dahl, Ragna Breda, John Eklöf, Tor Borong

Liliom
A play by Ferenc Molnár, adapted by Benjamin Glazer
Produced by Vinton Freedley
Staged by Benno Schneider
Opened at the Forty-fourth Street Theater, New York, March 25, 1940
Cast: Burgess Meredith, Ingrid Bergman, Margaret Wycherly, John Emery,
   Ann Mason, Elia Kazan, Beatrice Pearson, Elaine Perry

Adam Had Four Sons
Columbia, 1941
Produced by Robert Sherwood
Directed by Gregory Ratoff
Screenplay by William Hurlbutt and Michael Blankfort
Cast: Ingrid Bergman, Warner Baxter, Susan Hayward, Fay Wray, Richard
   Denning, Johnny Downs, Robert Shaw, Charles Lind, Helen Westley, June
   Lockhart, Pete Sosso, Gilbert Emery, Renie Riano, Clarence Muse, Billy
   Ray, Steven Muller, Wallace Chadwell, Bobby Walberg

Rage in Heaven
Metro-Goldwyn-Mayer, 1941
Produced by Gottfried Reinhardt
Directed by W. S. Van Dyke II
Screenplay by Christopher Isherwood and Robert Thoeren, based on the
   novel by James Hilton
Cast: Robert Montgomery, Ingrid Bergman, George Sanders, Lucile Watson,
   Oscar Homolka, Philip Merivale, Matthew Boulton, Aubrey Mather, Fred-
   eric Worlock, Francis Compton, Gilbert Emery, Ludwig Hart

Dr. Jekyll and Mr. Hyde
Metro-Goldwyn-Mayer, 1941
Produced and directed by Victor Fleming
Screenplay by John Lee Mahin, based on the story by Robert Louis Stevenson
Cast: Ingrid Bergman, Spencer Tracy, Lana Turner, Ian Hunter, Donald
   Crisp, Barton MacLane, C. Aubrey Smith, Sara Allgood, Peter Godfrey,
   Frederick Worlock, William Tannen, Francis Robinson, Denis Green, Billy
   Bevan, Forrester Harvey, Lumsden Hare, Lawrence Grant, John Barclay

Anna Christie
A play by Eugene O'Neill
Produced by the Selznick Company
Directed by John Houseman and Alfred de Liagre, Jr.
Opened at the Lobero Theater, Santa Barbara, July 30, 1941; also played in
   San Francisco and New Jersey
Cast: Ingrid Bergman, Damian O'Flynn, Jessie Bosley, J. Edward Bromberg,
   John Miller, Peter Bronte, Edmund Glover, Walter Brooke, William Alland

Casablanca
Warner Brothers, 1942
Produced by Hal B. Wallis
Directed by Michael Curtiz
Screenplay by Julius J. and Philip G. Epstein and Howard Koch, from the play *Everybody Comes to Rick's* by Murray Burnett and Joan Alison
Cast: Humphrey Bogart, Ingrid Bergman, Paul Henreid, Claude Rains, Conrad Veidt, Sydney Greenstreet, Peter Lorre, S. Z. Sakall, Madeleine LeBeau, Dooley Wilson, Joy Page, John Qualen, Leonid Kinsky, Helmut Dantine, Curt Bois, Marcel Dalio, Corrina Mura, Ludwig Stossel, Ilka Gruning, Charles La Torre, Frank Puglia, Dan Seymour

Swedes in America
Office of War Information, 1943
Produced by the Office of War Information's Overseas Bureau
Directed by Irving Lerner
Cast: Ingrid Bergman and the Charles Swensons and their family of Chisago, Minnesota, and neighbors.

For Whom the Bell Tolls
Paramount, 1943
Produced and directed by Sam Wood
Screenplay by Dudley Nichols, from the novel by Ernest Hemingway
Cast: Gary Cooper, Ingrid Bergman, Akim Tamiroff, Katina Paxinou, Joseph Calleia, Vladimir Sokoloff, Arturo de Cordova, Mikhail Rasumny, Eduardo Ciannelli, Fortunio Bonanova, Duncan Renaldo, Alexander Granach, Leonid Snegoff, George Coulouris, Frank Puglia, Pedro de Cordoba, Michael Visaroff, Konstantin Shayne, Martin Garralaga, Jean Del Val, Jack Mylong, Feodor Chaliapin, Mayo Newhall, Michael Dalmatoff, Antonio Vidal, Robert Tafur, Armand Roland

Gaslight
Metro-Goldwyn-Mayer, 1944
Produced by Arthur Hornblow, Jr.
Directed by George Cukor
Screenplay by John Van Druten, Walter Reisch, and John L. Balderston, based on the play *Angel Street* by Patrick Hamilton
Cast: Charles Boyer, Ingrid Bergman, Joseph Cotten, Dame May Whitty, Angela Lansbury, Barbara Everest, Emil Rameau, Edmund Breon, Halliwell Hobbes, Tom Stevenson, Heather Thatcher, Lawrence Grossmith

Saratoga Trunk
Warner Brothers, 1945
Produced by Hal B. Wallis
Directed by Sam Wood
Screenplay by Casey Robinson, based on the novel by Edna Ferber
Cast: Gary Cooper, Ingrid Bergman, Flora Robson, Jerry Austin, Florence Bates, John Warburton, John Abbott, Curt Bois, Ethel Griffies, Minor Watson, Louis Payne, Fred Essler, Adrienne D'Ambricourt, Helen Freeman, Sophie Huxley, Maria Shelton, Sarah Edwards, Jacqueline de Wit, Thurston Hall, William B. Davidson, Theodore Von Eltz, Glenn Strange, Monte Blue, Georges Renavent, Alice Fleming, Alan Bridge, Ruby Dandridge, Ralph Dunn

The Bells of St. Mary's
RKO Radio, 1945
Produced and directed by Leo McCarey for Rainbow Productions
Screenplay by Dudley Nichols, from a story by Leo McCarey
Cast: Bing Crosby, Ingrid Bergman, Henry Travers, William Gargan, Ruth Donnelly, Joan Carroll, Martha Sleeper, Rhys Williams, Dickie Tyler, Una O'Connor, Bobby Fresco, Aina Constant, Gwen Crawford, Matt McHugh, Edna Wonacott, Jimmy Crane, Minerva Urecal, Pietro Sosso, Cora Shannon, Joseph Palma, Jimmy Dundee, Dewey Robinson

Spellbound
Selznick–United Artists, 1945
Produced by David O. Selznick
Directed by Alfred Hitchcock
Screenplay by Ben Hecht, adapted by Angus MacPhail from the novel *The House of Doctor Edwardes* by Francis Beeding
Cast: Ingrid Bergman, Gregory Peck, Michael Chekhov, Jean Acker, Donald Curtis, Rhonda Fleming, Leo G. Carroll, Norman Lloyd, John Emery, Paul Harvey, Steven Geray, Erskine Sanford, Janet Scott, Victor Kilian, Wallace Ford, Dave Willock, Bill Goodwin, George Meader, Matt Moore, Harry Brown, Art Baker, Regis Toomey, Joel Davis, Clarence Straight, Teddy Infuhr, Richard Bartell, Addison Richards, Edward Fielding

Notorious
RKO Radio, 1946
Produced and directed by Alfred Hitchcock
Screenplay by Ben Hecht
Cast: Cary Grant, Ingrid Bergman, Claude Rains, Louis Calhern, Madame Konstantin, Ivan Triesault, Reinhold Schunzel, Moroni Olsen, Alex Minotis, Wally Brown, Ricardo Costa, Sir Charles Mendl, Eberhard Krumschmidt, Fay Baker

Joan of Lorraine
A play by Maxwell Anderson
Presented by The Playwrights Company
Directed by Margo Jones
Alvin Theater, New York, 1946
Cast: Ingrid Bergman, Sam Wanamaker, Kenneth Tobey, Gilmore Brush,
  Romney Brent, Roger De Koven, Kevin McCarthy, Joseph Wiseman

Arch of Triumph
Enterprise–United Artists, 1948
Produced by David Lewis for Enterprise Studios
Directed by Lewis Milestone
Screenplay by Lewis Milestone and Harry Brown, based on the novel by Erich
  Maria Remarque
Cast: Ingrid Bergman, Charles Boyer, Charles Laughton, Louis Calhern,
  Roman Bohnen, Stephen Bekassy, Ruth Nelson, Curt Bois, J. Edward
  Bromberg, Michael Romanoff, Art Smith, John Laurenz, Leon Lenoir,
  Franco Corsaro, Nino Pepitoni, Vladimir Rashevsky, Alvin Hammer, Jay
  Gilpin, Ilia Khmara, Andre Marsauden, Hazel Brooks, Byron Foulger, William Conrad, Peter Virgo, Feodor Chaliapin

Joan of Arc
Sierra Pictures–RKO Radio, 1948
Produced by Walter Wanger
Directed by Victor Fleming
Screenplay by Maxwell Anderson and Andrew Solt, adapted from the play
  Joan of Lorraine by Maxwell Anderson
Cast: Ingrid Bergman, José Ferrer, George Coulouris, Richard Derr, Selena
  Royle, Jimmy Lydon, Francis L. Sullivan, Irene Rich, Gene Lockhart,
  Nicholas Joy, Richard Ney, Colin Keith-Johnston, Leif Erickson, John
  Emery, John Ireland, Ward Bond, J. Carroll Naish, Hurd Hatfield, Cecil
  Kellaway, Philip Bourneuf, Sheppard Strudwick, Taylor Holmes

Under Capricorn
Warner Brothers, 1949
Produced by Transatlantic Pictures
Directed by Alfred Hitchcock
Screenplay by James Bridie, from Hume Cronyn's adaptation of the play by
  John Colton and Margaret Linden and the novel by Helen Simpson
Cast: Ingrid Bergman, Joseph Cotten, Michael Wilding, Margaret Leighton,
  Cecil Parker, Denis O'Dea, Jack Watling

Stromboli
RKO Radio, 1950
Produced and directed by Roberto Rossellini
Story by Roberto Rossellini in collaboration with Art Cohn and Renzo Cesana
Cast: Ingrid Bergman, Mario Vitale, Renzo Cesana, Mario Sponza

The Greatest Love/*Europa '51*
I.F.E. Releasing Corp., 1951; 1954 (U.S.A. release)
A Ponti–De Laurentiis Production
Produced and directed by Roberto Rossellini
Screenplay by Roberto Rossellini, Sandro de Leo, Mario Pannuzio, Ivo Perilli, and Brunello Rondi, from Roberto Rossellini's original story
Cast: Ingrid Bergman, Alexander Knox, Ettore Giannini, Giulietta Masina, Teresa Pellati, Sandro Franchina, William Tubbs, Alfred Browne

Joan of Arc at the Stake
Oratorio by Arthur Honegger, written by Paul Claudel
Produced and directed by Roberto Rossellini
Teatro San Carlo, Naples, 1953, and elsewhere
Cast: Ingrid Bergman, Tullio Carminati, Marcella Pobbe, Florence Quartarar, Miriam Pirazzini, Giacinto Prandelli

We, the Women/*Siamo Donne*
Titanus, 1953
The Chicken, the third of five segments, stories and screenplays by Cesare Zavattini; Luigi Chiarini collaborated on the screenplay
Directed by Roberto Rossellini
Cast: Ingrid Bergman, Anna Magnani, Isa Miranda, Alida Valli, Emma Danieli, Anna Amendola

Joan at the Stake/*Giovanna d'Arco al Rogo*
1953
Produced and directed by Roberto Rossellini
Screenplay by Roberto Rossellini, based on the story and dialogue of Paul Claudel and the oratorio of Paul Claudel and Arthur Honegger
Cast: Ingrid Bergman, Tullio Carminati, Giacinto Prandelli, Augusto Romani, Plinio Clabassi, Saturno Meletti

Journey to Italy/*Viaggio in Italia*
Titanus, 1954
Produced by Roberto Rossellini in association with Sveva-Junior Films
Directed by Roberto Rossellini
Story and screenplay by Roberto Rossellini and Vitaliano Brancati
Cast: Ingrid Bergman, George Sanders, Paul Muller, Anna Proclamer, Maria Mauban, Leslie Daniels, Natalia Rai, Jackie Frost

Fear/*Angst*
Minerva Films, 1955
Produced by Minerva Films
Directed by Roberto Rossellini
Screenplay by Roberto Rossellini, Sergio Amidei, and Franz Graf Treuberg, based on the novel *Der Angst* by Stefan Zweig
Cast: Ingrid Bergman, Mathias Wiemann, Renate Mannhardt, Kurt Kreuger, Elise Aulinger

Anastasia
20th Century-Fox, 1956
Produced by Buddy Adler
Directed by Anatole Litvak
Screenplay by Arthur Laurents, adapted by Guy Bolton from a play by Marcel Maurette
Cast: Ingrid Bergman, Yul Brynner, Helen Hayes, Akim Tamiroff, Martita Hunt, Felix Aylmer, Sacha Piteoff, Ivan Desny, Natalie Schafer, Gregoire Gromoff, Karel Stepanek, Ina De La Haye, Katherine Kath

Tea and Sympathy
A play by Robert Anderson, French adaptation by Roger-Ferdinand
Presented by Elvire Popesco and Hubert de Malet
Directed by Jean Mecure
Opened at Théâtre de Paris, December 2, 1956
Cast: Ingrid Bergman, Jean-Loup Philippe, Yves Vincent, Georges Berger, Simone Paris, Bernard Lajarrige, Guy Sarrazin, Guy Kerner, Bernard Klein, Jean Mondani, Pierre Derone

Paris Does Strange Things/*Elena et les Hommes*
Warner Brothers, 1957
Produced and directed by Jean Renoir
Screenplay by Jean Renoir, based on his story
Cast: Ingrid Bergman, Mel Ferrer, Jean Marais, Juliette Greco, Marjane, George Higgins, J. Richard

Indiscreet
Warner Brothers, 1958
Produced and directed by Stanley Donen for Grandon Productions
Screenplay by Norman Krasna, based on his play *Kind Sir*
Cast: Cary Grant, Ingrid Bergman, Cecil Parker, Phyllis Calvert, David Kossoff, Megs Jenkins, Oliver Johnston, Middleton Woods

The Inn of the Sixth Happiness
20th Century-Fox, 1958
Produced by Buddy Adler
Directed by Mark Robson
Screenplay by Isobel Lennart, based on the novel *The Small Woman* by Alan Burgess
Cast: Ingrid Bergman, Curt Jurgens, Robert Donat, Michael David, Athene Seyler, Ronald Squire, Moultrie Kelsall, Richard Wattis, Peter Chong, Tsai Chin, Edith Sharpe, Joan Young, Lian Shin Yang, Noel Hood, Burt Kwouk

The Turn of the Screw
NBC-TV, 1959
Executive producer, Hubbell Robinson, Jr.
Directed by John Frankenheimer
Adapted for television by James Costigan, from the novella by Henry James
Cast: Ingrid Bergman, Hayward Morse, Alexandra Wager, Isobel Elsom, Laurinda Barrett, Paul Stevens

Goodbye Again/*Aimez-Vous Brahms?*
United Artists, 1961
Produced and directed by Anatole Litvak
Screenplay by Samuel Taylor, based on the novel *Aimez-vous Brahms?* by Françoise Sagan
Cast: Ingrid Bergman, Yves Montand, Anthony Perkins, Jessie Royce Landis, Jackie Lane, Pierre Dux, Jean Clarke, Peter Bull, Michele Mercier, Uta Taeger, Andre Randall, David Horne, Lee Patrick, A. Duperoux, Raymond Gérôme, Jean Hebey, Michel Garland, Paul Uny, Colin Mann, Diahann Carroll

Twenty-four Hours in a Woman's Life
CBS-TV, 1961
Executive producer, Lars Schmidt
Directed by Silvio Narizzano
Screenplay by John Mortimer, based on a story by Stefan Zweig
Cast: Ingrid Bergman, Rip Torn, John Williams, Lili Darvas, Helena de Crespo, Jerry Orbach

Hedda Gabler
A play by Henrik Ibsen, translated by Gilbert Sigaux
Produced by Lars Schmidt
Directed by Raymond Rouleau
Opened at Théâtre Montparnasse, Paris, December 10, 1962
Cast: Ingrid Bergman, Claude Dauphin, Jean Servais, Jacques Dacomine

Hedda Gabler
CBS-TV, 1963
Produced by David Susskind, Lars Schmidt, and Norman Rutherford
Directed by Alex Segal
Adapted for television by Phil Reisman, Jr., from Eva Le Gallienne's translation of the Henrik Ibsen play
Cast: Ingrid Bergman, Michael Redgrave, Ralph Richardson, Trevor Howard, Dilys Hemlett, Ursula Jeans, Beatrice Varley

The Visit
20th Century–Fox, 1964
Produced by Julian Derode
Directed by Bernhard Wicki
Screenplay by Ben Barzman, based on the play by Friedrich Duerrenmatt
Cast: Ingrid Bergman, Anthony Quinn, Irina Demick, Valentina Cortese, Ernest Schroeder, Paolo Stoppa, Hans-Christian Bleck, Romolo Valli

The Yellow Rolls-Royce
Metro-Goldwyn-Mayer, 1965
Produced by Anatole De Grunwald
Directed by Anthony Asquith
Screenplay by Terence Rattigan
Cast: Ingrid Bergman, Omar Sharif, Joyce Grenfell, Wally Cox

A Month in the Country
A play by Ivan Turgenev
Produced and directed by Michael Redgrave
Opened at the Yvonne Arnaud Memorial Theatre in Guilford, England, in June 1965, before moving to the Cambridge Theatre in London
Cast: Ingrid Bergman, Michael Redgrave, Fay Compton, Daniel Massey, Max Adrian, Jennifer Hilary, Geoffrey Chater, Peter Pratt

Stimulantia
Omnia Films, 1967
An eight-part film. Ingrid Bergman appeared in the episode *The Necklace* (*Smycket*), written and directed by Gustav Molander from the story by Guy de Maupassant
Cast: Ingrid Bergman, Gunnar Björnstrand, Gunnel Brostrom

More Stately Mansions
A play by Eugene O'Neill
Staged by José Quintero
Opened at the Ahmanson Theater in Los Angeles, September 1967, and at the Broadhurst Theater in New York, October

Cast: Ingrid Bergman, Colleen Dewhurst, Arthur Hill, Fred Stewart, Barry McCallum, Vincent Dowling, Helen Craig, John Marriott, Lawrence Linville, Kermit Murdock

The Human Voice
ABC-TV, 1967
Produced by David Susskind and Lars Schmidt for Stage 67
Directed by Ted Kotcheff
Adapted for television by Clive Exton, from a translation by Carl Wildman of a story by Jean Cocteau
Cast: Ingrid Bergman

Cactus Flower
Columbia, 1969
Produced by M. J. Frankovich
Directed by Gene Saks
Screenplay by I. A. L. Diamond, from the play by Abe Burrows
Cast: Ingrid Bergman, Walter Matthau, Goldie Hawn, Jack Weston, Rick Lenz, Vito Scotti, Irene Hervey, Eve Bruce, Irwin Charone, Matthew Saks

A Walk in the Spring Rain
Columbia, 1970
Produced by Stirling Silliphant
Directed by Guy Green
Screenplay by Stirling Silliphant, from the novel by Rachel Maddux
Cast: Ingrid Bergman, Anthony Quinn, Fritz Weaver, Katherine Crawford, Tom Fielding, Virginia Gregg, Mitchell Silberman

Captain Brassbound's Conversion
A play by George Bernard Shaw
Produced in the United States by Roger Stevens and Arthur Cantor
Played in England and the United States, 1971 and 1972
American Cast: Ingrid Bergman, Leo Leyden, Geoff Garland, Yusef Bulos, Eric Berry, Zito Kozan, Joss Ackland

From the Mixed-up Files of Mrs. Basil E. Frankweiler
Cinema 5, 1973
Produced by Charles G. Mortimer, Jr.
Directed by Fielder Cook
Screenplay by Blanche Hanalis, based on the novel by E. L. Konigsburg
Cast: Ingrid Bergman, Sally Prager, Johnny Doran, George Rose, Georgann Johnson, Richard Mulligan, Madeline Kahn

Murder on the Orient Express
Paramount Pictures, 1974
Produced by John Brabourne and Richard Goodwin
Directed by Sidney Lumet
Screenplay by Paul Dehn, based on the novel by Agatha Christie
Cast: Ingrid Bergman, Albert Finney, Lauren Bacall, Martin Balsam, Jacqueline Bisset, Jean-Pierre Cassel, Sean Connery, John Gielgud, Wendy Hiller, Anthony Perkins, Vanessa Redgrave, Rachel Roberts, Richard Widmark, Michael York, Colin Blakely, George Coulouris, Denis Quilley

The Constant Wife
A play by W. Somerset Maugham
Produced by Arthur Cantor
Directed by John Gielgud
London and Shubert Theater, New York, 1975
Cast: Ingrid Bergman, Jack Gwillim, Brenda Forbes, Carolyn Lagerfelt, Marti Stevens

A Matter of Time
American International Pictures, 1976
Produced by Jack H. Skirball and J. Edmund Grainger
Directed by Vincente Minnelli
Screenplay by John Gay, based on the novel *The Film of the Memory of Maurice Druon*
Cast: Ingrid Bergman, Liza Minnelli, Charles Boyer, Isabella Rossellini, Spiros Andros, Tina Aumont, Fernando Rey

Autumn Sonata
New World Pictures, 1978
Producted, written, and directed by Ingmar Bergman
Cast: Ingrid Bergman, Liv Ullmann, Lena Nyman, Halvar Björk, Arne Bang-Hansen, Georg Lokkeberg, Gunnar Björnstrand, Erland Josephson, Linn Ullmann, Knut Wigert, Evan von Hanno, Marianne Aminoff, Mimi Pollak

Waters of the Moon
Played at Chichester Theatre's summer season and at Haymarket Theatre, London, 1979
Produced by Duncan C. Weldon and Louis Michaels
Directed by Patrick Garland
Cast: Ingrid Bergman, Wendy Hiller, Doris Hare, Frances Cuka, Derek Godfrey, Charles Lloyd Pack, Paul Hardwick, Brigette Kahn, Carmen Silvera, Paual Geoffrey

A Woman Called Golda
Paramount Television, 1982
Executive Producer: Harve Bennett
Associate Producer: Marilyn Hall
Producer: Gene Corman
Written by Harold Gast and Steven Gethers
Cast: Ingrid Bergman, Ned Beatty, Franklin Cover, Judy Davis, Anne Jackson, Roberto Loggia, Leonard Nimoy, Jack Thompson, Anthony Bate, Ron Berglas, Bruce Boa, David de Keyser, Barry Foster, Nigel Hawthorne, Louis Mahoney

Research Notes

In researching *As Time Goes By*, I believe that I talked to almost every major living figure in Ingrid Bergman's life. I have relied primarily on interviews that I conducted and on documents such as letters, diaries, contracts, etc. that I have personally seen. I have occasionally quoted from books, newspapers, and magazines. Although I have read most of the celebrity journalism, gossip columnists, and fan magazines about Ingrid, I have used such sources only as examples of Ingrid's image.

I have used Miss Bergman's autobiography as my primary source for her own version of herself, for there she is quoted accurately.

In the notes that follow I have highlighted the sources of important facts, quotes, and material. To keep this to a reasonable length, I have not cited each instance that I have quoted a major figure from my interviews. Letters and memos from the Selznick organization are from the Selznick archives at the University of Texas. Newspaper and magazine articles are cited below. Books are listed by authors' names and are fully cited in the selective bibliography.

THE STAR WHO HAD EVERYTHING

page

2 **She talked amiably:** interview with Ellen Neuwald, New York City.
3 **"Italy had just . . .":** interview with Federico Fellini, Rome.

CHAPTER 1: "PAPA, PAPA, THAT'S WHAT I'M GOING TO DO"

4 Description of Strandvägen in nineteenth century: Soder, pp. 76–81.
4 **the silver shoe and the photo constituted:** interview with Disa Lauhren, Stockholm.
4 Biographical information about the Bergman family from family history and genealogy in Swedish in Miss Bergman's possession at the time of her death.

page
5   **rejoiced in:** quoted in *Sweden: Historical and Statistical Handbook.*
5   **Friedel's senior:** Although Ingrid told Steele that her father was 18 years older, her tombstone in Stockholm and family genealogical records show that Justus was born in 1871 and Friedel in 1884.
5   **No. 21, modeled after a palace:** Soder, p. 81.
6   **"That's the devil . . .":** quoted in Bergman and Burgess, p. 20 (henceforth called BB).
6   **"Is Mrs. . . .":** interview with Lauhren, Stockholm.
7   **"She was a . . .":** interview with Lauhren, Stockholm.
8   **"I think . . .":** interview with Greta Danielsson, Stockholm. Danielsson was then called by her maiden name, Haugran.
8   **"Do you know . . .":** quoted in BB, p. 23.
8   **"We fell in love and . . .":** interview with Danielsson.
9   **He handed:** interview with Danielsson.
10   **"In our house . . .":** interview with Britt Engstrom, Stockholm.
10   **Description of the Red Mill:** interview with Torsten Jungstedt, Stockholm.
11   **"one day I would . . .":** IB diary, quoted in BB, p. 27.
11   **"If you remember . . .":** interview with Lauhren, Stockholm.
11   **"My father was . . .":** interview with Engstrom, Stockholm.
12   **"I never had . . .":** interview with Engstrom, Stockholm.
12   **"I think she . . .":** interview with Danielsson.
12   **ostrich farm:** interview with Jungstedt.
12   **"age of lethargy":** quoted in Béranger.
12   **the cinema was:** interview with Rune Waldekranz, Stockholm.
14   **the boy in:** Steele, p. 18.
14   **"A run and a leap . . .":** quoted in BB, pp. 14–16.
14   **"with only minor slips":** "Smorgasbord Circuit," by Irving Wallace, *Collier's,* Dec. 21, 1946, pp. 12, 96.

CHAPTER 2: "OH, SHE STARTS WELL, DOESN'T SHE?"

16   **"I like your . . .":** quoted in BB, p. 32.
17   **"When I was . . .":** interview with Dr. Petter Lindstrom. Unless noted otherwise, all quotes from Lindstrom are from a series of interviews conducted in Santa Monica and San Diego.
18   **"She was absolutely . . .":** interview with Engstrom.
19   **"I was so hated . . .":** quoted in BB, p. 34.
19   **few memories:** interviews with Hasso, Los Angeles; Sundstrom and Bjornstrand, Stockholm.
19   **"I really should have . . .":** quoted in BB, p. 34.
20   **"I didn't look very . . .":** quoted in BB, p. 37.
21   **"had destroyed a scene . . .":** quoted in Adolphson, pp. 213–214.
21   **"I was crushed . . .":** quoted in Tengroth, pp. 111–117.

page

22 "**And who's this?**": quoted in Adolphson, pp. 213–214.

22 "**Edvin says . . .**": quoted in BB, p. 38.

22 "**More as an . . .**": interview with Dahlqvist, Malmo.

23 "**I don't see . . .**": quoted in BB, p. 40.

28 "**How happy I . . .**": quoted in Tengroth, pp. 111–117.

29 "**Little golden kitten . . .**": quoted from undated letter, IB to PL.

29 "**How many hours . . .**": quoted from *Dagens Nyheter* article by Barbro Alving, July 11, 1937.

30 "MOST BEAUTIFUL AND . . .": quoted from Alving, op. cit.

CHAPTER 3: DESTINED FOR HOLLYWOOD

31 "**Men make . . .**": quoted in BB, p. 51.

32 "**I had the . . .**": interview with Holm, Stockholm.

32 "**Gustav Molander, the director . . .**": interview with Dahlqvist.

34 "**rubber truncheons and . . .**": quoted in Crick, p. 364.

34 "**Karl Fröhlich took . . .**": quoted in BB, pp. 51–52.

35 "**I suddenly realized . . .**": quoted in BB, p. 50.

36 "**As I recall it . . .**": interview with Kay Brown, New York.

36 "**I reported on . . .**": quoted in BB, p. 59.

36 "**Miss Reissar has long . . .**": letter Brown to David O. Selznick (henceforth DOS) July 26, 1938, Selznick archives (henceforth SA).

37 "**Keep it most . . .**": memo DOS to Brown, Aug. 15, 1938, SA.

37 "**would still be . . .**": cable DOS to Brown, Aug. 16, 1938, SA.

37 "**a cold shudder . . .**": DOS to Brown, Aug. 16, 1938, quoted in Behlmer, p. 123.

37 "**thrusts her head . . .**": memo Lewton to DOS, May 6, 1938, SA.

38 Description of Stockholm and "**This feeling of . . .**": letter Jenia Reissar to Brown, SA.

38 "**It was as soon . . .**": interview with Reissar, London.

38 "**Under no circumstances . . .**": letter Reissar to Brown, Oct. 4, 1938, SA.

39 "**To almost every question . . .**": letter Reissar to Brown, Jan. 28, 1939, SA.

40 **angry and frustrated**: Steele, p. 24.

40 "**when I arrived in . . .**": letter Brown to O'Shea, Feb. 24, 1939, SA.

40 Terms of contract: contract dated Feb. 14, 1939, SA.

41 "SOMEWHAT UNATTRACTIVE AND . . .": cable DOS to Brown, Feb. 12, 1939, SA.

41 "**You can't conceive . . .**": quoted in BB, p. 60.

41 "**You know you've . . .**": quoted in BB, p. 60.

42 "**utterly disappointed**": quoted in cable Brown to O'Shea, Mar. 16, 1939, SA.

42   "My wife, who since . . .": letter Lindstrom to Brown, Mar. 15, 1939, SA.

42   "IF WE ARE . . .": cable DOS to Brown, Apr. 6, 1939.

CHAPTER 4: "A FIGURE TO TAKE INTO ACCOUNT"

43   **April 20, 1939:** Although IB wrote in her autobiography that she arrived May 6, 1939, the Selznick archives show otherwise.

43   "I think that . . .": letter DOS to Brown, Feb. 27, 1939, SA.

43   "eligibles": letter Brown to DOS, Apr. 24, 1939, SA.

44   "I got in . . .": interview with Neuberger, New York City.

45   "How do you . . .": quoted in BB, pp. 64–65. Irene Selznick says that this story is not true and that Miss Bergman told her she made up the story to give Alan Burgess a good anecdote in her autobiography. Burgess denies this and indeed Ingrid told the story to reporters years before her autobiography was written.

46   Description of first meeting with Selznick based on BB, pp. 65–69.

47   "revolutionary instructions . . .": letter DOS to IB, Nov. 3, 1945, SA.

48   "We have enough trouble . . .": quoted in Irene Selznick, p. 225.

48   "Don't let this . . .": quoted in BB, p. 70.

48   "Understand this . . .": quoted in BB, p. 69.

49   "a combination . . .": quoted in "Big Girl," by Kyle Crichton, *Collier's*, Sept. 14, 1940, p. 13.

49   "Yi! Yi!": quoted in Crichton, p. 13.

49   "I used to . . .": interview with Finnochio, Los Angeles.

50   "This in turn . . .": memo DOS to Ratoff/cc Toland, June 22, 1939, SA.

50   "Ingrid was here . . .": interview with LeBorg, Hollywood.

51   "His judgment was . . .": quoted in BB, p. 81.

51   "I don't hear . . .": letter Brown to Lewton, July 17, 1939, SA.

51   "I was told . . .": interview with Sandler, Los Angeles.

52   "She was the most . . .": letter DOS to Brown, July 28, 1939, SA.

53   "I've got to have . . .": quoted in BB, p. 78.

53   **That had all been called off:** memo DOS to Calvert, July 28, 1939, SA.

53   **To avoid:** memo Calvert to Hebert, July 31, 1939, SA.

53   "THANKS FOR THE . . .": cable IB to DOS, Aug. 9, 1939, SA.

CHAPTER 5: A WILLFUL IGNORANCE

54   **Pia cried and would not:** letter IB to Irene Selznick, Sept. 7, 1939, SA.

54   **Parsons alleged:** *Los Angeles Examiner*, Sept. 21, 1939.

page

54 "this thing could . . .": memo DOS to Birdwell, Sept. 26, 1939, SA.

54 neither any political: cable IB to Selznick, Sept. 29, 1939, SA.

54 "they have a claim . . .": memo Brown to O'Shea, Oct. 11, 1939, SA.

55 "frightening American . . .": letter IB to DOS, Sept. 29, 1939, SA.

55 "but this does . . .": letter DOS to IB, Oct. 16, 1939, SA.

56 "her angelic nature . . .": memo DOS to Brown, Oct. 17, 1939, SA.

56 she did not feel: letter IB to Brown, Oct. 28, 1939, SA.

56 "I think it . . .": quoted in BB, p. 83.

57 Description of the *Rex* based on *The New York Times*, Jan. 13, 1940.

57 Gellhorn noticed: interview with Martha Gellhorn, England.

57 "I AM BOLD . . .": quoted in memo Brown to Selznick, Jan. 10, 1940, SA.

57 "Don't talk too much . . .": quoted in BB, p. 83. Also Myer Beck from memo Brown to DOS, Feb. 9, 1940, SA.

59 "I noticed a distinct . . .": memo DOS to Brown, Feb. 6, 1940, SA.

59 "I can't see . . .": memo Brown to DOS, Feb. 9, 1940, SA.

60 According to Kay: interview with Brown, New York City.

60 "not unduly . . .": cable Brown to DOS, Mar. 20, 1940, SA.

60 "Would my mouth . . .": quoted in BB, p. 87.

61 "Thank God . . .": letter IB to DOS, Mar. 27, 1940, SA.

61 "The theater was . . .": *New York World Telegram*, Mar. 30, 1940.

62 "Oh, you've . . .": Crichton, p. 30.

63 "reluctance about . . .": O'Shea to DOS, May 23, 1940, SA.

63 "stubborn as . . .": memo O'Shea to DOS, June 21, 1940, SA.

63 "It is outrageous . . .": memo DOS to O'Shea, June 24, 1940, SA.

CHAPTER 6: "THE BARS OF MY CAGE ARE BROKEN"

65 "You have heard . . .": letter IB to Selznick, July 15, 1940, SA.

65 They assumed that: cable O'Shea to DOS, June 25, 1940, SA.

66 "At last something . . .": quoted in BB, p. 91.

66 "addicted to . . .": interview with Pober, Hollywood.

66 seven hours later: MGM archives.

67 "There are people . . .": interview with Isherwood, Santa Monica.

67 "I know I can . . .": interview with Dr. Ray Daum, Austin, Tex.

67 "Why didn't you . . .": quoted in BB, p. 94.

68 "Couldn't we switch . . .": quoted in BB, p. 98.

69 Ingrid was the: memo DOS to Brown, Dec. 10, 1940, SA.

69 Selznick commissioned: memo DOS to Brown, Dec. 10, 1940, SA.

70 "I suggested . . .": interview with Gellhorn.

70 "dumb": memo DOS to Brown, Jan. 31, 1940, SA.

72 "shy and . . .": interview with Schram, Los Angeles.

72   **in 1934:** "Cameraman Asks for Divorce After Love Balm Suit," *Los Angeles Daily News,* Mar. 14, 1934.

72   **"was deeply . . .":** quoted in BB, p. 102.

72   **"I watched . . .":** interview with Houseman, Brentwood.

72   **"that in all his career . . .":** quoted in letter DOS to Benny Thau, Mar. 4, 1941, SA.

72   **"Shall I . . .":** quoted in BB, pp. 102–103.

73   **"he wasn't in . . ":** quoted in BB, p. 102.

73   **"Six years is . . .":** letter Fleming to IB, undated 1947.

73   **"He adored . . .":** interview with de Havilland, Venice, Italy.

74   **"like the Ideal . . .":** *New York Journal American,* Aug. 26, 1941.

74   **"Garbo of the 40s":** *New York Post,* Aug. 26, 1941.

74   **"EVERY EVENING . . .":** cable Lindstrom to DOS, Sept. 5, 1941, SA.

CHAPTER 7: MONEY, FAME, AND POWER

76   **"really sweet":** letter IB to Ruth Roberts, quoted in BB, p. 106.

76   **"I think I . . .":** letter IB to Roberts, quoted in BB, p. 107.

77   **"The Lindstroms had . . .":** by Homer C. Hosmer, *Rochester Times-Union.*

77   **"Don't get upset . . .":** letter IB to DOS, Sept. 29, 1941.

77   **"a very poor loser . . .":** memo O'Shea to DOS, Oct. 11, 1941, SA.

77   **"was all wrong . . .":** cable DOS to O'Shea, Oct. 31, 1941, SA.

77   **"another reason . . .":** letter IB to DOS, Nov. 7, 1941, SA.

78   **"I really feel . . .":** letter Lindstrom to Brown, Oct. 24, 1941, SA.

78   **"With your . . .":** letter IB to DOS, Nov. 7, 1941, SA.

79   **"Is it true . . .":** quoted in BB, p. 109.

79   **"We talked about . . .":** interview with McCann, Rochester, N.Y.

80   **"Are you really . . .":** letter IB to Brown, quoted in BB, p. 109.

80   **"a frightening one . . .":** memo Selznick to Brown, Jan. 28, 1942, SA.

80   **"only half . . . alive . . .":** BB, p. 110.

80   **for four days:** letter IB to Roberts, Feb. 21, 1941, quoted in BB, p. 111.

80   **"I should be very . . .":** letter Lindstrom to Brown, Oct. 24, 1941, SA.

80   **"all the indecent . . .":** letter IB to Roberts, quoted in BB, p. 113.

81   **"genius of . . .":** memo Brown to DOS, Mar. 16, 1942, SA.

81   **"I've heard some . . .":** SA, Mar. 24, 1942.

81   **"I wish you . . .":** memo DOS to Brown, Mar. 31, 1942, SA.

81   **"squawking about . . .":** memo DOS to Brown, Mar. 31, 1942, SA.

81   **"she was so . . .":** memo Brown to DOS, Apr. 2, 1942, SA.

82   **"that Swedish . . .":** memo DOS to Brown, Apr. 7, 1942, SA.

82   **"fainting . . .":** cable IB to DOS, Apr. 20, 1942, SA.

CHAPTER 8: A TIGRESS WHO HAS MADE A KILL

page

94   "Ingrid, you are . . .": quoted in BB, p. 117.
94   "triumphant vitality . . .": quoted in Henreid, p. 131.
95   "Edith Head, the . . .": Chierichetti, p. 62.
95   "happy to . . .": cable Roberts to O'Shea, Aug. 7, 1942, SA.
95   "climbed on all . . .": letter IB to O'Shea, Aug. 10, 1942, SA.
96   "beautiful man": quoted in BB, p. 214.
96   "Really, Ingrid . . .": quoted in BB, p. 119.
96   "Tell him . . .": letter IB to O'Shea, Aug. 10, 1942, SA.
97   "you don't . . .": letter IB to Irene Selznick, Aug. 29, 1942, SA.
97   "In a lifetime . . .": unsent cable DOS to Lindstrom, Aug. 6, 1942, SA.
98   "I must handle . . .": cable DOS to Flagg, Dec. 28, 1942.
99   "deepest appreciation": cable Steele to MacFadden, Feb. 15, 1943, SA.
99   One young boy: interview with Larry Ashmead, New York.
99   "Dear Boss!": letter IB to DOS, Dec. 31, 1942, SA.
99   *Cosmopolitan* poll: WA.
99   "I never . . .": quoted in BB, p. 124.
100 Terms of deal: memo Obringer to Wallis, May 19, 1943, WA.
100 "Cooper wanted . . .": interview with Wallis.
100 in January: letter IB to DOS, Jan. 20, 1943, SA.
100 "I feel rather . . .": memo DOS to Flagg, Dec. 29, 1942, SA.
101 "self-effacement": Steele, p. 4.
101 "tall, goodlooking": IB to Roberts, quoted in BB, p. 127.
101 "Sometimes I . . .": quoted in "Bergman, the Beautiful," *Movieland,* January 1944.
101 The censors: letter from Obringer to Jack Warner, Mar. 19, 1943, WA.
102 driving together: interview with Frank Barrena, Los Angeles.
102 "I want to . . .": Warner publicity release, WA.
103 "In my whole . . .": quoted in Bacon, p. 60.
103 "I enjoyed it . . .": quoted in BB, p. 122.
103 "hit the *Bell* . . .": *Time,* Aug. 2, 1943.
104 "Ingrid was . . .": interview with Keyes.
104 "I am going . . .": letter IB to DOS and Irene Selznick, Aug. 29, 1943, SA.
104 "flesh-peddler": quoted in Irene Selznick, p. 258.
105 Selznick wrote: letter DOS to Lindstrom, Nov. 17, 1943, SA.
106 "The worst . . .": letter IB to DOS, Dec. 27, 1943, SA.

CHAPTER 9: A HOLLYWOOD CAREER

107 number one actress: letter from *Box Office Digest* to DOS announcing IB as No. 1 actress for previous year, July 27, 1944, SA.
107 "This is impossible . . .": quoted in BB, p. 136.

page

108   **little Pia:** interview with Dido Renoir, Beverly Hills.
109   **"Peter was a . . .":** interview with Gregory Peck, Los Angeles.
110   **"I got out . . .":** interview with Pia Lindstrom, New York.
110   **"Lindstrom is . . .":** quoted in Davidson, pp. 158–159.
110   **"Ingrid always . . .":** interview with Kjellin, Los Angeles.
111   **sent the script:** note, June 14, 1944, SA.
111   **"getting herself . . .":** memo DOS to Colby, June 22, 1944, SA.
112   **somewhat upset:** BB, pp. 159–160.
112   **"didn't believe . . .":** quoted in Spoto, p. 275.
112   **first shot:** interview with Norman Lloyd, Los Angeles.
112   **"rather erotic story":** Spoto, p. 248.
113   **permission to stay:** quoted in "Portrait of Ingrid Bergman," by Joseph Henry Steele, *Photoplay*, April 1945, p. 36.
113   **"imperious, like . . .":** interview with William, Los Angeles.
114   **Selznick did not:** memo DOS to O'Shea, Dec. 9, 1944, SA.
115   **RKO deal:** memo, RKO archives; also interview with Peck.
115   **extra $25,000:** memo DOS to O'Shea, Jan. 23, 1945, SA.
116   **arrested twice:** Los Angeles newspaper clippings for Feb. 25, Mar. 30, and Apr. 13, 1945, in files of Academy of Motion Picture Arts and Sciences.
116   **"Goodbye, goodbye . . .":** letter IB to DOS, June 13, 1945, SA.
117   **"That is such . . .":** interview with Adler, London. See also Adler, p. 140.
117   **"Ingrid wasn't . . .":** interview with Adler.
117   **Scene in** hunting lodge based on interview with and letter from Robert L. Orbach.
118   **"What a pity . . .":** interview with Adler; and Adler, p. 141.
118   **"Ah, now you're . . .":** quoted in BB, p. 151.
119   **Description of** Capa's career based on Whelan and Capa.
120   **"The fabrication . . .":** quoted in Whelan, p. 100.
120   **"The next day . . .":** interview with Adler.
120   **One evening:** interview with Adler.
121   **"I'm shot! . . .":** interview with Adler; and BB, p. 152.
121   **"I'm going to . . .":** quoted in BB, p. 153.
121   **"One evening . . .":** interview with Adler.

CHAPTER 10: THE LONELINESS OF A BAD MARRIAGE

124   **"I hear you're . . .":** interview with Adler.
124   **"Ingrid said . . .":** interview with Neuwald.
125   **"Hitchcock said . . .":** interview with Grant, Beverly Hills.
125   **"a fiction, fresh . . .":** Spoto, p. 292.
126   **$175,000 and:** Steele, p. 286.
127   **"fantastic distortion":** letter DOS to O'Melveny, Oct. 26, 1945, SA.

page

127 **"was extremely . . .":** memo Hungate to O'Shea, SA.

127 **frantically wired:** cable Reissar to DOS, Nov. 16, 1945, SA.

127 **"without moving . . .":** cable O'Shea to DOS, Dec. 16, 1945, SA.

128 **"sometimes not . . .":** interview with Neptune, Santa Monica.

129 **"psychic subterfuge":** Steele, p. 79.

130 **"What do you . . .":** quoted in Davidson, p. 160.

130 **"Should we . . .":** quoted in Laurence Stallings, *Esquire*, August 1950.

130 **One evening:** interview with Grant.

131 **"I'm so lonely":** quoted in BB, p. 200.

131 **"One evening":** Steele, p. 90.

132 **"Thank you . . .":** quoted in BB, p. 201.

132 **Ingrid made:** interview with Machu, Los Angeles.

133 **Even Bertolt Brecht:** interview with Lloyd.

133 **"Ingrid loved . . .":** interview with Lloyd.

133 **"I'm sure . . .":** interview with Michel Bernheim.

134 **"Why aren't . . .":** interview with Lloyd.

134 **"One day . . .":** interview with Adler.

134 **"That's Ingrid . . .":** quoted in "My Mother, Ingrid Bergman," by Pia Lindstrom as told to George Christy, *Good Housekeeping*, October 1964.

135 **"I thought . . .":** quoted in BB, p. 310.

CHAPTER 11: A SECULAR SAINT

137 **"aura . . . partly . . .":** quoted in "Sonnet to a Lady," by Sam Wanamaker, in unnamed magazine, circa 1947, in Ingrid Bergman collection at Lincoln Center Library of the Performing Arts.

138 **"Shame on . . .":** quoted in BB, pp. 170–171.

138 **For several weeks:** interviews with Frederick O'Neal and Billy Rowe, New York.

138 **"If I had . . .":** AP, Oct. 28, 1946.

138 **emotional crisis:** Steele, p. 115.

138 **"My white rose . . .":** quoted in Whelan, p. 233.

139 **"Sometimes I think . . .":** quoted in "Ingrid of Lorraine," by Lincoln Barrett, *Life*, Mar. 24, 1947.

139 **"so pure, so . . .":** "How Ingrid Became Joan," by Maxwell Anderson, *Photoplay*, April 1947.

139 **"as Miss Bergman . . .":** "Backstage with Miss Bergman," by S. J. Woolf, *New York Times Magazine*, Dec. 29, 1946.

139 **"Why are you . . .":** quoted in BB, p. 340; also interview with Warren Thomas, New York.

139 **a large group:** interview with Frank Edwards, Beverly Hills, and Warren Thomas.

page

140   **One evening:** interview with Lloyd.

140   **15 percent:** "Miss Bernstein Promises to Return," *New York Times*, May 11, 1947.

141   **"putting more trust . . .":** letter Fleming to IB, quoted in BB, p. 177.

141   **"Come back . . .":** interview with Bernheim, Los Angeles.

141   **"It's not . . .":** interview with Pia Lindstrom.

142   **"find no champagne":** letter Capa to IB, quoted in BB, p. 176.

142   **"I would like . . .":** letter Lindstrom to Wyler, Jan. 31, 1947.

142   **"Lindstrom really was . . .":** quoted in Davidson, p. 158.

142   **$175,000 plus:** deal memo in RKO archives.

142   **"Tears are just . . .":** letter Fleming to IB, undated 1947.

143   **"damn embarrassing":** quoted in Steele, p. 139.

143   **"go back into . . .":** letter IB to Roberts, quoted in BB, p. 174.

143   **"Don't think . . .":** letter IB to Roberts, quoted in BB, p. 177.

144   **"There's no fool . . .":** letter Fleming to IB, quoted in BB, p. 180.

144   **fifteen or so:** interviews with Edwards and Thomas.

144   **Ingrid put:** Steele, p. 148.

145   **Charades were:** interview with Celeste Holm, Washington, D.C.

145   **"That little . . .":** quoted in Steele, p. 155.

145   **"Ingrid was supposed . . .":** interview with Adler.

146   **"David, your . . .":** quoted in Lambert, p. 86.

146   **"She's a girl . . .":** interview with Noel Howard, Los Angeles.

146   **One evening:** "The Real Ingrid Bergman Story," by Laurence Stallings, *Esquire*, August 1950.

147   **Fleming deferred:** production notes in RKO archives.

147   **"I remember . . .":** interview with Jose Ferrer, Los Angeles.

147   **The horse:** interview with Howard.

148   **"Every actress . . .":** interview with Ferrer.

148   **for Christmas:** memo Heniigson to Wanger, Dec. 17, 1947, RKO.

149   **"He's just . . .":** quoted in BB, pp. 190–191.

150   **"The part . . .":** quoted in BB, p. 165.

150   **"I would not . . .":** interview with Adler.

150   **"I know . . .":** letter IB to Roberts, quoted in BB, p. 191.

CHAPTER 12: "TI AMO"

151   **"the realism . . .":** BB, p. 1.

151   **"Petter, we . . .":** quoted in BB, p. 1.

151   **"And I was . . .":** BB, p. 3.

151   **"I want . . .":** quoted in BB, p. 4.

152   **The film was not:** based on an examination of Los Angeles newspapers for the spring of 1948 at the Los Angeles Public Library.

152   **She saw it:** Steele, p. 92, and *New York Times* film advertisements for spring 1946. Also PL says that he never saw the film with IB.

152   **"She told me . . .":** quoted in Irene Selznick, pp. 374–375.

152   **"If you need . . .":** quoted in BB, p. 4.

152   **signed a letter:** letter IB to Milestone, Apr. 19, 1947, in archives at Library of Academy of Motion Picture Arts and Sciences.

152   **"beautiful present":** quoted in Overbey, pp. 102–103.

153   **"I JUST . . .":** quoted in BB, p. 7.

153   **sister Marcella:** interview with Marcella Mariani, Rome.

153   **"turning round . . .":** quoted in BB, pp. 7–10.

154   **"From the time . . .":** interview with Reissar, London.

154   **particularly thrilled:** letter Rossellini to DOS, SA.

154   **"This danger . . .":** letter DOS to Reissar, June 19, 1948, SA.

155   **"Let's go . . .":** BB, p. 184.

155   **one of those:** BB, pp. 165–166; also interview with Howard.

156   **"What a . . .":** letter IB to Lindstrom, July 19, 1948.

156   **"I'm going . . .":** letter IB to Roberts, Aug. 6, 1948, quoted in BB, p. 185.

156   **"He creates . . .":** quoted in *No Innocence Abroad,* by Michael Stern, p. 171.

157   **"a phenomenon of . . .":** interview with Father Lisandrini, Rome.

157   **One day Roberto:** interview with Helen Tubbs, New York.

158   **congratulating her:** cable Rossellini to Jones, SA.

158   **"Personally, I . . .":** letter Reissar to DOS, Sept. 28, 1948, SA.

158   **"We were . . .":** quoted in BB, p. 194.

159   **"Swedish women . . .":** quoted in Steele, p. 168.

159   **"I am sure . . .":** quoted in BB, p. 196.

159   **George Gallup's:** *The Hollywood Reporter,* Nov. 16, 1948.

160   **"Ingrid was . . .":** interview with Veger.

160   **Steele could:** Steele, p. 159.

161   **"Probably, subconsciously . . .":** quoted in BB, p. 211.

161   **"I'm going . . .":** quoted in Steele, p. 168; also interview with Lindstrom quoting Lopart.

162   **One evening:** interview with Helen Tubbs.

162   **"I JUST ARRIVE . . .":** quoted in BB, p. 197.

162   **Ingrid had prepared:** interviews with Veger and Lindstrom.

162   **"I was uncontrollably . . .":** quoted in Davidson, p. 162.

163   **"As time wore . . .":** quoted in Hedy Lamarr, pp. 101–102.

163   **"I can't understand . . .":** interview with Sam Goldwyn, Jr., Los Angeles.

164   **"Roberto was . . .":** quoted in Davidson, p. 162.

164   **"every time . . .":** quoted in BB, p. 200.

164   Ingrid's and Roberto's contracts on *Stromboli,* based on Steele, p. 169, plus divorce proceedings in 1950.

164   **a Hollywood column:** "The Bergman Bombshell," by Louella Parsons, *Photoplay,* July 1949.

164   **One evening:** interview with Celeste Holm.

165   **"I'd like . . .":** quoted in BB, p. 204.

165   **"I'd like to come . . .":** quoted in BB, pp. 204–205.

CHAPTER 13: THE PRINCE OF DISORDER

167   **"There has already . . .":** letter IB to Rossellini, quoted in BB, p. 206.

167   **Visiting with:** interview with Ferrer.

167   **"I gave you . . .":** quoted in "News of the Screen," *New York Herald Tribune,* Mar. 14, 1949.

167   **"was not . . .":** quoted in Selznick, p. 375.

167   **"She fell . . .":** quoted in Irene Selznick, p. 375; also interview with Irene Selznick.

168   **"We talked . . .":** interview with Neuwald.

168   **most popular:** Tannenbaum, p. 237.

168   **The American:** Painter-Downs, *The New Yorker,* Nov. 20, 1948.

168   **"it was a . . .":** BB, p. 207.

169   **"Here is . . .":** interview with Tubbs.

169   **"Did Ingrid . . .":** interview with d'Amicos.

169   **Roberto scheduled:** "Ingrid Bergman Meets the Press in Rome, and Near-Riot Ensues," Associated Press, Mar. 22, 1949.

170   **She saw only:** interview with d'Amicos.

170   **"charming like a . . .":** interview with Marcella Mariani.

171   *Petter lilla:* letter IB to Lindstrom, Exhibit A, 1952 trial.

172   **"I was worried . . .":** interview with Marcella Mariani.

172   **"Sure, we . . .":** quoted in Davidson, p. 163.

173   **nine of every:** "Letter from Rome," by Genet, *The New Yorker,* Mar. 19, 1949.

174   **"a spectacular . . .":** BB, p. 220.

174   **"I have seen . . .":** quoted in "Ingrid's Love Affair," by Michael Wilson in the British *People,* Dec. 3, 1950.

174   **"Start of . . .":** quoted in BB, p. 230.

175   **"The actors . . .":** interview with Neuwald.

175   **"You can . . .":** quoted in BB, p. 230.

175   **"A little higher . . .":** quoted in Wilson, Dec. 3, 1949.

175   **April 9 and 12:** quoted in BB, p. 221.

175   **Pia was anticipating:** interview with George Diehl, Arizona, and Lindstrom.

175   **"I had to be . . .":** interview with Cassini, Milan.

page

176 "A wife that . . .": letter Lindstrom to IB, quoted in BB, p. 221.
176 "I think . . .": interview with Neuwald.
177 "Sometime afterward . . .": Stern, pp. 174–175.
177 "endangering my . . .": cable Wanger to IB, quoted in BB, p. 237.
178 "Such stories . . .": letter Breen to IB, quoted in BB, p. 236.
178 "Kay is . . .": interview with Marcella Mariani.
178 "The whole thing . . .": quoted in BB, pp. 243–244.
178 "At Stromboli . . .": interview with Brown, New York.
179 A century earlier: Berenson, pp. 67–68.
179 cold and dominating: Steele, p. 183.
180 "Petter and I . . .": quoted in BB, p. 245.
180 "an Italian farce": interview with Brown.
181 "How I managed . . .": quoted in BB, p. 247.
181 "She looked . . .": quoted in Davidson, p. 163.
181 Not until: "Ingrid's Mate Boards Plane," United Press, Rome, May 6, 1949.
182 "Petter called . . .": interview with Engstrom, Stockholm.
183 "I don't know . . .": letter IB to Lindstrom, quoted in BB, p. 248.
183 "My mission was . . .": court testimony quoted in *Los Angeles Examiner*, June 17, 1952.
183 "I said . . .": court testimony quoted in *Los Angeles Times*, June 18, 1952.
184 "Ingrid took no part . . .": quoted in Wilson, in *People*, Nov. 27, 1950.
184 She showed Ingrid: interview with Neuwald.
185 He told her: Steele, p. 205.
185 "When they . . .": interview with Father Lisandrini.
186 "In the beginning . . .": letter IB to Steele, quoted in Steele, p. 255.
186 "in the midst . . .": quoted in Overbey, p. 107.
187 "was trembling . . .": Wilson, *People*, Dec. 4, 1950.
187 "NO ONE REALIZES . . .": Steele, p. 205, and BB, p. 255.
188 Steele stayed up: Steele, pp. 207–213.

CHAPTER 14: THE EDGE OF A VOLCANO

189 Steele pointed: Steele, p. 219.
190 It *was not:* quoted in BB, p. 257.
190 "Wait till . . .": quoted in BB, pp. 139–140.
191 "I took a . . .": quoted in "Ingrid Bares Her Troubles," *Los Angeles Times*, Aug. 10, 1949.
191 "What's all this . . .": quoted in BB, p. 258.
192 the conversation fell: Steele, p. 229.
192 even refused: *Los Angeles Daily News*, Aug. 16, 1949.

page

193   *you know if:* letter IB to Anna-Britta, Sept. 3, 1949, quoted in "Ingrid and Pia Tell Their Own Stories," article in Lewis Sweyd Collection at U.S.C.

193   **"From what . . .":** interview with Franco Rossellini, Rome.

193   *Since her:* "The Real Love Story," by Cholly Knickerbocker, *New York Journal American,* Sept. 21, 1949.

194   **"friends in . . .":** interview with Cassini.

194   **Strangely unaffected:** Steele, p. 238.

195   **wrote an article for *Collier's*:** interview with Sandler.

195   **"spokesman for . . .":** *Los Angeles Herald Examiner,* Sept. 23, 1949.

195   **"You say . . .":** letter IB to Lindstrom, quoted in BB, p. 261.

195   List of assets based on court documents in divorce proceedings.

196   **As Steele learned:** Steele, p. 283.

196   **"I feel . . .":** letter IB to Lindstrom, quoted in BB, p. 261.

197   **"STRANGE . . .":** *New York Mirror,* Oct. 10, 1949.

197   **Steele thought:** Steele, p. 242.

197   **and admonished:** Steel, p. 242.

197   **Pia asked:** letter IB to Steele, quoted in Steele, p. 250.

198   **"The experience . . .":** interview with Pia Lindstrom.

198   **None of:** letter IB to Steele, Dec. 1, 1949, quoted in Steele, p. 257.

198   **"There is . . .":** letter IB to Steele, Nov. 25 and 26, 1949, quoted in Steele, pp. 254–255.

199   **he warned:** letter Steele to IB, Steele, pp. 256–257.

199   **Steele said:** Steele, pp. 259–260.

199   **"Few women . . .":** *Los Angeles Examiner,* Dec. 12, 1949.

200   **As Gregory:** interview with Peck.

201   **"Whether she . . .":** *The New York Times,* Dec. 15, 1949.

202   **"contemplated suicide":** *International News Service,* by Michael Chinigo, Rome, Feb. 3, 1949.

202   **"What's the matter . . .":** BB, p. 264.

202   **She told Ingrid:** letter IB to Steele, quoted in Steele, p. 275.

202   **"terrible presentiment":** quoted in BB, p. 264.

203   *I am going:* letter IB to Pia, Feb. 2, 1950, quoted in BB, pp. 266–268.

203   **"The guards . . .":** letter IB to Steele, quoted in Steele, p. 277.

204   **"five-million-lire . . .":** "Letter from Rome," by Genet, *The New Yorker,* Apr. 8, 1950.

CHAPTER 15: A CHILD OF LOVE

206   **"How nice is . . .":** interview with Father Lisandrini.

206   **"living publicly . . .":** "Vatican Attack on Rossellini," *Daily Telegraph,* Feb. 16, 1950.

206   **"while thousands . . .":** quoted in *London News,* Feb. 12, 1950.

page

207 **In Annapolis:** *Washington Post,* Feb. 10, 1950.

207 **"Mr. President . . .":** quoted in BB, pp. 273–274.

207 **"low level . . .":** quoted in *The Worker,* Feb. 22, 1950.

209 **almost hysterical:** BB, p. 276.

209 **"Most of the . . .":** letter IB to Steele, quoted in Steele, p. 284.

210 **"*Maestro!*":** quoted in BB, pp. 280–281.

210 **On another occasion:** interviews with Ann Todd, London, and David Lean, Beverly Hills.

210 **"I saw her . . .":** interview with Fellini, Rome.

211 **"Ingrid's reaction . . .":** interview with Masina, Rome.

211 **"We were like . . .":** interview with Fiorella Mariani, Rome.

211 **"with a very . . .":** letter DOS to Reissar, June 13, 1950, SA.

212 **She said that:** letter IB to Steele, Steele, p. 295.

212 **"Let's go . . .":** interview with a prominent Italian director. The story of Rossellini's sexual unhappiness with Ingrid was confirmed in separate interviews with two of his closest associates.

212 **"a woman without passion":** interview with Rodolfi.

212 **"While she was . . .":** interview with Father Lisandrini.

214 **"express to her . . .":** deposition, August 1980.

215 **$80,000 in:** Steele, p. 282, and newspaper accounts.

215 **property settlement:** property settlement filed in court documents.

215 **in court proceedings:** *Los Angeles Examiner,* June 24, 1952.

215 **"of August 9 . . .":** letter Pacht to Bautzer, Aug. 17, 1950.

216 **"I think you can . . .":** letter IB to Lindstrom, Oct. 6, 1950, quoted in BB, p. 287.

216 **"No, I have no . . .":** *The New York Times,* Nov. 2, 1950.

217 **"Mr. Borre . . .":** letter Brinn to Lindstrom, Nov. 17, 1950.

217 **"You and your . . .":** letter Lindstrom to IB, Mar. 20, 1951.

218 **Ingrid remembered:** BB, p. 289.

218 **Fiorella Mariani:** interview with Fiorella Mariani.

218 **Roberto did:** newspaper clipping from unnamed London paper for July 7, 1951, in British Film Institute library.

218 **"Dr. Lindstrom . . .":** quoted in BB, p. 290.

218 **"I had . . .":** interview with Todd.

219 **"I recall . . .":** affidavit filed in Superior Court of California, June 4, 1952.

219 **"calm":** letter IB to Irene Selznick, Sept. 10, 1951, quoted in BB, p. 292.

220 **"Yes, this is . . .":** UPI, Aug. 30, 1951, *Los Angeles Daily News,* p. 4.

220 **"I remember . . .":** quoted in Davidson, p. 159.

220 **One evening:** AP, "Rome Crowd Boos Ingrid," *Los Angeles Herald,* June 16, 1951.

221 **"Ingrid was like . . .":** interview with Masina.

page

235 *My editor:* quoted in Davidson, p. 171.
236 **"When you did . . ."**: interview with Father Lisandrini.
236 *Miss Bergman and:* quoted in Quirk, pp. 143–144.
237 **"If a good . . ."**: letter IB to Steele, quoted in Steele, p. 315.
237 **"I give you . . ."**: interview with Dido Renoir.
237 **"splitting artistically"**: quoted in AP, *Citizen News,* June 7, 1955.
237 **"could stop . . ."**: quoted in BB, p. 282.
237 **"never seen . . ."**: *Los Angeles Times,* June 29, 1955.
238 **"I don't talk . . ."**: quoted in BB, p. 282.
238 **"From the beginning . . ."**: interview with Fellini.

CHAPTER 17: "WELCOME HOME, MISS BERGMAN"

239 **"Why are . . ."**: interview with Ferrer, Beverly Hills.
240 **"I think . . ."**: interview with Brown.
240 **a figure of:** *Variety,* Dec. 21, 1955; *Mirror,* Dec. 21, 1955.
240 **"I had . . ."**: quoted in BB, pp. 332–333.
240 **he soon left:** *Daily Mail,* June 27, 1956.
241 **"I tried . . ."**: letter IB to Gigi Girosi, quoted in BB, p. 330.
241 **"Roberto's India . . ."**: interview with Fiorella Mariani.
242 **"I think that . . ."**: interview with Helen Hayes, New York.
243 **"You won't . . ."**: quoted in BB, p. 335.
243 **fifteen curtain calls:** AP, *New York Times,* Dec. 4, 1956.
243 **"I looked toward . . ."**: quoted in Davidson, p. 173.
243 **"They were standing . . ."**: quoted in BB, p. 335.
244 **"Phyllis and I . . ."**: interview with Anderson, New York City.
245 **"When I look . . ."**: interview with Rossellini, Monte Carlo.
246 **"Now I know . . ."**: quoted in *The New York Times,* Aug. 5, 1956.
246 **The results:** *Newsweek,* Aug. 13, 1956.
246 **"I was very sad . . ."**: interview with Pia Lindstrom.
247 **"Then we'll . . ."**: letter IB to Steele, quoted in Steele, p. 326.
247 Description of Alvin gang based on interviews with Frank Edwards, Los Angeles, and Warren Thomas.
248 **"Miss Bergman . . ."**: quoted in PBS documentary on Ingrid Bergman.
248 **"at least 50 . . ."**: quoted in "Dick Williams," *New York Mirror-News,* Jan. 23, 1957.
249 **"well-nigh rhapsodic"**: "Ingrid's Return," *Newsweek,* Jan. 28, 1957.
249 **"I had given . . ."**: interview with Anderson.
249 **"I tried to . . ."**: quoted in BB, p. 346.
249 **"nice"**: UP, Jan. 21, 1957.
250 *Dear Bob:* letter IB to Anderson.
250 **"I seldom went . . ."**: interview with Grant.

page

251 **"Isn't it strange . . .":** quoted in BB, pp. 350–351; also interview with Schmidt, Paris.

251 **He said that:** quoted in Steele, p. 331.

252 **Indian film starlet:** quoted in UPI, *Los Angeles Herald Express*, May 27, 1957.

252 **"There was . . .":** interview with Tonti, Rome.

252 **"My wife and . . .":** quoted in *Los Angeles Times*, May 21, 1957.

253 **"There were nights . . .":** quoted in Davidson, p. 173.

253 **She wrote Steele:** letter IB to Steele, quoted in Steele, p. 332.

253 **"Now it's all . . .":** quoted in BB, p. 353.

253 **"Ingrid rang . . .":** interview with Todd.

254 **"My husband . . .":** quoted in BB, p. 354.

254 **"That summer . . .":** quoted in "My Mother, Ingrid Bergman," by Pia Lindstrom as told to George Christy in *Good Housekeeping*, October 1964.

255 **"As I look back . . .":** quoted in BB, p. 347.

255 **"Of course . . .":** letter IB to Irene Selznick, quoted in BB, p. 348.

255 **"I've brought . . .":** interview with Donen.

255 **"It is rubbish . . .":** INS and AP, Oct. 21, 1957.

256 **she went to see:** interview with Sonali Senroy, Rome.

256 **"So what's the . . .":** quoted in BB, pp. 356–357.

256 **$976 a month:** *New York Times*, Nov. 8, 1957.

256 **"Ingrid, take also . . .":** interview with Father Lisandrini.

CHAPTER 18: A MAN OF PERFECT MANNERS

258 **"Why don't you . . .":** UP, "Ingrid Sad on Arrival in London," Nov. 12, 1957.

258 **Ingrid's deal:** production memo, WA.

258 **"Mother had . . .":** interview with Isotta Rossellini, New York.

258 **"By the time . . .":** letter IB to Steele, quoted in Steele, p. 338.

259 **"She was so . . .":** interview with Donen, Beverly Hills.

259 **"We had . . .":** interview with Grant.

259 **Anderson wrote:** interview with Anderson.

260 **She flew to Rome:** *New York Times*, Dec. 24, 1957.

260 **They greeted the:** publicist's letter, WA.

260 Biography of Schmidt based primarily on "Hardly Anybody Knows Him—That's the Way He Wants It," by Dora Jane Hamblin, *Life*, Oct. 16, 1964; interview with Hamblin, Rome; and interview with Schmidt, Paris.

261 **"The house was . . .":** interview with Schmidt.

261 **"I love your . . .":** quoted in BB, p. 362.

261 **"Ingrid said . . .":** interview with Schmidt.

page

262   **She believed:** letter IB to Steele, Steele, p. 343.

262   **"We reach . . .":** UPI, *Los Angeles Times,* July 12, 1958.

262   **"The children . . .":** UPI, *Los Angeles Times,* July 12, 1958.

263   **"How would you . . .":** quoted in BB, p. 364.

263   **"Mama? Does . . .":** quoted in BB, pp. 365–366.

263   **"Rossellini never . . .":** interview with Schmidt.

263   **suspicious of a:** letter IB to Liana Ferri, Oct. 5, 1958, quoted in BB, p. 368.

263   **"some of . . .":** interview with Franco Rossellini, Rome.

264   **For months:** "Inside Hollywood," by Herb Stein, *Daily Racing Form,* Los Angeles, June 3, 1959; also *The Morning Telegraph,* June 22, 1959.

264   **privately she condemned:** interview with Danny Selznick, Washington, D.C.

264   **"I met an . . .":** interview with Schmidt.

266   **"My sense was . . .":** interview with Hamblin.

266   **"We were . . .":** interview with Schmidt.

266   **"I may . . .":** interview with Isabella Rossellini.

267   **"Separation is not . . .":** interview with Schmidt.

267   **The court ruled:** AP, *The New York Times,* Jan. 25, 1959.

267   **To ensure:** AP, Jan. 24, 1959.

267   **"In many ways . . .":** quoted in BB, p. 386.

268   **"We lived . . .":** interview with Isabella Rossellini.

268   **One weekend he:** interviews with Isabella and Isotta Rossellini.

268   **"That's something . . .":** quoted in *Los Angeles Times,* Apr. 4, 1959.

269   **In April she:** AP, Apr. 17, 1959.

269   **Description of court hearings** based on *Washington Post,* Sept. 10, 1959; *Newsweek,* Sept. 21, 1959; AP, Sept. 9, 1959.

269   **She went up:** *The New Yorker,* Oct. 10, 1959.

269   **"It's no good! . . .":** quoted in *Newsweek,* Oct. 19, 1959.

270   **"I don't see . . .":** quoted in *New York News Syndicate,* Oct. 14, 1959.

270   **flew out of:** Reuters, Oct. 17, 1959.

271   **"Everyone swam . . .":** interview with Isabella Rossellini.

271   **"I would have . . .":** quoted in *Los Angeles Times,* Nov. 25, 1960.

271   **"he could steal . . .":** quoted in "Hedda Hopper," *Los Angeles Times,* Nov. 25, 1960.

271   **"I wanted . . .":** quoted in "Erskine Johnson" column, *Los Angeles Mirror,* Feb. 10, 1961.

271   **"Ingrid started . . .":** interview with Perkins, Los Angeles.

272   **"She would have . . .":** quoted in "Psycho II," by Brad Darrach, *People,* June 13, 1983.

272   **"a presumably . . .":** interview with Perkins. Brad Darrach, the author of the *People* article, stands by his story.

272   **"What's the . . .":** interview with Perkins.

page

273 **It was Anthony:** interview with Anthony Quinn conducted by Vesna Obradovic Leamer, Washington.

274 **"Ingrid begged . . .":** interview with Quinn.

274 **"Somehow in . . .":** interview with Nichols, Boston.

275 **"At the Cannes . . .":** *Daily Express,* June 27, 1964.

275 Salaries on *The Yellow Rolls-Royce* based on figures in the production file, WA.

275 **"She said to . . .":** interview with Nichols.

276 **"My uncle . . .":** interview with Fiorella Mariani.

276 **"Roberto was a . . .":** interview with Senroy, Rome.

276 **She charged:** UPI, Dec. 12, 1961.

277 **"I was a . . .":** quoted in *Newsweek,* Nov. 25, 1963.

277 **"My mother asked . . .":** interview with Pia Lindstrom.

277 **"Her beauty . . .":** quoted in *New York Daily News,* June 27, 1964.

277 **"Pia was . . .":** interview with Quinn.

277 **"no doubt . . .":** *New York Daily News,* June 27, 1964.

278 **"undue publicity . . .":** quoted in *Good Housekeeping,* October 1964.

278 **"I don't want . . .":** interview with Pia Lindstrom.

279 **"I thought that maybe . . .":** interview with Pia Lindstrom.

279 **"Many things . . .":** interview with Marcella Mariani, Rome.

279 **"I felt . . .":** interview with Pia Lindstrom.

279 **Pia received:** *Los Angeles Herald-Examiner,* July 31, 1965.

279 **"I am sincerely . . .":** quoted in *Modern Screen,* November 1965.

CHAPTER 19: AN ELEGANT FACADE

280 **She called Lars's:** interview with Gérôme, Paris.

280 **His take on:** *Life,* Oct. 16, 1964.

281 **"Sometimes it was . . .":** interview with Isabella Rossellini.

282 **"one of the happiest . . .":** quoted in BB, p. 403.

283 **"where nobody . . .":** quoted in BB, p. 406.

283 **"Where does it . . .":** Interview with Schell, Venice.

284 **"Here! . . .":** interview with Isabella Rossellini.

284 **"How can you . . .":** quoted in BB, p. 414.

284 **"I turned to . . .":** quoted in BB, p. 415.

285 **"He came . . .":** interview with Isabella Rossellini.

286 **"Why is everyone . . .":** quoted in *Los Angeles Times West Magazine,* Sept. 10, 1967.

286 **"You come running . . .":** quoted in BB, p. 422.

287 **"I drove poor . . .":** letter IB to Schmidt, quoted in BB, p. 423.

287 **"You mustn't . . .":** BB, p. 424.

287 **Ingrid's reception:** *The New York Times,* Sept. 14, 1967.

288 **"I hope you . . .":** PBS documentary on Ingrid Bergman.

page

289 **"I showed her . . ."**: interview with Thomas.

289 **Isotta insists:** interview with Isotta Rossellini.

289 **"you are always . . ."**: letter Schmidt to IB, quoted in BB, p. 427.

289 **On at least:** interview with Stig Nahlbom.

289 **"the most urbane . . ."**: interview with Silliphant, Beverly Hills.

290 **"Ingrid said she . . ."**: interview with Todd, London.

291 **"We weren't close"**: interview with Matthau, Venice.

291 **"What movie . . ."**: quoted in "Ingrid Bergman: The New Happiness in Her Life," by Muriel Davidson, *Good Housekeeping*, May 1969.

291 **"I knew it . . ."**: interview with Quinn.

292 **"They were like . . ."**: interview with Silliphant.

292 **"the 'love bag' . . ."**: quoted in *Los Angeles Herald-Examiner*, June 7, 1969.

293 **"The romance was . . ."**: interview with Veitch, Los Angeles.

293 **"One of my . . ."**: interview with Quinn.

294 **"I have calmed . . ."**: letter IB to Schmidt, quoted in BB, pp. 432–433.

CHAPTER 20: "DARLING, THAT IS YOU CRYING"

295 **"At first I . . ."**: quoted in BB, p. 435.

296 **"Lars is a . . ."**: interview with Fiorella Mariani.

296 **"Ingrid and Lars . . ."**: interview with Anderson.

297 **"Well, Lady . . ."**: interview with Banbury, London.

297 **"You're late"**: interview with James.

297 **"She would only play . . ."**: interview with Ackland, London.

298 **Louie watched out:** interview with Hollis, London.

299 **"Walter, it's me . . ."**: interview with Matthau.

300 **Ingrid arrived:** *Washington Post*, Mar. 28, 1972.

301 **"Miss Bergman . . ."**: interview with Daly, Venice.

301 **"From an early . . ."**: interview with Fiorella Mariani, Rome.

301 **"This was the . . ."**: interview with Isotta Rossellini.

302 **"She gave . . ."**: interview with Todd.

303 **No, it can't:** BB, p. 446.

303 **"Am I insured . . ."**: interview with James, and BB, p. 446.

303 **"Yes, you must . . ."**: quoted in BB, p. 447; also *The Daily Express* four-part series on the death of Ingrid Bergman by Michael Thornton, Sept. 27, 1982, to Sept. 30, 1982.

303 **"Miss Bergman's . . ."**: *Los Angeles Times*, Jan. 16, 1974.

303 **"I'm sorry . . ."**: interview with James.

304 **"Do you think . . ."**: interview with Evans, London.

304 **"Well, I've got . . ."**: quoted in BB, p. 449.

304 **"I have to . . ."**: interview with Isotta Rossellini.

CHAPTER 21: INGRID'S GREAT PERFORMANCE

320   "People like you . . .": based on the dubbed English-language version of *Autumn Sonata*. The English-language printed version of the script is substantially different and somewhat wooden in places.

321   "Ingrid was . . .": interview with Ingmar Bergman.

CHAPTER 22: "OH, WENDY, IT'S ONLY A PLAY"

322   "She'd enter . . .": interview with James.

322   Once, from: interview with Schmidt.

323   "Obviously, I loved . . .": interview with Van Eyssen.

323   "Oh, Wendy": interview with Garland.

323   "If anyone . . .": interview with Hiller.

324   "Louie, they're . . .": interview with Hollis.

324   "It was a bit . . .": interview with Hiller.

324   "You must . . .": interview with Garland.

325   "Whatever is . . .": interview with Hollis.

326   Peek talked: interview with Peek.

326   "She was very . . .": interview with Fiorella Mariani.

326   "Mother thought . . .": interview with Isabella Rossellini. Pia Lindstrom has no comment to make about this incident.

327   talked to Ingrid: interview with Todd.

327   Steele and his collaborator: interview with Davidson and Lindstrom.

327   Benjamin called: interview with Benjamin, Beverly Hills.

328   Carla knew: interview with Carla Benjamin.

328   "We must leave you now . . .": videotape of tribute viewed at American Film Institute in Los Angeles.

328   She was holding: interview with Isabella Rossellini.

329   "He took my hands": quoted in Spoto, p. 552.

329   "As soon as . . .": interview with Burgess, Houston.

329   "Dear Grandma": letter Lindstrom to IB.

330   "Stöde is just . . .": letter IB to Lindstrom.

330   "Does he move . . .": interview with Isabella Rossellini.

331   He was playing: interview with Scorsese, New York.

331   "the only reality . . .": quoted in Todd, p. 220.

331   Isabella took: interview with Isabella Rossellini.

331   "Don't you give . . .": interviews with Todd and Isabella Rossellini.

331   "Ingrid worked . . .": interview with Engstrom.

332   "I thought . . .": videotape of tribute.

333   Griff turned: interview with James.

333   "Where's the . . .": interview with Burgess.

333   "Kay mentioned . . .": letter Lindstrom to Burgess.

333   "I had no . . .": interview with Burgess.

334   been a "joy": letter IB to Lindstrom.

page

334 **he was sorry:** letter Burgess to Lindstrom.

335 **"The past . . .":** letter Lindstrom to IB, Mar. 26, 1980.

335 **it was the publisher:** interviews with Ross Claiborne and Jeanne Bernkopf, New York.

335 **"to say what . . .":** interview with Burgess.

336 **"Ingrid said that . . .":** interview with Claiborne.

336 **"We were writing . . .":** interview with Bernkopf.

336 **Irene Selznick was upset:** IB diary, viewed at home of Isabella Rossellini.

CHAPTER 23: "I DON'T WANT THE FILM TO BE OVER"

338 **got together:** interviews with Harve Bennett and Silvia Rubinstein, Los Angeles.

338 **She phoned:** interview with Hall, Beverly Hills.

339 **Ingrid couldn't help:** interview with Engstrom.

339 **he was stunned:** interview with Corman, Los Angeles.

340 **Laurence Evans:** interview with Evans.

340 **"From what I . . .":** letter IB to Bennett, Apr. 9, 1981.

341 **"You know, I . . .":** interview with Hall, Beverly Hills.

341 **"But why?":** interview with Bennett.

341 **Pia came:** interview with Pia Lindstrom.

342 **"There's no way . . .":** interview with Gibson, London.

342 **He had saved:** interview with Schneiderman, London.

343 **"I have only . . .":** interview with Bennett.

343 **"I've gone through . . .":** interview with Johnstone, London.

344 **"was a good hater . . .":** "An Unworthy Script," by Philip Gillon, *The Jerusalem Post International Edition,* undated clipping obtained from Paramount Studios.

345 **Schneiderman used:** interview with Schneiderman, London.

345 **For Alan Greenberg:** interview with Greenberg, Los Angeles.

346 **"There was concern . . .":** interview with Nimoy, Hollywood.

346 **"I think . . .":** interview with Corman, Los Angeles.

347 **"You'll have to . . .":** interview with Monty Hall.

348 **Several times:** interview with Schmidt.

348 **"See, you're standing . . .":** interview with Isabella Rossellini.

CHAPTER 24: "I'M ALONE"

350 **Lars phoned:** interview with Johnstone.

350 **"She was very . . .":** interview with Isabella Rossellini.

350 **Although Dr. Edward MacLellan:** Thornton, *Daily Express,* Sept. 30, 1982.

page

351   "I want . . .": interview with James.

351   "Isn't there . . .": interview with Engstrom.

352   "She was . . .": interview with Todd.

352   "They wait . . .": interview with Fiorella Mariani.

352   arrived to: interview with Green, Beverly Hills.

353   "her little day . . .": interview with Franka, London.

353   "Is that . . .": interview with Isotta Rossellini.

353   "We talked about . . .": interview with Weiss, New York.

353   a hard time: interview with Van Esseyen.

353   Thomas was there: interview with Thomas.

354   "A lot of . . .": letter IB to Alving, July 6, 1982, reproduced in the Swedish magazine *Saxons*.

354   "He died . . .": interview with Fiorella Mariani.

354   "Ingrid had . . .": interview with Johnstone.

354   "At the end . . .": interview with Isabella Rossellini.

355   "For Mama . . .": interview with Isotta Rossellini.

355   "When the girls . . .": interview with Engstrom.

355   "Margaret has . . .": interview with Hall.

356   "How are you . . .": interview with Todd.

356   "She started . . .": interview with Schmidt.

356   "Ingrid's bad . . .": interview with Lasse Lundberg, Fjällbacka.

357   "When he was . . .": interviews with Lasse and Ingela Lundberg.

357   Pavo closed: interview with Turtiainen.

357   "She often . . .": interview with Engstrom.

358   Greta thought: interview with Danielsson.

358   "I said goodbye . . .": interview with James.

358   "I'm so . . .": interview with Todd.

359   "Do I look . . .": interview with Johnstone.

CHAPTER 25: THE ENDLESS SEA

360   they came: *The Times of London*, Oct. 15, 1982.

361   They walked: interviews with Schmidt and Lasse and Ingela Lundberg.

Selected Bibliography

Magazine and newspaper articles are cited in the notes.

Adler, Larry. *It Ain't Necessarily So.* London: Collins, 1984.

Adolphson, Edvin. *Ea berätar.* Stockholm: Bonniers, 1972.

Anobile, Richard, Jr. *Casablanca.* New York: Universe Books, 1974.

Arce, Hector. *Gary Cooper.* New York: Bantam Books, 1980.

Austin, Paul Britten. *On Being Swedish: Reflections Towards a Better Understanding of the Swedish Character.* London: Secker and Warburg, 1968.

Avallone, Michael. *A Woman Called Golda.* New York: Leisure Books, 1982.

Bacon, James. *Made in Hollywood.* New York: Warner Books, 1977.

Barnett, Lincoln. *Writing on Life: Sixteen Close-Ups.* New York: William Sloane Associates, 1951.

Barzini, Luigi. *From Caesar to the Mafia: Sketches of Italian Life.* New York: The Library Press, 1971.

Behlmer, Rudy. *America's Favorite Movies Behind the Scenes.* New York: Frederick Ungar, 1982.

Behlmer, Rudy, ed. *Memo from Selznick.* New York: Grove Press, 1972.

Benchley, Nathaniel. *Humphrey Bogart.* Boston: Little Brown, 1975.

Béranger, Jean. *La Grande Aventure du Cinéma Suédois.* Paris: La Terrain Vague, 1956.

Berenson, Bernard. *The Passionate Sightseer: From the Diaries 1947–1956.* New York: Simon & Schuster, 1960.

Bergman, Ingmar. *The Marriage Scenarios.* New York: Pantheon Books, 1974.

Bergman, Ingrid, and Burgess, Alan. *Ingrid Bergman: My Story.* New York: Delacorte, 1981.

Boccardi, Luciana, ed. *Dossier Ingrid Bergman: Una Vita per il Cinema.* Venice, 1983.

Bondanella, Peter. *Italian Cinema from Neorealism to the Present*. New York: Frederick Ungar, 1983.

Bowers, Ronald. *The Selznick Players*. New York: A. S. Barnes, 1976.

Brown, Curtis F. *Ingrid Bergman*. New York: Galahad, 1973.

Capa, Robert. *Slightly out of Focus*. New York: Henry Holt, 1947.

Chierichetti, David. *Hollywood Costume Design*. New York: Harmony Books, 1977.

Cowie, Peter. *Ingmar Bergman, A Critical Biography*. New York: Scribner, 1982.

———. *Swedish Cinema*. London: A. Zwemmer, 1966.

Davidson, William. *The Real and the Unreal*. New York: Harper, 1961.

Dyer, Richard. *Stars*. London: British Film Institute, 1982.

Francisco, Charles. *You Must Remember This . . . The Filming of Casablanca*. Englewood Cliffs, N.J.: Prentice-Hall, 1980.

Frank, Gerold. *Zsa Zsa Gabor: My Story*. Cleveland and New York: World, 1960.

Guarner, Luis José. *Roberto Rossellini*. Translated by Elisabeth Cameron. New York: Praeger, 1970.

Henreid, Paul, with Fast, Julius. *Ladies' Man: An Autobiography*. New York: St. Martin's Press, 1984.

Higham, Charles, and Greenberg, Joel. *Hollywood in the Forties*. New York: A. S. Barnes, 1968.

Hotchner, A. E. *Choice People*. New York: Morrow, 1984.

Hyams, Joe. *Bogie: The Biography of Humphrey Bogart*. New York: New American Library, 1966.

Ibsen, Henrik. *Plays: Two*. London: Methuen, 1982.

Katz, Roberto. *Death in Rome*. New York: Macmillan, 1967.

Koch, Howard. *As Time Goes By*. New York: Harcourt Brace Jovanovich, 1979.

———. *Casablanca: Script and Legend*. Woodstock: Overlook Press, 1973.

Lamarr, Hedy. *Ecstasy and Me: My Life as a Woman*. New York: Bartholomew House, 1966.

Lambert, Gavin. *GWTW: The Making of Gone With the Wind*. Boston: Little Brown, 1973.

Liehm, Mira. *Passion and Defiance: Film in Italy from 1942 to the Present*. Berkeley: University of California Press, 1984.

Locock, C. D., trans. *A Selection from Modern Swedish Poetry*. New York: Macmillan, 1929.

Madsen, Axel. *William Wyler, the Authorized Biography*. New York: Thomas Y. Crowell, 1973.

McBride, Joseph, ed. *Persistence of Vision*. Madison: Wisconsin Film Society Press, 1968.

Millichap, Joseph R. *Lewis Milestone*. Boston: Twayne Publishers, 1981.

Moberg, Vilhelm. *A History of the Swedish People: From Prehistory to the Renaissance*. New York: Pantheon, 1972.

———. *A History of the Swedish People: From the Renaissance to the Revolution*. New York: Pantheon, 1973.

Oakley, Stewart. *A Short History of Sweden*. New York: Praeger, 1966.

Orwell, George. *A Life: Bernard Crick*. New York: Penguin, 1982.

Overbey, David, ed. and trans. *Springtime in Italy: A Reader on Neo-Realism*. Hamden, Conn.: Anchor Books, 1978.

Procaci, Giuliano. *History of the Italian People*. New York: Harper & Row, 1968.

Quirk, Lawrence J., ed. *The Films of Ingrid Bergman*. Secaucus, N.J.: Citadel Press, 1970.

Ranvaud, Don. *Roberto Rossellini*. London: Blackrose Press, 1981.

Rhode, Eric. *A History of the Cinema from Its Origins to 1970*. Middlesex, Eng.: Penguin Books, 1979.

Roncoroni, Stefano, ed. *The War Trilogy of Roberto Rossellini*. Translated by Judith Green. New York: Grossman, 1973.

Rosenzweig, Sidney. *Casablanca and Other Major Films of Michael Curtiz*. Ann Arbor, Mich.: UMI Research Press, 1982.

Sanders, George. *Memoirs of a Professional Cad*. New York: Putnam, 1960.

Scott, Franklin D. *Sweden: The Nation's History*. Minneapolis: University of Minnesota Press, 1977.

Selznick, Irene. *A Private View*. New York: Alfred A. Knopf, 1983.

Shipton, David. *The Great Movie Stars: The Golden Years*. New York: Hill and Wang, 1979.

Sklar, Robert. *Movie-Made America: A Cultural History of American Movies*. New York: Vintage, 1975.

Skoglund, Gunnar. *God Min I Brokigt Spel*. Stockholm: Norstedt, 1983.

Smith, Dennis Mack. *Mussolini: A Biography*. New York: Vintage, 1983.

Spoto, Donald. *The Dark Side of Genius: The Life of Alfred Hitchcock*. Boston: Little Brown, 1983.

Steele, Joseph Henry. *Ingrid Bergman: An Intimate Portrait*. New York: Delacorte, 1959.

Stern, Michael. *No Innocence Abroad*. New York: Random House, 1952.

Strindberg, August. *Plays: Two*. Translated by Michael Meyer. London: Methuen, 1982.

Swindell, Larry. *The Reluctant Lover: Charles Boyer.* Garden City, N.Y.: Doubleday, 1983.

Tannenbaum, Edward R. *The Fascist Experience: Italian Society and Culture 1922–1945.* New York: Basic Books, 1972.

Taylor, John Russell. *Ingrid Bergman.* New York: St. Martin's, 1983.

———. *Strangers in Paradise: The Hollywood Émigrés 1933–1950.* New York: Holt, Rinehart & Winston, 1983.

Tengroth, Birgit. *Livs Levande.* Stockholm, 1952.

Thomas, Bob. *Selznick.* New York: Doubleday, 1970.

Todd, Ann. *The Eighth Veil.* New York: Putnam, 1981.

Trevelyan, Raleigh. *Rome '44: The Battle for the Eternal City.* New York: Viking, 1982.

Verdone, Mario. *Roberto Rossellini.* Paris: Éditions Seghers, 1963.

Von Heidenstam, O. G. *Swedish Life in Town and Country.* New York: Putnam, 1904.

Von Zaneigbergk, Eva. *Stockholm to Delight You.* Stockholm: Bonniers, 1960.

Walker, Alexander. *Stardom: The Hollywood Phenomenon.* New York: Stein and Day, 1970.

Wallis, Hal, and Higham, Charles. *Star Maker.* New York: Berkley, 1981.

Warner, Marina. *Joan of Arc: The Image of Female Heroism.* New York: Penguin Books, 1981.

Welch, David. *Propaganda and the German Cinema.* Oxford: Clarendon Press, 1983.

Whelan, Richard. *Robert Capa.* New York: Alfred A. Knopf, 1985.

Winquist, Sven, and Jungstedt, Torsten. *Svenskt Filmskadespelar Lexikon.* Sweden: Bokfolaget Forum AB, 1973.

Yeadon, David. *Backroad Journey of Southern Europe.* New York: Harper & Row, 1981.

Acknowledgments

$\mathcal{A}$lthough this is not an authorized biography, almost everyone close to Ingrid Bergman cooperated. For thirty-five years, journalists and authors have asked Dr. Petter Lindstrom for interviews, and he has always backed away. He agreed to talk to me with only the promise that I would attempt to write about Ingrid's and his marriage in an objective fashion.

Miss Bergman's third husband, Lars Schmidt, was extremely helpful, as well. Not only did I have two worthwhile interviews with Mr. Schmidt in Paris, but he invited me to visit the island of Danholmen in Sweden.

Miss Bergman's children were equally forthcoming. I met Robertino at the tribute to his mother at Venice on the first anniversary of her death. Isabella, Isotta, and Pia all put up with my endless questions. I would like especially to thank Isabella, who spent many hours with me, and could not have been more helpful.

There are journalists in five countries who shared their expertise with me. Costanzo Costantini, of Il Messaggero, is a distinguished journalist and author, a congenial host and guide to Roman culture and life. Logan Bentley, an American journalist in Rome, was very generous too. In Paris, Gisele Galante opened the files of Paris Match. In Stockholm, Marie Anne Jansson was a wonderful guide to Sweden; Stig Nahlbom, the well-known columnist for Expressen, was generous with his time and insights. Torsten Jungstedt, the film historian and television personality, was extraordinarily helpful. He even arranged to fly to Stöde, in southern Sweden, to do a radio interview with Åke Dahlqvist, the cameraman, at a time when he could act as my translator. Alan Burgess, the author of Ingrid's autobiography, spent a long afternoon and evening with me in Houston, Texas; many authors would not have been so gracious to a colleague involved in a project similar to their recent book. In Hollywood, Bill Davidson talked about his experiences writing about Ingrid. Tag Gallagher, a film scholar writing a biography of Roberto Rossellini, was very kind.

407

I made two lengthy trips to Europe, and wherever I traveled, Ingrid's family and friends were helpful. In Rome, Fiorella Mariani, Marcella Mariani, and Franco Rossellini were marvelous introductions to the Rossellini side of the family. Federico Fellini was full of brilliant metaphor, and was gracious enough to invite me to his home to interview his wife, the distinguished actress Giulietta Masina. In Paris, Raymond Gérôme provided memorable insights into Ingrid. In London, Griff James, Margaret Johnstone, and Ann Todd were generous with their time and memories, as were many others. In Stockholm, I particularly remember time spent with Greta Danielsson and Britt Engstrom, but I cannot possibly thank all the people there or anywhere else for their help. I would also like to thank Iris Love, the archaeologist, for help in Venice.

There is a voluminous printed record of Ingrid's life and career, and I explored archives and libraries in four countries. It took me ten days to go through the Bergman material at the David O. Selznick collection at the Humanities Research Center of the University of Texas, a time made infinitely more enjoyable and easier thanks to Dr. Ray Daum. The staff at the Lincoln Center Library for the Performing Arts was helpful. So was the staff at the Margaret Hedrick Library of the Academy of Motion Picture Arts and Sciences in Beverly Hills. I received gracious assistance at the Warner Brothers collection at the University of Southern California, the archives of RKO Pictures, Inc., in Los Angeles, and the American Film Institute in Los Angeles. I would also like to thank MGM for allowing me to look at their archival material, and Mary Anne Dolan, editor of the *Los Angeles Herald-Examiner*, for permitting me to see the newspaper's files. I did useful research at the Library of Congress, the graduate research library at UCLA, the Santa Monica Public Library, and the Los Angeles Public Library. I also received help from the Rochester Public Library and the Rochester *Times-Union* library. The Warner Brothers retirees organization allowed me to solicit their members for memories of Ingrid.

I was able to screen several rarely seen Ingrid Bergman films at the UCLA film archives. Ollie Rosberg was very helpful at the Swedish Film Institute in Sweden, as was the staff at Svensk Filmindustri. Material at the British Film Institute in London was very useful. I also would like to thank William Hifner, the librarian at the *Washington Post,* for his assistance.

My wife, Vesna Obradovic Leamer, was my researcher in the United States and my interpreter in Italy, as well as my first and finest critic. That the book was such a pleasure to write has much to do with her, and I have dedicated the book to her. Any author would dream of having Larry Ashmead as an editor, and this is the second time that I have been so fortunate. Craig Nelson, a young editor at Harper & Row, offered his uniformly perceptive comments on the manuscript, as well. Margaret Wimberger, now herself an assistant editor at Harper & Row, handled all the details of this project with acumen and good cheer. I also must thank Kenneth P. Norwick, my literary attorney, who is both an outstanding attorney and a man of highest principle. And I am grateful to my agent, Carol Mann, for her work on the book.

When I finished interviewing Ingmar Bergman, he said: "I could have told you stories, but I told you the truth." I am indebted to the Swedish director for his perceptions and for allowing me to view his private documentary on the making of *Autumn Sonata*.

I am grateful to all Ingrid Bergman's other friends, associates, relatives, who told me not only stories but what they considered the truth. They include: Joss Ackland, Larry Adler, Robert Anderson, Frith Banbury, Frank Barrena, Kate Barrett, Greg Bautzer, Ben and Carla Benjamin, Harve Bennett, Michel Bernheim, Jeanne Bernkopf, Gunnar Björnstrand, Kay Brown, Igor Cassini, George Christy, Ross Claiborne, Richard Coe, Claudette Colbert, Bob Colman, Gene Corman, Åke Dahlqvist, Joe Daly, Silvia d'Amicos, Suso Cecchi d'Amicos, Brad Darrach, Olivia de Havilland, Giuseppe De Santis, Madame De Sica, George Diehl, Stanley Donen, Frank Edwards, Julius Epstein, Laurence Evans, José Ferrer, Mel Ferrer, Armiene Field, Silvia Field, Rhonda Fleming, Joan Fontaine, Franka, Charles Futoran, Patrick Garland, Martha Gellhorn, Alan Gibson, David Golding, Sam Goldwyn, Jr., Cary Grant, Shirley Green, Alan Greenberg, Marilyn and Monty Hall, Dora Jane Hamblin, Doris Hare, Signe Hasso, Helen Hayes, Charlton Heston, Wendy Hiller, Louie Hollis, Celeste Holm, Elsa Holm, John Houseman, Noel Howard, Paul Hume, Christopher Isherwood.

Marion Keyes, Alf Kjellin, David Ladd, Disa Lauhren, David Lean, Reginald LeBorg, Francesco Leseur, Judge Mildred Lillie, the late Father Antonio Lisandrini, Carlo Lizzani, Norman and Peggy Lloyd, Gina Lollobrigida, Lasse and Ingela Lundberg, Marcel Machu, Aldo Martini, Giulietta Masina, Ella McCann, Fiorella Mariani, Marcella Mariani, Walter Matthau, Liza Minnelli, Gunilla Mohlin, Roger Moore, Stig Nahlbom, Elsa and Vincent Neptune, Elsa Neuberger, Ellen Neuwald, Mark Nichols, Leonard Nimoy, Tom J. A. Olsson, Frederick O'Neal, Roberto Orbach, Guya Palavachini, Malcolm Peattie, Gregory Peck, Major Peek, Mimi Pollak, Anthony Quinn, Senator Charles Percy, Anthony Perkins, Rae Pober.

Jenia Reissar, Madame Renoir, Tony Reyes, Don Roberts, Francisco Rodolfi, Toby Rowland, Franco Rossellini, Lina Rossellini, Renzo Rossellini, Billy Rowe, Silvia Rubinstein, Åke Sandler, Carl Schaeffer, Wally Schneiderman, Maximilian Schell, Martin Scorsese, Phyllis Seaton, Danny Selznick of Monday Productions, Irene Selznick, Sonali Senroy, Ralph Serpe, Stirling Silliphant, Catharine Stackelberg, Frank Sundstrom, Warren Thomas, Umberto Tirelli, Eva Tissell, Aldo Tonti, Helen Tubbs, Pavo Turtiainen, Raf Vallone, John Van Eyssen, Peter Veger, John Veitch, Rune Waldekranz, Hal Wallis, Stephen Weiss, Sandra Westin, Richard Whelan, Bob William.

Index

PHOTO CREDITS

Following page 184:

The transcendent beauty of Ingrid Bergman (*Theater Arts Library, Harry Ransom Humanities Center, University of Texas at Austin*); Ingrid and her father (*Svenska Filminstitutet*); Ingrid as an extra (*Svenska Filminstitutet*); At the Swedish Royal Dramatic School (*Svenska Filminstitutet*); Ingrid and Petter at the Lutheran church in Stode, Sweden (*Sture Gewert*); Ingrid and Petter as man and wife (*Sture Gewert*); In *The Count of the Monk's Bridge*, with Edvin Adolphson (*Svenska Filminstitutet*); In the Swedish *Intermezzo*, with Gösta Ekman (*Svenska Filminstitutet*); Ingrid in 1937 (*Svenska Filminstitutet*); A pregnant Ingrid making a film in Nazi Germany in 1938 (*private collection*); With Pia (*private collection*); In *The Four Companions* (*Svenska Filminstitutet*); Taking direction from Gregory Ratoff in the American *Intermezzo* (*Theater Arts Library, Harry Ransom Humanities Center, University of Texas at Austin*); In Hollywood in 1939 (*Selznick archives*); Publicity shot, 1939 (*Selznick archives*); With Leslie Howard in Selznick's *Intermezzo* (*Selznick archives*); With Burgess Meredith in *Liliom* (*Phototeque*); With Humphrey Bogart and Dooley Wilson in *Casablanca* (*Memorabilia*); The most famous goodbye (*Memorabilia*); Sam Wood directs Ingrid and Gary Cooper in *For Whom the Bell Tolls* (*A.M.P.S.*); Cooper, Ruth Roberts, and Ingrid during the making of *For Whom the Bell Tolls* (*A.M.P.S.*); Petter and Pia (*private collection*); Behind Alfred Hitchcock's back, Ingrid jokes for the camera (*private collection*); With Gary Cooper and Clark Gable on the ski slopes (*private collection*); Gable with an eagle shot on a trip with Ingrid and Petter (*private collection*); Ingrid and Pia in the house on Benedict Canyon (*private collection*); Ingrid and Petter's bedroom (*private collection*); Pia, Petter and Ingrid (*private collection*); A very rare publicity shot (*private collection*); A costume test for *Saratoga Trunk* (*private collection*); Reunited with Cooper in *Saratoga Trunk* (*Memorabilia*); With Gregory Peck in *Spellbound* (*Selznick archives*); With Cary Grant in *Notorious* (*Selznick archives*).

Following page 248:

At Hampshire House during *Joan of Lorraine* (*Svenska Filminstitutet*); With Sam Wanamaker in *Joan of Lorraine* (*Phototeque*); Director Victor Fleming adjusts Ingrid's armor for *Joan of Arc* (*A.M.P.S.*); Joan burns at the stake (*A.M.P.S.*); With *Arch of Triumph*'s director Lewis Milestone (*A.M.P.S.*); With Charles Boyer in *Arch of Triumph* (*A.M.P.S.*); Ingrid and Roberto as she arrives in Rome (*Wide World Photos*); With Roberto at the Excelsior Hotel (*Wide World Photo*); Shooting *Stromboli* (*Phototeque*); A pregnant Ingrid leaving her apartment (*Wide World Photos*); With Giulietta Masina in *Europa '51* (*Aldo Tonti*); With the newborn twins (*David Seymour/Magnum*); Ingrid, Roberto, and their three children, Isotta, Robertino, and Isabella (*David Seymour/Magnum*); In the Honegger-Claudel oratorio *Joan at the Stake* (*H. Roger-Viollet*); With Pia Lindstrom, 1957 (*Wide World Photos*); With Oscar, 1957 (*Wide World Photos*); Reunited with her children Isabella, Isotta, and Robertino (*Wide World Photos*); New York press conference, 1957 (*Paris Match*); With Helen Hayes in *Anastasia* (*Phototeque*); With Lars Schmidt, 1958 (*Paris Match*); Accompanying her three children back to Italy (*Wide World Photos*); With Lars (*Associated Press*); With Pia and Hugh O'Brian (*Wide World Photos*); With Goldie Hawn in *Cactus Flower* (*Larry Edmunds*); With Anthony Quinn in *A Walk in the Spring Rain* (*Larry Edmunds*); With Isabella, Pia, and Edgar Lansbury at premiere of *Godspell* (*Wide World Photos*); With Lauren Bacall in *Murder on the Orient Express* (*The Memory Shop*); Rossellini in his last years (*Francesca Rodolfi*); Directed by Ingmar Bergman in *Autumn Sonata* (*Svenska Filminstitutet*); With director Alan Gibson (*Harve Bennet*); Ingrid in April 1982 (*Paris Match*).